I0198521

Discovering Christ

In

The Gospel Of Matthew

Discovering Christ In The Gospel Of Matthew

Don Fortner

Go *publications*

Go Publications
The Cairn, Hill Top, Eggleston, Co. Durham, DL12 0AU, ENGLAND

First Published 2009

British Library Cataloguing in Publication Data available

ISBN 978-095486247-3

Printed and bound in Great Britain
By Lightning Source UK Ltd.

To

Walter and Betty Groover

Faithful Servants of Our God in Mexico

Cherished Friends

Contents

Chapter **Page**

Foreword

I hope if you do not already know him, that very soon you will discover the Lord Jesus Christ as your Master and Friend, your Redeemer and Rest, your Substitute and Saviour. I am confident that such a discovery will change your life and open to you a whole new experience of grace and truth.

Unfortunately, the book you have in your hand cannot do this, for such a discovery of grace is the Holy Spirit's work, not yours or mine, or Don Fortner's. But should the Holy Spirit choose to reveal the Lord to you through the pages of this book then I for one will not be surprised. Here is a faithful word for sinners; a gospel message *par excellence* for the weary and heavy laden; a signpost, clear and direct, to the Saviour himself.

Discovering Christ as Lord and Saviour is the most important matter you will face in your life and Matthew's gospel is an excellent place to begin looking. As an apostle and evangelist, Matthew supplies first-hand documentary evidence of the Lord's doctrine and miracles. He reveals the Lord Jesus as the Messiah, long sought for and eagerly anticipated by the Old Testament saints and prophets.

Today, many know the name of Jesus Christ, and some even know his words and works. But many who know about Jesus do so without truly knowing the joy and peace that comes from experiencing sovereign grace in personal terms. To discover this requires that we acknowledge our need as a sinner, that we hear and understand the gospel message of salvation by grace, and that these discoveries are applied to our hearts by faith.

In Matthew 21:42 the evangelist records the Lord's words concerning the stone the builders rejected and Don Fortner shows us how this stone is a picture of the Lord Jesus Christ. In 1864, William Parks of Openshaw in Manchester preached a sermon and also used Matthew's account to underline the necessity of personally discovering Christ as the foundation stone of our lives. Here is what he said:

> It signifies little that we acknowledge Christ in name, if we do not know him as the prophets and Apostles did, namely, as the great Covenant-Head of His Church, as her Representative, her Law-fulfiller, her Atoner, and her Saviour. If we do not know Christ thus, we might as well be worshippers of an idol! Then again, if we do know Christ as all these in relation to His Church, and instead of letting our souls down upon Him with all their burden, weight, sin, and guilt, we set to, and place our works upon Him, our convictions, our prayers, repentance, tears, and obedience, we are deriving no benefit from Him, for we, to all intents and purposes, are not on Him, not built upon Him, not knit unto Him, not in union with Him. Let me illustrate this for you. Suppose a huge stone in the midst of a plain; and suppose a rushing mighty flood to threaten that plain, and suppose you are warned to place yourself upon that huge stone, and you will be saved from the rush of waters; and suppose further that instead of getting upon that stone, you begin first to put your watch, and then your money, and then your garments, and then your shoes upon it, and the flood comes 'ere you yourself can get upon it, would it be thought extraordinary that you had been swept away? Surely not. Yet this is actually the position that the sinner occupies with regard to Christ, who instead of flinging himself, just as he is, upon Him, sets to and places the wretched rags of his self-righteousness upon the foundation Stone, and keeps off it himself!

I am confident that all who consider the discoveries made of Jesus Christ in Matthew will be challenged to think of the Saviour in a new and fresh way. Whether you are only beginning to think about the Christian faith or already confess Christ as Lord, I earnestly pray you will be much blessed and spiritually enriched by the experience of Christ so discovered.

Peter L Meney

Introduction

Christ The King

I cannot stress this fact often enough or forcefully enough: the Bible, the Word of God, is in its entirety a book about Christ. It is all about Him who loved us and gave himself for us. I do not mean by that that the Bible is a Christ centred Book. I do not mean that Christ is the primary aspect of divine revelation in these pages. I mean that Christ is the message of holy scripture.

This is exactly what God the Holy Spirit tells us in Luke 24:27. Our Saviour said to those two disciples on the Emmaus road, "O fools and slow of heart to believe all that the prophets have spoken" (v. 25). Then, we read in verse 27, "And beginning at Moses and all the prophets, he expounded unto them in all the scriptures the things concerning himself".

The message of this Book is Jesus Christ and him crucified. This Book is not a book about history, or a book about morality, or a book about religious dogma. This is a Book about Christ and redemption by his blood. This is what the apostle Peter tells us in Acts 10:43. The apostle Paul states exactly the same thing, declaring that the one message he preached, everywhere to all people, was Jesus Christ and him crucified. This message, he declares, is "all the counsel of God", the whole of divine revelation.

Read 1 Corinthians 2:1, 2: "And I, brethren, when I came to you, came not with excellency of speech or of wisdom, declaring unto you the testimony of God. For I determined not to know any thing among you, save Jesus Christ, and him crucified." Now, look at Acts 20: Paul is about to leave his brethren at Ephesus, never to see them again. They urged him not to go to Jerusalem for fear that the Jews would kill him. Yet he declares, "I go bound in the spirit unto Jerusalem … that I might finish my course with joy, and the ministry which I have received of the Lord Jesus". And he tells us exactly what his course and ministry were, which he had received from the Saviour. It was "to testify the gospel of the grace of God" (Acts 20:22-24). Now, look at verses 26 and 27. Here

Paul defines what it is to preach the gospel. "Wherefore I take you to record this day, that I am pure from the blood of all men. For I have not shunned to declare unto you all the counsel of God".

The Book of God is a Book about Christ. In the Old Testament, the law, the prophets, and the Psalms declare, "Someone is coming". When we open the book of Matthew, that blessed Someone steps onto the stage and is identified as the incarnate God, our Saviour (1:18-23).

One Object Of Faith

The Old Testament saints believed God just as we do, trusting Christ just as we do, and were saved by grace, trusting the crucified Lamb of God in exactly the same way we are. Christ was not then fully revealed. He was not personally identified. Yet, he was known and trusted as God the Saviour, the Christ, the Anointed One, the promised Seed.

Beginning with the Gospel of Matthew, we move from the realm of shadow, type, and prophecy into the full sunshine of the Sun of Righteousness, the Son of God. As we have seen, the Old Testament speaks of him on every page, but speaks in shadows, in types, in symbols, and in prophecies, all looking forward to the coming of that Someone whom Abel, Enoch, Noah, and Abraham trusted. You cannot read the Old Testament without a sense of anticipation, thinking to yourself, this Book is talking about Someone who is yet to appear, who is a woman's Seed, an Ark of salvation, a sin-atoning Lamb, a man who is God, a Redeemer, a King like David, a Prophet like Moses, a Priest like Melchizedek, a divine Substitute, and a Saviour.

Matthew, Mark, Luke, and John say, "Here he is"! When we come to read the four gospels, we say with Andrew and Phillip, "We have found the Messiah … the Christ … We have found him of whom Moses in the law, and the prophets did write, Jesus of Nazareth, the son of Joseph" (John 1:41-45). "And the Word was made flesh, and dwelt among us, (and we beheld his glory, the glory as of the only begotten of the Father,) full of grace and truth" (John 1:14). "Thou shalt call his name JESUS: for he shall save his people from their sins" (Matthew 1:21).

Here we see Christ as he is. Remember, what he was is what he is; and what he is, is what we have. All the fulness of his character and being and life and glory is ours (John 17:22). That makes the four gospels uniquely important. They tell us exactly who our Saviour is.

The Sun of Righteousness has arisen with healing in his wings (Malachi 4:2). In the 39 books of the Old Testament we have been watching the unfolding of the dawn of that day which Abraham rejoiced to see, the rising of that Star of whom Balaam spoke, and of the great Light promised in Isaiah. We have been watching one cloud after another dissipate by the rising Sun. Now, the King of Glory, of whom David sang, has come. "We have seen his star in the east" (in the Old Testament) "and are come" (in the New Testament) "to worship him". We have "seen the Lord's Christ". As we pick up the New Testament, we say with old Simeon, who waited for the Consolation of Israel, our "eyes have seen thy salvation, which thou hast prepared before the face of all people; a light to lighten the Gentiles, and the glory of thy people Israel" (Luke 2:30-32).

Why Four Gospels?
People sometimes wonder why we have four gospel narratives. The reason is really very simple. Matthew, Mark, Luke, and John show us our Saviour's full character, his full person and work from four angles. They do not give us four different pictures, but four different views of the same picture. Really, they present the Lord Jesus like a statue, each allowing us to view the statue from a different side. I say that because in some ways a statue is better than a picture. A statue allows us to see the image it represents from all sides. The four gospels have been compared to the four cherubim of Ezekiel and Revelation. Matthew shows Christ as the King, as the Lion of the Tribe of Judah, who has come to save his people from their sins. Mark presents him as Jehovah's Servant, who has come to fulfil his Father's will, the ox ready to serve and ready to be sacrificed upon the altar. Luke, the beloved Physician, presents him as the Son of Man, full of human sympathy and tenderness, as the cherub with the face of a man suggests. John, like the eagle soaring into the heavens, sets the Saviour before us as the Son of God, with a majesty that transcends our thought and imagination.

Christ the King
Let us take a brief overview of Matthew's gospel, and worship our King. Here we see the royal majesty of our heavenly King and his great kingdom. Matthew, more so than all the other gospel writers, sets forth the Mosaic law, referring constantly to the Old Testament scriptures, and shows that both the law and the scriptures of the Old Testament find their fulfilment in Christ, the King.

The Genealogy
Matthew 1:1-17 gives us our Lord's genealogy, tracing it back to Abraham. We read in verse 1, "The book of the generations of Jesus Christ, the Son of David,

the Son of Abraham". He is set before us in verse 1 as the Son of Abraham to show us that he is that One with whom God's covenant was made, and as Abraham's promised Seed in whom all the covenant is fulfilled. He is set before us as the son of David (v. 6) to show us that he is the rightful Heir to David's throne, and that he has come to take possession of David's true kingdom and throne.

The Jews carped about many things, raised many questions, and made many accusations in their attempts to discredit our Saviour's claims as the Christ, as God's Messiah; but never once did they question his genealogy. Why? Because it was a matter of public and biblical record that could not be disputed.

The Sinner's Saviour

There is something especially precious in our Saviour's genealogy that is commonly overlooked. Here, just before we are told that he came to save his people from their sins, three of his ancestral mothers are named who had a smear upon their names. Thamar was Judah's daughter-in-law, who played the harlot and committed incest. Ruth was a Moabitess, a woman of a cursed race, a race that came into existence by Lot's incestuous behaviour. Bathsheba was the adulteress wife of Uriah. Add to that the fact that our Saviour is here identified specifically as the son of David by Bathsheba; and you can almost hear him saying, "Behold, I have come to save poor sinners"!

The Incarnation

Our Saviour's wondrous divinity is immediately presented in Matthew's record of the incarnation and virgin birth (1:18-25). Here is a picture of the New Birth. The Lord Jesus Christ was conceived in a sinner, conceived by the work of God the Holy Spirit, and conceived without the aid of a man. That is exactly how Christ is formed in us in the new birth.

Here is our Saviour's name "Jesus". Here is his mission "He shall save his people from their sins". Here's the character of his people Sinners; and they were his people before he came to save them, chosen in eternal election, and given to him as a Surety. Here is his divinity, the certainty of his success. Our Saviour is himself God in human flesh, Emmanuel!

Old Testament Prophecies

Matthew 1 and 2 set before us a number of Old Testament prophecies fulfilled by our Saviour's incarnation. He is Immanuel, the virgin-born Saviour (Isaiah 7:14;

Matthew 1:22, 23). He is a Nazarene (Judges 13:5; 1 Samuel 1:11; Matthew 2:23). He fulfilled Jeremiah's prophecy of weeping in Ramah (Jeremiah 31:15; Matthew 2:17, 18). He was called out of Egypt (Hosea 11:1; Matthew 2:15). He was born at Bethlehem (Micah 5:2; Matthew 2:5, 6).

Wise Men

Matthew alone describes the visit of the wise men (2:1-13). The whole world at this time was expecting the advent of some Great One. These wise men came to Jerusalem asking, "Where is he that is born King of the Jews?" Their adoration of the newborn King foreshadowed his universal dominion (John 17:2; Romans 14:9). Matthew alone tells us how Herod, the usurper of David's dominion, sought to slay the heir to David's throne (2:14-23).

John The Baptist

In this Gospel John the Baptist appears preaching repentance and introducing the Lord Jesus as the mighty Judge who shall purge his floor with tremendous judgment (3:10-17). Our Lord Jesus Christ was immersed by John to fulfil all righteousness. At first John was reluctant to immerse the Saviour because he recognized who it was that stood before him, and was humbled in his presence. But, when the Master said, "Suffer it to be so now: for thus it becometh us to fulfil all righteousness. Then he suffered him", and immersed the incarnate God in the Jordan River.

The question is sometimes asked, "How did Christ's baptism fulfil all righteousness?" There can be but one answer. By his baptism, and by believer's baptism today, righteousness is fulfilled symbolically. By our baptism (immersion), we symbolically testify how it is that sinners are made righteous before God. Our sins are washed away and we are made righteous by our death, burial, and resurrection with Christ, our Substitute.

This man is owned at his immersion as the Son of God. When our Lord was baptized John saw the Spirit of God descending and abiding upon him, thereby identifying him as the Son of God and the Messiah. And this is he in whom the Father is well pleased. When he came up out of the watery grave, the Father spoke from heaven, declaring, "This is my beloved Son in whom I am well pleased". This same word from heaven was heard at the transfiguration (17:5). By these two things, the Lord God tells us that Christ, our ascended, exalted Saviour, is that One in whom alone we find acceptance with God. As the Holy Lord God is well pleased with his Son, so he is well pleased with his elect in his Son, our Substitute.

The Temptation

Matthew's account of the temptation is detailed and instructive (4:1-11). He was tempted in all points like as we are, yet without sin. The devil came and found nothing in him. The word "tempted" would be more accurately translated "tested". Temptations (tests and trials) do not make any change in anyone. They simply reveal what the person is.

There is some debate about whether our Lord's temptations were real, and whether it was possible for him to sin. The temptations were real. Yet, there was no possibility of the holy, incarnate God sinning. The temptations proved that there was no evil in him (John 14:30). If you run a test on water, the test is real; but the fact that the test is real does not imply that there is impurity in the water. The test will simply show the water pure or corrupt. So it was with our Master's temptations. They showed that he is, indeed, "holy, harmless, undefiled, and separate from sinners".

Christ's Kingdom

Beginning in Matthew 4:17, our Lord began to preach, saying, "Repent, for the kingdom of heaven is at hand". The word "kingdom" appears fifty-three times in Matthew. Thirty-five times Christ's kingdom is called, "the kingdom of heaven", an expression found nowhere else in the Gospels.

Chapters 5-7 give us our Saviour's Sermon on the Mount. Here he tells us the nature of his kingdom. The Jews, because of their perverted understanding of the Old Testament, expected the Messiah to establish a physical, Jewish kingdom in the earth. Our Saviour dispelled that notion at the very outset of his public ministry in this tremendous sermon.

He opens his sermon (5:3-13) with the beatitudes, declaring that those who are his servants, his people, those who enter into his kingdom are identified not by outward ceremonies but by inward grace (Philippians 3:3). The kingdom of heaven is inward, not outward.

The service of his kingdom (chapter 6) is inward, heart service, not an outward show. Every form of religion with which I am familiar tells its adherents to show their religion to men by outward deeds. The Son of God tells his disciples never to attempt to show their religion by outward deeds that are seen, approved of, and applauded by men. Our giving, our prayers, our fastings are to be things arising spontaneously, kept in strict secrecy, and performed for God and before God.

True religion is a matter of faith in Christ, a matter of the heart. The only thing our Saviour tells us to show is mercy, love, and grace. That is what is discussed in the latter part of this chapter. The law of his kingdom is love; and love is best displayed in forbearance, forgiveness, and uprightness.

Chapter 7 continues with the same subject, teaching us to guard against rash judgment concerning others. We ought to embrace as brethren all who profess faith in Christ (who profess to believe the gospel of God's free and sovereign grace in him), without doubtful disputations (Romans 14:1). Then, our Lord brings his message to a pointed conclusion, urging us all to make certain we trust him alone, to make certain we have entered in "at the strait gate".

Miracles

In chapters 8 and 9 our Lord performed numerous, unparalleled miracles, displaying his omnipotent grace. He healed a leper, who came worshiping him, with a touch. He healed the centurion's servant by the mere exercise of his will. He touched Peter's mother-in-law and raised her from her sickbed. "When the even was come, they brought unto him many that were possessed with devils: and he cast out the spirits with his word, and healed all that were sick: That it might be fulfilled which was spoken by Esaias the prophet, saying, Himself took our infirmities, and bare our sicknesses" (8:16, 17).

He calmed the raging tempest by his mere word, healed a paralyzed man and forgave his sins, raised a man's daughter from the dead, healed a woman who had been diseased with an issue of blood for twelve years, and gave two blind men their sight. There can be no question about it, this man was and is God the Son!

Conversion

In chapter 10 our Lord names his apostles and sends them out to preach the gospel. In chapter 11 he confirms himself to John the Baptist's disciples. In chapter 12 he shows himself to be Jehovah's Servant spoken of in Isaiah 42:1-4, that is the Lord of the sabbath, and declares that the sabbath was made for man, not man for the sabbath. Healing the man with a withered hand on the sabbath, he hints that the sabbath of the Old Testament portrayed the believer's experience of grace, finding life and rest in him. Then, our Lord shows us that conversion is nothing less than his own entrance into a man's heart, casting Satan out, and setting up his own throne in the heart by omnipotent grace.

The Parables

We have eight parables of the Kingdom in chapter 13, each beginning with "The kingdom of heaven is like", except that of the sower, where we have the word "kingdom" in verse 11. Numerous other parables are recorded by Matthew, all describing the spiritual nature of Christ's kingdom, and the establishment of it by grace alone.

The parable of the sower tells us of the necessity of the Holy Spirit's work, making the heart as good ground to receive the gospel, and warns us of those things that rob men's souls of the blessings of the gospel. The parable of the tares teaches us that we must never try to separate the tares from the wheat. That work is performed by Christ himself, through the preaching of the gospel.

The mustard seed and leaven parables tell us that the kingdom of God grows secretly, almost imperceptibly, but constantly until all God's elect are gathered into it by his grace. The parable of the treasure hid in the field speaks of Christ's purchased dominion over, and possession of, the whole world as the God-man Mediator (John 17:2), that he might obtain the treasure of it, his elect.

The parable of the pearl of great price teaches that we must forsake all for Christ, who is the Pearl of great price. The parable of the great net, like that of the tares, tells us that as long as time stands the kingdom of heaven (the outward, visible kingdom and every local church) is a mixed multitude of good fish and bad, true believers and those who merely profess to be believers.

The parable of the lost sheep (18:10-14) portrays our Saviour's determination to save his elect and his joy in saving them. That of the wicked servant (18:23-35) portrays our Redeemer's teaching (18:15-22) on the necessity and blessedness of believers forgiving those who offend them.

The parable of the labourers (20:1-16) is our Lord's picture of grace, displaying the fact that all God's elect are perfectly accepted in him. This parable is preceded by (chapter 18) and followed by (20:20) strife among the disciples regarding who shall be greatest in the kingdom of God. Because salvation is by grace alone, because there are no degrees of acceptance with God, because the whole of our salvation is bestowed freely for Christ's sake, there can be no degrees of reward in heaven.

The parable of the vineyard (21:33-45) portrays the wrath of God to be visited upon the Jewish nation for slaughtering his Son. The marriage supper parable sets before us the freeness of grace proclaimed by the gospel (22:2-14).

Christ The King

The parable of the ten virgins warns us of the danger of religion without Christ, outward religion without inward grace, and the great need of diligence in personally watching over our own souls (25:1-13).

The parable of talents (25:14-30) shows us our responsibility to be faithful stewards of that which the Lord God has put in our hands to use for his glory.

Divine Sovereignty

In all these parables the absolute sovereignty of God our Saviour over all things is clearly exemplified. Our Saviour declares that he has the right to do with his own what he will (20:15; Romans 9:15-18). In this opening book of the New Testament he asserts that he came specifically to redeem and that he effectually calls the many in this world who are his own elect (20:28; 22:14; 1:21), and only them.

Promises To The Church

In Matthew 16 and 18 the Lord Jesus identifies himself as the only Foundation upon which his church is build, and that the building of his church is his work alone. Immediately after making this declaration, he tells us that the way he would build his church is by the merit, power, and efficacy of his sin-atoning sacrifice (16:13-21). Then in chapter 18:20 he promises that he is always with his assembled saints when they gather for worship in his name. This church, this kingdom that Christ builds, he protects, provides for, and shall make triumphant over hell itself.

Transfiguration

Along with Mark and Luke, Matthew tells us of the unveiled glory of the King in his transfiguration, foreshadowing his resurrection glory as Zion's King. He adds this touch, "His face did shine as the sun", and these words, "in whom I am well pleased", showing how perfectly our Lord fulfilled God's Law as a Representative Man (17:1-13; Mark 9:2-13; Luke 9:28-36).

Meaningless Questions

In chapter 22 the Pharisees, Sadducees, and lawyers came asking meaningless questions about political matters, the resurrection, and the law. Their questions were made meaningless by the fact that they ignored the one great question "What think ye of Christ?" (v. 42). In chapter 23 our Lord condemns them and all who follow their path.

The Crucifixion

Chapters 26 and 27 give us a brief account of our Lord's betrayal, his mock trial, and the agony of his crucifixion and death as our sin-atoning Substitute. Forsaken by heaven and earth, alone he endured all the wrath of God for us when he was made to be sin. Darkness covered the earth for three hours. Upon the cursed tree, he vanquished sin, death, Satan, and hell. As Paul puts it in Colossians, he made a show of them openly, triumphing over them, and leading them behind him as a conqueror would lead a train of captives in open display before the people. When at last he gave up the ghost, the veil of the temple was ripped apart, showing that he has opened the way for sinners to come to God; and many were raised from their graves, showing that the sentence of death can never be executed upon those for whom he died. Substitution is beautifully portrayed in the fact that Christ died in the place of Barabbas. Barabbas went free because a substitute died in his place; and God's elect must and shall go free because Christ died in their place (Romans 8:1, 33, 34).

The Resurrection

In his account of the resurrection (chapter 28) Matthew tells of the great earthquake, the angel whose face was like lightning, for fear of whom the keepers did shake and became as dead men, and of the Lord's bodily appearance to his disciples after he arose. He was sent to the tomb as a guilty criminal, worthy of death. He was released as a free man, without sin, "justified in the Spirit" and "declared to be the Son of God" our Saviour, because he had accomplished our justification by the sacrifice of himself (Romans 4:25).

Our Commission

Finally, this Gospel gives us, as no other, our Lord's last royal commission. The risen Lord says to you and me, "Go tell the world what I have done". "And Jesus came and spake unto them, saying, All power is given unto me in heaven and in earth. Go ye therefore, and teach all nations, baptizing them in the name of the Father, and of the Son, and of the Holy Ghost: teaching them to observe all things whatsoever I have commanded you: and, lo, I am with you alway, even unto the end of the world. Amen" (28:18-20).

Chapter 1

The Genealogy Of Christ

"The book of the generation of Jesus Christ, the son of David, the son of Abraham. Abraham begat Isaac; and Isaac begat Jacob; and Jacob begat Judas and his brethren; And Judas begat Phares and Zara of Thamar; and Phares begat Esrom; and Esrom begat Aram; And Aram begat Aminadab; and Aminadab begat Naasson; and Naasson begat Salmon; And Salmon begat Booz of Rachab; and Booz begat Obed of Ruth; and Obed begat Jesse; And Jesse begat David the king; and David the king begat Solomon of her *that had been the wife* of Urias; And Solomon begat Roboam; and Roboam begat Abia; and Abia begat Asa; And Asa begat Josaphat; and Josaphat begat Joram; and Joram begat Ozias; And Ozias begat Joatham; and Joatham begat Achaz; and Achaz begat Ezekias; And Ezekias begat Manasses; and Manasses begat Amon; and Amon begat Josias; And Josias begat Jechonias and his brethren, about the time they were carried away to Babylon: And after they were brought to Babylon, Jechonias begat Salathiel; and Salathiel begat Zorobabel; And Zorobabel begat Abiud; and Abiud begat Eliakim; and Eliakim begat Azor; And Azor begat Sadoc; and Sadoc begat Achim; and Achim begat Eliud; And Eliud begat Eleazar; and Eleazar begat Matthan; and Matthan begat Jacob; And Jacob begat Joseph the husband of Mary, of whom was born Jesus, who is called Christ. So all the generations from Abraham to David are fourteen generations; and from David until the carrying away into Babylon are fourteen generations; and from the carrying away into Babylon unto Christ are fourteen generations."
(Matthew 1:1-17)

The New Testament begins with the history of the earthly life, death, resurrection, and ascension of the Lord Jesus Christ. It is given four times, by four different men (Matthew, Mark, Luke, and John), from four points of view. Yet, in these four narratives there is one complete story, without a single contradiction. Four distinct gospel narratives tell the blessed story of Christ's doing and dying as the sinners' Substitute. Four times we read of his precious words, works, and worth as our God-man Mediator. How thankful we ought to be for the four gospels! Each one compliments and reinforces the others. J. C. Ryle said, "To know Christ is life eternal. To believe Christ is to have peace with God. To follow Christ is to be a true Christian. To be with Christ is heaven itself. We can never hear too much about the Lord Jesus Christ."

God's Word

The verses in this study are the opening lines of the New Testament, the beginning of the story of the Lord Jesus Christ. At first glance it may appear to be just a list of names. But it is much, much more. These lines are given, not by the pen of men alone, but by the direct arrangement and inspiration of God the Holy Spirit. Read them with serious thought. What we have before us is "not the word of man, but of God" (1 Thessalonians 2:13; 2 Timothy 3:16). Let us cherish the Book of God. It is "The Holy Bible"! We should, each of us, constantly give thanks to God that he has given us his Word in our native tongue. This Book is able to make us wise unto salvation (2 Timothy 3:15). This Book is able to thoroughly furnish us for every good work in this world (2 Timothy 3:17). It is our responsibility to search, and study, and seek to understand the message of this Book, and to govern our lives by it (John 5:39; 2 Timothy 2:15). In the last day we will be judged out of this Book and required to give account to God for our use or neglect of the light he has given us.

Wise they are who follow the counsel of J. C. Ryle, "Read the Bible reverently and diligently, with an honest determination to believe and practise all we find in it. It is no light matter how we use this Book. Above all, let us never read the Bible without praying for the teaching of the Holy Spirit. He alone can apply truth to our hearts, and make us profit by what we read."

The Gospel of Matthew is thought by some to have been written as early as within eight years after our Lord's ascension. Others think it was written later, 15 to 20 years after the ascension. It was written by Matthew, whose name means, "gift of the Lord". Here he proves that Jesus of Nazareth is the Christ of God by giving us his genealogy and, at the same time, shows us that the Son of God has graciously identified himself with the people he came to save.

The passage now before us (1:1-7) contains the genealogy of our Lord Jesus Christ, in the time of Joseph his reputed father, tracing his genealogy through Joseph. Luke's genealogy differs from Matthew's simply because Luke traces the Saviour's genealogy through his mother, Mary. Frequently, when reading the genealogical records of scripture, there is a tendency to neglect them because many fail to see any meaning or value in them. That should never be the case. Clearly, there are five lessons to be learned from these seventeen verses.

The Importance Of The Genealogy Itself
First, let us recognize the importance of this genealogical record. Matthew was directed by the Holy Spirit to begin his Gospel with a long list of names. Sixteen verses are taken up with tracing out the family tree of the Lord Jesus Christ as a man, from Abraham to David, from David to Jechonias, and from Jechonias to Joseph. The seventeenth verse divides the genealogy into three groups of fourteen generations. Do not foolishly imagine that these verses are useless. Nothing in God's creation is useless; and nothing in God's Word is useless. These lines were not written by a man alone, but by a man who wrote as he was inspired by God the Holy Spirit. They are to be read with serious thought. We have before us a very important document, a record of monumental significance. Robert Hawker shows the importance of this record in his comments on the opening verse, "The book of the generation of Jesus Christ, the son of David, the Son of Abraham". He wrote …

> The Old Testament begins with the account of the Creation. The New Testament begins with the account of Him, by whom all things were created (Hebrews 1:1, 2). The great design of this pedigree concerning Christ after the flesh, is to prove Christ's lineal descent from Abraham. For unless this be proved, the evidence that Christ is the promised seed, would be wanting. "For to Abraham and his seed were the promises made. He saith not to seeds as of many, but as of one, and to thy seed which is Christ. Compare Galatians 3:16 with Genesis 12:3 and Genesis 22:18. Hence, therefore, the importance of this pedigree is evident. And the correctness of the one here given, is striking … Perhaps it were a thing impossible in any other instance, but in the genealogy of Christ, to find among all the pedigrees of the Jews, from the days of our Lord to this hour, a correct genealogy of any one house, or tribe, or family, even for fourteen generations together. Whereas in this of Christ, we have three times fourteen. What can more decidedly manifest the overruling providence and watchfulness of God!

This genealogical record is important because it is an irrefutable proof that Jesus of Nazareth is indeed the Christ of God, the Son of David, the promised Seed of Abraham. The Jews, from the very beginning of their history, kept precise genealogical records. The scribes and Pharisees studied those records with great care. They constantly raised questions about "endless genealogies" (1 Timothy 1:4). If they could have disproved his genealogy, that alone would have been sufficient ground for their rejection of Jesus as the Christ; but they could not do it. Though the Jews argued about many things and constantly accused the Lord Jesus of horribly evil deeds, they never once brought up his ancestry. In fact, to this day, though religious heretics abound who try to undermine our faith in Christ, I know of none who have ever attempted to discredit his genealogy. The reason should be obvious to anyone. It is flawless! Though Luke's record of the genealogy gives additional details and omits others, there is not a single point of disagreement between the two.

God's Faithfulness To His Word

Second, in this long list of names we are made to see that God is faithful to his Word. He always keeps his Word. He promised long ago that all the nations of the earth would be blessed in the Seed of Abraham (Genesis 12:3); and Jesus Christ is Abraham's Seed in whom all nations are blessed (Matthew 1:1; Galatians 3:13-16). God promised that he would raise up One out of the family of David to be the Saviour of his people (Isaiah 11:1); and Jesus Christ is David's great Son and his Lord (Matthew 1:1; Acts 2:25-36).

These seventeen verses are a demonstration of the fact that God always keeps his Word. Let every thoughtless scoffer remember this and tremble! Though men imagine that because God does not immediately punish sin he will never punish sin, it is not so. The righteous Lord, because he loves righteousness, will destroy the wicked with his everlasting wrath (Psalm 7:11; 11:5-7). Let every believer remember this and be comforted! Our heavenly Father will be true to all his promises. "He is not a man, that he should lie" (Numbers 23:19). "He abideth faithful: he cannot deny himself" (2 Timothy 2:13). "God, who cannot lie" (Titus 1:2), has made some promises to his people; and all his promises in Christ Jesus are yea and amen (2 Corinthians 1:20). He has promised saving grace to all who believe on the Lord Jesus Christ (Acts 16:31), sufficient grace to his tried saints (2 Corinthians 12:9), sustaining grace to those who are tempted (1 Corinthians 10:13), strengthening grace to those who are weak (Isaiah 41:10), restoring grace to those who are fallen (Psalm 37:24; Proverbs 24:16), dying grace at the time appointed (Exodus 15:16; Hebrews 2:15), and crowning grace to all who enter into heaven's glory (2 Timothy 1:12; James 1:12). And what he has promised he will perform (2 Corinthians 1:20).

The Sinfulness And Corruption Of Man

Third, our Saviour's genealogy is one of many almost incidental revelations of the universal depravity of our race. It is humbling, but instructive for us to observe how many in this list of names were godly parents who had wicked and ungodly sons. Roboam, Joram, Amon, and Jechonias were all terribly wicked men, though they had believing, godly fathers. Two lessons are obvious.

Grace does not run in blood lines (John 1:13). Salvation is not inherited. There are some families in which several are the objects of grace, many families in which none are the objects of grace, and very few families in which all are the objects of grace. But in all cases salvation comes to chosen sinners according to God's sovereign prerogative (Romans 9:11-24).

Fathers are responsible to train their children in the nurture and admonition of the Lord; but they are not responsible for the salvation of their children, or even for their behaviour beyond childhood. David was a good father. He loved his children and trained them in the fear of God. However, for the most part, his children did not heed his instruction. David was not required for that reason to relinquish his calling, either as the king of Israel or as the prophet of God.

The simple fact is it takes more than a good example, good instruction, and faithful training to save our sons and daughters. It takes the grace of God (Ephesians 2:8, 9). It takes the Father's sovereign election (2 Thessalonians 2:13), the Son's blood atonement (Hebrews 9:22), and the Holy Spirit's effectual call (Psalm 65:4).

Christ's Great Compassion

Fourth, we see here something of the great mercy, grace, compassion, and condescension of our Lord Jesus Christ. This is the genealogy of the humanity of the Lord Jesus Christ, of the people from whom our Lord descended according to the flesh. Wonder of wonders, the eternal Son of God, the infinite, the almighty, the incomprehensible God assumed our nature! God took humanity into union with himself and identified himself with the sinners he came to save! Some of the names in this genealogy remind us of some of the saddest, most shameful events in history. Some of those here named are mentioned nowhere else in the Bible. But the last name in the list is the name of our Saviour, Christ. So that he might save fallen men, the Son of God became a man (Philippians 2:6-8; 2 Corinthians 8:9). "Thanks be unto God for his unspeakable gift" (2 Corinthians 9:15).

It is worthy of observation that in the genealogy of Christ four of the five women mentioned were women with a reputation or a blemish that most would like to hide from their family tree. Our Saviour chose to be numbered with transgressors, even in his genealogy. Tamar was guilty of incest. Rahab was a harlot. Ruth was a Moabitess, a child of a cursed race. Bathsheba was the adulterous wife of Uriah.

We know that the Lord Jesus was made "sin for us, who knew no sin" (2 Corinthians 5:21). He who was made in the likeness of sinful flesh (Romans 8:3) was also made "a curse for us" (Galatians 3:13). But here, as the New Testament opens, the Spirit of God tells us that our holy Saviour came into this world through such channels of sin and uncleanness as none could ever have imagined. He who was "holy, harmless, undefiled and separate from sinners" and "made higher than the heavens" (Hebrews 7:26) came into the world through a family of sinners. What humiliation! Truly, he of whom this genealogy speaks is the Friend of sinners! He came into the world to save sinners!

Notice this, too. Two of the women named in our Lord's earthly lineage were Gentiles. Ruth was from Moab and Rahab was from Jericho. Yet, they were as much a part of our Saviour's family as Abraham and David. Surely, this is intended to show that it was ever the purpose of God that the Israel of God, his holy nation, the church of Christ was to be made up of Jew and Gentile (Isaiah 49:6; Galatians 3:28).

Divine Sovereignty

The fifth thing we see in this record is the great sovereignty of God's saving grace in Christ. No one can read this genealogical record and fail to see God's sovereignty, unless he just does not want to see it. Most families and nations were passed over; but Abraham was chosen. Isaac was chosen, but not Abraham's other son, Ishmael. Jacob was chosen, but not Esau. Among all the families of Israel, the house of Jesse was chosen. From among all Jesse's sons, David was chosen. Even Manasses is named in the line of those who were chosen of God and called. Therefore, it must be concluded that no human being is beyond the reach of Christ's saving arm or sympathetic heart. Our sins may have been as many and as vile as any who are here named; but they shall never be remembered against us by God if we trust him who is the Christ, the Son of the living God.

Chapter 2

"The Birth Of Jesus Christ"

"Now the birth of Jesus Christ was on this wise: When as his mother Mary was espoused to Joseph, before they came together, she was found with child of the Holy Ghost. Then Joseph her husband, being a just man, and not willing to make her a public example, was minded to put her away privily. But while he thought on these things, behold, the angel of the Lord appeared unto him in a dream, saying, Joseph, thou son of David, fear not to take unto thee Mary thy wife: for that which is conceived in her is of the Holy Ghost. And she shall bring forth a son, and thou shalt call his name JESUS: for he shall save his people from their sins. Now all this was done, that it might be fulfilled which was spoken of the Lord by the prophet, saying, Behold, a virgin shall be with child, and shall bring forth a son, and they shall call his name Emmanuel, which being interpreted is, God with us. Then Joseph being raised from sleep did as the angel of the Lord had bidden him, and took unto him his wife: And knew her not till she had brought forth her firstborn son: and he called his name JESUS."
(Matthew 1:18-25)

The subject of this passage is "the birth of Jesus Christ", the Messiah, the King, our Saviour. In these verses Matthew, being inspired by the Holy Spirit, declares the deepest, most profound truths of sacred theology in simple, unmistakable terms. He tells us that Jesus Christ; the man who was born at Bethlehem, reared in Nazareth, and crucified at Calvary two thousand years ago is God. He tells us that this One who is God assumed our nature and became a man in a most remarkable way, by a miraculous, supernatural birth. His mother was a virgin!

These are holy, mysterious things, noble objects of holy, reverent faith and adoration. They are things that can be defiled only by speculative curiosity. Those who deny either the deity of Jesus Christ or his miraculous virgin birth do not know God and cannot be persuaded by human reason to believe that which they will not receive as a matter of divine revelation. Consequently, nothing can be gained by the feeble, though well intended, efforts of men to prove these glorious and essential truths of holy scripture.

We believe that which is recorded here. We adore it. We rejoice in it. We proclaim it. And we sing about it. But, we will not try to prove it. No man knows the way of the Spirit in the formation of any ordinary human being in the womb (Ecclesiastes 11:5). How then can we expect to understand and explain the virgin birth of Jesus Christ? It is enough for the believing heart to know that nothing is impossible with our God. It is enough for us to simply be informed that we may admire the wonderful works of our God. Like Moses of old, as he stood before the burning bush, when we read Matthew 1:18-25, we have entered upon holy ground. Let us put off the shoes of carnal curiosity and seek to hear what God the Lord will say.

Here the Holy Spirit tells us how Christ came into this world and why: He came by divine incarnation through the womb of the virgin Mary, to save his people from their sins. Every word in these verses needs to be carefully studied. Each line is worthy of diligent, prayerful study.

Mary's Pregnancy
"Now the birth of Jesus Christ was on this wise: When as his mother Mary was espoused to Joseph, before they came together, she was found with child of the Holy Ghost" (v. 18). God the Holy Spirit prepared in the womb of the virgin Mary a body for the Son of God (Hebrews 10:5). His human nature was conceived in the womb of the chosen virgin by the Holy Spirit, without the aid of a man (Luke 1:35). There was no other way for the Christ to come into this world. He must be born of a virgin, conceived by the Holy Spirit. Had he been conceived by the seed of a fallen, sinful father, he could not have been a sinless substitute of sinners. C. H. Spurgeon comments, "He was born of a woman that he might be human; but not by man, that he might not be sinful."

Our Lord Jesus was born of a virgin that he might be brought into this world as one "made of a woman" (Galatians 4:4), but of an espoused, or lawfully betrothed virgin, so that he might both show the sanctity of marriage and protect the honour of his mother's name. "Marriage is honourable in all and the bed undefiled" (Hebrews 13:4). Only those whose doctrine is the doctrine of devils prohibit men from marriage (1 Timothy 4:1-4). At the same time, he took care to protect Mary's name. Though he was born of a virgin, she was a married virgin. Mary's Son was also her Saviour and he took care to protect her reputation, justifying her pregnancy in the eyes of the world. Matthew Henry suggests that three lessons are to be drawn from this verse.

First, those in whom Christ is formed will show it; and it will be found to be a work of God, which he will own (Colossians 1:27; Ephesians 2:8-10). Second, after great and high advancements, lest we be puffed up with them, we must expect something or other to humble us, some reproach, as a thorn in the flesh. Third, those who take care to keep a good conscience may cheerfully trust God with the keeping of their good names, and have reason to hope that he will clear up, not only their integrity, but their honour, as the sun at noon day. You can imagine what a problem Mary's pregnancy presented to Joseph. Here he was engaged to a woman who showed up pregnant; and he knew with certainty that he was not the father of her child. What will he do?

Joseph's Behaviour

"Then Joseph her husband, being a just man, and not willing to make her a public example, was minded to put her away privily" (v. 19). Joseph's behaviour exemplifies godliness, wisdom, and compassion. He saw in Mary what appeared to be a horribly evil thing. But he did not behave rashly. He patiently weighed his options as a man who sought to glorify God and do his will in all things. According to the law he could do any of three things: 1. He could privately give her a bill of divorcement before two or three witnesses (Deuteronomy 24:1). 2. He could make a public example of her and have her stoned to death (Deuteronomy 22:23, 24). 3. He could go ahead with his plans and marry her. No doubt, Joseph weighed the matter carefully with much prayer before the Lord. "Being a just man", a man who sought always to do what was right, Joseph chose not to expose what he thought to be sin in his espoused wife. Though he felt he could not marry her, he chose to put her away quietly.

C. H. Spurgeon wrote, "When we have to do a severe thing, let us choose the tenderest manner. Maybe we shall not have to do it at all." What an example Joseph is to us in his behaviour. Having been forgiven, he was willing to forgive. Having reason to suspect the worst of Mary, his love for her compelled him to cover and refuse to expose what he thought to be sin in her. As Shem and Japheth covered their father's sin, Joseph was determined to cover that which he thought was Mary's sin. May God give us grace to behave like Joseph in our dealings with others, especially in our dealings with his people. In all things be as lenient as possible with others. Always be ready to forgive the faults of others (Matthew 6:14), and seek what is best for the fallen, erring brother or sister. No matter the fault, seek restoration, not retribution (Galatians 6:1). In all things show love and grace, not judgment and condemnation.

The Angel's Message

"But while he thought on these things, behold, the angel of the Lord appeared unto him in a dream, saying, Joseph, thou son of David, fear not to take unto thee Mary thy wife: for that which is conceived in her is of the Holy Ghost. And she shall bring forth a son, and thou shalt call his name JESUS: for he shall save his people from their sins" (vv. 20, 21). Joseph's patience was abundantly rewarded. He sought God's will and found it. He sought divine direction and he received it. The angel of the Lord appeared to Joseph and gave him a message directly from God regarding the thing that troubled him. Blessed are they who wait on the Lord, who cast their cares upon him in the prayer of faith, and wait for him to direct their paths (Proverbs 3:5, 6). God sent his angel to speak to his servant in a dream. The angel of the Lord assured Joseph that Mary had not sinned, but had been highly favoured of God and reminded him of his royal descent as a "son of David".

What comfort the angel's words must have brought to Joseph. The Lord's "fear not" was a matter of great relief to him. He was a man appointed by God to be the foster-father of the Son of God who, as the Son of Man, would come into this world through the womb of Mary. Thus, it became his privilege and honour, as well as his duty, to take Mary into his home and lovingly care for her.

No doubt, Mary had great apprehensions. Would her story of the angelic visitation be believed? It certainly seemed improbable. No doubt, her faith sustained her. But she had a great trial for her faith. How relieved she must have been when Joseph told her of the angel's message to him.

JESUS

More importantly, the angel's message to Joseph was a message of grace, redemption, and salvation to sinners. The Lord of glory came into this world as the Son of Man. As the Son of God he was not born but given. As the Son of Man he was born through the womb of a chosen virgin (Isaiah 9:6). By God's command he was named, "JESUS", the Saviour, because he was sent of God to save his people from their sins. What he is called, that he is, our Saviour[1].

---

[1] Jesus is the Greek form of the Hebrew Yeshua (Joshua) which means Jehovah is Salvation, or the Lord of Salvation. It is a compound of Y'hovah, God's name, and shuá meaning salvation, deliverance, victory, help.

“The Birth Of Jesus Christ”

The Lord Jesus came into the world to save “his people” from their sins. Those he came to save were his people before he came to save them, his by eternal election. There are some people in this world, an elect multitude, chosen in him before the world began, who are peculiarly and distinctively his people, chosen in him unto salvation (Ephesians 1:2-6; 2 Thessalonians 2:13) and given to him as sheep to the shepherd (John 6:39).

It is the office, work, and responsibility of Christ, the Son of God, as the God-man our Mediator, as the Surety of his people, and as Jehovah’s righteous Servant to save all who were given to him in the covenant of grace (John 10:16-18). And save them he shall. The Lord Jesus Christ is an almighty, effectual Saviour. The angel said to Joseph, “He shall save his people from their sins”! He saves his people from the penalty of their sins by his blood atonement (Romans 3:24-26), from the dominion of their sins by his regenerating Spirit (John 3:5-8; Romans 6:18), from the being of their sins when he takes them out of this world (John 14:1-3; Romans 7:25), and from all the evil consequences of their sins in resurrection glory (1 Corinthians 15:51-56). It is written of him, “He shall not fail” (Isaiah 42:4), “He shall save his people from their sins”!

“Jesus” is our Saviour’s Mediatorial name. It is the same as Joshua in the Old Testament. Jesus is our Saviour, our Redeemer, our Deliverer, our Salvation. “Neither is there salvation in any other: for there is none other name under heaven given among men, whereby we must be saved” (Acts 4:12).

“Jesus” is the name of encouragement and hope for guilty, heavy-laden sinners. Sinners may draw near and come to God, with confident hope of finding mercy, grace, and forgiveness through faith in Jesus Christ (John 3:16, 17). It is the name of him who is peculiarly sweet and precious to believers (1 Peter 2:7). “Thy name is as ointment poured forth” (Song of Solomon 1:3). We breathe our Saviour’s name in prayer, trusting his blood, his righteousness, his grace, his power, and his intercession. Trusting him we have peace with God. Calling on his name we are saved, justified, forgiven of all sin, and forever accepted with God. John Newton wrote:

How sweet the name of Jesus sounds in a believer’s ear!
It soothes his sorrows, heals his wounds, and drives away his fear!

Prophecy Fulfilled

“Now all this was done, that it might be fulfilled which was spoken of the Lord by the prophet, saying, Behold, a virgin shall be with child, and shall bring forth a son, and they shall call his name Emmanuel, which being interpreted is, God with us" (vv. 22, 23). Who would ever have imagined that the prophecy found in Isaiah 7:14 had reference to the Lord Jesus Christ? We are so spiritually dull in this body of flesh that, before we are capable of understanding prophecy, we must see it fulfilled. When we know even as we are known, we will see how that all the scriptures speak of him whose name is Emmanuel (Luke 24:27, 44).

This name, "Emmanuel", is only found three times in the Word of God (Isaiah 7:14; 8:8; and Matthew 1:23). But it is a name full of instruction and comfort to believing hearts. Emmanuel is God with us. Emmanuel declares the union of two natures in the Person of our Saviour. He is both God and man in one glorious Person, as perfectly God as though he were not man, and as completely man as though he were not God. We must never lose sight of this great, foundation truth of the gospel. Jesus Christ is a man, just like us, only without sin. Yet, he "is over all, God blessed forever" (Romans 9:5), "God manifest in the flesh" (1 Timothy 3:16). He must be both God and man, or he could not be our Saviour.

Someone said, "God could not suffer, and man could not satisfy; but the God-man both suffered and satisfied". Our Saviour is a man. Therefore he is sympathetic with us. But he is not at all limited by his humanity. "In him dwelleth all the fulness of the Godhead bodily" (Colossians 2:9). Therefore he is able to save all who trust him.

Joseph's Obedience

"Then Joseph being raised from sleep did as the angel of the Lord had bidden him, and took unto him his wife: And knew her not till she had brought forth her firstborn son: and he called his name JESUS" (vv. 24, 25). Having received instruction from the Lord, Joseph was immediately obedient. He took Mary into his home as his wife, but refrained himself from all the privileges of their conjugal relationship until after "she had brought forth her firstborn son: and he called his name JESUS". Thus the Son of God came into this world and became one of us, that he might be our Saviour. "The word was made flesh and dwelt among us" (John 1:14). He became obedient unto death, even the death of the cross, that he might redeem us. Now, he has ascended up to heaven again and is seated upon the throne of grace that he might "save his people from their sins". "Thanks be unto God for his unspeakable gift"

Chapter 3

Lessons From The Saviour's Birth

"Now when Jesus was born in Bethlehem of Judaea in the days of Herod the king, behold, there came wise men from the east to Jerusalem, Saying, Where is he that is born King of the Jews? for we have seen his star in the east, and are come to worship him. When Herod the king had heard these things, he was troubled, and all Jerusalem with him. And when he had gathered all the chief priests and scribes of the people together, he demanded of them where Christ should be born. And they said unto him, In Bethlehem of Judaea: for thus it is written by the prophet, And thou Bethlehem, in the land of Juda, art not the least among the princes of Juda: for out of thee shall come a Governor, that shall rule my people Israel. Then Herod, when he had privily called the wise men, inquired of them diligently what time the star appeared. And he sent them to Bethlehem, and said, Go and search diligently for the young child; and when ye have found him, bring me word again, that I may come and worship him also. When they had heard the king, they departed; and, lo, the star, which they saw in the east, went before them, till it came and stood over where the young child was. When they saw the star, they rejoiced with exceeding great joy. And when they were come into the house, they saw the young child with Mary his mother, and fell down, and worshipped him: and when they had opened their treasures, they presented unto him gifts; gold, and frankincense, and myrrh. And being warned of God in a dream that they should not return to Herod, they departed into their own country another way."
(Matthew 2:1-12)

The first to take notice of and come to Christ after his birth were the shepherds, who heard of him by the angel of the Lord (Luke 2:8-20). After that, Simeon and Anna saw him in the temple and spoke of him by the Spirit of God, telling all who would hear who he is and what he had come to accomplish (Luke 2:21-40). Then, for nearly two whole years, no one else took notice of the fact that God had come into the world in human flesh! Apparently no one in Jerusalem, Bethlehem, or all of Judea believed the messages Simeon and Anna had declared or the word of Joseph and Mary concerning the Christ of God. Then, about two years after the birth of our Saviour, "wise men came from the east to Jerusalem, saying, where is he that is born King of the Jews?" Let us carefully observe the spiritual lessons conveyed to us in this inspired record of the visit of the wise men who came to Jerusalem seeking Christ. The history of these wise men and their visit to our Saviour, like everything else in holy scripture, is recorded for our learning and our comfort and hope as we seek to glorify our God in this world (Romans 15:4).

An Inspired Book

The first thing that strikes me as I read Matthew 2 is the fact that the Book, the Word of God, must be as it claims an inspired Book, a Book written by the very finger of God. This one chapter is Matthew's complete account of our Saviour's infancy. Mark and John tell us nothing, and Luke tells us very little about it.

Why do Matthew, Mark, Luke, and John tell us so little about our Saviour's infancy and childhood? Surely, this lack of information places a stamp of inspiration upon their writings. What they wrote was not their word, but God's. Had they written only as men giving the record of a man highly esteemed by them, there would have been much more recorded about the Saviour's earliest years. What biographer has ever failed to do so, when those who could supply the information were at hand?

If the Gospel writers did not write "as they were moved by the Holy Ghost" (2 Peter 1:21), they could not have restrained themselves from giving us greater details about the holy childhood of the "holy child Jesus". The ancient Jews placed great importance upon childhood. They had eight different words to mark its various stages of development, ranging from conception to adulthood. For Matthew, who was a Jew and wrote specifically to identify Christ to his own countrymen, to omit everything about our Saviour's infancy and childhood, except what we have in these twenty-three verses, is remarkable. His silence cannot be explained by anything except the fact that he wrote this Gospel narrative by divine inspiration.

Lest any should think I am making a fanciful stretch to demonstrate an evidence of the fact that the Word of God is just that *The Word Of God*, inspired and inerrant, it should be noted that those things which have been written about Jesus of Nazareth by other men confirmed it. Such writings (ancient and modern) are filled with speculations about his childhood. Matthew, Mark, and Luke, writing by divine inspiration, tell only enough to demonstrate that this man is the Christ promised and prophesied of in the Old Testament scriptures.

Prophecy Fulfilled

Second, let us realize that every Old Testament prophecy concerning the advent of the Messiah has been fulfilled by the Lord Jesus Christ, in every detail. Let anyone honestly study the Old Testament scriptures in which the person, advent, and accomplishments of the Messiah are foretold and then study the person and work of Jesus of Nazareth, and he will be forced to acknowledge this fact: Jesus of Nazareth is the Christ of whom Moses and the prophets spoke (John 1:45).

The Old Testament tailors a garment that will fit only one man. Find that man and you will have found the Christ of God, the Messiah. In this passage only one thing is mentioned in this regard. But this fact of fulfilled prophecy is sufficient to demonstrate the point. According to the Old Testament, Messiah must be born in Bethlehem of Judea prior to the destruction of the Temple at Jerusalem "But thou, Bethlehem Ephratah, though thou be little among the thousands of Judah, yet out of thee shall he come forth unto me that is to be ruler in Israel; whose goings forth have been from of old, from everlasting" (Micah 5:2).

The Jews fully expected the Messiah to be born at Bethlehem (Matthew 2:4-6; John 7:41, 42). However, Joseph and Mary were not residents of Bethlehem at the time she conceived or at the time she gave birth to the Lord Jesus. They were living in Galilee, in the city of Nazareth at the time (Luke 2:4). Yet, the scripture must be fulfilled. Messiah must be born at Bethlehem. So God, who directs the thoughts of the king's heart (Proverbs 21:1), moved Caesar Augustus to make a decree requiring that every man return to his hometown to pay his taxes (Luke 2:1-4). To my knowledge no such decree had ever been made before and none after. It was an absurd thing to do. But the scriptures must be fulfilled. Thus, while Joseph and Mary were in Bethlehem to pay taxes, the Lord Jesus, the Messiah, was born (Matthew 2:1; Luke 2:4-7).

John Gill writes, "Bethlehem signifies the house of bread, and in it was born, as an ancient writer observes, the Bread which comes down from heaven: and it may also signify the house of flesh, and to it the allusion may be in 2 Timothy 3:16, 'God was manifest in the flesh'". In the light of this one fact, only one who is a wilfully blind and wilfully ignorant fool would deny that Jesus of Nazareth is indeed the Christ of God, the Saviour of the world.

God's Hidden Ones

Third, we see here that our Saviour has many "hidden ones" (Psalm 83:3) in the earth. We sometimes foolishly imagine that we know all that God is doing in the world and that we either know or know about all his people in the world. But nothing could be more absurd and further from the truth.

Holy Spirit tells us of wise men who came from the east to worship the Son of God. We know no more about their lives than we do of Melchizedek, Jethro, or Job. But they were the servants of God. So it is today. Our God has a people scattered throughout the earth who are altogether unknown to us; but their names are in the book of life. We need to remind ourselves of this fact. We sometimes think the earth is barren because our own gardens are fruitless, but it is not so. The grace of God is not limited to certain races, tied to certain places, or restricted to certain families (Revelation 5:9). Certainly, God has an appointed means of grace by which he saves his elect (Romans 10:17; 1 Corinthians 1:23; 1 Peter 1:23-25). But he does not always act openly and obviously. He sometimes hides the means he uses and only shows us the result of his work.

Sinners, like these wise men, are sometimes born of God in the dark places of the earth and made wise unto salvation. No doubt there are some travelling to heaven now of whom the church and the world know nothing. They are the Lord's "hidden ones". They know Christ, and Christ knows them, and nothing else really matters! We must never imagine that God has left himself without a witness anywhere (Romans 11:1-5). We must never attempt to measure the length and breadth of God's kingdom by our own yardstick. And we must never imagine that God is not working because we do not see him work, or that our labour is in vain because we do not see its fruit (1 Corinthians 15:58; Isaiah 55:11).

The Objects Of Grace

Fourth, this passage demonstrates, as the scriptures constantly teach, that the least likely are often the most likely objects of God's saving grace. The word here translated, "wise men", would be better translated, "magi". It is almost always used in a bad sense in the scriptures. It refers to pagan astrologers, soothsayers, sorcerers, magicians, wizards, and fortune-tellers. We are not told who these men were, or where they lived, or how they learned of Christ, only that they were from the east. Perhaps they had learned to expect Christ from the ten tribes who were once carried away into captivity. Maybe some prophet had passed through their land expounding the words of Isaiah, or Daniel, or David. We simply do not know. But, as Matthew Poole wrote, "These were the first fruits of the Gentiles owning Christ as King of the Jews, whilst he came among his own, and they received him not; nor do I know anything more worthy of our observation concerning them."

God often passes by those who have, but neglect, the greatest privileges and opportunities, and saves those who seem to be beyond the reach of mercy (Luke 4:25-27). We would have thought the scribes and Pharisees, those men so learned in the facts of scripture and religion, would have been the first to go down to Bethlehem as soon as the Saviour's birth was rumoured; but it was not so (John 1:11). It is a sad fact, but a fact often confirmed by experience, that the hardest people on earth to reach with the gospel are gospel hardened rebels (2 Corinthians 2:14-16). Those who neglect the privileges and opportunities set before them to hear the gospel and learn of God court reprobation and judgment (Proverbs 1:23-33). God graciously saves those who are esteemed by men to be the least likely candidates for mercy (1 Samuel 16:1-12; 1 Corinthians 1:26-30). He passed by self-righteous Pharisees and self-complacent scribes, and saved some pagan magicians from a far eastern land.

Knowledge Without Grace

Here is a fifth lesson that must not be overlooked. Many have heads full of knowledge whose hearts are altogether void of grace. When King Herod asked the chief priests and scribes where Christ should be born, they answered him immediately, demonstrating an accurate knowledge of the letter of the scriptures (vv. 4-6). They knew where Christ was to be born; but they never went to Bethlehem to seek him! Their heads were full; but their hearts were empty. What a sad condition! The wise intellectual foolishly imagines that if he stores the barn of his brain with knowledge he has won God's salvation, never realizing that "The Lord looketh upon the heart"! Great knowledge is good; but grace is better. Knowledge alone saves no one. It is grace that carries men and women to glory. The Pharisees had knowledge, but no grace. Judas had knowledge, but no grace. Demas had knowledge, but no grace. Diotrephes had knowledge, but no grace. Knowledge, no matter how accurate, that does not reach, and change, and rule the heart with grace is useless, damning knowledge!

Faith And Works

Sixth, we are here reminded that faith in Christ always shows itself by works. "Faith worketh by love" (Galatians 5:6). "Faith without works is dead" (James 2:18). Faith in Christ is more than mental assent to facts, doctrines, and propositions. Faith is a principle of life. These wise men are set before us as striking examples of faith. They believed God's Word without any outward evidence to support it. They trusted Christ, though they had never seen him. They came to him, though the scribes and Pharisees believed him not. They worshipped him as their God, Saviour, and King when he was a baby on Mary's knee! There was no halo over his head. There were no signs or miracles to convince them. They had nothing but the naked Word of God and the inner witness of the Holy Spirit. Yet, when they saw the Christ, they fell down and worshipped him (not Mary, but him) as their Saviour and God (v. 11). We read of no greater faith in all the Bible than this. Blessed are those who thus believe God, who dare to take God at his Word (without evidence) and walk accordingly!

Believing God's Word concerning his Son, these wise men were diligent in seeking him. They had made up their minds that they would go to Jerusalem to see him "that was born king of the Jews"; and never rested until they had seen him. When they came to worship Christ, they brought prepared gifts of worship, praise, and gratitude to him. C. H. Spurgeon wrote, "These choice offerings, especially the gold, would help Joseph and Mary to provide for the Royal Child, who was so soon to be exiled. God brought providers from the far East to supply the needs of his Son. Remember, Omnipotence has servants everywhere. Before the babe starts for Egypt, Oriental sages must pay his charges". All who worship Christ consecrate their substance to him, and worship him with sacrifices of love and gratitude. Such worship requires faith (Proverbs 3:9, 10).

Our Father's Rule

Seventh, we have in this passage a demonstration of that which ought to make our hearts rejoice. Our heavenly Father rules all things in providence to accomplish his purpose of grace (Romans 8:28-30; 11:33-36). He made a star to guide these chosen men to Christ the Saviour. He moved Caesar Augustus to make his decree concerning taxation. He prevented Herod from following these men to Bethlehem. He provided what Joseph and Mary needed to flee to Egypt. He warned these men in a dream not to return to their own country through Jerusalem. As he cared for Joseph and Mary, his servants, and our Saviour who came into the world as his righteous Servant, so God's servants in this world are the objects of his special and unceasing care. All who are his are the apple of his eye. You may safely cast all your care upon him, for "he careth for you"!

These are the lessons the Holy Spirit here teaches us by recording this brief event in the history of these wise men and their Saviour. The Holy Bible is God's inspired Word, cherish it as such. Every Old Testament prophecy concerning the advent of the Messiah has been precisely fulfilled in every detail by our Lord Jesus Christ.

Chapter 4

Satan's First Assault

"And when they were departed, behold, the angel of the Lord appeareth to Joseph in a dream, saying, Arise, and take the young child and his mother, and flee into Egypt, and be thou there until I bring thee word: for Herod will seek the young child to destroy him. When he arose, he took the young child and his mother by night, and departed into Egypt: And was there until the death of Herod: that it might be fulfilled which was spoken of the Lord by the prophet, saying, Out of Egypt have I called my son. Then Herod, when he saw that he was mocked of the wise men, was exceeding wroth, and sent forth, and slew all the children that were in Bethlehem, and in all the coasts thereof, from two years old and under, according to the time which he had diligently inquired of the wise men. Then was fulfilled that which was spoken by Jeremy the prophet, saying, In Rama was there a voice heard, lamentation, and weeping, and great mourning, Rachel weeping for her children, and would not be comforted, because they are not. But when Herod was dead, behold, an angel of the Lord appeareth in a dream to Joseph in Egypt, Saying, Arise, and take the young child and his mother, and go into the land of Israel: for they are dead which sought the young child's life. And he arose, and took the young child and his mother, and came into the land of Israel. But when he heard that Archelaus did reign in Judaea in the room of his father Herod, he was afraid to go thither: notwithstanding, being warned of God in a dream, he turned aside into the parts of Galilee: And he came and dwelt in a city called Nazareth: that it might be fulfilled which was spoken by the prophets, He shall be called a Nazarene."
(Matthew 2:13-23)

From the beginning of time Satan has opposed his Creator. When God made known to his holy angels his intention to save sinful men by the blood and righteousness of Christ and thus to exalt manhood to the place of highest dominion over all creation, so that even the angels would be servants to chosen, redeemed sinners, Lucifer said, "No, I will not be servant to man. I will be like the Most High" And he led one third of the heavenly host in rebellion against

God and against the purpose of God. From the beginning of time Satan has been opposed to Christ and has attempted to nullify the purpose of God. So it shall be until time is no more and the old serpent, the devil, is cast into the lake of fire.

In the passage of scripture now before us the Holy Spirit describes Satan's first assault against the incarnate Christ, his first attempt to destroy the Saviour and keep him from accomplishing the redemption of his people. But there is no cause for alarm or fear. Though Satan goes about the earth as a roaring lion, seeking whom he may devour, all his devices and plans are easily foiled by our omnipotent God. Our God is so infinitely and totally sovereign that he is not only beyond the reach of Satan and able to foil the old serpent's plans; but he even makes Satan's deeds and devices subservient to his own great purpose of grace, as we shall see in this passage.

The Narrative

Matthew's narrative of the historical events here recorded are easily and quickly perceived by the most casual reader. Verses 13-15 describe our Saviour's flight into Egypt. Being commanded by the angel of the Lord to do so, Joseph took the young child and his mother and fled into Egypt to escape the fury of Herod.

In verses 16-18 Matthew describes Herod's slaughter of the infants in the realm of Bethlehem. Many translations and editions of the Bible place a caption above this passage and call it "the slaying of the innocents". But that is not accurate. Though babies are innocent of wilful transgression and have not sinned after the similitude of Adam's transgression, they are far from innocent. All are born in sin and spiritual death (Psalm 51:5; Romans 5:12). Adam's transgression is imputed to all and his nature imparted to all, so that from infancy we are estranged from God (Psalm 58:3) and full of enmity toward God (Romans 8:7).

In his fury and jealousy Herod gave command that every infant in Bethlehem two years old and under be slain. It is almost beyond conception that such an order could be given, much less carried out. Greater, more barbaric cruelty cannot be imagined. Yet, in our day thousands of mothers murder their unborn children in their own wombs, not to protect a crown like Herod, but to avoid the inconvenience of an unwanted child!

Verses 19-23 tell us of our Redeemer's return from Egypt and settlement of his family in Nazareth. After Herod died, the angel of the Lord appeared to Joseph and told him to return with his family from Egypt, which he did and settled in the little town of Nazareth, where our Lord was raised as the carpenter's son.

Those are the historic events covered by these verses. But what do these verses teach us? What lessons do they unfold? What spiritual truths do they illustrate?

The Angels

The very first thing that confronts us in this passage is the ministry of the angels of God. Again and again in these first two chapters we are told, "the angel of the Lord appeared" to Joseph (1:20; 2:13; 2:19). In those days angels of God were frequently used by God to be special messengers of grace. I do not hesitate to avow that God does not speak to men today by angels. He has spoken and speaks to us by his Word. We need no other Word from him (2 Peter 1:19-21).

But that does not at all imply that the angels of God are inactive, or that they no longer serve God's elect. I do not pretend to know a great deal about angels. However, I do know that the angels of God reverently wait at the throne of God to do his will (Isaiah 6:1-4). They encamp round about God's saints to protect them (Psalm 34:7; 2 Kings 6:17). The angels of God are ministering spirits sent forth to minister to those who shall be the heirs of salvation (Hebrews 1:14). They attend the worship of God's saints and the preaching of the gospel with keen interest, hoping to learn from us the wonders of redeeming, saving grace and love (Ephesians 3:10, 11). And the angels rejoice every time a sinner repents of his sin, trusting Christ as his Saviour and Lord (Luke 15:10).

Inspiration

Second, these verses of scripture stand as an irrefutable testimony to the inspiration and divine origin of the Bible. I am fully aware of the fact that many today and throughout history have given vague words of prophecy that might be fulfilled in many different ways. And foolish men and women are certain that these lying dreamers and fortune-tellers are inspired of God. But Bible prophecies are not vague representations of what might be. Prophecy in the Bible gives names and details with such clarity that, when the prophecies have been fulfilled, they stand as irrefutable proofs that the Bible is of divine origin and is divinely inspired, as it claims to be.

Matthew, more than any of the other gospel writers, takes notice of the fulfilling of the Old Testament scriptures by Christ. He does so because his gospel was the first to be published among the Jews, who held the Old Testament alone to be the Word of God. Everything he has told us thus far has been the unfolding of Old Testament prophecy. The birth of Christ at Bethlehem (v. 6) fulfilled Micah 5:2. The flight of Joseph into Egypt with the young child and his mother was necessary for the fulfilment of Numbers 24:8 and Hosea 11:1.

Matthew Henry wrote, "It is no new thing for God's sons to be in Egypt. They may be hid in Egypt, but they shall not be left there." Though often found in the strange land and house of bondage, at the time appointed they are fetched out by almighty grace. All God's elect, being children of wrath by nature, were born in a spiritual Egypt. But in conversion they are called out by effectual power. Even so, as Israel was brought out of Egypt and highly honoured, Christ Jesus was brought out of Egypt that he might be brought up to glory. Thus the scriptures were fulfilled.

The slaughter of the infants by Herod (cf. vv. 17, 18) fulfilled the words of Jeremiah 31:15. The fact that the Lord Jesus was raised in Nazareth as a Nazarene (v. 23) fulfilled the universal consensus of the prophets that he would be despised and rejected of men. "Can any good thing come out of Nazareth?" (John 1:46). Perhaps reference is here made to Isaiah 11:1. The word Branch is Natzar, from which the word Nazareth comes, which means a shoot, or a sprout.

Being the divinely inspired, inerrant Word of God, the Bible alone is our rule of faith and practice (2 Timothy 3:16, 17; Isaiah 8:20). "Thus saith the Lord", is the standard by which all things in the church of God must be judged and determined. Believing men and women bow to the authority of holy scripture in all things. Our doctrine, the ordinances we observe, and the rules of conduct by which we live arise directly from the Book of God. We must neither add to the scriptures by imposing upon God's saints the customs of men's creeds, confessions, and opinions, nor take anything away from the scriptures by refusing anything taught in them.

Enmity Against God

Third, Herod stands before us as an example of the enmity of man's heart against God and his opposition to Christ and his cause. The Lord Jesus came down from heaven to save poor sinners. What could be more noble and beneficial? But as soon as he came into the world Satan had Herod in place and inspired his heart with barbaric cruelty to "seek the young child to destroy him".

Reprobate interpreters of history tell us that Christianity has been the cause of great cruelty and bloodshed. But if they were honest they would say, "It has not been Christianity, but man's opposition to Christianity that has been the cause of great cruelty and bloodshed." Here are three things that we must never forget, or expect to change …

1. The cross of Christ and the gospel of God's free grace in him are an offence and stumbling block to unregenerate men (1 Corinthians 1:21-23; Galatians 5:11). While on earth, our Saviour said, "They hated me without a cause", and nothing has changed. The offence of the cross has not ceased. Men do not object to Christ being a Saviour. The offence of the cross is that the gospel insists that Christ is the only Saviour. Men do not object to Christ being a partial Saviour. The offence of the cross is that the gospel declares that Christ alone is Saviour.

2. The gospel of God, the gospel we believe runs in direct opposition to the religious world in which we live. The gospel of God's free and sovereign grace in Christ is contrary to all the natural religious sentiments of all men. To all men by nature, to all lost, unregenerate men, religious or irreligious, the cross of Christ is an offence. It is not possible to make the gospel palatable to lost men. Every attempt to do so, of necessity, involves compromise. It is not possible to faithfully preach the message of salvation by God's free and sovereign grace through the merits of Christ's sin-atoning death and imputed righteousness without offending those who reject and deny it.

3. The great, powerful, influential men of this world, though they are almost always religious, are the foes, not the friends of righteousness. Josiahs are few. Herods are legion. The cause of Christ does not depend upon and must never seek the power and patronage of political figures and civil government.

It is written, "Put not your trust in princes" (Psalm 146:3). It is common today, as it has been throughout history, for churches and religious leaders to seek approval and authority from political leaders and by civil law. While we are and should be happy to be free from the fear of political persecution, believers ought to quietly submit to civil authority and never seek to promote and build the church and kingdom of God by civil law (Romans 13:1-7). Let those whose god is such a pigmy, that he needs the laws and swords of men to give him power, do what they will, we are to do everything within our power to lead a quiet and peaceable life with all men (1 Timothy 2:1, 2).

Divine Providence

Fourth, in all that is recorded in these verses we are again reminded of the sovereign rule and wondrous mystery of divine providence. Satan wanted the Christ child destroyed. So he moved Herod with the rage of petty jealousy to kill him. But God had other purposes and designs, which he used Herod to accomplish (Psalm 76:10).

Herod's wrath forced Joseph to flee with the young child and his mother into Egypt to fulfil holy scripture. Herod's slaying of the infants in Bethlehem, his hell-inspired, hell-bent slaughter of babies, was the means of God's mercy to those who were slaughtered, the means by which he brought multitudes of elect infants into glory.

Men often accuse those who believe the teaching of holy scripture with regard to election and predestination of teaching that babies go to hell. Such accusations are without foundation. C. H. Spurgeon comments on verses 17 and 18:

> Our Rachels still weep; but holy women who know the Lord Jesus, do not now say concerning their little ones that 'they are not'. They know that their children are, and they know where they are, and they expect to meet them again in glory. Surely, if these women had but known, they might have been comforted by the fact, that though their little ones were slain, The Childrens' Friend has escaped and still lives to be the Saviour of all who die before committing actual transgression.

I will leave it to the theologians to wrangle over their points of logical deduction and theological calculation. I simply tell you what I know. All God's elect are saved and all babies dying as such are elect, chosen in eternal love, redeemed by precious blood, and saved by omnipotent, free grace. I cannot help thinking, "How good it was of our God to keep these maliciously slaughtered children from ever experiencing personal sin". Robert Hawker's comments on this passage are excellent.

> In relation to the infants themselves; they were only removed from the evil to come. Had they lived to old age, they would have lived to have seen the siege and destruction of Jerusalem, which the Lord Jesus so mournfully foretold, when they would have said, "blessed are the barren and the wombs that never bare, and the paps which never gave suck". If those sweet babes who died for Christ died also in Christ; were they not such as John heard a voice from heaven concerning, saying, "blessed are the dead which die in the Lord" (Revelation 14:13)? And is it not said, "precious in the sight of the Lord is the death of his saints" (Psalm 116:15)? And may we not

> without violence to the words suppose, that these little ones of Christ's fold, were among that holy army John saw on Mount Zion, when he said, "I looked, and lo, a Lamb stood on the Mount Zion, and with him an hundred and forty and four thousand, having his Father's name written in their forehead (Revelation 14:1-5)?

I do not mean to suggest that infants are not sinners. They are. We are all born in sin. As the sons and daughters of Adam, we all have his nature. But the scriptures speak of small children as those who have not sinned "after the similitude of Adam's transgression" (Romans 5:14). I certainly do not want you to think, as ignorant people often do, that the Lord took those children to make them angels! No! He took them to give them all the fulness of grace and glory with Christ, beloved of God, chosen by grace, redeemed by his precious blood, and born again by the power of his Spirit.

Three Reasons

Let me give you three reasons why I am confident that those children dying in infancy are saved by God's grace. I mean by that that they are chosen, redeemed, sanctified, justified, and born of God.

1. Our God is good (Exodus 34:5, 6).
2. No child will ever go to hell and suffer the wrath of God because of the sins of its fathers. God does not send people to hell because of Adam's transgressions, but because of their own (Ezekiel 18:20, Revelation 20:12, 13).
3. The only example we have in scripture of a child's death, with comment concerning its state after death, is that of David's son. David's words concerning his son assure us that he was completely confident the child went to glory when he died (2 Samuel 12:23).

Obedient Faith

Fifth, Joseph here stands before us as an example of the obedience of faith. When the angel of the Lord said to Joseph, "Arise, take the young child and his mother, and flee into Egypt", he did not pause to pack his bags, go on deputation to raise support, or solicit funds to make it possible for him to do what God commanded. He simply took his family to Egypt. When the angel of the Lord told him to return to the land of Israel, he returned. Matthew Poole wrote, "True faith always produceth obedience to the precept of it ... They indeed believe not the scriptures to be the Word of God, who take no care to live up to the rule of life prescribed in them." "Whatsoever he saith unto you, do it" (John 2:5), conferring "not with flesh and blood" (Galatians 1:15, 16). The only thing that causes disobedience is unbelief. Precisely to the degree that we believe God we obey him.

Christ's Humiliation

Sixth, this passage shows us a great example of the humiliation of our Lord Jesus Christ as our Mediator. When the Son of God lived on this earth he spent 30 of his 33 years in Nazareth, a small, obscure, despised town in Galilee. No one lived in Nazareth except those who could not afford to live anywhere else. This is where the Son of God chose to reside. Let us learn from his example.

We must never seek great things for ourselves (Jeremiah 45:5). It is not nearly as important as people imagine it is to have property, position, power, praise, and money. It is a very great sin to be covetous and proud. But it is no sin to be poor. As J. C. Ryle put it, "It matters not so much what money we have, and where we live, as what we are in the sight of God. Where are we going when we die? Shall we live forever in heaven? These are the main things which we should attend."

The fact is great wealth is a great danger to any man's soul. Those who seek the riches of this world know not what they seek. They are likely to fill our hearts with pride and chain our affections to this world. Our Master said, "It is easier for a camel to go through the eye of a needle than for a rich man to enter into the kingdom of God", "How hardy shall they that have riches enter into the kingdom of God" (Matthew 19:24, Luke 18:24). Seek not riches, but righteousness. Seek not money, but mercy. Seek not greatness, but grace.

Death

Seventh, we see in this passage that death is a great leveller. "Herod was dead"! Death enters the palace of kings just as it does the dens of paupers. None can resist its power. The murderer of helpless infants was himself helpless before the Lord God when the hour of his departure from this world had come. At the hour appointed, we too shall die. After death, we shall stand before God in judgment. After judgment we shall spend eternity somewhere, either in heaven, or in hell. Where will you spend eternity? Are you prepared to meet God? Am I? The only way to be accepted with the Holy Lord God is to be washed in Christ's precious blood and robed in his perfect righteousness. For that, we must trust him. May God the Holy Spirit give us grace to "Believe on the Lord Jesus Christ".

Chapter 5

John the Baptist: A Faithful Preacher

"In those days came John the Baptist, preaching in the wilderness of Judaea, And saying, Repent ye: for the kingdom of heaven is at hand. For this is he that was spoken of by the prophet Esaias, saying, The voice of one crying in the wilderness, Prepare ye the way of the Lord, make his paths straight. And the same John had his raiment of camel's hair, and a leathern girdle about his loins; and his meat was locusts and wild honey. Then went out to him Jerusalem, and all Judaea, and all the region round about Jordan, And were baptized of him in Jordan, confessing their sins. But when he saw many of the Pharisees and Sadducees come to his baptism, he said unto them, O generation of vipers, who hath warned you to flee from the wrath to come? Bring forth therefore fruits meet for repentance: And think not to say within yourselves, We have Abraham to our father: for I say unto you, that God is able of these stones to raise up children unto Abraham. And now also the axe is laid unto the root of the trees: therefore every tree which bringeth not forth good fruit is hewn down, and cast into the fire. I indeed baptize you with water unto repentance: but he that cometh after me is mightier than I, whose shoes I am not worthy to bear: he shall baptize you with the Holy Ghost, and with fire: Whose fan is in his hand, and he will thoroughly purge his floor, and gather his wheat into the garner; but he will burn up the chaff with unquenchable fire".
(Matthew 3:1-12)

Here the Holy Spirit gives us a description of John the Baptist, the forerunner of our Lord Jesus Christ, and his ministry. It is a ministry that deserves careful study. John was a faithful servant of God, a preacher worthy of imitation by all who would be faithful preachers of the gospel. He is a standard by which all who are called and ordained to this holy office must be measured. The Lord Jesus called him "a burning and shining light" (John 5:35) and said, "among them that are born of women there hath not risen a greater than John the Baptist" (Matthew 11:11).

The Time
Matthew describes the time of John's ministry as being "in those days". About 28 years had passed from the close of Matthew 2 to the opening of Matthew 3. "Those days" were the time appointed by God for the beginning of this gospel age and its ministry. The prophet Daniel speaks of a time when Messiah the Prince would confirm the covenant with many (Daniel 9:27). "Those days" were the beginning of the latter half of Daniel's seventieth week.

The Place
The place where John preached was "in the wilderness". John was an open-air preacher because the organized religion of his day would have nothing to do with him and he would have nothing to do with it. In times of apostasy and judgment, such as had now seized Israel, God's prophets are always found outside the mainstream of religion, "in the wilderness", so to speak. This world is a dark, barren wilderness spiritually. So, too, are the hearts of men, desolate, empty, and void.

The Voice
John is described as "The voice of one crying in the wilderness". And that is how he described himself (John 1:23). Christ is "the Word of God" (John 1:1), the Revelation of the Triune God (John 1:18). A gospel preacher is simply a voice conveying the Word of God, a voice echoing the message God has given. "And what is a voice?" asked Robert Hawker. "It is a nonentity, a mere sound, light as air, and so short in its being and existence, if it can be called by such a name, that when it hath performed its office, it dies away in the air, is dissolved, and is known no more. Such said John am I, when considered in any comparative view with my Lord and Master."

Yet, the voice is not indifferent. He is found "crying in the wilderness", arousing and awaking sinners with the claims of God. His garments were plain and simple. His diet was plain and simple. His companions were simple wilderness people (v. 4). Like John, God's servants are ordinary men. They are not pampered, self-serving men of luxury and ease.

The Purpose
The purpose of John's life and ministry was to "prepare the way of the Lord". That is what preachers are sent to do, to prepare the way for Christ to come to men. John was Elijah (Malachi 3:1; Isaiah 40:3). In a sense all gospel preachers,

like him, are forerunners of Christ. Blessed are those people to whom God sends a faithful preacher. That is an indication that he intends to send his Son on a mission of mercy!

John's Success

The success of John's ministry was phenomenal (v. 5). Very few preachers in history, that is very few faithful preachers have been so widely received and heard as the messengers of God. It had been 350 years since the last prophet of God (Malachi) had spoken on the earth. When John came, the multitudes thronged to hear him. Truly, in all things John the Baptist was a remarkable servant of God. As such, he is held before us by Matthew, Mark, Luke, and John. He is here set before us as an example of what every preacher should be and what every preacher who is sent from God preaches.

John's Message

What did John preach? What were the leading themes of his ministry? What subjects did he dwell upon and expound most constantly? With what message did he prepare the way of the Lord? John the Baptist spoke plainly about sin and repentance (v. 2).

No man is faithful to your soul or faithful to God who does not expose your sin and proclaim to you the necessity of repentance toward God and faith in the Lord Jesus Christ. Because we are all sinners, except we repent we must all perish. We are all sinners by divine imputation (Romans 5:12). We are all sinners by birth and nature (Psalm 51:5). We are all sinners by choice and practice (Psalm 58:3; Romans 3:9-19). We are all sinners at heart (Jeremiah 17:9; Matthew 15:19). We are all so thoroughly sinful that even our righteousness must be repented of (Isaiah 64:6). John the Baptist was a preacher of repentance who faithfully exposed and reproved the sins of his hearers.

Repentance

John was not a silver tongued orator, or a refined pulpiteer, or a man-pleaser. John the Baptist was a prophet, the voice of God crying to men (v. 7). He plainly declared the necessity of repentance, warning religious men not to rest in their religious privileges and services. He was no less faithful in preaching to the great and mighty than to the meek and lowly (Luke 3:10-14, 18-20).

It is commonly thought that everyone understands what repentance is. In reality very few do. Repentance, like faith, is the gift of God. It is that which God gives to us and works in us. Not until the Ethiopian can change his skin and the leopard his spots can a sinner turn himself to God (Jeremiah 13:23). The Lord Jesus "is exalted a Prince and a Saviour, for to give repentance to Israel and forgiveness of sins" (Acts 5:31). That which Christ gives cannot be the work of man. There is a false repentance with which multitudes are deluded. False repentance is that which springs from a sorrow for the consequences, not the causes of sin. True repentance is that which flows from the consciousness of sin itself. False repentance is sorrow that arises because a person fears the punishment of sin. True repentance is a godly sorrow for having offended God. False repentance arises from fear of judgment. True repentance rises from the revelation of justice satisfied by Christ (Zechariah 12:10).

Kingdom Of Heaven

John the Baptist preached the kingdom of heaven (v. 2). The argument and motive by which he urged sinners to repent was this: "The kingdom of heaven is at hand". John did not preach an earthly, carnal millennium, but a spiritual, gospel millennium. He did not say, "The kingdom of heaven will come in a few thousand years". He said, "The kingdom of heaven is at hand". He was saying that when Christ dies and is raised again, when he has ascended back to heaven and pours out his Spirit upon all flesh, the kingdom of heaven will be here.

The kingdom of heaven is the church of God. It is the kingdom of which Christ is the sovereign King. Its origin is heaven. Its character is heavenly, spiritual, not carnal and material. And its end is in heaven. It is a kingdom into which a son must be born (John 3:5-7). Yet, it is a kingdom, which must be willingly entered by personal repentance and faith. Surrender to Christ must be a willing surrender (Luke 14:23-33; Mark 8:35, 36).

God's Greatness

John the Baptist preached plainly and forcefully the sovereign independence of God almighty (v. 9). He told his hearers, "God does not need us. He can do without us. But we cannot do without him". John the Baptist did not pass out invitation cards, begging people to come hear him preach, that read, "We can't spell 'church' without 'u'". He said to the Pharisees and Sadducees, "God does not need you to fulfil his promise to Abraham. He can raise up these stones from the Jordan River and make them the heirs of his grace."

What does that mean? Simply that God does not need man. Man needs God! It means that no earthly privilege, performance, or pedigree is a guarantee of divine favour. God has mercy on whom he will. And it means that it is no problem for God to transform hearts as hard and cold as stone into hearts of love and faith. The children of Abraham are not Abraham's natural descendants, but those who, like Isaac, are children of promise and of grace.

Useless Religion

John the Baptist faithfully exposed the utter uselessness of false religion (v. 10). Judaism had degenerated into nothing but an outward, ceremonial system of works religion that God was determined to cut down and destroy as a fruitless tree. How his message needs to be heard in our day! All freewill, works religion is useless religion. All ceremonial, ritualistic religion is useless religion. All useless religion will one day be destroyed. There is only one way to deal with useless religion "Come out of her"! (Revelation 18:4; 2 Corinthians 6:14; 7:1).

Christ The Saviour

John the Baptist constantly preached Christ. He talked to men and women about the Lord Jesus Christ and pointed them to him (v. 11). He sent men directly to Christ. He did not seek to draw men to himself. He said, "I am just his servant. You need him. I can only baptize you in water. He can baptize you in the Holy Ghost. I can only warn you of judgment. He is your Judge"! The subject of John's ministry was "Jesus Christ and him crucified". He preached our Saviour's eternal existence (John 1:15) and deity (John 1:34), and his substitutionary, sin-atoning, effectual sacrifice (John 1:29).

Holy Spirit

John the Baptist spoke in plain terms about the person and work of God the Holy Spirit (v. 11). He preached that there is such a thing as baptism in the Holy Spirit, and that it is the special office of the Lord Jesus Christ to baptize his church into the Holy Spirit. The baptism in the Holy Spirit is not a second work of grace, but a primary work of grace. It is not something we work up by frenzied ecstasy, but something we enter into when we are born of God.

The Lord Jesus Christ baptized his church into the Holy Spirit at Pentecost (Acts 2:1-4). That was a one time act. It can no more be repeated than his crucifixion can be repeated. There is no need for a repetition. However, just as we receive the benefits of Christ's death by the new birth, so when sinners are born of God they are born into a spiritual kingdom and forever live in the realm of the Spirit (Romans 8:3-17). "Ye are not in the flesh, but in the Spirit". The Spirit of

God dwells in us and we dwell in the Spirit. All believers walk in the Spirit. We are led by the Spirit. We are taught of the Spirit. We have the Spirit's witness.

Believer's Baptism

John the Baptist preached the necessity of believer's baptism, too (vv. 5-8). Baptism was not a matter of indifference or insignificance to John. He was the Baptizer because he insisted that all who believed his message be baptized. He immersed (baptized) those who believed God, and only those. John baptized no one except those who brought forth "fruits meet for repentance". Neither he, nor anyone else in the New Testament immersed believers and their children. The notions of infant baptism and some other mode of baptism, other than immersion, are mere human fabrications, utterly without foundation or precedent in the Book of God. When John baptized people, there was need for "much water" (John 1:28; 3:23), because it takes more than a font will hold to immerse a man. The ordinance of baptism is a burial in water (Romans 6:4-6; Colossians 2:12). John Gill pointed out that this was the common practice of early believers. "The Christians of Christ's time were called by the Jews, in a way of contempt, apostates, that received the doctrine of baptism, and were dipped in Jordan."

Divine Judgment

John the Baptist spoke plainly about the danger of unbelief and the certainty of divine judgment (v. 12). He told his hearers of "wrath to come", "unquenchable fire", and "chaff" that must be burned. John spoke of forgiveness; but he also spoke of judgment. He spoke of mercy; but he did not fail to tell sinners of wrath, and of hell, and of eternal torment. It is no kindness for a preacher to keep back what the Bible teaches about hell. Every unconverted sinner needs to be plainly warned and convinced that he is hanging over the brink of hell by a thin and frayed thread. One more breath, and he may fall headlong into destruction.

Absolute Security

John the Baptist told his hearers of the safety and security of all true believers in Christ and by Christ (vv. 11, 15). As surely as Christ will burn up the chaff in hell, so surely also he will gather his wheat into his garner at the day of his appearing. All who are preserved in Christ from eternity by God the Father (Jude 1) were redeemed at Calvary by God the Son, and shall be born again, called and sealed in time by Holy Spirit (Ephesians 1:13, 14). They are kept through faith in Christ (1 Peter 1:5), who declares, "They shall never perish" (John 10:27-30).

Chapter 6

The Baptism Of Our Lord

"Then cometh Jesus from Galilee to Jordan unto John, to be baptized of him. But John forbad him, saying, I have need to be baptized of thee, and comest thou to me? And Jesus answering said unto him, Suffer it to be so now: for thus it becometh us to fulfil all righteousness. Then he suffered him. And Jesus, when he was baptized, went up straightway out of the water: and, lo, the heavens were opened unto him, and he saw the Spirit of God descending like a dove, and lighting upon him: And lo a voice from heaven, saying, This is my beloved Son, in whom I am well pleased."
(Matthew 3:13-17)

Our Lord Jesus spent the first thirty years of his life on this earth in obscurity. But the time had come for him to embark upon his public ministry and prophetic office. He did so by coming from Galilee to Jordan to be baptized by John the Baptist. We have Matthew's account of this momentous event in this passage. As the Jewish priests of the Old Testament, when they entered the priestly office, consecrated themselves to God by being washed with water (Exodus 29:4), so our great High Priest began the great work, which he came into the world to accomplish, by consecrating himself to God in public baptism. Being baptized by John the Baptist, our Lord Jesus here sits before us an example of obedience to God, which he later commanded all his disciples to follow.

An Honoured Ordinance
"Then cometh Jesus from Galilee to Jordan unto John, to be baptized of him" (v. 13). Do any imagine that baptism is an insignificant thing? Do any dare assert that this ordinance of Christ is a "non-essential"? The Son of God did not look upon it as such. The journey from Nazareth to Jerusalem took three days. Yet, our Saviour took that long journey so that he might be baptized by John the Baptist. I

take it, from such an example, that this ordinance of divine worship is not to be lightly esteemed. If Christ our Lord, the Head of the Church, honoured the ordinance of baptism by submitting to it, surely all who profess to follow him must do the same.

Two words of caution are necessary because this ordinance has been greatly perverted by lost religious men. 1. Let us throw away the creeds and confessions of men and simply obey the Word of God as it stands, without addition or alteration. Whenever men begin to tamper with the Word of God souls are ruined. 2. We must never attach any idolatrous, superstitious importance to the ordinance of baptism. Baptism is a picture of redemption; but baptism is not redemption. Baptism is a picture of the remission of sins; but baptism is not the remission of sins. Baptism is a picture of salvation; but baptism is not salvation.

We are redeemed by the blood of Christ. We are born again by the Spirit of God. We are saved by the grace of God. Baptism pictures and confesses these blessings of grace. But baptism has absolutely no redeeming, saving merit and efficacy!

Yet, we must never dishonour the ordinance of baptism by refusing to submit to it, by making it a mere ritual without meaning, or by altering its form. And we must never allow inconvenience or trouble to keep us from the worship of our God, or from observing this ordinance of divine worship as prescribed and practised by our Saviour.

The Lord Jesus went to considerable trouble and inconvenience to observe this ordinance of worship. Today, multitudes who call themselves believers and followers of Christ quickly justify themselves in the neglect of worship. But you will find no justification for it in the Word of God. The Shunammite woman rode on horseback every sabbath day to hear God's prophet at Carmel, though her husband hindered her (2 Kings 4:23). In David's time the saints of God "passed through the valley of Baca" to worship God at Zion (Psalm 84:6). In Daniel's day believers ran to and fro "to increase knowledge", to know more of the Lord God (Daniel 12:4). In Zechariah's day the inhabitants of one city went to another, saying, "Let us go speedily to pray before the Lord and to seek the Lord of hosts" (Zechariah 8:21). In the Book of Acts we read of the eunuch who journeyed from Ethiopia to Jerusalem to worship God (Acts 8:26-28). Any man or woman who talks about being a Christian, who talks about worshipping God, who talks about being a believer and yet wilfully neglects the worship of God ought to blush with shame!

The Baptism Of Our Lord

Our Lord's Humility

"But John forbad him, saying, I have need to be baptized of thee, and comest thou to me? And Jesus answering said unto him, Suffer it to be so now: for thus it becometh us to fulfil all righteousness. Then he suffered him" (vv. 14, 15). It was a great act of condescension and humility for the Son of God to come to John the Baptist to be baptized.

In all things our Saviour constantly strikes a blow at our foolish pride. He never misses an opportunity to expose and condemn it, both by his words and by his actions. He constantly teaches all who follow him to walk in humility. Our Saviour was ever the meek and lowly one. He was born to lowly parents, laid in a manger, and raised in obscurity. When he rode into Jerusalem as the King of Zion, he rode not upon a white charger, but a lowly ass. And when he began his public ministry, it was not with pomp and pageantry, but by being immersed by a man in a muddy river (2 Corinthians 8:9; Philippians 2:5-8).

His servant, John the Baptist, though bold as a lion, was also a man of true humility. When the Lord came to John for baptism, John forbad him. He strenuously objected, not out of a spirit of rebellion, but out of a spirit of reverence and awe. John knew who Christ is. He knew that the man standing before him was the infinite God, his Redeemer and Saviour. And he knew himself, too. He knew that he was a sinner in need of grace and a sinner saved by grace, through the merits of the Lamb of God who stood before him.

Though he was conscious of his personal sin and unworthiness to do so, when the Lord commanded him to do it, John baptized him. No man is worthy to do anything in the worship and service of the holy Lord God. Our only worthiness before God is Christ. It is his blood and righteousness alone that makes us "meet to be partakers of the inheritance of the saints in light" (Colossians 1:12). And it is Christ who makes us worthy to approach our God in all acts of worship. We have no right, in a pretence of humility, to refuse any command or duty clearly set before us by our God.

"To Fulfil All Righteousness"

Why did the Lord Jesus insist upon being baptized by John? He had no sins to confess. He had no transgressions of which to repent. He had no iniquities to be washed away. Yet, he told John that it was necessary for him to be baptized "to fulfil all righteousness". But what did his baptism have to do with the fulfilment of all righteousness?

We know that our blessed Saviour fulfilled all the righteous requirements of God's holy law for us as our Representative, freeing us from its curse and condemnation by his obedience unto death (Romans 5:18-21). And he fulfilled all the will of God as the God-man, our Mediator, by which we are forever sanctified (Hebrews 10:5-14).

By his baptism, our Saviour symbolically fulfilled all righteousness and established as a standing ordinance in his Church that by which believing men and women publicly confess the fulfilment of all righteousness by him. By his baptism the Lord Jesus symbolically demonstrated how he would fulfil all righteousness as our sin-atoning Substitute. And by our baptism we confess the same. "The baptism of Christ", wrote C. H. Spurgeon, "was the picture, the type, the symbol of the work, which he afterwards accomplished. He was immersed in suffering; he died, and was buried in the tomb; he rose again from the grave; and all that is set forth in the outward symbol of his baptism in the River Jordan."

Believer's baptism typically fulfils "all righteousness". It is an ordinance full of meaning when rightly observed. It is to be reverently observed by all who follow Christ. If our Lord himself submitted to it, we cannot follow him and refuse to submit to it. I quote Spurgeon again. "Shall I refuse to follow my Lord? Shall I think that there is nothing in an ordinance of which he said, 'Thus it becometh us to fulfil all righteousness'?"

When the Lord Jesus was made sin for us, he was slain under the wrath of God, and buried. When he had put away sin, he rose from the dead because he had accomplished our justification. When believers follow Christ into the watery grave, we publicly acknowledge that our only hope before God is that which he accomplished for us in his death and resurrection as our Substitute. Rising up out of the watery grave, we symbolically avow our allegiance to Christ, walking with him in the newness of life, in hope of the resurrection (Romans 6:4-6).

Immersion Only

"And Jesus, when he was baptized, went up straightway out of the water: and, lo, the heavens were opened unto him, and he saw the Spirit of God descending like a dove, and lighting upon him" (v. 16). While I fully recognize that many oppose our insistence upon baptism as an ordinance for believers only and upon the fact that baptism can only be performed by immersion, it would be treasonous of me not to declare the obvious from this verse. Baptism is immersion. Immersion is not "the Baptists' mode of baptism". Immersion is baptism. "Sprinkling" is sprinkling. And "pouring" is pouring. Baptism is immersion.

The Baptism Of Our Lord

"Jesus, when he was baptized, went up straightway out of the water." There is absolutely no reason for Matthew to make that statement except to show us that baptism must be performed by immersion. Without immersion, there is no baptism. John Gill argues:

> We learn this from it, that since it is said, that he came up out of the water, he must first have gone down into it; must have been in it, and was baptized in it ... That Christ should go down into the river, more or less deep, to the ankles, or up to the knees, in order that John should sprinkle water on his face, or pour it on his head, as is ridiculously represented, can hardly obtain any credit with persons of thought and sense.

Baptism is always represented in the scriptures as a burial (Romans 6:3-6; Colossians 2:12). When you bury a corpse in the earth, you do not throw a few grains of sand on its face. You put it beneath the ground. Nor is a man buried in baptism by sprinkling a few drops of water in his face. He must be immersed in water. Any alternation of the baptismal mode is a perversion of the ordinance and a denial of what it represents: the gospel of redemption and righteousness by Christ alone.

The Trinity

"And Jesus, when he was baptized, went up straightway out of the water: and, lo, the heavens were opened unto him, and he saw the Spirit of God descending like a dove, and lighting upon him: And lo a voice from heaven, saying, This is my beloved Son, in whom I am well pleased" (vv. 16, 17). Here we see the interest of the triune God in the work of redemption. Here is a display of the Holy Trinity, an identification of our Lord Jesus as the Messiah, and a declaration from heaven, "this is my beloved son, in whom I am well pleased".

Here is everything that is solemn, sublime, and glorious. The scene before us ought to be contemplated with utmost reverence, awe, and adoration. "For there are three that bear record in heaven, the Father, the Word, and the Holy Ghost: and these three are one" (1 John 5:7). Here the three Persons of the triune God distinctly manifest themselves. God the Father speaks by a voice from heaven. God the Son, incarnate in human flesh, stoops to the watery grave. And God the

Holy Spirit descends from heaven in the form of a Dove, lighting upon our blessed Saviour.

Here we have a most majestic meeting of the three Persons of the Holy Trinity about the work of redemption. As in the beginning of creation, the triune God said, "Let us make man"; so in the beginning of redemption, he said, "Let us redeem man"! The salvation of our souls is the united work of the Triune God. It was planned and purposed by God the Father. It was purchased and obtained for us by God the Son. And it is performed and sealed in us by God the Holy Spirit (Ephesians 1:3-14).

Fully God

It is very significant that the man Christ Jesus is here declared to be God the Son, even as he portrays his death, burial and resurrection as our Substitute. He is as fully God in his lowest humiliation as he is in his highest eternal glory. The glory and perfection of our Saviour as God in his essential divinity was not even slightly diminished by his incarnation, obedience, and death as our Surety. Whenever we read anything about him in the Book of God that appears to limit his knowledge, power, or being, we must never fail to recognize that such limitations only reflect genuineness of his humanity and his voluntary subjection to the will of God as Jehovah's righteous Servant for the accomplishment of our redemption. He who is God our Saviour is God and man in one glorious person. He is truly and fully and perfectly God. And he is truly and fully and perfectly man. It is he, the GODMAN our Mediator, in whom, and through whom, and by whom we have access to and everlasting acceptance with the eternal God.

Well-Pleased

There is one more sweet and rapturous fact revealed in verse 17. The declaration of God on this occasion is, "This is my beloved Son in whom I am well-pleased." God the Father is well-pleased with Christ and only with Christ. He is well-pleased with his person, with his obedience, and with his sacrifice pictured in his baptism. God the Father is eternally and infinitely pleased with his Son as his Son. He is eternally pleased and satisfied with his Son as his Servant (Isaiah 42:1). He is infinitely and eternally well-pleased with the sacrifice of his Son as the Lamb slain from the foundation of the world (Revelation 13:8). He was well pleased with his assumption of our nature, with his obedience to the law, his bringing in everlasting righteousness; with him being made sin for us, bearing our sins in his own body on the tree, enduring the penalty and curse of his holy law against sin to the full satisfaction of justice as our Substitute. Yes, the Father is well-pleased with his person, his righteousness, his satisfaction, and his atonement, by which his law is magnified and honoured and his justice is satisfied.

But the Voice from heaven did not say, "This is my beloved Son *with* whom I am well-pleased." The Voice from heaven said, "This is my beloved Son *in* whom I am well-pleased." How thankful we ought to be for that. The God of Glory is well-pleased with all who are in his Son because of his Son. He is well pleased with us in Christ, for he has made us "the righteousness of God in him". God is not only well pleased with his Son and in his Son, he is well-pleased with all his people in his Son. In him he loves us with an everlasting love. As the Son, our Surety, was delighted with us from eternity (Proverbs 8:31), so the Father took delight in us, rejoiced over us, accepted us, and blessed us with all spiritual blessings in his Son before the world began (Ephesians 1:3-6). And as the Father's delight in his Son is immutable, so his delight with and pleasure with his elect in his Son is immutable. He shall rejoice over them with joy and singing forever, resting in his love (Zephaniah 3:17). Robert Hawker's reflections on this passage ought to be the reflections of our hearts after reading it.

> May the Lord mercifully grant, that the whole church of God, through divine teaching, may be enabled to keep in unceasing remembrance, the Father's testimony to his dear Son. And while my soul, and the souls of all his redeemed, are thus continually hearing, and receiving, the precious assurance of God's being well pleased with his dear Son, for his redeeming love to his church, and his finished salvation for his people; oh, for grace to love him, whom JEHOVAH, in all the persons of the Godhead, loves; and to delight in Him, in whom JEHOVAH delighteth. Precious Lord Jesus! I would say, 'Whom have I in heaven but thee; and there is none upon earth my soul desireth but thee. My flesh and my heart faileth: but thou art the strength of my heart, and my portion for ever.'

Chapter 7

The Temptation Of Christ

"Then was Jesus led up of the Spirit into the wilderness to be tempted of the devil. And when he had fasted forty days and forty nights, he was afterward an hungered. And when the tempter came to him, he said, If thou be the Son of God, command that these stones be made bread. But he answered and said, It is written, Man shall not live by bread alone, but by every word that proceedeth out of the mouth of God. Then the devil taketh him up into the holy city, and setteth him on a pinnacle of the temple, And saith unto him, If thou be the Son of God, cast thyself down: for it is written, He shall give his angels charge concerning thee: and in their hands they shall bear thee up, lest at any time thou dash thy foot against a stone. Jesus said unto him, It is written again, Thou shalt not tempt the Lord thy God. Again, the devil taketh him up into an exceeding high mountain, and sheweth him all the kingdoms of the world, and the glory of them; And saith unto him, All these things will I give thee, if thou wilt fall down and worship me. Then saith Jesus unto him, Get thee hence, Satan: for it is written, Thou shalt worship the Lord thy God, and him only shalt thou serve. Then the devil leaveth him, and, behold, angels came and ministered unto him".
(Matthew 4:1-11)

As soon as our Lord was baptized, as soon as he began to publicly identify himself in this world as the Son of God, he was tempted of the devil. While he stayed in the carpenter's shop, chipping away at wood, the devil was undisturbed. But as soon as he began to lay the axe to the root of Satan's kingdom, our Lord was tempted by the devil. The very first thing that is recorded concerning our Lord's public ministry is his temptation.

Notice the order of things. Our Lord was baptized. He was owned to be the Son of God. He was anointed by the Spirit of God. Then he was tempted. Here is a fact of life, from which there is no escape in this world. If you are a child of God, if the Spirit of God is in you, you will be tempted of the devil.

The Temptation of Christ is a subject so deep and mysterious that no sensible man would imagine being able to understand, much less explain the facts that are clearly revealed concerning it. It is a subject shrouded in mystery. In fact, mystery is a vital aspect of all divine truth. Any doctrine that is not mysterious is not divine in its origin. That which God has revealed about himself in holy scripture is infinitely beyond human conception and comprehension. The infinite God cannot be comprehended by the puny mind of finite man.

So, when we come to meditate upon, think about, and discuss the temptation of our Lord, we must begin with an acknowledged inability to comprehend the things we have before us. No man can understand what occurred in our Saviour's heart when he was tempted. But there is much revealed in the Book of God that we do not understand. Who can explain how sin originated in the sinless heart of Adam, how the eternal God can be one God in three distinct persons, or how our Saviour can be both the omniscient, omnipresent, omnipotent God and a man in a physical body that needed both rest and nourishment, and from whom some things are hidden? Yet these things are plainly revealed in the Sacred Volume.

The basis of our faith is not our understanding of God's Word, but the Word of God itself. Because the Bible is the Word of God, we recognize that it is infinitely superior to human reason. Therefore, we gladly submit our reason to God's revelation.

This much we understand Our Lord Jesus was tempted in all points like as we are, so that he might be touched with the feeling of our infinities; but he never succumbed to the temptation. He never sinned. There are five things that we need to learn from this passage of holy scripture.

A Real Adversary

First, learn that Satan is a real adversary to our souls. "Then was Jesus led up of the Spirit into the wilderness to be tempted of the devil" (v. 1). Matthew understood that the devil is real, a personal adversary, a mighty foe with whom we must do battle continually. The fiend of hell is not afraid to assault the very throne of God, or the Son of God! In these eleven verses we are told three times that Satan attacked the Lord of glory. Our Saviour was "tempted of the devil".

It was the devil who brought sin into the world in the beginning. It was he who vexed Job, deceived David, and caused Peter to fall so miserably. The Word of God calls him a "murderer", a "liar", and a "roaring lion" (John 8:44; 1 Peter 5:8). The world is ruled by the wicked influence of Satan (Ephesians 2:1-3). Unbelieving men and women are taken captive by the devil at his will (2 Timothy 2:26). His goal is the everlasting destruction of our souls. He ever seeks whom he may devour. His malice is unrelenting. His hatred against us never abates. For nearly 6000 years he has been trying to destroy and draw into hell those men and women he was created to serve. As it was with our glorious Head, so is it with his members. No sooner is the work of grace wrought in the hearts of God's elect than all hell is up in arms.

We must constantly watch and pray that we be not taken by his devices. His cunning and subtlety are greater than we can imagine. The prince of darkness often transforms himself into an "angel of light" and his ministers into "preachers of righteousness" (2 Corinthians 11:13, 14). Satan is with us wherever we live. He goes wherever we go. He never tires. He never sleeps. He never quits. If he can, he will destroy our souls! If we would be saved, we must crucify the flesh and overcome the world; but we must also "resist the devil".

God Rules

Second, we see in this passage the fact that the Lord our God rules all things absolutely. We know that God cannot be tempted to do evil and that he will never tempt any man to do evil (James 1:13-15). But everyone who reads the Bible with understanding knows that God rules even in the temptations of his people (Psalm 76:10). Neither the fall of Satan nor the temptation and sin of our father Adam took God by surprise.

Notice the language of verse 1. Our Lord Jesus was led (Mark 1:12 says "driven") into the wilderness by the Holy Spirit "to be tempted of the devil". Why? Because we need a tempted Saviour, one who can be and is touched with the feeling of our infirmities. He was tempted of the devil because, as a man, he needed to be tempted, that he might perform the work of perfect righteousness for us, faithfully doing the will of God in the face of temptation, thereby fulfilling all righteousness as our Representative and Mediator. And he needed to be tempted, as he entered his public ministry, that he might learn obedience by the temptations he endured. Martin Luther wrote, "Three things make a preacher: meditation, prayer, and temptation." Therefore, our Redeemer was led into the wilderness to be tempted of the devil.

Our Saviour's temptations were also necessary on our account. "For in that he himself hath suffered, being tempted, he is able to succour them that are tempted" (Hebrews 2:18). This account of our Redeemer's temptations in the wilderness is specifically recorded for our comfort. Not only does our blessed Saviour know what our temptations are, his personal knowledge of them by experience was such that he now knows both what we feel when we are tempted and how to minister to us the very help that will exactly suit our case and circumstances.

As his temptations were in complete accordance with the will and purpose of our God, so are ours. The Lord our God is in control of our temptations just as fully as he is in control of everything else in this world (1 Corinthians 10:13; 1 Thessalonians 5:16-24). Robert Hawker made the following observation in commenting on our Lord's temptation. "What a sweet thought is it, that the Lord Jesus was in all points tempted as his people are, yet without sin! Precious Lord! Was it not intended to prompt thy redeemed to come to thee with more confidence from fellow feeling?"

Our Defence

Third, our Lord's example in this passage teaches us that the best defence we have in times of temptation is the Word of God. Three times Satan tempted our Lord with great offers that strongly appealed to his human nature. But three times our Lord foiled Satan's temptations by asserting some portion of holy scripture as his reason for not doing as the devil suggested. This is just one of many reasons why we ought to make ourselves intimately and constantly familiar with holy scripture. It is not enough to have a Bible. Read it! It is not enough to carry a Bible to church. Make yourself familiar with its contents. Seek to understand its doctrine (2 Timothy 3:15-17).

J. C. Ryle wrote, "Knowledge of the Bible never comes by intuition. It can only be got by hard, regular, daily, attentive, wakeful reading." You cannot fight the good fight of faith if you cannot use the sword of the Spirit (Ephesians 6:17). You cannot walk in the King's highway if you do not walk by the light of His Word, which is "a lamp unto our feet and a light unto our pathway" (Psalm 119:105). If we would know the way of salvation, let us seek to know the Word of God. If we would live in this world for the glory of God, let us seek to know his Word. If we would escape the temptations of Satan, let us bury ourselves in the Word of God and the worship of God.

Our High Priest

Above all else these eleven verses are written to teach and assure us that we have a great High Priest in heaven who is touched with the feeling of our infirmities (Hebrews 2:17, 18; 4:14-16). The sympathy of the Lord Jesus with us is a truth which ought to be peculiarly precious to every believer.

Here is a treasury of consolation for tempted souls! We have a great, almighty Friend and Advocate in heaven, who intercedes for us in all our temptations, is touched with our infirmities, and enters into all our spiritual troubles and fears.

The Temptation Of Christ

Are you ever tempted by Satan to distrust God's providence? So was Christ! Are you ever tempted by Satan to presume upon God's promises? So was Christ! Are you ever tempted by Satan to some act of evil for worldly gain? So was Christ!

The Lord Jesus Christ is just the Saviour that tempted people need! Let us flee to him for help and spread our troubles before him. You will always find that his ear is ready to hear, his heart is ready to feel, and his arm is ready to help. He understands our sorrows, temptations, and troubles!

Though he is exalted to heaven, this Man, who is God our Saviour, still possesses "the tongue of the learned" and knows how "to speak a word in season to him that is weary" (Isaiah 50:4). For this purpose he is wakened every morning throughout the ages of time with the ear of the learned. Yes, our dear Redeemer is a Son who has learned obedience by the things he suffered. He has learned what it is to wrestle with Satan's temptations and assaults. He has learned what it is to endure malicious slander. He has learned what it is to be bereaved of a loved one. He has learned what it is to be betrayed by a friend. He has learned what it is to be made sin! He has learned what it is to have a broken heart. He has learned what it is to be forsaken of God! He has learned what it is to die! And he has learned what it is to be raised from the dead! He is able to comfort and help his tempted people, because God has given him "the tongue of the learned ... to speak a word in season to him that is weary". He can speak a word in season to our weary souls, because he is touched with the feeling of our infirmities. How thankful we ought to be to know that he who is God our Saviour was once "led of the Spirit into the wilderness to be tempted of the devil."

Questions

Certain questions are constantly asked by men when discussing the temptation of Christ, which I suppose I should answer. Some ask, "Was it possible for our Saviour to sin?" The answer is "No. Absolutely, no"! He was without sin and without the ability to sin (Isaiah 53:10; John 8:46; 14:30; 2 Corinthians 5:21: Hebrews 7:26). When that is stated, the question is raised, "If it was not possible for the Lord Jesus to sin, was the temptation real?" The answer is "Yes. Absolutely, yes"! (Hebrews 4:15). He heard Satan's voice. The things Satan tempted him with were things he desired: food, divine protection, and dominion over the world. But there was no inward urge or desire to disobedience and sin!

The Temptations

Satan tempted our Lord to four things. He tempted him to an act of unbelief, to distrust God (vv. 3, 4). C. H. Spurgeon wrote, "A true son will not doubt his father, and undertake to provide his own bread. He will wait to be fed by his father's hand." And our Saviour, as a true Son, trusted his Father. May he give us grace to do the same.

Then the devil tempted him to an act of presumption and to suicide (vv. 5-8). The devil even sought to justify the temptations from scripture and talked freely about angels, about God, and about grace.

Finally, the prince of darkness tempted our blessed Saviour to an act of idolatry (vv. 8-10). We cannot conceive of Christ worshipping at the devil's feet. Yet the church bows itself before Satan every time the gospel of God is supported and promoted by theatrical performances, bingo games and worldly attractions rather than relying on the truth of Christ preached in the power of the Holy Spirit.

Should we ever hunger and be in poverty, as our Lord was, we must never yield to the temptation to do wrong to gain wealth, honour, or even a pressing need! Though we may have to endure seasons of apparent barrenness, the church of God must never seek to advance Christ's kingdom by any means other than simple gospel preaching after the pattern of the New Testament!

As our Lord Jesus was tempted so we shall be. Satan will not treat us better than he treated our Master. Believers often find evil thoughts rising in their minds, which they truly hate, doubts and sinful imaginations against which we honestly revolt, and there is in us an ungodly nature that yearns for the very things we hate and revolt against.

Our greatest temptations will usually come after times of greatest privilege, communion, and usefulness. So it was with our Lord. Ever be aware of your weakness in the flesh and your tendency to evil. Ever keep in mind that our peace and comfort is in Christ our Substitute, not in some imaginary, inward, personal goodness. He who was tempted and triumphant for us will also cause us to be triumphant over the tempter and his temptations (John 10:27-30; 17:15; Romans 8:35-39; Philippians 1:6; 1 Thessalonians 5:24; 1 Corinthians 10:13).

Chapter 8

"Jesus Began To Preach"

"Now when Jesus had heard that John was cast into prison, he departed into Galilee; And leaving Nazareth, he came and dwelt in Capernaum, which is upon the sea coast, in the borders of Zabulon and Nephthalim: That it might be fulfilled which was spoken by Esaias the prophet, saying, The land of Zabulon, and the land of Nephthalim, by the way of the sea, beyond Jordan, Galilee of the Gentiles; The people which sat in darkness saw great light; and to them which sat in the region and shadow of death light is sprung up. From that time Jesus began to preach, and to say, Repent: for the kingdom of heaven is at hand. And Jesus, walking by the sea of Galilee, saw two brethren, Simon called Peter, and Andrew his brother, casting a net into the sea: for they were fishers. And he saith unto them, Follow me, and I will make you fishers of men. And they straightway left their nets, and followed him. And going on from thence, he saw other two brethren, James the son of Zebedee, and John his brother, in a ship with Zebedee their father, mending their nets; and he called them. And they immediately left the ship and their father, and followed him. And Jesus went about all Galilee, teaching in their synagogues, and preaching the gospel of the kingdom, and healing all manner of sickness and all manner of disease among the people. And his fame went throughout all Syria: and they brought unto him all sick people that were taken with divers diseases and torments, and those which were possessed with devils, and those which were lunatic, and those that had the palsy; and he healed them. And there followed him great multitudes of people from Galilee, and from Decapolis, and from Jerusalem, and from Judaea, and from beyond Jordan."
(Matthew 4:12-25)

When we read the four gospels, we must not imagine that each of the evangelists recorded things in the same chronological order. They did not. Each one wrote out the history of our Lord's earthly life and ministry, as he was led by the Holy Spirit, to best serve the purpose of his own gospel narrative. So the fact that Matthew's history is not consecutive is of no concern to us. It was not his design to make it so.

Several things happened between our Lord's temptation in the wilderness and his appearance on the shores of Galilee preaching the gospel.

His Appearance to John (John 1:29).
The Calling of His First Disciples (John 1:39-51).
The Marriage Feast at Cana (John 2:1-11).
The Passover at Jerusalem (John 2:13-22) "The Scourge"!
The Discourse with Nicodemus (John 3).
The Samaritan Woman (John 4).

Many months had passed, probably more than a year, since our Lord's temptation and the calling of his first disciples. At any rate, Matthew begins his account of our Lord's public ministry in Galilee. In these verses we see the Lord Jesus preaching in the synagogues and along the streets of Galilee after the imprisonment of John the Baptist. "These are sweet views", wrote Robert Hawker, "of Jesus in his humbleness of character. And what a blessed proof they become in proof of his mission (Isaiah 9:1, 2)."

Our Lord Jesus was the first Preacher of that great salvation which he accomplished (Hebrews 1:3); and as such he is held before us as the great Pattern and Example all true gospel preachers must follow.

A Singular Message

Unlike the religious world in his own day and more especially in this day, the Lord Jesus began his public ministry with the utmost simplicity: without pomp and pageantry, without press conferences, advance men, and announcements, he just began to preach. Without calling attention to himself at all, he just began to preach!

The time when he began to preach was "when Jesus had heard that John was cast into prison" (v. 12). When John the Baptist had done his work, he was laid aside. Like the two witnesses in Revelation 11:7, when he had borne his testimony, John was slain, and not a moment before. Mortals are immortal here, until their work is done!

God never leaves himself without a witness. He never leaves his church in the wilderness without guides. When John's work was finished, the Lord God raised up other faithful witnesses to proclaim the gospel of his grace and glory. He who raised up Moses can raise up Joshua. There is no lack with our God.

"Jesus Began To Preach"

The place where our Lord began his ministry was in Capernaum, in Galilee of the Gentiles (vv. 13-16). He left Nazareth because the people there rejected his message and had rejected him (Luke 4:28-30). He came to Galilee because some of God's elect were to be found there. He came to Capernaum because the scriptures had to be fulfilled (Isaiah 9:1, 2).

Like the inhabitants of Capernaum, like the Gentiles of Galilee long ago, you and I were in gross darkness. We sat in darkness because we loved it. We did not seek the light, but upon us great light has come. The light of Christ and the grace and glory of God in him has shined into our hearts, creating in us life and faith in Christ (Genesis 1:1-3; John 1:1-14; 2 Corinthians 4:4-6). When the gospel comes, light comes (Luke 1:78-79; John 3:19). When the gospel comes into the heart in the grace and power of God the Holy Spirit, we are made new creatures in Christ (2 Corinthians 5:17).

He came to Capernaum because Capernaum in Galilee, the place of Gentile "nothings" and "nobodies", was the place from which he would fetch trophies of his grace (1 Corinthians 1:26-30). Galilean speech was crude. Galilean people were poor, illiterate, and uncouth. Galileans were the rough-necks on the other side of the tracks. These are the people from whom our Lord would call out a people to serve him, by whom he would build his church and kingdom.

The message our Lord preached was the same as that of John the Baptist. "From that time Jesus began to preach, and to say, Repent: for the kingdom of heaven is at hand" (v. 17). Our Lord Jesus could have dazzled the brains of men with deep, profound theology, or by unravelling the hidden mysteries of prophecy, or by opening up the intricate complexities of the law. But he chose not to do so. He preached one message. He preached the necessity of repentance, the necessity of trusting him alone for acceptance with God (Acts 20:21). He preached that message constantly (Luke 13:1-5). And he preached that message urgently, "For the kingdom of heaven is at hand"! The Lord of Glory was a preacher. Let all who claim to be preachers follow his example and reiterate his message. J. C. Ryle comments:

> There is no office so honourable as that of the preacher. There is no work so important to the souls of men. It is our office, which the Son of God was not ashamed to take up. It is an office to which he appointed his twelve apostles. It is an office to which Paul in his old age specially directs Timothy's attention. He charges him with almost his last breath to 'preach the Word' (2 Timothy 4:2). It is the principle

> means which God has always been pleased to use for the conversion and edification of souls. The brightest days of the church have been those when preaching has been honoured. The darkest days of the church have been those when it has been lightly esteemed.

His Chosen Messengers

When our Lord began to preach, he began to gather disciples. In these verses we see our Lord's calling of two sets of brothers to himself (vv. 18-22). Here we have an example of the effectual call. Do not overlook the sovereignty of our Lord's call. What marvellous light and omnipotent grace must have accompanied his words! The effectual, or irresistible call of God the Holy Spirit (2 Timothy 1:9; 2 Peter 1:10) is that which he performs by the preaching of the gospel (Romans 10:13; Hebrews 4:12; 1 Peter 1:23-25). It is this gracious call of omnipotent mercy by which sinners who are dead in trespasses and sins are born of God and given faith in Christ.

We also have in these verses an example of the call to the gospel ministry. Peter and Andrew, and probably James and John, had been called to Christ earlier (John 1:40-42). They were now called to be preachers of the gospel. They were called by the Lord Jesus Christ himself, not by mere men, but by the Son of God, to be "fishers of men". What a great privilege this is! These rough, unlearned, Galilean fishermen were chosen and gifted of God to preach the gospel.

What were they doing when the Lord Jesus called them? They were taking care of business in their given sphere of life and responsibility. They were fishing. They were mending their nets. Spurgeon says, "They were busy in a lawful occupation when he called them to be ministers. Our Lord does not call idlers, but fishers"!

What did the Master call these men to do? "Follow me, and I will make you fishers of men" (v. 19). As ordinary disciples they had been following the Lord, as such it was proper for them to continue in the pursuit of their careers. But now the Lord calls them to the work of the gospel ministry. He separates them to the work of the gospel. God's preachers are fishers of men. And Christ alone can make men fishers of men.

In order for a man to be a fisher of men, in order for a man to be a gospel preacher he must be separated unto the gospel (Romans 1:1). That means that he must follow Christ. His life must be ruled by the Word of God and the direction of God the Holy Spirit. He must drop all earthly interest and concerns. These men left their boats and their nets. Like Peter and Andrew, and these sons of Zebedee, all who are called of God to the great work of preaching the gospel must separate themselves from all earthly concerns, being entirely devoted to the work of the gospel. As James and John left their father Zebedee sitting in the boat, bewildered I imagine, so God's servants must not allow their dearest relations to keep them from obeying him.

Yes, that means that a man who is called of God to preach the gospel is to abandon other occupations, living upon the generosity of those whose souls they serve. God's preachers are to be supported by the free gifts of God's people. The Word of God is crystal clear in teaching this (Matthew 10:7, 9, 10; Luke 10:7; 1 Corinthians 9:1-14; 2 Corinthians 11:7-9; Galatians 6:1-6; 1 Timothy 5:17, 18).

The Master's Miracles

Concerning the miraculous cures the Lord Jesus wrought among men such as those recorded in vv. 23-25, let me simply point out four things about them. First, they were many. Our Saviour was no religious charlatan. He cured every disease known to men. He cured men of the palsy, the greatest weakness of the body. He healed lunatics of their great mental disorders. He cast out devils. And this man, who is God, even raised people from the dead by the mere word of his power. Second, they were miraculous. All were wrought in such an open and public manner that no one questioned their supernatural power. Third, they were merciful. The cures of Christ's hand were all acts of mercy, free and gratuitous. And, fourth, they were mysterious.

Our Lord's miraculous healings of bodily disease were meant to teach us his power, to typify his great and miraculous works of grace, to show us the tenderness of his heart, and to give indisputable evidence that he is the Christ (Luke 4:16-22).

What a delightful, comforting picture the Holy Spirit has here drawn of our blessed Saviour. Remember, this is the same Saviour who now intercedes for us in heaven and rules all the universe for our everlasting good. Though our Lord Jesus is now exalted, he is the same "yesterday, and today, and forever" (Hebrews 13:8). He is yet able and willing to heal. He is yet able and willing to save (Hebrews 7:25). He is yet moved by the needs of his people.

Remember what was written of him in Isaiah 63:7-9. "I will mention the lovingkindnesses of the LORD, and the praises of the LORD, according to all that the LORD hath bestowed on us, and the great goodness toward the house of Israel, which he hath bestowed on them according to his mercies, and according to the multitude of his lovingkindnesses. For he said, Surely they are my people, children that will not lie: so he was their Saviour. In all their affliction he was afflicted, and the angel of his presence saved them: in his love and in his pity he redeemed them; and he bare them, and carried them all the days of old."

While he walked on this earth in all the days of his humiliation, we are told, "having loved his own which were in the world, he loved them unto the end." And nothing has changed. Follow the Lord Jesus up to heaven itself and behold "the Lamb which is in the midst of the throne" feeding his own and drying all tears from their eyes forever (Revelation 7:17). Let every believing soul be assured that this Saviour will never forget you and will never leave you. It behoved him to be made like unto his brethren, that he might be a merciful and faithful High Priest for us; and that is what he is. "For we have not an high priest which cannot be touched with the feeling of our infirmities; but was in all points tempted like as we are, yet without sin. Let us therefore come boldly unto the throne of grace, that we may obtain mercy, and find grace to help in time of need" (Hebrews 4:15, 16).

I insert Robert Hawker's reflections on this fourth chapter of Matthew, hoping that his prayer may be yours and mine each time we read these verses.

> Behold on the close of this chapter, how he, who in the opening of it, is said to have been assaulted by hell, is here manifesting forth his sovereignty as God. Oh! that that dear Lord, who thus in the days of his flesh, went about preaching his gospel, and healing the bodies of the diseased, would now, in the day of his almighty power, come forth in a preached gospel, and heal the souls of his redeemed. Precious Lord Jesus, behold the diseased state of thy church, and in compassion to Zion take the glorious cause into thine own almighty hand. And as then, so now, Lord, cause the multitudes of thy people to come to thy standard, until thou shalt have brought all thy blood-bought children home to thy church, and all the blessed purposes of thy temptations and ministry be abundantly answered in the salvation of thy chosen. Amen.

Chapter 9

Who Is Blessed Of God?

"And seeing the multitudes, he went up into a mountain: and when he was set, his disciples came unto him: And he opened his mouth, and taught them, saying, Blessed are the poor in spirit: for theirs is the kingdom of heaven. Blessed are they that mourn: for they shall be comforted. Blessed are the meek: for they shall inherit the earth. Blessed are they which do hunger and thirst after righteousness: for they shall be filled. Blessed are the merciful: for they shall obtain mercy. Blessed are the pure in heart: for they shall see God. Blessed are the peacemakers: for they shall be called the children of God. Blessed are they which are persecuted for righteousness' sake: for theirs is the kingdom of heaven. Blessed are ye, when men shall revile you, and persecute you, and shall say all manner of evil against you falsely, for my sake. Rejoice, and be exceeding glad: for great is your reward in heaven: for so persecuted they the prophets which were before you."
(Matthew 5:1-12)

According to the Book of God, there are some people in this world who are truly blessed, blessed of God, blessed from eternity, blessed now, and blessed forever in Christ, blessed with all the blessings of grace here and all the blessings of everlasting glory hereafter (Ephesians 1:3). There are some sons and daughters of Adam who truly are blessed of God. Who are they?

Those who were chosen in Christ in eternal election (Ephesians 1:3-6).
Those who trust the Lord (Jeremiah 17:7; Luke 11:27, 28).
Those who fear the Lord (Psalm 128:1; Matthew 10:28).
Those whose sins are forgiven (Psalm 32:1, 2; Romans 4:8).
Those who are not offended by Christ (Luke 7:23).
Those who endure temptation (James 1:12).

There are some in this world who are blessed of God. Are you among these blessed ones? Am I? Let us look to the Word of God and see. I am calling for each of us to examine ourselves in the light of holy scripture (2 Corinthians 13:5). In these twelve verses the Lord Jesus sets before us the character of those men and women who are blessed of God.

Our Prophet

These verses are from the first part of our Lord's Sermon on the Mount. The sermon itself continues in chapters 6 and 7. "And seeing the multitudes, he went up into a mountain: and when he was set, his disciples came unto him: And he opened his mouth, and taught them" (vv. 1, 2).

The preacher is the Lord Jesus Christ himself, the true Prince of preachers, the Prophet of his church. He of whom the prophets spoke is now the preacher. The voice we hear in these verses is the voice of our Master. It is the voice of him who "spoke as never a man spake".

The place was a mountain in Galilee. It was not Mount Sinai, or Mount Olivet, or Mount Calvary, but a common Galilean hillside. But on that common hillside the Son of God met with and instructed his disciples. That made the place a holy place!

The congregation was his disciples. The sermon was addressed to those who professed to be his followers. Others were present and heard the message. But the message was particularly addressed to men and women who had publicly avowed their faith in Christ by baptism and hoped that they would live with Christ forever in heaven. In a word, this sermon was addressed to people just like you and me.

Look at verse 2 again. "He opened his mouth, and taught them". When our Saviour's mouth was closed, he taught by example. Yet, he did not refrain from speaking, as well as living the truth. And when he spoke, he spoke earnestly. He "opened his mouth and taught". He did not mumble, mutter, or stutter. When he opens his mouth let us open our ears!

We have a blessed scene before us! As the law was given from the Mount, the Lord Jesus went up on the Mount to proclaim the gospel. But there is a great contrast. At Mount Sinai boundaries were set, which the people were not allowed to cross. When our great Saviour came preaching the gospel, he set no boundaries sinners could not cross. He said, "Come ye near unto me, hear ye this; I have not spoken in secret from the beginning; from the time that it was, there am I: and now the Lord God, and his Spirit, hath sent me. Thus saith the Lord, thy Redeemer, the Holy One of Israel; I am the Lord thy God which teacheth thee to profit, which leadeth thee by the way that thou shouldest go" (Isaiah 48:16, 17). What gracious words proceeded out of his mouth!

The Beatitudes

Now, let us look at the beatitudes given in verses 3-12. Here the Son of God describes his people by eight distinct characteristics, and pronounces eight beatitudes, eight blessings of grace upon them. If we fit the character of those described in the blessing, then the blessing is ours and we are blessed. If we do not fit the character of the ones described, then we have no right to claim the blessing. Our Master begins this great sermon by pronouncing blessings upon his people. He is himself the great comprehensive blessing of all blessings and the blessedness of his people.

In these verses our Saviour gives us eight distinct characteristics of blessed people, eight things found in all who are saved by his matchless grace. They are poor in spirit, people who mourn, the meek of the earth, people who hunger and thirst after righteousness, the merciful, the pure in heart, peacemakers, and those who are persecuted for righteousness' sake.

When I read these verses, the question immediately arises in my mind, "Where are such people to be found?" It is certain that none among the fallen sons and daughters of Adam possess such traits. Among all the people of our fallen race, there are none who are good, none who do good, and none who seek after God (Psalm 14:1-3. Romans 3:10-18). Obviously, those who are here described are the redeemed of the Lord, his own elect who were given to him by the Father, made blessed in the righteousness of the Son, and regenerated and sanctified by the Holy Spirit.

Poor In Spirit

"Blessed are the poor in Spirit". He did not say, "Blessed are the poor". He said, "Blessed are the poor in spirit". Those who are poor in spirit are men and women who, in their own judgment and esteem, are spiritually poor. Their souls are barren and empty before God. They have no righteousness of their own, no good works, no good thoughts, nothing with which to commend themselves to God. As John Gill wrote, "Being sensible of their poverty, they place themselves at the door of mercy and knock there. Their language is, 'God be merciful … ' They are importunate, will have no denial, yet receive the least favour with thankfulness."

Before God lifts us up by his grace, he brings us down. Until we are poor in spirit, we will not seek mercy in Christ. It is painful, but blessed work when God puts a soul into a bankrupt state! The Laodiceans of this world will never seek mercy (Revelation 3:17-19). Jacob was brought down (Genesis 32:24, 25). Isaiah was brought down (Isaiah 6:1-8). Gomer was brought down (Hosea 2:6-23). The woman with an issue of blood was brought down (Luke 8:43, 44, 47, 48). Onesimus was brought down (Philemon 10-16). The prodigal son was brought down (Luke 15:11-32). God knows how to make proud, self-sufficient sinners poor in spirit. He knows how to bring sinners down (Psalm 107).

Those who are poor in spirit are people who have been made to know their desperate need of free grace in and by Christ, their all-sufficient Saviour. They have nothing. They can do nothing. They must have someone to atone for their sins. They must have someone to make them righteous before God. They need pardon and grace for their countless sins. Rowland Hill said, "Poverty of spirit is the bag into which Christ puts the riches of his grace." Saved sinners are men and women who know their utter poverty of soul before God. They are people convinced of their sin by God the Holy Spirit.

"Blessed are the poor in spirit: For theirs is the kingdom of heaven." "The sacrifices of God are a broken spirit, a broken and contrite heart, O God, thou wilt not despise" (Psalm 51:17). The Lord God declares, "To this man will I look, even to him that is poor, and of a contrite spirit, and trembleth at my word" (Isaiah 66:2). If a person is ever brought to the place that he has nothing in himself, he will have everything by grace in Christ. But as long as a person imagines that he has something in himself, he has nothing. Nothing is more painful to our proud flesh; but nothing is more needful than that we be made "poor in spirit" before God. Are you poor in spirit? If you are, you are blessed. God made you poor. And he has made you an heir of his kingdom in Christ.

Mourn

"Blessed are they that mourn". There is a mourning that is sinful, as when Jonah mourned over a withered gourd. There is a mourning that is natural, as when we mourn over the death of a loved one. And there is mourning that is the result of God's operations of grace in the heart. Those who mourn in this sense, our Lord Jesus declares are blessed.

The mourners our Saviour here declares to be blessed are those who mourn over their sins (Psalm 51:1-17). No sooner is grace poured into our hearts, giving us the knowledge of Christ as our Saviour, than we are made to see and know the wretchedness that is ours by nature (Zechariah 12:10). When Christ is revealed in us, our hearts melt before him. "I do not understand", wrote John Owen, "how a man can be a true believer, in whom sin is not the greatest burden, sorrow and trouble." Indwelling sin is to the believing soul a constant source of bitterness and sorrow. Like Paul, the believer cries out, "O wretched man that I am! Who shall deliver me from the body of this death?" This mourning over sin, the sin that is in us, is a lifelong experience, causing God's saints to be in a state of continual repentance, ever looking to Christ alone for redemption and righteousness.

The more fully we are made aware of our sin, the more we mourn over it, the more we are compelled to look out of ourselves to Christ alone for righteousness, and the more he is endeared to our hearts. "Unto you therefore which believe, he is precious."

How delightful it is to hear our Saviour declare, "Blessed are they that mourn for they shall be comforted"! Those who mourn because of their sin shall be comforted here by the revelation of Christ in their hearts. Though we mourn because of our sin and utter corruption, we are comforted by the knowledge and assurance of Christ's all-sufficiency as our Surety, Substitute, and Saviour. His righteousness is ours. His satisfaction is ours. He has, by his one great sacrifice, put away our sins forever. How comforting it is to hear the gospel of God's free grace in his darling Son! How comforting it is to hear him speak to our hearts by his Holy Spirit through the scriptures! How comforting it is to remember our dear Saviour as we eat the bread and drink the wine at the Lord's table! How comforting it is to fetch grace and mercy from the throne of grace in every time of need, by prayer and supplication! How comforting it is to know that he who loved us and gave himself for us rules all things for our good; ordering all the affairs of providence according to his infinite wisdom and goodness, and according to his own infinite eternal love for us!

Yes, those who are taught of God to mourn over their sin are comforted here. And when we drop this robe of flesh in the grave and are brought into heavenly glory, dwelling forever in the presence of our God and Saviour, we shall be fully and eternally comforted (Luke 16:25; Jeremiah 50:20). In that great day, our God shall wipe all tears from our eyes. Then we shall be free from sin, free from all the evil consequences of sin, free from sorrow, and made possessors of all the glory the Father has given to the Son as our Mediator (John 17:5, 22).

The Meek

"Blessed are the meek". Someone once said, "Meekness is the mark of a man who has been mastered by God." The meekness our Lord here pronounces is a blessed thing. It is not that which men call meekness. It is not an outward show of pretended humility. It is that which is wrought in the heart by grace. Meekness is a realization of who I am before God. Meekness is submission to the will of God. Meekness is obedience to God. Meekness causes us to esteem others better than ourselves (Philippians 2:1-5).

Matthew Henry wrote, "They are meek who are rarely and hardly provoked, but quickly and easily pacified; and who would rather forgive twenty injuries than avenge one, having the rule of their own spirits." John Gill describes the meek as those who "have the meanest thoughts of themselves, and the best of others; do not envy the gifts and graces of other men; are willing to be instructed and admonished, by the meanest of the saints; quietly submit to the will of God, in adverse dispensations of providence; and ascribe all they have, and are, to the grace of God."

Moses was the meekest man on earth in his day; but no man looking at his behaviour would have thought so. He was meek before God. He knew he was God's servant, responsible to do God's will. Therefore, he was as bold as a lion. The Lord Jesus lived on this earth in meekness. It was this meekness that caused him to speak with authority and drive the money-changers out of the temple. Robert Hawker explains:

> The meekness the Son of God pronounced blessed, is the meekness inwrought in the soul, by the gracious influence of God the Holy Ghost. It is learnt of Jesus (Matthew 11:29). It is wholly from Jesus (John 15:4, 5). And it is his regenerated members of whom he saith, the Lord will "beautify the meek with salvation" (Psalm 149:4). This meekness of the Lord's own creating in the soul is of great price (1 Peter 3:4).

"They shall inherit the earth". They shall inherit all the blessings of the earth, all things working together for their good. And they shall inherit all the new earth, when our God shall make all things new. "The meek shall inherit the earth; and shall delight themselves in the abundance of peace" (Psalm 37:11).

Hunger And Thirst

"Blessed are they which do hunger and thirst after righteousness". Many imagine that our Lord Jesus is here telling us that those who greatly desire to make themselves righteous are blessed and shall have their hunger satisfied and their thirst quenched. Such teaching is totally foreign to the scriptures. Mere morality is not righteousness. The scribes and Pharisees of our Lord's day prided themselves in the performance of such.

The Son of God did not come to preach a righteousness that men can perform. He did not teach men to trust in themselves, but just the opposite. He preached grace. His gospel demands that sinners count all personal righteousness but dung (Philippians 3:7, 8), and look to Christ alone for righteousness. Those are blessed of God who hunger and thirst for his righteousness, the only righteousness by which a sinner can be justified in the sight of God.

The souls that hunger and thirst for him who is "the Lord our Righteousness" are blessed of God with grace, salvation, and eternal life. They desire to be found in him, not having their own righteousness, but the righteousness of God established and brought in by Christ's obedience to God as their Substitute. Righteousness that can be obtained only by faith in him. Hungering and thirsting after Christ's righteousness, we acknowledge and confess that we have no righteousness of our own. Therefore, we long to be clothed with Christ's robe of righteousness and garment of salvation. Christ is that righteousness and holiness we must have, without which no man shall see the Lord (Hebrews 12:14).

Not only does our Saviour pronounce those blessed who hunger and thirst after him, he promises, "they shall be filled" (Isaiah 55:1; John 7:37). We shall not hunger in vain. All who abandon their own righteousness, seeking righteousness before God in Christ alone, who is "the end of the law for righteousness to everyone that believeth" (Romans 10:4), shall be filled (Psalm 132:9-16; Isaiah 61:1-3, 10, 11). God's elect shall be filled with (completely satisfied with) Christ's righteousness and never seek any other righteousness. And being filled with Christ's righteousness, they shall be filled "with all other good things in consequence of it" (John Gill).

Merciful

"Blessed are the merciful". The merciful are those who show mercy to others, having obtained mercy themselves from God. Those who are merciful have been made merciful by the experience of God's mercy bestowed upon them in Christ. They are loving and charitable (1 Corinthians 13:4-7), kind and gracious (Ephesians 4:32-5:1), and forgiving (Matthew 6:14, 15). These graces within are the fruits and effects of God's saving grace and the believer's vital union with Christ in regeneration.

"For they shall obtain mercy". This is not a suggestion that our obtaining mercy is in some way dependent upon or determined by our mercifulness to others. Rather, it is the declaration and assurance that all who have obtained mercy in the gift of God's grace shall continue to obtain mercy all the days of their lives in this world and in the world to come (2 Timothy 1:16-18).

Pure In Heart

"Blessed are the pure in heart". Almost everything I have read or heard by theologians, preachers, teachers, and religious leaders on Matthew 5:8 is totally contrary to the scriptures. Men use this verse of holy scripture to teach that if we will make our hearts pure, we shall see God in heaven. Very few leave out God's work altogether. Most try to make their doctrine of works appear to be the doctrine of grace. They tell us, of course that God must first make our hearts new in regeneration; but we must make our hearts pure by the discipline of grace in self-denial and the mortification of our sins in sanctification.

I ask all who give and all who attempt to follow such counsel, "Have you succeeded? Have you made yourself pure in heart? So pure that you can now, by reason of your heart purity, confidently hope to see God himself face to face in heaven's glory?" If we have even a shred of honesty in us, we must hang our heads with shame and confess No! What, then, does this mean? "Blessed are the pure in heart: for they shall see God".

These words, lofty and remote as they seem, are in fact among the most hopeful, comforting, and radiant that ever came from our Master's lips. They proclaim the certain, sure realization of something that seems impossible. They promise the possession of an apparently impossible vision. They soothe our corrupt, sinful hearts: hearts so sinful that we most naturally shrink from, and tremble at, the thought of seeing God in all the splendour of his radiant glory. These words assure us that seeing God shall be our highest, ultimate blessedness.

Our hearts, yours and mine, are by nature horribly evil (Genesis 6:5; Psalm 12:2; 101:4; Isaiah 44:20; Jeremiah 17:9; Mark 7:20-23). The promise of grace is, "I will take away the stony heart out of your flesh, and I will give you a heart of flesh" (Ezekiel 36:26). Do you see this? Has God taught you the evil, the horrid corruption of your hard, cold, dead, unfeeling, unmoved, heart of stone? Well may we look within and sigh, "The rocks can rend, the earth can quake, the seas can roar, the mountains shake; of feeling all things show some sign, but this unfeeling heart of mine."

Who Is Blessed Of God?

If this is the state of my heart, if this is the condition of every man, woman, and child by nature, how can we ever hope to know the blessedness of which the Son of God speaks, when he declares, “Blessed are the pure in heart: for they shall see God”? Such hearts cannot see God. Such hearts can never see God. Indeed, such hearts as these, the heart of man, cannot see the things of God, much less God himself. Did not the Lord Jesus say to Nicodemus, “Except a man be born again, he cannot see the kingdom of God” (John 3:3)? The natural man simply cannot see God, cannot see Christ, and cannot see the things of God (1 Corinthians 2:14).

That is the state and condition of every man’s heart by nature. It is anything but pure. Yet, our Lord speaks of “the pure in heart”. What does our Lord mean by this statement? “Blessed are the pure in heart”. This purity of heart is, not the external varnish of a Pharisee, or the boasted perfection of a hypocrite, or the empty dream of the carnally secure. They are pure in their own eyes; but they are not pure (Proverbs 30:12).

The pure in heart are not those vain, religious fools who convince themselves that they are pure. They shall never see God. They are an irksome smoke in his nose (Isaiah 65:5; Jude 16-19). Purity of heart certainly does not imply sinlessness of heart. Those who think that they have no sin are yet dead in sin (1 John 1:7-10). Heart purity is not accomplished by the imaginary self-sanctification of those multitudes who delude themselves into thinking they make themselves pure by their slight, occasional conformity to selected points of the law in their outward behaviour (Isaiah 66:16, 17). And that which our Lord speaks of as a pure heart is not a changed heart. When I was a young man, before God saved me, people would often ask me to give my heart to the Lord. Even then, in my utter ignorance, I thought, “What on earth would God want with that filthy thing?” Salvation is not you giving God your old, wretched heart. Salvation is God giving you a new heart (Jeremiah 32:37-40; Ezekiel 36:26). There are multitudes who talk about conversion as “a change of heart”. Nothing could be further from the truth. Salvation is God giving us a new heart.

Those who are blessed of God are those whose hearts the Lord has made new, those who are holy and pure in the cleansing and justifying purity and holiness of the Lord their Righteousness. They are a people who know their own, personal corruption and groan under its weight. They see God in Christ in all the blessedness of salvation here in the life that now is, and they shall see him in the complete enjoyment of him in the life of glory that is to come.

This purity of heart stands in having the heart sprinkled from an evil conscience by the sprinkling of Christ's precious blood (Hebrews 9:11-14). What is the meaning of this word "pure"? There are three words translated "pure" in the New Testament. The word used here is the word from which we get the name "Katherine". It is also the word from which we get the term used in psychology, "catharsis", which means, "the purging of emotions, the release of pent up emotions, and the relief of guilt". Actually, that is pretty close to the meaning of the word "pure" in Matthew 5:8. The word means "purified by fire", "purified as a vine that is pruned and made fit to bear fruit", "free from corruption, sin, and guilt", "blameless, innocent", "unstained with the guilt of anything", "transparent and undiluted".

When our Lord speaks of those who are "pure in heart", he is talking about a people who have in their hearts an honest, transparent consciousness of perfection, righteousness, innocence, sinlessness, and stainlessness before God, without pretence or hypocrisy. In Titus 2:14 the Holy Spirit tells us that it was the intention, design, and purpose of Christ in his death to make us pure before God. In Acts 15:8, 9 we are told that God the Holy Spirit purifies the hearts of chosen, redeemed sinners by the blessed gift of faith in Christ. When Christ is revealed and the sinner looks to him alone for complete atonement, for all righteousness, for acceptance with God, looking on Christ, his heart is sprinkled with the blood of Christ and his conscience is purged of all guilt before God. William Huntington wrote:

> Men who are destitute of this faith, and who never received this atonement, are as destitute of internal purity as the prince of devils. "Unto the pure all things are pure, but unto them that are defiled and unbelieving is nothing pure, but even their mind and conscience is defiled." The man whose sins are forgiven him, and whose conscience is purged from guilt and dead works, who is renewed by the Spirit, who is a believer in Jesus, and holds fast the truth of the gospel as it is in Christ, is the man that holds the mystery of faith in a pure conscience. These are the people to whom the Lord turns a pure language, and such bring to the Lord a pure offering.

The pure in heart are those who, looking to Christ, are convinced of God the Holy Spirit concerning sin, and righteousness, and judgment (John 16:7-11).

They are those who openly, frankly, honestly confess their sin to God, trusting Christ alone for the forgiveness of sin (1 John 1:9; Psalm 51:1-10).

These, and only these, are truly blessed of God, "for they shall see God"! Has the Lord God given you a pure heart? Has he given you a tender, feeling heart? A broken and contrite heart? A heart that is crushed under the awareness of your utter sin and depravity? A heart that mourns over sin and hungers and thirsts for righteousness? A heart that looks for grace, righteousness, merit before God, and eternal life altogether outside yourself? A heart that pours out the painful, bitter confession of sin before God, acknowledging that there is nothing you want more than purity and that there is in you no purity at all? If he has given you such a heart, this is the blessedness that is yours. "Blessed are the pure in heart: for they shall see God"! "God who commanded the light to shine out of darkness hath shined in our hearts, to give the light of the knowledge of the glory of God in the face of Jesus Christ."

This is nothing less than seeing him who is invisible. It is seeing him as he is in his true character, as he reveals himself to your soul in Christ, and seeing him forever. The promise is that you shall never be separated or banished from God and his presence. You shall see him with acceptance, and with approbation as your dear and everlasting Father. You shall see his face without a cloud, and hear his voice without a proverb. The promise here given is that you shall have an eternal abiding with him, in whose favour is life, in whose presence is fulness of joy, and at whose right hand are pleasures for evermore. This is the promise of complete salvation in Christ in the glorious liberty of the sons of God in heaven, when "the righteous shall shine forth as the sun in the kingdom of their Father", forever and ever. We shall then see as we are seen, and know as we are known (1 John 3:1, 2; Revelation 22:3-5). "Blessed are the pure in heart, for they shall see God"!

Peacemakers

"Blessed are the peacemakers". Again, I ask, "Of whom does Christ speak?" Clearly, he is not talking about men who make peace with God. That is impossible. Christ alone makes peace between God and men. Our peace with God is found in the blood of his cross. The peacemakers are those men and women whose hearts are ruled by the Prince of Peace, in whose hearts the peace of God rules. They are peaceful themselves. They strive to live peaceably with all men, especially with those who are of the household of faith. They strive to make all men love one another by preaching the gospel of peace.

"They shall be called the children of God". Their adoption as the children of God by grace is made manifest and they are known to be God's children by the grace of God that is wrought in them, making them peaceful before God. And those who are at peace with God, by faith in Christ, are at peace with all things and with all men.

Persecuted For Righteousness

"Blessed are they which are persecuted for righteousness' sake". Many suffer greatly because they are haughty and self-righteous (1 Peter 2:19; 4:16). But God's people are now, have been throughout history, and shall be so long as time shall stand, persecuted and reviled by a self-righteous world "for righteousness' sake"; because they trust Christ alone as the Lord their Righteousness and assert that there is no righteousness to be found in the world except the righteousness of God in Christ.

To my knowledge, no one has ever been persecuted or reviled for living a good life, for doing what men call works of righteousness. No one is going to persecute you for being honest, being a faithful husband, a good wife, or an exemplary citizen. God's saints are persecuted for declaring that no man can produce righteousness and asserting that salvation is by the obedience and righteousness of Christ alone. When we declare that salvation is by a righteousness given to sinners freely in Christ, not by a righteousness performed by sinners, we are reviled as promoters of licentiousness (Romans 3:8). They are persecuted for believing and preaching free justification by the righteousness of Christ, which all men naturally despise because it excludes all boasting. Though persecuted and reviled as the offscouring of the earth, these are a truly blessed people, "for theirs is the kingdom of God". "Blessed are ye, when men shall revile you, and persecute you, and shall say all manner of evil against you falsely, for my sake. Rejoice, and be exceeding glad: for great is your reward in heaven: for so persecuted they the prophets which were before you" (vv. 11, 12).

How different real Christianity is from that which the world looks upon as Christianity! The very characters the world despises and ridicules, Christ honours and calls blessed. The blessedness pronounced upon believing sinners in this world and in the world to come is the blessedness of pure, free grace: it is gospel blessedness, which is altogether the gift of God.

Chapter 10

Lessons From Salt, Light, And The Law

"Ye are the salt of the earth: but if the salt have lost his savour, wherewith shall it be salted? it is thenceforth good for nothing, but to be cast out, and to be trodden under foot of men. Ye are the light of the world. A city that is set on an hill cannot be hid. Neither do men light a candle, and put it under a bushel, but on a candlestick; and it giveth light unto all that are in the house. Let your light so shine before men, that they may see your good works, and glorify your Father which is in heaven. Think not that I am come to destroy the law, or the prophets: I am not come to destroy, but to fulfil. For verily I say unto you, Till heaven and earth pass, one jot or one tittle shall in no wise pass from the law, till all be fulfilled. Whosoever therefore shall break one of these least commandments, and shall teach men so, he shall be called the least in the kingdom of heaven: but whosoever shall do and teach them, the same shall be called great in the kingdom of heaven."
(Matthew 5:13-19)

Our Lord Jesus Christ was truly the Prince of preachers. He who is the subject of all true preaching is also the example all true preachers should follow. He wisely used common, ordinary, simple things, with which all his hearers were familiar, to illustrate and enforce the doctrine he taught. In the passage now before us he used salt, light, and the law to show us the characteristics of true Christianity. He shows us in these verses that the grace of God changes people from the inside out, making them both righteous before God and useful to one another. In these eight verses of Inspiration our Saviour teaches us three very important lessons. May the Holy Spirit of God now seal them to our hearts.

True Christianity
First, our Saviour here demonstrates the character of true Christianity (vv. 13-16). All that glitters is not gold. "They are not all Israel which are of Israel". And not all who profess to be Christians truly are Christians. Christianity radically

changes men and women. Grace gives men and women new motives and principles of life that set them apart from the rest of the world.

Believers are the salt of the earth. “Ye are the salt of the earth: but if the salt have lost his savour, wherewith shall it be salted? it is thenceforth good for nothing, but to be cast out, and to be trodden under foot of men” (v. 13).

Salt has a peculiar taste and quality. Nothing can really imitate it well. When mingled with other things, it imparts some of its taste and preserves other things from corruption. It is useful as long as it retains its savour, its saltiness. But once that is lost, it is useless. But how do these things apply to us?

There is clearly an application here to those who preach the gospel. The preaching of the gospel preserves society from total corruption. It preserves God’s saints from the corrupting influence of the world. And when a preacher departs from the preaching of the gospel, he is utterly useless. However, these words must not be restricted to gospel preachers.

Our Lord’s intention was that these words be applied by every believer to himself. C. H. Spurgeon correctly noted, “In the believer’s character there is a preserving force to keep the rest of society from utter corruption … There is a secret something, which is the secret of the believer’s power. That something is savour. It is not easy to define it, but yet it is absolutely essential to usefulness.”

This teaches us the necessity of perseverance. If the savour of God’s grace could be lost, it could never be restored (Hebrews 6:1-6). Thank God that grace cannot fail to save a man; but if grace could fail to save a man, there would be no hope for any! You can salt meat. But no one can salt salt. If grace fails, everything fails! Thank God for grace that cannot fail, for salt that cannot lose its savour (2 Corinthians 12:9).

Believers are the light of the world. “Ye are the light of the world. A city that is set on an hill cannot be hid. Neither do men light a candle, and put it under a bushel, but on a candlestick; and it giveth light unto all that are in the house. Let your light so shine before men, that they may see your good works, and glorify your Father which is in heaven” (vv. 14-16). J. C. Ryle says,

> It is the property of light to be utterly distinct from darkness. The least spark in a dark room can be seen at once. Of all things created, light is the most useful: it fertilizes; it guides; it cheers. It was the first thing called into being (Genesis 1:3). Without it, the world would be a gloomy blank.

Again, there is clearly a reference to those who preach the gospel of Christ (2 Corinthians 4:3-6). Christ himself is the Light of the world (John 1:4; 8:12; 9:5). The gospel of Christ is the means by which that Light shines in the world. It is our responsibility to give out the Light. Our object is that chosen sinners, being converted by the light of the gospel, may glorify God, our Father, by repentance and faith in Christ.

Again, these words must not be applied only to gospel preachers. You who trust Christ are the light of the world. The church of Christ is the light of the world. As the moon reflects the light of the sun, so those who trust him reflect the light of Christ, the Sun of Righteousness.

We are to dispel the darkness of ignorance, sin, and sorrow by proclaiming the glorious gospel of Christ (v. 14). God intends for us to be conspicuous in our testimony regarding his grace and his Son (v. 15). Yet, the light of the gospel shines forth, not in our words, but in our works (v. 16). The works by which the light shines forth from God's elect are not religious works of self-righteousness, or displays of religious devotion (Matthew 6:2, 3, 5, 6, 16-18), but works of faith and love in the daily affairs of life. Christianity is not a show of religion, but a life of devotion to Christ.

C. H. Spurgeon says, "True shining is silent, but yet it is so useful, that men ... are forced to bless God for the good which they receive ... when they mark the good works of his saints." It ought to be our constant prayer and desire before God that he would give us grace to be useful to others, to improve the lives of those whose paths we cross, to make them happier and better for having come into contact with us.

The emblems our Lord used here of salt and light are instructive. Christ is the salt of the covenant (Leviticus 2:13; Numbers 18:19; Mark 9:49). Our Saviour, as we have already observed, is the light of the world. It is because Christ is in his redeemed (Colossians 1:27), and only because Christ is in us that believers are the salt of the earth and the light of the world. Were it not for the fact that Christ's seed are in the earth, the whole world would be in a state of putrefaction and utter darkness (Philippians 2:15).

Scripture Unity

Second, in verses 17-19 our Lord shows us the unity of the Old Testament and the New. "Think not that I am come to destroy the law, or the prophets: I am not come to destroy, but to fulfil. For verily I say unto you, Till heaven and earth pass, one jot or one tittle shall in no wise pass from the law, till all be fulfilled. Whosoever therefore shall break one of these least commandments, and shall teach men so, he shall be called the least in the kingdom of heaven: but whosoever shall do and teach them, the same shall be called great in the kingdom of heaven."

This is a point of great importance. The Bible is one Book, not two. The religion of the Old Testament and the religion of the New Testament are the same. Totally disregard as false any religious teacher or any doctrinal system that would teach you to despise, disregard, or ignore any part of holy scripture, suggesting that it applies only to people of another age. The Book of God was written for you and me (Romans 15:4). Be sure you grasp and firmly hold to the unity of God's holy Word.

The Lord Jesus Christ fulfilled all the types and requirements of the law and all the promises and predictions of the prophets. He fulfilled all the Old Testament prophecies, all the types of the ceremonial law, and all the requirements of the moral law as our Mediator (Matthew 2:6; Luke 4:16-22; Acts 4:27, 28; Luke 24:25-27, 44-47; Romans 10:4). In all things he magnified the law of God and made it honourable by his obedience and death as our Substitute (Isaiah 42:21). Nothing can be more blessedly comforting than beholding the Son of God by faith as our law-surety, and our law-fulfiller. As such he is the Lord our Righteousness, and is the "end of the law for righteousness to every one that believeth".

Let me be perfectly clear. God's people do not, in any way, despise or disregard his holy law. We rejoice in the fact that in Christ we are free from the law. The scriptures plainly declare that believers are not under the law (Romans 6:14, 15; 7:1, 9; 10:4). We have no curse from the law (Galatians 3:13), no covenant with the law (Hebrews 8:10-12), and no constraint by the law (2 Corinthians 5:14).

Yet, every believer loves and delights in God's holy law (Romans 7:22). The law is God's measure, the only measure of right and wrong (Romans 7:7). The law shows men their sin and their need of Christ as their Redeemer and Saviour (Romans 3:19, 20; Galatians 3:19-22). And the law restrains wicked men from the wickedness that is in them (1 Timothy 1:8, 9).

Let no one imagine that the gospel lowers either the law of God or the holiness of his saints. Nothing can be further from the truth. The only person who truly fulfils and honours the law is the sinner who is saved by grace, through faith, without the law (Romans 3:31). And the constraint of grace in the heart is far more powerful than the constraints of the law written in stone (Romans 12:1, 2; 1 Corinthians 6:19, 20; 2 Corinthians 8:9).

Our Substitute

Third, in verses 19 and 20 our Saviour demonstrates to all the necessity of an infinitely meritorious substitute. "Whosoever therefore shall break one of these least commandments, and shall teach men so, he shall be called the least in the kingdom of heaven: but whosoever shall do and teach them, the same shall be called great in the kingdom of heaven. For I say unto you, That except your righteousness shall exceed the righteousness of the scribes and Pharisees, ye shall in no case enter into the kingdom of heaven." Robert Hawker, in his commentary on these two verses, wrote:

> These are very strong expressions of Christ, in proof that nothing short of a whole and complete obedience to the law, can justify a soul before God. And hence the presumption of the scribes and Pharisees. Oh! the folly of the Pharisees of the present hour! Oh! the blessedness of being found, as Paul was (Philippians 3:8, 9), in Christ's righteousness!
>
> The scribes and Pharisees were, in their day, the most highly respected and admired religious leaders in the world. Everyone stood in awe of them. But our Lord Jesus said to his disciples, "Except your righteousness shall exceed the righteousness of the scribes and Pharisees, ye shall in no case enter into the kingdom of heaven.

Those words must have been astounding to the people who first heard them. The scribes were the religious scholars of the day. They were the men who copied and expounded the scriptures. They gave their lives entirely to this one great work for God and his people. They consecrated themselves to this one noble work.

The Pharisees were the strictest sect of the Jews. No one exceeded the Pharisee in outward morality, obedience to the law, saying of prayers, tithing, sabbath keeping, scripture memory, personal righteousness, and public approval. Yet, our Lord declares, "Except your righteousness shall exceed the righteousness of the scribes and Pharisees, you cannot be saved"!

Is the Son of God here telling us that we must do more and be better than the scribes and Pharisees? Is he saying that we must gain a greater measure of personal holiness than those men had? Not at all. In fact, he is saying just the opposite.

The Master is telling us that it is utterly impossible for any man to gain favour with God on the basis of his own, personal righteousness. There never has been a child of Adam upon this earth good enough, righteous enough, holy enough to inherit or inhabit the kingdom of heaven, and there never shall be.

You and I must get every thought of personal righteousness out of our minds, and the very word "good" out of our vocabulary, when we think or speak of any human being in God's sight! We have no righteousness of our own before God, and no ability to produce righteousness. Indeed, "all our righteousnesses are as filthy rags" (Isaiah 64:6) before the holy Lord God.

If we would be saved, we must have the righteousness of God in Christ imputed and imparted to us. It is this righteousness that exceeds the righteousness of the scribes and Pharisees! Do what you may, without the righteousness of God in Christ, you cannot enter into the kingdom of heaven. And the only way anyone can get that righteousness is by faith in Christ. Only God can give us the righteousness of God. Let me show you five things from the Word of God about this matter of righteousness.

1. God demands perfect righteousness (Leviticus 22:21). He says, "Walk before me and be thou perfect" (Genesis 17:1). He will accept nothing less. Without perfect righteousness no one can ever enter into heaven (Revelation 21:27; 22:11-14).

2. You and I have no righteousness and no ability to produce righteousness. We used to be righteous; but we lost it in Adam's fall. We cannot do righteousness (Romans 3:9-19). Even our imaginary righteousness is sin (Isaiah 64:6).

3. The Lord Jesus Christ, by his obedience to God as our Representative and by his sacrificial death as our Substitute, has established and brought in everlasting righteousness for God's elect (Jeremiah 23:6; Daniel 9:24). In his obedience to God as our Representative he lived the life we could not live. In his sin-atoning death as our Substitute he paid the debt we could not pay, making full satisfaction to divine justice for us. In order to enter that perfect kingdom we must be made perfectly righteous by the righteousness of Christ (Romans 5:19; 2

Corinthians 5:21). It is Christ himself who is that Holiness we must have, without which no one shall ever see God and live (Hebrews 12:14).

4. The righteousness of Christ is imputed to God's elect in justification (Romans 4:3-8). Our sin was imputed to Christ at Calvary. Though he never committed sin, he was made to be sin, and became responsible under the law for our sins as our Substitute. In exactly the same way the righteousness of Christ has been imputed to all who trust the Lord Jesus Christ, though we never have performed a righteous deed. Just as the law punished Christ for our sin, which was legally imputed to him, the law of God rewards every believer for the righteousness of Christ imputed to us.

5. The righteousness of Christ is imparted to redeemed sinners in regeneration (2 Peter 1:2-4; 1 John 3:4-9). "If any man be in Christ, he is a new creature: old things are passed away; behold, all things are become new" (2 Corinthians 5:17). If I am born again by the Spirit of God, I have a new nature created in my soul; a righteous nature is imparted to me, by which I reign as a king over the lusts and passions of my flesh. Yes, God's people do sin. Sin is mixed with all we do so long as we live in this body of flesh. But sin no longer reigns over us. We are no longer under the dominion of sin (Romans 6:14-16; Galatians 5:22, 23). The believer's life is a life of faith, godliness, and uprightness.

The Amen

In verse 18 our Lord Jesus uses the word "amen", here translated "verily", for the first time. Our Master's use of this word is very significant. This is one of his precious names, by which he distinguishes himself as the Christ, our God-man Mediator (Revelation 3:14). Using it as he did throughout his earthly ministry, the Lord Jesus puts his name to that which he declares (Isaiah 65:16). He is declaring that the thing stated is certain, sure, and true, as certain, sure, and true as him who is "the Amen, the Faithful and True Witness, the beginning of the creation of God".

Our Lord frequently began his discourses with this word and often repeated it "Verily, verily, I say unto you". Yet, no one else in the scriptures ever used this word as he did, introducing a statement with it, as if to give what he was about to say his own divine oath, attaching his honour as our God-man Mediator to the certainty of what he was about to declare. All the promises of God are "yea and amen" in Christ Jesus (2 Corinthians 1:20.) Strictly and properly speaking, they are his promises, for he is himself the one great promise of the Bible. Therefore, it is written of God's elect in Isaiah 65:16, "That he who blesseth himself in the earth shall bless himself in the God of truth". That is to say, "in the Amen".

Whenever we use this sacred name by which our Saviour identifies himself, in public worship and in private, let us remember our blessed Saviour with faith, love, adoration, and gratitude. No one should say "Amen" in the church ignorantly (1 Corinthians 14:16).

Chapter 11

Six Aspects Of Righteousness

"For I say unto you, That except your righteousness shall exceed the righteousness of the scribes and Pharisees, ye shall in no case enter into the kingdom of heaven".
(Matthew 5:20)

The scribes and the Pharisees were regarded by the ancient Jews as the most devoted, most spiritual, and most holy of all men. Had anyone at that time thought of calling any man "his holiness", they would have been called "most holy, holiness". They were men of such high esteem and reputation that the Jews had a saying about them. It went like this, "If be two of all the world were to go to heaven the one would be a scribe and the other a Pharisee."

In so far as outward, religious righteousness was concerned no one excelled these two groups of men. In works of piety they made long public prayers on the corners of streets, so that all could see and hear their devotion. In works of charity they gave alms, blowing the trumpet, so that all would be impressed by their generosity. In works of equity they paid their tithes, counting out ten percent on their gross income. In works of courtesy and hospitality they often held banquets, even for Christ and his disciples (Luke7:36-50).

Yet, the Lord Jesus declares that our righteousness must exceed, not match but exceed, the righteousness of the scribes and Pharisees. If it does not, we cannot be saved. The text clearly teaches us these three things:

1. There will be no admission into heaven without righteousness.
2. A legal, pharisaical righteousness will never be accepted of God.
3. The only hope any sinner has of being saved is through the righteousness of a divinely appointed and accepted Substitute and Representative. And that Substitute and Representative is the Lord Jesus Christ, the Lord our Righteousness (Jeremiah 23:6; 1 Corinthians 1:30, 31; 2 Corinthians 5:21; Romans 9:31-10:4). The only way a guilty sinner can be saved and obtain righteousness before God is through faith in Jesus Christ, Jehovah-tsidkenu, The Lord our Righteousness.

Righteousness Lost

All the sons and daughters of Adam are all sinners. We lost all righteousness before God in the garden of Eden. We are all totally depraved. We have all gone astray from the womb speaking lies. We all drink iniquity like water. So thorough and complete is the depravity of man that even our works of righteousness are filthy rags before the holy Lord God; and we are all at our best estate altogether vanity! But these things were not always so.

God created man in righteousness and holiness. We were all created in the image and likeness of God himself. One aspect of that created image of God was an uprightness of nature (Ecclesiastes 7:29). How long Adam lived in this state, we do not know. But it appears to have been a relatively short period of time. Then something happened. Our father Adam sinned against God and plunged the entire human race into sin, death, and condemnation (Romans 5:12; Psalm 14:2, 3). Because Adam was our divinely appointed representative and federal head, his sin was imputed to us in divine judgment. And his sin nature was imparted to us by natural generation (Psalm 51:5; Jeremiah 17:9; Matthew 15:19).

By the sin and fall of our father Adam we all suffered a threefold loss of righteousness. This is a loss that simply cannot be denied. First, when Adam sinned in the garden, he lost his righteous nature, and we did too. Before the fall man was righteous. After the fall, he had no righteousness (Matthew 15:19). We are all, by nature, sinful, guilty, condemned, and lost.

Second, Adam lost all legal righteousness, and we did too. Because man is sinful, he cannot approach God. Adam was expelled from the garden and separated from God. Because our sins have separated us from God, we cannot approach him (1 Timothy 6:15, 16).

Third, once he sinned, fallen man lost all knowledge and understanding of righteousness. As soon as he did he went about to establish righteousness for himself, sewing fig leaves together to make himself presentable to the holy Lord God; and man has been doing the same ever since (Romans 9:31-10:4). The natural man has absolutely no idea what righteousness is, where it is to be found, or how it can be obtained. But he thinks he does (Luke 16:15). This is the first thing to be established. We have no righteousness, and no ability to produce it.

Yet, our Lord said, "Except your righteousness shall exceed the righteousness of the scribes and Pharisees, ye shall in no case enter into the kingdom of heaven". In making that statement our Lord declared that there has never been one son or daughter of Adam on this earth good enough, righteous enough, or holy enough to inherit and inhabit the kingdom of heaven. There is not now and never will be one person in heaven who is there because he was good, righteous, and holy in this world. Man at his best estate is altogether vanity. Our righteousnesses are as filthy rags in God's sight.

We must get the idea of "righteousness" out of our minds and get the word "righteousness" out of our vocabulary, insofar as any human works are concerned in God's sight. Our righteousness is filthy rags before the holy Lord God! (Isaiah 64:6; Isaiah 1:16-20). Every imagination of the thoughts of man's heart is only evil continually (Genesis 6:5). Read the Book of God and you will discover that every man in the Book who knew God, who knew the righteous character of God and had been made righteous in Christ, lamented his own utter wickedness.

Righteousness Required

God is holy. Being perfectly holy, he demands perfect holiness. He requires perfect righteousness. Anything and anyone that is not perfectly holy will be consumed by the fire of his glorious holiness. He declares, "I am Almighty God; walk before me and be thou perfect" (Genesis 17:1). "It shall be perfect to be accepted; there shall be no blemish therein" (Leviticus 22:21). "Be ye holy; for I am holy" (1 Peter 1:16). There is a holiness to be pursued, without which no man shall see the Lord (Hebrews 12:14).

God demands character holiness. We are required to be holy on the inside, in heart, at the very core of our being. "The Lord looketh on the heart" (1 Samuel 16:7). He demands conduct holiness. We must be holy on the outside, in behaviour. "Be ye holy in all manner of conversation" (1 Peter 1:15). In a word, God demands complete holiness. We must be entirely without sin "The soul that sinneth, it shall die" (Ezekiel 18:20).

God demands holiness; but we cannot produce holiness. Not one of us can do one good thing before God. It is written, "There is none that doeth good, no not one" (Romans 3:12). Purity cannot come from our corrupt nature. We cannot even seek the Lord on our own, much less correct our past record, change our present wretchedness (Psalm 51:1-5), or control our future thoughts and deeds (Galatians 3:10). The whole purpose of God's law is to show us our utter inability to keep it and to convince us of our need of a Substitute (Galatians 3:24). And the first work of God the Holy Spirit in a sinner's heart is to convince him of sin, of his need of a Substitute (John 16:9).

A man's definition of righteousness depends entirely upon his understanding of who God is. The problem with this religious generation is that they have never seen the holy, righteous, just character of God almighty. They have never seen the absolute holiness of God. And no one will ever see the holy character of God until he sees what happened at Calvary (Isaiah 6:1-5).

How good does a person have to be to get to heaven? He must be as good as God. It must be perfect to be accepted. God cannot and will not accept anything short of perfection. "Who shall ascend into the hill of the Lord? or who shall stand in his holy place? He that hath clean hands, and a pure heart; who hath not lifted upon his soul unto vanity, nor sworn deceitfully" (Psalm 24:3, 4), and no one else. Yet, it is written, "They that are in the flesh cannot please God" (Romans 8:8). "Cursed is everyone that continueth not in all things written in the book of the law to do them" (Galatians 3:10).

Still, the fact that we cannot produce righteousness does not mean that righteousness cannot be produced. God can do it. Man cannot please God; but God can please God. Man cannot produce righteousness; but God can.

Righteousness Established

The Lord Jesus Christ came into this world to fulfil all righteousness, not for himself, but for us (Matthew 3:15; 5:17). "The LORD is well pleased for his righteousness' sake; he will magnify the law, and make it honourable" (Isaiah 42:21). Our Saviour did for us exactly what Daniel 9:24 said he would do. He finished the transgression and made an end of sin for us, putting away our sins by the sacrifice of himself. He made reconciliation for iniquity by satisfying the justice of God as our Substitute. And he brought in everlasting righteousness by his obedience to the will of God in all things as our Representative and Federal Head. By his obedience to the will of God as our Representative and Substitute, the Lord Jesus Christ brought in an everlasting righteousness of infinite worth and merit for God's elect (Hebrews 10:5-14).

According to the Book of God, it is the life obedience of Christ that constitutes that righteousness, with which we are clothed, that righteousness we are made to become before God. His death washed away our sins, and his life covers us from head to foot. His death was the sacrifice to God, and his life is the gift to man, by which all God's elect have satisfied the demands of the law.

Only in this way is it possible for the law to be honoured and our souls accepted by God. Many who appear to be perfectly clear about the merits of Christ's death, do not seem to understand the merits of his life. Remember, from the moment that our blessed Saviour left his mother's womb, until the hour that he ascended up on high, he was at work for his people. From the moment that he was seen in Mary's arms, until the moment that he was in the arms of death, when "he bowed his head and gave up the ghost", he was performing the work of our salvation.

The Lord Jesus Christ completed the work of his obedience in his life, and said to his Father, "I have finished the work which thou gavest me to do" (John 17:4). Then, he finished the work of his atonement in his death. And, knowing that all things were accomplished, he cried, "It is finished" (John 19:30). Throughout his earthly life, the Saviour was spinning the fabric of that royal, priestly garment in which we are robed, and in his death he dipped that garment in his blood. In his life he was gathering precious gold, and in his death he hammered it out to make for us a garment of wrought gold. We have as much to be thankful for in the life of Christ as we do in his death. In his life Christ Jesus rendered perfect obedience to the law as our Substitute. And in his death he satisfied the claims of the law as our Substitute. Therefore, the prophet of God declares of Christ, "This is the name whereby he shall be called, the Lord our Righteousness".

That is the message that is set before us in 2 Corinthians 5:21. The Lord Jesus Christ is our only righteousness, and it is our joy to confess that he is. "Of him are ye in Christ Jesus, who of God is made unto us wisdom, and righteousness, and sanctification, and redemption: That, according as it is written, He that glorieth, let him glory in the Lord" (1 Corinthians 1:30, 31).

Righteousness Imputed

The only way a sinner can be made righteous is by the holy Lord God imputing righteousness to him. In justification God imputes the righteousness of Christ to his people in exactly the same way as he imputed the sins of his people to Christ (Romans 5:18, 19; 2 Corinthians 5:21). How are sinners made to become the righteousness of God in Christ? I appeal to the Word of God alone for the answer to that question. The opinions of men are totally irrelevant. What does the Book say? Nothing else matters.

When Christ was made sin, that was a one time, once and for all act accomplished in the past, a work in which he was personally involved. But when the Holy Spirit speaks of us being "made the righteousness of God in him", the word he uses for "made" is another word altogether. It is a present tense, passive verb, implying total passiveness on our part, and means "continually cause to become". He is telling us that those for whom Christ was made sin God continually causes to become the righteousness of God in him without doing a thing. Let me show you how he has done it and is doing it.

Eternally

Our great, all-wise, eternally gracious God made us righteous before the world was made, in his sovereign, eternal purpose of grace in Christ, the Lamb slain from the foundation of the world, (Romans 8:28-30; Ephesians 1:3-6; 2 Timothy 1:9, 10; Jude 1). If we were blessed of God with all spiritual blessings before the world began and accepted in the Beloved, it was not as unrighteous but as the righteousness of God in Christ.

Judicially

We were made to become the righteousness of God judicially, in a legal sense, when the Lord Jesus died as our Substitute under the wrath of God, satisfying divine justice for us. When he had put away sin by the sacrifice of himself, he obtained eternal redemption for us, and we were made to become the righteousness of God in him by divine imputation in justification (Romans 4:25; 5:12, 17-21).

Experimentally

But this matter of being made the righteousness of God in Christ, while it is something with which we have no involvement, is not just a matter of law, any more than Christ's being made sin was just a matter of law. It is not something that takes place altogether outside our experience, any more than Christ being made sin was outside his experience.

Sinners are made the righteousness of God in Christ experimentally in the new birth, when we are made "partakers of the divine nature" (2 Peter 1:4). That holy thing in us that is born of God, that John tells us cannot sin, is "Christ in you, the hope of glory" (Colossians 1:27). We experience this blessed thing (being made the righteousness of God) in the inmost depths of our souls, in the constant assurance of our access to, acceptance with, and forgiveness of our sins by our God (1 John 1:7-2:2).

We are in Christ, in whom alone God is well pleased. That means he is well pleased with us (Matthew 17:5). Our sacrifices are accepted of God as a sweet-smelling savour in Christ (1 Peter 2:5). Our sins are never imputed to us, but perpetually forgiven because we are one with him who was once made sin for us, in whom we are perpetually made to become the righteousness of God.

Absolutely
Believing on the Lord Jesus Christ, every sinner who trusts him is made to become the righteousness of God in him absolutely (2 Corinthians 5:17; Colossians 1:12). Discerning the Lord's body, that is to say, knowing our need of a Substitute and knowing the Substitute himself, trusting his finished work and trusting him, sinners like you and me are worthy to enter his church, worthy to call upon his name, worthy to receive the Lord's table, and worthy to enter into and possess forever his glory! Tobias Crisp wrote:

> Mark it well, Christ himself is not so completely righteous, but we are as righteous as he was. Nor are we so completely sinful, but he became (being made sin) as completely sinful as we. Nay more, the righteousness that Christ hath with the Father, we are the same, for we are 'made the righteousness of God'. And that very sinfulness that we were, Christ is made before God. So that here is a direct change. Christ takes our persons and condition, and stands in our stead. We take his person and condition, and stand in his stead. What the Lord beheld Christ to be, that he beholds his members to be. What he beholds them to be in themselves, that he beheld Christ himself to be.
>
> So that if you would speak of a sinner, supposing him to be a member of Christ, you must not speak of what he manifests, but of what Christ was.
>
> If you would speak of one completely righteous, you must speak and know that Christ himself is not more righteous than he is. And that that person is not more sinful than Christ was when he took his sins on him. So that if you will reckon well, beloved, you must always reckon yourself in another's person, and that other in yours. And until the Lord find out transgressions of Christ's own acting, he will never find one to charge upon you.

Everlastingly
We shall be made to become the righteousness of God everlastingly in the last day in resurrection glory. We shall be raised in righteousness. We shall be declared righteous according to the record book of heaven at the Day of Judgment

(Revelation 20:11-15; Jeremiah 50:20). We shall be declared righteous to wondering worlds to the glory of our God forever (Ephesians 2:7). Then, we shall forever begin to enjoy, in such experimental reality, as words cannot describe, the blessedness of being made to become the righteousness of God in Christ (Revelation 21:2-5; 22:1-6).

I am lost in wonder. All this, all that Christ has as the God-man, the Mediator, we have in him. All that he is, we are in him. All that he enjoys, soon, we shall enjoy forever in him, because …

If any man be in Christ, he is a new creature: old things are passed away; behold, all things are become new. And all things are of God, who hath reconciled us to himself by Jesus Christ, and hath given to us the ministry of reconciliation; To wit, that God was in Christ, reconciling the world unto himself, not imputing their trespasses unto them; and hath committed unto us the word of reconciliation. Now then we are ambassadors for Christ, as though God did beseech you by us: we pray you in Christ's stead, be ye reconciled to God. For he hath made him to be sin for us, who knew no sin; that we might be made the righteousness of God in him (2 Corinthians 5:17-21).

"He that spared not his own Son, but delivered him up for us all, how shall he not with him also freely give us all things?" (Romans 8:32).

Righteousness Imparted

In regeneration we are sanctified, made holy, by righteousness being imparted to us by the Spirit of God (Galatians 5:24, 25; 2 Peter 1:4; Colossians 1:27; 1 John 3:4-9). Believers are people with two natures (Romans 7:14-24), that holy seed which is born of God and cannot sin (1 John 3:9), and the flesh which is nothing but sin (Romans 7:18). These two natures, the flesh and the spirit, are constantly at war with one another so long as we live in this world (Galatians 5:21).

When God saves a sinner, he does not renovate, repair, and renew the old nature. He creates a new nature in his elect. Our old, Adamic, fallen, sinful nature is not changed. The flesh is subdued by the spirit; but it will never surrender to the spirit. The spirit wars against the flesh; but it will never conquer or improve the flesh. The flesh is sinful. The flesh is cursed. Thank God, the flesh must die! But it will never be improved.

This dual nature of the believer is plainly taught in the Word of God. It is utterly impossible to honestly interpret this portion of Paul's epistle to the Galatians, chapter seven of Romans, and 1 John 3 without concluding that both Paul and John teach that there is within every believer, so long as he lives in this world, both an old Adamic nature, that can do nothing but sin, and a new righteous nature, that which is born of God, that cannot sin, that can only do righteousness. The Holy Spirit's work in sanctification is not the improvement of our old nature, but the maturing of the new, steadily causing the believer to grow in the grace and knowledge of Christ and bring forth fruit unto God.

Every believer knows the duality of his nature by painful, bitterly painful, experience. Ask any child of God what he desires above all things and he will quickly reply, "That I may live without sin in perfect conformity to Christ, perfectly obeying the will of God in all things." But that which he most greatly desires is an utter impossibility in this life. Is it not so with you? Though you delight in the law of God after the inward man, there is another law of evil in your members, warring against you. You would do good; but evil is always present with you, so that you cannot do the things that you would. Even your best, noblest, most sincere acts of good, when honestly evaluated, are so marred by sin in motive and in execution that you must confess, "All my righteousnesses are filthy rags"!

It is this warfare between the flesh and the spirit more than anything else that keeps the believer from being satisfied with life in this world. Blessed be God, we shall soon be free! When we have dropped this robe of flesh, we shall be perfectly conformed to the image of him who loved us and gave himself for us!

This conflict is caused by and begins in regeneration because the righteousness of Christ is imparted to us in the new birth. C. H. Spurgeon said, "The reigning power of sin falls dead the moment a man is converted, but the struggling power of sin does not die until the man dies." A new nature has been planted within us; but the old nature is not eradicated.

Do not think for a moment that the old nature dies in regeneration, or even that it gets better. Flesh is flesh, and will never be anything but flesh. Noah, Lot, Moses, David, and Peter, like all other believers, had to struggle with this fact. We need no proof of the fact that God's people in this world have two warring natures within beyond an honest examination of our own hearts and lives. Our best thoughts are corrupted with sin. Our most fervent prayers are defiled by lusts of the flesh. Our reading of holy scripture is corrupted by carnal passions. Our most spiritual worship is marred by the blackness within. Our most holy aspirations are vile. Our purest love for our Saviour is so corrupted by our love of self and love for this world that we can hardly call our love for Christ love. From time to time we have all found, by bitter experience, the truthfulness of the hymn:

Prone to wander, Lord, I feel it!
Prone to leave the God I love:
Here's my heart, O take and seal it,
Seal it for Thy courts above.

Righteousness Rewarded

In the last day, every believer shall enter into heaven and obtain the inheritance of everlasting glory; and that will be righteousness rewarded. Immediately after the resurrection we must all be judged by God, according to the record of our works (Revelation 20:12, 13). "It is appointed unto men once to die, but after this the judgment" (Hebrews 9:27). The Judge before whom we must stand is the God-man, whom we have crucified (John 5:22; Acts 17:31; 2 Corinthians 5:10). We will be judged out of the books, according to the record of God's strict justice.

In the scriptures God is often represented as writing and keeping books. And, according to these books, we all shall be judged. I realize that this is figurative language. God does not need books to remember man's sins. However, as John Gill wrote, "This judgment out of the books, and according to works, is designed to show with what accuracy and exactness, with what justice and equity, it will be executed, in allusion to statute-books in courts of judicature."

What are the books? The Book of Divine Omniscience (Malachi 3:5); the Book of Divine Remembrance (Malachi 3:16); the Book of Creation (Romans 1:18-20), the Book of God's Providence (Romans 2:4, 5), the Book of Conscience (Romans 2:15), the Book of God's Holy Law (Romans 2:12), and the Book of the Gospel (Romans 2:16).

But there are some against whom no crimes, no sins, no offences can be found, not even by the omniscient eye of God himself! "In those days, and in that time, saith the LORD, the iniquity of Israel shall be sought for, and there shall be none; and the sins of Judah, and they shall not be found: for I will pardon them whom I reserve" (Jeremiah 50:20). Their names are found in another book, a book which God himself wrote and sealed before the worlds were made. It is called, "The Book of Life". In this book is a record of divine election, the name of Christ our divine Surety, a record of perfect righteousness (Jeremiah 23:6, cf. 33:14-16), a record of complete satisfaction, and the promise of eternal life.

The question is often raised, "Will God judge his elect for their sins and failures committed after they were saved, and expose them in the Day of Judgment?" The only reason that question is ever raised is because many retain a remnant of the Roman Catholic doctrine of purgatory, by which they hope to hold over God's saints the whip and terror of the law. There is absolutely no sense in which those who trust Christ shall ever be made to pay for their sins! Our sins were imputed to Christ and shall never be imputed to us again (Romans 4:8). Christ paid our debt to God's law and justice; and God will never require us to pay. God, who has blotted out our transgressions, will never write them again. He who covered our sins will never uncover them!

The perfect righteousness of Christ has been imputed to us. On the Day of Judgment, God's elect are never represented as having done any evil, but only good (Matthew 25:31-40). The Day of Judgment will be a day of glory and bliss for Christ and his people, not a day of mourning and sorrow. It will be a marriage supper. Christ will glory in his Church. God will display the glory of his grace in us. And we will glory in our God. Those who are found perfectly righteous, righteous according to the records of God himself, shall enter into eternal life and inherit everlasting glory with Christ. They that have done good, nothing but good, perfect good, without any spot of sin, wrinkle of iniquity, or trace of transgression, shall enter into everlasting life (Revelation 22:11).

Who are these righteous ones? They are all who are saved by God's free and sovereign grace in Christ (1 Corinthians 6:9-11; Romans 8:1, 33, 34). Though there shall be degrees of punishment for the wicked in hell, because there are degrees of wickedness, there shall be no degrees of reward and glory among the saints in heaven, because there are no degrees of redemption and righteousness.

Heaven was earned and purchased for all God's elect by Christ. We were predestined to obtain our inheritance from eternity (Ephesians 1:11). Christ has taken possession of heaven's glory as our forerunner (Hebrews 6:20). We are heirs of God and joint-heirs with Jesus Christ (Romans 8:17). Our Saviour gave all the glory he earned as our Mediator to all his elect (John 17:5, 20). And in Christ every believer is worthy of heaven's glory (Colossians 1:12).

Glorification shall be but the consummation of salvation; and salvation is by grace alone! That means no part of heaven's bliss and glory is the reward of our works, but all the reward of God's free grace in Christ! All spiritual blessings are ours from eternity in Christ (Ephesians 1:3), and all shall be ours forever in Christ, by Christ, and with Christ.

Jehovah-tsidkenu

Read Jeremiah 23:5, 6 and Jeremiah 33:15, 16. In both places Jeremiah is describing for us this blessed gospel day in which the Branch of Righteousness has grown up unto David and his seed. That Branch is Christ. And that David is Christ our King. Our David is now seated on his throne in glory, having grown up righteously, by bringing in everlasting righteousness. He now executes judgment and justice throughout the earth in the salvation of his people by the gospel. That is what the Lord our God declares in these two passages.

> Behold, the days come, saith the LORD, that I will raise unto David a righteous Branch, and a King shall reign and prosper, and shall execute judgment and justice in the earth (Jeremiah 23:5).
>
> In those days, and at that time, will I cause the Branch of righteousness to grow up unto David; and he shall execute judgment and righteousness in the land (Jeremiah 33:15).
>
> In his days Judah shall be saved, and Israel shall dwell safely: and this is his name whereby he shall be called, THE LORD OUR RIGHTEOUSNESS (Jeremiah 23:6).
>
> In those days shall Judah be saved, and Jerusalem shall dwell safely: and this is the name wherewith she shall be called, The LORD our righteousness (Jeremiah 33:16).

That is not a mistranslation. Every word is translated with exact accuracy. This is what the Lord God tells us about the work of Christ in this day of grace in which we live. Judah, the tribe of God's choice, shall be saved. Israel, God's holy nation, his chosen generation, his royal priesthood, shall dwell safely. And this is the name whereby that Righteous Branch our King shall be called, Jehovah-tsidkenu, "The Lord Our Righteousness". And this is the name wherewith every saved sinner shall be called: Jehovah-tsidkenu! "The Lord Our Righteousness".

Christ is our Righteousness. He is that righteousness that exceeds the righteousness of the scribes and Pharisees. And, if we trust him, he is ours! Because his righteousness is ours, we shall enter into the kingdom of heaven. He is that Holiness without which no man shall see the Lord. If we believe on the Son of God, that Holiness is ours and we shall see the Lord our God face to face in Christ. Then, (O blessed day!) he shall wipe all tears from our eyes!

Chapter 12

How Can I Come To God's Altar?

"Ye have heard that it was said by them of old time, Thou shalt not kill; and whosoever shall kill shall be in danger of the judgment: But I say unto you, That whosoever is angry with his brother without a cause shall be in danger of the judgment: and whosoever shall say to his brother, Raca, shall be in danger of the council: but whosoever shall say, Thou fool, shall be in danger of hell fire. Therefore if thou bring thy gift to the altar, and there rememberest that thy brother hath ought against thee; Leave there thy gift before the altar, and go thy way; first be reconciled to thy brother, and then come and offer thy gift. Agree with thine adversary quickly, whiles thou art in the way with him; lest at any time the adversary deliver thee to the judge, and the judge deliver thee to the officer, and thou be cast into prison. Verily I say unto thee, Thou shalt by no means come out thence, till thou hast paid the uttermost farthing."
(Matthew 5:21-26)

How can I come to God's Altar? How are we to understand our Saviour's words in these verses? What do they mean? Since the fall of our father Adam, God has never allowed man to approach him without an altar and a sacrifice of blood. In the old days of the patriarchs, from Adam to Moses, the people of God built altars of stone, upon which they offered sacrifices to God. Whenever men drew near to God, whether to offer praise or to seek mercy, they built an altar and offered a sacrifice of blood. Even in those days, men of faith knew that God's justice could only be satisfied for sin by blood, even the blood of God's own Son, the Redeemer who must come into the world to put away sin.

One Altar
Then, when God called Moses up into the mount and spoke to him face to face, he appointed one altar of sacrifice to be built, and appointed a place for that one altar in Israel alone. One spot was selected, and only one. All the rest of the world was left without an altar and without a sacrifice.

At first the altar was placed in the tabernacle; and later it was placed in the temple at Jerusalem. This was the only altar of sacrifice, by which men might approach unto God. From time to time, the prophets of God, by God's special command, raised up other altars. But for all others the rule was unbending. One altar! All other altars which men erected were erected in defiance of God's command; and their pretended sacrifices to God were an abomination to him.

As in the typical, legal dispensation, so it is now. There is but one altar upon which the holy Lord God meets sinners in mercy, one altar where God can and will be worshipped; that Altar is Christ. "We have an altar, whereof they have no right to eat which serve the tabernacle" (Hebrews 13:10). The altar of sacrifice, in the tabernacle and in the temple, was typical of our Lord Jesus Christ, (his Person, his work, and his merit), as our Substitute before God. This is what God the Holy Spirit teaches us in Hebrews 13:10. The only access which sinners have to God, and the only acceptance we have with God is Christ, our Altar.

Our Altar is in heaven. We recognize no altar upon the earth. He who has an Altar in heaven needs none on earth. He who has an altar on earth has no altar in heaven. The Holy Spirit tells us this. "We have an altar, whereof they have no right to eat which serve the tabernacle." We cannot approach God without a Mediator, without an Altar, and without a Sacrifice. We are all sinners by nature. Our best and most righteous acts are but the deeds of sinful men. Our purest worship is but the worship of depraved hearts. "Who can bring a clean thing out of an unclean? Not one" (Job 14:4). Before we can ever be accepted with God, before we can ever bring an acceptable offering or service to God, there must be a shedding of blood for the removal of our sin and guilt. We must come to God by way of the Altar and Sacrifice he has appointed, the Lord Jesus Christ.

There is no door of acceptance for us except through the merit of our great Surety, who laid down his life for us. There is but one way by which we who are washed in the blood of Christ can offer unto God our prayers, our gifts, our praises, or our service, and that is by the Lord Jesus Christ, who alone is our Altar. We must give ourselves to him, as living sacrifices to God, because only in him will God accept our reasonable service.

One Altar Still

There is still but one Altar by which sinful men may approach the Holy God. In the Old Testament there was but one altar of sacrifice by which men could ceremonially approach God; and that one altar finds its fulfilment in the Person of the Lord Jesus Christ. The only altar, which can sanctify us and make us acceptable to God, is Christ. In this Gospel Day all physical, carnal, ceremonial altars are instruments of idolatry. Use anything as an altar for acceptance with God, other than Christ, and you have no right to the merits of Christ. If you have another altar, your altar will drag your soul down to hell.

There are many who think of the cross upon which our Saviour died as an altar. I have heard it said that the cross was the altar upon which our Lord offered himself as a sacrifice for sin. But it is not so. That cross upon which our Lord was crucified was nothing more than the instrument of his torture. It is no more to be reverenced as an altar than the whips of Pilate's soldiers or the spit of those Jews, which defiled his holy face. I would no more wear a cross around my neck than I would take the dagger a murderer used to kill my wife and wear it on my belt.

Sometimes men talk of the heart as an altar to God. I know what they mean. They mean that sincerity makes our service to God acceptable. It is true that there must be sincerity in our service to God, or it will never be acceptable. But sincerity itself will never make our most solemn devotion acceptable to God. Nothing but blood will ever make a man acceptable to God. Only the blood of Christ, shed for the atonement of our sin can make us accepted with God.

It is common for men to talk of having a family altar. It is good to worship God in your home, with your family. But your family devotions will never make you acceptable to God. The church of God is our family, and we have a family altar. His name is Jesus Christ our Substitute. In many churches, the table used for serving the Lord's supper is looked upon as an altar. But the scriptures never speak in such a way. The table spread before you at the Lord's supper is a table of communion; not a table of sacrifice; it is a place of remembrance, not a place of atonement; it is a solemn feast, not a sanctifying feast. Perhaps the most deceptive of all idolatrous notions is the idea of an altar of salvation at the front of the church. You can no more obtain salvation by walking down the aisle of a Baptist church to an altar than the papists can by making a pilgrimage to Rome and climbing the stairs to the pope's seat of infamy.

There is but one Altar. There is but one place of salvation. That Altar is Christ. He is God's salvation. God only meets with men in his Son. Christ is the Altar of God's making, not man's (Exodus 20:23-26). If you lift up your tool upon it, that is to say, if you attempt to make any contribution to salvation, you have polluted it altogether. All forms of carnal worship, all forms of physical things that men call "holy", all attempts to place any merit of any kind or any reverence of any kind in material things is base idolatry (Exodus 20:23; John 4:23, 24; Philippians 3:3). Let us put away every form of idolatry (2 Kings 18:4).

The Altar's Use

Christ our Altar fulfils all that was symbolically portrayed in the Old Testament altar of sacrifice. Moses describes the altar of sacrifice for us in Exodus 27:1-8. All that the altar of the tabernacle and the temple signified typically is fulfilled for us really and truly in the Lord Jesus Christ. The altar of sacrifice typified Christ in the use for which it was made. The altar sanctified the gift, the sacrifice, which was placed upon it, and made it acceptable to God (Matthew 23:19). Christ sanctifies us. He makes the believing soul and our sacrifices acceptable to God (1 Peter 2:5). There was one altar for all the people, one altar for all their sins, one altar for all their sacrifices. There is one Altar for sinners; and that Altar is Christ.

The altar bore the violent heat of divine wrath, so that the sinner might go free. While the fire consumed the sacrifice on the altar, the altar itself was not destroyed. Even so, Christ our Altar bore the violent heat of God's wrath. He poured out his soul unto death for our sins as a sacrifice to God of a sweet-smelling savour. Yet, he is not destroyed. This sacrifice, rather than being consumed by the wrath of God, has consumed the wrath of God (Romans 8:1).

The altar was a place of refuge for guilty men. Both Adonijah and Joab had fled to the altar in the temple; yet they were subsequently slain (1 Kings 1:50; 1 Kings 2:28-30). What else can a guilty man do but take hold of the horns of the altar? But Christ the true Altar of Refuge for guilty sinners, is an Altar at which no sinner shall ever be slain by God. There were four horns on the altar. Those horns represent the extent of Christ's redemption, reaching to the four corners of the earth. "Whosoever shall call upon the name of the Lord shall be saved". You will be wise to lay hold of the horns of the Altar, and plead for God's mercy.

The Altar's Form

The altar of sacrifice was typical of Christ in its form. The altar was four square, suggesting the fulness, completion, and perfect symmetry of God's boundless grace and love for his elect in Christ (Ephesians 3:8, 19) and the firmness and stability of all things in Christ, who changes not (2 Samuel 23:5; Hebrews 13:8)

There were no steps going up to the altar because there is no possibility of approaching God by the steps of your own works. There are no steps of preparation before you come to the Altar. When the priest approached the altar, no nakedness could be seen. His robe completely covered him. All who come to God by Christ are covered with his blood and righteousness. The altar itself was completely covered with blood, because justice must be satisfied (Hebrews 9:22).

How Can I Come To God's Altar?

The Altar's Position

The altar of Sacrifice was typical of Christ in its position. The moment the sinner entered the door of the tabernacle, the first, the most important, most prominent thing he saw was that huge brazen altar. As he approached God, the first thing he saw was the altar. As he left the tabernacle, and went out to live in the world, the last thing he saw was the altar. Christ is pre-eminent. All fulness dwells in him. In order to approach God, we must come by the Altar, Christ Jesus (Hebrews 7:25). As we attempt to live in the world, we must live with Christ, the Altar of Sacrifice, before our heart's eye. Every aspect of life is affected by this Altar.

The Altar's Materials

The altar of sacrifice was typical of Christ in its materials. The shittim wood represented the incorruptible humanity of Christ. The brass represented his eternal Godhead. The shittim wood overlaid with brass shows the eternal duration and efficacy of Christ's sacrifice. The fire, which continually burned upon the altar of sacrifice, represents the eternal love of Christ for his people, the zeal of Christ for the glory of God, the purifying of God's elect by the blood of Christ, and the unfailing intercession of Christ for us.

Come To The Altar

I am a needy sinner and need to come to God's Altar for forgiveness. And the only way I can offer up my gifts of praise and thanksgiving to my God is upon his Altar. But how can I come to God's Altar? Our Lord Jesus tells me exactly how I can and must come to God's Altar in Matthew 5:21-26.

Our Saviour, in the Sermon on the Mount, in which these verses are found, is not telling us how we ought to live in this world. He is telling us what God absolutely requires of all who find acceptance with him. He states this fact clearly in the last verse of chapter five. "Be ye therefore perfect, even as your Father which is in heaven is perfect." This is precisely what he said in verse 20, "For I say unto you, That except your righteousness shall exceed the righteousness of the scribes and Pharisees, ye shall in no case enter into the kingdom of heaven." He is not telling us that we ought to try to be as good as we can. He is telling us that we cannot come to God and find acceptance and everlasting life with him, except we stand before him in the perfection of righteousness, without so much as a trace of sin upon us. In the passage before us, our Lord is showing us how we can, the only way we can, come to God and obtain this perfect righteousness.

Thou Fool

The letter of the law says, “Thou shalt not kill; and whosoever shall kill shall be in danger of the judgment” (v. 21). In the next verse he explains the depth of those words. “But I say unto you, That whosoever is angry with his brother without a cause shall be in danger of the judgment: and whosoever shall say to his brother, Raca, shall be in danger of the council: but whosoever shall say, Thou fool, shall be in danger of hell fire.” Who is that “brother” against whom we have all been angry without a cause, to whom we have all said, “Raca” and “Thou fool”? These words cannot possibly have reference to any fallen, sinful person. The Lord Jesus is here describing the hatred of man for himself (Romans 8:7). He is the only man who ever lived who was hated without a cause (John 15:25). Though he may not be aware of it, anyone who knows me has reason to hate me; and the same is true of you (Matthew 15:17-20).

The word “raca” is a contemptible term. It means “graceless”. The word “fool” is a much more so. It means more than we commonly associate with it. It does not just mean, “moron”, “stupid”, “ignorant”, and “senseless”. The word means “godless”. And that is exactly what unbelief says with regard to Christ. Man’s unbelief declares the Son of God to be an impostor and a liar, a godless reprobate who deserves to be put to death (John 10:33; 1 John 5:10). Unbelief says that gospel of Christ is “foolishness” (1 Corinthians 1:18). In a word, our Master is declaring that every unbeliever continually murders the Son of God, hating him without a cause, calling him a fool, and is in danger of hell fire.

Be Reconciled

The opening word of verse 23, “Therefore”, points us back to what our Lord has just stated. “If thou bring thy gift to the altar … first be reconciled to thy brother” (vv. 23, 24). Grace does what law can never do. Grace causes people to love each other. The law requires that we love one another, but it can never produce love. In fact, as the Pharisees attested by their conduct, those who claim to live by the law commonly manifest the judgmental hatred our Lord has just condemned. Those who give up all hopes of law righteousness and trust Christ alone are taught by the grace they experience to love one another (Galatians 5:22, 23).

As we bring our gifts and sacrifices of praise and thanksgiving to our God by Christ Jesus and recall some offence we have given to a brother, believers (men and women who walk in the Spirit and so fulfil the law of Christ) seek to be reconciled to the one they have offended. There is a true, sweet union in Christ.

All who are in Christ are one with Christ and one with one another. When we come to him in adoration, love, and worship, we come with all our brethren (Hebrews 12:22-24). As Robert Hawker put it, "His members come to him as the Head and bring with us, by faith, the whole body in our arms to the Lord (John 17:21. 1 Corinthians 12:25-27)."

Our Lord's words in this passage may be properly applied to the necessity of brotherly love; but that is not what is taught here. The context points us in another, higher, more profitable direction. Our Saviour is, in this entire chapter, showing us the demands of God's holy law and our complete inability to meet those demands. Is he not here telling us that we cannot come to God except upon that one Altar he has made (Exodus 20:24-26; 25:22), which is Christ himself?

The Brother we have offended above all others is God our Saviour. He is that Brother with whom we have been angry without a cause. It is the Lord Jesus to whom unbelief says, "Raca", "Thou fool". There is no coming to God until we are reconciled to him in and by Christ, reconciled to Christ as our only God and Saviour, our only atonement for sin. Once we are reconciled to Christ our Brother, once we trust him alone for acceptance with God, we may, and can, and do come to God upon the merits of Christ, and he accepts us, and our gifts, by the merits of his dear Son (1 Peter 2:5).

How can we be reconciled to our Brother, the Lord Jesus? We must take our place as fools before him. The word fool is found many times in holy scripture; but the exact word that is here translated "fool", from which we get our word "moron", is only used in one other place in the New Testament, in 1 Corinthians 3:18. In that passage the Holy Spirit tells us that the Lord Jesus Christ is the only foundation God has laid (v. 11), the Foundation upon which we must be built. Then, in verse 18, we read, "Let no man deceive himself. If any man among you seemeth to be wise in this world, let him become a fool, that he may be wise." If we would be spiritually wise, we must take our place before God as fools, godless sinners, in danger of hell fire without Christ.

Our Adversary

The words of verse 24, "First be reconciled to thy brother", and the words of verse 25, "Agree with thine adversary quickly", obviously refer to the same person. Our "brother" and our "adversary", in this passage, speak of the same person, the Lord Jesus Christ. Those words simply cannot be applied to a mere earthly adversary. Try as we may, there is no way in the world that you can agree with an adversary or get an adversary to agree with you. Besides, if I am your brother in Christ, I cannot be your adversary and you cannot be mine. Brothers are friends, not adversaries.

These verses, which have been a source of great trouble for many sensitive souls (simply because they have been so terribly misinterpreted), are truly a source of great consolation and joy, when we rightly understand them. This passage is not at all talking about us suing one another for mercy. Our Lord is telling us how we can and must, as ignorant, godless sinners, in danger of hell fire, sue for mercy at the throne of grace.

Yes, our adversary, the devil, seeks to destroy us (1 Peter 5:8); and many are in league with him as adversaries to our souls. It is good to try to quieten them and live peaceably, as much as is possible, with such men (Romans 12:18). But it is utterly impossible for us to agree with such adversaries or persuade them to agree with us. Our Lord must, therefore, be speaking of something else and of someone else.

An adversary is not always one who is intent upon hurting or ruining us. In Exodus 23:22 the Lord our God declares, "I will be an adversary to thine adversaries". Christ, our Brother, the sinners' Friend, is an Adversary for us against our enemies! But there comes a day in the life of every eternally loved, elect and blood bought sinner when his eye "is dim by reason of sorrow" (Job 17:7). In that day, when a sinner is convinced of his sin, the Lord stands as an adversary, with his bow bent like an enemy, who pours out his fury like fire (Lamentations 2:4). In that hour of sorrow, the needy soul is sweetly forced by omnipotent grace to cry in the depths of his soul for an advocate with God, saying, as Job did, "O that one might plead for a man with God, as a man pleadeth for his neighbour (friend)"! (Job 16:21).

Take Sides

As an adversary, the Lord our God has a controversy with his people by reason of sin. Here our blessed Saviour and Advocate, the Lord Jesus, tells us to make up the breach quickly while we are in the way. That is to say, "Be reconciled to God quickly by Christ, who is himself the Way, the only way of reconciliation." The only way a sinner can be reconciled to God is to agree with him when he appears as our adversary, threatening judgment. If we would agree with our Adversary, we must takes sides with him, agreeing with him about everything, confessing our sin and worshipping him alone as God our Saviour, our only Righteousness and Redemption (1 John 1:9; Romans 3:23, 24; 1 Corinthians 1:30).

Chapter 13

Seven Vital Lessons

"Ye have heard that it was said by them of old time, Thou shalt not kill; and whosoever shall kill shall be in danger of the judgment: But I say unto you, That whosoever is angry with his brother without a cause shall be in danger of the judgment: and whosoever shall say to his brother, Raca, shall be in danger of the council: but whosoever shall say, Thou fool, shall be in danger of hell fire. Therefore if thou bring thy gift to the altar, and there rememberest that thy brother hath ought against thee; Leave there thy gift before the altar, and go thy way; first be reconciled to thy brother, and then come and offer thy gift. Agree with thine adversary quickly, whiles thou art in the way with him; lest at any time the adversary deliver thee to the judge, and the judge deliver thee to the officer, and thou be cast into prison. Verily I say unto thee, Thou shalt by no means come out thence, till thou hast paid the uttermost farthing. Ye have heard that it was said by them of old time, Thou shalt not commit adultery: But I say unto you, That whosoever looketh on a woman to lust after her hath committed adultery with her already in his heart. And if thy right eye offend thee, pluck it out, and cast it from thee: for it is profitable for thee that one of thy members should perish, and not that thy whole body should be cast into hell. And if thy right hand offend thee, cut it off, and cast it from thee: for it is profitable for thee that one of thy members should perish, and not that thy whole body should be cast into hell. It hath been said, Whosoever shall put away his wife, let him give her a writing of divorcement: But I say unto you, That whosoever shall put away his wife, saving for the cause of fornication, causeth her to commit adultery: and whosoever shall marry her that is divorced committeth adultery. Again, ye have heard that it hath been said by them of old time, Thou shalt not forswear thyself, but shalt perform unto the Lord thine oaths: But I say unto you, Swear not at all; neither by heaven; for it is God's throne: Nor by the earth; for it is his footstool: neither by Jerusalem; for it is the city of the great King. Neither shalt thou swear by thy head, because thou canst not make one hair white or black. But let your communication be, Yea, yea; Nay, nay: for whatsoever is more than these cometh of evil. Ye have heard that it hath been said, An eye for an eye, and a tooth for a

tooth: But I say unto you, That ye resist not evil: but whosoever shall smite thee on thy right cheek, turn to him the other also. And if any man will sue thee at the law, and take away thy coat, let him have thy cloak also. And whosoever shall compel thee to go a mile, go with him twain. Give to him that asketh thee, and from him that would borrow of thee turn not thou away. Ye have heard that it hath been said, Thou shalt love thy neighbour, and hate thine enemy. But I say unto you, Love your enemies, bless them that curse you, do good to them that hate you, and pray for them which despitefully use you, and persecute you; That ye may be the children of your Father which is in heaven: for he maketh his sun to rise on the evil and on the good, and sendeth rain on the just and on the unjust. For if ye love them which love you, what reward have ye? do not even the publicans the same? And if ye salute your brethren only, what do ye more than others? do not even the publicans so? Be ye therefore perfect, even as your Father which is in heaven is perfect."
(Matthew 5:21-48)

When I say that something is vital, I mean that it is crucial, imperative and essential. Here are seven things we must learn. We must each personally learn them, or we cannot live before God. These things are vital. In the passage before us we have a picture of Christianity as it ought to be. No child of God can read these verses without painful feelings of inadequacy, unworthiness, and deep conviction. None of us measures up to the standard that is here set before us. In these twenty-eight verses our Lord Jesus Christ shows us that grace experienced in the heart makes people gracious. These verses deserve our closest attention. A proper understanding of the lessons they contain lies at the very root of all true Christianity.

God's Law

First, our Lord here teaches us the spirituality of God's holy law. In verses 17 and 18 he declared that he came not to destroy the law, but to fulfil it; and fulfil it he did. What a blessed thing it is to know that Christ is both our law-surety, and our law-fulfiller. As such he has become the Lord our Righteousness, and "is the end of the law for righteousness to every one that believeth" (Romans 10:4).

Here he explains that his gospel does nothing to lower the standard of God's law, but only magnifies and honours the law. To the Jews of his day and to the religious of our day the law of God is nothing more than a standard of moral conduct, a regulatory rule of life and behaviour. So our Lord selected three of the commandments regarding murder, adultery, and taking God's name in vain and expounded them to show us that the law requires more than outward conformity. The law of God requires inward, spiritual perfection, perfection in heart, in thought, and in mind, as well as outward perfection.

Murder And Faith

"Thou shalt not kill" (vv. 21, 22) requires more than not committing murder. It forbids all unjustified anger, all malice, ill-will, and cruel, mean-spirited speech. Many who would cringe at the thought of wringing a chicken's neck are mass murders at heart, for they slay thousands with their angry words. Worse by indescribable measure is unbelief. Unbelief, rebellion, and sin are nothing less than the outworking of man's heart enmity against God, nothing less than the murder of God himself in the heart of man.

As we have seen, the word "Raca" was used by the Jews to imply utter abhorrence and contempt. To say to another, "Raca", was to call him a graceless wretch. The word "Fool", as our Lord uses it here, was even worse. The word is sometimes used to refer to someone who lacks understanding (Luke 24:25; 1 Corinthians 15:36; Galatians 3:1; James 2:20). That is not a good thing to say. But, as our Lord uses it here, the word "Fool" implies one who is in a state of reprobation, predestinated to everlasting misery, a child of hell (Matthew 23:33; Jude 4). The Son of God, the great Searcher of hearts, who knows the heart, who knows them that are his and knows all things, did say to some of his day that they were of the generation of vipers, and who could not escape the damnation of hell. But no mere mortal has the right or ability to make such judgment. We ought never to imagine that we know the state of a man's soul before God, much less declare that we do.

"If thou bring thy gift to the altar … first be reconciled to thy brother" (vv. 23, 24). Here our Saviour teaches us that grace does what law can never do. Grace actually causes people to love each other. The law requires that we love one another, but it can never produce love. In fact, as the Pharisees attested by their conduct, those who claim to live by the law commonly manifest the judgmental hatred our Lord has just condemned. Those who give up all hopes of law righteousness and trust Christ alone for righteousness are taught by the grace they experience to love one another (Galatians 5:22, 23).

"Agree with thine adversary quickly" (vv. 25, 26). "These are sweet verses", writes Hawker again, "if referred to that lawsuit we all have, by reason of sin and transgression, with God." Yes, our adversary, the devil, seeks to destroy us (1

Peter 5:8); and many are in league with him as adversaries to our souls. It is good to try to quiet them and live peaceably, as much as is possible, with such men (Romans 12:18). But it is utterly impossible for us to agree with such adversaries or persuade them to agree with us. Our Lord must, therefore, be speaking of something else and of someone else.

As an adversary, the Lord God has a controversy and a lawsuit with his people by reason of sin. Here our blessed Saviour and Advocate, the Lord Jesus, tells us to make up the breach quickly while we are in the way. That is to say, "Be reconciled to God quickly by Christ, who is himself the Way, the only way of reconciliation"; Christ is our peace. It is written, "This man shall be the peace" (Micah 5:5). "God was in Christ reconciling the world unto himself" (2 Corinthians 5:19). "There is therefore now no condemnation to them that are in Christ Jesus" (Romans 8:1). But to those who live and die in enmity against God, Christ will soon come as the Judge. Into his hands the ungodly shall be delivered (John 5:22). Christ the great Judge shall send his angels to execute his wrath against his enemies (Matthew 13:41, 42). And the prison into which they shall be cast forever is the place of everlasting darkness, torment, and separation from God called "Hell" and "the lake of fire" (2 Peter 2:4; Revelation 20:15).

Adultery And Faith

"Thou shalt not commit adultery" (vv. 27-33) requires much more than marital fidelity. Adultery and fornication are horrible crimes against God and against man. One of the saddest indications of God's judgment upon our society is the freedom of conscience, with which men and women commit licentious deeds of immorality. These are abominable evils that ought never be named among God's saints. But the God with whom we have to do looks beyond actions to thoughts, attitudes, and looks! Multitudes who march in protest against pornography run a constant porno shop in their own evil minds. Yet, should I ask, "Who is not guilty?" No one could, with honesty, claim innocence, neither the reader nor the writer of these lines.

The law of God looks beyond words and deeds. It looks to the depths of our hearts, and requires perfection there, in the inward parts, in the very core of our being. All the actions of the body are but the outworkings of the heart. It matters not whether our continually evil imagination breaks out in actual deeds. Before God's holy, piercing eyes, the imagination is the deed and renders us guilty before his holy law. In other words, every human being is by nature "guilty before God" (Romans 3:19). The silliest thing on earth is the notion of fallen men that exemption from certain acts of evil constitutes righteousness before God. All are not alike evil in their deeds. God providentially restrains many, as he did Abimelech (Genesis 20:6), from performing much of the evil that is in their hearts. But at heart, in the core and essence of our being, all are alike, sinful before God. The debased harlot and the devoted housewife, the murderer and the minister, the obedient child and the rebel are all alike at heart. "They are all gone out of the way, they are together become unprofitable; there is none that doeth good, no, not one" (Romans 3:12).

In the law God gave to Israel provision was made for a man to divorce his wife in specific circumstances (Deuteronomy 24). The Lord Jesus tells us that this provision was made because of the hardness of man's heart, but from the beginning it was not so (Mark 10:5-7). We who believe are married to Christ and he to us. Painful as it is to acknowledge, we are constantly an adulterous, fornicating wife, ever sinning against our utterly devoted Husband. Yet, such is his love for and devotion to us that he will never put us away, but ever calls for us to return to him; and graciously forces us to do so (Isaiah 54:5, 6; Jeremiah 3:1; Hosea 2:19, 20). How we ought to love, adore, and praise him, "for he hateth putting away" (Malachi 2:14-16); and he will never allow us to leave him (Hosea 2:7; Jeremiah 32:37-40). May he give us grace to willingly part with that which we consider dearest and most needful to us (even the right eye and right hand), by which we are tempted to abandon him.

God's Name And Faith

"Thou shalt not take the name of the Lord Thy God in vain" (vv. 33-37) requires much more than not using God's name in an oath (vv. 33-37). It forbids all vain, light thoughts and words about God and his work. It compels simple honestly. Honest men do not have to take an oath before people who know them.

Our Lord is not here forbidding us to take a lawful oath, as one might be required to do in a court of law. He is forbidding the rash use of God's name in common speech, which reveals a lack of reverence for and contempt of God. Believers reverence God upon his throne and, reverencing him as God, walk before him and their fellow mortals upon the earth in honesty. If I believe God, I have no reason to be dishonest before men; and if I am honest before God, I am honest before men. As John Gill stated, "A righteous man's yea, is yea, and his no, is no; his word is sufficient." The common use of an oath to reinforce a simple "yes" or "no" "cometh of evil". Such oaths arise from an evil and dishonest heart.

Law Is Spiritual

The second thing taught by our Saviour in this passage is the fact that the law of God is spiritual. "The law is spiritual" (Romans 7:14). "The Lord looketh upon the heart" (1 Samuel 16:7). He requires "truth in the inward parts" (Psalm 51:6). God did not punish Adam for eating an apple, but for the rebellion and treason of his heart. Sin is not an outward problem, but an inward problem, a heart problem.

Man's Ignorance

Third, our Lord's words in this portion of holy scripture demonstrate the complete ignorance of man regarding spiritual things (1 Corinthians 2:11-14). The natural man, no matter how devotedly religious, is completely ignorant of God's character, his own character, and the requirements of God's holy law. Most professing Christians, I fear, know no more about God's law and true holiness than the spiritually ignorant scribes and Pharisees of our Lord's day. They know the letter of the law, and try to live by it. Because they are not outwardly immoral, they presume, like the rich young ruler, that they have kept God's law (Matthew 19:20), and see nothing terribly obnoxious and sinful about themselves. That is the reason for man's natural pride, self-righteousness, and easy contentment with an outward form of godliness.

That person who knows the proper place of the law and the glory of God's free grace, the person who can rest in Christ alone for all that the law requires and all that justice demands, knows the gospel. But that person who mixes law and grace, in any measure whatsoever, as a matter of acceptance before God has not yet learned the gospel.

There are no two things in the world more completely opposed to one another than law and grace. They are as opposite as light and darkness. They can no more agree than fire and water. Like oil and water, law and grace simply will not mix. The scriptures are explicitly clear (Romans 11:5, 6).

Yet, there is an amazingly well established opinion in the distorted minds of men that law and grace will mix! Though law and grace are diametrically opposed to one another, the depraved human mind is so void of spiritual understanding and so thoroughly turned away from God that the most difficult thing for man to do is to discriminate between law and grace. Man insists on mixing that which God has positively put asunder. Because of his foolish ignorance, man wants to find some legal standing before God. This is the thing

Paul opposes throughout all of his epistles. He expends every effort to destroy every remnant of legalism among God's people.

"Ye are not under the law, but under grace ... We are not under the law, but under grace ... Wherefore, my brethren, ye also are become dead to the law by the body of Christ; that ye should be married to another, even to him who is raised from the dead, that we should bring forth fruit unto God ... For what the law could not do, in that it was weak through the flesh, God sending his own Son in the likeness of sinful flesh, and for sin, condemned sin in the flesh: That the righteousness of the law might be fulfilled in us, who walk not after the flesh, but after the Spirit ... For Christ is the end of the law for righteousness to every one that believeth" (Romans 6:14, 15; 7:4; 8:3, 4; 10:4). "Wherefore the law was our schoolmaster to bring us unto Christ, that we might be justified by faith. But after that faith is come, we are no longer under a schoolmaster" (Galatians 3:24, 25). "But we know that the law is good, if a man use it lawfully; Knowing this, that the law is not made for a righteous man, but for the lawless and disobedient" (1 Timothy 1:8, 9).

Do those assertions mean that Paul was opposed to the law; or that he thought the law was an evil thing? Certainly not. In his seventh chapter of Romans the apostle shows us the believer's attitude toward God's holy law. The true believer recognizes the purpose of the law, delights in the law, and reverences the law. It is his desire to live in perfect compliance with the law. And recognizing the law's perfection, he refuses to seek acceptance with God on the basis of legal obedience. The only way sinners can honour, fulfil, and establish the law is by faith in Christ (Romans 3:31).

A Needed Saviour

Fourth, our Saviour's object in these verses is to teach us the necessity of a divine, sin-atoning Saviour. God requires perfect righteousness, a righteousness we can never produce (v. 20). He requires complete satisfaction for sin, a satisfaction we can never give. But, blessed be his name, all that God requires, God provides in the Lord Jesus Christ (2 Corinthians 5:21).

God requires eye for eye and tooth for tooth (vv. 38-42). And his righteous and just requirements have been perfectly met in Christ as our Surety, who, having fulfilled all the law's requirements for us, died under the penalty of the law, suffering all the fury of God's holy wrath to the full satisfaction of justice, when he was made sin for us, that we might be made the righteousness of God in him. Thus, "Christ is the end of the law for righteousness to everyone that believeth" (Romans 10:4).

Constant Watchfulness

We know that we can never meet God's demands. We trust Christ alone as our Saviour (1 Corinthians 1:30). But that does not make us indifferent to sin. The fifth thing our Lord teaches us throughout this passage is the importance of constant watchfulness and diligence over our lives (Ephesians 4:17-32). It is your responsibility and mine to put on Christ Jesus and be renewed in the inward man day by day, to make no provision for the flesh, and walk not as other Gentiles walk in the vanity of their minds. Let men call us straight-laced, puritanical, and peculiar if they please; but if we want to walk with God and glorify Christ, we must labour to crucify the flesh and mortify our members. We must walk in the Spirit, ever looking to Christ alone for righteousness and acceptance with our God, so that we do not fulfil the lusts of the flesh.

Grace And Love

Sixth, in verses 38-47 the Lord Jesus teaches us the blessedness of grace and love. J. C. Ryle wrote, "He that would know how he ought to feel and act towards his fellow-man, should often study these verses." We must always be ready to make up quarrels and disagreements. Our Saviour forbids everything like retaliation, revenge, malice, and an unforgiving spirit (vv. 38-42). Our God and Saviour shows us that we who claim to be his disciples are to practise indiscriminate, universal love (vv. 43-47). We are to put away malice. When cursed, we are to bless. When we receive evil, we are to return good. We are not to love in word only, but in deed. We are to deny ourselves and take the trouble to be kind and courteous. We are to put up with much and bear much, rather than hurt another, or give offence. Unfailing courtesy, kindness, tenderness, and thoughtful consideration of others are things that all men can understand, even if they cannot understand our doctrine. Rudeness, roughness, bluntness, and incivility are not spiritual graces, but reflect the absence of spiritual grace (Ephesians 4:32-5:1).

Our Lord uses two very weighty arguments to enforce these principles of grace and love. First, it is the character of God to be merciful and kind (v. 45). If God is my Father, I will reflect his character. Second, it is the character of worldlings to be selfish, self-serving, and self-centred. If that is my character, I am yet of the world! (vv. 46, 47).

In a word, our Lord tells us to walk in love, to love our neighbour as ourselves, even to love our enemies. That is what the law requires and what grace teaches. And that which he requires he has done, and done for us. And that which he has done for us as our Surety and Substitute, we have done in him perfectly. None but Christ ever truly loved his neighbour as himself. None but Christ ever loved his enemies, or could love his enemies (Romans 5:5-8). Try as we may, want to as we may, we simply cannot love our neighbour as ourselves and love our enemies. Thanks be unto our God, we have a Substitute who has fulfilled the law for us, in and by whom we fulfil the law.

Perfection Demanded

The seventh lesson in the passage is one that needs to be constantly brought before our minds. God demands perfection. "Be ye therefore perfect, even as your Father which is in heaven is perfect" (v. 48).

Throughout this chapter our Lord has been teaching us that God demands perfection. In this last verse he states it plainly. By all means, let us ever strive to live in perfection, in perfect holiness and obedience to the will of God and for the glory of God. We cannot settle for less than absolute perfection. We cannot attain it here. But we must strive to attain it. Let us ever seek total commitment to Christ, total conformity to Christ, and total communion with Christ. But we must never imagine that we can attain perfection in this world, or ever make the slightest progress toward doing so.

There is no such thing as partial holiness, partial righteousness, or partial perfection. "All our righteousnesses are as filthy rags". If we would be perfect, we must trust Christ. There is no perfection in this world except that which he is and he gives. Men may call sincerity perfection, improved behaviour righteousness, and religious devotion holiness, but God never will. "That which is highly esteemed among men is abomination in the sight of God" (Luke 16:15).

Yet, as the members of the body possess all that belongs to the head, so the members of Christ's body are perfect in him. And when our Saviour says, "Be ye perfect", his meaning is, "Be ye perfect in me." And all who know him gladly acknowledge, "In the Lord have I righteousness" (Isaiah 45:24). We glory in him "who of God is made unto us wisdom, and righteousness, and sanctification, and redemption" (1 Corinthians 1:30), rejoicing in the perfection that is ours in him (Colossians 1:28), and anxiously looking for that day when he shall present us "faultless before the presence of his glory with exceeding joy" (Jude 24).

Chapter 14

Alms, Prayers, And Fasting

"Take heed that ye do not your alms before men, to be seen of them: otherwise ye have no reward of your Father which is in heaven. Therefore when thou doest thine alms, do not sound a trumpet before thee, as the hypocrites do in the synagogues and in the streets, that they may have glory of men. Verily I say unto you, They have their reward. But when thou doest alms, let not thy left hand know what thy right hand doeth: That thine alms may be in secret: and thy Father which seeth in secret himself shall reward thee openly. And when thou prayest, thou shalt not be as the hypocrites are: for they love to pray standing in the synagogues and in the corners of the streets, that they may be seen of men. Verily I say unto you, They have their reward. But thou, when thou prayest, enter into thy closet, and when thou hast shut thy door, pray to thy Father which is in secret; and thy Father which seeth in secret shall reward thee openly. But when ye pray, use not vain repetitions, as the heathen do: for they think that they shall be heard for their much speaking. Be not ye therefore like unto them: for your Father knoweth what things ye have need of, before ye ask him. After this manner therefore pray ye: Our Father which art in heaven, Hallowed be thy name. Thy kingdom come. Thy will be done in earth, as it is in heaven. Give us this day our daily bread. And forgive us our debts, as we forgive our debtors. And lead us not into temptation, but deliver us from evil: For thine is the kingdom, and the power, and the glory, for ever. Amen. For if ye forgive men their trespasses, your heavenly Father will also forgive you: But if ye forgive not men their trespasses, neither will your Father forgive your trespasses. Moreover when ye fast, be not, as the hypocrites, of a sad countenance: for they disfigure their faces, that they may appear unto men to fast. Verily I say unto you, They have their reward. But thou, when thou fastest, anoint thine head, and wash thy face; That thou appear not unto men to fast, but unto thy Father which is in secret: and thy Father, which seeth in secret, shall reward thee openly."
(Matthew 6:1-18)

Matthew 6 is a continuation of our Redeemer's Sermon on the Mount. In chapter 5 our Lord taught us that while the Pharisees were very good at avoiding outward deeds of lawlessness and wickedness, they understood nothing of heart-sins or of righteousness. He taught us that it is not enough that we avoid evil acts, we must also avoid evil attitudes. "The Lord looketh on the heart." In this chapter our Saviour teaches us that while the Pharisees were very meticulous in observing their outward acts of worship, to be seen and applauded by men, they did not worship God. In all their religion, there was no heart worship. It was all an outward show. They convinced themselves that it was real; but their religion was, nonetheless, nothing but an outward show. He is teaching us the necessity of heart-worship, the necessity of doing what we do from an inward principle of grace, for the glory of God.

In these verses (1-18), our Lord Jesus Christ is warning us to be aware of and studiously avoid hypocrisy in all acts of worship and service in the name of God. Hypocrisy is the leaven of the Pharisees, the leaven of outward religion. If it reigns in us, it will ruin us. So we are warned to beware of it. Hypocrisy is religion that is only skin deep. It is a religion of words and works, but not of grace, heart, and spirit. Hypocrisy is a form of godliness, an outward show of religion, without the life and power of God in the soul.

Specifically, our Master calls our attention to three areas of religious activity that are easily perverted into mere acts of religious showmanship; three areas of religious service where hypocrisy shows itself: the giving of alms, the matter of prayer, and the practice of fasting. Alms, prayer, and fasting were prominent areas of religious activity among the Jews of our Lord's day. In fact, wherever men practise religion of any kind, it is most natural to make these three things matters of prominence. Judaism, Islam, Hinduism, Christianity, Protestant as well as Catholic, all religions encourage alms, prayers, and fasting. Man naturally associates these things with religion. By these three things, it is assumed that we serve God with our whole being. In the giving of alms we serve him with our estates, in prayer with our souls, and in fasting with our bodies.

While encouraging the practice of outward piety, in this chapter, our Lord gives us a much needed and commonly ignored warning: in all our acts of worship, devotion, and service to God, we must avoid seeking to be seen of men and seek only to be seen of and to glorify the Lord God.

Alms, Prayers, And Fasting

Alms

In verses 1-4 our Lord talks about the giving of alms. All that is said here may be applied to giving in the house of God and giving in support of the gospel ministry. But that is not what is primarily intended. Almsgiving is charity giving. It is giving to the poor. Without question, this kind of giving is prescribed by the law of God written upon the hearts of all men by nature, the law given by the pen of Moses, and by the grace of God experienced in the soul. Wherever grace and righteousness is established in the heart, charity flows generously from the hand (Psalm 112:5, 9). That which is given to the poor is said by God to be their due (Proverbs 3:27, 28). Almsgiving is the essence of what James describes as the practice of pure, undefiled religion (James 1:27). Those who profess to be the followers of Christ should, above all other people, be charitable, generous, giving people. Give to the poor. Give to the cause of Christ. Give to the church of God. And give to the servants of God.

In all our giving, let us give as unto the Lord. A giving God is worthy of a giving people. I make this promise to you, as you exercise generosity for the glory of Christ and the good of your fellowmen you will never impoverish yourself by generosity! Do not give by the force of legal constraint. And do not give from a spirit of covetousness, hoping to get more. But God will never allow a generous soul to lack the means to be generous (Proverbs 3:9, 10; 11:24, 25; 19:17; 28:27; Malachi 3:10-12; Luke 6:38; Philippians 4:19). Let every child of God give according to his own means, "as God hath prospered him" (1 Corinthians 16:2). Two words of warning: 1. Do not be stingy, but generous (2 Corinthians 9:6-8). 2. Do not do anything in a public show (Matthew 6:1-4). Be as quiet and unobservable as possible in giving. Never tell anyone how much you give, or even that you give alms to those in need.

Alms giving, when done with an eye to God's glory and from a principle of real love for others, is the gift of the heart. Therefore, it seeks neither applause nor direction from men. "What flows from God", wrote Robert Hawker, "will tend to God. Jesus is then in all, and a respect to him is the aim of all."

Prayer

In verses 5-15, the Lord Jesus gives us very simple, but very needful, instructions about prayer. Our Saviour here assumes that all Christians pray. As soon as Saul of Tarsus was converted, we read, "Behold, he prayeth." All who are godly, all who are born of God pray (Psalm 32:6). I do not say, "They say their prayers". Saul of Tarsus did that all his life. There is a huge difference between saying a prayer and praying! Yet the Word of God does declare that every regenerate soul prays. "You may as soon find a living man that does not breathe", wrote Matthew Henry, "as a living Christian that does not pray." In these verses, our Lord does not teach his people to pray. There is no need for that. He teaches us how not to pray and how to pray.

In verses 5 and 6, he says, "Do not pray to be seen of men". Do not use a posture in prayer that causes people to look at you or calls attention to yourself. In public places, other than places of public worship, we are not to engage in public prayer. Prayer is between you and God. As much as possible, let your prayers be unobserved and unheard by men.

Do not use vain repetitions (v. 7). That prohibition extends to all memorized prayers, pious sounds and voice tones, religious jargon, and "Hail Marys". It even includes the mere repetition of the words contained in these verses. This is a prohibition against much speaking in prayer, too. God does not need to be informed or argued with, but acknowledged, sought and honoured. The prophets of Baal put on a show when they cried aloud to their deaf god. The servant of God simply uttered the desire of his heart (1 Kings 18:36, 37). That is what prayer is.

True prayer is an act of faith. Place, position, and posture are meaningless. Words are really insignificant. Prayer is the acknowledgment of God as my Father with the confidence that he knows and will supply all my needs. In prayer, the believer simply and confidently seeks the glory of God (v. 9), the increase of God's kingdom (v. 10), the will of God (v. 10), daily provision (v. 11), daily mercy (v. 12), daily preservation (v. 13), and the praise of God (v. 13). Let men talk all they will about prayer, unless our prayers arise from sincere hearts of faith and love, they amount to nothing but meaningless noise, sounding brass and tinkling cymbals. That is what the Lord Jesus says in verses 14 and 15.

Prayer Meetings

What about prayer meetings? When our Lord tells us that we are to enter into our closets to pray to our Father, is he forbidding public prayer meetings? Of course, the answer to that question is "No". We read, in Acts 1:14, that the saints in the early church "all continued with one accord in prayer and supplication, with the women, and Mary the mother of Jesus, and with his brethren." When our Lord says, "When thou prayest, enter into thy closet, and when thou hast shut thy door, pray to thy Father which is in secret", he is simply telling us that true prayer is intensely private, between us and our Father. In the passage before us (Matthew

6:5-15), our Lord is principally talking about the private prayers of individuals. Yet, what he says certainly has application to the public prayers of God's saints in the house of worship.

After the ascension, the Apostles of our Lord met together with their wives, with Mary, and with the other brethren, continuing "with one accord in prayer and supplication". Then, at the appointed time and according to the promise of God, the Holy Spirit was poured out upon the infant church on the Day of Pentecost.

Acts 1:14 is often referred to as an example of and basis for what is called "prayer meetings", meetings particularly for the purpose of praying, especially with reference to revival. Generally, these are not public worship services, but meetings of the "spiritually elite", usually men, in which one man after another leads the others in "prayer". In some cases all join in audibly, making it a time of senseless confusion. The hope is that many men praying together can twist the arm of the omnipotent God and get him to send revival.

Is that what took place in the early church? Not likely. Acts 1:14 speaks of the church meeting in public worship. They "continued with one accord in prayer and supplication, with the women". The women also prayed and made supplication, but certainly not audibly (1 Corinthians 14:34, 35).

I am occasionally asked, "Why don't you have prayer meetings in your church?" My answer is, "We have prayer meetings at least three times every week. All our worship services are prayer meetings." Our men meet in my office before every service for scripture reading and prayer. The public reading of holy scripture and prayer are also a central part of all our worship services. I encourage the men who read and lead us in prayer to read a brief passage, with little or no comment. Then the man appointed to do so leads the rest of us in prayer. But we do not have the kind of prayer meetings that are common in most conservative churches, because I see no basis for them in scripture and see no value in them. In fact, I see them as detriments, rather than helps.

Most of what goes on in the religious world is nothing but the practice of sentimentalism, designed and intended to make people feel religious and spiritual. People who call, asking to be put on our "prayer list", are shocked when I tell them "We don't have a prayer list." I do not want to be put on anyone's prayer list. I want to be remembered before the throne of grace as God enables his people to pray. Churches advertise "prayer lines", as though we could get in contact with God by a dial-up connection. Such tom-foolery is as absurd and perverse as anything I can imagine. I would rather have a dial-up wife than have a dial-up god! Others start “prayer chains”. There is no more power in a prayer chain than there is in one of those chain letters ladies get from superstitious friends. We often get letters with an “urgent prayer request”. But we are not going to get God almighty to do what we want him to do by trying to twist his arm! And multitudes engage in “group prayers”, or what is called “prayer meetings”. Groups cannot twist God’s arm any better than an individual can.

Anything commonly practised and promoted by the whole religious world ought to be marked with a skull and cross bones. It is nothing but poison to our souls.

I said that those things called “prayer meetings” are real detriments rather than helps, because they tend to much evil. Those who join in the group are looked upon (and, if the truth be told, usually look upon themselves) as the spiritual leaders of the church, considering others less spiritual. And such meetings are looked upon as forerunners to revival. After all, all the histories of revival tell us that before revival came, men (and usually women) had great prayer meetings in which they worked themselves up into a frenzy, calling it God’s work.

Frankly, I am not impressed by most of what has been called revival in church history. That which is commonly called revival appears to me to be more demonic than heavenly. Most would call the events recorded in 1 Kings 18:26, 28, and 29 revival, if they were to occur today, and the word Jesus were used instead of Baal. But true revival came in verse 39. When God works his wonders in the midst of his people, he does not cause a fleshly, charismatic show of emotional frenzy. Rather, he causes sinners to be awed before him in worship, bowing before the throne of his sovereign majesty (read Isaiah 6, Joel 2 and Acts 2). Whatever revival is, it is not a spasmodic fit of religion, with only temporary results. Rather, it is Christ seizing the hearts of men and women by his omnipotent grace.

I do not want to discourage prayer. Let us pray more, not less! But we ought to take this matter of speaking to God seriously (Ecclesiastes 5:2). I am desperately afraid of being pretentious before God! Too often when I speak to God my words are too many and my thoughts too few.

Rather than getting people worked up in “prayer meetings” I offer this suggestion to pastors and churches. Let us, like the church in Acts 1:14, continue “with one accord in prayer and supplication”, worshipping God. As we meet together in God’s house, with his people, in our Saviour’s name, let our hearts be focused on worshipping our God, pouring out our hearts to him in prayer and supplications, as we preach and hear the blessed gospel of his free, saving grace in the Lord Jesus Christ. It is by the preaching of the gospel that Christ is honoured, his people are edified, and sinners are converted. It is by this means, not religious excitement, that God is pleased to pour out upon his church his Spirit and his grace.

In his day during the 18th century, Robert Hawker commented about prayer, "How little understood by the great mass of what the world calls worshippers"! How much more might we make the same lamentation today!

The Pattern

Look more closely at the pattern of prayer by which our Saviour teaches us how we are to pray. "After this manner therefore pray ye: Our Father which art in heaven, Hallowed be thy name. Thy kingdom come. Thy will be done in earth, as it is in heaven. Give us this day our daily bread. And forgive us our debts, as we forgive our debtors. And lead us not into temptation, but deliver us from evil: For thine is the kingdom, and the power, and the glory, for ever. Amen" (vv. 9-13).

The Lord Jehovah, our great God, in the three persons of the Blessed Trinity, is our Father. Our Saviour said, as he was leaving this world, once his work of redemption was finished, "I ascend to my Father and your Father, to my God and your God" (John 20:17). As we adore him on his throne in heaven, we pray that his name may be "hallowed" (sanctified and honoured) on earth as it is in heaven.

We desire that all his elect be saved, that his kingdom of grace be established on earth among all his redeemed, as his kingdom of glory is and will be established in heavenly glory to all eternity.

The bread for which we seek a daily supply, is not simply the bread of the body that perishes, but the bread of the soul that endures to life everlasting, the Lord Jesus himself, "the living Bread which came down from heaven ... He that eateth of this Bread shall live forever" (John 6:51, 58). The cry of hungry souls is, "Lord, evermore give us this bread" (John 6:34). We need and feed upon his blood and his obedience daily, as sinners in constant need of pardon by his blood and righteousness by his obedience as our Surety.

As we delight to forgive the trespasses of others against us, so we seek forgiveness from our God by the merits of Christ continually.

Because he alone can keep us in the hour of temptation, our Saviour here teaches us to pray that our Father will keep us from the evil one who goes about "as a roaring lion, seeking whom he may devour" (1 Peter 5:8).

In the last part of verse 13, our Lord teaches us to ascribe all the glory and praise to God alone; and every heaven-born soul delights to do so. "For of him, and through him, and to him, are all things, to whom be glory forever" (Romans 11:36).

With the last word of verse 13, our Saviour puts his name to the prayer, saying, "Amen". Had he not done so, our amen would be nothing. Every time we pronounce that blessed word, it should be done with the greatest reverence and with an eye of faith toward Christ. To say "Amen" is not simply saying, as is commonly thought, "so be it". To say "Amen" at the end of our prayers is not simply giving our confirmation to what has been spoken. It is also calling upon and worshipping the Lord Jesus who is "the Amen" (Revelation 3:14) by one of his great names, to confirm what has been said. To quote Hawker again, "We should feel the striking nature of the expression, if at the end of sermons, or prayers, or in any other part of our ordinances, we were solemnly to close all with saying 'Jesus'. But yet in fact we do this when we say 'Amen'. For this is as truly the name of the Lord Jesus as any other. May the Lord give both to Writer and Reader a right understanding in all things"!

In verses 14, 15, our Saviour declares, "For if ye forgive men their trespasses, your heavenly Father will also forgive you: But if ye forgive not men their trespasses, neither will your Father forgive your trespasses". These two verses have caused great confusion to some; but there is no reason for the confusion. It is utterly heretical to imagine, as many do, that our Lord here conditions our forgiveness by his blood and his free grace upon our forgiving of others. Our pardon and acceptance with God is entirely on Christ's account. Our forgiveness of others is a blessed result and evidence of our own experience of forgiveness by God's boundless, free grace. It is a sweet token of the love of Christ ruling our hearts when we are enabled of God to be "kind one to another, tender-hearted, forgiving one another, even as God for Christ's sake hath forgiven" us (Ephesians 4:32).

Fasting

Look at verses 16-18, "Moreover when ye fast, be not, as the hypocrites, of a sad countenance: for they disfigure their faces, that they may appear unto men to fast. Verily I say unto you, They have their reward. But thou, when thou fastest, anoint thine head, and wash thy face; That thou appear not unto men to fast, but unto thy Father which is in secret: and thy Father, which seeth in secret, shall reward thee openly." Here our Saviour gives a word of instruction about fasting.

Though religious people today talk a good bit about fasting, the Word of God says very little about it. Fasting is subjecting the desires of the body and the needs of the body to the burden of the heart and the longings of the spirit in prayer. Our Lord is not giving us instructions about the value of dietary or medical fasting, but about the spiritual significance of religious fasting. What is fasting? What does the Word of God teach about fasting? Should we fast today? If so, how? Let us hear what of our Lord Jesus Christ says in his Word about the matter.

Fasting is an occasional abstinence from food and carnal pleasures. It is subjecting the needs and desires of the body to the burden of the heart and longings of the spirit in prayer. We read of many in the Word of God who fasted in prayer when greatly concerned about a specific matter (David, when his child was dying; Daniel, when he sought the mind of the Lord; Esther, before going in to Ahasuerus; the Lord Jesus, before he was tempted; and the church at Antioch, when they ordained Paul and Barnabas to preach the gospel).

Yet, there is no direct command given in the Word of God requiring anyone to fast or teaching us that we should fast. It is left to each believer to decide whether he will fast, when, and for how long. This is a matter about which no man should sit in judgment over another.

There are some poor people in this world who never have enough to eat. It would be utter cruelty to require them to fast. Sickly people, whose frames must be sustained by a very strict diet, would be acting foolishly if they fasted. If you choose to fast, you may do so freely. And, if you choose not to fast, you may do so freely.

The only thing our Lord requires is that no one is to know, but you and the Lord, whether you fast or do not fast. If you fast, "do not appear unto men to fast". That is the only rule given in the Word of God about fasting.

Having said that, I am confident that our Lord intends for us to understand that fasting is not really a matter of depriving ourselves of physical food and pleasure. He does not condemn fasting, but he reproves all outward, Pharisaic and hypocritical displays of mortification and self-denial. All outward displays of "godliness", "devotion", and "spirituality" are but displays of corrupt hearts. The Pharisees attempted to cast reproach upon our Lord and his disciples, when they asked our Saviour, "Why do the disciples of John fast often, and make prayers, and likewise the disciples of the Pharisees, but thine eat and drink?" (Luke 5:33).

The mere abstinence from food is not a fasting of the soul before God. "The kingdom of God is not meat and drink, but righteousness and peace, and joy in the Holy Ghost" (Romans 14:17). "Meat commendeth us not to God, for neither if we eat are we the better, neither if we eat not are we the worse" (1 Corinthians 8:8). It is an astonishing indication of the pride and corruption of our sinful hearts and vile nature that inclines us (as is so constantly the case) to substitute physical acts in the place of real vital godliness and heart worship. This inclination is strong among all the fallen sons and daughters of Adam because that which we do gratifies the flesh. Our proud flesh will bring anything to God but Christ, trust anything but Christ, and find consolation and hope in anything but Christ. To trust the person, work, and finished salvation of the Lord Jesus none will ever do, except those who are taught of God the Holy Spirit and made willing to do so by the power of his grace. All outward shows of "godliness", "devotion", and "spirituality" the Spirit of God declares, are nothing but "a show of wisdom in will worship, and humility, and neglecting of the body" (Colossians 2:23). Instead of directing us to Christ, they lead us away from him into everlasting ruin (Colossians 2:16-23).

Do nothing in the worship and service of God to be seen of and applauded by men. Yes, we are to let our light shine before men, that they may see our good works and glorify our Father which is in heaven. But we are never to do anything that others my see and applaud us! Our Lord Jesus, in this weighty, instructive passage teaches us that we are never to attempt to do anything to show people our faith in him, our love for him, or our devotion to him. Rather, we are to simply walk before God in faith, devotion, and love. The hypocrite is one who lets his light so shine before men that they cannot see what is going on backstage! The Lord God cares nothing about how much money we give, how long we pray or how often, and whether we fast. He is interested in only one thing. "The Lord looketh on the heart"! When God looks on the heart, he looks for faith in and love for the Lord Jesus Christ. He will not accept us, and he will not accept anything we give to or do for him, no matter how costly, no matter how zealous we are, unless we are washed in the blood of his dear Son, robed in his righteousness, and sanctified by his Spirit (1 Peter 2:7).

Sinners cannot be accepted by the holy Lord God upon any grounds, for any reason, other than the person and work of the Lord Jesus Christ. We cannot give anything to God, worship him in prayer, or fast before him until we are in Christ by faith, until we are born again by his almighty grace. The real test of Christianity is not what we do for God, but what God in Christ has done for us.

Chapter 15

"Lord, Teach Us To Pray"

"After this manner therefore pray ye: Our Father which art in heaven, Hallowed be thy name. Thy kingdom come. Thy will be done in earth, as it is in heaven. Give us this day our daily bread. And forgive us our debts, as we forgive our debtors. And lead us not into temptation, but deliver us from evil: For thine is the kingdom, and the power, and the glory, for ever. Amen. For if ye forgive men their trespasses, your heavenly Father will also forgive you: But if ye forgive not men their trespasses, neither will your Father forgive your trespasses."
(Matthew 6:9-15)

Volumes have been written about prayer. In fact, many volumes have been written about these few, brief words of instruction, which our Saviour gave about prayer. I suppose there are more silly "how to" books on prayer than on any other Bible subject. I fear they do more harm than good. Yet, I know there is need for clear, biblical instruction about prayer. Every believer feels like our Lord's disciples at times, when they cried, "Lord, teach us to pray". In this passage our blessed Saviour does just that. He teaches us how to pray.

Still, when I take it upon myself to say or write anything on the subject of prayer, I do so with great reluctance because I fully and shamefully acknowledge that I know so little about the subject. My own prayers are so sinful that they are matters of constant repentance before my God. What hypocrisy there is in my petitions, when there should be honesty! What arrogant seeking of my own will, when there should be submission to my God's will! What vain repetitions I make, when there should be nothing but the cries of a broken heart! How little I feel the sins I confess! How little I sense my deep need for the mercies I seek! How I long for the "Spirit of grace and supplication" to teach me how to pray!

> I often say my prayers, but do I ever pray?
> Or do the wishes of my flesh dictate the words I say?
> I might as well kneel down and worship gods of stone,
> As offer to the living God a prayer of words alone!

"After This Manner Therefore, Pray Ye"

First, it must be stated clearly that this is not, as it is commonly called, "The Lord's Prayer". Our Lord Jesus did not, should not have, and could not have prayed for divine forgiveness! John 17 might properly be called "The Lord's Prayer", though really that is a mistake. John 17 records just one of the many prayers uttered by our blessed Saviour while he walked on this earth.

And this is not a prayer to be memorized and recited. Never do we find the disciples reciting this prayer. In fact, the only other reference made to it is in Luke 11. And Luke studiously avoids giving us an exact replica of it. There is nothing spiritual or worshipful in the mere repetition of words. Rather, this is a word of instruction about how we are to pray and for what we are to pray. Here our Lord Jesus, knowing that we do not know what to pray for as we ought, helps our infirmities by showing us what we are to pray for and how to do it.

In these few, short statements our Lord teaches us all the vital aspects of prayer. Our prayers should be simple, sincere, sagacious, spiritual, and short, avoiding everything like pretence, formality, and show. When our Master says, "After this manner therefore, pray ye", he is telling us to pray like this, and proceeds to teach us to pray without the use of vain repetitions, but in brief, simple expressions, according to the pattern given in the few words that follow. He does not tell us to use the words he here uses, but the pattern he here gives.

In prayer believers simply spread before God, our heavenly Father, the great desires and needs of their hearts, trusting him to fulfil those desires and meet those needs by his grace for the glory of his name. What are the great desires of the believer's heart? What are the great needs we have, which cause us to wait in utter helplessness before God. Let us look at this model prayer, by which our Lord teaches us how to pray, line by line.

"Our Father, Which Art In Heaven"

We are not to pray to saints or angels, but to God our Father, the God and Father of our Lord Jesus Christ, the God of glory, who is in heaven. Our God and Father is the God and Father of all men as their Creator (Acts 17:28). Because he is the God and Father of all men by creation, it is proper for all men to praise him and pray to him. We must never forbid anyone to pray, or in any way discourage anyone. Rather, we ought to encourage all men to pray.

Many quote John 9:31, where it is written, "We know that God heareth not the prayer of sinners", pointing to it as a reason why we ought not teach our children and others to pray. In doing so I fear they reveal their true character. This statement, "We know that God heareth not the prayer of sinners", was made by the man born blind, having been healed by Jesus – though he may have been repeating a popular teaching of the Pharisees. This man born blind was quoting their own doctrine to the Pharisees in justification of Jesus' miraculous powers to restore sight, and thus must be from God and not a sinner. The fact is, God never hears the prayers of anyone except sinners.

The God of glory is the Father of all men as their Creator; but he is the God and Father of his elect in a very distinct and very special sense, by grace. Our Lord Jesus Christ made peace through the blood of his cross and reconciled "all things unto himself; whether they be things in earth, or things in heaven. And you, that were sometime alienated and enemies in your mind by wicked works, yet now hath he reconciled in the body of his flesh through death, to present you holy and unblameable and unreproveable in his sight" (Colossians 1:20-22). We are the children of God by adoption, by election, by redemption, by reconciliation, by regeneration, and by faith. We call God our Father by "the Spirit of adoption whereby we cry, Abba, Father" (Romans 8:15).

Do you trust the Lord Jesus Christ? If you do, it is right for you to call God almighty your Father, and to come to him as such in prayer. "Let us therefore come boldly unto the throne of grace, that we may obtain mercy, and find grace to help in time of need" (Hebrews 4:16). We pray to God in heaven as our Father. What a great privilege! And there is something especially sweet about that little word "our". When we pray collectively in our public worship services or anytime two believers pray together, we pray as the children of God. Nothing unites hearts like mutual prayer. How can two be divided who together call the God of all grace, "Our Father"?

We are to call upon God as our Father in heaven, both expressing our reverence for him and our complete liberty to speak to him, as sons would speak to their father on earth. We ought to always approach our great and glorious God, our Father in heaven, with complete confidence and freedom. Oh, that he might, by his blessed Spirit, teach us to do so!

The fact that he is here described as "our Father which art in heaven", may well be intended to teach us that we are to set our hearts on things above, not on things on the earth. This earth is not our homeland. Heaven is. Let us set our hearts upon it.

"Ye are come unto mount Sion, and unto the city of the living God, the heavenly Jerusalem, and to an innumerable company of angels, To the general assembly and church of the firstborn, which are written in heaven, and to God the Judge of all, and to the spirits of just men made perfect, And to Jesus the mediator of the new covenant, and to the blood of sprinkling, that speaketh better things than that of Abel" (Hebrews 12:22-24).

"Hallowed Be Thy Name"

The name of God represents all his attributes by which he reveals himself to us. His name represents his Being, all that he is! When we say, "Hallowed be thy name", we are simply praying, like the Lord Jesus did, "Father, glorify thy name" (John 12:28). The word "hallowed" simply means "sanctified". God created the world for his glory (Revelation 4:11; Proverbs 16:4). All providence tends toward his glory (Romans 11:36). God's object in saving sinners is his glory (Psalm 106:8). The object of Christ in his death was, above all else, the glory of God (John 12:28). And it is the heart desire of every believer, above all else, that God's name be honoured, magnified, and glorified (Psalm 35:27; 40:16; 70:4; 1 Peter 4:11). Therefore, this is set before us as the first thing we are to seek in prayer.

We pray as children to a Father, and we pray as brothers and sisters in Christ to "Our Father". "Our Father" is a family term. The words, "which art in heaven", suggest our Father's majesty and the reverence with which we are to approach him. The God of Glory is "our Father", though he is "in heaven". And though he is "in heaven", he is "our Father". His name is ever to be treated with reverence. Indeed, all that concerns him is to be treated with reverence. His Word, his gospel, his church, and his ordinances should always be regarded with the utmost awe! Let us walk humbly before him, seeking his honour in all things and above all things, praying, "Hallowed be thy name", as we hallow it ourselves. Our heart's highest wish is for God's honour, dominion, and glory.

"Thy Kingdom Come"

Our first concern is and must be the glory of God himself. Our second concern is for the kingdom of God. We seek in all our prayers that the Lord God will be pleased to establish and enlarge his church and kingdom in this world (Psalm 122:6, 7). To pray "thy kingdom come" is simply to pray, "Lord, save your people, establish your kingdom in this world." Our concern is for the kingdom of God, his sheep, his people, his elect, and his church. We pray for the kingdom of grace to be filled (Romans 11:26). We pray for the kingdom of glory to be established (2 Peter 3:13).

Our hearts ought not be consumed with care for the kingdoms of this world, but with concern for the kingdom of God. Our Lord Jesus here teaches us to ever seek the mighty operations of his grace in the hearts of sinners, causing them to be willing servants to him in the day of his power (Psalm 110:3), subduing the hearts of chosen, redeemed sinners before him in willing, loyal obedience. We long for the coming of Christ our King. Until he comes we pray to our Father, "Thy kingdom come".

"Thy Will Be Done In Earth As It Is In Heaven"

Prayer is not us trying to get God to do our will. Rather it is a voluntary leaving of our will to his will. "Our truest happiness", wrote J. C. Ryle, "is perfect submission to God's will". We want to obey God's revealed will. We want all men everywhere to surrender to and obey God's revealed will. But here, our Lord is teaching us to sincerely and heartily surrender everything to and earnestly desire that God's will be done in this world exactly as it is in heaven, knowing that it is (Ephesians 1:11).

Our Lord teaches us always to pray, "thy will be done". No matter what our circumstances are, no matter what we think needs to be done, no matter how much we think we want something, wisdom and faith bows to the throne of God and says, "thy will be done". We are so sinful and ignorant that we simply do not know, we never know, what is best. Our Father does. Let us, therefore, gladly bow our will to his will. "The Spirit also helpeth our infirmities: for we know not what we should pray for as we ought: but the Spirit itself maketh intercession for us with groanings which cannot be uttered" (Romans 8:26).

"Who knoweth what is good for man in this life?" (Ecclesiastes 6:12) "We know not what we should pray for as we ought." Do we really believe that? Generally, going by what they say, people think they know exactly what to pray for. Yet, the Book says, "We know not what we should pray for as we ought." What a flesh-humbling declaration! "We know not what we should pray for as we ought." "If we ask any thing according to his will, he heareth us" (1 John 5:14). But to ask something which is not according to God's will is not praying, but presuming. We have reason, then, to cry with the disciples, "Lord, teach us to pray" (Luke 11:1). And this is how he teaches us to pray, "thy will be done in earth as it is in heaven."

In all that we have seen thus far, the concern of true prayer is altogether spiritual. Our Lord Jesus teaches us to pray for the glory of God, the people of God, and the will of God. He teaches us to submit all things to those things!

"Give Us This Day Our Daily Bread"

What an instructive word this is! J. C. Ryle wrote, "We are here taught to acknowledge our entire dependence on God, for the supply of our daily necessities. As Israel required daily manna, so we require daily 'bread'. We confess that we are poor, weak, needy creatures, and beseech him who is our Maker to take care of us. We ask for 'bread', as the simplest of our needs, and in that word we include all that our bodies require."

We are to seek God's providential supplies for ourselves and our brethren "Give us". We seek our daily food as a gift from God knowing, that if we have bread to eat, we are fed by the hand of God. Here we are taught to seek no more than is needful for us. "Bread", not gold, just bread. And we are taught to seek no more than our daily provision of bread, "Give us this day", or as Luke phrases it, "day by day our bread". It is no less spiritual to look to our Father in heaven for the daily provision of our daily needs than it is to pray, "Hallowed be thy name". Faith looks to the hand of God for all things, and seeks only that which is the will of God, for the glory of God, and needed by us.

Yet, as we saw in the previous chapter, just as we look to God to provide the needs of our bodies, we must also look to him to give us daily bread for our souls. That bread is Christ. He is truly the Bread we need, the Bread upon which we must feed day by day. Yet, we are such sinful wretches that we cannot feed upon this Bread from heaven, except the Father give us our Bread. Only he can cause our souls to hunger for Christ; and only he can satisfy our hungry souls. "Lord, evermore give us this bread" (John 6:34).

"Forgive Us Our Debts"

We must especially remember this. Our Lord here teaches us to constantly acknowledge our sinfulness, and to constantly seek forgiveness through his blood. We are to confess our sins continually, not in the ear of an earthly priest, or in the ear of a counsellor, or in the ear of a preacher, but in the ear of our Father in heaven, seeking forgiveness by the merit of our great High Priest, who is in heaven, the Lord Jesus Christ. "If we confess our sins, he is faithful and just to forgive us our sins, and to cleanse us from all unrighteousness" (1 John 1:9).

Our sins are here described as debts, which we have incurred. They have made us debtors to God, who demands of us both righteousness and satisfaction. The Lord Jesus Christ fully paid our debt. He brought in righteousness for us by his obedience in life. And he satisfied divine justice for us by his obedience in death, putting away or debts forever by the sacrifice of himself.

Our great God, holy and just, freely forgives our debts through the merits of Christ. He has forgiven them; and he forgives them. He forgave our debts before they were ever incurred, in eternity, accepting us in Christ our Surety (Romans 8:28-30; Ephesians 1:3-6). He forgave our debts when Christ, by his blood, washed them away at Calvary (Hebrews 9:12). And he is faithful and just to forgive us our debts, our sins, day by day and moment by moment, as we confess them before his throne of grace.

We constantly need forgiveness because we constantly sin; and we constantly have it through the infinite, perpetual merit of Christ's blood. No, our confession of sin does not, in any way, cause God to forgive our sin. Yet, as we confess sin, he speaks forgiveness in our souls through Jesus Christ the righteous One, our blessed Substitute, who is "the propitiation for our sins".

We must never forget the next part of this sentence. "Forgive us our debts, as we forgive our debtors." This is the only part of this prayer that our Lord expands and explains. He does so because this is the part we are most apt to overlook. The explanation is given in verses 14, 15. "For if ye forgive men their trespasses, your heavenly Father will also forgive you: But if ye forgive not men their trespasses, neither will your Father forgive your trespasses." Our Lord here teaches us that if we are unforgiving, we are yet unforgiven. If we are not gracious, it is because we have not yet experienced grace. Spurgeon wrote:

> This yoke is easy. This burden is light. It may be a blessing to be wronged, since it affords us an opportunity of judging whether we are indeed the recipients of the pardon that comes from the throne of God. Very sweet it is to pass by other men's offences against ourselves; for thus we learn how sweet it is to the Lord to pardon us.

Ephesians 4:32-5:1 contains one of the sweetest and most important admonitions given to the children of God in this world. May God the Holy Spirit, whose words these are, give us grace to heed them. "Be ye kind one to another, tender-hearted, forgiving one another, even as God for Christ's sake hath forgiven you. Be ye therefore followers of God, as dear children; And walk in love, as Christ also hath loved us, and hath given himself for us an offering and a sacrifice to God for a sweetsmelling savour." Without forgiveness, forbearance, and brotherly love our prayers are nothing but noise, the hollow echoes of empty hearts! If we cannot forgive, we have not been forgiven.

"Lead Us Not Into Temptation"
As long as we are in this world, we are liable to temptation. As long as we are in this body of flesh, we may be drawn away of our own lust, enticed by our own nature, tempted and overcome by the snare of Satan. Here our Saviour says, "You need to be constantly aware of your weakness and Satan's strength. You need to be constantly aware of your helplessness, so that you will constantly look to me for help." Prayer, in its essence, is the conscious spreading out of my helplessness before God! Wise people seek to avoid danger. And we ask God who rules all things to keep us from the danger of temptation. May he who orders our steps order them away from temptation.

"Deliver Us From Evil"
Let us ever pray that our God will graciously deliver us from all the evil present in the world. From Satan, who inspires all evil, that he might destroy our souls. From all the evil that is the result of sin. And the greatest of evils, the evil that is in our own hearts!

Blessed be his name, our God will deliver us from evil (Jude 24, 25). He will deliver us from every evil temptation we face in this world (1 Corinthians 10:13), giving us grace sufficient in the time of trial. He will deliver us from sin and all the evil of this world in the moment we drop our robe of flesh (John 14:1-3; 2 Corinthians 5:1-9). And he will deliver us from all the evil consequences of sin in resurrection glory at the last day (Ephesians 5:25-27). "And God shall wipe away all tears from their eyes; and there shall be no more death, neither sorrow, nor crying, neither shall there be any more pain: for the former things are passed away" (Revelation 21:4).

"For Thine Is The Kingdom, And The Power, And The Glory, Forever"
Here our Saviour teaches us that all prayer is to be an ascription of praise to God "For thine is the kingdom, and the power, and the glory, forever. Amen." All the kingdoms of the world belong to God. All power belongs to God. And all glory belongs to God alone. These are the words David used to ascribe praise to our Father in heaven, by which he "Hallowed" his holy name. "Thine, O LORD, is

the greatness, and the power, and the glory, and the victory, and the majesty: for all that is in the heaven and in the earth is thine; thine is the kingdom, O LORD, and thou art exalted as head above all" (1 Chronicles 29:11).

What an encouragement this is for us to walk before our God in confident faith, trusting him in all things and for all things! What an encouragement to prayer! He who is our Father in heaven, the God of all grace, omnipotent and omniscient, ever wise and ever-good, will hallow his own great name, save all his elect, perform all his will, give us our daily bread, forgive all our sins, preserve us from all harm by our temptations, support us in them, deliver us from them, and deliver us from all evil. Should he fail to do all that is implied in these words of instruction about prayer, how could his name be hallowed, sanctified, and glorified?

"Amen"

"Amen" is a word of assent, expressing confident faith. It means, "so be it", or "so it shall be". John Gill wrote, "This word being retained, and kept the same in all languages, signifies the unity of the spirit, and faith in prayer, in all the saints, in all ages." And, as we have seen before, "Amen" is one of our Saviour's names.

When our Lord Jesus teaches us to pray, "after this manner", he is teaching us to pray in his name. To use the word "Amen" when we pray, if we pray as we ought, in the spirit and with understanding, is to pray in Christ's name. When we gather to worship with God's saints, we are to gather in Christ's name. If we do so, we are assured of his presence (Matthew 18:20). And if we pray in his name, we are assured that we have what we desire of God. "Whatsoever ye shall ask in my name, that will I do, that the Father may be glorified in the Son. If ye shall ask any thing in my name, I will do it" (John 14:13, 14). "Verily, verily, I say unto you, Whatsoever ye shall ask the Father in my name, he will give it you" (John 16:23). "And this is the confidence that we have in him, that, if we ask anything according to his will, he heareth us: and if we know that he hear us, whatsoever we ask, we know that we have the petitions that we desired of him" (1 John 5:14, 15).

But what is it to worship and pray in Christ's name? It is not simply tacking the word "Amen", or the words "in Jesus' name" onto the end of our prayers, as if they were magical words like "abracadabra". It is coming to God, as needy sinners, trusting the merits of Christ's blood, righteousness, and mediation alone for acceptance with him. To pray in Christ's name is to come to God in faith, trusting Christ, bowing before his throne, bowing to his will, seeking his glory.

If, when we pray, we truly bow to and seek the will of God, we have what we desire of him. God will do his will! Contrary to popular opinion, prayer is not a mighty instrument for getting God to do our will, but a mighty instrument by which God performs his will in this world. As A. W. Pink put it, "To ask in the name of Christ is to set aside our own will and bow to the perfect will of God." To pray in Christ's name and according to the will of God is to want what God wills for his glory. Prayer is not, as so many vainly imagine, a blank check made out to us, waiting for us to fill in the amount. Prayer is the cry of broken spirits to our Father in heaven, saying, "Thy will be done". "Lord, teach us to pray".

I bend my knees and bow my head,
And shut my eyes to all without;
But still my heart, so cold and dead,
Is full of sin and fear and doubt.
I say the words I ought to say,
Confess my sin, and long for thee;
But still, I fear, I seldom pray:
Teach me to pray, O Lord, teach me.
Cause me to know thy grace and power,
Spirit of God, awake my heart,
Within my soul create a prayer:
Give me, O Lord, a fervent heart.
Here at thy throne of grace I lie,
Trusting the merits of thy Son;
"Father, Abba, Father", I cry,
And hope that I am heaven born.
"Thy kingdom come, thy will be done",
These things, with earnest heart, I say:
My only hope is in thy Son:
But still, I ask, "Teach me to pray".

Chapter 16

A Cure For Care

"Lay not up for yourselves treasures upon earth, where moth and rust doth corrupt, and where thieves break through and steal: But lay up for yourselves treasures in heaven, where neither moth nor rust doth corrupt, and where thieves do not break through nor steal: For where your treasure is, there will your heart be also. The light of the body is the eye: if therefore thine eye be single, thy whole body shall be full of light. But if thine eye be evil, thy whole body shall be full of darkness. If therefore the light that is in thee be darkness, how great is that darkness! No man can serve two masters: for either he will hate the one, and love the other; or else he will hold to the one, and despise the other. Ye cannot serve God and mammon. Therefore I say unto you, Take no thought for your life, what ye shall eat, or what ye shall drink; nor yet for your body, what ye shall put on. Is not the life more than meat, and the body than raiment? Behold the fowls of the air: for they sow not, neither do they reap, nor gather into barns; yet your heavenly Father feedeth them. Are ye not much better than they? Which of you by taking thought can add one cubit unto his stature? And why take ye thought for raiment? Consider the lilies of the field, how they grow; they toil not, neither do they spin: And yet I say unto you, That even Solomon in all his glory was not arrayed like one of these. Wherefore, if God so clothe the grass of the field, which to day is, and to morrow is cast into the oven, shall he not much more clothe you, O ye of little faith? Therefore take no thought, saying, What shall we eat? or, What shall we drink? or, Wherewithal shall we be clothed? (For after all these things do the Gentiles seek:) for your heavenly Father knoweth that ye have need of all these things. But seek ye first the kingdom of God, and his righteousness; and all these things shall be added unto you. Take therefore no thought for the morrow: for the morrow shall take thought for the things of itself. Sufficient unto the day is the evil thereof."
(Matthew 6:19-34)

Years ago I heard Pastor Henry Mahan make several statements in a message he preached. As I sat in the congregation, I could easily have been convinced that he was preaching to no one but me. Like barbed arrows, these five statements pierced my heart. I wrote them down because I hoped never to forget them.

1. "We have entirely too many fears for a people to whom the Lord has said, 'Fear thou not; for I am with thee; be not dismayed, for I am thy God; I will strengthen thee, yea, I will uphold thee with the right hand of my righteousness.'"

Why can't we believe God? Has he not proven himself faithful to us? David heard God's promise and believed him. His faith in Christ quietened his fears. He said, "Yea, though I walk through the valley of the shadow of death. I will fear no evil for thou art with me; thy rod and thy staff, they comfort me."

2. "We have far too many doubts and fears concerning God's mercy, love, and grace for a people to whom the Lord has said, 'Him that cometh to me I will in no wise cast out … I give unto them eternal life, and they shall never perish.'"

I know that some who read these lines have trouble in this area. And I acknowledge my own shameful, baseless, sinful doubts. But I will not excuse them! On what grounds dare we call into question the mercy, love, and grace of our God? We have absolutely no reason to entertain the slightest shade of doubt! Did he not promise? Will he not perform it? "God is not a man that he should lie" (Numbers 23:19). Mr Spurgeon reasoned like this, "The scripture says, 'He that believeth on the Son of God hath everlasting life!' I believe the Son of God. I have life"! Why should we ever question that? Paul did not (2 Timothy 1:12; 4:6-8). Believing God, he raised these four challenges confidently: "If God be for us, who can be against us? … Who shall lay anything to the charge of God's elect? … Who is he that condemneth? … Who shall separate us from the love of Christ?" (Romans 8:31, 33-35).

I refuse to doubt God's love because of something I have thought, or said, or done. His love is free and unconditional! I refuse to question his grace because of my sin. While I acknowledge the abundance of my sin, I will rejoice in the superabundance of God's free grace in Christ. I am not going to be suspicious of his mercy because I do not deserve his mercy. Mercy is for the undeserving!

3. "We spend entirely too much time grumbling and complaining about our trials and troubles for a people to whom the Lord has said, 'In the world ye shall have tribulation but be of good cheer; I have overcome the world.'"

We should not be surprised when troubles come. We ought to expect them. Every ounce of gold that has been perfected and made valuable has been refined by fire. Every diamond that sparkles with beauty has been broken out of the earth, cut by sharp blows, and polished by rough rubbing. God has chosen us in the furnace of affliction (Isaiah 48:10). He will break, and cut, and polish his jewels. "Beloved, think it not strange concerning the fiery trial which is to try you, as though some strange thing happened unto you" (1 Peter 4:12). Trouble is not strange. For the believer, the absence of trouble is strange!

4. "We have entirely too much attachment to this world and to this present life for a people who are looking for a city whose Builder and Maker is God (Hebrews 11:8-10)".

"We know that if our earthly house of this tabernacle were dissolved, we have a building of God, a house not made with hands, eternal in the heavens" (2 Corinthians 5:1). The sooner, the better! We know that "to be absent from the body is to be present with the Lord". We have a desire to depart and be with Christ, which is far better. Believers are people who long to be with Christ. Yet, it is so difficult for us to turn loose of this world and this present existence. I cannot explain that. I just know it is so. The only way for us to be delivered from these carnal principles, and saved from our fears, concerns, and attachment to this world is to find something better. Our religious works will be dropped like a hot potato if we ever truly see Christ's finished work. Our "good deeds" will be of no value if we see what Christ has done for sinners by his incarnation (2 Corinthians 8:9), his obedience to God as our Representative (Philippians 2:5-7), and his accomplished redemption in his death as our Substitute (2 Corinthians 5:21).

Our "righteousnesses" will appear to us as they really are, "filthy rags", when we behold the righteousness of God in Christ. Our "goodness" will wither and die when God shows us his goodness, grace, and glory in Christ (Isaiah 6:1-8). Find me a sinner who has seen Christ, and I will show you a sinner who has quit arguing about his goodness, debating over his worthiness, and fussing about the power of his will! Our fears, doubts, grumblings, and complaints against our little trials, against God's purpose and his providence, will disappear in proportion to the faith we have in his promises (Isaiah 43:1-5; 46:4). The more I believe God, the less I will live in fear. The less I believe God, the more I will live in fear.

5. "We have far too much anxiety, care, and fear, far too much concern for earthly, material things for a people to whom the Lord has said, 'Your heavenly Father knoweth that ye have need of all these things'" (Matthew 6:32).

It is written, "My God shall supply all your need according to his riches in glory by Christ Jesus" (Philippians 4:19). Why should I fret when my God has promised to provide? Why should I concern myself about that which God has promised to do?

These five, heart-piercing statements are the very matters addressed in our Redeemer's message to us in Matthew 6:19-34. If we seek the kingdom of God and his righteousness, if we truly seek the will of God, the glory of God, and the kingdom of God in Christ, we have no reason to concern ourselves with earthly things.

Worldliness

The passage before us begins with a warning against worldliness (vv. 19-21). One of the greatest dangers we face is worldliness. It is one of Satan's most cleverly disguised snares. It seems an innocent thing to pay close attention to business and seek happiness and prosperity in this world, so long as we avoid open sins of immorality. Yet, our Lord warns us that worldliness is the rock on which many a man has made shipwreck of his soul. Worldliness is the love of this world (1 John 2:15). Worldliness is conformity to the principles, aspirations, and behaviour of unregenerate men. Griffith Thomas said, "Worldliness is a spirit, an atmosphere, an influence permeating the whole of life and human society, and it needs to be guarded against constantly and strenuously."

The only way to lay up treasure in heaven is to trust Christ. He is our Treasure! Where your treasure is, there will your heart be (Colossians 3:1-3). Learn, ask God to teach you, to look upon everything in the light of eternity. Value nothing here more than you will value it when you have to leave it. Beware of worldliness (Matthew 13:21, 22). J. C. Ryle wrote, "Open transgression of God's law slays its thousands, but worldliness its tens of thousands." "There is no surer evidence of an unconverted state", wrote Joseph Alleine, "than to have the things of the world uppermost in our aim, love, and estimation."

Light or Darkness

Next, our Saviour warns us against light that is darkness and the folly of a divided heart (vv. 22-24). "The light of the body is the eye: if therefore thine eye be single, thy whole body shall be full of light. But if thine eye be evil, thy whole body shall be full of darkness. If therefore the light that is in thee be darkness, how great is that darkness"! There are multitudes who have light that is nothing but darkness. The light they have is nothing but an acquired head-knowledge of sacred things, without the experience of grace. It is knowledge that puffs up, having no influence upon the heart. Like the devils, they have a clear apprehension of some of the great truths of holy scripture, but no love for them. That is the kind of knowledge Balaam possessed. Few men have understood the things Balaam stated in Numbers 23 so clearly as he did (Numbers 23:8-10, 19-24). His eyes were opened (Numbers 24:3, 4), but not his heart. He knew who the Lord God is, but did not know him. He knew many great things about him, but not him. He knew much about God's grace, but had no experience of grace. There was no love created in his heart for the God he professed to serve. He possessed great knowledge about God, but he hired himself out to curse the people of God.

While our Saviour walked upon the earth, the devils gave the same testimony concerning him as Balaam gave. "We know thee who thou art, the Holy One of God (Luke 4:33, 34). Yet, they are devils still, devils with the full knowledge and conviction that our Lord Jesus Christ is himself the eternal God! That is just the condition our Lord is describing. What a terrible condition it is! That knowledge men may acquire, be it ever so great, that is nothing but factual knowledge, never reaching the heart, knowledge without grace, void of life, is great darkness, indeed! In this world it is blinding. In the world to come it will be utter darkness and everlasting torment.

"No man can serve two masters: for either he will hate the one, and love the other; or else he will hold to the one, and despise the other. Ye cannot serve God and mammon." Where such darkness rules, the heart is always divided. It is impossible to serve Christ and the world at the same time. The ark of God and Dagon cannot stand in the same house. Christ must be King in our hearts, ruling over us, so that his will, his glory, his kingdom receives the devotion and commitment of our hearts. Unless our lives are so ordered, everything is confusion. "Thy whole body shall be full of darkness"!

Let us be people of one thing, having our eyes fixed on one thing; let that one thing be the one thing needful, the Lord Jesus Christ! Decisive consecration to Christ is the secret of happiness for any believer. God make us a people of one thing (Psalm 27:4; Luke 10:42; John 9:25; Philippians 3:13; Colossians 3:1-3).

Jesus is the one thing needful,
Our precious Lord and Saviour!
Ever true and ever faithful,
We'll sing His praise forever.
In Him a boundless fulness dwells
Of grace to all His chosen,
And like a flooding river swells
To weary sinners broken.

What mercy from His bosom flows
To every true believer!
He put away the countless woes
Of us poor, needy sinners.
Oh, blessed are His saints, indeed,
Christ Jesus is our Saviour!
And everything that we can need
Is ours in Him forever!

Cure For Care

Our Lord knows our hearts. He knows how quickly we turn off warnings against worldliness and how easily we excuse our pursuit of earthly things. Knowing our hearts, our Lord here nips in the bud every excuse we might offer for these things in verses 25-34. Here is a cure for our earthly cares.

First, our Saviour tells us in verse 25 that we ought never be possessed of an overly anxious spirit. "Therefore I say unto you, Take no thought for your life, what ye shall eat, or what ye shall drink; nor yet for your body, what ye shall put on. Is not the life more than meat, and the body than raiment?" Four times in these verses he says, "Take no thought". Prudent provision and care about earthly responsibilities is right. We are to work and provide for our families. But greed, worry, and tormenting care over earthly things is wrong.

To cure us of care and teach us to trust him, the Lord Jesus here reminds us of God's providential care of everything he has created. He sends us to the birds of the air for instruction. "Behold the fowls of the air: for they sow not, neither do they reap, nor gather into barns; yet your heavenly Father feedeth them. Are ye not much better than they?" In verse 27 he reminds us of the utter uselessness of worry, "Which of you by taking thought can add one cubit unto his stature?" Then, in verses 28-30 he sends us to the fields to observe the flowers to rebuke our unbelief. "And why take ye thought for raiment? Consider the lilies of the field, how they grow; they toil not, neither do they spin: And yet I say unto you, That even Solomon in all his glory was not arrayed like one of these. Wherefore, if God so clothe the grass of the field, which to day is, and to morrow is cast into the oven, shall he not much more clothe you, O ye of little faith?" In verses 31 and 32 our blessed Saviour tells us that any failure to implicitly trust our heavenly Father is utterly shameful. "Therefore take no thought, saying, What shall we eat? or, What shall we drink? or, Wherewithal shall we be clothed? (For after all these things do the Gentiles seek:) for your heavenly Father knoweth that ye have need of all these things." In verse 33 he gives us a great, precious promise. "But seek ye first the kingdom of God, and his righteousness; and all these things shall be added unto you." "For the LORD God is a sun and shield: the LORD will give grace and glory: no good thing will he withhold from them that walk uprightly" (Psalm 84:11). "And we know that all things work together for good to them that love God, to them who are the called according to his purpose" (Romans 8:28).

In verse 34 our Saviour seals up his instruction on this subject with a universally known and acknowledged fact, saying, "Sufficient to the day is the evil thereof." Why carry trouble before it comes? Attend to today's business and leave tomorrow's worries to tomorrow's troubles. If tomorrow comes, the Lord will be with you. If he sends trouble, he will give you grace sufficient. "Take therefore no thought for the morrow: for the morrow shall take thought for the things of itself. Sufficient unto the day is the evil thereof."

Any attempt to explain the wondrous things here declared by our Lord would be, at least on my part, utter folly. They are too sweet and delightful to need comment. Rather, let them be rolled over in our hearts, praying that God the Holy Spirit will effectually seal them to our hearts. Contemplate with joy the eternal love of God in Christ to our souls. All that is contained in creation, providence, redemption, grace, and glory to come, are countless tokens of that love and goodness! Loved in Christ with an everlasting love (Jeremiah 31:3), chosen in Christ by immutable grace, blessed in Christ with all blessings of grace and salvation from eternity, accepted in Christ from everlasting (Ephesians 1:3-6; 2 Timothy 1:9), preserved in Christ and called (Jude 1). Surely, his goodness to us in time, in every work of providence, cannot be doubted. His compassions never fail. His faithfulness is indescribably great. His mercies are new every morning. Yes, "the Lord is good to them that wait for him, to the soul that seeketh him" (Lamentations 3:22-25). He who redeemed us with his precious blood will never forget to take care of us. May he give us grace to leave all our concerns with him and be anxious only to be found in his kingdom, robed in his righteousness, and accepted as one with him. Let us take no thought for tomorrow, knowing that "whether we live, we live unto the Lord; and whether we die, we die unto the Lord: whether we live therefore, or die, we are the Lord's" (Romans 14:8).

Chapter 17

Needful Exhortations And Warnings

"Judge not, that ye be not judged. For with what judgment ye judge, ye shall be judged: and with what measure ye mete, it shall be measured to you again. And why beholdest thou the mote that is in thy brother's eye, but considerest not the beam that is in thine own eye? Or how wilt thou say to thy brother, Let me pull out the mote out of thine eye; and, behold, a beam *is* in thine own eye? Thou hypocrite, first cast out the beam out of thine own eye; and then shalt thou see clearly to cast out the mote out of thy brother's eye. Give not that which is holy unto the dogs, neither cast ye your pearls before swine, lest they trample them under their feet, and turn again and rend you. Ask, and it shall be given you; seek, and ye shall find; knock, and it shall be opened unto you: For every one that asketh receiveth; and he that seeketh findeth; and to him that knocketh it shall be opened. Or what man is there of you, whom if his son ask bread, will he give him a stone? Or if he ask a fish, will he give him a serpent? If ye then, being evil, know how to give good gifts unto your children, how much more shall your Father which is in heaven give good things to them that ask him? Therefore all things whatsoever ye would that men should do to you, do ye even so to them: for this is the law and the prophets. Enter ye in at the strait gate: for wide *is* the gate, and broad *is* the way, that leadeth to destruction, and many there be which go in thereat: Because strait *is* the gate, and narrow *is* the way, which leadeth unto life, and few there be that find it. Beware of false prophets, which come to you in sheep's clothing, but inwardly they are ravening wolves. Ye shall know them by their fruits. Do men gather grapes of thorns, or figs of thistles? Even so every good tree bringeth forth good fruit; but a corrupt tree bringeth forth evil fruit. A good tree cannot bring forth evil fruit, neither *can* a corrupt tree bring forth good fruit. Every tree that bringeth not forth good fruit is hewn down, and cast into the fire. Wherefore by their fruits ye shall know them. Not every one that saith unto me, Lord, Lord, shall enter into the kingdom of heaven; but he that doeth the will of my Father which is in heaven. Many will say to me in that day, Lord, Lord, have we not prophesied in thy name? and in thy name have cast out devils? and in thy name done many wonderful works? And then will I profess unto them, I

never knew you: depart from me, ye that work iniquity. Therefore whosoever heareth these sayings of mine, and doeth them, I will liken him unto a wise man, which built his house upon a rock: And the rain descended, and the floods came, and the winds blew, and beat upon that house; and it fell not: for it was founded upon a rock. And every one that heareth these sayings of mine, and doeth them not, shall be likened unto a foolish man, which built his house upon the sand: And the rain descended, and the floods came, and the winds blew, and beat upon that house; and it fell: and great was the fall of it. And it came to pass, when Jesus had ended these sayings, the people were astonished at his doctrine: For he taught them as *one* having authority, and not as the scribes."
(Matthew 7:1-29)

In this chapter, our Lord Jesus concludes his Sermon on the Mount. Throughout this sermon (Matthew 5-7), our Saviour draws a clear, unmistakable distinction between true and false religion, between outward ceremonialism and inward godliness, between religious hypocrisy and true spirituality. In chapter 5 he showed us the character of his people and the necessity of holiness. In chapter 6 he showed us the character of true worship and the necessity of faith. Here in chapter 7 he brings his sermon home to all who heard him (and to all who read his words today) by making general, but pointed, exhortations and warnings, that we all need to be reminded of continually. May God the Holy Spirit, who has preserved these exhortations and warnings for us upon the pages of holy scripture, graciously apply them to our hearts.

Kindness

This chapter opens with a gracious exhortation to kindness (vv. 1-5). I do not know of any text in all the Bible that has been more twisted, abused, and misapplied by men than Matthew 7:1. Those who despise absolute values, absolute standards of right and wrong, absolute doctrinal truths and dogmatism, even if they cannot quote any other text in the Bible, recite these words to condemn as divisive bigots all who press upon them the doctrinal and spiritual demands of holy scripture. With sweet sounding piety and complete seriousness they will look you right in the eye and say, "Judge not, that ye be not judged."

Our Lord does not here teach us that we ought never to exercise judgment about anything. Indeed, we are taught of God to "prove all things" (1 Thessalonians 5:21). He is not here telling us that we must never condemn as evil the opinions, behaviour, and doctrines of men. If the Sermon on the Mount teaches anything, it teaches us the necessity of spiritual discernment (vv. 15, 16). We are to "try the spirits" (1 John 4:1). We are to mark those who cause division. We are to be a people of decided values and dogmatic doctrine. Here our Lord is condemning a censorious, fault-finding spirit. As J. C. Ryle wrote, "A readiness to blame others for trifling offences or matters of indifference, a habit of passing rash, hasty judgments, a disposition to magnify the errors and infirmities of our neighbours, and make the worst of them, this is what our Lord forbids."

That "faith which worketh by love" teaches us not to be rash, critical, nit-pickers, but to be patient, longsuffering, forbearing, and forgiving of one another (1 Corinthians 13:4-7). We must never put ourselves in the place of God, sitting in judgment over our brethren, acting as though we have the ability, or the right to condemn (v. 1). That is God's prerogative alone. This principle applies to our attitude regarding all people; but it is particularly applicable to our attitude toward other believers (Romans 14:4). Any time we set ourselves up as judges over others, we set ourselves up to be judged (v. 2). We have work enough to do in taking care of our own souls (vv. 3-5).

We cannot look into another person's heart or judge the motives of others. Far too many are quick to condemn another believer's conduct and to tell a brother or sister what they should or should not do, not with the authority of God's Word, but merely by the measure of their own opinions. We would be wise to recognize that none of us have the ability to discern what God the Holy Spirit would have another to do, unless we can point to a specific passage of scripture that gives specific instructions regarding the matter at hand. We have no right to even form an opinion relating to the conduct of a brother or sister in Christ, apart from the Word of God. Rather, let us pray that God the Holy Spirit will supply both ourselves and our brothers and sisters in Christ with wisdom and grace to do his will in all things; and leave it to him to do so. In all our judgments of others let us be kind, gentle, and lenient (v. 12). If we must err in our judgment concerning others, let us err on the side of lenience, not on the side of severity.

Wisdom

Here is a word of wisdom concerning the way we are to deal with those who oppose our God and Saviour and the gospel of his grace (v. 6). Dogs and swine are terms used in the scriptures to refer to unclean things and to refer to wicked, reprobate men. Just after telling us not to be rash in judgment, our Lord tells us that in preaching and witnessing to men, we must make a judgment, deciding when to work with men in patience and when to dust off our feet as a witness against them (Matthew 10:14; Acts 18:6; Titus 3:10, 11). "Reprove not a scorner, lest he hate thee" (Proverbs 9:8). We must never be reluctant to confess Christ before men; but there are some, like Nabal, to whom none can speak concerning the things of God (1 Samuel 25:17). If you speak to someone about the things of God, and they do not want to hear what God has revealed, leave them alone.

Grace

In verses 7-11 our Saviour gives us a blessed promise of grace. Here our Lord encourages us to pray. There is nothing so plain and simple as prayer. Our Lord assures us of God's readiness to hear and answer the prayers of his children (Hebrews 4:16). Using the illustration of an earthly father, our blessed Redeemer assures us that our heavenly Father is predisposed to bless his children. Is a fallen, sinful man naturally predisposed to give good things to his children, simply because they are his children? If so, how earnest the great Father of mercies must be to give his Holy Spirit to his children. Our Father, who, though unasked, has already given the greatest of all blessings in giving us his darling Son, will not withhold any good thing from us (John 14:16, 17; Romans 8:32).

Golden Rule

In verse 12 our Master lays down that which has been, in my opinion, very properly called "the golden rule". "Therefore all things whatsoever ye would that men should do to you, do ye even so to them: for this is the law and the prophets." These words summarize all that our Lord has said in this Sermon on the Mount. By this golden rule, let us mould our behaviour toward all. Let this be the measure of our judgment and reproof, our charity and severity, and of our thoughts and conduct with regard to all men. This is the essence of all that is taught in the Word of God concerning our treatment of others, both of believers and unbelievers. May God give us grace to live by this blessed rule. There is nothing that would make us more useful to others.

Strait Gate

Next, our Lord Jesus calls sinners to enter in at the strait gate (vv. 13, 14). The strait gate is Christ himself. He is the Door of life and salvation (John 10:7-9). By him alone we have access to and acceptance with the Father. The strait gate is exactly as wide as Christ, and exactly as narrow. The wide gate is as broad as anything and everything added to Christ (Galatians 5:2, 4). Most people are on the broad way to destruction. Therefore, our Lord graciously urges us to strive to enter in at the strait gate. "Because strait is the gate, and narrow is the way, which leadeth unto life, and few there be that find it." Salvation is by grace alone, through faith alone, in Christ alone.

False Prophets

Having just urged us to trust him alone for righteousness and redemption, in verses 15-20 the Lord Jesus warns us to "beware of false prophets". Few words have ever been spoken that are so universally needed and so universally ignored. Nothing in this world is more sinister, nothing more dangerous, and nothing more universally accepted than the false religion promoted by false prophets.

False prophets come in sheep's clothing, professing to be sheep. But they are ravening wolves, whose only object is the destruction of the sheep. They creep into the church, as Jude puts it, "unawares", undetected. But they can always be detected and known by their fruits. Their fruits do not refer to their outward conduct and behaviour; but to the doctrines they teach in opposition to the gospel. All false prophets and all false religion teach a mixture of works with grace. They deny the only Lord God and our Lord Jesus Christ by denying the efficacy of his redemption, righteousness, and grace. They turn the grace of God into lasciviousness, asserting that the teaching of salvation by grace alone, without works, opens the floodgates to immorality (Jude 4). Augustus Toplady wrote:

> Every religion except one puts upon you doing something in order to recommend yourself to God. It is only the religion of Christ (which runs counter to all the rest by affirming that we are saved and called with a holy calling, not according to our works, but according to the Father's own purpose and grace) which was not sold out to us on certain conditions to be fulfilled by ourselves, but was given us in Christ before the world began. It was long ago remarked by a good man that, 'It is the business of all false religion to patch up a righteousness in which the sinner is to stand before God. But it is the business of the glorious gospel to bring near to us, by the hand of the Holy Spirit, a righteousness ready wrought, a robe of perfection ready made, wherein God's people, to all the purposes of justification and happiness, stand perfect and without fault before the throne.'

Presumption

Here is a warning against presumption (vv. 21, 22). Grace that does not make a person obedient to God is not the grace of the gospel. Faith that does not make a man faithful is not the faith of God's elect. Salvation that does not transform sinners into the image of the Saviour is not Bible salvation. Salvation is more than a religious profession, an emotional experience, and the performance of religious duties. Salvation is doing the will of God, believing on, and trusting in, the Lord Jesus Christ (John 6:29). Salvation is the voluntary surrender of our lives to Christ the Lord (Luke 14:26-33).

Preaching or prophesying in the name of Christ, and even performing miracles in his name, are not evidences of grace and salvation. If there is no union with Christ here, there can be no communion with Christ in eternity. The Lord Jesus does not say that few, but many will be found in the day of judgment who lived and died in religion without Christ. What a solemn fact this is to consider! Let us "strive to enter in at the strait gate", that we may be found among the blessed few who have Christ, "the hope of glory", formed in them.

True And False Faith

In verses 24-29 our Lord Jesus draws a clear distinction between true and false faith. Christ is the Rock upon which we must be built. He is the precious Corner Stone the Lord has laid in Zion. Those who believe on him shall never perish, but have everlasting life. Those who build on the sand of their own works shall be buried in the everlasting ruins of their own confusion in hell.

Faith in Christ is compared to the building of a house of refuge (v. 24). Sooner or later, our house will be tested by earthly trials, spiritual trials, rains of trouble, floods of sorrow, and winds of adversity (v. 25). If your house is built on Christ the Rock, it will endure the trial and stand the test of time. If your house is built on the sand, anything other than Christ, sooner or later the rains and floods and winds will bring it crashing down around you.

Throughout his Sermon on the Mount, our Saviour exemplified the way gospel preachers are to preach. He taught "as one having authority". He did not propose questions for debate. He declared truth. He did not offer an opinion to consider. He taught doctrine to be believed. He did not defend a religious system. He taught a righteous salvation. He did not mutter with uncertainty about speculative theories. He taught matters of absolute certainty "as one having authority".

As we read Matthew 5-7 and hear the Lord Jesus Christ teaching the gospel, showing us the way of holiness and perfection before God, let us rejoice to know that he has fulfilled all for us as our blessed Surety and Substitute. He is all our Salvation. He is "all in all" to his redeemed. Let us, by faith, build upon him who alone is the Foundation laid by God and the whole Superstructure, both of the law and the prophets. In that great day, when the Lord God shakes the whole earth in judgment, let us be found in him and built upon him as upon a rock, as that Rock against which the gates of hell shall never prevail! Robert Hawker concluded his comments on the Sermon on the Mount with a prayer worthy of repetition:

> Precious, blessed Lord Jesus! A stone of stumbling and rock of offence; yet to me be thou more precious than the mountains of spices. In thy person, work and offices; in thy character and relations, in thy complete righteousness and salvation; be thou my Lord, my hope, and everlasting portion. Lord grant that I may never build on the sandy performance of any thing of my own, or mix up with thy complete work the hay and the stubble of any legal righteousness, which can stand no wind of the day of God's wrath; but be thou the all in all, of all grace here, and of glory for ever.

Chapter 18

Seven Lessons From A Day Of Miracles

"When he was come down from the mountain, great multitudes followed him. And, behold, there came a leper and worshipped him, saying, Lord, if thou wilt, thou canst make me clean. And Jesus put forth his hand, and touched him, saying, I will; be thou clean. And immediately his leprosy was cleansed. And Jesus saith unto him, See thou tell no man; but go thy way, show thyself to the priest, and offer the gift that Moses commanded, for a testimony unto them. And when Jesus was entered into Capernaum, there came unto him a centurion, beseeching him, And saying, Lord, my servant lieth at home sick of the palsy, grievously tormented. And Jesus saith unto him, I will come and heal him. The centurion answered and said, Lord, I am not worthy that thou shouldest come under my roof: but speak the word only, and my servant shall be healed. For I am a man under authority, having soldiers under me: and I say to this man, Go, and he goeth; and to another, Come, and he cometh; and to my servant, Do this, and he doeth it. When Jesus heard it, he marvelled, and said to them that followed, Verily I say unto you, I have not found so great faith, no, not in Israel. And I say unto you, That many shall come from the east and west, and shall sit down with Abraham, and Isaac, and Jacob, in the kingdom of heaven. But the children of the kingdom shall be cast out into outer darkness: there shall be weeping and gnashing of teeth. And Jesus said unto the centurion, Go thy way; and as thou hast believed, so be it done unto thee. And his servant was healed in the selfsame hour. And when Jesus was come into Peter's house, he saw his wife's mother laid, and sick of a fever. And he touched her hand, and the fever left her: and she arose, and ministered unto them. When the even was come, they brought unto him many that were possessed with devils: and he cast out the spirits with his word, and healed all that were sick: That it might be fulfilled which was spoken by Esaias the prophet, saying, Himself took our infirmities, and bare our sicknesses. Now when Jesus saw great multitudes about him, he gave commandment to depart unto the other side. And a certain scribe came, and said unto him, Master, I will follow thee whithersoever thou goest. And Jesus saith unto him, The foxes have holes, and the birds of the air have nests; but the Son of

man hath not where to lay his head. And another of his disciples said unto him, Lord, suffer me first to go and bury my father. But Jesus said unto him, Follow me; and let the dead bury their dead. And when he was entered into a ship, his disciples followed him. And, behold, there arose a great tempest in the sea, insomuch that the ship was covered with the waves: but he was asleep. And his disciples came to him, and awoke him, saying, Lord, save us: we perish. And he saith unto them, Why are ye fearful, O ye of little faith? Then he arose, and rebuked the winds and the sea; and there was a great calm. But the men marvelled, saying, What manner of man is this, that even the winds and the sea obey him! And when he was come to the other side into the country of the Gergesenes, there met him two possessed with devils, coming out of the tombs, exceeding fierce, so that no man might pass by that way. And, behold, they cried out, saying, What have we to do with thee, Jesus, thou Son of God? art thou come hither to torment us before the time? And there was a good way off from them an herd of many swine feeding. So the devils besought him, saying, If thou cast us out, suffer us to go away into the herd of swine. And he said unto them, Go. And when they were come out, they went into the herd of swine: and, behold, the whole herd of swine ran violently down a steep place into the sea, and perished in the waters. And they that kept them fled, and went their ways into the city, and told every thing, and what was befallen to the possessed of the devils. And, behold, the whole city came out to meet Jesus: and when they saw him, they besought him that he would depart out of their coasts."
(Matthew 8:1-34)

The great miracles which our Lord Jesus performed while he walked on this earth were, without question, supernatural works. They were, indisputably, miraculous works. The Jews made every false accusation imaginable against our Lord's claims as the Christ, the Son of God. But they never raised even the slightest hint of a question about either his genealogy or the validity of the miracles he performed. Both were matters of public record beyond dispute. They could not be denied, or even called into question. Our Lord's numerous, unprecedented miracles served two purposes: First, they proved him to be the Christ, the Messiah, the Son of God (Matthew 11:2-6). Second, the miracles, like all the supernatural works of God in the deliverances of his people in the Old Testament, were designed to be pictures of God's saving grace and were intended to teach us spiritual lessons.

Seven Lessons From A Day Of Miracles

In this chapter Matthew briefly describes some of the miracles performed by our Lord in a single day. Our Lord's miracles are both pictures of his grace and object lessons full of spiritual instruction for those who have eyes to see and ears to hear the things that are here revealed. J. C. Ryle wrote, "There is a beautiful fitness in this. It was fitting that the greatest sermon ever preached should be immediately followed by mighty proofs that the preacher was the Son of God."

Repentance

In verses 1-4 we are given a lesson about repentance. Would you know how to come to Christ? Do you want to know how a sinner can come to Christ and obtain mercy from him? If you are interested, learn from the leper.

This poor wretch is representative of every poor sinner, convinced of the leprosy of sin by God the Holy Spirit, coming to Christ. Being convinced of Christ's ability to heal him, this man came to Christ as he was, a leper! He was an unclean, unworthy, legal outcast. Death was in his breath. He had an incurable disease. He had no right to approach the Lord Jesus. But he knew that no one else could do anything for him. So he came out of the crowd to the Saviour.

He worshipped Christ as Lord, bowing down in humble reverence before a man whom he acknowledged to be his rightful, sovereign Lord. There is no other way to come to the Saviour (Luke 23:42; Acts 9:5, 6). The leper freely acknowledged Christ's sovereign right to give or withhold grace according to his own sovereign pleasure as Lord. "If thou wilt, thou canst make me clean."

There may have been great weakness in his faith. He seems to have been confident that the Lord Jesus was able to heal him, but not that he was willing to do so. Yet, the apparent weakness of his faith did not prevent Christ's mercy. Be sure you do not fail to see this. It is not the strength of our faith, but Christ the Object of our faith, that saves us.

Trusting Christ, he obtained mercy. "And Jesus put forth his hand, and touched him, saying, I will; be thou clean. And immediately his leprosy was cleansed." The Master tenderly touched him with his hand, as if to indicate his loving sympathy with the poor leper; and he still reaches out the hand of tender omnipotence to touch the needy soul coming to him. Then he healed him by the power of his word. He said, "I will"; and with a word of grace the Son of God made this vile son of Adam clean. "Be thou clean." If we would obtain mercy, if we would be saved, we must come to Christ, just like this leper did.

Faith

In verses 5-13 we are given a lesson about faith. While the scribes and Pharisees and the people of Israel despised the Lord Jesus and his gospel, this unnamed Roman officer fully believed that the Man standing before him was the only Lord God, sovereign over all things, with whom nothing is impossible.

This centurion shows what a great and precious gift the gift of faith is (v. 10). To believe Christ, to trust him, is a rare and precious gift of God's saving grace (Ephesians 2:8, 9; Philippians 1:29). How thankful we should be if we have this gift of grace, for few do! Few are willing to come to Christ as helpless, lost sinners, and commit their souls to him. Few will forsake their own righteousness and trust Christ alone as the Lord our Righteousness. Few will come to Christ, trusting him alone to save them.

Faith in Christ appears to be a small and insignificant thing in the eyes of the world. But true faith, that faith that "worketh by love", is the highest privilege, greatest gift, and rarest jewel in the world. Many have religion. But few have faith. This centurion had faith. So great was his faith in Christ, that the Lord Jesus "marvelled" at it.

I cannot help asking, "Why is that fact recorded by divine inspiration?" Why did the Lord Jesus who gave this man the faith he exercised marvel at the display of it? Why has the Holy Spirit recorded it here in his Word? Was it not to emphasize the fact that true faith in Christ is a personal thing? True, God gave the centurion faith. We rejoice in the knowledge of that fact. Yet, the faith given was the centurion's. It was his because God gave it to him.

Faith in Christ is not a notion, or a doctrine, or a principle. It is the heart confidence of every needy sinner who looks to Christ as his only Saviour, that causes him to confess, "My Lord, and my God" (John 20:28). Yes, it is God's gift and God's operation in us. Faith is the fruit of the Holy Spirit (Galatians 5:22). Yet, it is our faith. If God gave it to me, that makes it mine.

The breath in my lungs is God's gift. He enables me to breathe. Yet, it is my breath and my breathing that is the evidence that God still gives me life. And the breathing of my body is as necessary to my living as God's gift of life. The two cannot be separated. If you doubt that, try putting a plastic bag over your face and see if you can live without breathing!

So it is with faith. We "are the children of God by faith in Christ Jesus" (Galatians 3:26). The Holy Spirit tells us plainly that the faith you have by his grace is "your faith in the Lord Jesus" (Ephesians 1:15; 1 Corinthians 1:4; 2:5). It is God's gift; and because God gave it to you, it is "your faith".

And your faith in Christ is just as necessary, just as vital to your everlasting salvation, and just as precious (2 Peter 1:1) as God's decree of election, Christ's accomplished redemption, and the Holy Spirit's effectual call. "Without faith it is impossible to please him: for he that cometh to God must believe that he is, and that he is a rewarder of them that diligently seek him" (Hebrews 11:6).

Do you, like the Philippian jailer of old, ask, "What must I do to be saved?" I do not hesitate to answer with Paul and Silas, "Believe on the Lord Jesus Christ, and thou shalt be saved" (Acts 16:30, 31). Do not look to yourself and your experience. Allow no one to put you off. "Believe on the Lord Jesus Christ", and salvation is yours.

Do you ask, "How can I know that I am saved?" Answer this one question. "Dost thou believe on the Son of God?" The question is not, "What did you know when you first professed faith in Christ?" or, "Was the man preaching a sound gospel preacher?" or, "When did you believe?" It does not matter whether you can answer these questions. They are totally irrelevant. This is the only question to be answered, "Dost thou believe on the Son of God?" If you *now* trust the Lord Jesus Christ, salvation is yours.

This centurion is held before us as a picture of God's elect among the Gentiles who must be saved (vv. 11, 12). Some, who vainly imagine that they have obtained "new light", vehemently assert that anyone who uses such terms as "saving faith" and "effectual faith" is a blaspheming heretic. Were such assertions not so serious and deluding, they would be laughable. The Lord Jesus tells us that this man's faith in him was effectual faith. "Go thy way; and as thou hast believed, so be it done unto thee." Then, Matthew tells us, "And his servant was healed in the selfsame hour" (v. 13). Be assured, that which men call "new light" is old satanic darkness!

Sickness

In verses 14-17 there is a lesson about sickness. Indeed, there is much to be learned in these verses. And the things taught are so obvious that only wilfully ignorant people can miss the meaning of Matthew's words. Certainly, it was the intent of the Holy Spirit in this passage to give us a clear, indisputable record of the fact that the Apostle Peter was a married man. This was recorded by divine design long before the idolatrous papists arose promoting the notion that celibacy is required for true spirituality.

We see too, in this passage a clear demonstration of the fact that faith in Christ and faithfulness to Christ do not prevent sickness and disease, pain and sorrow, or bereavement and death. These things are all the results of sin, and the results of sin ran through Peter's house, just as it does any other man's.

Those who are the objects of God's mercy should be diligent in the Lord's service. As soon as Peter's mother-in-law was healed, "She arose and ministered unto them", unto the Lord Jesus, unto Peter, and unto all who were with them. Nothing so effectually inspires love for, and devotion to, the Lord Jesus Christ and his people as gratitude for grace experienced.

Our great Saviour, our sovereign Lord, is in complete control of all things, including sickness and disease. He sends it. He controls it. And he removes it. It takes no more than his word or his touch to relieve his suffering child.

What could be sweeter, more comforting, or more honouring to our blessed Lord than the statement given in verse 17 that the Lord Jesus Christ, "Himself took our infirmities, and bare our sicknesses"? Our Saviour so completely identifies himself with us that he takes our infirmities and sicknesses to be his own, just as surely as he bare our sin in his body on the tree. This verse does not teach that there is healing from sickness and disease in the atonement. It teaches that there is sympathy in the Saviour, who sends sickness and death or healing and life, as he sees fit, to the people he loves.

Robert Hawker observed, "What a beautiful representation is here made of the lovely, and all-loving Jesus"! What a display this is of his sovereignty! What a display of his grace! Christ Jesus "Himself took our infirmities, and bare our sicknesses". There was no possibility of him ever becoming sick. Sickness is the result of sin; and he "knew no sin". Yet, as he was made sin for us and bore our sins in his body on the tree, so here we see that by sympathy he bore our sicknesses. In this sense, he knew and felt more what sin and the sorrows of sin and sickness are than we for whom he suffered. He who felt the whole weight and burden of our sins, and the wrath of God as our Surety, must have known more and felt more, both of the bitterness of sin itself, and all the horrid consequences of sin, than we can ever imagine. If righteous Lot vexed his soul day by day with the filthy deeds of the Sodomites (2 Peter 2:7), what must have been the feelings of our blessed Lord Jesus as he beheld the sins of his redeemed? Thus, throughout the days of his earthly life, our dear Saviour "bore our sicknesses", until at last he gave himself a ransom for us, to redeem us from sin and all its consequences.

Usefulness

Verse 16 provides a fine lesson about usefulness. Throughout the four gospels we see frequent mention of the fact that men and women brought other needy men and women to the Lord Jesus to be healed by him. Those involved were always commended for doing so. Some may think, "God does not need man." I could not agree with you more. God does not need us. But I rejoice in the fact that God has chosen and ordained the use of saved sinners for the saving of other sinners.

The highest, greatest, most useful service we can perform for the souls of men is to bring them to Christ. I will leave for you to make of it what you will, but it is a fact that no one in the New Testament ever brought a needy soul to the Saviour who did not obtain for their friend the mercy they sought. What a hopeful thought! God honours the faith that brings sinners to Christ. In fact, we are told in Luke 5:20 that when our Saviour saw the faith of those four men who carried their friend to him, he said to the man, "Thy sins are forgiven thee".

Discipleship

In verses 18-22 our Lord Jesus teaches us a lesson about discipleship. Our Master was not one of our modern, slick, polished, soul-winning evangelists, who will use every trick imaginable to get people to make a profession of faith. When the scribe came and said, "I will follow thee", and one who professed to be his disciple said, "I will follow just as soon as I have buried my father", our Master replied with solemn words of warning and reproof (vv. 20, 22).

If we would be faithful to God and to the souls of men, we must keep back nothing from those who say they want to follow Christ. Yet we must never enlist souls in the cause of Christ under false pretences. Let all who would follow Christ sit down first and count the lost. Before any can wear the crown of glory, he must daily take up his cross and follow the Master. That may mean giving up earthly comfort. It may mean neglecting ordinary, but unnecessary, duties of life. Someone will bury the dead! Discipleship means Christ is all and Christ is first!

This is the first place in the New Testament in which we meet with the phrase "Son of Man", in reference to the Lord Jesus Christ. It is a phrase our Saviour frequently used. He seems to have particularly delighted in calling himself by this title. It is the title by which he sets forth his wonderful condescension and his great love in assuming our nature. He who "thought it not robbery to be equal with God" was delighted to become one of us, that he might redeem us. "For ye know the grace of our Lord Jesus Christ, that, though he was rich, yet for your sakes he became poor, that ye through his poverty might be rich."

Fear

In verses 23-27 we see the disciples with the Lord Jesus crossing the Sea of Galilee and learn a lesson about fear. Fear is inconsistent with faith. Yet, the two often live together in the same heart. True saving faith is often mingled with fear, weakness, and infirmity. This is a humbling lesson, but a needful one. Many standing upon the shore may chide and laugh at these terrified disciples. But experience tells me that very few behave more confidently when they are in the storm themselves.

Many who believe Christ and love him, who gladly and truly forsake all to follow him, are full of fear in the face of danger. Many have faith enough to cry out, "Lord save us, we perish", who do not have faith enough to ride out the hurricane at sea in the little fishing boat with tranquillity. We never know the weakness of our faith until it is tried. Yet weak faith is not false faith. I have often been made to rejoice in reading David's words in Psalm 56:3, even as my own heart broke with the acknowledgement of my fear and unbelief. "What time I am afraid, I will trust in thee."

If you have the strong faith of Job that can say, "though he slay me, yet will I trust him" (Job 13:15), do not despise that weak, trembling, fearful faith that cries, "Master, carest thou not that we perish?" (Mark 4:38). The Lord Jesus did not despise such faith, but nurtured it. Let us do the same.

Let us give thanks to God for a great high Priest who is compassionate and tender-hearted. He knows our frame. He remembers that we are dust. He considers and is touched with the feeling of our infirmities. He does not cast us off because of our defects. He reproves, certainly, but he pities those whom he reproves. And even the prayer of fearful "little faith" does not go unheard and unanswered by him.

In these verses we are given a beautiful, clear, and instructive picture of our Saviour's two-fold nature as the God-man, our Mediator. Here is Christ the man sleeping because he is tired. And here is Christ our God, the One by whom all things were made, rebuking the wind and sea. Who but the Creator could thus command the mighty waters?

What sweet consolation this passage ought to bring to our souls in every time of trouble to hush all the winds and storms of life. Our God and Saviour sometimes appears to be asleep, inattentive, and uncaring when our little boats are filling with water and our distressed souls cry, "Lord, save us: we perish"! Ever remember, he is with you in the midst of your storms. He will keep your little boat safe. And, at the appointed time, he will deliver you. He will arise and rebuke wind and sea, and there shall be a great calm. Storms of fear, and storms of temptation must all subside at the command of our omnipotent God and Saviour.

Unbelief

In verses 28-34 the Holy Spirit uses two demon possessed men, a heard of hogs, and a group of worldly business men to teach us a lesson about unbelief. In these last seven verses Matthew describes, with unusual fulness and detail, our Saviour casting out devils. These verses cannot be overlooked and ignored.

The devil and the demons of hell are real. I do not pretend to know much about the subject of demonology. Frankly, I do not want to know much about it. But I warn all who read these lines. The devil is a real adversary to our souls. Demons are real. Only a fool will deny their existence. And only a fool will investigate their operations.

I rejoice to assert that Satan, the demons of hell, and the powers of darkness are under the total control of the Lord Jesus Christ. We are no match for them. But the Son of God holds the chain that binds them. They can go only where he leads them, and do only what he commands them to do (John 12:30; Revelation 20:1-3). Powerful as he is, Satan is not omnipotent. He only operates by divine permission (Job 1:1-2:7).

Learn this, too, none but Christ can deliver lost souls from the power of Satan (Acts 10:38; Hebrews 7:25). He who bruised the serpent's head is the only one who can bind the strong man, cast him out of his house, and dispossess him (Genesis 3:15; Matthew 12:28, 29).

And here we see a clear demonstration of the fact that there is no greater hindrance to faith in Christ, and no greater power to keep sinners in the darkness and death of unbelief, than the love of the world demonstrated by these Gergesenes. God walked their shores in human flesh yet they believed not! Demon possessed lunatics were retrieved from the clutches of Satan before their very eyes, yet, they believed not! The sovereign Master of heaven, earth, and hell stood before these men, yet, they believed not, and even begged him to go away! Why? The "hope of their gains was gone" (Acts 16:19).

What multitudes perish in unbelief, under the wrath of God for the same reason as these Gergesenes! Their only concern is for money. They care nothing for Christ, his Word, their souls, or the glory of God. A terrible, infectious, spreading disease has entered their hearts. It is a disease from which we ought ever to pray for deliverance. It is called "worldliness". Worldliness is the love of the world.

"Love not the world, neither the things that are in the world. If any man love the world, the love of the Father is not in him. For all that is in the world, the lust of the flesh, and the lust of the eyes, and the pride of life, is not of the Father, but is of the world. And the world passeth away, and the lust thereof: but he that doeth the will of God abideth for ever" (1 John 2:15-17).

"Behold the wonders of our wonder-working God", was Robert Hawker's admonition in his reflections on Matthew 8. "See the leprous man cleansed; the paralytic healed; the raging fever subdued; yea, the winds, sea, and devils, in a moment brought under the word of our Jesus. But let us not stop here. He that cleansed the poor leper in his body, can and will cleanse all the leprosy of soul in his people. He that gave strength to the palsy of nature, can and will make the crippled in soul to leap as a hart; and all the feverish lusts of his redeemed Jesus will subdue! Oh! thou gracious God of our salvation! No storms of hell, nor storms of indwelling corruption, nor storms of the world, shall drown thy people! Jesus, for a while may appear to our impatient minds as inattentive, but he hath said, 'For the sighing of the poor, and the oppression of the needy, now will I arise!' And oh! with what tenderness and fellow-feeling the Lord Jesus enters into all the concerns of his redeemed. Truly Lord, it may be said of thee, thou dost thyself take our infirmities, and bare our sicknesses! Oh! vouchsafe thy continual presence with us! and never, never Lord, do thou depart out of our coasts!"

Chapter 19

"Learn What That Meaneth"

"And he entered into a ship, and passed over, and came into his own city. And, behold, they brought to him a man sick of the palsy, lying on a bed: and Jesus seeing their faith said unto the sick of the palsy; Son, be of good cheer; thy sins be forgiven thee. And, behold, certain of the scribes said within themselves, This man blasphemeth. And Jesus knowing their thoughts said, Wherefore think ye evil in your hearts? For whether is easier, to say, Thy sins be forgiven thee; or to say, Arise, and walk? But that ye may know that the Son of man hath power on earth to forgive sins, (then saith he to the sick of the palsy,) Arise, take up thy bed, and go unto thine house. And he arose, and departed to his house. But when the multitude saw it, they marvelled, and glorified God, which had given such power unto men. And as Jesus passed forth from thence, he saw a man, named Matthew, sitting at the receipt of custom: and he saith unto him, Follow me. And he arose, and followed him. And it came to pass, as Jesus sat at meat in the house, behold, many publicans and sinners came and sat down with him and his disciples. And when the Pharisees saw it, they said unto his disciples, Why eateth your Master with publicans and sinners? But when Jesus heard that, he said unto them, They that be whole need not a physician, but they that are sick. But go ye and learn what that meaneth, I will have mercy, and not sacrifice: for I am not come to call the righteous, but sinners to repentance."
(Matthew 9:1-13)

The Gadarenes, resenting the loss of their hogs, were disgusted with the Son of God and urged him to "depart from their coasts". So he did. He entered into a ship and crossed over the Sea of Galilee, and came into the city of Capernaum. Capernaum is here designated "his own city", because, at present it was the principle place of his residence and the principle city of his ministry. All that is recorded in this chapter took place in Capernaum. In this instructive chapter we see a clear display both of our Lord's justice and of his mercy.

Here is his justice. When the Gadarenes bid him depart from their coasts, he did! Not only did he depart, he departed never to return! The Son of God will not tarry where he is not wanted. In righteous judgment he forsakes those places and those people where he is neglected. Those who become weary of him will not be bothered by him. Here is his mercy. The Gadarenes who spurned him, by their hardness of heart and unbelief, sent the Saviour of the world to Capernaum, where he performed all the mighty works described in this chapter upon chosen sinners for the glory of God. The miracles performed by Christ and the events recorded in this chapter are designed to teach us who Jesus Christ is, and what he came to do. Let me show you five things in verses 1-13. May God the Holy Spirit be our teacher. I pray that he will take the things of Christ and show them to us.

The Man Who Is God

The first thing clearly demonstrated in this ninth chapter is the fact that the man Christ Jesus is the God of grace, forgiveness, and everlasting salvation. "And, behold, they brought to him a man sick of the palsy, lying on a bed: and Jesus seeing their faith said unto the sick of the palsy; Son, be of good cheer; thy sins be forgiven thee" (v. 2). Here the Lord Jesus publicly declares himself to be God by absolving the sins of the paralyzed man who lay before him.

"They brought to him a man sick of the palsy, lying on a bed". Here is a sick man with caring friends. They could not heal their friend. But they knew he could be healed. So they brought him to the Master in hopes that he would heal him. And he did what they hoped he would do. What an encouragement this should be to us to bring sinners to hear the gospel. With regard to the souls of men, the sphere of our ability is the sphere of our responsibility. We cannot save anyone; but we can bring sinners to the place where the gospel is preached and Christ is worshipped, laying them at the Saviour's feet, praying for him to have mercy upon them.

Those standing by Lazarus' tomb could not raise Lazarus from the dead; but they could take the stone away from the tomb. Therefore, the Lord Jesus graciously commanded them to do so, and gave them the privilege of doing so (John 11:39-41). So it is with us. We cannot perform the miracle of grace. Yet, the Lord commands us to proclaim his grace to poor, needy sinners, and gives us the privilege of being instruments in his hands, by which he calls out his own elect (vv. 42-45).

Faith And Forgiveness

"Jesus seeing their faith said unto the sick of the palsy; Son, be of good cheer; thy sins be forgiven thee." I find that statement remarkable. God honours faith. When the Lord Jesus saw their faith, the faith of those four friends and of the man who lay before him, he granted forgiveness. Wherever there is faith in Christ, there is assurance of adoption. The Saviour called this man "Son". It is a word that implies sonship. Here, the Master publicly owned this sinner as his own child (Galatians 4:6; 1 John 3:1; Romans 8:16, 17). Wherever there is assurance of sonship, there is cause for cheer.

The Saviour said, "Son, be of good cheer". Even before healing him, before giving any indication that he would heal him! If I am a child of God I have reason to be of good cheer, no matter what my earthly condition is (Philippians 4:4, 11). Wherever there is faith, there is forgiveness. "Thy sins be forgiven thee". All who trust Christ are forgiven of all their sins. And this forgiveness is complete, immutable (Romans 10:8-11), just (1 John 1:9), and perpetual (1 John 2:1, 2). The Lord God will never charge the believing sinner with his sins (Romans 4:8).

He who forgives sin is God our Saviour. The Jews said, "This man blasphemeth". And any mere man who pronounces the forgiveness and absolution of sin is a blasphemer. It matters not whether that man is a pope, an imaginary priest, or a Baptist preacher. But this man is God! He forgave the sins of men while on this earth; and he still forgives the sins of men on earth from his lofty throne in heaven. It is not insignificant that the first act by which the Lord Jesus demonstrated his eternal power and Godhead was to pardon this man's sins. The reasoning of the scribes, though formed in malice, was well founded. None but God himself can forgive sins. Robert Hawker wrote, "the Lord Jesus, by the exercise of this authority, and in the cure of the body, which immediately followed, proved that he was God".

The Omniscient God

Another demonstration of our Redeemer's divinity was the fact that he knew their thoughts, and acted upon that knowledge, by telling them what they thought. Again, no one knows the thoughts of a man but God (Jeremiah 17:10. Revelation 2:23). The Lord Jesus Christ, the God of all grace and forgiveness, also demonstrated himself to be the God of perfect and total omniscience, from whom nothing can be hidden.

This is he of whom David in the Psalms spoke (Psalm 139:1-6). Jesus Christ is the omniscient, all-seeing, all-knowing God (Hebrews 4:12, 13). What do you think of in private, when no man sees you? What do you think of in Church, when you are most solemn in appearance? What are you thinking at this moment? The Son of God hears it all perfectly. So strict is his justice that God will judge the very thoughts of men (Romans 2:16). To the unbeliever, the Lord's omniscience is terrifying. To the believer, the Lord's omniscience is most comforting (John 21:17). How we ought to thank God for the blood of Christ that "cleanseth us from all sin". Let us ever pray for grace to reign even over the thoughts of our minds (Psalm 19:14).

The Healing

Then, after speaking forgiveness to this man who was "sick of the palsy" and demonstrating that he knew the thoughts of the Pharisees, the Lord Jesus demonstrated his eternal Godhead by healing the man of the palsy (vv. 5-8). By performing this miracle, the Lord Jesus asserted plainly that he was and is the Messiah (the Christ) by calling himself "the Son of Man". This was, perhaps, the most common title by which the Jews referred to the Messiah. When John sent his disciples to ask the Master whether he was the Christ who should come, the Lord Jesus referred John's disciples to those things by which it was unquestionably demonstrated that he was and is the very Son of Man (Isaiah 61:1; Matthew 11:2-6). When the Jews attacked him for healing on the sabbath day, our Saviour declared that all authority was given to him to execute judgment, because he was the Son of Man. In all the miracles of mercy performed by our great Saviour he acted both as our God and our Saviour, as the God-man our Mediator, and thereby manifested both who he is and the great mission upon which he came into the world (Matthew 1:21). He who is our Saviour is God and man in one person (John 5:17; 17:2, 3; Matthew 26:62-65; Colossians 2:9, 10; 1 Timothy 3:16).

Take joyful notice of our Saviour's tenderness and compassion, as it is set before us here. Though unasked, he pardoned this man's sins and healed his body. No one can be surprised that the astonished crowd expressed thankfulness to God. But it is, or should be, surprising to all who read this inspired record that after such a great, public demonstration of divine grace, omniscience, and power there appears to have been no saving faith in those who saw and heard these things. But those who are taught of God understand this, too. Faith in Christ is the gift and operation of God the Holy Spirit. Spiritually dead sinners cannot believe, except God the Holy Spirit give them life and faith in Christ (Isaiah 6:9, 10; Matthew 13:14; Mark 4:12; Luke 8:10; John 12:40; Acts 28:26, 27; Romans 11:8). Let us never read such passages as this without lifting our hearts in praise and thanksgiving to our great God for his great grace in giving us faith in his darling Son (Ephesians 2:8, 9; Philippians 1:29).

This man proved himself to be born of God by his unhesitating obedience to his Master's word. He who was "justified freely by his grace through the redemption that is in Christ Jesus" (Romans 3:24), was like "Abraham our father, justified by works" (James 2:21). That is to say, he proved his faith by his works. Obedience is always the fruit of faith. Believers are men and women who are obedient to Christ. That is the tenor and character of their lives.

Irresistible Grace

In the calling and conversion of Matthew we are given an illustration of the fact that our Saviour's call is the irresistible, effectual, saving call of almighty, invincible grace. Matthew's given name was Levi. But he is called Matthew in the New Testament because he was given by God the Father to the Son. His name means "gift of God". He was given to Christ in the covenant of grace before the world began. Now he is given to Christ in saving grace (John 6:37-45).

Matthew was a publican, a tax-collector. He was thoroughly absorbed with his good career. He thought of nothing but money, how to get it, how to spend it, and how to get more. Matthew was not seeking the Lord. He appears not even to have any consciousness of need in his soul. There were no preparations that preceded the Saviour's call. Matthew did not first experience deep feelings of guilt, a great time of mourning and repentance, or even acquire great knowledge. The Saviour called; and, as the result of the Saviour's call, Matthew followed him. What grace there is here; surprising, omnipotent, free grace! He who said, "I am found of them that sought me not" (Isaiah 65:1), found Matthew, and caused Matthew to find him by the effectual, distinguishing call of his omnipotent mercy.

How surprised Matthew must have been the day grace conquered him! God's saving grace is always surprising in the experience of it. Here is the blessed, sovereign, intervention of grace. The Lord Jesus passed by, he saw Matthew and he called him. That is the way he still works, even today. Here is the blessed choice and decision of faith. "He arose and followed him." Because he followed Christ, this worthless, useless, hated man became a useful man of indescribable benefit to the souls of men. Effectual grace always produces effects in the lives of saved sinners. Matthew wrote this gospel narrative known the world over. He became a blessing to millions. He left a name never to be forgotten. He was a man used of God for much good to many souls. As soon as the Saviour called, he obeyed. No sooner did the Lord Jesus open his heart to receive him than Matthew opened his house to the Saviour; and this publican who obtained mercy from the Lord invited other publicans to come and find mercy also (v. 10).

The Saviour's Mission

We are here told what the mission and message of Jesus Christ is. He came to save sinners. His message is mercy, grace, and salvation for sinners. He came to show mercy. He came to teach us to show mercy. Let us never forget what we are: sinners! Let us never forget who Jesus Christ is: The Saviour of sinners!

How delightful it is to see our great Redeemer, encircled at Matthew's table, with publicans and sinners! The grumbling of the Pharisees was exactly what might have been expected then, and expected today. Such is the activity of Pharisees in all ages. But our Lord's response to their attempted slander is as delightful as it is instructive. The very character of Christ as the Physician of our souls, Robert Hawker wrote, "naturally led him to haunts of sickness for the exercise of his profession". By quoting Hosea 6:6, when he said, "I will have mercy, and not sacrifice", and applying the passage to himself and his great work of saving sinners, our blessed Saviour declared himself to be Jehovah-Rophe, "The Lord that healeth thee" (Exodus 15:26).

"Go ye and learn what that meaneth". Charles Spurgeon wrote, "Our Lord, having gloriously defended himself from the insinuations of the proud Pharisees, now carries the war into the enemies' territory. He says to them, 'Go ye and learn.'" That alone would be galling to men who thought they knew everything already. The Pharisees were a crowd of snobbish, know-it-all, self-righteous religionists. Nothing could have been more offensive to the know-it-all crowd than for the Master to have said, "Go ye, and learn what that meaneth". Like most, these men never shut up long enough to learn anything, because they presumed that they knew everything. The Lord Jesus told them that they did not even know the meaning of the scriptures they claimed to believe and defend.

They were told to learn the meaning of Hosea 6:6. Then, the Lord Jesus told them the meaning. To have mercy upon sinners is a work more pleasing to God than the offering of sacrifices and the performance of religious duties. The Son of God prefers to be merciful himself and prefers for us to be merciful. Religion and religious activity without mercy is but a cloak of hypocrisy.

The Lord Jesus came into this world not to be served by the good, but to save the wicked. He had come to call to repentance those who needed repentance, and not those who imagine that they are righteous and therefore need no repentance. The Son of God came to save sinners, real sinners. And it is sinners he calls to repentance.

Chapter 20

What A Wonderful Saviour!

"Then came to him the disciples of John, saying, Why do we and the Pharisees fast oft, but thy disciples fast not? And Jesus said unto them, Can the children of the bridechamber mourn, as long as the bridegroom is with them? but the days will come, when the bridegroom shall be taken from them, and then shall they fast. No man putteth a piece of new cloth unto an old garment, for that which is put in to fill it up taketh from the garment, and the rent is made worse. Neither do men put new wine into old bottles: else the bottles break, and the wine runneth out, and the bottles perish: but they put new wine into new bottles, and both are preserved. While he spake these things unto them, behold, there came a certain ruler, and worshipped him, saying, My daughter is even now dead: but come and lay thy hand upon her, and she shall live. And Jesus arose, and followed him, and so did his disciples. And, behold, a woman, which was diseased with an issue of blood twelve years, came behind him, and touched the hem of his garment: For she said within herself, If I may but touch his garment, I shall be whole. But Jesus turned him about, and when he saw her, he said, Daughter, be of good comfort; thy faith hath made thee whole. And the woman was made whole from that hour. And when Jesus came into the ruler's house, and saw the minstrels and the people making a noise, He said unto them, Give place: for the maid is not dead, but sleepeth. And they laughed him to scorn. But when the people were put forth, he went in, and took her by the hand, and the maid arose. And the fame hereof went abroad into all that land."
(Matthew 9:14-26)

As I read this passage of holy scripture, my heart's response to this display of our Saviour's wisdom, goodness, and power is, "What a wonderful Saviour"! I am certain that Matthew was inspired by God the Holy Spirit to record these events as he did, without any interpretive comment, so that we might see in these things something of the grandeur, greatness, and glory of our Lord Jesus Christ. The man of whom Matthew speaks is God; and this great God-man is our Saviour. His name is called "Wonderful", because everything about him is wonderful.

Wonderful In Grace
He is a wonderful Saviour, indeed, who is longsuffering, patient, gentle, kind and gracious to such sinful disciples as all his disciples are in this world.

It is a painful and shameful fact, but a fact none the less, that all the Lord's people in this world are sinners still. And being sinners we often behave as such. Nothing more betrays the evil that remains in us than the strife and division that exists among true believers. All too often, throughout the history of God's church, those who truly are brethren have behaved as though they were not!

Paul and Barnabas were both faithful servants of God; but they had such a strong division over John Mark that they never worked together again. The conflict was needless; but the division was permanent (Acts 15:36-41). How sad! How painful! How shameful! Yet, that is what happened then; and that is what still happens far too often today. Brethren here are sometimes incapable of living and working together peaceably. That it is so reveals much about our fallen nature and depraved hearts. Division is horribly dishonouring to our testimony and to our God. Blessed Saviour, hasten the day when every breach in Zion shall be healed! Until then, let us strive to avoid strife among God's saints.

In verse 14, disciples of John the Baptist, who were also followers of the Lord Jesus, came to the Master with a word of reproof because they presumed that he and his disciples did not fast. "Then came to him the disciples of John, saying, Why do we and the Pharisees fast oft, but thy disciples fast not?"

While there is much in their behaviour that is reprehensible, it must be acknowledged that these disciples of John did behave with integrity. They did not murmur and gossip like the scribes and Pharisees. They had a problem that greatly concerned them; and rather than sitting around in a stew, talking about it, they came directly to the Lord with it. One of their number must have said, "Wait a minute, brethren. If we've got a problem with what appears to be a matter of grave error, there must be some explanation for it. Let us go talk to the Master". Much evil could be avoided if men and women would behave like this today!

Yet, there is much in the conduct of these men that is blameworthy. Like the Pharisees, they proclaimed their own goodness (Proverbs 20:6). They judged their brethren by the yardstick of their own rules. Fasting was one of the customs of the Pharisees, a custom they had accepted as a required display of godliness. Because they did not see the disciples fasting, they presumed that they did not fast. And they appear to cast a slur upon the Lord Jesus because of the presumed bad conduct of his disciples.

However, neither Matthew, Mark, nor Luke indicate that the Lord Jesus was angry or upset with these men. That fact is as instructive as it is comforting. "For he knoweth our frame: He remembereth that we are dust" (Psalm 103:14). Our God and Saviour is the one of whom it is written, "He delighteth in mercy" (Micah 7:18). Let us imitate him (Ephesians 4:32-5:1).

We should never presume anything evil concerning God's saints. We should never presume that we know what goes on in the heart of another believer. We should never presume that we know what another person's private life is like. God's people are his people, not ours. His servants are his servants, not ours. They stand or fall before him. We must not set ourselves up as judges over them (Romans 14:4, 13).

How thankful we ought to be that our Saviour's grace is immutable, indestructible, and effectual. He who gives no indication of anger toward John's disciples for their evil presumption is our great God, who will never charge his own with sin (Romans 4:8). Having pardoned us of all our transgressions through the blood of Christ, our God beholds no evil in his people (Jeremiah 50:20). Rather, he beholds us in Christ as perfect, complete, and holy. If he beholds all his people this way, how much more we ought to do so! "In lowliness of mind let each esteem other better than themselves" (Philippians 2:3).

Wonderful In Identification

In verse 15 the Lord Jesus graciously and tenderly identifies himself with his disciples. "And Jesus said unto them, Can the children of the bridechamber mourn, as long as the bridegroom is with them? but the days will come, when the bridegroom shall be taken from them, and then shall they fast."

Rather than getting into a dispute with these men about a matter of insignificance, our Lord seized the opportunity to identify himself with us in one of the most tender, intimate, and suggestive ways imaginable. He calls himself the Bridegroom. John's disciples could not have missed the significance of this (John 3:29). It was true that his disciples were not known to fast. Here the Lord Jesus comes to their defence and explains why that was the case.

In Bible times marriages were arranged; and the glorious marriage of the Lord Jesus Christ has been arranged. The marriage has been arranged and the bride chosen by God the Father in eternal election. The bride chosen is the church of God (Ephesians 5:25-27). The children of the bride chamber, the friends of the Bridegroom, are God's servants, all true gospel preachers. In those days of old the centre of attention in a wedding was not the bride but the bridegroom; and our Lord Jesus is our Bridegroom! Let him have all the attention and adulation!

What the bridegroom is to the bride, the Lord Jesus Christ is to every sinner who trusts him. He loves us with deep, everlasting, unchangeable love. He has taken us into an indissoluble union with himself (Ephesians 4:30). By his death as our Substitute, he paid all our debts with his blood. He supplies all our needs. He sympathizes with us in all our troubles. He bears all our affronts, sins, and horrible thoughts and acts of unfaithfulness towards him. With this Bridegroom there is no divorce, no putting away! And all the glory that he has received from his Father he has given to his bride, the church, the Lamb's wife (John 17:5, 22; Revelation 19:7). Spurgeon's explanation of verse 15 is excellent:

> He is 'the Bridegroom' who came to woo and win his bride, those who followed him were the guests, the Bridegroom's best men and attendants, it was for them to rejoice while the Bridegroom headed their company, for sorrow is not suitable for wedding-feasts. Our Lord is that Bridegroom of whom Solomon sang in the Song of Songs, and we who enjoy his fellowship are one with him in his joy. Why should we fast while he is near? Can we allow little things to kill our great joy? Can we, in consistency with reason, and in harmony with respect for our Lord, mourn as long as the Bridegroom is with us?
>
> But Jesus was to go. He says himself, 'The Bridegroom shall be taken from them.' Here first he speaks about his death. Did his disciples note the warning word? When their Beloved was gone, they would have fasting enough. How true was this! Sorrows crowded in upon them when he was gone. It is the same with us. Our Lord is our joy: his presence makes our banquet, his absence is our fast, black and bitter. All Ritualistic fasting is the husk: the reality of fasting is known only to the child of the bridechamber when his Lord is no more with him. This is fasting indeed, as some of us know full well.
>
> There is no wedding without a Bridegroom, no delight without Jesus. In his presence is fulness of joy, in his absence is depth of misery. Let but the heart rest in his love and it desireth nothing more. Take away a sense of his love from the soul, and it is dark, empty, and nigh unto death.

Wonderful In Teaching

In verses 16, 17 our Lord Jesus shows himself to be a tender Master and teaches us how to deal with young disciples. "No man putteth a piece of new cloth unto an old garment, for that which is put in to fill it up taketh from the garment, and the rent is made worse. Neither do men put new wine into old bottles: else the bottles break, and the wine runneth out, and the bottles perish: but they put new wine into new bottles, and both are preserved."

In the family of God there are "little children", "young men", and "fathers" (1 John 2:12-14). Little children are not to be dealt with as young men, or fathers, but as little children. Sometimes those who should be fathers are still just little children, and must be dealt with as such (Hebrews 5:12-14). Just as a seamstress would never put a new piece of cloth into and old pair of trousers to patch them, so we must not expect from babes the maturity of fathers and must not put them in the place of fathers. If we do, we are sure to regret it. Just as a winemaker would never put new wine in an old bottle, lest it burst, so we must not impose upon young converts the rigid discipline we ought to impose upon ourselves, lest we do them great harm. We must not impose upon men what they are not able to bear. We must never neglect the doctrines of the gospel. We must not fail to teach the ordinances of the gospel. We must take care to train young believers in the way of Christ. But we must be patient with the Lord's little children. They are usually more harsh and hasty in their judgments than they will be in time, more strict and unbending in their thoughts of others than they will be when they have more experience in grace, more highly opinionated than they will be when they know more, more susceptible to error than they will be when they have been made to know their own weakness, and more rash and erratic in their behaviour than they will be when they have been through heavy trials (2 Timothy 2:24, 25).

These parabolic statements given by our Saviour also demonstrate the folly of man in substituting anything and everything for a real work of grace and true godliness. Throughout history, in every part of the world, it is ever the trait of fallen man to attempt to gain favour with God by doing something. In his proud self-righteousness man will readily fast, give alms, attend church, perform disciplined religious duties, reform his life, and make great sacrifices in the hope of attaining salvation by his own works. He sews the new cloth of religion into the old garment of nature, and puts the new wine of religion into the old bottle of nature. But, seeking righteousness by their own works, they will not submit to Christ and trust him for the whole of their acceptance with God. That makes their religion both foolish and harmful. The old creature is only dressed up in a new form; but no transformation has taken place, there has been no regeneration, no work of grace in the soul. Robert Hawker wrote:

> Jesus makes use of two beautiful similitudes to shew the folly of it. The new cloth put into the old garment; and the new wine into old bottles neither of which can receive into union what is altogether the reverse of themselves. The strength of the new cloth will only tend to rend the old; and the old dried skins of bottles must burst if new fermenting wine is put into them. In like manner, the new robe of Jesus' righteousness cannot be joined to patch up our filthy rags, neither can the new wine of the Gospel be received into the old, unrenewed skin of nature. But when the Holy Ghost hath by regeneration made all things new, and Christ's righteousness is received as the new robe of salvation; and the blood of Christ as the wine that maketh glad the heart of man; both then are preserved and blessed.

Wonderful In Salvation

In verses 18-26 our blessed Redeemer shows himself wonderful in the salvation he performs by two great miracles of grace. Matthew shows us two examples of the Lord honouring faith. He blends these two great miracles together by the direction of God the Holy Spirit, because the one runs into the other, and both serve mutually to illustrate the glory of Christ and the omnipotence of his saving grace. Try to picture the scene drawn for us by the pen of the inspired writer.

First we see a man whose daughter is dead, asking the Lord Jesus to come, lay his hand on his dead child, and restore her life. To this great request, which exemplified great faith, the Lord Jesus readily complied and started to go with the man. Can you imagine the hope and joyful anticipation that must have flooded that father's heart as the Son of God was going to raise his darling child to life? But as he was going, a woman with an issue of blood interrupted the procession, touching the Lord Jesus with a hand of faith. When she touched him, the procession came to a halt. The Lord Jesus paused to cure that poor woman, honouring and commending her faith.

Mark adds a little colour that Matthew omits. He tells us that, while the Lord Jesus was speaking to this woman, "there came from the ruler of the synagogue's house certain which said, Thy daughter is dead, why troublest thou the master?" Luke tells us the same thing (Mark 5:35; Luke 8:49). What a trial that must have been to the man's faith! He must have thought to himself, "Now it is too late. My daughter is at the point of death." Had he such fears, they were ill-founded. He who had begun his good work would finish it. He had started to the ruler's house to heal his daughter who was dying. And he would go on to the place to raise his daughter from the dead. Our increasing need is not a hindrance to Christ's power and grace, but only a better background upon which he will display his grace and power.

In the healing of this woman we are given a tremendous, instructive picture. Mark and Luke, in their more detailed accounts of this event, inform us that she had been in this sorrowful condition of weakness and uncleanness for twelve long years, and that she had spent all her living on physicians of no value, hoping to obtain a cure. Yet, she was no better, but only grew worse. How anxious sinners are to make any sacrifice, try any religious medicine, and submit to the tortures of religious rehabilitation at the hands of quack religious physicians! All the while their condition just gets worse. Until the sin-sick soul comes to Christ, there is no hope. All the attempted cures of religious experience and religious works are vanity. But as soon as the sinner in desperate need comes to the Saviour in faith, his malady is gone!

Truly this daughter of Abraham was a woman of remarkable faith. Her faith honoured the Lord Jesus; and the Lord Jesus honoured her faith. He said, "Daughter, be of good comfort; thy faith hath made thee whole." Obviously, it was Christ who made her whole, not her faith. Yet, it was her faith in Christ that fetched his healing power to her body and to her soul. So, while we admire her faith, let us admire and honour him who gave her faith. As Spurgeon put it, "Thus he put the crown upon the head of her faith, because her faith had already set the crown on his head." Though she did not know it at the time, the Lord Jesus had given her this lively faith, just as he gave her the blessing of grace she needed. "And the woman was made whole from that hour."

Immediately, the Lord Jesus went on to the ruler of the synagogue's house. His darling daughter was now dead. By all human reason, all hope was gone. But that was not the case. He who is the Resurrection and the Life had come to give life to a dead child; and she must live again. With the ease of omnipotence, "he went in, and took her by the hand, and the maid arose". By his omnipotent grace "the dead are raised up" still (Matthew 11:5). With the ease of omnipotent, irresistible grace, still he raises up those who are dead in trespasses and in sins.

With that same ease of omnipotent grace, he is able to raise up and revive our languishing souls; and he will (Hosea 6:1-3).

Faith honours God and God honours faith. The Lord Jesus honoured the ruler's strong faith by doing what he desired. And he honoured the woman's, perhaps, weaker faith, doing for her what she desired. It is not the measure of our faith, but the Object of our faith that saves us.

Without question, the Man who performed these wonders of mercy is the omnipotent God. All power is his (Matthew 28:18-20). He who is God our Saviour has power over all flesh (John 17:2), all events (Romans 8:28), and Satan, too (Revelation 20:1-3). "He that is our God is the God of salvation; and unto GOD the Lord belong the issues from death" (Psalms 68:20). Let his fame go abroad into all the earth!

Chapter 21

"Believe Ye That I Am Able To Do This?"

"And when Jesus departed thence, two blind men followed him, crying, and saying, Thou Son of David, have mercy on us. And when he was come into the house, the blind men came to him: and Jesus saith unto them, Believe ye that I am able to do this? They said unto him, Yea, Lord. Then touched he their eyes, saying, According to your faith be it unto you. And their eyes were opened; and Jesus straitly charged them, saying, See that no man know it. But they, when they were departed, spread abroad his fame in all that country. As they went out, behold, they brought to him a dumb man possessed with a devil. And when the devil was cast out, the dumb spake: and the multitudes marvelled, saying, It was never so seen in Israel. But the Pharisees said, He casteth out devils through the prince of the devils. And Jesus went about all the cities and villages, teaching in their synagogues, and preaching the gospel of the kingdom, and healing every sickness and every disease among the people. But when he saw the multitudes, he was moved with compassion on them, because they fainted, and were scattered abroad, as sheep having no shepherd. Then saith he unto his disciples, The harvest truly is plenteous, but the labourers are few; Pray ye therefore the Lord of the harvest, that he will send forth labourers into his harvest."
(Matthew 9:27-38)

In the passage before us two blind men and one who was possessed by an evil spirit and could not speak were healed by the Word of our Lord Jesus Christ and by the power of his touch. The two blind men who were healed came to the Lord Jesus seeking mercy. These two men, who had been companions in misery, were about to be made companions in mercy. The things written in these verses of scripture are here recorded by divine inspiration to teach us about the mercy, grace, and compassion of our Lord Jesus Christ and about our responsibilities before him. Notice what Matthew tells us about these men.

They were blind – as all men are spiritually. They were earnest and they meant business. They were determined to give the Son of God no rest until he gave them rest. They followed the Saviour through the streets and on into the house, crying for mercy. They believed on the Lord Jesus Christ. They believed him to be the Messiah, the Christ, the Son of David. They acknowledged and confessed him as "Lord". And they believed he was able to give them their sight. They believed him! They believed him to be both omnipotent and merciful. They sought mercy! They cried, "Thou Son of David, have mercy on us." All who seek for God to deal with them on the basis of what they deserve shall have what they deserve, everlasting ruin. But all who seek mercy shall obtain mercy (Jeremiah 29:13, 14). They obtained the thing they desired. "Their eyes were opened."

The two blind men came seeking the Lord; but the poor demon-possessed man who could not speak was brought to the Master (v. 32). Notice the word "behold". This is a striking case. This man was not himself. A demon had taken possession of him. He does not cry for help. He does not come to Christ. But someone cared enough for his wretched state to bring him to Christ. Let us do the same. God will create a need in some to be in the place of worship. But others will not come until gracious souls go out and bring them into the house of mercy.

The Experience Of Grace

The experience of grace is vividly portrayed in these three men. The examples are set before us, one following the other, to teach us that the manifestation of grace is as varied and diverse as the recipients of grace. All three of these men needed mercy. All three obtained mercy. All three obtained mercy through Christ the Mediator. But they did not obtain it the same way. Mercy came to the blind men only after they actively, earnestly sought it. But mercy came to the dumb, demon-possessed soul by such immediate power that he never even thought about it before he had obtained it. Salvation is the same wherever it is found. It is the same in the experience of all who are saved. Every true child of God has experienced the same salvation. All are saved by grace alone, through faith alone, in Christ alone. But we do not all experience grace the same way. Paul's experience was not the same as Lydia's. Both experienced the same grace, but not the same way. The experience of grace is not always the same. Our needs are the same, the grace is the same, and the results are the same; but the experience is not the same. Yet, all who are saved have a "common salvation" (Jude 3). We have a common Saviour. We are born into a common family. We have a common Father, a common hope, a common blessedness, and a common inheritance.

We must never put God in a box and imagine he must work in the way we think. As "the wind bloweth where it listeth" (John 3:8), the God of all grace works as he will. We must not attempt to determine the validity of one person's experience of grace by comparing it with someone else's, our own or another's.

“Believe Ye That I Am Able To Do This?”

A Gift And A Responsibility

Faith is frequently found where it is least expected by us. Who would have thought two blind men, or that poor, demon-possessed wretch would have believed on Christ? The multitudes marvelled (v. 33). The Pharisees blasphemed (v. 34). But these three needy souls believed and obtained mercy. The two blind men could not have seen the miracles the Lord Jesus had performed. They were blind. But having heard the common reports of Christ, they believed him. And believing him, the eyes of their understanding were enlightened. It is written, “Faith cometh by hearing” (Romans 10:17).

The Word of God teaches us, with unmistakable clarity, that faith is the gift of God. Faith in Christ is not something we muster up in ourselves by the exercise of our freewill. Faith is something God the Holy Spirit gives to and produces in chosen, redeemed, called sinners (John 1:12, 13; Romans 9:16; Ephesians 2:8; Colossians 2:12). It is a gift which God sovereignly gives to some and withholds from others (John 10:25, 26). It is a gift that God works in sinners by the preaching of the gospel (Romans 10:17). And the object of God-given, saving faith is the Lord Jesus Christ.

The scriptures also tell us that faith in Christ is the commandment of God (1 John 3:23). Being God’s commandment to us, it is the responsibility of all who hear the gospel to believe on his Son. Many appear to be incapable of seeing that both these facts are true. When we assert that faith is God’s gift and God’s operation we are denounced by some as hardshells and hyper-Calvinists. When we declare that it is the responsibility of sinners to trust Christ we are denounced by others as Arminians and freewillers, teachers of “duty faith”, and accused of teaching that faith is a work of man.

I will leave it to others to beat the winds they blow. The Word of God is crystal clear. If any sinner believes God and is saved by his grace, it is because God gives him faith in Christ (Ephesians 2:8, 9). If any abide under the wrath of God, it is because they do not believe on the Son of God (John 3:36).

Another thing clearly set before us in these miracles performed by our Saviour is the fact that there is a direct correlation between our faith and God’s work. Our Lord asked the blind men, “Believe ye that I am able to do this? They said unto him, Yea, Lord. Then touched he their eyes, saying, According to your faith be it unto you” (vv. 28, 29). Spurgeon wrote, “He touched them with his hand; but they must also touch him with their faith … If we do not in very truth trust our Lord, we shall die in our sins.” How thankful we are that it is not always true, that the measure of our mercies is our faith, or our lack of faith in our God (Isaiah 48:18, 19; Mark 6:5, 6; John 11:40). We must never blame on God's sovereignty that which is the result of our own shameful unbelief. I often wonder what God might do, if we simply believed him.

Inexcusable Disobedience

The Lord Jesus commanded these men not to tell anyone what he had done for them. We are not told why he did this. It is obvious that our Master was not like the self-serving, glory seeking preachers of our day. He did not seek and did not want worldly fame. And he who is God our Saviour is under no obligation to give us the reasons for that which he does or commands us to do. Our Saviour's language was clear and emphatic. In fact, it was a stern command. But they disregarded his command. He left them no option: he demanded complete silence on their part.

Such disregard for the word of our God is inexcusable. I am sure these men convinced themselves that their disobedience was really what the Master wanted them to do; but they were wrong. We are never doing right if we disobey Christ. Even if the results turn out to be advantageous, disobedience is not to be excused. "Behold, to obey is better than sacrifice" (1 Samuel 15:22). In all things it is our responsibility to submit to and obey the revealed will of God.

I have no doubt that these men did not disobey the Saviour contemptuously. They were, I am sure, filled with gratitude and joy, and desired to give him glory for the wondrous work of mercy he had performed for them and in them. Their love for Christ was the thing that moved them to speak forth his praise. But our affections, emotions, and thoughts are not to be our guide, or the rule of our behaviour. Our only guide, our only rule is and must be the revealed will of God our Saviour. And his Word is his revealed will.

Omnipotent Mercy

When the Lord Jesus cast the devil out of the man in verses 32 and 33, "The Pharisees said, He casteth out devils through the prince of the devils." Then, we read in verse 35, "And Jesus went about all the cities and villages, teaching in their synagogues, and preaching the gospel of the kingdom, and healing every sickness and every disease among the people." That was our Saviour's answer to their blasphemous slander. He simply ignored them and went on doing what he was sent of the Father to do. We would be wise to follow his example. Nothing is ever gained, and much lost, by answering the slanderous accusations of men.

We see in the miracles that are described in this passage that none are beyond the reach of Christ's omnipotent mercy. We must never despair of anyone's salvation, merely because he lives in unfavourable circumstances. Grace is stronger than circumstances! We must never despair of any because they are blind, or because they are under the yoke of Satan, or because they obstinately refuse to come to Christ. Our Lord's arm is not shortened that it cannot save. His omnipotent arm of mercy can both break the power of Satan and break the power of man's obstinate rebellion (Psalm 110:3).

Matthew tells us that the Lord Jesus healed "every sickness and every disease". None were too loathsome for him to touch. None were too far gone for him to cure. The Son of God is indeed "The Great Physician". All physical healing is his work. We use medicine, doctors, and hospitals, just as we look both ways before crossing a busy street. But we look to our God for life and health.

The healing of our souls is altogether his work, too. As we read the succession of miracles performed by our Saviour in this chapter, remembering that all the maladies and woes of Adam's fallen race are the result of sin, we ought to be moved to adore and praise him who came into this world to "put away sin by the sacrifice of himself". How thankful we ought to be for our all-glorious Christ who came here to destroy the works of the devil! He is the Balm of Gilead. He is the Sun of Righteousness who has risen with healing in his wings. "With his stripes we are healed." There is no disease of soul he cannot, or will not completely cure (1 Corinthians 6:9-11; 1:30, 31).

Moved With Compassion

Verse 36 shows us that the Lord Jesus is a Saviour full of compassion for needy souls. I cannot imagine why anyone would feel obliged to try to make this say less than it does. We have here a great display of our Saviour's great compassion. We ought to rejoice in it and pray for grace to emulate his compassion. When our Saviour saw the lost multitudes before him, he was overcome by sympathy. What he saw with his eyes affected his heart. His whole being was stirred by the sight of perishing souls. "He was moved with compassion on them"!

What are our thoughts when we see the lost multitudes around us? Multitudes are seen on every side, Muslims and Jews; Papists and Protestants; intellectuals and scoffers; who are spiritually blind, ignorant, unconverted, lost, and perishing! They are as sheep without a shepherd, unfed, exposed, unguarded. What will become of them? Do you feel their destitution? Do you long to see their predicament relieved? These are serious questions; and they ought to be honestly answered. Those who are unmoved by perishing souls do not have "the mind of Christ" (1 Corinthians 2:16).

Great Harvest

There is a great harvest of souls to be gathered by grace for which we are responsible (vv. 37, 38). The harvest of souls to be gathered out of all the earth is a great multitude, which no man can number. They are God's elect, Christ's redeemed ones; and they must and shall be gathered. The Lord of the harvest is the triune God. He owns the field and controls it. The plants to be gathered are his; and the labourers are his. Our Saviour here calls faithful gospel preachers "labourers" because the faithful performance of their work involves arduous labour. God's servants labour in the Word and in the doctrine, labour in prayer and the study of holy scripture, devoting themselves to the work as workmen that need not be ashamed, for the glory of Christ and the salvation and edification of God's elect. But such labourers, men who are willing to spend and be spent for Christ, are in every place and generation few.

"Pray ye therefore the Lord of the harvest, that he will send forth labourers into his harvest." None but God himself can send them forth. Man-made preachers are not just useless; they are in the way. Only God can, by the power and grace of his Spirit, gift a man for the work of the gospel ministry, incline his heart to the work, and enable him to perform it faithfully.

Yet, it is the responsibility of every believer to make God's harvest a matter of prayer and personal concern. Our Saviour says to his disciples, "Pray ye therefore the Lord of the harvest, that he will send forth labourers into his harvest." You may not be called and gifted of God to perform the work of a pastor, evangelist, or missionary; but there are many things you can and should do. You can give generously to support the preaching of the gospel. You can bring people to hear the gospel preached. You can distribute tapes and literature proclaiming the gospel. And you can pray. Pray for those God has sent forth as labourers in his vineyard. Pray that he will raise up and send forth others. And pray that he will give his church a time of reaping.

Our Lord Jesus asked the blind men, and I put the question to myself and to you, "Believe ye that I am able to do this?" Do we believe that he is able to heal the blind, free the possessed, and gather in his lost ones scattered through all the earth? This much I know, if we believe him, we will act accordingly.

Chapter 22

Labourers Sent Forth

"And when he had called unto him his twelve disciples, he gave them power against unclean spirits, to cast them out, and to heal all manner of sickness and all manner of disease. Now the names of the twelve apostles are these; The first, Simon, who is called Peter, and Andrew his brother; James the son of Zebedee, and John his brother; Philip, and Bartholomew; Thomas, and Matthew the publican; James the son of Alphaeus, and Lebbaeus, whose surname was Thaddaeus; Simon the Canaanite, and Judas Iscariot, who also betrayed him. These twelve Jesus sent forth, and commanded them, saying, Go not into the way of the Gentiles, and into any city of the Samaritans enter ye not: But go rather to the lost sheep of the house of Israel. And as ye go, preach, saying, The kingdom of heaven is at hand. Heal the sick, cleanse the lepers, raise the dead, cast out devils: freely ye have received, freely give. Provide neither gold, nor silver, nor brass in your purses, Nor scrip for your journey, neither two coats, neither shoes, nor yet staves: for the workman is worthy of his meat. And into whatsoever city or town ye shall enter, inquire who in it is worthy; and there abide till ye go thence. And when ye come into an house, salute it. And if the house be worthy, let your peace come upon it: but if it be not worthy, let your peace return to you. And whosoever shall not receive you, nor hear your words, when ye depart out of that house or city, shake off the dust of your feet. Verily I say unto you, It shall be more tolerable for the land of Sodom and Gomorrha in the day of judgment, than for that city."
(Matthew 10:1-15)

In the last verse of chapter 9 our Lord urged his disciples to pray that the Lord God would send forth labourers into his field to gather in his harvest. Here in chapter 10 the Lord Jesus demonstrates that he is "the Lord of the harvest" by sending forth his labourers into his field to reap his harvest.

Matthew 10 is a chapter of holy scripture that ought always be read with peculiar solemnity. In these forty-two verses we have the first ordination sermon ever preached. Those being ordained and set apart for the work of the gospel ministry are the twelve apostles. The ordination preacher is the Lord Jesus Christ, the Son of God. The solemn charge here given by Christ to the first gospel preachers of the New Testament era is the charge he gives to all who are sent of God to preach the gospel.

Let us carefully examine the first fifteen verses of this chapter. The apostolic office ceased with the calling of the Apostle Paul and the death of the last Apostle, probably John. Yet, every believer, every church, and every man who claims to be, or hopes to be, a preacher of the gospel ought to be interested in the things recorded in these verses. There are no apostles today in the official sense of that word. However, like the word "angel", the word "apostle" simply means, "messenger". In that sense every true gospel preacher is an apostle, a messenger, an ambassador for Christ (2 Corinthians 5:20), sent from God himself with the message of grace and salvation in the Lord Jesus Christ.

Twelve Men

These twelve men who were called to be Christ's Apostles, his messengers, were first his disciples. "And when he had called unto him his twelve disciples, he gave them power against unclean spirits, to cast them out, and to heal all manner of sickness and all manner of disease" (v. 1). It seems ridiculous that I should have to say so, but in these days when people who claim to worship and serve God both ignore and wilfully pervert holy scripture, it must be said: The messengers of Christ were all men! No woman has ever been called of God to preach the gospel. The teaching of holy scripture in this matter is crystal clear (1 Corinthians 14:34; 1 Timothy 2:11, 12). The ordination of women for the work of the gospel ministry, including pastors, elders, missionaries, and deacons, is totally contrary to the teaching of the Bible.

These men were first called to be Christ's disciples, then called to be his Apostles. No man is fit for the work of the gospel ministry who has not experienced God's saving grace. We cannot know the hearts of men. Therefore, we deal with them upon the basis of their professed faith in Christ. But none are to be put into the gospel ministry who are not followers of Christ. Those who are set apart by local churches for the work of the gospel ministry must be men of proven faithfulness (1 Timothy 3:10). They who would be teachers of others must first be learners, taught of God. No man is apt to teach, or able to teach others who has not first learned the mysteries of the kingdom of heaven (1 Timothy 3:2; 2 Timothy 2:2, 24).

Labourers Sent Forth

Twelve men were chosen to be apostles. The number twelve is significant. It has reference to the twelve sons of Jacob, the twelve tribes of Israel. The Church of God is the Israel of God. These twelve apostles are the twelve stars that make up the church's crown (Revelation 12:1), the twelve foundations of the New Jerusalem (Revelation 21:12, 14), typified by the twelve precious stones in Aaron's breastplate, the twelve loaves on the table of showbread, and the twelve wells of water at Elim. The Lord Jesus speaks of them as sitting upon thrones to judge the twelve tribes of Israel (Luke 22:30).

These men were called by Christ. First, they were called to follow him. Then, they were called to be his messengers. The call of every disciple of Christ is the same. The Holy Spirit teaches us in 1 Peter 1:2 and 2 Peter 2:9, 10 that our election in Christ and our redemption by him is made manifest by this call. He has saved us and called us (2 Timothy 1:9). All who are justified by Christ's blood are called (Romans 8:30). And all who are sanctified by God the Father and preserved in Christ are called by God the Holy Spirit (Jude 1). Gospel preachers are called and sent forth by Christ, "the Lord of the harvest". Being called and sent forth by him, the fruit of their labour is sure. God's Word proclaimed by them is triumphant over unclean spirits; and in the name of Christ, by the power of the gospel preached, diseases and sicknesses of immortal souls are healed.

Their Names

Matthew was inspired of God to list the names of these twelve men for us. "Now the names of the twelve apostles are these; The first, Simon, who is called Peter, and Andrew his brother; James the son of Zebedee, and John his brother; Philip, and Bartholomew; Thomas, and Matthew the publican; James the son of Alphaeus, and Lebbaeus, whose surname was Thaddaeus; Simon the Canaanite, and Judas Iscariot, who also betrayed him" (vv. 2-4).

There are some apostles of whom we virtually know nothing more than their names (Bartholomew and Simon the Canaanite). Some are famous. Some are obscure. But it matters not to them. They are God's messengers! Peter is mentioned first because he was one of the Master's first two disciples (John 1:35-42) and (perhaps) because he rose to be the leader and chief spokesman for the rest. Matthew calls himself "the publican", acknowledging his debt to the grace of God, and puts himself in the list with obscurity, preferring to promote his fellow labourers rather than himself. These were truly blessed men. Their names were first written in the book of life before the world began, except for Judas

Iscariot. Yet his place was also marked out from eternity (Psalm 41:9; Acts 1:25; John 17:12). Matthias was chosen by the others to take the traitor's place (Acts 1:26). But their choice of a replacement was not God's choice. The Lord's intention was for his church to have twelve apostles, twelve and only twelve. David's prophecy (Psalm 69:25; Acts 1:20) must be fulfilled. Another apostle must take Judas' place. But, like the others, he must be personally chosen and ordained to the office by Christ himself. The Lord had not chosen Matthias for this office. He had chosen Paul (1 Corinthians 15:8).

Yes, one of the chosen Apostles was a devil. The scriptures do not hide the fact that Judas was among the original twelve; and we must never forget it. This fact is prominently displayed in the Word of God to teach us never to pin our faith on the sleeve of a man. Not all preachers are believers. Even those who preach the "truth" are not all genuine Christians. Yet, the fact that one preacher is a devil is no indication that all are devils. Faithful gospel preachers are to be followed and obeyed (Hebrews 13:7, 17). Yet, we must follow them only as they follow Christ.

A Great Work

These twelve men were called and commissioned by Christ to do a very great work. "And when he had called unto him his twelve disciples, he gave them power against unclean spirits, to cast them out, and to heal all manner of sickness and all manner of disease." He sent them forth saying, "Heal the sick, cleanse the lepers, raise the dead, cast out devils: freely ye have received, freely give" (vv. 1 and 8).

The purpose of the gospel ministry is the healing of men's souls (v. 1). The design of the gospel is to conquer the world, the flesh, and the devil. Christ gave these men power to cast demons out of men's bodies, to show that Christ has come to destroy the power of Satan and his works. He gave them power to heal all manner of sickness and disease to show that none are beyond the reach of God's omnipotent grace, because the blood of Christ effectually cleanses from all sin (1 John 1:7, 9).

The miracles performed by Moses, who represented the law, were for destruction and judgment. These miracles of the apostles were all wrought for comfort, edification, and life, portraying the power of the gospel. These miracles were an affirmation of Christ as the Messiah and these men as his messengers (Hebrews 1:3). Now that we have the full revelation of God in holy scripture, God's servants need no miraculous signs to confirm their message. Faithful men do not come with a new word (revelation) from God, but simply declare the revelation of God in holy scripture. “That which is perfect” has come. We have a “more sure Word of prophecy”. Those who pretend to work miracles, speak in tongues, and have a word of prophecy or revelation from God are saying, “Christ is not enough”! “The Bible is not enough”! “Salvation is not enough”! “The Gospel is not enough”!

“He gave them power” to do the work he sent them to do. The Lord Jesus Christ never called anyone to do anything for him without giving them the power to do it. Whatever the work is to which God calls a person, he will give him the power (ability, opportunity, and means) to do it.

Their Message

God’s messengers, like these twelve apostles, are sent of God into this world to preach the gospel of his sovereign, saving grace in the Lord Jesus Christ. “And as ye go, preach, saying, The kingdom of heaven is at hand” (v. 7). This was the Apostles’ commission. They were to preach, “The kingdom of heaven is at hand”, the near approach of Christ’s kingdom; that is of his Person, his work and his salvation. God’s messengers all have one message to declare. We have been sent of God to preach, and to preach Jesus Christ and him crucified, to preach Christ is the King. He has brought in and established the Kingdom of Heaven. Salvation is finished. God’s salvation, the Kingdom of Heaven is at hand, right before you (Psalm 85:9-11). The kingdom of grace and the kingdom of glory, to which that grace leads, is distinguished from the law by the preaching of the gospel (John 1:15-18).

Let every man sent of God to preach the gospel of Christ ever be mindful that he is to be turned aside to no other message. It does not matter what Satan gets you off on, if he gets you off Christ, he has won the day. Our message is not prophecy, morality, politics, the home, or any other matter but “Jesus Christ and him crucified” for, “The Kingdom of Heaven is at hand”.

Lost Sheep

God’s servants are sent to the lost sheep of the house of Israel (vv. 5, 6). It never was our Lord’s purpose to save all men. And he never has sent the gospel to all men. These two verses must be interpreted literally. The Lord Jesus sent the gospel to the Jews first and then to the Gentiles. He later commands that we go into all the world and preach the gospel to every creature, saying, “He that believeth and is baptized shall be saved; he that believeth not shall be damned.”

But, whether preaching to Jews or to Gentiles, we are sent of God to seek out the lost sheep of the house of Israel: God's elect! We are on the trail of Christ's sheep. We are seeking the Lord's sheep. We have good news for the Lord's sheep. Redemption is accomplished! Forgiveness is free! Salvation is forever! When we find them, these lost sheep will hear the Shepherd's voice and follow him. These sheep are the house of Israel, the Israel of God scattered among the nations who must and shall be gathered. John Gill wrote:

> These are called 'sheep' because they were chosen of God, and given to Christ to be redeemed, looked up, sought out, and saved by him; and 'lost' ones, not only because lost in Adam, and by their own transgressions, so that neither they themselves, nor any mere creature, could save them from eternal ruin and destruction; but also, because they were made to go astray, and were lost through the negligence and errors of their pastors, the scribes and Pharisees: and this character is the rather given of them, partly to reflect upon the characters of the shepherds of Israel: and partly to magnify the grace of God, in having regard to such ruined and miserable creatures; and also to excite the compassion and diligence of the apostles, to preach the Gospel to them: respect seems to be had to Jeremiah 1:16.

Freely Give

What a beautiful view is here given of those faithful men going forth with their lives in their hands to preach Christ, having neither gold, nor silver, nor money in their purse, making no provision for themselves (vv. 7-10).

God's servants are not greedy, covetous men who seek to enrich themselves. Gospel preachers are not hirelings. They make it their business to freely give as they have freely received. Our Lord Jesus specifically tells his disciples not to provide anything for themselves and not to beg (Luke 10:4-7). God's ambassadors never grovel before men! I cannot imagine any of these men announcing that the Lord Jesus had called them to preach the gospel and then grovel like hungry dogs before men, declaring that they must have so much money, or assistance from others before they can do the Lord's work!

Yet, those who preach the gospel are to live by the gospel. Those who benefit from the gospel are to maintain those who preach the gospel in an honourable way (1 Corinthians 9:11; Galatians 6:6-10; 1 Timothy 5:17, 18). Those men who faithfully preach the gospel of God's free and sovereign grace in Christ are to be supported and maintained by the people to whom they minister. Faithful missionaries should be as fully and generously supported by the churches that send them out as the pastors of those local churches.

There were times when Paul and his companions were required to make tents to support themselves in the work of the gospel. It was an honourable thing for them to do. Paul tells us that his goal was not to enrich himself, but to avoid being a burden to young churches (1 Thessalonians 2:9), and to avoid causing an offence to young, weak believers (1 Corinthians 9:15-19). But the fact that God's messenger had to spend his time and effort making tents was a shameful reproach upon the churches. Those churches that were established in the gospel should have assumed the responsibility of supplying Paul's needs and the needs of his companions as they travelled from place to place preaching the gospel. The New Testament clearly makes it the responsibility of every local church to provide for the financial, material support of those who preach the gospel of Christ.

Shake Off The Dust

"And into whatsoever city or town ye shall enter, inquire who in it is worthy; and there abide till ye go thence" (v. 11). The word, "worthy", obviously refers to hospitable people, willing to receive God's messengers. God's servants are not to be difficult and demanding, but content with such things as gracious people are able and willing to provide for them. C. H. Spurgeon, commenting upon the words "there abide", wrote, "Keep to those good people with whom your mission begins. It may be that richer people will turn up, but never forget the worthy men and women who first entertained you."

The presence of God's servants in any home ought to be a great blessing to the household. We should never enter a home without desiring to be a blessing to it. When we leave it, the family ought to be better off because of our influence. That is true with regard to all God's people. How much more God's servants ought to seek grace to be a blessing to others, wherever they go!

Wherever we go, we ought to think well of men until their conduct forces us to do otherwise. When we enter a home, let us enter it determined to bring good to the house. If the blessing we bring by the gospel is despised, we must not be discouraged.

Shaking off the dust of your feet in v. 14 is not to be viewed as a matter of spite, or mean-spirited retaliation, or even as a physical act to be performed. Our

Lord is simply telling us that when people refuse the gospel we preach, we are to leave them alone. Because they will not have our King and will not worship our God, we cannot walk in fellowship with them.

However, it is a very dangerous thing to despise and reject the gospel of God's free grace. The Lord Jesus sends forth his royal ambassadors to call sinners to repentance, calling for rebels to bow to him as Lord and King. But for those who will not bow to him, who will not receive his gospel, nothing but judgment awaits them. In the day of judgment "it shall be more tolerable for the land of Sodom and Gomorrha" than for those who hear, but will not believe the gospel. What solemn words of warning these are! The preaching of the gospel is to all who hear it either a savour of life unto life, or a savour of death unto death (2 Corinthians 2:15, 16).

Chapter 23

Ten Important Lessons From The Master

"Behold, I send you forth as sheep in the midst of wolves: be ye therefore wise as serpents, and harmless as doves. But beware of men: for they will deliver you up to the councils, and they will scourge you in their synagogues; And ye shall be brought before governors and kings for my sake, for a testimony against them and the Gentiles. But when they deliver you up, take no thought how or what ye shall speak: for it shall be given you in that same hour what ye shall speak. For it is not ye that speak, but the Spirit of your Father which speaketh in you. And the brother shall deliver up the brother to death, and the father the child: and the children shall rise up against *their* parents, and cause them to be put to death. And ye shall be hated of all *men* for my name's sake: but he that endureth to the end shall be saved. But when they persecute you in this city, flee ye into another: for verily I say unto you, Ye shall not have gone over the cities of Israel, till the Son of man be come. The disciple is not above *his* master, nor the servant above his lord. It is enough for the disciple that he be as his master, and the servant as his lord. If they have called the master of the house Beelzebub, how much more *shall they call* them of his household? Fear them not therefore: for there is nothing covered, that shall not be revealed; and hid, that shall not be known. What I tell you in darkness, *that* speak ye in light: and what ye hear in the ear, *that* preach ye upon the housetops. And fear not them which kill the body, but are not able to kill the soul: but rather fear him which is able to destroy both soul and body in hell. Are not two sparrows sold for a farthing? and one of them shall not fall on the ground without your Father. But the very hairs of your head are all numbered. Fear ye not therefore, ye are of more value than many sparrows. Whosoever therefore shall confess me before men, him will I confess also before my Father which is in heaven. But whosoever shall deny me before men, him will I also deny before my Father which is in heaven. Think not that I am come to send peace on earth: I came not to send peace, but a sword. For I am come to set a man at variance against his father, and the daughter against her mother, and the daughter in law against her mother in law. And a man's foes *shall be* they of his own household. He that loveth father or mother more than me is not worthy of me: and he that loveth son or daughter more than me is not worthy of me. And he

that taketh not his cross, and followeth after me, is not worthy of me. He that findeth his life shall lose it: and he that loseth his life for my sake shall find it. He that receiveth you receiveth me, and he that receiveth me receiveth him that sent me. He that receiveth a prophet in the name of a prophet shall receive a prophet's reward; and he that receiveth a righteous man in the name of a righteous man shall receive a righteous man's reward. And whosoever shall give to drink unto one of these little ones a cup of cold water only in the name of a disciple, verily I say unto you, he shall in no wise lose his reward."
(Matthew 10:16-42)

God's servants in this world are sheep in the midst of wolves, needing wisdom, grace, and strength that only God can give to do his will. In these verses of scripture our Lord Jesus Christ gives his servants words of instruction to sustain and comfort them as they endeavour to serve the interest of his kingdom and the souls of men in this world. These words of instruction, in their primary application, were given to the apostles of our Lord. However, they are equally applicable to every gospel preacher in this world. And they are just as properly applied to you who seek to serve the Lord Jesus Christ in your day by day lives. We are God's servants.

To the selfish and unbelieving, who care for nothing but their own ease and comfort, these verses of scripture are meaningless. To you who serve God and the souls of men, they will be of great interest. To serve God and do good to men's souls in this world is hard work. Satan fights to maintain his kingdom. The hearts of men are far more wicked than any of us imagine. Our Lord Jesus knows this. Therefore, he takes care, when he sends us out to do his service, to supply us with instructive and encouraging words that we might be prepared for the trials, temptations, and troubles we must face in this world.

Here are ten lessons that we must learn, as we endeavour to serve God and our generation by the will of God.

Be Modest In Our Expectations

If we serve God, if our object is the glory of God, we must not make success our goal. "Beware of men". We are "as sheep in the midst of wolves". If you set your heart to serve God, you must make up your mind to be hated, abused, misunderstood, slandered, and persecuted by men. Even your nearest relations will oppose you if they do not know God (vv. 16-23). Whether you preach, or teach, or visit, or pass out tracts, or write, or give witness to others, whatever you do, for Christ, you must expect nothing from the world but opposition.

Many who once seemed full of zeal have turned back because they had extravagant expectations. Many a preacher has been taken in Satan's snare of "success" and has compromised the gospel to get it! Our only ambition ought to be the glory of God. Our only duty is the will of God. Our only guide is the Word of God. The only success we should desire is the approval of God. We must endure the hatred and opposition of men throughout the days of our lives; "but he that endureth to the end shall be saved".

Be "Wise As Serpents And Harmless As Doves"
That simply means we must pray for God to give us wisdom, good sense, a sound mind, and sincerity of heart. The word "harmless" means "simple". We are to be simple, honest, sincere as God's servants. Yet, we must have wisdom and good sense. We must never seek to avoid persecution by cowardice or compromise. The Lord allows his servants to flee from one city to another. But he does not allow us to hold our tongues. Yet, we must never foolishly court persecution by being obnoxious, arrogant, or even out of order and place. There is a proper time and place for witnessing and bearing testimony to the gospel; but there are times when it is out of place to do so. When someone is paying you to work for him, it is evil, not spiritual, to rob him of the labour for which you are being paid to discuss religious matters with your co-workers.

To state the matter simply, our God does not require us to throw out common sense when we are engaged to do his will. The offence of the cross we must bear. But we are not to be offensive. Let us "strive to walk circumspectly, not as fools but as wise" (Ephesians 5:15).

Do Not Expect To Receive Better In This World Than Did Our Saviour
If we leave men alone, they will probably leave us alone; but we dare not leave men alone. We must, as our Saviour did, expose man's sin, proclaim God's righteousness in and by Christ, and call sinners to repentance and faith in Christ. If we follow our Master, we will, in the ordinary course of events, experience what he experienced. He was slandered and rejected by those among whom he ministered. Men "called him Beelzebub", a devil, a glutton, a winebibber, and a sinner. Few believed his message. Let us not be surprised if we experience the same (vv. 24, 25). C. H. Spurgeon wrote:

> If the Master of the family is likened to Beelzebub, the fly-god of the Philistines, and named after the prince of demons, by what names will they call us? Doubtless malice will quicken wit, and sarcasm will invent words which pierce as daggers, and cut like knives … God was slandered in Paradise, and Christ on Calvary, how can we hope to escape? Instead of wishing to avoid bearing the cross, let us be content to endure dishonour for our King's sake.

Be Content To Wait For Him Whom We Serve

God will bring everything to light in his time. "Fear them not therefore: for there is nothing covered, that shall not be revealed, and hid, that shall not be known" (v. 26). Vengeance belongs to him. If we are his servants, he will both vindicate and avenge our names and our work in the last day. Either here or there God will vindicate his servants. And he will do it by judgment (Psalm 37:5, 6; 1 Corinthians 4:1-5). Wicked men, under cover of religion and devotion, may cover their malice and hatred for a time, but it will be revealed at God's appointed time and in God's appointed way to their everlasting shame.

Fear God Rather Than Man

Like Daniel and his friends, we must be willing to surrender anything and everything, even life itself, rather than compromise the glory of God, violate the truth of God, or go against the Word of God. The wrath of man may be hard to bear, but it is infinitely easier to bear than the wrath of God. Let us ever be faithful to our God.

Our Master here tells us to blow the trumpet of the everlasting gospel, to loudly and publicly proclaim to all the truths and mysteries of God's free grace, which he has made known to us. In quiet meditation, prayer, and study let every servant of Christ seek and receive God's message. Let none speak until spoken to by God; but once God speaks we are to proclaim his message everywhere. Receive the message like a whisper in your ear. Then sound it forth from "the housetops". Like the town-criers of old, get to the highest point possible and sound out the Word of the Lord. As Spurgeon put it, "Keep the study and the closet out of sight, and there in secret meet with Jesus, and then set the pulpit of testimony in as conspicuous a place as you can find." We are responsible to preach the gospel of Christ as fully and as widely as possible by every means at our disposal in the generation in which we live (vv. 27, 28).

Trust The Providential Care Of God

The path of duty may lead us into danger. Our lives may seem to be in peril if we go forward. But we must ever realize that everything is in God's hand. Whatever fearful thing we meet, as we serve our God, we may say to it, as our Lord did to Pilate, "Thou couldest have no power at all against me, except it were given thee from above" (John 19:11).

If our heavenly Father observes the death of even a sparrow (vv. 29-31), we ought to be confident that he will take care of us, even of the most minute concerns of our lives. His care for use extends even to the numbering of the hairs on our heads. Every circumstance of our lives is controlled by the arrangement of our heavenly Father's eternal love and grace toward us. Let us never look upon anything as a matter of chance. That which we experience day by day is but the fulfilling of our God's eternal purpose of grace for our everlasting good (Romans 8:28).

Live Constantly In The Anticipation Of Judgment And Eternity

It may cost you the sneers and frowns of men to confess Christ in this world. But it will cost you the frown of God in eternity to refuse to confess him (vv. 32, 33). Without question, these words extend to the whole of our lives. We must never blush to confess Christ and his gospel before the world that hates him. But the confession of Christ before men begins in baptism.

Believers confess Christ before men in believer's baptism. In baptism we confess our union with Christ and our confidence in him as our representative before God (Galatians 3:27). Being buried with Christ symbolically in the waters of baptism, we acknowledge our sin and its just punishment. We testify also of our faith in Christ's substitutionary death for the satisfaction of justice, by which our sins have been put away (Romans 6:3). Rising up from the watery grave, we confess our faith in the resurrection of Christ, our representative resurrection in Christ, our spiritual resurrection by Christ, and our bodily resurrection in the likeness of Christ (Romans 6:4; Colossians 2:12). Being raised up from spiritual death by the grace of God in regeneration, through the merits of Christ's obedience, we confess to God and all the world that we will henceforth "walk in newness of life', for the glory of our God. Our confession of faith is a confession of Christ. What an honour it is to confess him before men! What a reward it shall be to be confessed by him before his Father's throne in the last day!

To "deny" Christ is not to confess him. While baptism has nothing whatever to do with the accomplishment of our salvation, it is essential as a matter of obedience to our God and Saviour. I am often asked, "Can a person be saved without baptism?" The answer is obvious. Of course! All of God's people are saved without baptism. Salvation is by grace alone (Ephesians 2:8, 9). But refusal to be baptized is rebellion against the plain command of God. In the New Testament all who were received as brethren and regarded as believers were those who had been baptized. I cannot find one person regarded as a believer in the New Testament who refused baptism.

Here, our Lord warns us that those who refuse to confess him before men, he will refuse to confess before his Father's throne in heaven. What a solemn warning! To be disowned by the Son of God before his Father who is in heaven is to perish forever in hell!

Understand The Need To Separate From This World

If we would serve our God and the souls of men, we must understand the gospel of Christ is the cause of constant irreconcilable divisions among men (vv. 34-36). Wherever Christ comes there is a "division because of him". The gospel of Christ divides men and often divides families. Unity, peace, and harmony are great blessings. We ought to earnestly seek them, pray for them, and sacrifice anything to obtain them anything except the truth of God! Peace that is purchased at the expense of truth is purchased at a rate that ought never to be paid!

Take Up Our Cross And Follow Him Every Day

Faith in and obedience to Christ is nothing less than the surrender of my life to his rule as my Lord, my Saviour, and my King (vv. 37-39). Christ will not have me unless he has all of me. Spurgeon said, "No man has truly given himself to Christ unless he has said, 'My Lord, I give thee this day my body, my soul, my powers, my talents, my goods, my house, my children, and all that I have. Henceforth, I hold them at thy will, as a steward under thee. Thine they are. As for me, I have nothing. I have surrendered all to thee!'"

The Lord Jesus Christ is the Pearl of great price. If we would have him, we must sell all to get him (Matthew 13:45, 46). He said, "Whosoever he be of you that forsaketh not all that he hath, he cannot be my disciple" (Luke 14:33). If we would have Christ, we must surrender all to him.

Christianity, true Christianity, true saving faith involves a total surrender to Christ the Lord. Either you will be a servant under the dominion of King Jesus, voluntarily giving up all to his claims, or you will go to hell! You may not have to give up anything in actuality. But surrender to Christ must be just as real and complete in your heart as if you had actually given up everything, even down to life itself. Our Lord Jesus Christ requires total and unreserved surrender to himself. Christ will be Lord of all, or he will not be Lord at all. Is Jesus Christ, the Son of God, your Lord? Is he truly your Lord?

Do Not Expect Reward In This World, But In The World To Come

Whosoever shall give to drink unto one of these little ones a cup of cold water only in the name of a disciple, verily I say unto you, he shall in no wise lose his reward." (vv. 40-42).

What a blessed word this is! God's people are so thoroughly and completely one with Christ that to receive one of his is to receive him. There is a special word of encouragement here to those who are sent by Christ to preach his gospel. Gospel preachers are God's ambassadors to men. To receive Christ's messengers is to receive the Lord Jesus himself, and to receive the Lord Jesus is to receive God himself. That which is done to God's servants in this world, good or evil, is treated by our Lord as being done to him. And that which is done to Christ's redeemed ones, good or evil, is considered by our Redeemer as being done to him (Matthew 25:31-46).

The least service done for our Lord is observed by him and shall be honoured by him. He that gives but "a cup of cold water" to one of his little ones, as a disciple, "shall receive a righteous man's reward", and shall never lose it.

The eyes of our God and Saviour are always upon those who serve him. We may be unnoticed by others; but we are not insignificant in the eyes of our God. He observes those who oppose and oppress us. And he takes notice of those who help. He took notice of Diotrephes, who opposed John. And he took notice of Lydia, who assisted Paul. All these things are written down in the great book of his remembrance, and will be brought to light at the last day. The chief butler forgot Joseph when he was restored to his place. But the Lord Jesus never forgets any of his people and counts the least, most insignificant service done for his honour and in his name as the greatest (Mark 14:3-9). It matters not whether we preach the gospel to great multitudes, or open our homes to his children, or give a cup of cold water in his name, all are the same in his sight. We are responsible only to do that which he gives us opportunity and ability to do. And all that is done for him is accepted and honoured by him (1 Samuel 2:30).

Are we helpers or hinderers in the cause of Christ? Do we assist God's servants, or do we impede their labours? Do we aid his little ones, or do we stand in their way? These are serious questions that ought to be considered by us. God give us grace, as often as we have opportunity, to give "a cup of cold water", or "receive a prophet", or "receive a righteous man", in the name of Christ, labouring together in the Lord's vineyard to gather in his harvest. We should, each of us, make it our business to leave this world better than it was when we entered it. If we follow Christ, if we serve God, if we serve the souls of men, we shall.

Make me a channel of blessing today,
Make me a channel of blessing, I pray;
My life possessing, my service blessing,
Make me a channel of blessing today.

Chapter 24

A Vindication, A Warning, And An Invitation

"And it came to pass, when Jesus had made an end of commanding his twelve disciples, he departed thence to teach and to preach in their cities. Now when John had heard in the prison the works of Christ, he sent two of his disciples, And said unto him, Art thou he that should come, or do we look for another? Jesus answered and said unto them, Go and shew John again those things which ye do hear and see: The blind receive their sight, and the lame walk, the lepers are cleansed, and the deaf hear, the dead are raised up, and the poor have the gospel preached to them. And blessed is he, whosoever shall not be offended in me. And as they departed, Jesus began to say unto the multitudes concerning John, What went ye out into the wilderness to see? A reed shaken with the wind? But what went ye out for to see? A man clothed in soft raiment? behold, they that wear soft clothing are in kings' houses. But what went ye out for to see? A prophet? yea, I say unto you, and more than a prophet. For this is he, of whom it is written, Behold, I send my messenger before thy face, which shall prepare thy way before thee. Verily I say unto you, Among them that are born of women there hath not risen a greater than John the Baptist: notwithstanding he that is least in the kingdom of heaven is greater than he. And from the days of John the Baptist until now the kingdom of heaven suffereth violence, and the violent take it by force. For all the prophets and the law prophesied until John. And if ye will receive it, this is Elias, which was for to come. He that hath ears to hear, let him hear. But whereunto shall I liken this generation? It is like unto children sitting in the markets, and calling unto their fellows, And saying, We have piped unto you, and ye have not danced; we have mourned unto you, and ye have not lamented. For John came neither eating nor drinking, and they say, He hath a devil. The Son of man came eating and drinking, and they say, Behold a man gluttonous, and a winebibber, a friend of publicans and sinners. But wisdom is justified of her children. Then began he to upbraid the cities wherein most of his mighty works were done, because they repented not: Woe unto thee, Chorazin! woe unto thee, Bethsaida! for if the mighty works, which were done in you, had been done in Tyre and Sidon, they would have repented long ago in sackcloth and ashes. But I

say unto you, It shall be more tolerable for Tyre and Sidon at the day of judgment, than for you. And thou, Capernaum, which art exalted unto heaven, shalt be brought down to hell: for if the mighty works, which have been done in thee, had been done in Sodom, it would have remained until this day. But I say unto you, That it shall be more tolerable for the land of Sodom in the day of judgment, than for thee. At that time Jesus answered and said, I thank thee, O Father, Lord of heaven and earth, because thou hast hid these things from the wise and prudent, and hast revealed them unto babes. Even so, Father: for so it seemed good in thy sight. All things are delivered unto me of my Father: and no man knoweth the Son, but the Father; neither knoweth any man the Father, save the Son, and he to whomsoever the Son will reveal him. Come unto me, all ye that labour and are heavy laden, and I will give you rest. Take my yoke upon you, and learn of me; for I am meek and lowly in heart: and ye shall find rest unto your souls. For my yoke is easy, and my burden is light."
(Matthew 11:1-30)

Our Master sent his original preachers out in pairs to preach the gospel in all the cities of Israel. Then, it seems, he followed them in person, to confirm their message by his own word of instruction. Thus, in the mouth of two and three witnesses, every word was established (Matthew 18:16; Deuteronomy 17:6).

Notice the words "their cities". That is an unusual expression. It appears that wherever the Lord sent a pair of gospel preachers, he gave the city to them. That city became their responsibility and their possession in a strictly spiritual sense, as the peculiar and particular domain of their labours. As the Lord Jesus entrusted Jerusalem to the hands of Peter and James, so he entrusts to each of his servants the care of his church wherever he places them (Acts 20:28; 1 Peter 5:1-4). Then, at the time appointed, Christ will come to take his sheep from the hands of his servants into his own hands. What a privilege that man has to whom the Son of God entrusts the care of his people, and what a responsibility!

In this chapter we will hear the Lord Jesus speaking to a great mixed multitude, of genuine believers, of curious, questioning people, of religious hypocrites, of unconcerned unbelievers, and of weary sinners in need of his mercy and grace. In these thirty verses our Lord Jesus vindicates the ministry of John the Baptist, warns men against despising the gospel, and graciously invites weary, heavy-laden sinners to come to him for rest.

A Word For A Troubled Disciple

"Now when John had heard in the prison the works of Christ, he sent two of his disciples, And said unto him, Art thou he that should come, or do we look for another? Jesus answered and said unto them, Go and show John again those things which ye do hear and see: The blind receive their sight, and the lame walk, the lepers are cleansed, and the deaf hear, the dead are raised up, and the poor have the gospel preached to them. And blessed is he, whosoever shall not be offended in me" (vv. 2-6).

John the Baptist was in prison for honestly telling Herod that his intention of taking his brother Philip's wife was unlawful (Matthew 14:4). He must have realized, perhaps by special revelation from God, that he would never be released. He was soon to be executed. Because of his testimony for Christ, the greatest preacher the world had ever known, except for the Lord Jesus himself, was beheaded.

Perhaps, in his low condition, when his heart was heavy, John began to doubt everything he had believed and preached. I know some strongly object to the idea that true believers sometimes have doubts and fears. They confidently assert, "He who doubts is damned". But that is not so. Many of God's dear saints have a weak faith that is often troubled with doubts and fears. And many who are very strong in faith are sometimes weak. Gideon asked for a sign because he doubted. Elijah fled from Jezebel because he feared. Peter temporarily went back to his fishing career because he thought all hope for him was lost.

It is not our faith that saves us, but Christ, the Object of our faith. Weak faith is not necessarily false faith. And strong faith is not necessarily true faith. What, or rather, *who* is the object of your faith? That is the question! If your faith is pitched upon the Lord Jesus Christ alone, be it weak or strong, it is true faith.

To give John the assurance that he sought, he pointed this troubled heart to three things. First, the Lord Jesus pointed John and his disciples to himself and to his works (vv. 4, 5). Then he pointed them to the scriptures, the holy Word of God (Isaiah 29:18; 35:4-6; 42:6, 7; 61:1). Finally, he pointed John the Baptist to his own persevering allegiance to him (v. 6). Those who endure to the end, who follow Christ unto death, who are not offended at him, with him, or in him, have evidence of grace in them.

Yet, I am of the opinion that John's question was intended not for himself, but for the benefit of his disciples. Perhaps he sent his disciples to the Lord Jesus because he wanted to have them see for themselves the power and glory of Christ. Perhaps he wanted to put an end to the jealousy that had arisen between his disciples and the Lord's disciples. Perhaps he sent his disciples to the Lord Jesus, as his dying act, to urge them to cleave to Christ alone. Whatever his reason, I cannot imagine that John himself had any doubts concerning Christ. He had given clear testimony to the Redeemer's person and work, being convinced of God regarding him (Matthew 3:13-17; John 1:29-34). He sent his disciples to the Lord Jesus that they might be personally convinced of him.

Whether John's action here indicates a time of doubt and unbelief on his part, or on the part of his disciples, what a gracious testimony the Lord Jesus provides for his poor, doubting, fearful disciples, who, in the absence of other evidences, can still say they love him, even when their behaviour suggests otherwise (John 21:17). The Lord God says, "When I see the blood, I will pass over you". He does not say, "When you see the blood". He saw the blood before you did. He saw the blood when you did. He sees the blood now. He sees the blood better than you ever can. And he will see the blood, even if the time comes, through sickness, trouble or age, when you cannot see it!

A Word Of Vindication For His Prophet

"And as they departed, Jesus began to say unto the multitudes concerning John, What went ye out into the wilderness to see?" (vv. 7-15).

People are always curious about a preacher who is a bit unusual, who does not fit the mould of what men think a preacher should be, or who creates a stir among men. The same thing was true in that day. People were curious about John the Baptist. When they went out to hear him, they expected to see and hear a preacher just like the others they knew, perhaps one who could preach a little better than the others. They expected to see a timid, unstable, vacillating "reed shaken with the wind" (v. 7). They went out to hear John, expecting to see a worldly, pampered, easy living man (v. 8). But when they met and heard John the Baptist, for the first time in their lives, they met and heard a prophet of God. John was a bold preacher of repentance. He was a self-denying prophet of God, content to wear camel's hair, rather than gorgeous robes. More than a prophet, John was the forerunner of Christ. He was that Elijah of whom Malachi spoke (vv. 9-15). Robert Hawker's comments on verse 10, as compared with Malachi's prophecy are excellent:

> I conceive the 10th verse to be the most weighty. If the reader will turn to the scripture, which the Lord Jesus quotes from his servant, the Prophet Malachi (Chapter 3:1), he will discover a very striking

> difference in the manner in which Jesus useth the words, from what, they are there. In the words of the Prophet, it is Jehovah the Lord of Hosts speaking to the Church concerning John: He shall prepare the way before *me*. But here, as the Lord of his temple, Christ is spoken *to* on the same subject; and now the words are, "Behold I send my messenger before thy face, which shall prepare thy way before thee." What a decisive proof of the Oneness in the divine nature, in the *me* and *thee*; Jehovah's *way* and Christ the Mediator's *way* is one and the same. And what can be more full in pointing to the Godhead of Christ? And hence it must undeniably follow, that the way of both, being one and the same; He who is the Lord of his temple, and the Angel of the covenant, is One, with the other Persons of Jehovah, in nature, in essence, in way, will, and work; in property, honour, and worship; and in all the divine attributes, perfections, and glory! Hail! thou Almighty Jesus, whom all thy people delight in! Oh! for ears to hear what the Spirit saith concerning thee to the Churches!

All God's prophets are the forerunners of Christ. As the Lord Jesus vindicated John, so he will vindicate and honour all who serve his interests in this world (1 Samuel 2:30). He will honour his servant in time by honouring his labours, blessing them to the hearts of his people. And he will vindicate and honour his servant in the day of judgment (Matthew 25:34; 1 Corinthians 4:1-5). Let no servant of God despise "the day of small things". At his own appointed time and in his own appointed way, God honours those who honour him (2 Corinthians 2:14-17).

A Word About Preacher Critics

In every generation (and in most local churches) there are many carping critics who are convinced that it is their unique calling to nit-pick everything a faithful gospel preacher declares. They are totally unconcerned about the glory of God, the gospel of his grace, and faith in Christ. They can never be taught anything, because they know everything. In a word, they are lost religious men and women, acting like peevish, pouting children playing games (vv. 16, 17). They always find convenient excuses for not hearing God's messengers. The Pharisees thought

John was too strict, so they refused to hear him. They thought the Lord Jesus was too loose, so they refused to hear him (vv. 18, 19).

The fact is neither the sweet melody of grace and salvation by Christ, nor the terrible thunders of the law of Moses have the least influence on the unregenerate heart. The silly behaviour of ignorant children is a striking illustration of a lost religious man's obstinacy to the things of God. From such obstinacy only God the Holy Spirit, by omnipotent grace, can deliver a sinner.

A Word To Those Who Hear The Gospel

"Then began he to upbraid the cities wherein most of his mighty works were done, because they repented not: Woe unto thee, Chorazin! woe unto thee, Bethsaida! for if the mighty works, which were done in you, had been done in Tyre and Sidon, they would have repented long ago in sackcloth and ashes. But I say unto you, It shall be more tolerable for Tyre and Sidon at the day of judgment, than for you. And thou, Capernaum, which art exalted unto heaven, shalt be brought down to hell: for if the mighty works, which have been done in thee, had been done in Sodom, it would have remained until this day. But I say unto you, That it shall be more tolerable for the land of Sodom in the day of judgment, than for thee" (vv. 20-24).

Every time I read these verses of holy scripture, two striking facts are forcibly driven home to my heart by the Spirit of God. First, God almighty is totally sovereign in providence and grace. He sends the gospel to whom he will! And second, the most heinous wickedness in this world is the sin of unbelief! Those people who hear the gospel and yet believe it not are guilty of the greatest evil in the world. They may be moral, descent, and respectable in behaviour before men; but before God they are guilty of crimes far more abominable than the idolatries of Tyre and Sidon, and more vile than the homosexuality of Sodom. That crime is wilful unbelief (Proverbs 1:23-33; 29:1). In the light of what is said here of Chorazin and Bethsaida, and the great woe pronounced upon those cities, which were favoured with such high privileges and regarded them not, I cannot help thinking, "What horrid condemnation awaits this generation in hell"!

A Word Of Praise And Thanksgiving

Now the Lord Jesus gives thanks to his Father and ours for the distinguishing grace bestowed upon chosen sinners. "I thank thee, O Father, Lord of heaven and earth, because thou hast hid these things from the wise and prudent, and hast revealed them unto babes" (vv. 25, 26).

While hiding the wonders of redemption from "the wise in their own eyes, and prudent in their own sight" (Isaiah 5:21), the Lord reveals his mercy unto the humble and the lowly. Salvation comes by divine revelation. But this revelation of grace never comes to any but those who receive the Word of God by faith as humble children. God will never lift up any by his grace until he has brought them down to need his grace. He will never teach any until they are made to see that they need to learn of him.

Our Saviour here assigns to God's own appointment, decree, and sovereign pleasure alone the cause of salvation. "To all the bold and presumptuous reasonings of the human mind, which have been or may be hereafter brought forward, against the exercise of Jehovah's sovereignty", Robert Hawker wrote, "the answer is direct. 'Shall not the Judge of all the earth do right?' Surely the Lord is not called upon to give account of the motives of his holy will and pleasure to any of his creatures. One thing we know, namely, that 'his counsel and purpose must stand, and he will do all his pleasure', and that all He doeth is right. His conduct towards his creatures is by an unerring standard. His mercy is not moved by any good in us, neither is it kept back by our undeservings; for neither our merit, nor our misery, can be said to have had any hand in disposing the purposes of his sovereign will towards us. That the Lord hath taken occasion from our misery to magnify the abounding riches of his mercy, is true; but then his mercy was before our misery, and his own everlasting love the sole cause of our blessedness in Christ, therefore our Lord's own words are most blessed in point: 'Even so Father! for so it seemed good in thy sight!'"

A Word For Needy Souls

We usually think of the words of verses 27-30 as being a gospel invitation addressed to the lost, "Come unto me, all ye that labour and are heavy laden, and I will give you rest". But we must not place such a limitation upon them. They are gospel words addressed to needy souls, both the lost and the saved. Here is a declaration of our blessed Saviour's greatness. "All things are delivered unto me of my Father: and no man knoweth the Son, but the Father; neither knoweth any man the Father, save the Son, and he to whomsoever the Son will reveal him" (v. 27). This is to be understood of Christ, as our Mediator. As God nothing was delivered to him. In his essential divinity the Son possesses all things eternally with the Father and the Spirit. As our Mediator all creatures, all men and angels, good and bad were delivered into his hands. Indeed, all creation was put in his hands to be ruled and disposed of by him for the glory of the triune God in the salvation of his people (John 17:2). All God's elect were delivered to him to be kept and saved by him. They are all "preserved in Jesus Christ" (Jude 1) from all eternity. All power in heaven and in earth are his. All the treasures of wisdom and knowledge are in him. All the blessings of grace, all the promises of mercy in the everlasting covenant, and all the glory and happiness of his people are in his hands.

So infinitely great are the mysteries here spoken of that our Saviour says, "and no man knoweth the Son, but the Father". No mere mortal knows the transcendent glories and perfections of the Son of God, or the fulness of his works and offices as our covenant Surety and Mediator, or all that is committed to his charge from eternity as Jehovah's righteous Servant. We shall spend eternity discovering all that he was commissioned and volunteered to do, and suffer for us, all that he has done for us, and all that he has bestowed upon us as the blessings of his grace from eternity as our Saviour (Ephesians 1:3).

"Neither knoweth any man the Father, save the Son". No man knows the infinite, eternal glory and essence of God as God, except that Man who is God our Saviour. None know the mind and will of the triune God, none know his purposes and decrees, none know his infinite grace and fulness of love toward chosen sinners, and none know the things he has prepared and laid up for us, the things he will give us in our eternal inheritance with Christ, except Christ himself "and he to whomsoever the Son will reveal him". What sweet, sweet words of grace and assurance these are! There is among the fallen sons and daughters of Adam a people to whom the Lord Jesus Christ reveals all the glory and grace of the triune God by his Spirit, according to his own sovereign will and pleasure.

"It pleased the Father that in him should all fulness dwell" (Colossians 1:19). It is the purpose and pleasure of the triune God that all the fulness of grace and glory dwell in the Lord Jesus Christ, our God-man Mediator and Saviour. Whatever we get from God we receive of his fulness (John 1:14-16). All things were created by him. All things were created for him. He is before all things. By him all things consist. God the Father has given him pre-eminence in all things. And all things shall be reconciled to God by him. Dwelling forever in the Lord Jesus Christ there is a superlative, infinite, immeasurable wealth of grace and glory. He is an artesian well of fulness. Everything is in him.

In verses 28-30 Jesus Christ, the Son of God, the Saviour of the world, commands, invites, and persuades sinners to come to him, promising salvation and eternal life to all who do. "Come unto me". The Lord Jesus calls sinners to come to him. He does not call us to come to an altar, the church, a priest, a preacher, a baptistery, the Lord's table, the law of Moses, or even to his doctrine. He says, "Come unto me"! What does that mean? What is it to come to Christ? He does not leave us to guess about that. He explains his meaning in John 6:35. To come to Christ is to believe on him. It is an act of faith.

"Come unto me, all ye that labour and are heavy laden". The word that is here translated "labour" means "toil with weariness". All who toil with weariness and are heavy laden, burdened down with a load they cannot get rid of, are bidden to come to Christ. Some labour and are heavy laden, seeking salvation by their own righteousness, by their own works. They are engaged in an impossible task.

If that is your case, quit trying to save yourself, and come to Christ (1 John 1:7, 9; Romans 10:1-4; Galatians 3:10-13). Are you labouring and are heavy laden with the temptations of the devil, inward corruption, unbelief, or worldly care? Come to Christ (Hebrews 2:18). The Lord Jesus Christ promises that he will, without exception, receive all who come to God by him (John 6:37).

"And I will give you rest"! This word "rest" expresses much more than relaxation. It also has in it the idea of refreshment. This is the rest our Saviour gives to sinners, both a cessation from labour and a reviving of life. It is *given* rest. It cost him dear but he gives it to us freely. He earned it and bought it for us. Now he gives it freely to all who trust in him. It is a present rest. All who believe do, when they believe, enter into rest, the rest of faith (Hebrews 4:3). And this is a satisfying rest because it is a rest from all guilt and fear, a rest from all toil and legal work, a rest from all curse and condemnation, a complete rest from the law (Romans 7:4; 8:1; 10:4). And the rest promised in this passage is, also, a future rest (Hebrews 4:9). It is a rest beyond all that can be experienced here. It is the perfect rest of complete salvation: a rest from all sin, a rest from all afflictions, a rest from all temptations, a rest from all sorrow, a rest from all unsatisfied desires!

"Take my yoke upon you". This is a call to voluntary submission and obedience. It is something we must do. We must bow to and slip upon ourselves the yoke of his profession, the yoke of his precepts, the yoke of his providence.

"And learn of me for I am meek and lowly in heart". Here is the appointed means by which sinners are enabled to bear this threefold yoke. He has given us an example to follow. He endured great hardship for us (Hebrews 12:3). He became obedient to God to save us (Philippians 2:5-8). He submitted to the will of God for us (John 18:11). In all these things, our Redeemer has left us an example that we should follow his steps (1 Peter 2:21-25).

"And ye shall find rest unto your souls." Trusting Christ alone as Saviour and Lord, God's elect find rest for their souls. Trusting his obedience unto death as our only righteousness and redemption, we obtain the rest of a good conscience. Following his steps, trusting and obeying his revealed will, we obtain the rest of a faithful servant. Trusting his providence, we obtain the rest of a believing heart.

"For my yoke is easy and my burden is light." All who come to Christ find it to be so. The easiest, most pleasant, most tranquil existence in this world is the life of faith in, submission to, and obedience to the Lord Jesus Christ. He calls you now to this life in him. Christ's yoke, to a believer, is no more of a burden than feathers are to a bird. His commandments are not grievous. His ways are the ways of pleasantness. All his paths are peace (1 John 5:3; Proverbs 3:17). Oh for grace to be always coming to Christ! Always free, yet ever bearing his yoke, always enjoying his rest, yet always finding more! This is the experience of those who are ever coming to Christ for everything. Blessed heritage of grace, and it is ours in and by our great God and Saviour, the Lord Jesus Christ!

Chapter 25

The Lord Of The Sabbath

"At that time Jesus went on the sabbath day through the corn; and his disciples were an hungred, and began to pluck the ears of corn, and to eat. But when the Pharisees saw it, they said unto him, Behold, thy disciples do that which is not lawful to do upon the sabbath day. But he said unto them, Have ye not read what David did, when he was an hungred, and they that were with him; How he entered into the house of God, and did eat the shewbread, which was not lawful for him to eat, neither for them which were with him, but only for the priests? Or have ye not read in the law, how that on the sabbath days the priests in the temple profane the sabbath, and are blameless? But I say unto you, That in this place is one greater than the temple. But if ye had known what this meaneth, I will have mercy, and not sacrifice, ye would not have condemned the guiltless. For the Son of man is Lord even of the sabbath day. And when he was departed thence, he went into their synagogue: And, behold, there was a man which had his hand withered. And they asked him, saying, Is it lawful to heal on the sabbath days? that they might accuse him. And he said unto them, What man shall there be among you, that shall have one sheep, and if it fall into a pit on the sabbath day, will he not lay hold on it, and lift it out? How much then is a man better than a sheep? Wherefore it is lawful to do well on the sabbath days. Then saith he to the man, Stretch forth thine hand. And he stretched it forth; and it was restored whole, like as the other. Then the Pharisees went out, and held a council against him, how they might destroy him."
(Matthew 12:1-14)

The subject which stands out pre-eminently in these fourteen verses is that of the sabbath day. It is a subject about which the Jews of our Lord's day were very sensitive and held many strange and absurd opinions. Many today are just as sensitive as they were and hold opinions just as bizarre as theirs. The Pharisees had added their traditions to the teachings of scripture and made Sabbath day observance the control and primary part of their religious legalism, as it is unto this day. This is a subject about which many, throughout the history of the church, have held different opinions, and held them very strongly, even to the point of having no fellowship with those who disagreed with them. This is a subject about which we need to have a clear understanding.

When our Lord's disciples began to pick corn and eat it, as they walked through the fields, the Pharisees became enraged. When they did, the Lord Jesus seized the opportunity to give words of clear instruction regarding the sabbath, about himself, and concerning the uselessness of legalistic, graceless religion. In these fourteen verses our Saviour shows himself to be the Lord of the Sabbath.

The Fallacy Of The Pharisees

Sabbath observance was the very heart of Jewish religion. When the Lord Jesus gave tacit approval to what the Jews considered a violation of sabbatical law, he touched a raw nerve. Several things need to be observed here.

Our Saviour never violated God's law regarding the Sabbath, or anything else. He perfectly fulfilled the law. Our Lord's disciples here violated Jewish tradition, not Mosaic law. People were allowed by law to take ears of corn as they walked through the fields. The objection of the Pharisees was to the Lord's disciples doing so on the sabbath day. To their hypercritical minds plucking was reaping, and rubbing the grain from the husk was threshing.

They regarded their customs and traditions and fancies as a code of law. According to their traditions, the disciples were doing "that which is not lawful to do upon the sabbath day". It is not insignificant to take notice of the fact that our Lord and his disciples were poor men, and that he who fed the multitudes used no miraculous power to feed his own followers. They were compelled to get a little food for their stomachs the way other poor people would, by walking through fields belonging to others and picking corn. The Son of God bribes none into following him with the promise of wealth.

This incident was not accidental. The words "at that time" direct our attention to the preceding verses. Our Lord is about to demonstrate that he is the Sabbath in whom sinners find rest for their souls (11:28-30).

The word "sabbath" carries the idea of ceasing from work: of rest, and inactivity (Genesis 2:2, 3; Exodus 20:9-11). Like all other aspects of Old Testament law, the sabbath was a picture of Christ, and pointed men to him in whom we find rest (Hebrews 4:1-10).

The fallacy of the Pharisees here was the same as it is now. They made the Word of God of none effect by their traditions (Matthew 15:6). The Old Testament law was still in effect when our Lord began his ministry. He and his disciples honoured the law. But this breach of religious tradition, the Pharisees considered a breach of God's law. We are told that just one section of the Jewish Talmud contains twenty-four chapters of sabbatical laws!

Instead of being a day of rest, the sabbath had become a day of incredible burden because of all the man-made restrictions imposed by the rabbis in the name of God. As one man observed, "It was harder to rest on the sabbath than it was to work the other six days of the week." The sabbath was anything but a day of rest. It had become a day of frustration, anxiety, fear, and religious manipulation, imposed by ungodly, religious legalists, who had made the people "Weary and heavy-laden" (Matthew 11:28). The Lord's disciples were not reaping on the sabbath. They were simply eating as they walked. But the Talmud (the written traditions of the Jews) forbade the rubbing of corn on the sabbath!

The Significance Of The Sabbath

In verses 3 to 8 our Lord Jesus shows how contemptuous he was of the Pharisees and their religious traditions. His questions (vv. 3 and 5) are scathingly sarcastic! They cut deep into the Pharisees' pride. One can almost see them wincing with pain and anger.

Like the other commandments, the sabbath day was intended to promote love to God and to one another. But the scribes and Pharisees knew nothing of love. These legalists lived only to fulfil lifeless, loveless duties, which made them feel good about themselves.

The laws regarding the sabbath were never intended to restrict deeds of necessity (vv. 3, 4; 1 Samuel 21:6), restrict service to God (vv. 5, 6), or restrict acts of mercy (vv. 7, 8). We should always choose mercy and compassion when there is a question between that and dogma, ritual, and religious ceremony (v. 7).

In verses 6 and 8 our Saviour, the Son of Man, claims divinity, supremacy, and sovereignty as he who is greater than the temple and "Lord even of the sabbath". He is Lord of everything, even of the law and all that concerns God and man. As the Son of Man, our divine Mediator, into whose hands the Father has delivered all things (Matthew 11:27), arranges and disposes of sabbaths as he pleases. He declares that even in the legal dispensation the sabbath was not profaned by works of necessity, devotion, and mercy. Certainly, in this gospel day we should never pay the least measure of attention to the sharp speeches of hypercritical legalists who strain the sabbatical law and make a yoke of bondage of that which was intended to point us to the holy rest of faith in Christ.

The Manifestation Of Mercy

The Lord Jesus showed great honour to the matter of public worship (v. 9; Hebrews 10:25). He had nothing to gain from it and nothing to learn by it; synagogue worship was a perverted form of worship. Yet, our Lord attended the worship of God for the glory of God and the benefit of others. If our Saviour made it his business to be in the house of God on the appointed day of worship, how dare we neglect this blessed ordinance of our God?

The Pharisees sought to entrap the Master (v. 10). They chose a man whose hand was withered, not one who was dying. Then, they raised a question, not to learn, but to condemn. "They asked him, saying, Is it lawful to heal on the sabbath days? that they might accuse him." Such behaviour is common among religious legalists. They seek to entrap, that they might accuse and condemn.

The Lord Jesus shamed the Pharisees into silence (vv. 11, 12). Not even a Pharisee would contend that sheep are more valuable than men, who are created in the image of God. Yet, in practice they treated other men with less respect than they did brute beasts in the name of religion. Our Lord answered their question emphatically by saying to them, "It is lawful to do well on sabbath days". Then, he showed himself to be God by an act of omnipotent mercy. "Then saith he to the man, Stretch forth thine hand. And he stretched it forth; and it was restored whole, like as the other."

There are important spiritual lessons to be gleaned from this incident. This man with a withered hand was found in the house of God. Though his hand was withered, he came to the place where God promised to meet with men. He was found waiting on the Lord in the place of the Lord's own appointing. There is no indication that he knew the Lord Jesus, much less that he sought his merciful intervention. Prevenient grace put him in the way of grace. The Lord Jesus knew this poor man was in the synagogue. And he, of whom it is written that "he must needs go through Samaria", because there was a poor woman there for whom "the time of love" had come (John 4:4), went to this particular synagogue on this particular sabbath day, because "the time of love" had come for this poor man with a withered hand. Here our Saviour had come to fulfil his own words, "I am found of them that sought me not" (Isaiah 65:1).

With the command of grace, "Stretch forth thine hand", came the power of grace to obey the command. "Christ's biddings are enablings", says Robert Hawker. It was impossible for this man to do what the Master here called him to do. Yet, he did it, because he who called him is God with whom all things are possible. So it is with the call of Christ by his Spirit to poor sinners. When he says to those who cannot and will not come to him, “Come unto me”, they come to him, being enabled and compelled by omnipotent mercy to obey his call. Did he not mysteriously and secretly communicate the ability to obey, none ever could or would obey his call. This blessed truth applies to every aspect of our lives. Without him we can do nothing (John 15:5). Yet, because it is God who works in us to will and to do of his own good pleasure, when he bids us work out our own salvation with fear and trembling, we can do all things through Christ who strengthens us (Philippians 2:12, 13; 4:13). The same grace that calls gives ability to obey.

The Rage Of The Religionists

“Then the Pharisees went out, and held a council against him, how they might destroy him” (v. 14). Mark tells us (Mark 3:6) that these Pharisees joined forces with the Herodians, their archenemies, the worldly political party who supported Herod, in order to destroy Christ. They were determined to rid the world of him at any cost. Why? Because he exposed their inward emptiness and sin. He denounced their outward religious rituals. He disregarded the traditions of their fathers. And he taught salvation by grace alone!

Legalism is the implacable enemy of grace (Galatians 3:3; 5:2-4). There is no room for sabbath keeping in this dispensation of grace. Christ is our Sabbath (Colossians 2:16, 17). Christians have, since the earliest days of church history (Acts 20:7; 1 Corinthians 16:2), set aside Sunday, the first day of the week, as a special day of worship, fellowship, and divine service, because that is the day our Lord was raised. John called it “The Lord’s Day” (Revelation 1:10); but it is not, in any way, a “Christian sabbath”.

Christ Our Sabbath

Allow me to conclude this study by giving that which I believe to be the clear teaching of holy scripture with regard to sabbath keeping. I do so because multitudes are still here in bondage to the law who have no reason to be. In Isaiah 58:13 the Lord God tells us to “call the sabbath a delight”.

When can we, when do we, “Call the sabbath a delight”? We can and do call the sabbath a delight only when we are brought to the blessed rest of faith in Christ, who is our Sabbath, when we keep the sabbath of faith, ceasing from our own works and resting in Christ alone for our entire acceptance with God.

When a person turns from his own way, from his sin, from the pleasure of his depraved heart, and from this world, to the Lord Jesus Christ, finding rest in him, he finds that Christ, in whom he rests, is a delight, a luxury, and that faith in him is an honour. Indeed, all who trust Christ delight in him, triumph over all their foes in him, and shall at last obtain the full heritage of the heavenly Canaan called, "the heritage of Jacob". "For the mouth of the Lord hath spoken it".

The Legal Sabbath

We need to understand that the Sabbath, which God required the Jews to keep, was only a temporary, typical ordinance, which represented Christ and our redemption by him. When the Lord God instituted sabbath keeping to the Jews in the legal dispensation, he gave two reasons for it.

First, the sabbath was to be kept as a symbol of God's rest (Exodus 20:8-11). It represented the completion of God's creation and the satisfaction of God in his work. Though God's work of creation has been marred by the sin and fall of our race, the sabbath day portrayed a blessed day of glorious rest called "the times of restitution of all things" (Acts 3:21; Colossians 1:20; Ephesians 1:10), when all things shall be restored to God.

Second, the sabbath day was a constant reminder of Israel's redemption out of Egypt. Hence, it was a picture of our redemption by Christ (Deuteronomy 5:15). In other words, the sabbath day, like all other aspects of the Mosaic law, was a picture prophecy of our perfect redemption by Christ. As the Jews rested on the seventh day of the week from all their works, so believers find perfect rest and peace in the Lord Jesus Christ.

Christ Our Sabbath

We can and will call the sabbath a delight only when we understand that Christ is our Sabbath. We do not observe a literal, legal sabbath day, because Christ is our Sabbath, and we rest in him. I know many who pretend to keep a literal sabbath day. Many try their best to delight in legal sabbath work. But I do not know a sabbatarian in the world who really delights in his attempts at sabbath keeping, not a single one. Every sabbatarian I know finds the yoke of their legal observance oppressive and galling. It is a spiritual flagellation they feel they must perform in order to be holy.

Sabbath keeping, like animal sacrifices, was a part of the Old Testament law. It has nothing to do with New Testament worship. I know that the sabbath day is frequently mentioned in the four gospels and the Book of Acts during that transitional period in which the church of God passed from the Old Testament era into the New. However, it is always mentioned in connection with the Jews and

Jewish worship in the temple, or in their synagogues. But it is mentioned only two times in all the Epistles (Romans through Revelation).

In Colossians 2:16, 17 we read, "Let no man therefore judge you in meat, or in drink, or in respect of an holyday, or of the new moon, or of the sabbath days: Which are a shadow of things to come; but the body is of Christ." Here the apostle Paul forbids the observance of legal sabbath days. He does so on the basis that in Christ, God's elect are entirely free from the law (Romans 7:4; 10:4).

In Hebrews 4:3, 4, 9-11 the sabbath that remains in this gospel age is called "rest". Here the Apostle shows us that all who believe on the Lord Jesus Christ keep the sabbath in a spiritual way. That is to say, they, and they only, truly keep the sabbath by faith in him, and by resting in him.

Finished Work

We can and will call the sabbath a delight when we realize that our all glorious Saviour, the Lord Jesus Christ, our Mediator, has entered into his rest, and his rest is glorious, because he has finished his work (Hebrews 4:10; Isaiah 11:10). Our Saviour's rest in heaven is glorious and it is his glory. "His rest shall be glory"! As God rested on the seventh day, because his work of creation was finished, so the God-man our Mediator has entered into his rest in heaven, because he has made all things new for his people, having finished his work of redemption (Romans 8:34; 2 Corinthians 5:17-21; Hebrews 10:10-14).

Behold our exalted Saviour! Do you see him seated upon his throne in heaven? There he sits in undisturbed and undisturbable sovereign serenity! His rest is his glory (John 17:2; Philippians 2:9-11). That exalted God-man, as our divinely appointed Representative, has fulfilled all the legal sabbath requirements for us, even as he did all the other requirements of the law. Now, in heaven, he is keeping an everlasting sabbath rest (Isaiah 53:10-12). And his rest, which is his glory, tells us that he has finished his work (John 17:4; 19:30), the salvation of his people is certain (Hebrews 9:12), and all his enemies shall soon be made his footstool (Hebrews 10:13). There is no more work to be done. Christ did it all! And when all the work was done for us, our blessed Saviour entered into his rest. Now, all who find rest in him call that sabbath a delight.

Sabbath Rest

All who believe on the Lord Jesus Christ keep the sabbath by faith (Hebrews 4:3), because we have entered into his rest; and we call this blessed sabbath rest of faith in Christ a delight, the delight of our souls. We do not yet keep the sabbath perfectly, because we do not yet trust our Saviour as we should. We do not yet trust him perfectly. But we do keep the sabbath truly and sincerely by faith. Our sabbath observance is not a carnal, literal thing. We do not keep a sabbath day. God forbids that (Colossians 2:16, 17). We keep the sabbath spiritually by faith.

Remember, the sabbath day was ordained by God in the ceremonial worship of the Jews in the Old Testament as a symbol of God's rest after creation and as a reminder of Israel's redemption out of Egypt. The essence of sabbath observation was self-denial and consecration to God. Anything personally profitable or pleasurable was expressly forbidden (Isaiah 56:2; 58:13; Ezekiel 20:12, 21). Sabbath observance was, in its essence, an unconditional, all-encompassing, self-denial. It was a renunciation of self and a dedication of one's self to God. That is exactly the way we observe the sabbath spiritually by faith in Christ, not one day in seven, but all the days of our lives. The believer's life is a perpetual keeping of the sabbath!

The Lord Jesus Christ gives rest to every sinner who comes to him in faith. He says, "Come unto me, all ye that labour and are heavy laden, and I will give you rest" (Matthew 11:28). Are you labouring and heavy-laden under the load of sin and guilt? Do you long for rest? In your inmost soul do you struggle hard with sin, longing to find peace with God? Will you hear what the Lord Jesus says? "Come"! That is: believe, trust, rely upon me. "Come unto me"! Not to the preacher. Not to my church. Not even to my doctrine. But "Come unto me, and I will give you rest"! When a sinner comes to Christ, he quits working for God's favour, because he rests his soul upon the finished work of his Substitute (1 Corinthians 1:30, 31).

Yet, this sabbath of faith involves more than a ceasing from our works and the remembrance of our redemption by Christ. It also involves, in its very essence, the consecration of our lives to our dear Saviour (Matthew 11:29, 30). We keep the sabbath of faith and find rest unto our souls as we wilfully, deliberately, wholeheartedly surrender to Christ as our Lord. If we would keep the sabbath, truly keep the sabbath, it will take considerably more than going to church on Sunday and reserving one day a week for religious exercises! We keep the sabbath by putting ourselves under the yoke of Christ's dominion, submitting to his will in all things, learning of him what to believe, how to live, and how to honour God. As we do, we find that his yoke is easy and his burden is light. When we submit to Christ's dominion, when we bow to his will, we find rest for our souls and "call the sabbath a delight"!

Chapter 26

Our Mediator, Jehovah's Servant

"Then the Pharisees went out, and held a council against him, how they might destroy him. But when Jesus knew it, he withdrew himself from thence: and great multitudes followed him, and he healed them all; And charged them that they should not make him known: That it might be fulfilled which was spoken by Esaias the prophet, saying, Behold my servant, whom I have chosen; my beloved, in whom my soul is well pleased: I will put my spirit upon him, and he shall shew judgment to the Gentiles. He shall not strive, nor cry; neither shall any man hear his voice in the streets. A bruised reed shall he not break, and smoking flax shall he not quench, till he send forth judgment unto victory. And in his name shall the Gentiles trust."
(Matthew 12:14-21)

In the first part of this chapter our Lord Jesus demonstrated his eternal deity and his great dignity as God, both by declaring himself to be Lord even of the sabbath and by healing the man with a withered hand. In the passage now before us the Holy Spirit shows us our Saviour's great humiliation as Jehovah's Servant, while at the same time demonstrating him to be himself Jehovah God and our great Saviour. Matthew Henry wrote in his introduction to this paragraph:

> As in the midst of Christ's greatest humiliations there were proofs of his dignity, so in the midst of his greatest honours, he gave proofs of his humility; and when the mighty works he did gave him an opportunity of making a figure (a name for himself), yet he made it appear that he emptied himself, and made himself of no reputation.

The Bond-Slave

When the Lord God began to give his judgments (civil statutes) to Israel, by which he typified and portrayed redemption, grace, and salvation by Christ,[2] the very first civil statute given to Israel was a blessed picture of redemption and grace by Christ in the law of the bond-slave (Exodus 21:1-6).

> Now these are the judgments which thou shalt set before them. If thou buy an Hebrew servant, six years he shall serve: and in the seventh he shall go out free for nothing. If he came in by himself, he shall go out by himself: if he were married, then his wife shall go out with him. If his master have given him a wife, and she have born him sons or daughters; the wife and her children shall be her master's, and he shall go out by himself. And if the servant shall plainly say, I love my master, my wife, and my children; I will not go out free: Then his master shall bring him unto the judges; he shall also bring him to the door, or unto the door post; and his master shall bore his ear through with an awl; and he shall serve him for ever.

The Servant spoken of in this passage of scripture, by type and picture, is the Lord Jesus Christ our Saviour. The Lord Jesus Christ, the Son of God, became the Servant of God, that he might redeem and save sinners chosen of God from the foundation of the world (Matthew 1:21). The text is not just talking about men who became the servants of men among the ancient Israelites. Those men were but pictures of another man, the Man Christ Jesus. How blessed it is to see and know Christ in this relationship! The eye of faith sees the Servant and rejoices in all his work.

Though he is himself God almighty, one with the Father and the Spirit in the Holy Trinity, in order to save us from our sins the Lord Jesus Christ, the Son of God, voluntarily became the servant of God and became obedient unto death, even the death of the cross, to do the will of God. In the passage before us God

[2] Ever remember, the law of God, these civil statutes, ceremonial rites, and all the commandments were messianic. They were given to Israel alone and applied to Israel alone. The law of the Old Testament has absolutely nothing to do with Gentiles. It was never given to Gentiles. The law was messianic. It pointed to Christ, who is the fulfilment and the end of the law.

the Holy Spirit calls for us to behold our great Saviour in his mediatorial office as Jehovah's Servant as he was described by the prophet Isaiah in Isaiah 42:1-4.

The Pharisees' Council

This passage opens with the Pharisees holding a council. "Then the Pharisees went out, and held a council against him, how they might destroy him" (v. 14). Religious councils throughout history have almost always proved to be "council against him". The Spirit of God here calls our attention to the hatred of these religious hypocrites toward Christ, because it is something that never changes.

These men pretended to have great reverence for the law and, particularly, for the sabbath day. Yet, they seem to have had no reluctance in gathering a religious council for the purpose of finding a way to murder One who lived among them in perfect righteousness, doing good to others. They had no qualms about pursuing a plot to murder the Lord of Glory on the sabbath day! Pharisees are always the same. They want everyone to admire their righteousness, piety, devotion, and spirituality. But they are unmasked by him who reads their hearts. He tells us that they shall receive the greater damnation (Matthew 23:14). And, it should be observed, their greater damnation is not because they behave in an outwardly reprehensible way, but because they, "going about to establish their own righteousness", refuse to submit themselves to the righteousness of Christ (Romans 9:31-10:4). All who pretend that they are righteous are hypocrites. Therefore, our Saviour warns us, "Beware ye of the leaven of the Pharisees, which is hypocrisy" (Luke 12:1).

Self-righteousness is but a religious covering by which men attempt to hide their hatred of God. "The carnal mind is enmity against God; for it is not subject unto the law of God, neither indeed can be" (Romans 8:7). The heart of man is not neutral or indifferent toward God. All natural men, all unregenerate people, at the core of their beings, in their hearts hate God! When the Lord Jesus both claimed to be "Lord even of the sabbath day" and proved his power as God by miraculously healing the man with a withered hand, the Jews, the religious leaders of the day, were so enraged against him that they sought to destroy him. No charge could be brought against his character. He was holy, harmless, undefiled, and separate from sinners. No charge could be levelled against his doctrine. He proved his teachings by the scriptures, irrefutably. But it mattered not how perfectly he lived or how perfectly he taught. He was hated by those people who claimed most loudly that they loved God!

J. C. Ryle wrote, "This is human nature appearing in its true colours! The unconverted heart hates God"! This is the reason why God's servants have been persecuted and martyred throughout the centuries. It must never surprise us when we meet with the same treatment that our Saviour received in this world. "Marvel not, my brethren, if the world hate you" (1 John 3:13). It is not our weaknesses, infirmities and faults, even our obedience, that stir up the wrath of reprobate men, but our doctrine, the gospel of Christ (John 3:19, 20; Galatians 5:11).

All Healed

"But when Jesus knew it" (v. 15). Here is another of the many, very casual assertions of our Saviour's divinity that are scattered throughout the gospel narratives. Matthew makes no attempt to prove what needed no proof to those who know and worship Christ. Knowing that he who redeemed us is God over all, we recognize and rejoice in our Saviour's divine omniscience. The omniscient God knew what the Pharisees were up to; and "when Jesus knew it, he withdrew himself from thence".

Our Lord did not flee from the Jews and the synagogue in fear, but because his hour was not yet come. The time had not yet come when he must suffer and die as our Substitute. He had other work yet to do to glorify his Father. Therefore, he rightly and wisely left the synagogue. As he left, "great multitudes followed him". Though some believe not, others will. The Pharisees and religious leaders in the synagogue hated him; but great multitudes followed him.

"And he healed them all". What a gracious word this is! As it was in Bethsaida, so it was here. When the multitudes followed him, "he received them, and spake unto them of the kingdom of God, and healed them that had need of healing" (Luke 9:11). Our Master came not to contend with carping religionists who (in their own opinion) needed nothing from him, but to bestow mercy upon needy souls. Happy is the preacher who, following the Master's example, has learned to ignore carping critics and refuses to be deterred from the Master's business, even momentarily, by them.

Our Master came to heal needy souls. While he was here in the flesh, he received all who came to him with bodily ailments, "and he healed them all". He has not changed. Great multitudes followed him from all parts of the country. And not one of those who followed him, even in this physical, carnal sense, lacked anything. When the multitudes were hungry, he fed them. If they were diseased, he healed them. If they were possessed by devils, he cast them out. "He that hath ears to hear, let him hear." Jesus Christ is merciful, gracious, and kind.

Our Saviour's mercy is coupled with omnipotence. All who follow him find all they need in him. His promise is, "Him that cometh unto me I will in no wise cast out."

Yes, this mighty, gracious, saving God-man still receives sinners and heals all who come to him. Because the Lord Jesus Christ, Jehovah's Righteous Servant, has fully obeyed his Father's will in putting away our sins by the sacrifice of himself, because he was made sin for us, because he bore our sins in his own body on the tree, because he paid all the debt for our sins and put them away completely and forever, he now assures sinners everywhere of this glorious truth by the gospel. "Him that cometh to me I will in no wise cast out" (John 6:37-40).

Come to Christ, no matter who you are, no matter how vile your transgressions are, and he promises that he will receive you, just as you are, and that he will never cast you out, that he will give you eternal life, that you shall never perish. "Come unto me, all ye that labour and are heavy laden, and I will give you rest. Take my yoke upon you, and learn of me; for I am meek and lowly in heart: and ye shall find rest unto your souls. For my yoke is easy, and my burden is light" (Matthew 11:28-30).

"And charged them that they should not make him known" (v. 16). The Son of God never courted the praises of men. He sought only to do the will of God. What a sermon that is! "To him", Spurgeon asserted, "popularity became a hindrance." Our Saviour deliberately "made himself of no reputation" (Philippians 2:5-8). He had no desire for the approval and applause of men, but only for the glory of God.

Scripture Fulfilled

This deliberate act of humiliation was "that it might be fulfilled which was spoken by Esaias the prophet" (v. 17). The prophecy to which Matthew refers is found in Isaiah 42:1-4. Here the Spirit of God gives us an undeniable evidence of inspiration and the infallibility of holy scripture (2 Timothy 3:16, 17; 2 Peter 1:20, 21). All that our Lord Jesus performed on this earth as our Substitute, from his incarnation to his ascension, was in perfect accord with the prophesies of the Old Testament. When he finished his work, "the scripture was fulfilled" (Mark 15:28). Here are 38 of the Old Testament prophecies relating to the Messiah which were fulfilled by our Lord Jesus Christ, and can never be fulfilled by anyone else. To anyone, except those who are wilfully ignorant, these are indisputable proofs that Jesus of Nazareth is the Christ of God.

The woman's seed	(Genesis 3:15; Galatians 4:4; Revelation 12:5; Luke 2:7).
Abraham's seed	(Genesis 18:18; 12:3; Acts 3:25; Matthew 1:1; Luke 3:34; Galatians 3:16).
Isaac's seed	(Genesis 17:19; Matthew 1:2; Luke 3:34).
Jacob's seed	(Numbers 24:17; Genesis 28:10-16; Luke 3:34; Matthew 1:2).
The Tribe of Judah	(Genesis 49:10; Luke 3:33; Matthew 1:2; Revelation 5:5).
Heir to David's throne	(Isaiah 9:7; 11:1-5; 2 Samuel 7:13; Matthew 1:1, 6; Acts 2:29-36).
Born in Bethlehem	(Micah 5:2; Matthew 2:1, 2; Luke 2:4-7).
Time of his birth	(Daniel 9:25; Luke 2:1-7).
Born of a virgin	(Isaiah 7:14; Matthew 1:18; Luke 1:26-35).
Massacre of children	(Jeremiah 31:15; Matthew 2:16-18).
Flight to Egypt	(Hosea 11:1; Matthew 2:14, 15).
Galilean ministry	(Isaiah 9:1, 2; Matthew 4:12-16).
A Prophet like Moses	(Deuteronomy 18:15; John 1:45; 6:14; Acts 3:19-26).
Melchizedek	(Psalm 110:4; Hebrews 5:5, 6; 6:20; 7:15-17).
King's triumphal entry	(Isaiah 62:11; Zechariah 9:9; John 12:12-16; Matthew 21:1-11).
Rejection by men	(Psalm 2:2; Isaiah 53:3; John 1:11; 5:43; Luke 4:28, 29; 17:25; 23:18).
Personal character	(Isaiah 11:2-5; Luke 2:52; 4:18).
Betrayal by a friend	(Psalm 41:9; Mark 14:10).
Thirty pieces of silver	(Zechariah 11:12, 13; Matthew 26:15).
Potter's field bought	(Zechariah 11:13; Matthew 27:6, 7).
Judas' office	(Psalm 109:7, 8; Acts 1:16-20).
False witnesses	(Psalm 27:12; 35:11; Matthew 26:59-61).
Silence when accused	(Isaiah 53:7; Psalm 38:13, 14; Matthew 26:62, 63; 27:12-14).
Smitten and spat upon	(Isaiah 50:6; Mark 14:65).
Hated without a cause	(Psalm 69:4; 109:3-5; John 15:23-25).
Vicarious sufferings	(Isaiah 53:4-6, 12; Matthew 8:16, 17; Romans 4:25; 1 Corinthians 15:3).
Crucified with sinners	(Isaiah 53:12; Matthew 27:38; Luke 23:33).
Pierced hands and feet	(Psalm 22:16; John 20:27).

Mocked of men	(Psalm 22:6-8; Matthew 27:39-44).
Gall, vinegar to drink	(Psalm 69:21; John 19:29).
Hears prophetic words	(Psalm 22:8; Matthew 27:43).
Intercedes for enemies	(Psalm 109:4; Luke 23:34).
Pierced side	(Zechariah 12:10; John 19:34).
Lots cast for his coat	(Psalm 22:18; Mark 15:24).
Not a bone broken	(Psalm 34:20; Exodus 12:46; John 19:33).
Buried with the rich	(Isaiah 53:9; Matthew 27:57-60).
His resurrection	(Psalm 16:10; Matthew 28:9; Luke 24:36-40).
His ascension	(Psalm 68:18; Luke 24:50, 51).

John Trapp wrote, "The Old Testament is the New Testament foretold. The New Testament is the Old Testament fulfilled."

Jehovah's Servant

Jesus of Nazareth is the Christ and he is Jehovah's Servant. Be sure you understand that verse 18, and all others relating to our Redeemer being the Servant of God, relate only to his humility and to his office capacity as our covenant Surety, Mediator, and Substitute. As such he was chosen by God the Father. He is beloved of God (John 10:16-18; Ephesians 1:6). He is well-pleasing to him. Our Redeemer's servitude was a matter of voluntary submission (Isaiah 50:5-7). He was equipped for his work by God, who said, "I will put my Spirit upon him" (Isaiah 42:1). Thus he came to reveal the righteousness of God through the gospel to the world, that is the Gentiles. As it is written, "He shall bring forth judgment to the Gentiles ... "He shall not fail ... " (Isaiah 42:1-9).

Matthew was inspired to translate Isaiah's prophecy as a declaration of the certain salvation of God's elect throughout the whole world, in every age, until the end of time. He will "send forth judgment unto victory. And in his name shall the Gentiles trust" (Matthew 12:20, 21; Romans 15:12). Our Lord Jesus came into this world as Jehovah's righteous servant for the purpose of saving his people from their sins; and to do so in a way that would make it manifest that he who is our God is "a just God and a Saviour" (Isaiah 45:21). And he finished what he came to do. He brought in everlasting righteousness (Daniel 9:24). He brought that righteousness to victory in the accomplishment of our redemption by the sacrifice of himself (Colossians 1:19, 20; 2:14, 15). And, now, upon the ground of his finished work, he gives life and faith to all God's elect among the nations of the world by omnipotent mercy and free grace (v. 21; Romans 11:26).

"A bruised reed shall he not break, and smoking flax shall he not quench" (v. 20). What sweet, consoling, encouraging words those are to poor, weak sinners! Mighty and great as our Saviour is, "He despiseth not any" (Job 36:5). Even those in whom grace is ever so weak, faith is ever so small, and repentance is ever so feeble, he is mighty to save! J. C. Ryle says, "There is life in the infant as truly as in the grown-up man. There is fire in a spark as truly as in a burning flame. The least degree of grace is an everlasting possession. It comes down from heaven. It is precious in our Lord's eyes. It shall never be over thrown."

The bruised reed and the smoking flax have reference to young converts, newly awakened souls. Like a "bruised reed", the newborn soul is bruised, broken, contrite, and tender in his soul because he is made to know his sin and vileness before God. Such souls, the Lord Jesus will never destroy. He binds up their broken hearts and heals their wounded spirits. The newborn soul is also compared to "smoking flax". The wick in an old oil lantern, when it is first lit, smokes and appears ready to go out, because it has little fire. So the newborn soul often has but little light and knowledge, but little faith and confidence and much darkness; but our tender Saviour will never quench the "smoking flax". He will give it more oil, and fire, and light by the abiding influence and grace of his Holy Spirit, "till he sends forth judgment into victory". The Apostle Paul says the very same thing in Philippians 1:6. "He which hath begun a good work in you will perform it until the day of Jesus Christ".

What sweet assurances of grace we have in this call of our God: "Behold my servant, whom I have chosen; my beloved, in whom my soul is well pleased". The Father calls us to behold his darling Son, commending him to us in his gracious office and work as the God-man Mediator and his faithful Servant. Nothing can be more blessed than that which God the Father says of him here, when his redeemed are enabled by his grace to look upon the Lord Jesus with the same delight, trusting him as our Saviour whom the Father trusted as his Servant. The Lord God said, "I will put my spirit upon him". The believing sinner says, "I will put my whole life into his omnipotent hands of grace." The Lord God says, "This is my Servant, whom I have chosen, my Beloved, in whom my soul is well-pleased." The heaven born soul, looking on him says, "This is my Saviour, who has chosen me, and he whom I have chosen, my Beloved, in whom my soul is well-pleased." The God of Glory says, "He shall show judgment to the Gentiles." We who are called from among the Gentiles rejoice to declare, "He has shown both judgment and mercy to me and has recovered me from sin and destruction. He has sent forth judgment to victory for my soul; and in his name I trust."

Chapter 27

Blasphemy Against The Holy Spirit

"Then was brought unto him one possessed with a devil, blind, and dumb: and he healed him, insomuch that the blind and dumb both spake and saw. And all the people were amazed, and said, Is not this the son of David? But when the Pharisees heard it, they said, This fellow doth not cast out devils, but by Beelzebub the prince of the devils. And Jesus knew their thoughts, and said unto them, Every kingdom divided against itself is brought to desolation; and every city or house divided against itself shall not stand: And if Satan cast out Satan, he is divided against himself; how shall then his kingdom stand? And if I by Beelzebub cast out devils, by whom do your children cast them out? therefore they shall be your judges. But if I cast out devils by the Spirit of God, then the kingdom of God is come unto you. Or else how can one enter into a strong man's house, and spoil his goods, except he first bind the strong man? and then he will spoil his house. He that is not with me is against me; and he that gathereth not with me scattereth abroad. Wherefore I say unto you, All manner of sin and blasphemy shall be forgiven unto men: but the blasphemy against the Holy Ghost shall not be forgiven unto men. And whosoever speaketh a word against the Son of man, it shall be forgiven him: but whosoever speaketh against the Holy Ghost, it shall not be forgiven him, neither in this world, neither in the world to come. Either make the tree good, and his fruit good; or else make the tree corrupt, and his fruit corrupt: for the tree is known by his fruit. O generation of vipers, how can ye, being evil, speak good things? for out of the abundance of the heart the mouth speaketh. A good man out of the good treasure of the heart bringeth forth good things: and an evil man out of the evil treasure bringeth forth evil things. But I say unto you, That every idle word that men shall speak, they shall give account thereof in the day of judgment. For by thy words thou shalt be justified, and by thy words thou shalt be condemned."
(Matthew12:22-37)

The passage we have read contains some "things hard to be understood". The principle thing that is dealt with in this text is "the blasphemy against the Holy

Ghost". This is a subject about which it must be acknowledged little is known. The best and fullest explanations of it are, in my opinion, far from being exhaustive and satisfactory. And I have no delusions about being able to fathom the depths of this subject. I will say no more about it than I am confident of as a matter of divine revelation, and no less.

We must never be surprised to find things in the Bible that are simply beyond the reach of our minds. If it had no deep places here and there, which no man is capable of understanding, much less explaining, it would not be the Word of the Infinite God. However, rather than stumbling and falling over the things we cannot understand, we ought to give thanks to God for those revelations of wisdom and grace, which even the simplest minds are able to grasp. When we find things written in the Word of God that we do not understand, or that appear to our puny brains to be inconsistent with matters of clear revelation, let us reverently bow to the scriptures, knowing that God is true, praying and waiting for clearer understanding that only God the Holy Spirit can give. Let us never speculate about divine truth, or offer opinions about things beyond our comprehension. There are five things in this paragraph that demand our attention.

The Prejudice Of The Pharisees

First, in verses 22-27 we see the prejudice of the Pharisees against Christ and his gospel, and learn that no slanderous speech is too vile and reprehensible for lost religious people to use against the gospel of Christ.

Whenever we read of our Lord's miracles in healing the bodies of people, we ought to view them as demonstrations of our Saviour's great compassion upon our immortal souls. It is the blind and dumb in spirit that he came to deliver.

When our Lord cast out devils, the Pharisees said, "He does that by Beelzebub"! It was an absurd charge, as our Lord demonstrated; but these men were blinded by religious prejudice. And none are so blind as those who will not see. When they could not refute his doctrine, could not deny the validity of his works, and would not acknowledge him as the Christ of God, the only way these men could justify their behaviour was to slander the Saviour's name and seek to cast reproach upon his character.

These Pharisees are not the only people who have lost reason, good sense, and civility when confronted with the Kingdom of God. The religious world called Athanasius a devil when he insisted upon the doctrine of the Holy Trinity. The pope called Martin Luther a devil when he proclaimed the doctrine of justification by faith alone.

This ought never to surprise us. When religious men are determined to reject the doctrine of the gospel, which they cannot refute, they attempt to defend themselves by blackening the character of those who preach the free grace of God in Christ. What an honour it is to God's faithful servants when such men speak evil of them for proclaiming the gospel of Christ. By their slanders they simply treat our Master's servants as they treated the Lord Jesus himself. I have been called a devil by more than a few of these Pharisees' sons over the years, and always count it my honour to be so treated (Matthew 10:25).

When the Holy Spirit tells us, "Jesus knew their thoughts" (v. 25), he gives clear testimony to our Saviour's eternal deity. None but the eternal God knows the thoughts of men. It is written, "I am he which searcheth the reins[3] and hearts" (Revelation 2:23). And there is in this passage a clear declaration of the three persons of the Holy Trinity as well. As all three Persons in the Holy Trinity are engaged in all the work of our salvation (Ephesians 1:3-14), so all three are here engaged in the work of "casting out devils". The Lord Jesus Christ, God the Son, said, "I cast out devils". He said that he did it "by the Spirit", by God the Holy Spirit. And he calls God the Spirit, "the Spirit of God", that is of God the Father. As it is written, "There are three that bear record in heaven, the Father, the Word, and the Holy Ghost: and these three are one" (1 John 5:7).

The Binding Of Satan

Second, verses 28 and 29 describe the work of Christ as the binding of Satan. In verse twenty-six the Lord Jesus speaks of Satan's kingdom. Here he speaks of the binding of Satan. The fact that Satan sets up and maintains an empire of sin in every human heart is a fact too obvious to be questioned by any rational person. The terrible effects of it are too well known to be denied. Here we have that fact plainly stated. "It was", Robert Hawker wrote, "the setting up of this kingdom against God and his Christ, for which the devil and his angels are said to have been cast out of heaven, and to have left their own habitation (Revelation 12:7-

---

[3] Reins is today an unfamiliar word. The Hebrew is kilyaw, the Greek is nefros, the Latin is renes, from which we get the word renal. In the three languages the word literally means kidneys, or region of the loins, an essential organ of the body. It is often linked with the word kardia or heart, from which we get the word cardiac. The biblical figurative meaning of reins refers to the inmost mind of a person, the deepest thoughts of the interior self, the seat of the feelings or affections. God is said to see, to know, to search, to try, and to possess the minds and hearts of all men (Psalm 2:23). Here in these verses of Matthew chapter 12 we have yet more evidence of the full and perfect deity of our Lord Jesus Christ; for only God can know and test the thoughts of men in such a way.

12; Jude 6)". It was by Satan's seduction of Eve that Adam was brought down, and by Adam's transgression that the whole human race was made a fallen, corrupt, sinful race (Romans 5:12). It is Satan who works in all the children of disobedience continually (Ephesians 2:2-4).

As Satan's kingdom of darkness, deception, and sin takes in the entire human race, he is called "the prince of this world" (John 16:11). He seeks to destroy our souls and seeks to destroy the church and kingdom of God, and is thus called "a roaring lion" (1 Peter 5:8) and "the dragon", "the devil" and "Satan" (Revelation 12:7, 9). He is "the strong man armed". So powerful is his influence over the unregenerate, that "men are taken captive by him at his will" (2 Timothy 2:26).

How happy and thankful we ought to be to read in the Book of God that "the Son of God was manifested that he might destroy the works of the devil" (1 John 3:8). One great purpose and design of the gospel is the overthrow of Satan and his kingdom and the restoration of perfect order in God's creation. Let us rejoice! The Son of God came into this world to "save his people from their sins" and "that he might destroy the works of the devil"; and all he came to accomplish shall be accomplished! The Word of God reveals a threefold binding of Satan.

By his death upon the cross; by the accomplishment of our redemption, and by his resurrection from the grave our Saviour bound Satan and broke the power of his usurped dominion over the nations of the world (John 12:31-33; Colossians 2:13-15; Hebrews 2:14, 15; Revelation 20:1-6). In regeneration and conversion, by the power of his grace, through the operations of his Holy Spirit in the new birth, the Son of God binds and casts out Satan from the hearts of chosen, redeemed sinners and takes possession of his house.

That is what is described in Matthew 12:28, 29. Our Saviour is the man stronger than the strong man armed. He comes by omnipotent mercy into the hearts of chosen sinners, binds Satan, casts him out, and spoils him of all. This is what happens every time he saves a sinner. He does not stand knocking at the door of the lost sinner's heart, hoping that the sinner might choose to let him enter. He knocks the door down, bolt and bar, enters the house of the ransomed soul, and sets up his throne in the heart, bringing his welcome with him. Thus it is that we have been "translated from the kingdom of darkness into the kingdom of God's dear Son" (Isaiah 49:24, 25; Mark 3:27; Luke 11:21, 22; John 12:31; 14:30; 16:7-11; Ephesians 2:1-5).

When he comes again to make all things new, the Lord Jesus will cast Satan out of this world into the lake of fire, where he shall have no more power (Revelation 20:10). There is a day coming, when Christ comes again in his glory, when the total and everlasting destruction of Satan's kingdom will take place. In that day we who are one with Christ will triumph over the prince of darkness in complete victory (Romans 16:20). There is no such thing as "a devil's hell". Hell belongs to God. It is his torture chamber, in which he will forever torment the devil and all who have followed him to destruction.

The Impossibility Of Neutrality

In verse 30 the Lord Jesus shows us the impossibility of neutrality with regard to him, his gospel, and his kingdom. "He that is not with me is against me; and he that gathereth not with me scattereth abroad." Multitudes try to straddle the fence, halting between two opinions, not wishing to deny Christ altogether and not wishing to serve him altogether, not wanting to engage in open rebellion to the Son of God, but not wanting to engage in the cause of Christ. But such neutrality is impossible.

There are, with regard to spiritual things, only two camps; only two sides. Either we are with Christ, committed to him and his cause, or we are against him, committed to the world, the flesh, and the devil. We cannot serve both God and mammon. If we do not serve Christ, we oppose him. There is no middle ground. The gospel of Christ demands decisiveness (Joshua 24:15). In his commentary on verse thirty John Gill wrote, "Since there is such an open war proclaimed and carried on between Christ and the devil, none ought to be neutral; whoever is not on the side of Christ, is reckoned as an enemy; and whoever is not concerned by prayer or preaching, or other means to gather souls to his word and ordinances, and to his church, and to himself, is deemed by him a scatterer of them."

Blasphemy Against The Holy Ghost

Verses 31 and 32 introduce us to what our Saviour calls "the blasphemy against the Holy Ghost", and warns us against the danger of what he declares is the only unpardonable sin. It is not difficult to show from the scriptures what this sin is not. The difficulty is showing clearly what it is.

Our Saviour declares the free, full, absolute, and everlasting forgiveness of all sin to all believers. "All manner of sin and blasphemy shall be forgiven unto men". "If we confess our sins", no matter what they are, no matter how vile they are, no matter how many they are, no matter how old or how new they are, the Lord God "is faithful and just to forgive us our sins", all of them, completely, and forever, "and to cleanse us from all unrighteousness" (1 John 1:9). For "the blood of Jesus Christ, his (God's) Son, cleanseth us from all sin" (1 John 1:7).

Yet, the Son of God does speak about one particular sin that is unpardonable. It is called "the blasphemy against the Holy Ghost". What is this "blasphemy against the Holy Ghost"? "The blasphemy against the Holy Ghost" does not involve sins of ignorance. The distinction drawn between speaking "against the Son of man" and speaking "against (blaspheming) the Holy Ghost" must not be overlooked. The sin against Christ as the Son of man was committed out of ignorance by those who did not know that he is the Messiah. Therefore, they did not receive him, believe him, and obey him, but opposed, persecuted, and even crucified him. But they did it ignorantly (1 Corinthians 2:8), as Saul of Tarsus did (1 Timothy 1:13).

This sin and blasphemy against the Holy Spirit, which our Saviour declares is unpardonable, is committed by men and women who wilfully persist in unbelief and obstinate impenitence, deliberately rejecting the counsel of God against themselves, and are therefore given up to a reprobate mind. J. C. Ryle accurately describes it as, "The union of the clearest head-knowledge of the Gospel with deliberate rejection of it, and deliberate choice of sin and the world". John Gill wrote, "It is a despiteful usage of the Spirit of grace, an opposing, contradicting, and denying of the operations wrought, or the doctrines revealed by him, against a man's own light and conscience, out of a wilful and obstinate malice, on purpose to lessen the glory of God, and gratify his own lusts. Such was the sin of the scribes and Pharisees; who, though they knew the miracles of Christ were wrought by the Spirit of God, yet maliciously and obstinately imputed them to the devil, with a view to obscure the glory of Christ, and indulge their own wicked passions."

This unpardonable sin is the wilful, deliberate rejection of Christ by one who is fully convinced that he is the Son of God and the only Saviour of sinners. It is a deliberate refusal to bow to him as Lord. It is choosing to save your life, rather than lose it to the dominion of the Son of God. It is nothing less than running over the top of the Son of God to get to hell!

Those who are troubled with the fear that they may have committed this unpardonable sin, most assuredly, have not done so! The one thing that always characterizes those people described in the scriptures as reprobate is a callousness and hardness, that is the result of a seared conscience. When God gives a man up in reprobation, that man is no longer concerned for the glory of God, the knowledge of Christ, and the things of God.

Lot's wife, Pharaoh, King Saul, Ahab, and Judas Iscariot stand out as beacons to warn all. Each of them had clear knowledge. Yet, each of them deliberately rejected Christ. They had light in their heads, but darkness in their hearts. Each of them today is in hell, suffering the wrath of God! Beware of despising the light God has given you. Do you know the truth? Then walk in the truth. Walk in the light God has given you. That is the best safeguard against the unpardonable sin.

Importance Of Words

Our Lord calls the scribes and Pharisees of his day and ours a "generation of vipers". The seed of the woman and the seed of the serpent are identified and defined throughout the Word of God as being at enmity toward each other (Genesis 3:15). On another occasion, our Saviour said to the same people, "Ye are of your father the devil, and the lusts of your father ye will do" (John 8:44). Because they are of their father, the devil, nothing but evil can be expected from such people. "How can ye, being evil, speak good things?" (v. 34). "Ye believe not, because ye are not of my sheep" (John 10:26). Such serpents, such a "generation of vipers", cannot escape "the damnation, of hell" (Matthew 23:33; 13:38; 25:33, 34, 41, 46; Acts 13:10; 2 Peter 2:12-14; 1 John 3:8, 9, 12).

"A good man out of the good treasure of the heart bringeth forth good things: and an evil man out of the evil treasure bringeth forth evil things." The scriptures plainly declare, "There is none righteous, no not one" (Romans 3:10). Yet, our Lord here speaks of "a good man". Obviously, he here distinguishes his own from the rest of the world. All who are born of God are made "good" before him by his own work of grace, by the righteousness of Christ imputed to them in justification and the righteousness of Christ imparted to them in regeneration (1 Corinthians 6:11; 2 Peter 1:4; 1 John 3:5-10). The "good man" differs from the natural man. He is a different man than he once was, because he is a new creature in Christ. He has a righteous nature imparted to him by the grace of God. "Out of the good treasure of his heart", by the graces of the Holy Spirit planted in him, he brings forth the sweet and precious fruit of the Spirit in his life and in his speech (Galatians 5:22, 23; Philippians 1:27). He speaks of Christ, his righteousness, his atonement, his forgiveness, and his grace, declaring what God has done for his soul (Psalm 66:16).

In verses 36 and 37 our Saviour shows us the immense importance of being careful about our words. He says, "every idle word that men speak, they shall give an account thereof in the day of judgment". Then he adds, "by thy words thou shalt be justified, and by thy word thou shalt be condemned". If there were nothing else in the Bible to do so, these statements of our Lord about the tongue should convince all who read them that we are all guilty before God and need the righteousness of Another, even the righteousness of Christ, to give us acceptance with him in the day of judgment (Philippians 3:9).

Our words reveal the state of our hearts. Words of grace, kindness, goodwill, and cheer give evidence of a heart renewed by grace. Words of envy, malice, slander, and gossip, words that are intended to hurt others reveal an evil, depraved, unregenerate heart (Ephesians 4:30-32). Idle words may seem frivolous to us; but they do permanent damage. "Death and life are in the power of the tongue" (Proverbs 18:21). Idle words often stick in the minds of those who hear them long after the one who speaks them is dead. No member of our bodies is more powerful to do good and to do evil than our tongues.

"For in many things we offend all. If any man offend not in word, the same is a perfect man, and able also to bridle the whole body. Behold, we put bits in the horses' mouths, that they may obey us; and we turn about their whole body. Behold also the ships, which though they be so great, and are driven of fierce winds, yet are they turned about with a very small helm, whithersoever the governor listeth. Even so the tongue is a little member, and boasteth great things. Behold, how great a matter a little fire kindleth! And the tongue is a fire, a world of iniquity: so is the tongue among our members, that it defileth the whole body, and setteth on fire the course of nature; and it is set on fire of hell. For every kind of beasts, and of birds, and of serpents, and of things in the sea, is tamed, and hath been tamed of mankind: But the tongue can no man tame; it is an unruly evil, full of deadly poison" (James 3:2-8). "Set a watch, O LORD, before my mouth; keep the door of my lips" (Psalm 141:3). "Let your speech be alway with grace, seasoned with salt, that ye may know how ye ought to answer every man" (Colossians 4:6).

We must not forget that our Saviour's words in verses 36 and 37 distinguish the believer from the unbeliever. Our words as well as our actions make manifest the state of our hearts and reveal whether we are born again by his grace or are yet unregenerate. The idle, sinful words of the unbeliever reveal the fact that he is unregenerate. Likewise, the gracious words of the believer reveal the work of grace in and upon him. As Abraham and Rahab justified their professed faith in Christ by their deeds, so, too, every believer justifies his professed faith in Christ by his daily conversation (James 2:19-26). For the believer, there is no condemnation. Those who are redeemed by Christ shall never be condemned (Romans 8:1, 33, 34; Song of Solomon 4:11; Malachi 3:16-18). The unregenerate and unbelieving, living and dying without Christ shall be condemned by their own words.

Chapter 28

"Behold, A Greater Than Solomon Is Here"!

"Then certain of the scribes and of the Pharisees answered, saying, Master, we would see a sign from thee. But he answered and said unto them, An evil and adulterous generation seeketh after a sign; and there shall no sign be given to it, but the sign of the prophet Jonas: For as Jonas was three days and three nights in the whale's belly; so shall the Son of man be three days and three nights in the heart of the earth. The men of Nineveh shall rise in judgment with this generation, and shall condemn it: because they repented at the preaching of Jonas; and, behold, a greater than Jonas is here. The queen of the south shall rise up in the judgment with this generation, and shall condemn it: for she came from the uttermost parts of the earth to hear the wisdom of Solomon; and, behold, a greater than Solomon is here. When the unclean spirit is gone out of a man, he walketh through dry places, seeking rest, and findeth none. Then he saith, I will return into my house from whence I came out; and when he is come, he findeth it empty, swept, and garnished. Then goeth he, and taketh with himself seven other spirits more wicked than himself, and they enter in and dwell there: and the last state of that man is worse than the first. Even so shall it be also unto this wicked generation. While he yet talked to the people, behold, his mother and his brethren stood without, desiring to speak with him. Then one said unto him, Behold, thy mother and thy brethren stand without, desiring to speak with thee. But he answered and said unto him that told him, Who is my mother? and who are my brethren? And he stretched forth his hand toward his disciples, and said, Behold my mother and my brethren! For whosoever shall do the will of my Father which is in heaven, the same is my brother, and sister, and mother."
(Matthew 12:38-50)

In these verses the Lord Jesus silences the cavilling Pharisees, demonstrates the validity of holy scripture and the danger of graceless religion, and gives great comfort to all who trust him.

Looking For A Sign

The first thing that confronts us in this passage is the fact that unbelief always looks for a sign. The Pharisees in their brazen, obstinate, self-righteousness arrogance and unbelief said, "Master, we would see a sign from thee" (v. 38). What sham pretence! They pretended that they merely wanted a little more evidence in order to be convinced and become his disciples. The healing of the sick, the cleansing of the lepers, the casting out of devils, and the raising of the dead was not quite enough evidence for them. It was not enough because they were determined not to believe the Son of God!

That is exactly the state of many today. They claim a willingness to believe if only they had enough evidence, or enough proof, or enough signs. But faith in Christ cannot be produced by signs, proofs, and arguments. Faith is the gift of God. It is wrought in men and women by hearing the Word of God (Ephesians 2:8, 9; Luke 16:31; Romans 10:17; 1 Corinthians 1:22-24). And the basis of faith is the naked revelation of God in holy scripture (1 John 5:9-13). The only way anyone can ever see the glory of God and be established in the peace of God and the truth of God, is by believing God (John 11:40).

One Book

Verses 39-42 demonstrate clearly that the authority of the Old Testament and the New Testament stand or fall together. "But he answered and said unto them, An evil and adulterous generation seeketh after a sign; and there shall no sign be given to it, but the sign of the prophet Jonas: For as Jonas was three days and three nights in the whale's belly; so shall the Son of man be three days and three nights in the heart of the earth. The men of Nineveh shall rise in judgment with this generation, and shall condemn it: because they repented at the preaching of Jonas; and, behold, a greater than Jonas is here. The queen of the south shall rise up in the judgment with this generation, and shall condemn it: for she came from the uttermost parts of the earth to hear the wisdom of Solomon; and, behold, a greater than Solomon is here."

In these verses the Lord Jesus, almost casually, displays the truth of the Old Testament scriptures. This is an important fact. The Bible is one Book, not two. It is one, united Word of divine revelation. Those who attempt to pick holes in the Old Testament are at the same time attempting to destroy the authority of the New (2 Timothy 3:16, 17; Romans 15:4; 2 Peter 1:20, 21).

The same Holy Spirit who inspired the Old Testament writers to tell us of Jonah, the Queen of Sheba, and Solomon inspired the writers of the New

Testament to tell us of Christ, his redemptive work, and his exaltation and glory. If one part of this Book is a lie, all of it is a lie. You cannot pick and choose what you want. You must either receive it all and believe it all, or reject it all as a lie, a falsehood, a fable, and a fabrication.

As Jonah really was in the belly of the whale for three days, so the Lord Jesus, when he was crucified as our Substitute, was buried in the earth and rose from the dead three days later. The men of Nineveh who believed Jonah's message and repented shall rise in judgment against all who refuse to believe the message of grace from the lips of the risen Christ. "Behold a greater than Jonah is here"! Christ is a greater Man with a greater message.

The Pharisees cast our Lord overboard, just as the sailors did Jonah. As the sea was calmed for those sailors by the sacrifice of Jonah, so our Lord's death made peace for us. As Jonah's mission and message were certified by his resurrection from the sea, so is our Lord's mission and message certified by his resurrection from the dead. That man who had come back from death and burial in the sea commanded the attention of all Nineveh. Even so, our risen Saviour demands and deserves the obedient faith of all who hear his message. The resurrection of Christ is the sign of the prophet Jonah; but it is supplemented by another, that in the mouth of two witnesses it might be established.

As the Queen of Sheba diligently sought Solomon and heard all his wisdom, so all who seek Christ shall find him and be taught of him all things pertaining to life and godliness. "Behold, a greater than Solomon is here"! This queen of the south shall rise in judgment against all who have Christ clearly set before them, but refuse to trust him.

The sign here spoken of displays our Lord's kingly wisdom. As the fame of Solomon caused the Queen of Sheba to seek him, so the doctrine of Christ commands the attention of the whole world. Though the Pharisees and lost religionists of our day refuse him who is the Wisdom of God, chosen multitudes, scattered over all the earth, gladly come to him, bow before his majesty, and gladly receive his Word.

The superlative excellence of Solomon's wisdom stands for our Lord as a second sign, a sign that cannot be disputed. Our Saviour's royal wisdom meets all the needs of men. Who else has revealed such grace and truth? Who but the Son of God could have revealed the Father to us?

Profession Without Possession

Verses 43-45 teach us that nothing is so dangerous and destructive to the souls of men as a profession of faith without the possession of grace. "When the unclean spirit is gone out of a man, he walketh through dry places, seeking rest, and findeth none. Then he saith, I will return into my house from whence I came out; and when he is come, he findeth it empty, swept, and garnished. Then goeth he, and taketh with himself seven other spirits more wicked than himself, and they enter in and dwell there: and the last state of that man is worse than the first. Even so shall it be also unto this wicked generation."

Faithful gospel preachers do not try to pump and twist professions of faith out of people, young or old, because we realize that nothing is more certain to destroy a person than religion without Christ. Such men want you to know Christ, to trust him, to be saved by him, and urgently press upon you the claims of Christ in the gospel. If God has given you faith in Christ, they will urge you to confess him in believer's baptism, identify yourself with his people, and publicly devote yourself to Christ, his gospel, and his cause, knowing that secret disciples are always suspect disciples. But they will not aid unconverted men and women in making a refuge of lies for themselves, professing faith without experiencing grace. None of God's elect are going to perish because we do not force professions of faith from people. Our only business is to faithfully preach the gospel, pray for God's blessing upon it, and wait for God to do his work.

In these verses the Lord Jesus describes what happens to men and women who are talked into religion despite never experiencing the grace of God. Men, women and children can be persuaded to make a profession of personal salvation amid a lost religious generation, They may even manifest a great moral change and outward religious sanctification; but their ultimate end will be everlasting ruin (Hebrews 4:6; 10:38; 2 Peter 2:20-22). J. C. Ryle wrote, "None prove so hopelessly wicked as those who after experiencing strong religious convictions have gone back again to sin and the world." The last state of that man is worse than the first. Do not be content with Christless, graceless religion!

"For", wrote Robert Hawker, "if while under the same awful influence of an unrenewed, unregenerated heart, the man is prompted to put on the appearance of an outside sanctity; and covers over the uncleanness that is *within*, with a seeming zeal for religion *without*: these are like the seven other spirits of the devil, more wicked than the former, because more desperately deceiving, both himself and the world; and of consequence, the end is more dreadful. And who shall calculate the numbers there are living under this most wretched of all delusions? Who shall say, the many, who go out of life well pleased with this whitening sepulchre-reform; in whose heart, no saving change hath been wrought; nor any acquaintance made with the person, work, or grace of God the Holy Ghost (John 3:3-9; Acts 19:2). Reader! see to it that no change satisfies your mind, but that which is wrought by the Holy Ghost and Christ, *formed in your heart the life of glory* (Romans 8:9-17; 2 Corinthians 5:17)".

God's Family

Verses 46-50 teach us that all true believers are the family of God. Sometimes the Church of God is called by one name and sometimes by another to show various aspects of our relationship to God and to one another. It is called "the church", "the body of Christ", "the bride", "the fold", "an holy nation", "a royal priesthood", "Jerusalem", "the church of the firstborn", "the kingdom of heaven", "the kingdom of God", and "the family of God". In this passage our Lord teaches us that all true believers are one in him, and that we are the family of God (Ephesians 3:15). All believers are counted by the Son of God as his relatives. He loves them. He feels for them. He cares for them, as members of his family, bone of his bone, flesh of his flesh. He provides for his family. He protects his family. He prays for his family. Some of his family have already gone home. Some of his family are yet in their pilgrimage. But all who do the will of his Father, all who trust him are members of his family. J. C. Ryle's observations on this passage are as precious and encouraging as they are instructive:

> Mark how He speaks of every one who does the will of His Father in heaven. He says, 'he is my brother, and sister, and mother.' What gracious words these are! Who can conceive the depth of our dear Lord's love towards His relations according to the flesh? It was a pure, unselfish love. It must have been a mighty love, a love that passes man's understanding. Yet here we see that all His believing people are counted as His family. He loves them, feels for them, cares for them, as members of His family, bone of His bone, and flesh of His flesh.
>
> There is a solemn warning here to all who mock and persecute true Christians on account of their religion. They consider not what they are doing. They are persecuting the near relations of the King of kings. They will find at the last day that they have mocked those

whom the Judge of all regards as His 'brother, and sister, and mother'.

There is rich encouragement here for all believers. They are far more precious in their Lord's eyes than they are in their own. Their faith may be feeble, their repentance weak, their strength small. They may be poor and needy in this world. But there is a glorious 'whoever' in the last verse of this chapter which ought to cheer them. 'Whoever' believes is a near relation of Christ. The elder Brother will provide for him in time and eternity, and never let him be cast away. There is not one 'little sister' in the family of the redeemed, whom Jesus does not remember (Song of Solomon 8:8). Joseph provided richly for all his relations, and Jesus will provide for His.

Are you a member of this family? Rejoice! Would you be? Trust Christ!

Chapter 29

"The Parable of the Sower"

"The same day went Jesus out of the house, and sat by the sea side. And great multitudes were gathered together unto him, so that he went into a ship, and sat; and the whole multitude stood on the shore. And he spake many things unto them in parables, saying, Behold, a sower went forth to sow; And when he sowed, some seeds fell by the way side, and the fowls came and devoured them up: Some fell upon stony places, where they had not much earth: and forthwith they sprung up, because they had no deepness of earth: And when the sun was up, they were scorched; and because they had no root, they withered away. And some fell among thorns; and the thorns sprung up, and choked them: But other fell into good ground, and brought forth fruit, some an hundredfold, some sixtyfold, some thirtyfold. Who hath ears to hear, let him hear. And the disciples came, and said unto him, Why speakest thou unto them in parables? He answered and said unto them, Because it is given unto you to know the mysteries of the kingdom of heaven, but to them it is not given. For whosoever hath, to him shall be given, and he shall have more abundance: but whosoever hath not, from him shall be taken away even that he hath. Therefore speak I to them in parables: because they seeing see not; and hearing they hear not, neither do they understand. And in them is fulfilled the prophecy of Esaias, which saith, By hearing ye shall hear, and shall not understand; and seeing ye shall see, and shall not perceive: For this people's heart is waxed gross, and their ears are dull of hearing, and their eyes they have closed; lest at any time they should see with their eyes, and hear with their ears, and should understand with their heart, and should be converted, and I should heal them. But blessed are your eyes, for they see: and your ears, for they hear. For verily I say unto you, That many prophets and righteous men have desired to see those things which ye see, and have not seen them; and to hear those things which ye hear, and have not heard them. Hear ye therefore the parable of the sower. When any one heareth the word of the kingdom, and understandeth it not, then cometh the wicked one, and catcheth away that which was sown in his heart. This is he which received seed by the way side. But he that received the seed into stony places, the same is he that heareth the word, and anon with joy receiveth it; Yet hath he not root in himself, but dureth for a while: for

when tribulation or persecution ariseth because of the word, by and by he is offended. He also that received seed among the thorns is he that heareth the word; and the care of this world, and the deceitfulness of riches, choke the word, and he becometh unfruitful. But he that received seed into the good ground is he that heareth the word, and understandeth it; which also beareth fruit, and bringeth forth, some an hundredfold, some sixty, some thirty."
(Matthew 13:1-23)

In this chapter our Lord Jesus Christ taught the gospel to his disciples by eight parables, eight distinct and striking illustrations of divine truth drawn from the book of nature. He calls these parables "the mysteries of the kingdom of heaven" (v. 11). When we study the parables, several things need to be kept in mind.

"Hear Ye Therefore The Parable Of The Sower"

We do not build our doctrine upon parables. Parables illustrate doctrine, they do not establish doctrine. Doctrine must be built upon the plain statements of holy scripture, contextually interpreted. Parables are earthly stories illustrating heavenly truths, earthly pictures of spiritual things. When the Lord Jesus preached the gospel, he gave people pictures and illustrations of his doctrine to fix it in their minds. Yet, he never gave a picture that was debasing to the gospel, or one that lowered the message of the gospel to make it more palatable to men. It is not necessary for everything in the parable to mean something, or even be compatible with the doctrine of the gospel. Like the types of the Old Testament, the parables of the New Testament were never intended to be perfect illustrations of gospel truth. They are just illustrations, yet, they are beautiful, instructive illustrations. Each parable is designed to illustrate and enforce only one thing. If we try to make the parables teach many things, we misuse them. Just as a preacher today uses a story only to illustrate one thing, so our Lord used his parables to illustrate, and drive home one particular thing, not two, or twenty.

The one thing taught in the parable of the sower (vv. 1-23) is the necessity of hearing the Word of the gospel with a believing heart. The message of this parable is a fact that is verified continually before our eyes. Wherever men and women gather to hear the Word of God preached and expounded, the sayings of our Lord in this parable are manifestly found to be true. It describes what goes on, as a general rule, in all congregations where the gospel is preached. Let me show you five things in this regard that are clearly established in these twenty-three verses of holy scripture.

"The Parable of the Sower"

Christ The Preacher

Before looking at the parable itself, it will be profitable to take notice of the ministry of our Saviour as the Servant of the Lord, as it is set before us by God the Holy Spirit in the opening verses of this chapter.

"The same day went Jesus out of the house, and sat by the sea side. And great multitudes were gathered together unto him, so that he went into a ship, and sat; and the whole multitude stood on the shore. And he spake many things unto them in parables, saying, Behold, a sower went forth to sow" (vv. 1-3).

Our Saviour was relentless in preaching the gospel. This was "the same day" in which he had preached the message contained in chapter twelve. He took no rest, though he was as weary as any other man would be after such labour. What a rebuke this should be to all who are called of God to this great work, but choose to pamper themselves, rather than be utterly consumed with the work of the ministry. All who are called and sent of God into the field of harvest should devote themselves completely to their work. I do not mean that pastors and gospel preachers should never rest. Our Saviour did, and so must we. But faithful men give themselves wholly to the work of the gospel (1 Timothy 4:15). Our Master said, "I must work the works of him that sent me, while it is day: the night cometh, when no man can work" (John 9:4). Let all who are called of him to preach the gospel follow his example.

Observe, too, the place where he preached. He was not now in the temple or synagogue, but the seaside. Robert Hawker wrote, "All places are sanctified when the Holy Ghost makes them so". And "great multitudes were gathered" to hear him. How anxiously they gathered to hear the Lord Jesus preach the gospel, "For he taught them as one having authority, and not as the scribes" (Matthew 7:29). Let every man who stands to speak to eternity bound sinners seek that authority that only God the Holy Spirit can give to deliver God's message to the hearts of those who hear him.

The Sower

"Behold a sower went forth to sow" (v. 3). Gospel preachers are like sowers. The preacher is a man who casts the bread upon the waters and waits for it to return only after many days (Ecclesiastes 11:1). He "goeth forth and weepeth, bearing precious seed", and "shall doubtless come again with rejoicing, bringing his sheaves with him" (Psalm 126:6).

Like the farmer, the preacher has to sow good seed if he wants to see fruit. The seed sown must be the pure Word of God, the gospel of God's free and sovereign grace in Christ. The man who does not preach the gospel does not preach the Word of God, though he may do nothing but recite scripture. To preach the Word of God is to preach Jesus Christ and him crucified (1 Corinthians 2:2). "We preach Christ crucified", not the traditions of the church, not a confession of faith, not the doctrines of men, and not the philosophy of the age, but "Christ crucified". Like the farmer who diligently sows his seed, the preacher must be diligent in the work of the gospel. He must spare no pains. He must use every means he has. He must seize every opportunity God gives, and earnestly labour in God's vineyard for the furtherance of the gospel. "Blessed are ye that sow beside all waters" (Isaiah 32:20). He must "be instant in season and out of season" (2 Timothy 4:2). He cannot be deterred by difficulties and discouragements. "He that observeth the wind shall not sow" (Ecclesiastes 11:4).

My wife and I raise a large garden every year. We are fully aware that we cannot cause the seed to germinate, and grow, and bear fruit. But if we do not plough the field, sow the seed, water it, and keep the garden weeded, we are not so foolish as to expect an ingathering of vegetables at the time of harvest. So it is with the preaching of the gospel. Success does not depend upon the preacher's labour and diligence; but success will not be attained without it. The preacher can no more give life to men than the farmer can cause the seed to germinate, and grow, and bear fruit. That is God's business and God's prerogative. But he can plough the ground, sow the seed, water it with prayer, and wait for God to give the increase as he sees fit, knowing all the while that "it is the Spirit that quickeneth; the flesh profiteth nothing" (John 6:63).

The Seed

"And when he sowed, some seeds fell by the way side, and the fowls came and devoured them up: Some fell upon stony places, where they had not much earth: and forthwith they sprung up, because they had no deepness of earth: And when the sun was up, they were scorched; and because they had no root, they withered away. And some fell among thorns; and the thorns sprung up, and choked them: But other fell into good ground, and brought forth fruit, some an hundredfold, some sixtyfold, some thirtyfold. Who hath ears to hear, let him hear" (vv. 4-9)

Luke tells us, "The seed is the Word of God" (Luke 8:11). The Word of God is the Seed of life (1 Peter 1:23-25; James 1:18; Romans 1:16; 10:17; Ephesians 1:13). I will not attempt to explain what I do not understand. But I know this. As sperm invading the egg brings forth life, so the Word of God invading the heart of a dead sinner, by the power of God the Holy Spirit, brings forth life. As the egg cannot be impregnated without sperm, so, too, a sinner cannot be born again without the Word of God. Why? Because God has so ordained it.

God's Prerogative

Salvation is the sovereign prerogative of God alone. If language has any meaning at all, verses 10-17 cannot possibly be read without concluding that there is such a thing as sovereign, distinguishing grace. God gives life, and faith, and understanding to his elect, and does not give it to others. "And the disciples came, and said unto him, Why speakest thou unto them in parables? He answered and said unto them, Because it is given unto you to know the mysteries of the kingdom of heaven, but to them it is not given." (vv. 10, 11). When people refuse to walk in the light God gives them, the light that is in them becomes darkness. "Take heed therefore how ye hear" (Luke 8:18). The seeing eye, the hearing ear, and the believing heart are gifts of God. "For verily I say unto you, That many prophets and righteous men have desired to see those things which ye see, and have not seen them; and to hear those things which ye hear, and have not heard them" (v. 17). Compare Romans 9:16; Ephesians 1:19; 2:8; Colossians 2:12.

Fruitless Hearers

Most people who hear the gospel preached receive no saving benefit from it. According to the passage before us, the vast majority, three out of four people, who hear the gospel preached do not profit by it. Our Lord is not talking about those who hear some false gospel, but those who hear the gospel of God's free and sovereign grace in Christ. The vast majority of those who hear the true gospel receive no spiritual, everlasting benefit from it.

Some are described as wayside hearers. "Hear ye therefore the parable of the sower. When any one heareth the word of the kingdom, and understandeth it not, then cometh the wicked one, and catcheth away that which was sown in his heart. This is he which received seed by the way side" (vv. 18, 19). Careless, thoughtless, and unconcerned, the gospel has no more effect on their hearts than a breeze upon rock. As fast as the Word falls on their ears, the devil plucks it away. They go out just like they came in, unaffected. Christ crucified means nothing to them (Lamentations 1:12).

When the Lord Jesus speaks of the devil, under the figure of the fowls of the air, catching away that which was sown in the heart, he is talking about the ministry of the word, and not the grace of God and the gracious operations of God the Holy Spirit, which are always effectual and irresistible. Satan does not and cannot take away what is sown by sovereign grace in the heart. That grace implanted by the Lord can never be taken away. Satan causes graceless hearers to forget what they heard. In them Isaiah's striking prophecy (Isaiah 6:9, 10), which is quoted no less than six times in the New Testament (Matthew 13:14, 15; Mark 4:12; Luke 8:10; John 12:40; Acts 28:26, 27; Romans 11:8), is fulfilled. "And in them is fulfilled the prophecy of Esaias, which saith, By hearing ye shall hear, and shall not understand; and seeing ye shall see, and shall not perceive: For this people's heart is waxed gross, and their ears are dull of hearing, and their eyes they have closed; lest at any time they should see with their eyes and hear with their ears, and should understand with their heart, and should be converted, and I should heal them."

Others are called stony ground hearers (vv. 20, 21). These people hear the sermon with pleasure. They are quickly excited. The message brings forth a plentiful crop of warm feelings and good resolutions. But the stony ground hearer's religion is religion without depth. As soon as the cold blasts of opposition or the hot sun of temptation and persecution come, their religion withers away. Many love to hear a gifted preacher preach good sermons, who have no interest at all in that which is preached. The mere love of good sermons and good preaching is not a sign of grace (Ezekiel 33:32).

The sun rising upon the stony ground hearer is not Christ, the Sun of righteousness, who rises "with healing in his wings", but the scorching, drying sun of opposition and persecution (Song of Solomon 1:6). The stony ground hearer was never rooted in Christ. The seed did not fall into the ground, but upon stony ground. Because they were never rooted in Christ and Christ was never in them, in time their interest and curiosity falls away and they disappear.

Then our Lord speaks of thorny ground hearers (v. 22). These people appear to be more hopeful than the others. They hang around much longer. They seem to really love the gospel. It appears that they really want to honour God and do his will. But other things constantly claim their affections. They know the truth. They hope one day to be decided and devoted followers of Christ; but they love the world! How many thorny ground hearers sit in the pews of our churches! They never make up their minds to "seek first the kingdom of God". They have real struggles trying to have both Christ and the world, not willing to give up either. But, in time, the care of the world and the deceitfulness of riches destroys them.

The Fruitful Hearer

Wherever the Word of God produces life, it brings forth fruit. "But he that received seed into the good ground is he that heareth the word, and understandeth it; which also beareth fruit, and bringeth forth, some an hundredfold, some sixty, some thirty" (v. 23). Because every human heart by nature is evil, we know that the "good ground", into which the seed is cast, is a heart renewed and made good by God's sovereign, saving grace.

God's method and order of grace is set before us in this parable, just as it is throughout the scriptures. First, he causes the chosen, redeemed sinner to hear the gospel. Then, by the hearing of the gospel, the sinner is born again by the incorruptible seed, the Word of God. And being born again, the believing sinner brings forth fruit unto God. We do not all bear fruit to the same degree. But all believers bear fruit; and the fruit they bear is the same (Galatians 5:22, 23; John 15:16). All is of the same quality, though not in the same quantity. A single drop of morning dew on a blade of grass is as truly water as the ocean. And fruits are fruits, be they small or great. It is all of Christ, and from Christ, and to Christ.

Grace in the heart produces heart fruit: repentance and faith, love, joy, peace. God the Holy Spirit causes the believing sinner to bring forth the lip fruit of prayer, confession, and praise. And Christ formed in the chosen sinner, being made partaker of "the divine nature", causes the believing sinner to bring forth the life fruit of love and consecration to Christ. "Take heed therefore how ye hear: for whosoever hath, to him shall be given; and whosoever hath not, from him shall be taken even that which he seemeth to have" (Luke 8:18).

Chapter 30

Three Instructive Parables

"Another parable put he forth unto them, saying, The kingdom of heaven is likened unto a man which sowed good seed in his field: But while men slept, his enemy came and sowed tares among the wheat, and went his way. But when the blade was sprung up, and brought forth fruit, then appeared the tares also. So the servants of the householder came and said unto him, Sir, didst not thou sow good seed in thy field? from whence then hath it tares? He said unto them, An enemy hath done this. The servants said unto him, Wilt thou then that we go and gather them up? But he said, Nay; lest while ye gather up the tares, ye root up also the wheat with them. Let both grow together until the harvest: and in the time of harvest I will say to the reapers, Gather ye together first the tares, and bind them in bundles to burn them: but gather the wheat into my barn. Another parable put he forth unto them, saying, The kingdom of heaven is like to a grain of mustard seed, which a man took, and sowed in his field: Which indeed is the least of all seeds: but when it is grown, it is the greatest among herbs, and becometh a tree, so that the birds of the air come and lodge in the branches thereof. Another parable spake he unto them; The kingdom of heaven is like unto leaven, which a woman took, and hid in three measures of meal, till the whole was leavened. All these things spake Jesus unto the multitude in parables; and without a parable spake he not unto them: That it might be fulfilled which was spoken by the prophet, saying, I will open my mouth in parables; I will utter things which have been kept secret from the foundation of the world. Then Jesus sent the multitude away, and went into the house: and his disciples came unto him, saying, Declare unto us the parable of the tares of the field. He answered and said unto them, He that soweth the good seed is the Son of man; The field is the world; the good seed are the children of the kingdom; but the tares are the children of the wicked one; The enemy that sowed them is the devil; the harvest is the end of the world; and the reapers are the angels. As therefore the tares are gathered and burned in the fire; so shall it be in the end of this world. The Son of man shall send forth his angels, and they shall gather out of his kingdom all things that offend, and them which do iniquity; And shall cast them into a furnace of fire: there shall be

wailing and gnashing of teeth. Then shall the righteous shine forth as the sun in the kingdom of their Father. Who hath ears to hear, let him hear."
(Matthew 13:24-43)

Our Lord Jesus here gives us three very instructive parables, comparing the kingdom of heaven to a field containing both wheat and tares, a grain of mustard seed, and leaven hidden in three measures of meal.

Why Jesus Spoke In Parables
In the middle of this passage (vv. 34-36) Matthew was inspired by God the Holy Spirit to give an explanation of why the Master spoke in parables. First, he tells us that it was our Lord's common habit in preaching to use parables. "All these things spake Jesus unto the multitude in parables; and without a parable spake he not unto them" (v. 34). The Master was a great story teller. He did not strive for spell-binding oratory, intellectual argument, or theological recitation. He deliberately spoke in plain, simple language to clearly set forth and illustrate gospel truth. That is the kind of preaching that should be cultivated among God's servants (1 Corinthians 2:3-5).

The word "parable" is the same word that is translated proverb in other places. Solomon's wise sayings and instructive similitudes are called proverbs, or parables, by which he taught us wisdom. "Behold, a greater than Solomon is here"! By his parables he teaches us wisdom "Who hath ears to hear, let him hear". Verse 34 shows us the manner, or method of Christ's preaching.

In verse 35 we see the subject matter of his parables. Speaking in parables, he fulfilled the prophecy of the Old Testament scriptures (Psalm 78:2). And the matter, the subject, the theme of these parables is "things which have been kept secret from the foundation of the world". The gospel of Christ and the purposes of God toward the Gentile world were wrapped up in the Old Testament by the types and shadows of the law, which have now been fulfilled by Christ, in whom God has revealed himself and made known his grace.

Then, in verse 36, we see something of our Saviour's sovereign majesty. Before explaining the parable of the wheat and the tares, he sent the multitudes away and entered into a house with his disciples. Here is God almighty exercising his sovereign mercy, giving grace to whom he would, and making a clear distinction among men. To some he revealed his Word. From others he hid the meaning of his words. That is his prerogative as God (Matthew 20:15; Exodus 33:19).

Three Instructive Parables

In these three instructive parables our Saviour shows us what we may expect to be the result of gospel preaching throughout the ages of time, and what both the righteous and the wicked may expect from God when time shall be no more.

Mustard Seed

First, let us read the parable of the mustard seed (vv. 31, 32). Though our Lord Jesus gave the parable of the wheat and the tares before those of the mustard seed and the leaven, he explained it afterward. So we will look at the parables in this order: first the mustard seed, second the leaven, and third the wheat and tares.

The parable of the grain of mustard seed is designed to teach us never to despise the day of small things (Zechariah 4:6-10). God's thoughts are not our thoughts and his ways are not our ways. God almost always does things exactly opposite of what we would and of what we might imagine he does. The gospel does not triumph all at once. The church and kingdom of God is not set up all at once, neither among us in the world, nor within us in our hearts.

The Church of God sprang from a very small seed sown in the earth. God's works almost always begin in obscurity, with what appear to be insignificant things. And the gospel has been spread through the nations of the world very gradually. Occasionally, there have been great, sudden out-pourings of grace upon multitudes, as on the day of Pentecost in Acts 2. But that has never been the normal method of God's workings among men, and is not now. Normally, God's church and kingdom grows and spreads gradually: consistently, but gradually. Like the grain of mustard seed sown in the ground, its growth is almost unobservable, but steady.

As the full grown mustard seed is the greatest and largest of all herbs, so the church and kingdom of God shall, in the end of the world, be immeasurably great and large. "Thou hast brought a vine out of Egypt: thou hast cast out the heathen, and planted it. Thou preparedst room before it, and didst cause it to take deep root, and it filled the land. The hills were covered with the shadow of it, and the boughs thereof were like the goodly cedars. She sent out her boughs unto the sea, and her branches unto the river" (Psalm 80:8-11). The number of God's elect shall be ten thousand times ten thousand, and thousands of thousands. Untold millions and billions of people shall inhabit heaven's glory with Christ!

Our Lord also compares faith to a grain of mustard seed. "If ye had faith as a grain of mustard seed, ye might say unto this sycamine tree, Be thou plucked up by the root, and be thou planted in the sea; and it should obey you" (Luke 17:6).

It begins small. It grows slowly. It becomes a great grace, honouring God and serviceable to men.

Leaven

"Another parable spake he unto them; The kingdom of heaven is like unto leaven, which a woman took, and hid in three measures of meal, till the whole was leavened" (v. 33). The parable of the leaven is misinterpreted by many. We are often told that the leaven refers to the ever-increasing evil of the world. But our Lord is not talking about the world. He is talking about "the kingdom of heaven". He is talking about his church. The parable of the leaven is very much the same in meaning as the parable of the mustard seed. It teaches us that the gospel prevails by degrees and works like leaven in the hearts of God's elect.

The woman, the weaker vessel, represents gospel preachers who have the treasure of the gospel in earthen vessels (2 Corinthians 4:7). The leaven was hidden in three measures of meal. The regenerate heart, like meal, is soft and pliable. Leaven will never work in corn, but only in ground meal. So the gospel has no effect upon the stony, unregenerate heart. It only works upon broken hearts that have been ground up by the Holy Spirit in conviction. Once the leaven is hidden in the dough, it works. So the word of God, hidden in the hearts of chosen, redeemed sinners by God the Holy Spirit, works and brings forth fruit (Hebrews 4:12). And the change it works, though it is universal, affecting the whole person (2 Corinthians 5:17), is gradual. This parable, like the parable of the mustard seed, is meant to show the wonderful works of God in and upon his elect. The grace of God in his children, like leaven, sanctifies them entirely, sanctifies the whole nature.

"As a little leaven leaveneth the whole lump", Robert Hawker wrote, "so the grace of God, when put by the Holy Ghost into the heart of a sinner, small and unnoticed as it is, produceth such vast things that angels look with wonder and astonishment at the change which is wrought (Luke 15:7)."

Wheat and Tares

Now, learn the parable of the wheat and the tares (vv. 24-30). "Then Jesus sent the multitude away, and went into the house: and his disciples came unto him, saying, Declare unto us the parable of the tares of the field. He answered and said unto them, He that soweth the good seed is the Son of man; The field is the world; the good seed are the children of the kingdom; but the tares are the children of the wicked one; The enemy that sowed them is the devil; the harvest is the end of the world; and the reapers are the angels. As therefore the tares are gathered and burned in the fire; so shall it be in the end of this world. The Son of man shall send forth his angels, and they shall gather out of his kingdom all things that offend, and them which do iniquity; And shall cast them into a furnace of fire: there shall be wailing and gnashing of teeth. Then shall the righteous shine forth as the sun in the kingdom of their Father. Who hath ears to hear, let him hear" (vv. 36-43).

I will not attempt to explain every detail of this parable, because our Saviour's explanation of it is crystal clear. Let me simply call your attention to the primary lessons to be learned from it. The first lesson here taught is so obvious that it is astonishing how slow we are to learn it. There is no such thing as a perfect or pure church in this world. Every local church, every assembly of professed believers is a mixed multitude of true believers and people who merely profess, but do not possess faith in Christ. In the professing church of Christ, the children of the wicked one are mingled with the children of the kingdom. They spring up together, and grow together. This has been the experience of God's saints in all ages.

In this parable, our Lord teaches us that it is not the business of God's servants to separate the wheat from the tares. We do not have the ability to do it. We are not authorized to do it. And we must not try to do it. We judge all things only by outward appearance. No mortal has the ability to look on the heart. That means that no human being has the ability to know who is saved and who is lost. If we try to separate the wheat from the tares, we will pull up the wheat and keep the tares every time.

Though we cannot discern one from the other, both are perfectly known to God from everlasting. The tares can no more become good seed, than good seed can become tares. They are a totally different race. Though they are "to grow together until the harvest", and though the Church of God in this world will never be free from tares, yet "the Lord knoweth them that are his". And blessed are those who, by the sweet and effectual operations of his grace, giving them life and faith in Christ, are made to know whose they are, and to whom they belong. What unspeakable mercy it is to be numbered by electing love among the seed of Christ, heirs of God and joint-heirs with Christ (Isaiah 44:3-5; 59:21; Romans 8:17; Galatians 3:16-29; 1 John 3:1, 2).

In the harvest time, at the end of the world, the Lord God will separate the wheat from the tares (vv. 40-43). "And another angel came out of the temple, crying with a loud voice to him that sat on the cloud, Thrust in thy sickle, and reap: for the time is come for thee to reap; for the harvest of the earth is ripe. And he that sat on the cloud thrust in his sickle on the earth; and the earth was reaped. And another angel came out of the temple which is in heaven, he also having a sharp sickle. And another angel came out from the altar, which had power over fire; and cried with a loud cry to him that had the sharp sickle, saying, Thrust in thy sharp sickle, and gather the clusters of the vine of the earth; for her grapes are fully ripe. And the angel thrust in his sickle into the earth, and gathered the vine of the earth, and cast it into the great winepress of the wrath of God. And the winepress was trodden without the city, and blood came out of the winepress, even unto the horse bridles, by the space of a thousand and six hundred furlongs" (Revelation 14:15-20).

None but God can tell tares from wheat until the harvest time. Then, at harvest time, all shall be made to know, because the tares will stand tall and the wheat will bows their heads (Matthew 25:31-46). C. H. Spurgeon, commenting on verses 40-42, wrote:

> What a description! The outgathering of 'all things that offend,' and of all persons who cause others to stumble, and who work evil, will be a consummation devoutly to be wished. Not only the outwardly wicked, but the false pretenders, the mock wheat, shall be removed … The fate of these ungodly ones will be fire, the most terrible of punishments, but this will not annihilate them, for they shall exhibit the surest tokens of a living woe 'wailing and, gnashing of teeth'. Sooner or later, this is what must come of evil men. Though in this world they flourish in the same field with believers, and can hardly be discerned from them, they shall be removed from such honourable association, and be cast, with the rubbish of the universe, into that great 'furnace of fire' whose smoke goeth up for ever and ever. This the Son of man will do with authority, the angels are simply the executioners of 'the wrath of the Lamb'.

"Then shall the righteous shine forth as the sun in the kingdom of their Father." The righteous are those sinners saved by the grace of God who have the righteousness of Christ imputed to them in free justification and imparted to them in regeneration. As Ralf Erskine put it, "If you would have righteousness, you must have it in and from Christ. He has to give you both an imputed righteousness for justifying you, and an imparted righteousness for sanctifying you." By faith in Christ we receive internally what Christ has done for us externally. Because we were justified by Christ's imputed righteousness at the cross, we are sanctified by his imparted righteousness in the new birth. "I will greatly rejoice in the Lord, my soul shall be joyful in my God; for he hath clothed me with the garments of salvation, he hath covered me with the robe of righteousness" (Isaiah 61:10).

Though, in this world, the righteous are slandered and reproached as evil, though they are incessantly opposed, afflicted, and persecuted, in that day they "shall shine forth", as John Gill wrote, "in the robe of Christ's righteousness, in perfect holiness of nature, in all felicity and prosperity of soul, and in the shining dazzling robes of glory, incorruption, and immortality, on their bodies." They "shall shine forth as the sun", having no spot in them or upon them, without any clouds of darkness. They will be as Christ himself, "the Sun of righteousness", with whom and in whose glory they shall appear, faultless, without spot or wrinkle, "before the presence of his glory"!

They "shine forth as the sun in the kingdom of their Father". When Christ our Mediator has "delivered up the kingdom to God, even the Father", when he has put all things under his (Christ's) feet, "that God may be all in all" (1 Corinthians 15:24-28). Then the righteous shall shine forth as everlasting monuments and trophies of grace (Ephesians 2:7) to the praise, honour, and glory of the triune God (Ephesians 1:6, 12, 14).

"Who hath ears to hear, let him hear". Our Redeemer calls us to pay attention to and reflect upon what he has taught us in these instructive parables. Blessed are they who, having ears to hear, hear and understand by his grace the things here declared by the Son of God.

Chapter 31

What The Kingdom Of Heaven Is Like

"Again, the kingdom of heaven is like unto treasure hid in a field; the which when a man hath found, he hideth, and for joy thereof goeth and selleth all that he hath, and buyeth that field. Again, the kingdom of heaven is like unto a merchant man, seeking goodly pearls: Who, when he had found one pearl of great price, went and sold all that he had, and bought it. Again, the kingdom of heaven is like unto a net, that was cast into the sea, and gathered of every kind: Which, when it was full, they drew to shore, and sat down, and gathered the good into vessels, but cast the bad away. So shall it be at the end of the world: the angels shall come forth, and sever the wicked from among the just, And shall cast them into the furnace of fire: there shall be wailing and gnashing of teeth."
(Matthew 13:44-50)

In these seven verses we have the parables of the treasure hidden in a field, the pearl of great price, and the net cast into the sea. Each of these three parables is full of rich, spiritual instruction for all who are taught of God. May God the Holy Spirit, who inspired Matthew to record these parables for us, be our Teacher as we study them together.

Treasure Hidden In A Field
The treasure hidden in a field is, in my opinion, the church of God's elect. Yes, we are the Lord's treasure, the portion of his inheritance, the apple of his eye, and the jewels of his crown. Though in ourselves, by nature and by birth, we are nothing but sinners, worthless and useless, because of God's sovereign love and distinguishing grace we are precious in his sight, so precious that he has sacrificed men and nations for us (Exodus 19:5, 6; Deuteronomy 32:8-10; Psalm 135:4; Isaiah 43:4). God's elect are so precious as the objects of his love and grace that he gave his own darling Son to redeem us and save us (John 3:16; Galatians 2:21; Titus 2:14; 1 John 3:16; 4:9, 10).

Roll this thought around in your heart. If you trust Christ as your Treasure, you are his treasure, the treasure of the Triune God! God's elect are like a treasure hidden in a field. The field in which they have been hidden is the world and the nations of it. Throughout the scriptures God's elect are spoken of as a people scattered among the nations, chosen from, redeemed out of, and called from the nations of the world.

This treasure was found by divine election (2 Thessalonians 2:13, 14). It was hidden by divine predestination and providence, the Lord God scattered and hid his elect among the nations of the world. He did so after the sin and fall of our father Adam (Genesis 3:24). He did so after the flood (Genesis 9:20-27). And he did so after the tower of Babel (Genesis 11:1-9). This scattering of the elect, hiding them in the earth, was God's work of judgment that he might gather them in everlasting mercy, love, and grace (Jeremiah 30:11; Ezekiel 11:16-18; Genesis 49:10; Isaiah 11:10; 56:8; 66:18; John 17:24).

The man in this parable, if I am not mistaken, is the God-man our Saviour, the Lord Jesus Christ. He bargained for us in old eternity as our Surety in the everlasting covenant of grace. He sacrificed everything he had that he might obtain the object of his love, his bride, the church, which he treasures above all things (2 Corinthians 8:9; Philippians 2:5-8). And he did it with joy! So great is his love for his elect that he joyfully came into this world to suffer the wrath of God for us to save us (Hebrews 12:2).

There was no joy in his sufferings. When our blessed Saviour anticipated being made sin for us, his heart was crushed within him in Gethsemane. If that which we read in Gethsemane displays the agony of our Saviour's holy soul in anticipation of the cross, how utterly inexpressible must have been his agony of soul when he was actually made sin for us and made to suffer all the unmitigated fury of the wrath of God at Calvary! Yet, he endured the cross, despising the shame, "for the joy set before him". What joy?" you might ask. The joy of seeing his seed with him in glory!

The scriptures clearly teach what is commonly called, "Limited Atonement", or "Particular Redemption", that the Lord Jesus Christ died and effectually redeemed his elect alone (Isaiah 53:8-11; 63:9; Daniel 9:24; Matthew 20:28; 26:28; John 10:11, 15, 26; 11:51, 52; Romans 5:11, 15, 19; 8:33, 34; 2 Corinthians 5:21; Galatians 3:13, 14; Ephesians 1:7; Colossians 1:14; Titus 2:14; Hebrews 1:1-3; 2:16; 9:12, 28; 10:10-14; 1 Peter 1:18-20; 2:21; 3:18; 1 John 3:16; Revelation 1:5, 6; 5:9, 10). Justice was not satisfied for the world. Christ did not put away everyone's sins. It was never the intention of the Son of God to redeem and save the whole world by his death. Christ died for God's elect. He satisfied divine justice for God's elect. He redeemed God's elect. And he put away the sins of God's elect.

Yet, as the God-man, as our Mediator, the Lord Jesus bought the world. Understand what I mean. I do not mean that the Son of God has redeemed every man in this world. Such an absurd pretence I have never made. But I do mean that Christ has purchased the right to rule this world as the mediator King for the salvation of his elect (John 17:2; Isaiah 53:10-12; 2 Peter 2:1). Our blessed Saviour has redeemed God's creation from the curse of sin (2 Peter 3:11-13; Romans 8:18-23). As a result of our Saviour's redemption work, this world shall be purged of all sin and restored to its pristine beauty. Not so much as a blade of grass shall be allowed to bear the curse brought upon it by sin. And when all things are created new, righteousness shall again flourish in the earth! The slime of the serpent's trail shall not be found in God's creation.

Our Lord Jesus bought the field (the world) that he might get the treasure hidden in the field. Our Lord Jesus, as a Man, bought the world that he might save his elect. This parable does not teach universal redemption. Not on your life! It teaches particular, effectual redemption. Christ did not make atonement for the world (the field). He made atonement for his elect (the treasure). But as a man he bought the right to rule the field and to dispose of the field, as he will, for the salvation of his elect (Psalm 2:8; John 17:2). When he has gathered his treasure out of this field, he will burn the field, destroy all that is evil in it, and make this field anew, making it a suitable habitation for his saints. The parable of the treasure hidden in the field is designed to show us a picture of Christ's love for his bride, the church of God's elect. Charles Wesley wrote:

> Amazing love! How can it be
> That Thou, my God, should'st die for me?

Pearl Of Great Price

"Again, the kingdom of heaven is like unto a merchant man, seeking goodly pearls: Who, when he had found one pearl of great price, went and sold all that he had, and bought it" (vv. 45, 46). The parable of the pearl of great price is intended to teach us how precious, highly valued and esteemed, and greatly loved, the Lord Jesus Christ is to God's elect. Christ is the believer's portion. "Unto you therefore which believe, he is precious" (1 Peter 2:7).

Some people object to the use of terms like “awakened sinners” and “sensible sinners”, and certainly the terms may be pressed to mean more than I intend by them; but I do not know how else to describe the merchantman in this parable than this. He represents a sinner who has been awakened to and made sensible of his need of salvation and acceptance with God. I do not say that he is regenerated, saved, or converted. But he is a person who knows he must meet God in eternity and he seeks to prepare for that awesome event.

Such men and women seek after a great variety of things, which, at first sight, seem to them to be “goodly pearls”: moral reformations; legal righteousness; religious ritualism; a profession of faith; church membership; works of zeal, devotion, and piety etc.. For these things they are willing to exchange many things and imagine that they have made a good trade, until Christ is revealed in all the fulness of his glory and grace. Then, when the seeking sinner finds the sovereign Saviour, he sees in the crucified Son of God everything he wants and needs (1 Corinthians 1:30; Ephesians 1:3; Colossians 3:11). Believing Christ, the sinner says, “He is precious”! And he is willing to part with anything and everything for Christ (Mark 8:34-37; Luke 14:25-33).

Gracious Lord, incline Thine ear,
My request vouch safe to hear;
Hear my never ceasing cry,
Give me Christ, or else I die!

Wealth and honour I disdain,
Earthly comforts all are vain,
These can never satisfy,
Give me Christ, or else I die!

Lord, deny me what Thou wilt,
Only ease me of my guilt,
Suppliant at Thy feet I lie,
Give me Christ, or else I die!

All to whom Christ is revealed in the fulness of his saving grace and glory willingly give up all things to win him and be found in him (Philippians 3:7-15). This parable, simple as it is, explains the life and behaviour of all true Christians.

The believer is what he is and does what he does because he is thoroughly convinced that "Christ is all". He comes out of the world. He says "No" to the lusts of the flesh. He puts off the old man and puts on the new. He hates sin and pursues righteousness. He counts all things but loss for Christ, because he sees Christ to be "the Pearl of great price" that he must have, for which he gladly sells all that he has.

Many years ago, I was sitting in a hospital waiting room reading J. C. Ryle's *True Christianity*, I was not trying to be obvious; but a man sitting next to me kept looking over, as if he wanted to talk. Finally, I laid the book on my lap for a few seconds and the man said to me, "I couldn't help noticing the title of the book you are reading. May I ask you something?" "Certainly", I said. "What does it take to be a true Christian?" the man asked. "Nothing *from* me, but all *of* me", I replied. Then I proceeded to tell him that faith in Christ is nothing more and nothing less than the surrender of myself to the Son of God as my Lord and Saviour. That is the doctrine of this parable.

This parable, simple as it is, also explains the life and behaviour of lost, unregenerate church members. Forgive me if I offend, but I must be plain if I am to help those who most need to understand our Lord's doctrine.

Many who have for years professed to be Christians are always halting between two opinions. They flinch from decisiveness. They shrink from taking up the cross and following Christ. They wear his name, but not his garments. They venture nothing for Christ. They simply cannot make up their minds to sell all for Christ. Why? The answer is obvious. They do not yet see that Christ is "the Pearl of great price". He is not precious to them because they do not trust him. Therefore, they cannot and will not forsake all that they may have him. They may sing with their lips, "Take the world, but give me Jesus", but everyday they say with their lives, "If it comes to that, I'll take the world, somebody else can have Jesus"!

The parable of the Pearl of great price is intended to show us that Christ is incomparably precious to all true believers. He is "the Pearl of great price", for which all who are born of God sell all that we may have him.

The Net

The parable of the net cast into the sea was given to show us the true nature of Christ's visible church and kingdom in this world. The preaching of the gospel is like the casting of a great net into the sea of this world. It is our business to cast the net. But as a net cast into the sea gathers a great multitude of fish, some good and some bad, so the preaching of the gospel gathers into Christ's visible church both genuine believers and carnal professors, both regenerate souls and unregenerate, both humble possessors of faith and hypocritical professors of faith. There is sure to be a time when the good fish are separated from the bad; but that is God's doing, not ours. And he will not do it until the end of the world.

We will look at this parable in more detail later. For now, I want to show you three things clearly revealed in it. First, all the churches of Christ in this world are mixed assemblies of good and bad fish. Throughout these parables, our Lord repeatedly stresses this point. There are good hearers and bad hearers, tares and wheat, good fish and bad fish. Why? He means for us to understand that there is no perfect church, no perfect body of believers in this world. If we try to make the church perfect and pure by separating the bad from the good, we will both be disobedient to our Master and instruments of great harm to his people.

Second, we must never be satisfied with an outward profession of faith and outward church membership. You may be in the net, and yet not be in Christ. Multitudes have been buried in the waters of baptism, who have never been crucified with Christ. Thousands around the world regularly eat and drink the bread and wine of the Lord's supper, who never feed upon Christ by faith.

Third, the true character of every person's religion will soon be revealed. "So shall it be at the end of the world: the angels shall come forth, and sever the wicked from among the just, And shall cast them into the furnace of fire: there shall be wailing and gnashing of teeth" (vv. 49, 50).

When the Lord God draws the net to shore, he will gather the good and throw away the bad. There will be an eternal separation between the wicked and the just. There is a heaven for the just and a furnace of fire for the wicked. Richard Baxter wrote, "These plain words need more belief and consideration than exposition". Have you bought "the Pearl of great price"? Are you in Christ?

Chapter 32

The Dragnet And The Householder

"Again, the kingdom of heaven is like unto a net, that was cast into the sea, and gathered of every kind: Which, when it was full, they drew to shore, and sat down, and gathered the good into vessels, but cast the bad away. So shall it be at the end of the world: the angels shall come forth, and sever the wicked from among the just, And shall cast them into the furnace of fire: there shall be wailing and gnashing of teeth. Jesus saith unto them, Have ye understood all these things? They say unto him, Yea, Lord. Then said he unto them, Therefore every scribe which is instructed unto the kingdom of heaven is like unto a man that is an householder, which bringeth forth out of his treasure things new and old."
(Matthew 13:47-52).

Matthew 13 contains the parables of the kingdom. Each parable is intended to convey a single specific spiritual truth. They are earthly illustrations of spiritual things, of things relating to the kingdom of heaven, that kingdom into which sinners are born when they are born again by God the Holy Spirit.

> The parable of the sower (vv. 3-23) illustrates the various effects the preaching of the gospel has upon those who hear it.
> The parable of the wheat and the tares (vv. 24-30, 37-43) illustrates the fact that God's visible church is a mixed multitude in this world, true believers and carnal professors.
> The parable of the mustard seed (vv. 31, 32) is a picture of faith, beginning as a very small thing, but growing into a strong and fruitful grace.
> The parable of the leaven hidden in meal (v. 33) portrays the gradual spread and influence of the gospel, both in the hearts and lives of God's elect and in the world.
> The parable of the treasure hidden in a field (v. 44) illustrates the love of Christ for his church, his elect bride.

> The parable of the pearl of great price (vv. 45, 46) displays the love of every believer for the Lord Jesus Christ "Unto you therefore which believe, he is precious"!

The last two of the eight parables of the kingdom given in this chapter illustrate the separation and judgment of unbelievers from the saints of God and the responsibility of God's servants in the work of the gospel ministry. The parable of the dragnet (vv. 47-50) is a warning of judgment, illustrating the separation of the wicked from God's elect and their everlasting destruction in the day of judgment. The parable of the householder (vv. 51, 52) shows us what God's servants are responsible to do as the ministers of Christ and stewards of the gospel.

The Dragnet

First, in verses 47-50 our Lord declares the parable of the dragnet. In this parable, our Saviour warns us that things will not always continue as they now are. Soon the kingdom of heaven will be full, the church of God will be complete, and there will be a day of judgment in which God will forever separate the righteous from the wicked. This parable is intended to be a warning to all men of the certainty of God's wrath and of the day of judgment.

To illustrate God's judgment our Lord used the activity of fishing, which all who heard him would surely understand, for it was a common, everyday activity around the Sea of Galilee. There were three basic methods of fishing employed in that day, just as there are today. A line and a hook were used to catch one fish at a time. That is the kind of fishing the Lord sent Peter to do when money was needed to pay taxes (Matthew 17:24-27). One man fishing by himself might use a one-man casting net. Peter and his brother Andrew were taking turns casting this kind of net when the Lord Jesus called them to be "fishers of men" (Matthew 4:18, 19). These small nets were used in shallow water. A man would wade out in the water. When a school of fish came near, he would cast the net upon the water. As the net's weights carried it down over the fish, he would draw it together and haul his catch to shore.

The third type of fishing was done by the use of a huge dragnet. A dragnet might be stretched out to cover as much as one half square mile. It required the labour of a team of fishermen. The dragnet was pulled in a giant circle by two boats, or by one boat if one end could be anchored to the shore. Floats were attached to the top of the net and weights to the sides, so that when it was cast, the dragnet formed a huge wall around everything it encompassed. Because the net permitted nothing to escape, it swept to shore everything in its path, fish of every kind, both good and bad. When the net was full, it would be dragged onto the beach by a huge team of men. At the end of the day, they gathered the good fish into containers to carry home or to market. And the bad fish, they simply discarded with all the useless trash that had been caught in their net. When our Lord said, "The kingdom of heaven is like unto a net", the word that he used specifically means dragnet.

Explanation

The fishermen in the parable are gospel preachers. The sea is the world. The net is the gospel we preach. The ship into which the fish are gathered is the church of God. The good fish are true believers. The bad fish are the false professors. The time of separation is the end of the world. John Gill puts it like this:

> The preaching of the gospel is the means of gathering souls to Christ, and into his churches. Those that are gathered into a visible gospel church are of every kind, of all nations in the world, Jews and Gentiles, all ranks and degrees of men, high and low, rich and poor, bond and free, all sorts of sinners, men good and bad. Some have the truth of grace in them. Others, that are only hypocrites, … have nothing but a form of godliness, and a name to live, and are dead.

We are to preach the gospel freely and indiscriminately to all men, as God gives us opportunity (Matthew 28:18-20; Romans 1:15, 16; 2 Corinthians 5:17-21). As long as we are in this world the visible church of God will be like the ark that Noah built, containing all kinds of creatures, both clean and unclean. Three times in these parables, in the parable of the sower, in the parable of the wheat and the tares, and again in this parable of the dragnet, our Lord tells us that his church in this world is a mixed congregation. He intends for us to learn and remember this lesson.

Separation

There is a day of separation coming (vv. 49, 50). When the fulness of the Gentiles has been brought in, when the last chosen, redeemed sinner has been saved, the Lord Jesus Christ will come again in judgment. In that day he will separate the bad fish from the good (Romans 11:25, 26; Revelation 20:11-15; John 5:28, 29; Acts 17:31).

Nothing in the Bible is more difficult to accept than the fact of hell. Nothing more difficult to talk or write about. But we cannot ignore it. We must not ignore it. It is clearly and constantly set before us in the Word of God. It was spoken of more often by the Lord Jesus than any other subject. He talked much more about hell and divine judgment than he did about the love of God (Matthew 5:22, 29, 30; 8:12; 11:23; 18:8, 9; 23:33; Mark 3:29; 9:43; Luke 10:15; 12:9, 10, 46; 16:23, 24; John 5:29; 15:6).

Hell is not merely the state of forever being separated from all that is good. It is not merely going out into nothingness. I do not pretend to know what hell is. The human mind simply cannot conceive the horrors of hell. Even the biblical representations of hell are only suggestive. Men argue about literal fire in hell. But the fire of God's wrath is infinitely more horrible than any inferno we ever imagined! No words can describe and no mind can imagine the pain, the agony, the torment of that "furnace of fire" where there is both "weeping and gnashing of teeth" forever.

This much is certain. Hell is a place of constant torment, misery, and pain (Matthew 22:13). The torments of hell will involve both body and soul. It is a place "where their worm dieth not, and the fire is not quenched" (Mark 9:44; cf. Hebrews 10:28, 29; Luke 12:47, 48). John Gerstner wrote, "Hell will have such severe degrees that a sinner, were he able, would give the whole world if his sins could be but one less"! And hell is forever! It is a state of total, eternal hopelessness (Matthew 25:46). John Bunyan wrote, "Forever"! will be the most tormenting word known in hell"! And C. H. Spurgeon said:

> In hell thou shalt have none but a company of damned souls with an innumerable company of devils to keep company with thee. While thou art in this world the very thought of the devil's appearing to thee makes thy flesh to tremble and thine hair ready to stand upright on thy head … Oh, what wilt thou do when all the devils of hell be with thee howling, roaring, and screeching in such a hideous manner that thou wilt be even at thy wit's end and ready to run stark mad again for anguish and torment? If after ten thousand years an end should come, there would be comfort. But here is thy misery: here thou must be forever!

The Householder

The parable of the householder portrays the great worth and importance of the gospel ministry. The question of verse 51 was put directly to our Lord's disciples, "Have ye understood all these things?" While the reference may include all that he had spoken in parables, I think it is best to see this question as referring to what he had spoken immediately before in verses 47-50 regarding the preaching of the gospel, the gathering of sinners to Christ, and the judgment to come.

Understanding these things, a great weight of responsibility is upon the shoulders of every believer and particularly upon the shoulders of all who are "scribes" in the kingdom, those men who are gifted and called by God as preachers of the gospel (2 Corinthians 5:1-21). They are men who have been instructed into the mysteries of the kingdom of heaven, the gospel of the grace of God. These men, God's servants, gospel pastors and preachers, are householders under Christ. They are responsible for the feeding of the family (Acts 20:28; Jeremiah 3:15), the rule of the family (Hebrews 13:7, 17), and the care and protection of the family of God (2 Timothy 4:12-16). John Gill says:

> Gospel ministers are deputies and stewards under him, and under him preside over the household, and have the government of it, provide food for it, and protect and defend it; all which require large gifts and abilities, great love and affection, both to Christ and his people; much wisdom, prudence, and knowledge; and great faithfulness and integrity, courage and firmness of mind.

Just as a faithful husband and father, who is a good provider for his family, lays up stores for his household, and brings them forth as needed, so the faithful pastor, by diligent labour in study and prayer, lays up good things for the family of God and brings them out as needed for their souls' good, comfort, and edification. The treasury from which we bring forth things old and new as they are needed is the Word of God. Every faithful gospel preacher knows that he carries the treasure of the gospel in an earthen vessel (2 Corinthians 4:7), and is humbled by the realization of that fact (Ephesians 3:8). Yet, like Elihu, he is full of the matter (Job 32:19). Like Jeremiah, he cannot forbear (Jeremiah 20:9). Like David, his tongue is the pen of a ready writer (Psalm 45:1).

But what does our Lord mean by "things new and old"? He certainly is not suggesting that the gospel preacher brings forth old doctrines and new. Someone once accurately stated, with regard to doctrine, "If it is new it is not true; and if it is true it is not new". By "things new and old", our Lord is referring to truths that are old in themselves, but newly made known to and experienced by his servants as they study the scriptures. To cite Gill again, this refers to "every new acquisition of knowledge and experience, added to the former stock and fund. The phrase seems to denote the plenty and variety of Gospel provisions, which the ministers of it are to bring forth, suited to the various cases of such who are under their care."

Some things are laid up to ripen in our hearts to be brought out in due season. Other things, like fresh vegetables gathered from the garden, are best served up immediately. But the faithful man keeps nothing back. He does not confine his provision for the family of God to a single aspect of gospel truth, but sets forth Christ crucified by declaring all the counsel of God. He is neither weary of the old, nor afraid of the new. Old truth is made new by a living experience; and the faithful man brings forth the old, old truths of holy scripture as new things, because he has experienced them new in his own soul.

The word "new" means "fresh". Faithful preachers do not serve up leftovers. They diligently seek God's message for his people, that they might feed them with knowledge and understanding. C. H. Spurgeon's comments on verse 52, in my opinion, precisely convey our Lord's intent.

> We must in our instruction of others cultivate variety, but we must not aim at it by poisoning the children with deadly drugs for the sake of giving them novel dishes. Only things worth putting into a treasury are worth bringing forth to the household. That scribe had need be well instructed who has to keep on handing out a variety of precious truth throughout a long life. Lord, make us sufficient for these things. Instruct us, that we may instruct our household. May we make no reserve for self, but bring out for thy people all that which thou hast put in our charge. Oh, to be accepted of thee in the day of thy return, because found faithful to our trust!

Chapter 33

The Power Of Unbelief

"And it came to pass, that when Jesus had finished these parables, he departed thence. And when he was come into his own country, he taught them in their synagogue, insomuch that they were astonished, and said, Whence hath this man this wisdom, and these mighty works? Is not this the carpenter's son? is not his mother called Mary? and his brethren, James, and Joses, and Simon, and Judas? And his sisters, are they not all with us? Whence then hath this man all these things? And they were offended in him. But Jesus said unto them, A prophet is not without honour, save in his own country, and in his own house. And he did not many mighty works there because of their unbelief."
(Matthew 13:53-58)

We often hear and read about the power of faith, and rightly so. Our Lord Jesus said, "If ye have faith as a grain of mustard seed, ye shall say unto this mountain, Remove hence to yonder place; and it shall remove; and nothing shall be impossible unto you" (Matthew 17:20). But in this closing paragraph of Matthew chapter thirteen the Holy Spirit sets before us the power of *unbelief.* Just as faith as a grain of mustard seed, looking to Christ, has the power to cast the mountains of our sins into the depths of the sea of God's grace, so unbelief has the power to ruin your soul, unleash the wrath of God, and drag your soul down to hell.

The power of faith in Christ is manifest throughout the scriptures. Abraham believed God and it was imputed to him for righteousness. Noah believed God and built an ark to the saving of his family. Israel believed God and walked through the Red Sea. David believed God and slew Goliath. Daniel believed God and stopped the mouths of lions. The centurion soldier believed God and saw his servant healed. Two blind men believed God and received their sight. The woman with an issue of blood believed God and was healed of her infirmity. Jairus believed God and saw his daughter brought back to life. The Philippian Jailer believed God and received everlasting life. The list could go on and on. The Bible says much about the power of faith.

The scriptures also shows us the power of unbelief. Adam, Noah's generation, Lot's wife, Pharaoh, Israel, Nebuchadnezzar, the scribes and Pharisees, the Rich young ruler, Felix, Festus, and Agrippa all stand out as beacons to warn us of the danger and power of unbelief. All unbelief is a matter of the will. Unbelief is a matter of choice. Unbelief is saying "no" to God in spite of the evidence. This is what we see in Matthew 13:53-58.

Capernaum had been the home base of our Lord's ministry for about a year (Matthew 4:13; 8:5-10). The people there had seen his miracles. They heard his word. They watched his life. But they did not believe on him. Therefore, the Lord departed, never to return (v. 53). The Lord Jesus never went back to Capernaum again, except to walk through it to go to another place.

When the Lord Jesus returned to Nazareth he met with opposition and unbelief in his own hometown and among his own kinsmen (vv. 54-57; Luke 4:16-32). The people who heard him preach and saw the miracles he performed were astonished by his doctrine and his divine power; but "they were offended in him". They fell at "the stumbling stone" of his gospel preaching. The presence amongst them of the incarnate Son of God, the sinner's Friend and Substitute, became "a Rock of offence".

Poor souls! Like multitudes today, the things they heard from his lips, by which they were astonished, made him to them "a savour of death unto death" (2 Corinthians 2:16). Because they only knew Christ after the flesh, and not after the Spirit (2 Corinthians 5:16), they despised him. He was, therefore, a prophet without honour in his own country and among his own people. The offence of the cross has not ceased; and it never shall.

Time and again our Lord came to Nazareth, yet "he did not many mighty works there because of their unbelief" (v. 58). J. C. Ryle wrote, "Behold in this single word the secret of the everlasting ruin of multitudes of souls! They perish forever, because they will not believe." Let me show you six things about unbelief. May God the Holy Spirit be our Teacher and give us understanding.

Unbelief Ignores The Obvious

Look again at verse 54. "And when he was come into his own country, he taught them in their synagogue, insomuch that they were astonished, and said, Whence hath this man this wisdom, and these mighty works?" Those who heard his doctrine and saw his miracles did not reject him for lack of evidence, but in spite of great evidence. They did not reject him because they lacked the truth, but because they rejected the truth. They despised the light because they preferred darkness (John 3:1-20).

When men and woman wilfully reject Christ, the most powerful arguments and the most convincing facts will not convince them of divine truth. These people, being left to themselves, would not and could not come to him. The most convincing preaching, the most unquestionable displays of divine power, and the most emotional experiences did not produce faith in them. Faith in Christ is the gift of God (Ephesians 2:8, 9). It is something that must be wrought in us by the omnipotent mercy of God the Holy Spirit (Colossians 2:12).

Unbelief Exalts The Irrelevant

"Is not this the carpenter's son? is not his mother called Mary? and his brethren, James, and Joses, and Simon, and Judas? And his sisters, are they not all with us? Whence then hath this man all these things?" (vv. 55, 56). These things were totally irrelevant. The Lord Jesus preached the gospel to these eternity bound sinners; and they began to quibble about his family, his education, and his qualifications as a preacher! C. H. Spurgeon says:

> They grew sarcastic, and harped upon the family names of James, and Joses, and Simon, and Judas. They hinted that he could not have learned much wisdom in a carpenter's shop, and as he had not been among the rabbis to obtain a superior education, he could not really know much. How could he have attained to such eminence? He was a mere nobody. Why, they knew him when his parents lost him when they went up to the feast at Jerusalem! They could not listen to the talk of the carpenter's son.

There are multitudes just like them today. As Paul described them, "Ever learning, and never able to come to the knowledge of the truth" (2 Timothy 3:7). There are countless armchair theologians, men, and women, who consider themselves the religious authorities of the age. They are determined to enlighten everyone they meet on spiritual matters they know little about. They contribute nothing to the cause of Christ or the souls of men. But they are always full of questions: questions spewed out under the pretence of sincerity, with no purpose except to exalt themselves and slander faithful men.

It is sad and tragic to see people exalting small, insignificant things and using them as great excuses for not believing the gospel. They like to discuss obscure texts, choosing to ignore the obvious. They value their opinions more highly than the revelation of God in holy scripture. They cling to personal experience, religious tradition, and religious creeds as coverings for their rebellion to divine authority. By their quibbles, they seek to divert attention from the gospel, escape the claims of Christ, and justify themselves. Pastor Chris Cunningham, in his commentary on John 9, described the know-it-all Pharisees of the religious world as "orang-utans with a vocabulary".

Unbelief Stumbles Over The Truth

"And they were offended in him" (v. 57). Read Romans 9:30-32; 10:3, 4, 1 Corinthians 1:21-24, and Luke 4:20-24. The fact is, all who are left to themselves in unbelief are offended by Christ and the gospel of Christ. In Matthew 11:6 our Saviour declares, "blessed is he whosoever shall not be offended in me". Truly they are blessed of God, blessed with grace and salvation in Christ, who, rather than being offended by the gospel, believe it and cannot part with it. Trusting Christ alone as our Saviour, we have peace, joy, and comfort in our souls and look for the mercy of our Lord Jesus Christ unto eternal life (Jude 21).

Unbelief Blocks The Supernatural

"And he did not many mighty works there because of their unbelief" (v. 58). Our Lord performed some miracles there, but not many, that they might be left without excuse. John Gill wrote, "He only 'laid his hands upon a few sick folk, and healed them.' Yet, these were such as raised their wonder and astonishment, but did not command their faith, and were rather stumbling blocks unto them. Such were their prejudices, their unbelief, and the hardness of their hearts. And the reason indeed why he did no more was, 'because of their unbelief'."

Mark tells us that "he marvelled because of their unbelief", and 'he could there do no mighty works' (Mark 6:5, 6). That does not mean that he lacked the power to perform them, or that their unbelief was too great and mighty for him (the omnipotent God) to overcome. Some of our Lord's miracles were performed in direct response to personal faith. But many, perhaps most of them, were performed without any expression of faith in those who benefited from them. Man's lack of faith does not bind the power of God. Man's unbelief does not hold dominion over God's omnipotence. God does what he will, whether man believes or not!

However, throughout his earthly ministry our Lord chose not to perform his miracles where men and women manifested a hardened, wilful unbelief. Unbelief became a barrier to divine blessings. In Matthew 13:58 the Holy Spirit specifically tells us that it was because of the unbelief of the people that our Saviour did no miracles of significance in Nazareth.

Unbelief Can Never See The Glory Of God

How unbelief robs us! I cannot help wondering, "What might have been, had I but believed God?" People sit around and debate the issue of God's sovereignty and man's responsibility as casually as they debate politics, so that they may appear very precise and orthodox in their theological opinions and excuse their rebellion, unbelief, sin, and disobedience, saying, "Well, God is sovereign. His purpose stands fast. His will is done." All of that is true enough; but their rationalization is wrong. In Isaiah 48:16-19 the Lord God expressly declares what might have been, had Israel simply obeyed his voice. As Martha stood before her brother's tomb, "Jesus saith unto her, Said I not unto thee, that, if thou wouldest believe, thou shouldest see the glory of God?" (John 11:40).

John Calvin wrote, "Our own unbelief is the only impediment which prevents God from satisfying us largely and bountifully with all good things." Too often we walk upon God's promises like children upon ice, always fearful of it breaking and us falling! How shameful! It is unbelief alone that prevents us from soaring in our hearts to the celestial city and walking by faith even now across the streets of gold.

Unbelief Alone Holds Lost Souls In Condemnation

If you perish, it will be for only one reason. It will be because you will not believe on the Lord Jesus Christ (John 3:13-18). There is nothing else in heaven or earth that will prevent you from being saved (John 5:40).

"There are three great enemies", J. C. Ryle, wrote, "against which God's children should daily pray: pride, worldliness, and unbelief." Of these three, none is greater than unbelief. Let us ever beware of unbelief, praying for grace to be delivered from it. Unbelief kept Moses out of the promised land, caused Aaron to fall under pressure, caused David to behave like a madman, and caused Peter to tremble before a little girl! I often wonder what blessings, privileges, and opportunities I have missed because of unbelief! "Lord, I believe, Help thou mine unbelief" (Mark 9:24).

Chapter 34

The Baptist Beheaded

"At that time Herod the tetrarch heard of the fame of Jesus, And said unto his servants, This is John the Baptist; he is risen from the dead; and therefore mighty works do shew forth themselves in him. For Herod had laid hold on John, and bound him, and put him in prison for Herodias' sake, his brother Philip's wife. For John said unto him, It is not lawful for thee to have her. And when he would have put him to death, he feared the multitude, because they counted him as a prophet. But when Herod's birthday was kept, the daughter of Herodias danced before them, and pleased Herod. Whereupon he promised with an oath to give her whatsoever she would ask. And she, being before instructed of her mother, said, Give me here John Baptist's head in a charger. And the king was sorry: nevertheless for the oath's sake, and them which sat with him at meat, he commanded it to be given her. And he sent, and beheaded John in the prison. And his head was brought in a charger, and given to the damsel: and she brought it to her mother. And his disciples came, and took up the body, and buried it, and went and told Jesus."
(Matthew 14:1-12)

What thoughts arise from this short narrative of the death of John the Baptist! The cruelty and hatred of Herodias toward that faithful prophet, the savagery of Herod, his guests, and his family are as disgusting as they are inexcusable. Yet, by the order of divine providence, they were but the executioners of God's appointed means of bringing one of his elect home to heaven.

It is written, "Precious in the sight of the Lord is the death of his saints" (Psalm 116:15). It matters not where they die, by what means they die, or when they die, "Precious in the sight of the Lord is the death of his saints." Here we are told about the death of one of his saints. John the Baptist was brutally beheaded by Herod. Why? He was beheaded for faithfully serving God and for being faithful to Herod as God's messenger. The things we have before us in these twelve verses are written for our learning. May God the Holy Spirit, whose Word this is, write its lessons upon our hearts.

Herod

Herod stands before us as a glaring example of human depravity. He was the vile son of a vile father. Faith and godliness never pass from generation to generation. Only God can give men faith. Only God makes men righteous. But ungodliness and wickedness do pass from fathers to sons, generation after generation.

The Herod mentioned in Matthew 14 was Herod the Tetrarch, also known as Herod Antipas. He was the son of Herod the Great, a Gentile, a descendant of Esau. Herod the Great was infamous for his cold-blooded atrocities. He murdered the entire Jewish Sanhedrin because they dared challenge his authority. He murdered one of his wives on a whim. He murdered two of his sons for fear that they might take his throne. And he had all the male children in Bethlehem slaughtered in a vain attempt to destroy the Lord Jesus in his infancy. Herod the Great was a vile, detested man.

His sons were just like him. After Herod's death, the Roman government divided his province into three parts, giving three of Herod's many sons authority. Archelaus was given the southern province of Judea and Samaria (Matthew 2:22). Philip was given the northern provinces of Trachonitis and Ituraea. And Herod Antipas was given the area that included Galilee and Porea. This Herod the Tetrarch, Antipas, was a ruthless, shameless, henpecked, lustful man, given to every imaginable evil. He was no less beastly than his father, only less defiant and courageous.

While visiting Rome with his half-brother Philip, Herod became involved with Philip's wife, Herodias, in a sordid, promiscuous affair. In order to have Herodias for himself, he betrayed his brother, divorced his own wife, and almost lost his kingdom. His enraged father-in-law, King Arêtes, would have killed him had not the Roman army intervened.

Let us ever be aware of our behaviour in our homes. Our sons and daughters will most likely imitate us in our most unbecoming traits. Godliness does not breed godliness. But wickedness does breed wickedness.

Shocking as it is to read of the sordidness and brutality of Herod, Herodias, and her daughter, all three stand before us as a glaring example of the depths of depravity to which all Adam's race has been reduced by the Fall. That which one person is capable of doing, all are capable of doing. If you and I do not act out the depravity of our hearts as fully as these did, it is only because of God's restraint. Robert Hawker wrote:

The seeds of every sin are in every heart, the same by the fall. Reader! do you believe this? Yes! if God the Holy Ghost hath convinced you of sin. And until this is feelingly known in the heart, never will the infinitely precious redemption by the Lord Jesus Christ be understood or valued. Oh! how precious to them that believe is Jesus! 1 Peter 2:7. Hence a child of God reads this account of Herod, therefrom to abhor himself, and to love Jesus! 1 Corinthians 4:7.

Herod's Marriage

Adultery is a crime against God and man. Herod's adulterous marriage to his brother's wife was a matter of public scandal and wickedness that had to be reproved. The gospel writers do not tell us how or where John and Herod were brought together. It is possible, even likely, that Herod summoned John to come to his court that he might hear him preach, or see him perform some miracle. Kings and rulers often summon religious leaders.

Had John in preaching to Herod not rebuked the king for his publicly known sin and demanded repentance of him, he would not have been faithful to God or to Herod. Whatever the occasion, John said to Herod, "It is not lawful for you to have your brother's wife." Herodias had been divorced from Philip for a number of years and insofar as Roman law was concerned, she was now Herod's wife. But John did not recognize Roman law when it contradicted God's law. She was sleeping with Herod but she was Philip's wife.

I would not be faithful to the Word of God and to you who read these lines if I did not reprove the same behaviour today. I am compelled to clearly state some things taught in the Word of God about marriage. They are not popular; but they are clearly revealed in holy scripture. The Word of God does not change because men do not receive it and bow to it. Marriage is for life. The marriage bond can only be broken by three things: death (Romans 7:1-4); adultery and fornication (Matthew 19:9); and abandonment (1 Corinthians 7:15).

I know that some have experienced things in the past that greatly disturb them. Some are divorced, others divorced and remarried. You have brought yourself to such circumstances by wilful rebellion against God and now are anxious about what you have done. As a pastor, I am often asked by believing men and women who are divorced and remarried, "What can I do?" My answer is "Forget the past. God has." This is the only reasonable and the only right answer.

It is the responsibility and the privilege of other believers also to forget the past with regard to their brothers and sisters in Christ, no matter what they have done, each esteeming his brother and his sister in Christ better than himself. Let every saved sinner rejoice to know that our sins are under the blood of Christ. All our sins: past, present, and future sins; sins before conversion and sins following conversion. If God has forgiven us, we are to reckon ourselves forgiven (Romans 6:11). If God has forgiven our brother and sister (and he has), we are to look upon them and treat them as forgiven, just as we are. All Christ's people are accepted, justified, and righteous in him. "Forgetting those things which are behind (with regard to ourselves and to one another), and reaching forth unto those things which are before, let us press toward the mark for the prize of the high calling of God in Christ Jesus" (Philippians 3:13, 14).

John The Baptist

John the Baptist stands before us as a faithful servant of God. The first Baptist preacher in history was John the Baptist. He was a faithful servant of God. He set the standard and laid down the example to follow for all who would come after him. His message was repentance toward God, calling upon all who heard him to "Behold the Lamb of God".

John's ministry was a ministry of preaching; not counselling, but preaching; not education, but preaching. John did not build shelters for the homeless or hospitals for the sick, he preached. If there is anything this generation needs to learn about the work of the ministry, it is this. Those who are called of God to the work of the ministry are called to preach, only to preach, and to preach the gospel of Christ, only to preach the gospel of Christ.

Let all who are called like John, be faithful like John (1 Corinthians 4:1, 2). He was faithful even unto death. He was neither a compromiser nor a diplomat. He was a faithful gospel preacher. He was no more reluctant to confront Herod and Herodias with the claims of God than he was the scribes and Pharisees. God's servant is God's servant everywhere. He does not consider the cost or the consequence of delivering God's message. Being God's servant, John the Baptist feared nothing, and no one, but God.

We must never look for reward or recognition in this world. If ever there was a case of godliness and faithfulness unrecognized and unrewarded by men, it was that of John the Baptist. But John was content to serve his generation by the will of God without recognition, and in the face of constant ridicule and scorn. Let us follow his example. There is a day of judgment appointed by God. In that great day God will set the record straight (1 Corinthians 4:3, 4). That great day will make amends for all these lesser days (Romans 8:17; 2 Corinthians 4:17).

John's Message

John's message to Herod exemplifies the necessity of repentance. John the Baptist was the forerunner of the Lord Jesus Christ. As such, his ministry was in some ways typical of the work of God the Holy Spirit in preparing the hearts of chosen, redeemed sinners to bow down to the claims of Christ Jesus. John the Baptist faithfully told sinners that God demands nothing less than all-out, unconditional surrender to the claims of Christ; and that only those who bow to the sceptre of King Jesus will know the pardon of their sins, and experience what we call salvation.

Herod knew that John the Baptist was a faithful prophet, "a just man and an holy". As such, he respected him; but he was also afraid of him, "and observed him". "He did many things" because of him, and "heard him gladly" (Mark 6:20).

John's faithfulness cost him his life. A. T. Robertson observed, "It cost him his head; but it is better to have a head like John the Baptist and lose it than to have an ordinary head and keep it"! John's message to Herod was a sermon about the demands of a holy God. It is a sermon on the character of God. John stood before Herod as God's mouthpiece.

John the Baptist faced the king of Judea, his ungodly wife, her ungodly daughter, and all the courtiers that stood about the court. Herod heard a message from God by the lips of God's preacher and prophet that it was not lawful for him to have his brother's wife. That sermon, that faithfulness to God's truth, cost John the Baptist his head. But it cost Herod his immortal soul, because he refused to hear and bow before the throne of God.

John the Baptist linked the Old Testament with the New. The Old Testament prophets from Genesis to Malachi demanded repentance toward God. From the beginning of John's ministry, throughout the New Testament, and throughout this gospel age, repentance has been the continuing demand of the gospel. Every prophet, the Lord Jesus Christ himself in his prophetic ministry, all the apostles, and every faithful gospel preacher in all ages declare that God is a holy God, that his demands have not lessened, and that everywhere men are called upon to repent toward God and believe on the Lord Jesus Christ.

In the Old Testament God's prophets constantly called the people they served to repent. When John the Baptist came as the forerunner of Christ, preparing the people's hearts to receive the Christ, he called all who heard him to repentance.

"Repent ye, for the kingdom of heaven is at hand" (Matthew 3:2). The first sermon the Lord Jesus ever preached on this earth was a call to repentance (Matthew 4:17). The message has not changed. "God commandeth all men everywhere to repent" (Acts 17:30).

Repentance is God's command. Repentance, turning to and coming to God by faith in Christ, is nothing other than the total surrender of our lives to Christ the King. It is rebels throwing up the white flag of surrender, stacking arms before him by whom they have been conquered, willingly resigned to the will of the sovereign Christ. Repentance (faith in Christ) involves taking up your cross and following Christ. It is not an act performed, but a life surrendered (Luke 14:25-33). "Except ye repent, ye shall all likewise perish" (Luke 13:3).

It was preaching repentance that cost John the Baptist his life. Like the rich young ruler, when Herod heard of John and his message, "he did many things and heard him gladly". Yet, he lacked one thing. He lacked repentance. He refused to bow to Christ as God his Saviour and King. John knew exactly where his point of rebellion was, and deliberately, boldly, and unmistakably put his finger on the spot. Herod betrayed his brother Philip and took his wife. The faithful Baptist told Herod that the relationship with his brother Philip's wife openly displayed his defiance of God. He said publicly to the king of his public sin, "It is not lawful for thee to have her." Herod was willing to do many things. He was happy to listen to good preaching, even the good preaching of a faithful man, so long as it cost him nothing. But when John touched that reprobate king's conscience, and told him God demands surrender, the old rebel had John the Baptist beheaded and his head brought to him on a charger!

Repentance is the wilful, deliberate surrender of my life to the sovereign Christ. The Lord Jesus says, "Whosoever will come after me, let him deny himself, and take up his cross, and follow me. For whosoever will save his life shall lose it; but whosoever shall lose his life for my sake and the gospel's, the same shall save it" (Mark 8:34, 35). Repentance is loosing your life to Christ.

Have you repented? Have you willingly put your life into the hands of the Son of God? Have you turned yourself over to his rule as your Lord? Have you renounced all hope of life and salvation in yourself, trusting Christ alone as your Saviour? If you have, your repentance toward God and faith in Christ are the fruit of his mighty and gracious work in you and for you (Acts 5:31). Your repentance and faith is his gift and his operation (Romans 6:23; Ephesians 2:8, 9; Philippians 1:29; Colossians 2:12). And he who began his work of grace in you will continue it and complete it (Philippians 1:6).

The Baptist Beheaded

Conscience

Herod shows us that the conscience of a man is a powerful thing. It had been more than a year since Herod had John beheaded and his head brought to Salome in a charger. But his conscience never let him forget John or his words. When he heard about the Lord Jesus, he thought John the Baptist had come back from the dead to get revenge! (vv. 1, 2).

God has given us all a conscience. Your conscience will always either accuse you or excuse you (Romans 2:15). God gives some over to a reprobate mind and a seared conscience, judicially hardening their hearts because of their wilful rebellion and unbelief (Romans 1:28). Someone said, "The conscience is the voice of God in a man's soul." I do not know whether that is true or not; but I do know that God has put a conscience in every person which either accuses or excuses him in all his actions.

Conscience is that voice inside us we simply cannot silence. We can muffle it. We can sear it. But we cannot silence it. Conscience is a faculty of the mind God has put in us all by which we judge the moral character of human conduct, our own and others. It is an inborn sense of right and wrong. All men have a sense of right and wrong which, to a greater or lesser degree, reflects the law of God written upon the heart in creation (Romans 2:14, 15). You cannot find a society anywhere in history which has not demonstrated this fact, no matter how barbaric. Even today, perverse as things are, men cannot escape God's law.

The conscience of a man often produces a sense of guilt, legal fear, which many mistake for Holy Spirit conviction (John 8:9). The conviction of sin is more than a sense of guilt and legitimate condemnation (John 16:7-11). The conviction of sin arises from the revelation of Christ in the heart (Zechariah 12:10), and is accompanied by a conviction of righteousness and of judgment. Holy Spirit conviction is a gracious work of God the Holy Spirit. He effectually applies the gospel to the hearts of chosen, redeemed sinners, causing them to see Christ alone as the object of faith. He convinces all who are called by his effectual grace "of sin, because they believe not on" Christ. He convinces them that righteousness has been established by the obedience of the God-man, "of righteousness, because I go to my Father". And he convinces them that justice has been satisfied by the sin-atoning blood of Christ, "of judgment, because the prince of this world is judged".

It was their conscience that caused Adam and Eve to hide from God after the Fall. It was their conscience that made them know their nakedness and filled them with shame. That they could, to some degree, appease their consciences with fig leaf garments, made by their own hands, shows that the conscience of fallen man is, like every faculty of human nature, perverted and depraved.

Knowing these things, we must not trust our consciences. The conscience can be trusted no more than the thoughts of the depraved mind or the emotions of the depraved heart. Let us ever be careful not to violate our consciences, not for anyone. But do not trust your conscience. He who trusts his own conscience, like he who trusts his own heart, trusts both a fool and a devil. Our guide in all things must be the Word of God alone! Not our feelings! Not our desires! Not the opinions of others! The Word of God alone! The total depravity of our nature has made us perverse in all our faculties, so perverse that even the conscience of fallen man is corrupt.

A Good Conscience

The scriptures tell us plainly that the conscience of fallen man is "an evil conscience", from which we must be cleansed by the blood of Christ (Hebrews 10:22). The consciences of lost religious men are "defiled" (Titus 1:15), so defiled that they may, in a sense, have a "good conscience" while performing abominable things (John 16:2; Acts 23:1; 26:9; Romans 9:1). The Apostle Paul, writing by divine inspiration, tells us that when he was persecuting the church his conscience was bearing him witness. He was fully convinced that he was doing the right thing. Some are so hardened by freewill, works religion and ungodly behaviour that they live with a "seared" conscience (1 Timothy 4:1, 2).

Some men and women, and even children have consciences which are so hardened that they are past feeling. They have no regard for the rightness or wrongness of what they say or do. They have no sense of evil. "Under a cloak of sanctity they commit the most shocking impieties" says John Gill. If a person works at it, if he holds down the truth of God (Romans 1:18) long enough and persistently enough, he can cauterize his conscience. You can sear your conscience to excuse your wickedness.

Yet we all want a good conscience, a quiet, peaceful conscience. What would you give to have a good conscience? A conscience to let you sleep at night. A conscience to allow you to draw near to God with full assurance, and give you ease of heart and peace of mind in the prospect of death, judgment, and eternity.

All the religion, ceremonies and sacrifices in the world cannot obtain a good conscience. All the gifts, works of charity and philanthropy imaginable cannot buy a good conscience. Good works of moral reformation and religious devotion, no matter how earnest and sincere, will never earn a good conscience.

Our consciences demand a perfection we cannot give. The conscience echoes God's holy law. Echoing the law, it demands the same thing God's law demands. The conscience demands perfection. It will only accept complete atonement for sin. It will only accept perfect righteousness. Perfect atonement and perfect righteousness is found only in Christ's obedience and death as our Substitute (Hebrews 10:1-22).

Horatius Bonar was right when he wrote, "In another's righteousness we stand, and by another's righteousness we are justified. All accusations against us, founded upon our unrighteousness, we answer by pointing to the perfection of the righteousness which covers us from head to foot, in virtue of which we are unassailable by law as well as shielded from wrath.

> Thy work alone, O Christ, can ease this weight of sin;
> Thy blood alone, O Lamb of God, can give me peace within.
> Thy love to me, O God, not mine, O Lord, to Thee,
> Can rid me of this dark unrest, and set my spirit free.

The only way for a sinner to have a peaceful conscience before God is by faith in Christ (Hebrews 9:14). Pastor Mark Daniel wrote:

> Peter speaks of some who have a guilt-free conscience, not only before men, but toward God Himself! How is that? It's not that they have no reason to have a bad conscience. No, quite the contrary. They view everything they do as offensive to God! But, with just one recollection, all the black stains of sin are completely cleared from their conscience – by the resurrection of Jesus Christ! That single glorious act is all the proof they need that their sins are gone, completely hidden from the all-seeing eye of God, under the blood of their successful Saviour. Now, that's a good conscience!

Go Tell Jesus

John's disciples show us by their example where we must go and do in times of trouble and need. We read in verse 12, "His disciples came and took up the body, and buried it, and went and told Jesus." Notice Matthew's inspired words. "His disciples came and took up the body, and buried it." They took up the body, not the man, but the body, and buried it. They buried it in hope of the resurrection. Then, with heavy, heavy hearts, they "went and told Jesus" (Hebrews 4:16).

Elisha Hoffman wrote of visiting one of God's troubled saints. "There was a woman to whom God had permitted many visitations of sorrow and affliction. Coming to her home one day, I found her much discouraged. She unburdened her heart, concluding with the question, 'Brother Hoffman, what shall I do?' I quoted from the Word, then added, 'You cannot do better than to take all of your sorrows to Jesus. You must tell Jesus.' For a moment she seemed lost in meditation. Then her eyes lighted as she exclaimed, 'Yes, I must tell Jesus.' As I left her home I had a vision of that joy-illuminated face. And I heard all along my pathway the echo, 'I must tell Jesus. I must tell Jesus.'" Hoffman wrote when he got home:

I must tell Jesus all of my trials;
I cannot bear these burdens alone;
In my distress He kindly will help me;
He ever loves and cares for His own.

I must tell Jesus all of my troubles;
He is a kind, compassionate friend;
If I but ask Him, He will deliver,
Make of my troubles quickly an end.

Tempted and tried, I need a great Saviour;
One Who can help my burdens to bear;
I must tell Jesus, I must tell Jesus;
He all my cares and sorrows will share.

O how the world to evil allures me!
O how my heart is tempted to sin!
I must tell Jesus, and He will help me
Over the world the victory to win.

I must tell Jesus! I must tell Jesus!
I cannot bear my burdens alone;
I must tell Jesus! I must tell Jesus!
Jesus can help me, Jesus alone.

Chapter 35

"They Need Not Depart"

"When Jesus heard of it, he departed thence by ship into a desert place apart: and when the people had heard thereof, they followed him on foot out of the cities. And Jesus went forth, and saw a great multitude, and was moved with compassion toward them, and he healed their sick. And when it was evening, his disciples came to him, saying, This is a desert place, and the time is now past; send the multitude away, that they may go into the villages, and buy themselves victuals. But Jesus said unto them, They need not depart; give ye them to eat. And they say unto him, We have here but five loaves, and two fishes. He said, Bring them hither to me. And he commanded the multitude to sit down on the grass, and took the five loaves, and the two fishes, and looking up to heaven, he blessed, and brake, and gave the loaves to his disciples, and the disciples to the multitude. And they did all eat, and were filled: and they took up of the fragments that remained twelve baskets full. And they that had eaten were about five thousand men, beside women and children."
(Matthew 14:13-21)

The miracle of the loaves and fish being so bountifully multiplied that five thousand men, besides women and children, were fed by them, so well fed that they were fully satisfied, is one of our Lord's most remarkable miracles. No other miracle is mentioned so often as this one. Evidently, the Holy Spirit intends for us to give it special attention.

The Holy Spirit inspired all the gospel writers to record these stories of our Lord's dealings with men upon the earth so that we might read them often, study them carefully, and learn from them continually. His miracles have not yet been fathomed. His words and his ways have not yet been comprehended. Like the cloud that Elijah's servant saw (1 Kings 18:44), these gospel stories seem to get bigger and bigger every time we look at them. Like the widow's barrel of meal (1 Kings 17:12-16), there is an inexhaustible fulness of spiritual instruction in this holy book. I read a lot of books. Most of them can be comprehended with one or two careful readings. But the more I read the Word of God, the more I am lost in the richness, fulness, and freshness of it.

I have said all this because I want you to realize that when I have finished this study, there will be much more that needs to be said. I will have only scratched the surface of this deep, deep mine. Yet, having scratched around the surface, I have found four, choice nuggets of gold I want to show you.

Christ's Compassion

First, this passage gives us a display of our Saviour's deep, deep compassion for man. "Jesus went forth, and saw a great multitude, and was moved with compassion toward them, and he healed their sick" (v. 14). This great feature in our Lord's character can never be remembered too often, esteemed too highly, or declared too frequently. The movement of his heart toward the sick and needy shows us how tender and affectionate our Saviour was and is. How often we read of our Saviour's compassion toward men! His heart was moved with compassion toward those whom he beheld as "sheep having no shepherd" (Matthew 9:36). The two blind men he saw as he left Jericho (Matthew 20:34), the leper who worshipped him (Mark 1:40, 41), and the widow of Nain who was going to bury her son (Luke 7:13) all benefited from his compassion. Truly, he is the Good Samaritan (Luke 10:33).

These accounts are not repeated to fill up space. They are written because the Lord intends us to understand that he who is our Saviour is a God full of compassion! The Holy Spirit intends us to know and be assured of the tenderness of Christ's love to his own. His are the mercies and compassions of a man who is himself God. The tender mercies of the eternal Trinity flow to chosen sinners through the God-man Christ Jesus! The mercies and compassions of our God and Saviour are the mercies and compassions of God, for he is "over all, God blessed for ever". But they are no less the mercies and compassions of the *man* Christ Jesus, for, "verily, he took not on him the nature of angels, but he took on him the seed of Abraham … that he might be a merciful and faithful High Priest in things pertaining to God, to make reconciliation for the sins of the people" (Hebrews 2:16, 17). In Christ, the God-man, our Saviour, there is both an infinite fulness of mercy and a tenderness of feeling toward his redeemed, the tenderness of perfect manhood. Being full of compassion, he forgives our iniquity and destroys us not; turns away his anger, and stirs not up all his wrath (Psalm 78:38).

When our Lord saw the sick, "he was moved with compassion toward them, and healed them". When he saw these thousands of people out in a desert place, ready to faint for hunger, he was moved with compassion for them and fed them.

The word, "compassion", is very expressive. It means, as Spurgeon put it, "His whole being was stirred to its lowest depth, and therefore he proceeded at once to work miracles of mercy among them." He knew that many in the crowd had no faith in him and no love for him. They followed him because of curiosity, because the crowds went after him, or because they wanted to see a miracle. Yet, our Master pitied them. All were fed. All were relieved. All were filled. Let no one ever question the gracious character of our God and Saviour (Exodus 34:6). He "delighteth in mercy" (Micah 7:18). Let all who profess to be followers of Christ follow him in his example of mercy and compassion (Matthew 18:33; Galatians 6:1, 2; Ephesians 4:32-5:1; James 1:27).

Christ's Omnipotence

Second, here is undeniable proof of our Saviour's omnipotence as the mighty God. It was promised by Isaiah that the Messiah would be both a man born of a woman (Isaiah 7:14) and "the Mighty God" (Isaiah 9:6). With five loaves and two small fish, the Lord Jesus fed 5,000 men, beside women and children. That means he fed many more thousands of people with five pieces of bread and two pieces of fish! The task was impossible for anyone other than God himself, who alone has creative power, who alone "giveth food to all flesh" (Psalm 136:25). Our Saviour, who is full of compassion toward us, is himself "the Mighty God", the Creator and Sustainer of all things, and nothing is too hard for him!

Faith

Third, this is a lesson about faith (vv. 15-18). The disciples wanted to "send the multitude away". They were ready to limit the Holy One. By their actions they were saying, like Israel of old, "Can God prepare a table in the wilderness?" They measured the Lord Jesus' ability by their own ability, or inability. They looked upon the Son of God as Naaman did the Jordan River, with Syrian eyes! Let us learn from their mistake and be warned. When we think of God, we must put down Hagar and raise up Sarah, silence human reason and act according to God-given faith. Faith believes without evidence, and even contrary to evidence, that "things which are impossible with men are possible with God". Two sentences in these verses are bursting with spiritual instruction. "Jesus said unto them, They need not depart." What a blessed word of grace and assurance! If there was no necessity for these hungry souls to depart from Christ for food, there can never be a reason for you and me to depart from him. There is no need for the bride of Christ to wander from beneath his banner of love. Mary may sit at Jesus' feet always! "They need not depart." There is never an excuse for compromising the gospel. There is never a reason for disobedience to Christ. There is never a cause for neglecting Christ, his worship, and his service. Whatever we need, our Saviour is ready to give to us or do for us (Hebrews 4:16; Proverbs 3:5, 6).

Then, in verse 18, "He said, Bring them hither to me". Bring all that you are and all that you have to Christ. He will remove the curse, add his blessing, and make our paltry loaves and fishes instruments of great usefulness and spiritual benefit to chosen sinners in his kingdom. Little is much in the Master's hands! It has always been God's delight and glory to use that which men consider useless. He used a baby's cry to move the heart of Pharaoh's daughter. He used a shepherd's crook to work miracles in Egypt. He used a boy and a slingshot to bring down Goliath. He used a poverty-stricken widow to feed his prophet. He used a little girl to lead Naaman to Elisha. He used Balaam's ass to teach him obedience. He used the jawbone of an ass to slay a thousand Philistines. He used a little child to teach his disciples humility. He used a boy's lunch to feed many thousands of hungry people. And he uses men, who are in themselves useless sinners, to call out his own elect (1 Corinthians 1:26-30; 2 Corinthians 4:7).

The Gospel

Fourth, this miracle serves as a beautiful and clear allegory of the gospel of God's grace. We must never attempt to make allegories where the Holy Spirit does not make them. We must never try to make the scriptures say what they obviously do not say. But just as Paul used Sarah and Hagar as an allegory to teach the distinction between law and grace (Galatians 4), so the Holy Spirit has given us these recorded miracles of Christ to teach us spiritual, gospel truths.

This hungry multitude in a desert place is a good representation of lost mankind in this world. All the sons of Adam are an assembly of perishing souls, lost, helpless, starving, and upon the verge of eternal ruin, without the gospel of Christ. There is but a breath between them and everlasting ruin. Their only hope of salvation is the gospel of Christ (Romans 1:15, 16).

The loaves and fishes, so readily despised as being inadequate to meet the needs of so many, might well be looked upon as representing the preaching of the gospel, Jesus Christ and him crucified, which God has ordained for the saving of his elect (1 Corinthians 1:21-23; John 6:33). Like the loaves and fish in this passage, the preaching of the cross of Christ meets all the spiritual needs of sinners in this world.

The disciples’ passing out the loaves and fishes to the crowd shows us the sphere of human instrumentality. I cannot make loaves and fish; but I can bring my lunch to the Master. I cannot multiply the loaves and fish; but I can pass them out. I cannot save anyone or do anything to help anyone get saved; but I can preach the gospel to eternity-bound sinners. And what I can do, and have the opportunity and means to do, I am responsible to do. And the same is true of you. Bring your lunch to Christ and watch him work! C. H. Spurgeon’s comments on verses 17 and 18 ought to be of great encouragement in this regard.

> ‘And they say unto him, We have here but five loaves, and two fishes’ (v. 17). See how they overhaul their provisions, and they report, ‘We have here but five loaves’. With what a gloomy ‘but’ they show how lean is the larder! Those two sardines make the stock seem positively ridiculous. It is a good thing for us to know how very poor we are, and how far from being able to meet the wants of the people around us. It is for our good to be made to confess this in so many words to our Lord. Truly, he who writes this comment has often felt as if he had neither loaf nor fish, and yet for some forty years and more he has been a full-handed waiter at the King’s great banquets.
>
> ‘He said, Bring them hither to me’ (v. 18). He will have us yield up what we have: we are to make no reserve. We must hand all over to Jesus: ‘Bring them hither to me’. He will accept what we bring: this is implied in the command to bring it. He will make a little go a long way: that which gets to Jesus will reach the needy by the surest route. The shortest way to procure provender for perishing souls is to go to Jesus about them.

The satisfaction of all the crowd and the baskets full leftover, appear to me to be a beautiful representation of the fulness of grace to be found in the Lord Jesus Christ. He freely gives all to all who trust him. All who come to him have all they want and need. Finding all in him, we find satisfaction for our souls. Drinking the water that he gives, we never thirst again. Yet, the storehouse of grace is never diminished. In our Father’s house there is “bread enough and to spare”!

Chapter 36

Deity Demonstrated

"And straightway Jesus constrained his disciples to get into a ship, and to go before him unto the other side, while he sent the multitudes away. And when he had sent the multitudes away, he went up into a mountain apart to pray: and when the evening was come, he was there alone. But the ship was now in the midst of the sea, tossed with waves: for the wind was contrary. And in the fourth watch of the night Jesus went unto them, walking on the sea. And when the disciples saw him walking on the sea, they were troubled, saying, It is a spirit; and they cried out for fear. But straightway Jesus spake unto them, saying, Be of good cheer; it is I; be not afraid. And Peter answered him and said, Lord, if it be thou, bid me come unto thee on the water. And he said, Come. And when Peter was come down out of the ship, he walked on the water, to go to Jesus. But when he saw the wind boisterous, he was afraid; and beginning to sink, he cried, saying, Lord, save me. And immediately Jesus stretched forth his hand, and caught him, and said unto him, O thou of little faith, wherefore didst thou doubt? And when they were come into the ship, the wind ceased. Then they that were in the ship came and worshipped him, saying, Of a truth thou art the Son of God. And when they were gone over, they came into the land of Gennesaret. And when the men of that place had knowledge of him, they sent out into all that country round about, and brought unto him all that were diseased; And besought him that they might only touch the hem of his garment: and as many as touched were made perfectly whole."
(Matthew 14:22-36)

Many who claim to be Christians and to worship God deny the deity of Christ. They deny that Jesus Christ is himself God. Others, who claim to believe Jesus Christ is God, ascribe to him attributes of weakness, frustration, and failure, which are a denial of his deity as much as the open denial of his eternal Godhead. The religion of such people, the religion of the liberal, or the Arian who denies Christ's deity, and the religion of the freewill, works religionist, whose doctrine denies Christ's deity, is nothing but a religion of moralisms and philosophy.

Trinitarians

We are Trinitarians. We worship one, holy, sovereign God in three separate, but equal persons, the Father, the Son, and the Holy Spirit. We do so because the Lord God has revealed himself from the beginning as One God subsisting of a plurality of divine Persons (Genesis 1:26; Deuteronomy 6:4; 1 John 5:7).

Not only are we Trinitarians, we fully believe that Jesus Christ of Nazareth, the man who walked this earth for thirty-three years and died by Roman crucifixion just outside Jerusalem more than two thousand years ago, is himself "over all God, blessed forever" (Romans 9:5). That man is "God manifest in the flesh" (1 Timothy 3:16). We believe that he is God because the Word of God declares that he is God, because he claimed to be God, because both angels and men worshipped him as God while he was upon the earth, and because our entire salvation stands and falls with his absolute deity. If Jesus Christ were not God, his righteousness, his atonement, his resurrection, his intercession, all that he has done could profit us nothing. To deny Christ's deity is to deny his honesty and integrity as a man, for he claimed to be God and received worship from men as God. The Jews took up stones to kill him because he, being a man, made himself equal with God! All he had to do to stop their wrath was to say, "Wait a minute, you misunderstood me. I did not mean to imply that I am God"!

Having said all that, I am fully aware that it is not possible to prove Christ's eternal power and Godhead to an unbeliever. I can no more prove the deity of Christ than I can prove the existence of God. Such proof cannot be given because God never made any attempt to prove his Being. The only way God can be proved is by faith. If you believe God, you know God. If you do not believe God, you cannot know him; and you hope that he is just a myth.

However, the Lord God has given us numerous demonstrations of his Being. He has given us such demonstrations of his Being, that no sane man can honestly deny that God is, and such demonstrations, that every believer simply laughs at those who do deny him. Even so, we have in the New Testament numerous demonstrations of the deity of Christ. They are given not to prove that Christ is God, but to reassure and strengthen the faith of all who know him, trust him, worship him, and love him as God our Saviour.

In the passage before us every thing is moving in one direction. The events before us come to a climax in verse 33, when the disciples "came and worshipped (the Lord Jesus) saying, Of a truth thou are the Son of God". The Father had declared this at his baptism (3:17). And the demons in Gadara confessed it in

Matthew 8:29. But this is the first time the twelve apostles unequivocally declared of Christ, "Thou art the Son of God". They made this declaration because our Lord Jesus had so powerfully demonstrated his deity that they simply could not refrain from worshipping him as their God. In Matthew 14:22-36 we are given six demonstrations of the fact that the man Christ Jesus is himself God.

Divine Authority

Here we have a clear demonstration of our Saviour's divine authority (vv. 22, 23). First, "Jesus constrained his disciples to get into a ship". Then, "he sent the multitudes away". He made the disciples take a ship across the Sea of Galilee that they did not wish to take. Then, he sent the multitudes away who wanted to take him by force and make him a king (John 6:14, 15).

Thus he demonstrated his authority as God over all things. He has authority over the lives and destinies of all men, including their final judgment (John 5:22). He has authority over all the supernatural world, including Satan and the fallen angels (Mark 1:27). He has sovereign authority over all the holy angels, whom he could have summoned at anytime to his aid (Matthew 26:53). Our Lord Jesus taught "as one having authority" (Matthew 7:29). He sent out his apostles with his authority over unclean spirits, to cast out demons and heal the sick (Matthew 10:1). It is his authority that inspires his church "to preach the gospel to every creature" (Matthew 28:18-20). Jesus Christ, because he is God, has control and authority over everything in heaven, earth, and hell. He commands and controls all men and all angels. He commands and controls all demons. He commands and controls all the elements of nature (Isaiah 45:7; Psalm 89:9; 107:28-30).

Yet, this great God is so much one with us in our nature that as a man he walked before God in perfect faith and was a man of prayer (v. 23). The gospel writers frequently remind us of those private seasons when our Redeemer "went up into a mountain apart to pray". Those sweet incidents are held before us as strong endearments of character. But were intensely private times. We are seldom given even the slightest indication about what was spoken from his holy heart to the Father in prayer. Our Master practised what he teaches us to practise. He entered into his closet, shut the door, and prayed to his Father in secret (Matthew 6:6). No effort should be made to describe the Master's times of private prayer. No mortal on earth knows (and none should guess) what words were uttered, or what groans were sighed by the Lord Jesus in his Mediator-character before the Father in those hallowed seasons. We are told about the transfiguration (Matthew 17:1-9). We read about his agony in the garden (Luke 22:41-45). And we are given details of his intercessory prayer in John 17. But here we must simply pause to adore him as our Mediator in prayer. The Lord Jesus always went somewhere to pray when he was tempted, when His disciples were in trouble, and when he was about to engage in some work as Jehovah's righteous Servant. And he tells us, by his Spirit, to follow his example (Hebrews 4:16).

Divine Omniscience

Now we see our Saviour's omniscience (vv. 24, 25). Try to imagine what was going through the minds of these men. They were in a terrible mess because the Lord made them get into the ship. He sent them right into the eye of a terrible storm! Truly, these disciples are to be admired for their obedience. But you can imagine the terror and confusion they must have felt. The Master was not with them this time! But, really, he was. They just did not know it!

"O LORD, thou hast searched me, and known me. Thou knowest my downsitting and mine uprising, thou understandest my thought afar off. Thou compassest my path and my lying down, and art acquainted with all my ways. For there is not a word in my tongue, but, lo, O LORD, thou knowest it altogether. Thou hast beset me behind and before, and laid thine hand upon me. Such knowledge is too wonderful for me; it is high, I cannot attain unto it" (Psalms 139:1-6).

In the time of the disciples' great need, "Jesus went unto them, walking on the sea". He knew where they were. He knew the trouble they were in. Yet, he waited a long time to come to them, because he knew infinitely better than they what they needed. When the storm arose and they were alone in the sea, these disciples forgot all they had seen and heard before. All they could think of was the storm. All they could see was danger. All they could see was fear. How much like them we are!

The ship tossed about with the waves and contrary winds remind us of our own situation in the world. In fact, in Isaiah 54:11-14 our Lord addresses us as a people in exactly this situation and speaks comfort to our hearts. "O thou afflicted, tossed with tempest, and not comforted … In righteousness shalt thou be established: thou shalt be far from oppression; for thou shalt not fear: and from terror; for it shall not come near thee". Our Saviour's name is Jehovah-jireh. He sees us. He knows our needs. He will provide. Commenting on verse 25, C. H. Spurgeon wrote:

> Jesus is sure to come. The night wears on and the darkness thickens, the fourth watch of the night draws near, but where is he? Faith says, 'He must come.' Though he should stay away till almost break of day, he must come. Unbelief asks, 'How can he come?' Ah, he will answer for himself: he can make his own way. 'Jesus went unto them, walking on the sea.' He comes in the teeth of the wind, and on the face of the wave. Never fear that he will fail to reach the storm-tossed barque: his love will find out the way. Whether it be to a single disciple, or to the church as a whole, Jesus will appear in his own chosen hour, and his time is sure to be the most timely.

Divine Protection

In verses 26 and 27 we see a clear display of our Saviour's divine care and protection. Being God full of compassion, he understood their frailty and came to them, "Walking on the sea". He did not come "walking on the sea" to teach them how to do it; but to teach them and us, that since he is God over all, we can and should trust him absolutely. Remember, he has absolute power and control over all things. He can and will do whatever is needed to protect us. We will never find ourselves a place where we are beyond his eye or beyond his reach. There is no storm from which he cannot save us! Though the disciples were in the midst of a terrible storm, they were in the place of obedience to their Master. The place of obedience to Christ is the place of safety (Proverbs 3:5, 6; Acts 27:22-26).

Divine Faithfulness

There is nothing more admirable about our great God than his everlasting faithfulness, and nothing more comforting (Lamentations 3:24-26). Here (vv. 28-31) Matthew gives us a beautiful picture of our Redeemer's divine faithfulness.

With great ease, being strong in faith, Peter stepped out onto the stormy sea. He walked upon the water as confidently as we might walk on concrete. Yes, faith may be, and is, very strong, when the almighty Giver of faith calls it forth. But, when he suspends (as it were) his omnipotent grace, when he takes away his support (even for a brief moment, and even after allowing us to do great things in his name), our faith is utter weakness! How we need to learn this lesson! No sooner had Peter, looking to Christ, stepped out of his boat, walking on the water to go to the Saviour, than he found himself looking at the storm, seized with fear, and sinking in unbelief!

Yet, in great faithfulness the Lord Jesus "stretched forth his hand" of omnipotent mercy and caught his sinking disciple, and gently rebuked him for his unbelief. How merciful, how gracious our blessed Saviour is to us, weak, unstable, unbelieving believers! Often, he leaves us to ourselves for brief moments, as he did Peter, and lets us begin to sink, to teach us that he alone is our Keeper. Yet, he ever stretches out his hand to save his fallen ones. He never leaves us to reap the fruit of our own weakness and unbelief. When sinking in deep waters, he seems only to consider our trouble, not our fault, and graciously delivers us. May he teach us and give us grace to follow his example (Galatians 6:1, 2; Ephesians 4:32-5:1).

Divine Omnipotence

"When they were come into the ship, the wind ceased." It always does, once the Saviour makes himself known (Isaiah 43:1-7). That the wind ceased when our Master came into the ship shows us his great omnipotence. Beholding this display of his omnipotence, "They worshipped him saying, of a truth thou are the Son of God"! These disciples, who had been rescued by their Lord's coming to them across the stormy sea, and calming the sea as he stepped into their little ship, were overwhelmingly convinced of his absolute omnipotence as the eternal God. Read (Psalms 139:7-18).

Divine Goodness

In verses 34-36 we are given a marvellous demonstration of Christ's Divine Goodness and Grace. What an endearing picture this is of our Saviour. Truly, this is he of whom the prophets spoke (Isaiah 35:4-6; Luke 4:17, 18). He delights in mercy. "Thou, O Lord, art a God full of compassion, and gracious, longsuffering, and plenteous in mercy and truth" (Psalm 86:15). He who bore our sins and carried our sorrows soothes the sorrows of needy souls. Though now enthroned on high, he is yet touched with the feeling of our infirmity and moved with compassion toward his needy people. "For in that he himself hath suffered being tempted: he knoweth how to succour them that are tempted" (Hebrews 2:18). And it is still true, "As many as touch him are made perfectly whole"!

Chapter 37

Empty Religion

"Then came to Jesus scribes and Pharisees, which were of Jerusalem, saying, Why do thy disciples transgress the tradition of the elders? for they wash not their hands when they eat bread. But he answered and said unto them, Why do ye also transgress the commandment of God by your tradition? For God commanded, saying, Honour thy father and mother: and, He that curseth father or mother, let him die the death. But ye say, Whosoever shall say to his father or his mother, It is a gift, by whatsoever thou mightest be profited by me; And honour not his father or his mother, he shall be free. Thus have ye made the commandment of God of none effect by your tradition. Ye hypocrites, well did Esaias prophesy of you, saying, This people draweth nigh unto me with their mouth, and honoureth me with their lips; but their heart is far from me. But in vain they do worship me, teaching for doctrines the commandments of men."
(Matthew 15:1-9)

In this passage the Lord Jesus confronts the religious system of his day head on. He confronts the scribes and Pharisees publicly, giving a scathing denunciation of their religion, its customs, traditions, and hypocrisy, drawing a clear line of distinction between false and true religion. This is a matter that God's servants must deal with, and deal with plainly, in every age.

It is written, "Thou shalt not take the name of the Lord thy God in vain" (Exodus 20:7). Obviously, that commandment prohibits profanity and vulgar language in which the name of God is used, as well as all flippant, irreverent usage of God's name. How often we hear men and women, and even children, taking God's name in vain, who would never think they are doing so! I cringe every time I hear someone say, "Gee", "Gees", "Gosh", "Golly", "Lord", "my Lord", "my God", or "oh God" as a by-word. The name of the Lord our God is not to be used as a by-word! But the commandment, "Thou shalt not take the name of the Lord thy God in vain", goes much, much deeper. It forbids all superficial, indifferent, insincere, half-hearted, hypocritical worship.

Someone said, "God's name is taken in vain more often inside the church than outside"! Most of what we see in religion today is nothing less than the blasphemy of God's name! The mechanical use of God's name in repetitious prayers, songs, and rituals, while having no thought and regard for his honour and genuine devotion to him, is taking his name in vain.

Empty religious rituals and ceremonies, even when the outward form conforms to the Word of God is but the taking of God's name in vain (Isaiah 1:13-18). And most religious practices today do not even attempt to be outwardly conformed to the Word of God. Malachi declares that the offering of blemished, unworthy sacrifices is taking God's name in vain (Malachi 1:6, 7). God will not accept any pretended worship of him that does not arise from a redeemed, regenerate, believing heart. The very sacrifices of the wicked are an abomination before him (Isaiah 66:2, 3; Amos 5:21-24; Proverbs 21:27).

Pharisees died out hundreds of years ago; but the spirit of the Pharisees thrives in every age. Most people think that religion is primarily an outward thing; but in our text and throughout the scriptures, the Lord Jesus shows us that true religion is more inward than outward (John 4:22-24; Philippians 3:3). Pharisees in all ages love to make religion a show. But our Saviour tells us plainly that we must never make a show of religion (Matthew 6:3-8, 16-18).

There are four things in these nine verses that need to be understood, remembered, and laid to heart. May God the Holy Spirit, who caused them to be written in his Word, now inscribe them upon our hearts.

Useless Religion

First, we see here that formal, ritualistic, ceremonial, outward religion, without heart faith, is empty, useless religion. The complaint of the scribes and Pharisees against the disciples was not that they were evil, corrupt, covetous men, but that they did not, in keeping with Jewish traditions, wash their hands before they ate!

Obviously, it is always good to wash your hands, the more often the better, as a matter of personal hygiene. But the practice of always washing one's hands before eating, as a show of religious devotion, had become a religious tradition with them, a tradition they would never dare to break, at least not in public. They washed their hands, whether they needed washing or not, because they vainly imagined that in doing so they showed spirituality and devotion to God. Our Lord's disciples, following his example and instruction, felt no compulsion to obey religious tradition. "They washed not their hands when they ate bread"!

Why should they wash them if they were clean? Tradition had no power over their consciences.

You may think, "What does that have to do with me? How does this apply to anyone today" There are multitudes who do much of what they do purely out of religious tradition, only to be seen of men, so that they will appear to others to be true Christians, spiritually minded, and devoted to Christ. How often have you heard people say, or said yourself, "I do that to show people that I am a Christian. I want people to know that I love the Lord"? The one thing our Lord Jesus tells us plainly that we are never to do is to try, by our dress, our public appearance, or our public behaviour, to show that we are Christians. Read Matthew 6:3-18. You may say, "But I want people to see Jesus in me." Lost, unbelieving people did not see Jesus in Jesus. They certainly are not going to see him in you and me.

Let us take care that we live as men and women who trust and worship the Lord Jesus Christ, in honesty, in labour, in conversation, in modesty, in love, and in patience. "Adorn the doctrine of God our Saviour" (Titus 2:10). But do nothing to be seen of men. Several years ago, I was in the company of several pastors in a restaurant. When his meal was served, the senior pastor among us began eating his meal without bowing to give thanks first (without publicly washing his hands). One of the younger men objected to his conduct, saying, "I could never do that. I always give thanks before I eat, especially in a public place." When my older friend asked, "Why", he said, "I want people to know that I'm a Christian." The older, wiser pastor smiled and said, "If you want people to know you're a Christian, leave the waitress a good tip."

No man has any more right to institute a new religious duty in the kingdom of God than to neglect an old one. The issuing of commands is for the King alone. Yet these religionists wanted to know why the Lord's disciples broke a law, which was never established by God as a law. Lost religionists in all ages love to invent traditions and then rest their souls upon them. Going about to establish their own righteousness, they refuse to submit themselves to the righteousness of God in Christ. They refuse to trust Christ alone for righteousness before God. They have a form of godliness, which they cherish, but deny the power of true godliness, which is the gospel of God's free, saving grace in Christ (Romans 1:16, 17). That which our Saviour said to the Pharisees of his day is yet true. "Ye are they which justify yourselves before men; but God knoweth your hearts: for that which is highly esteemed among men is abomination in the sight of God" (Luke 16:15).

The washing of hands, like all other religious tradition, is nothing. "Faith which worketh by love" is everything. The blood of Jesus Christ cleanseth us from all sin (1 John 1:7). All those things that men do to make themselves righteous is will-worship and "is abomination in the sight of God".

True Worship

Do not misunderstand either my doctrine or the doctrine of our Lord in this passage. I do not suggest that outward, public worship is insignificant. Nothing is more important in the activities of life than the worship of God (Hebrews 10:25). Neither do I suggest that the outward forms of public worship are insignificant.

God's saints vary in the way they conduct their assemblies of public worship. Some are more formal and some less formal than others. Some have instrumental music, and some do not. Some do not have music at all. But, with regard to the ordinances of public worship, if we fail to keep God's ordinances in God's way, we do but take the name of God in vain in our pretended worship.

Yet, even when the outward form of worship is right, that is not the principle thing. Heart worship is the principle part of worship. "This people draweth nigh unto me with their mouth, and honoureth me with their lips; but their heart is far from me" (v. 8). The heart is the principle thing in the relationship of a husband and wife, parents and children, friend and friend. And in our relationship with, service to, and worship of our God, the matter of chief concern is our hearts (Isaiah 29:13; Ezekiel 33:31; Romans 10:3; 14:17).

What must we have to be saved? A new heart! What sacrifice does God require from us? A broken and contrite heart! What is true circumcision? Heart circumcision! What does God call for from his sons? "My son, give me thine heart"! Where does Christ dwell? In our hearts!

J. C. Ryle wrote, "The bended knee, the bowed head, the loud Amen, the daily chapter, the regular attendance at the Lord's table, are all useless and unprofitable, so long as our affections are nailed to sin, or pleasure, or money or the world."

Our Rule Of Faith

Second, in the church and kingdom of God our only rule of faith and practice is and must be the Word of God alone. That religion which either adds to or diminishes from the Word of God is empty, useless religion. It does not matter how sincere, zealous, and well received a religious practice is, if it is something that adds to or diminishes the Word of God, it is useless (Deuteronomy 4:2; 12:32; Proverbs 30:6; Revelation 20:18, 19).

The Jews took this matter of washing hands before a meal very seriously (John 2:6). They had no biblical authority for it at all. It was nothing but the invention of some old Jewish rabbi. But it had become a matter of religious law and a test of righteousness in their eyes. The scribes and Pharisees asked, "Why do thy disciples transgress the tradition of the elders? for they wash not their hands when they eat bread. But he answered and said unto them, Why do ye also transgress the commandment of God by your tradition?" (vv. 2, 3). All who treat the Word of God with such contempt make the Word of God of none effect by their traditions. "For God commanded, saying, Honour thy father and mother: and, He that curseth father or mother, let him die the death. But ye say, Whosoever shall say to his father or his mother, It is a gift, by whatsoever thou mightest be profited by me; And honour not his father or his mother, he shall be free. Thus have ye made the commandment of God of none effect by your tradition" (vv. 4-6).

Our only authority is the Word of God (2 Timothy 3:16, 17). Our doctrine is false doctrine, if it is not the doctrine of holy scripture. Our ordinances of worship are an abomination to God, if they are not the ordinances established by our Saviour, performed as he performed them. All prescribed religious duties, in what people call "practical godliness", are but acts of ungodliness, if they are not prescribed in the New Testament (Isaiah 8:20). We must never allow ourselves to be put in subjection to the commandments of men (Colossians 2:16-23; 1 Timothy 1:1-6; Titus 1:14; 1 Thessalonians 5:22).

Practical Religion

Third, true religion, true spirituality is a very practical thing. False, empty religion will allow a man or woman to neglect and despise the most common duties of life. True religion, true Christianity causes people to cherish and faithfully perform the most common duties of everyday life for the glory of God.

In verses 5 and 6 our Lord declares that if a person refuses to take care of his parents, trying to excuse his selfishness, by saying that the only money he has has been devoted as a gift to God, he nullifies the Word of God, and proves himself a religious hypocrite (vv. 7, 8). The worship of God will cause a man to honour his parents, cause a father and husband to provide for his family, cause a believer to be a diligent employee, cause a Christian to be a faithful employer, and cause a woman to be a good wife and mother.

Spiritual Matter

Fourth, true religion, true Christianity, true worship is a spiritual matter (John 4:24; Philippians 3:3; Romans 14:17). It begins with the circumcision of the heart. It involves knowledge of and obedience to the truth. Christianity is a spiritual thing. It is, in its essence, rejoicing in Christ, believing him, loving him, and exalting him. It is a renunciation of all confidence in anything performed by or experienced in the flesh. "The Lord looketh on the heart." All acts of worship, whether in public or in private, are utterly vain, if our hearts are far from him.

Chapter 38

True Religion More Inward Than Outward

"And he called the multitude, and said unto them, Hear, and understand: Not that which goeth into the mouth defileth a man; but that which cometh out of the mouth, this defileth a man. Then came his disciples, and said unto him, Knowest thou that the Pharisees were offended, after they heard this saying? But he answered and said, Every plant, which my heavenly Father hath not planted, shall be rooted up. Let them alone: they be blind leaders of the blind. And if the blind lead the blind, both shall fall into the ditch. Then answered Peter and said unto him, Declare unto us this parable. And Jesus said, Are ye also yet without understanding? Do not ye yet understand, that whatsoever entereth in at the mouth goeth into the belly, and is cast out into the draught? But those things which proceed out of the mouth come forth from the heart; and they defile the man. For out of the heart proceed evil thoughts, murders, adulteries, fornications, thefts, false witness, blasphemies: These are the things which defile a man: but to eat with unwashen hands defileth not a man."
(Matthew 15:10-20)

In all aspects of worship, faith, and obedience to God, the most important thing is the attitude of our hearts. I do not suggest that outward obedience is insignificant. We must never become negligent in matters of worship and obedience to our God. Public worship, the ordinances of divine service, the reading of holy scripture, and prayer are matters of great importance, and must be meticulously observed in strict accordance with divine revelation. However, if we observe all things outwardly, but fail to approach God with grace, and faith, and love to Christ, the most careful and strict observance of outward duties is an abomination to God (Isaiah 66:3; Proverbs 15:8; 21:27).

Offensive Doctrine

Our Saviour turned from the Pharisees and called the multitudes, saying, "Hear, and understand: Not that which goeth into the mouth defileth a man; but that which cometh out of the mouth, this defileth a man" (vv. 10, 11). The Pharisees, by their tradition, taught that spiritual cleansing came from observing religious traditions and ceremonies, such as ceremonially washing their hands before they ate in public. Those who did not observe their traditions were considered unclean and unholy.

Our Lord Jesus had reproved them for their hypocrisy (vv. 1-9). Here he declares plainly that we do not defile ourselves by what we eat. All that we are and do is defiled by the corruption of our depraved hearts. He was not speaking to the Pharisees, but to the multitude. Yet, knowing that the Pharisees were listening, hoping to catch a word or phrase they could use against him, he gave them exactly what they wanted. "Hear, and understand: Not that which goeth into the mouth defileth a man; but that which cometh out of the mouth, this defileth a man." They now had a direct quote from the Master's own lips they could twist and use against him, to accuse him of teaching against the law.

In a word, he threw the goats a can to chew on. But that which is to goats a sharp can, is sweet food for the Lord's sheep. Sheep are not offended by having their inward depravity exposed. Sheep find in their depravity reason to look to Christ for mercy. Sheep are never offended by being told that their religious works are, at best, filthy rags. Knowing that to be true, they trust Christ alone for righteousness.

But the Pharisees were (and still are) offended by the Master's doctrine. "Then came his disciples, and said unto him, Knowest thou that the Pharisees were offended, after they heard this saying?" (v. 12). The disciples were far more concerned about offending lost religionist than the Lord Jesus was. It is obvious that our Lord deliberately offended the Pharisees. Let that be a lesson to us. We should never be fearful of offending those whose religion is an offence to our God. Spurgeon wrote, "They had come to him in a fawning manner, desiring to catch him in his speech: he was disgusted with their hypocrisy, and by this staggering statement he unmasked them, and they came out in their true colours. They could not further conceal their hate: henceforth they could not entrap the disciples by their professions of friendliness."

The Lord Jesus told the Pharisees, and told them plainly, that they transgressed the law of God, which they pretended to honour by their religious customs (v. 3), making the commandment of God "of none effect" (v. 6). He told them that they were nothing but hypocrites (v. 7). And he pointedly told them that Isaiah's damning words were specifically intended to describe them (vv. 8, 9). Then, when the Saviour publicly declared the depravity of their hearts (vv. 9, 10), that band of lost religious legalists was obviously offended and provoked to anger. The disciples were disturbed by that fact, but not the Master. Rather than retracting, or qualifying his words, the Lord Jesus declared their condemnation even more forcefully.

"Rooted Up"

We read in verses 13 and 14, "But he answered and said, Every plant, which my heavenly Father hath not planted, shall be rooted up. Let them alone: they be blind leaders of the blind. And if the blind lead the blind, both shall fall into the ditch." With those words, the Son of God declares that it is the duty of God's servants to oppose every doctrine that sets itself in opposition to Christ. The destruction of heresy is a matter of certainty. God's truth shall prevail (Matthew 16:18). All who teach that which is in opposition to Christ, his gospel, and his glory are to be forsaken by us! His standing command is, "Come out from among them"!

Without question, these stern words may be applied to individuals, to all who profess faith in Christ and are numbered with his people in this world. If our religion is not wholly of God, if our faith is not a God given faith, if our salvation is not a God wrought salvation, it shall be rooted up! It will come to an end. And that end will be everlasting destruction! "No matter how fair the flower, if the Father hath not planted it, its doom is sealed: It shall not be pruned, but 'rooted up'." said C. H. Spurgeon. It will be rooted up by the trials of providence (Matthew 13:21), by the temptations of Satan (Matthew 13:22), and by the preaching of the truth (John 6:66).

But, primarily, our Lord was talking about those who teach and preach another gospel. The disciples were shocked that the Lord had spoken bluntly to the Pharisees, and had offended them. But the Master shows us that he intended to offend them. He shows us that those who teach "for doctrines the commandments of men" are people to whom we are to show no mercy or kindness. It mattered nothing to him that they were planted in high office, if his Father had not planted them. It mattered nothing to him how highly esteemed they were in their own eyes or in the eyes of men.

Those who are the enemies of the cross are the enemies of men's souls (Philippians 3:18, 19). And those who are the enemies of our God must be accounted by us as our enemies. God commands us to love our enemies and pray for those who despitefully use us; but we are not to love and pray for his enemies (2 Chronicles 19:2; Psalm 139:21, 22). God's servants must expose, denounce, and condemn them and their doctrine. God's people must forsake them

(Revelation 18:4; 2 Corinthians 6:14-7:1). The Master's word is, "Let them alone". If we submit ourselves and our families to the counsel of the ungodly and the doctrines of antichrist, our blood and the blood of our children, and of all who are influenced by us will be upon our own heads. It is never right to follow the blind into a ditch!

God will overthrow that doctrine that opposes him, and those who preach it. Babylon must and shall fall: the sooner, the better (Revelation 18:1, 2, 20). By Babylon, I mean the religion of this world, Arminian, freewill, works religion. The weapons of our warfare, by which we must oppose Babylon, are spiritual, not carnal. We fight the forces of evil in this world, as our Lord did here, not with the sword, or even the ballot box, but with the gospel (2 Corinthians 10:4, 5).

Distinguishing Grace

The Lord Jesus said, "Every plant, which my heavenly Father hath not planted, shall be rooted up." God's elect are a people loved with an everlasting and unchangeable love, a people planted in Christ by sovereign, distinguishing grace. It is impossible for those who are thus planted by the Lord to fall from his grace and be rooted up. And everyone who is not planted in Christ is sure to be rooted up and fall into everlasting ruin. Robert Hawker says, "Oh! the blessedness of distinguishing grace. Lord! sweetly give grace to the improvement of thy people, that we may know where we are, and to whom we belong. And avert from thy redeemed, false teachers and false guides: that we may not be in danger of being led by the blind, and both fall into condemnation."

Source Of Defilement

Our Master teaches us that the source of all sin and defilement is the heart of man. "Then answered Peter and said unto him, Declare unto us this parable. And Jesus said, Are ye also yet without understanding? Do not ye yet understand, that whatsoever entereth in at the mouth goeth into the belly, and is cast out into the draught? But those things which proceed out of the mouth come forth from the heart; and they defile the man. For out of the heart proceed evil thoughts, murders, adulteries, fornications, thefts, false witness, blasphemies: These are the things which defile a man: but to eat with unwashen hands defileth not a man" (vv. 15-20).

The Pharisees of old, like the religionists of our day, taught that holiness, righteousness, and godliness depended upon abstaining from certain meats and drinks and carefully observing religious ceremonies of washing and purification. Our Saviour overthrows this doctrine by declaring three things.

First, it is not what you put in your body that defiles you, but what comes out of your mouth (Romans 14:17). Material things cannot defile your soul by using them. And material ceremonies cannot cleanse your soul by enduring them. Carnal things can neither corrupt nor cleanse the soul. If we would worship and serve God, we must have something more than a separated life and a form of godliness. We must have a heart that is clean and upright before God, a clean heart and a right spirit. Such a heart is the gift of God's grace, the work of his Spirit in the new birth (Psalm 51:10).

Second, all sin and defilement originates in and springs from the heart. It is not our environment that corrupts us, or our company, or our education, but our hearts.

"For out of the heart proceed evil thoughts, murders, adulteries, fornications, thefts, false witness, blasphemies." What a list! What must that heart be out of which so many evils pour forth! If these are the bees, what must the hive be! "Evil thoughts", evil devisings such as the Pharisees displayed, come from the heart. "Murders" begin not with the dagger, but with malice in the soul. "Adulteries" and "fornications" are committed in the heart before they are performed by the body. The heart is the cage from which every unclean bird flies forth into the world. "Thefts" are born in the covetousness of the heart. No man steals what he does not first covet. "False witness", lying and slander, is venom in the heart that is spewed out of the mouth. "Blasphemies" are the enmity of the heart expressed by the vile speech of the tongue. All these, and all other evils, ooze from the vile cesspool inside fallen man called, "the heart".

"These are the things which defile a man: but to eat with unwashen hands defileth not a man". It is the corruption of the heart that makes fallen man unfit for communion with God, not failure to pour water on your hands before you eat, or failure to observe religious duties. The heart of man is abominable before God. The evils gushing from the heart makes fallen man loathsome and revolting before God and expose all to shame and ruin. It is only the blood of Christ that can cleanse us from the pollution and guilt of our corrupt hearts and save us from the wrath of God, which we so fully deserve. Yet, those who know nothing of the corruption of their hearts, know nothing of God's saving grace, know nothing of repentance and faith in Christ, are horrified when they see one who worships God in Spirit and in truth neglecting the religious traditions by which their blind leaders lead them into hell. God looks on the heart. But we prefer outward things, because we are able to perform them and they call attention to us.

Third, few are able to grasp such elementary, but vital truths, because they are turned away from the simplicity that is in Christ by self-righteous, works religion. There is a vast difference between physical and spiritual defilement. What we eat and drink does not touch the soul. It passes through the body; but it does not reach our hearts. Material things cannot defile a person. That which is eaten is material substance, and cannot make anyone spiritually, or morally unclean. That fact is so obvious that no one would ever imagine otherwise, were it not for the man made dogmas of false religion.

True Religion

Our Lord's doctrine in this passage, and throughout holy scripture, is this: True religion is more inward than outward. The state of our hearts before God is the main thing. Do not be content with church attendance, religious duties, and outward behaviour. Make certain that your heart is right in the sight of God (Psalm 51:10; Proverbs 4:23; Acts 8:21; Romans 10:10). The Lord God receives the broken, contrite, believing heart (Psalm 51:17; Romans 10:9, 10). Let us never forget that our greatest enemy is our own heart. The world and the devil combined are not so dangerous as our hearts. So let us keep our hearts with all diligence! The only way to keep your heart is to keep it full of Christ (Philippians 4:1-8). May God graciously keep us so that we may keep our hearts for him. Remember, "He that trusteth in his own heart is a fool" (Proverbs 28:26).

Chapter 39

Lessons From The Canaanite Woman

"Then Jesus went thence, and departed into the coasts of Tyre and Sidon. And, behold, a woman of Canaan came out of the same coasts, and cried unto him, saying, Have mercy on me, O Lord, thou Son of David; my daughter is grievously vexed with a devil. But he answered her not a word. And his disciples came and besought him, saying, Send her away; for she crieth after us. But he answered and said, I am not sent but unto the lost sheep of the house of Israel. Then came she and worshipped him, saying, Lord, help me. But he answered and said, It is not meet to take the children's bread, and to cast it to dogs. And she said, Truth, Lord: yet the dogs eat of the crumbs which fall from their masters' table. Then Jesus answered and said unto her, O woman, great is thy faith: be it unto thee even as thou wilt. And her daughter was made whole from that very hour."
(Matthew 15:21-28)

Every word in this passage is rich in instruction, and deserves to be thoroughly studied, mediated upon, and laid up in our hearts. In these verses we see a woman with a great need, who shows great faith in our great Saviour, and obtained great mercy from him. The circumstances attending this miracle are both interesting and instructive. We will look at them in order and see what they are intended to teach us. This Canaanite woman is here held before us as an example of faith in Christ.

Sheep Found
The Lord Jesus Christ, the Good Shepherd, will seek and find his lost sheep wherever they may be. That is the first lesson set before us in this passage (vv. 21-23; Luke 15:3-7). The natural man, reading our text with spiritually blind eyes, might think, "This is not a story about Christ seeking the woman, but about a woman seeking Christ". Granted, this Canaanite woman came to Christ, earnestly seeking him. But she would never have come to him in verse 22 if he had not come to where she was in verse 21. Our Lord Jesus came into the coasts

of Tyre and Sidon because, as Mark says, there was "a certain woman" there to whom he must come. God, in his eternal decree, had marked out the spot where and the time when this needy soul would meet her all-sufficient Saviour. When "the time of love" arrived, he came to the spot to perform for her and in her his great purpose of grace (Ezekiel 16:8). In all his movements while upon the earth, and in all his movements now in providence and by his Spirit, the Son of God is on an errand of mercy. He is seeking and saving his people (Matthew 1:21; Luke 19:10). Wherever you find a seeking sinner you will also find a seeking Saviour (John 6:44, 45; 4:4).

Here we read that she was "a woman of Canaan". She was a Gentile. Mark tells us (Mark 7:26) that she was a Syrophenician. She was from that part of Phoenicia near Syria. She came seeking the Lord Jesus and his mercy, believing him to be the Christ, the Son of David. How did she know Christ? How did she come to trust him? No answer can be given except God revealed his Son in her and gave her faith in him by his omnipotent grace (Psalm 65:4; Isaiah 54:13; Matthew 16:16, 17; John 6:37-40; Romans 9:16). The Lord Jesus came "into the coasts of Tyre and Sidon" on an errand of mercy to meet this woman, as she was coming out of those coasts to meet Christ. It is written, "It shall come to pass that before they call, I will answer; and while they are yet speaking, I will hear" (Isaiah 65:24).

We have before us in this Canaanite woman a marvellous display of the sovereignty of God's free grace in Christ. Here is a chosen vessel of God's mercy taken from the coasts of Tyre and Sidon. She shows us that the church and kingdom of Christ is made up of God's elect gathered by him from all nations into which he has scattered them. They shall come from "the east, and from the west, and from the north, and from the south". And their coming is a matter of absolute certainty. "Thy people shall be willing in the day of thy power" (Psalm 110:3). He scattered them that he might gather them (Ezekiel 11:16-18).

Most Unlikely

Second, we see here, as we do throughout the scriptures, that God's elect are usually those we think are the most unlikely to be saved. Lay it to heart. It is a lesson that must never be forgotten. God's elect are often found where we least expect them. It is grace, not place, that determines who shall be saved. It is grace, not race, that determines who shall obtain faith. Remember, this was a Canaanite woman, a Syrophenician, from the coasts of Tyre and Sidon. She was a woman of a cursed race of idolaters (Genesis 9:22, 25; Deuteronomy 7:1, 2). But she was a chosen vessel of mercy (1 Corinthians 1:26-30; 4:7).

Many, like Elisha's servant, Gehazi, live in the homes of God's prophets, and yet live and die without Christ, without grace, without life, and without faith. Others, like this Canaanite woman, rise from the darkness and debauchery of idolatry, sin, and utter paganism to faith in Christ, righteousness, peace, joy, and eternal life. God's saving grace is not a family inheritance. It does not run in bloodlines (John 1:12, 13). No one has any claim upon God's grace by nature. And none are beyond the reach of God's grace.

Grace And Providence

A third lesson should be obvious to all who read this passage. That is the fact that God's providence is ordered according to his great purpose of grace toward his elect. This entire story is a commentary upon, and illustration of, Romans 8:28-30. What prompted this woman to come to Christ? Her daughter was grievously vexed with a devil. No one else could help her. The Son of God was manifested "that he might destroy the works of the devil" (1 John 3:8).

Love for her daughter, who was grievously vexed with a devil, compelled this broken-hearted mother to come to the Saviour, bringing her daughter's need to him. She asked the Lord Jesus to pity her daughter as an act of mercy to herself. "Have mercy on me", was her cry, bowing to Christ as her Lord. Her desperate need brought her to the Saviour and taught her how to pray. Let every believing mother and father follow her example.

The ground upon which she sued for mercy was her need. The ground upon which she hoped for and expected it, was that the man Christ Jesus is the Son of David, God incarnate, Emmanuel, God with us, God and man in one person. The multitudes who saw him had no idea who he was and did not trust him. This woman, being taught of God (John 6:45), knew him and trusted him. And, when she was in great need, she came to him for mercy.

Affliction is often a means of grace to God's elect, and proves a great blessing to a person's soul. Adversity will never produce faith. But God often uses adversity to bring chosen sinners to the Saviour. Carefully read Psalm 107:1-43.

This poor woman had been put through the wringer. Her heart was crushed. Her darling daughter, perhaps her only child, was grievously vexed with a devil. She was utterly helpless. There was nothing she could do to help her daughter. Yet, it was the very thing that caused her great pain, heartache, and sorrow that brought her to Christ and taught her to pray. If she could speak to us now from heaven, she would say, “It is good for me that I have been afflicted; that I might learn thy statutes” (Psalm 119:71).

Every trial, every providential adversity, every difficulty of life is a message from God. Our troubles in this world are sent by our heavenly Father and are intended to draw us to Christ, to wean us from the world, to send us to the scriptures, and to teach us to pray. As trials are used of God to bring us to Christ and cause us to trust him, so our trials are designed to keep us clinging to Christ, and to strengthen our faith in him (Hebrews 12:5-14). Commenting on this passage, J. C. Ryle wrote:

> Health is a good thing; but sickness is far better, if it leads us to God. Prosperity is a great mercy; but adversity is a greater one, if it brings us to Christ. Anything, anything is better than living in carelessness, and dying in sin. Better a thousand times to be afflicted, like the Canaanite mother, and like her to flee to Christ, than live in ease, like the rich ‘fool’, and die at last without Christ and without hope.

Sinners Still

Here is a fourth lesson. It is a sad lesson, but one we need to learn. God’s saints in this world are all sinners still, justified and sanctified in Christ, but sinners still. Sometimes we act as if we did not know the Lord at all. Here is a woman, a poor, broken-hearted woman, crying out for mercy. And here is a band of blood-washed sinners, who had themselves obtained mercy, looking down their noses upon this Canaanite, Syrophenician woman of Tyre and Sidon, as though she was not worthy of being identified with them! What a pity! They cried, “Send her away; for she crieth after us”!

She was not crying after them. She was crying after Him! Our Master is far more gracious than we are. How thankful we ought to be! Let us ever beware of, and guard against, our natural prejudices, pride, and hardness of heart toward those who are around us. Do not try to determine who is and who is not sincere and true, who is and who is not a believer. We have no way of knowing. We cannot look upon the heart. You and I should never be doubtful of those who profess faith in Christ (Acts 9:26; Romans 14:1).

Lessons From The Canaanite Woman

Great Faith

When we read that our Lord said to this woman, "O woman, great is thy faith", we learn that there are varying degrees of faith. Our Lord calls this woman's faith "great faith". He called the centurion's faith great faith, too. But he spoke of his disciples' faith, and even of Peter's faith, as "little faith". He would have us to understand that even little faith, if it is fixed upon him, is saving faith. Yet, he holds this woman who is newly converted before us as an example of great faith, so that we might seek to imitate her.

When I read these words, "O woman, great is thy faith", I want to know what this great faith is. I cannot say much about the matter, but of these six things I am certain. Great faith looks to Christ alone, trusting him alone for all mercy and grace (1 Corinthians 1:30, 31). Great faith is based upon the naked Word of God. She believed Christ Jesus to be the Christ, because he met the prophecy of the Old Testament and fulfilled it (Matthew 11:2-6). Great faith involves great repentance. Repentance and faith always go hand in hand. This woman turned from her sin, her religion, and her gods to Christ. Great faith bows to the Word of God. When Christ spoke of election (v. 24), she worshipped him. When he called her a dog (v. 26), she acknowledged it and used it as an argument for mercy (v. 27). Great faith cannot be driven from Christ. It never gives up. It never quits. Look how this poor soul hangs on to Christ. She had nowhere else to go (John 6:66-69; Hebrews 11:13). Great faith always gets what it wants: Mercy! Faith wants, needs, and seeks nothing else but mercy at the throne of grace. And if it must great faith will endure great trials to obtain it.

Nowhere else in the Book of God do we find a sinner coming to the Saviour discouraged by him; but this woman met with great discouragement. At first the Master did not even answer her. Then, he who calls every poor, weary, heavy-laden, broken-hearted soul to come to him, assuring all who come that they shall find rest, said to one coming to him, "I am not sent but unto the lost sheep of the house of Israel … It is not meet to take the children's bread, and cast it to dogs".

Does it sometimes appear that the Saviour refuses to hear your heart's cries? When that is the case, lie still before the throne of grace and wait for him. He sees you. He hears your cries. He knows all your sorrows. It is he who measures out your portion day by day. And, being touched with the feeling of your infirmities, he is infinitely more disposed to give you mercy than you are to ask for mercy. But he waits to be gracious at the best time, at the time that is best to fulfil his purpose and best too, for you.

Still the trial of her faith is not finished. When the Lord finally spoke to her, his words must have cut her to her heart. He said, "I am not sent but unto the lost sheep of the house of Israel ... It is not meet to take the children's bread, and cast it to dogs". Who can imagine how she must have felt when she heard those words? Yet, those are the first words the Saviour spoke to her. He who loved her infinitely and everlastingly, who was determined to do more for her than she asked or thought, made the trial of her faith even greater, because he desired to make her an everlasting monument and example of faith among his people, teaching us by her example to hope against hope, trusting him.

By all this, he sweetly and graciously forced her to publicly take her proper place before him, saying, "Truth, Lord: yet the dogs eat of the crumbs which fall from their master's table"! Just in proportion as we see Christ's glory, we will see and acknowledge our unworthiness of his grace.

"Then Jesus answered and said unto her, O woman, great is thy faith: be it unto thee even as thou wilt. And her daughter was made whole from that very hour" (v. 28). Robert Hawker wrote, "It is as if Jesus threw the reins of government into her hand, saying, as by the Prophet, 'Concerning my sons, and concerning the work of my hands command ye me' (Isaiah 45:11). And was there ever a more finished instance of grace and mercy, not only in following up this daughter of Abraham's petition; but planting such faith in her heart, as might sustain so long, and painful a trial."

Let us remember this woman when we try to witness to sinners. God's elect may be found anywhere. Let us remember this woman when we pray. "The effectual, fervent prayer of a righteous man availeth much" because our great God and Saviour waits to be gracious. Let us remember this woman when our faith is tried. The more greatly our God intends to bless us, the more greatly he tries our faith.

Chapter 40

"I Will Not Send Them Away"

"And Jesus departed from thence, and came nigh unto the sea of Galilee; and went up into a mountain, and sat down there. And great multitudes came unto him, having with them those that were lame, blind, dumb, maimed, and many others, and cast them down at Jesus' feet; and he healed them: Insomuch that the multitude wondered, when they saw the dumb to speak, the maimed to be whole, the lame to walk, and the blind to see: and they glorified the God of Israel. Then Jesus called his disciples unto him, and said, I have compassion on the multitude, because they continue with me now three days, and have nothing to eat: and I will not send them away fasting, lest they faint in the way. And his disciples say unto him, Whence should we have so much bread in the wilderness, as to fill so great a multitude? And Jesus saith unto them, How many loaves have ye? And they said, Seven, and a few little fishes. And he commanded the multitude to sit down on the ground. And he took the seven loaves and the fishes, and gave thanks, and brake them, and gave to his disciples, and the disciples to the multitude. And they did all eat, and were filled: and they took up of the broken meat that was left seven baskets full. And they that did eat were four thousand men, beside women and children. And he sent away the multitude, and took ship, and came into the coasts of Magdala."
(Matthew 15:29-39)

We have here another display of our Saviour's great compassion and grace, both to the souls and bodies of men. He manifested his power and Godhead and proved himself the Messiah, fulfilling that which had been prophesied of him (Isaiah 35:5, 6; 61:1). Here was a great throng of people gathered around the Lord Jesus. They had been with him for three days. He performed miracle after miracle, healing the sick, diseased, and impotent souls that were brought before him. His miracles were so astounding that all these thousands of people were utterly astonished by the power and grace of God. "And they glorified the God of Israel."

This great crowd of people, many thousand strong, was so taken up with Christ, his miraculous power, his infinite goodness, and his gracious word that they lost all track of other things. Three days had passed before they knew it. Now they were all hungry and faint. Having received great, great mercy and blessings, one on top of another, they were yet in great need. They needed food and strength.

Notice our Lord's response to their need in verse 32. He says to his disciples "I will not send them away"! Oh, how I love the sound of these words falling from the lips of the Son of God! He says, "Him that cometh unto me I will in no wise cast out" (John 6:37). That means there is nothing in any sinner in all the world that will keep Christ from receiving him, if he does but come to him. Come then to Christ! Come just like you are! Just come to Christ; and he will receive you". Charlotte Elliott summed this up beautifully when she wrote:

Just as I am, without one plea,
But that Thy blood was shed for me,
And that thou bidst me come to Thee,
O Lamb of God, I come!

Then, regarding those who have come to him, our Saviour says, "I will not send them away"! That means, having come to Christ, there is nothing in us that will cause him to send us away, and no need that might arise that can necessitate our going away from our Saviour. Come to Christ and he will never send you away, for this is his promise. "I will not send them away"!

Christ is all I need! Christ is all I need!
He is all I need. For me He died.
He was crucified. And He is all I need!

Needy Souls

In verses 29 and 30 we see great multitudes of needy souls coming to Christ. "And Jesus departed from thence, and came nigh unto the sea of Galilee; and went up into a mountain, and sat down there. And great multitudes came unto him, having with them those that were lame, blind, dumb, maimed, and many others, and cast them down at Jesus' feet; and he healed them".

What could be more difficult and troublesome than moving sick, impotent, diseased people, especially in those days? They had literally to be carried to the Saviour. But the hope of being healed was in sight. Such a hope inspired these needy souls and those who cared for them. No obstacle was considered. No cost was calculated.

When people are in desperate need, nothing will prevent them from seeking relief, if there is any hope. For bodily health, people will wait in a crowded doctor's office for hours, move from one place to another for purer air, give up jobs, and pay any price. But few are even slightly concerned about their souls' health. Yet, the Word of God teaches us that any sinner who knows his soul's need, will allow nothing to keep him from Christ, who alone can meet his needs. And anyone who knows the power of Christ and cares for the souls of others will do whatever he can to get sin sick souls to the Saviour. We saw that in the story of the Canaanite woman (Matthew 15:21-28).

I have been under a doctor's care for many years. He treats me for glaucoma. A while back, I got a little weary of going to his office every two months and paying the fees connected with his constant examination. So I asked if I might not be able to cut back on the number of visits. My doctor's reply was, "They are your eyes. You're the one that has glaucoma." I was embarrassed and immediately decided that the inconvenience and cost was far less significant than the possibility of losing my eyes! But that is nothing compared with losing my soul, and nothing compared with the thought of others perishing. Let all who value their souls make it their life's business to seek Christ. Let all who value the souls of others make it their life's business to bring sinners to the Saviour. Every believer ought to be like those four men who are described by Mark (Mark 2:1-4), who carried their needy friend up to the roof and tore the tiles off, so they could get their friend to the Master.

Omnipotent Mercy

Verse 31 displays the omnipotence of God's mercy. "The multitude wondered, when they saw the dumb to speak, the maimed to be whole, the lame to walk, and the blind to see: and they glorified the God of Israel."

Our Lord Jesus was not one of our modern false healers. He healed people with real infirmities. The word "maimed" means mutilated or cut off, as one whose limb had been cut off in an accident. What we have before us is a tremendous picture of our Lord's power to heal sin-sick souls. There is no plague of the heart that he cannot cure. There is no deformity of soul that he cannot overcome. There is no fever of lust that he cannot stop, no palsy of worldliness that he cannot heal, no cancer of indolence that he cannot remove. When the Son of God sends his Spirit, omnipotent grace is healing grace for our souls. He opens blind eyes, causes the dumb to sing his praise, the deaf to hear his Word, the blind to see his glory, and the lame to walk in paths of righteousness for his name's sake.

I have no hesitation in asserting that those who claim apostolic gifts of tongues and healing are deceitful workers. But do not imagine that the time of miracles has passed. Every conversion is a miracle of omnipotent mercy.

If you would be saved, go to Christ by faith. Cast your soul down before him. Call upon him for relief. He is still the same today as he was two thousand years ago. He is still "the great physician". He still "receiveth sinners". He is still "mighty to save".

Our Compassionate Saviour

Verse 32 shows us the compassionate character of our God and Saviour. "Then Jesus called his disciples unto him, and said, I have compassion on the multitude, because they continue with me now three days, and have nothing to eat: and I will not send them away fasting, lest they faint in the way."

It is striking to me that this word "compassion" is used more often in the four gospels to describe our Saviour than any other. Matthew, Mark, Luke, and John show us much about our Redeemer's feelings of joy and sorrow, thanksgiving and anger, holiness and zeal. But the word they most often use to describe him is this word "compassion". The word means, "to be moved from within". Our English word means, "co-passion", or "to suffer with". It is "a feeling of deep sympathy and sorrow, accompanied with a strong desire to alleviate the pain and remove its cause".

Our Lord's compassion for his elect extends to every aspect of our lives. Our spiritual and eternal needs are of indescribable importance to him, and so are our immediate, temporal needs. Let us never imagine that our Saviour is less concerned for our welfare than we are for the welfare of our own families!

And let no sinner question the tenderness and compassion of Christ. He will graciously receive all who come to him. He will freely, fully, and forever forgive all the sins of all who trust him. He will forever supply all the needs of all who call upon him. God's mercy in Christ is an infinitely vast, bottomless ocean. Though countless multitudes draw from it incessantly, its boundless fulness is never diminished.

What comfort there is for our souls in this great attribute of our God. "His compassions fail not" (Lamentations 3:22). He knows the world in which we live. He knows our temptations. He knows Satan's devices. He knows our frailties. He remembers that we are dust. And he pities us. If the Lord Jesus is full of compassion toward us, how much more compassionate we ought to be toward the needs of men (Ephesians 4:32-5:1; James 1:27; 1 John 3:17; Galatians 6:10).

Human Instrumentality

Our Saviour's employment of his disciples in the distribution of the loaves and fish teaches us something about the sphere of human instrumentality. Certainly the sovereign God does not need us for anything. Our Saviour does not need to use us. He could have distributed the loaves and fish far more easily and much, much faster than the disciples. But he chose not to do what they were perfectly capable of doing. What a privilege it was for the disciples to be allowed to pass out the bread and fish as he multiplied it! Serving Christ by serving the needs of others is the highest honour and greatest privilege in this world (Matthew 10:40-42; Ephesians 3:8).

Faith And Usefulness

"And his disciples say unto him, Whence should we have so much bread in the wilderness, as to fill so great a multitude?" (v. 33). The disciples' reply to the Saviour was not, as I see it, a matter of unbelief. They had not forgotten what happened in chapter 14. They were simply saying, "Lord, if this crowd is going to be fed, you will have to feed them. We do not have any bread and have no way of getting any bread." We are most useful, when we acknowledge that we are useless. We are most sufficient when we acknowledge our insufficiency. God never gives us a task to do without giving us the means and the ability to do (Acts 1:8). If we would serve our Saviour, if we would be useful to the generation in which we live, we must constantly acknowledge that we have nothing with which to serve him, except that with which he supplies us. "Our sufficiency is of God."

God's Glory

When I read the last line of verse 31, I am reminded that the glory of God, only the glory of God, must be our motive in all things. When our Lord Jesus healed the multitudes, "they glorified the God of Israel". The object and goal of everything we do in the service of Christ must be to bring eternity bound souls to glorify and worship the God of Israel. The goal of the preacher, the church, and the individual believer must never be success, fame, popularity, or the approval of men, but the glory of our God.

The Blessedness Of Giving

Read verses 34-37 and learn something about the blessedness of giving. "And Jesus saith unto them, How many loaves have ye? And they said, Seven, and a few little fishes. And he commanded the multitude to sit down on the ground. And he took the seven loaves and the fishes, and gave thanks, and brake them, and gave to his disciples, and the disciples to the multitude. And they did all eat, and were filled: and they took up of the broken meat that was left seven baskets full."

The word "baskets" here is not little lunch baskets as in Matthew 14:20, but huge baskets, the kind used by people carrying goods to the market, the kind that was used to lower Paul over the city wall in Damascus (Acts 9:25). These disciples handed the Lord Jesus just seven loaves and a few small fish. With that insignificant lunch, sufficient only to feed one or two men by us, the Son of God fed thousands; and the disciples gathered up seven grocery carts full of the Master's leftovers!

What an honour it is to give to Christ! What an honour for our great, glorious, all-sufficient God to take our loaves and fishes and use them! Let us leave this great display of Christ's goodness being convinced that it is impossible for anyone to impoverish himself by giving (Proverbs 3:9, 10; Malachi 3:10; Luke 6:38; 2 Corinthians 9:6).

Chapter 41

"Show Us A Sign"

"The Pharisees also with the Sadducees came, and tempting desired him that he would shew them a sign from heaven. He answered and said unto them, When it is evening, ye say, It will be fair weather: for the sky is red. And in the morning, It will be foul weather to day: for the sky is red and lowring. O ye hypocrites, ye can discern the face of the sky; but can ye not discern the signs of the times? A wicked and adulterous generation seeketh after a sign; and there shall no sign be given unto it, but the sign of the prophet Jonas. And he left them, and departed. And when his disciples were come to the other side, they had forgotten to take bread. Then Jesus said unto them, Take heed and beware of the leaven of the Pharisees and of the Sadducees. And they reasoned among themselves, saying, It is because we have taken no bread. Which when Jesus perceived, he said unto them, O ye of little faith, why reason ye among yourselves, because ye have brought no bread? Do ye not yet understand, neither remember the five loaves of the five thousand, and how many baskets ye took up? Neither the seven loaves of the four thousand, and how many baskets ye took up? How is it that ye do not understand that I spake it not to you concerning bread, that ye should beware of the leaven of the Pharisees and of the Sadducees? Then understood they how that he bade them not beware of the leaven of bread, but of the doctrine of the Pharisees and of the Sadducees."
(Matthew 16:1-12)

Since the beginning of time, unbelieving men and women have always demanded signs to corroborate the Word of God. Before he will believe God, the unregenerate, unbelieving man wants signs and evidences to convince him that what God says in his Word is true. The rich man in hell foolishly imagined that if his brothers could hear a preacher who was risen from the dead they would believe God. But God says, "If they hear not Moses and the prophets, neither will they be persuaded, though one rose from the dead" (Luke 16:31).

God often confirms his Word to those who believe him by special providential occurrences, even as he once confirmed it to his people by special miracles. He showed Noah the sign of his covenant by putting a rainbow in the sky. He showed Gideon a sign, using the fleece Gideon spread before him. He showed Elijah a sign on Mount Carmel. And our Lord performed many miracles himself and by his Apostles, called "signs and wonders" (Hebrews 2:4), by which he confirmed to us that he is the Christ.

But any faith that is built upon signs, miracles, and evidences is a false faith (John 2:23-25). Our faith must be based upon the Word of God alone, not upon signs and miracles, scientific evidence, human reason and learning, or even our own emotions and experiences. As Martin Luther puts it …

> Feelings come, and feelings go,
> And feelings are deceiving.
> I trust the Word of God alone;
> Naught else is worth believing!

Lost religionists as well as scoffing blasphemers have always demanded what God will never give them, a convincing sign from heaven, a carnal sign to convince their carnal minds that his word is true. That is exactly what we have before us in Matthew 16:1-12.

A Wicked Alliance

First, the Holy Spirit describes and sets before us the wicked alliance of the Pharisees and Sadducees. "The Pharisees also with the Sadducees came, and tempting desired him that he would shew them a sign from heaven" (v. 1). The Pharisees and Sadducees hated each other. Normally, they would have nothing to do with one another. The Pharisees were conservatives, fundamentalists, who would never consider working with the Sadducees, free-thinking liberals. And the Sadducees were just as adamant in their hatred of the Pharisees. But both the Pharisees and Sadducees so thoroughly despised Christ and the gospel of God's free grace in him that in order to oppose and persecute him, they laid aside their differences and formed the unholy alliance Matthew describes.

How often we see the exact same thing happening in our day. Men and women who despise each other, who have nothing to do with each other, will unite and work feverishly together to oppose the gospel of God's free and sovereign grace in Christ. I have often seen church members, who cared nothing for one another, unite in opposition to a faithful gospel preacher, and churches that are doctrinal opposites, unite to oppose a gospel church. "There is no new thing under the sun" (Ecclesiastes 1:9).

Notice the method employed by these pompous, religious, hypocritical friends of hell "Tempting desired him that he would show them a sign". Those words mean that these men came to Christ scrutinizing and testing him with questions. It is always the method of heretics to ask leading questions with the hope of entrapping the one whose doctrine they despise. They are never open and honest (Jude 4). God's servants are not of their mould. The heretic tries to entrap you. God's servant simply, forthrightly declares the truth to you. Lost religionists, like dogs, may bite and devour one another, but unite to pursue their common prey.

Commenting on this verse, John Trapp quotes Zanchius, who said of the heretic Socinus, "He was a learned man, and of unblameable behaviour, but full of heresies, which he never propounded to me otherwise than by way of question, as seeming desirous to be better informed. By this subtle means, he drew away many."

These Pharisees and Sadducees came asking the Lord Jesus to "show them a sign from heaven". They could not deny the miracles he had performed before so many. So they pretentiously acted as if they would believe him if he would prove himself to them by a sign from heaven. They were asking for some very unusual sight in the heavens as proof of his mission from God. They wanted him to produce a miracle in the visible heavens, to prove that he had come from heaven and that he is the Son of God, and the true Messiah. They wanted him to do something like God did when he set the rainbow in the sky, or dropped manna from heaven.

Of course, it was nothing but a hypocritical desire. Had our Lord suddenly formed fifty rainbows, turned upside down and covered the earth with manna, they would have found a very "obvious" and "reasonable" flaw in the sign. We would be wise, as our Lord did here, never to honour ungodly religionists with an answer to any of their "learned" objections to the gospel. "Foolish and unlearned questions avoid" (2 Timothy 2:23). If every question raised by carping infidels could be answered irrefutably, they would still be carping infidels. The best thing to do with them (always) is leave them alone.

A Wise Answer

He who is the Wisdom of God here gives us a great display of his great wisdom. Notice how he dealt with these people. First, he exposed their spiritual ignorance. "He answered and said unto them, When it is evening, ye say, It will be fair weather: for the sky is red. And in the morning, It will be foul weather to day: for the sky is red and lowring. O ye hypocrites, ye can discern the face of the sky; but can ye not discern the signs of the times?" (vv. 2, 3)

They could predict the weather with a fair measure of ease and accuracy by observing the sky. But they were so blinded by religious tradition that they could not see the fulfilment of all the law and the prophets when he stood square in their face. The natural man, no matter how thoroughly educated, no matter how religious he may be, is totally ignorant of all things spiritual (1 Corinthians 2:14-16). Every thought he has, every opinion he forms about man, sin, God, Christ, redemption, salvation, righteousness, faith, justice, truth, mercy, love, and grace is totally wrong. Faith in Christ is a matter of divine revelation (Matthew 16:16, 17). No man can see the things of God until he is born of God (John 3:5-7). That means the opinions of gainsayers who do not believe God are totally irrelevant, and should be looked upon with utter contempt by those who do believe God.

When our Saviour speaks about "the signs of the times", he is referring to the fact that all the signs given in the Old Testament of the times of the Messiah were fulfilled in him and by him. They have nothing to do with people today being able (as multitudes imagine they are) to discern the time when prophetic events connected with our Lord's second coming are to take place (Acts 1:8).

Second, the Lord Jesus exposed the utter hypocrisy of these pretentious, religious deceivers. "O ye hypocrites"! When it came to dealing with the deceivers of men's souls, the Son of God did not mince words. He frankly and publicly declared them to be "a wicked and adulterous generation" (v. 4), because they not only forsook God; but they attempted to justify their unbelief because they lacked sufficient proof.

Third, our Lord declared that one solemn, indisputable sign would be fulfilled by him, "The sign of the prophet Jonah" (v. 4). Jonah was sacrificed, one man for many, to save all who were in the ship with him from the wrath of God. So the Lord Jesus was sacrificed as our Substitute, one Man for many. He died to save all God's elect (John 11:47-52; 2 Corinthians 5:21; 1 Peter 1:18). As Jonah was in the belly of the whale for three days and three nights, so the Son of God was buried in the heart of the earth for three days and three nights. As Jonah was delivered from the whale's belly, so the Lord Jesus was raised up from the dead on the third day. Having put away our sins by the sacrifice of himself, he was "justified in the Spirit" when God raised him from the dead. As Jonah declared, so the Son of God declared, in all that he did and suffered for us, "Salvation is of the Lord" (Jonah 2:9).

Then, at last, "He left them" (v. 4). Oh, what a solemn word! "He left them and departed" and the people of that place saw him no more. Because they would not hear him and would not believe him, he left them to themselves! This is horrible to consider; but it is his just judgment upon men who will not receive his Word (Hosea 4:17; Proverbs 1:23-33). What great wrath our God heaps upon those who refuse to believe him! He orders his servants to preach no more to them. He allows none to tell them of the good news of life and salvation by him. He commands his prophets not even to pray for them. And should they try to do otherwise, they simply cannot.

What a solemn passage this is to read! Here is a band of lost men showing great concern for the things of God. There are multitudes in every age who amuse themselves and deceive others by falsely interpreting the scriptures to suit themselves, and by misrepresenting God's faithful servants to get people to follow them. Like Diotrephes, they love to have the pre-eminence. The cross of Christ is always an offence to them. They want something more, "a sign from heaven". But no sign shall be given them. And they shall only be offended more, if God has given them up to their reprobate minds.

A Warning Announced

In verses 6 and 12 our Saviour announces an ageless warning to his disciples. "Then Jesus said unto them, Take heed and beware of the leaven of the Pharisees and of the Sadducees … Then understood they how that he bade them not beware of the leaven of bread, but of the doctrine of the Pharisees and of the Sadducees."

If you will read the four gospels carefully, paying attention to what our Saviour taught, you cannot miss the fact that he warned us more often against false religion and false prophets than anything else. Nothing else is so dangerous to your soul. Nothing else is so deadly! Let us be wise and hear what Jesus says.

To whom is the warning given? "Then Jesus said unto them", his disciples, "take heed and beware". This is a warning given to the apostles themselves. If these men needed warning, how much more do we need it (1 Corinthians 10:12).

What is the danger against which the Son of God here warns us? "The doctrine of the Pharisees and of the Sadducees." The warning goes beyond the spirit of hypocrisy, self-righteousness, and ritualism in the Pharisees. It goes beyond the spirit of the free-thinking, compromising, half-infidel intellectualism and rationalism of the Sadducees. Our Lord warns us to take heed and beware of their doctrine.

But the doctrines of the Pharisees and the Sadducees were totally different. They did not agree about anything. Their creeds were as opposite to one another as any two religious creeds could be. That is how it appears; but that is not really the case. True, the Sadducees denied the authority of the prophets, which the Pharisees defended. The Sadducees denied the resurrection and future judgment, which the Pharisees vigorously maintained. Yet, the Pharisees and the Sadducees really believed the same thing. Their doctrine was the result of human tradition, the commandments of men, and the inventions of religious leaders being mixed with the Word of God. They taught the freewill of man, justification by works, and religious ritualism. The Holy Spirit calls it "the doctrine", not doctrines, "of the Pharisees and of the Sadducees".

There are many churches and denominations in this world. Some are liberal. Others are conservative. Some are large, wealthy, and influential. Others are small, poor, and insignificant. But, if you cut through all the trappings of them all and get to the heart of things, you will find that really there are only two religions in the whole world. The one is true. The other is false.

True religion, the religion of the Bible, is the religion of free grace. It traces salvation to God. It ascribes the entire work of salvation to God alone. It makes election, redemption, regeneration, preservation, and glorification to be the works of God's free grace alone. All false religion is the religion of freewill. No matter what denominational name it wears, freewillism traces salvation to man. It does not omit God altogether (Satan is too sly for that!) But it ascribes salvation to man, not to God. It makes the determining factor in salvation to be the will, work, and worth of man. Whereas the Word of God makes salvation to be determined by the will of God (Romans 9:11-18), the worth of Christ (1 Peter 3:18; Romans 3:24-26), and the work of God the Holy Spirit (John 6:63).

Is your religion true, or false? Think about it? Does your religion glorify God, or man? Read Proverbs 16:25. The religion of the Bible honours the triune God alone (1 Corinthians 1:30, 31).

What word does our Lord use to describe the doctrine of the Pharisees and the Sadducees? "Leaven". Leaven once admitted, even in the smallest quantity, works secretly, without noise, and gradually changes the whole character of the loaf. So false doctrine and heresy works in the church to corrupt it from "the simplicity that is in Christ" (2 Corinthians 11:3). If the church of Christ is to be strong and established in the faith of the gospel, the pulpit must be strong, relentlessly proclaiming the faith of the gospel. It is the responsibility of every faithful pastor to see to it that he faithfully preaches the doctrine of Christ. It is also his responsibility to see to it that everything taught in the assembly trusted to his care is consistent with and reinforces the message of God's free and sovereign grace that he proclaims in the pulpit. Every piece of literature in the assembly ought to reflect the message of the pulpit. If it does not, it is because the pastor is weak and irresponsible. The hymns sung must be gospel hymns. It is inconceivable to me that any pastor would preach free grace in the pulpit and then allow freewill hymns (if that title can be used for such trash) in the congregation. Yet, many do. If that is the case, it is because the pastor is weak and irresponsible. A faithful father would never allow poison to be served at the family table, no matter how much his wife and children were addicted to it.

This is a warning for all ages. We must add nothing to the gospel. We must take nothing from the gospel (Galatians 1:6-8). Any human additions or subtractions are "the leaven of the Pharisees and of the Sadducees".

A Wretched Assumption

In verses 5-12 we see our Lord's disciples make a wretched assumption. Because of the weakness of their faith, they assumed that the Lord Jesus was talking about their failure to bring food with them and almost missed the lesson he was teaching. How much we are like these poor disciples!

Their reasoning was carnal. "They reasoned among themselves" (v. 7). Such reasoning is always carnal and leads to error. The poor disciples had forgotten their past experiences (vv. 8-10). It was their lack of faith that caused them to misunderstand the Saviour's words. Spurgeon said, "If it were not for our wretched little faith and our reasoning among ourselves, the memory of our former deliverances would lift us beyond all tendency to mistrust God." But our Lord is always better to us than our fears. We have a gracious and faithful Saviour and Teacher who mercifully causes us to understand his Word, even as he did these disciples.

As we read and study holy scripture, we should always look for an obvious, personal and spiritual application, not merely the facts contained in the letter of the Word. "For whatsoever things were written aforetime were written for our learning, that we through patience and comfort of the scriptures might have hope" (Romans 15:4). Let us ever keep in memory the wondrous works of our God on our behalf, and review them often, so that we may learn to trust him implicitly. That which he has done, he will do. He will always care and provide for his own.

Chapter 42

"Thou Art The Christ"

"When Jesus came into the coasts of Caesarea Philippi, he asked his disciples, saying, Whom do men say that I the Son of man am? And they said, Some say that thou art John the Baptist: some, Elias; and others, Jeremias, or one of the prophets. He saith unto them, But whom say ye that I am? And Simon Peter answered and said, Thou art the Christ, the Son of the living God. And Jesus answered and said unto him, Blessed art thou, Simon Bar-jona: for flesh and blood hath not revealed it unto thee, but my Father which is in heaven. And I say also unto thee, That thou art Peter, and upon this rock I will build my church; and the gates of hell shall not prevail against it. And I will give unto thee the keys of the kingdom of heaven: and whatsoever thou shalt bind on earth shall be bound in heaven: and whatsoever thou shalt loose on earth shall be loosed in heaven. Then charged he his disciples that they should tell no man that he was Jesus the Christ."
(Matthew 16:13-20)

What is the meaning of our Lord's statement "Upon this rock I will build my Church"? Without question, the papists' fabrication that Peter was to be the foundation of the church is ludicrous. To speak of a fallen, sinful, depraved son of Adam as the foundation upon which God's holy temple is built is contrary to scripture. Such an exaltation of Peter above the rest of the Apostles would have been contrary to the plainest teachings of our Lord (Matthew 20:1-28). The rock upon which the Church of God is built is Peter's confession, not Peter (Ephesians 2:20-22; 1 Corinthians 3:11). Christ himself is the Rock God has laid in Zion (Isaiah 28:16). Peter himself, writing by divine inspiration, tells us this (1 Peter 2:6-8). When the Lord Jesus said, "Upon this rock will I build my church", he was, obviously, referring to himself. He is the Rock upon whom Peter and all true believers are built by God's saving grace (1 Peter 2:5). Being built on him, we are safe and secure. Hell itself can do us no harm.

What is the meaning of our Lord's promise, "I wilt give unto thee the keys of the kingdom of heaven?" Again, the papal doctrine that Peter and his successors, the popes, and priests of Rome (as they dream) have the power to admit souls into heaven is a delusion. Peter does not open and close the gates of heaven. That prerogative belongs to Christ alone (Revelation 1:18; 3:7). This sentence appears to have no greater meaning, and no less, than this. By God's special decree Peter was ordained to be the first messenger, the first preacher of the gospel after the resurrection, by whom (as God's mouthpiece and instrument) the doors of salvation were thrown open to both Jews and Gentiles (Acts 2, 10, 15:7-9).

What do the last words of verse 19 mean? "Whatsoever thou shalt bind on earth shall be bound in heaven; and whatsoever thou shalt loose on earth shall be loosed in heaven." Our Lord did not give Peter the power to forgive and absolve sins! And this promise of our Lord has nothing to do with church discipline. What the text does teach is this: Peter and the Apostles were commissioned to teach the way of salvation with inspired authority (Acts 15:9-11; 16:31; Romans 10:9-13). J. C. Ryle wrote, "As the Old Testament priests declared authoritatively whose leprosy was cleansed, so the apostles were appointed to 'declare and pronounce' authoritatively whose sins were forgiven."

As the Apostles of Christ they were inspired to lay down and establish the rules and regulations by which the church and kingdom of Christ must be governed. Those things which they made binding are binding. The doctrine of Christ's church and kingdom is the gospel, "Jesus Christ and him crucified". The ordinances of the kingdom are believer's baptism and the Lord's supper. The divinely appointed rulers of the kingdom are faithful pastors. All matters of indifference they left as matters of indifference. Those things they "loosed", so that each believer is free to decide what is best for himself (Acts 15:19; Romans 14:4, 5).

It is important to state that this authority and power to bind and loose things in the kingdom of heaven was confined to the apostles. It began with them. And it ended with them. It has never been given to anyone else. I am not an infallible teacher. Neither is any other man. No pastor, no church, no denomination has any right or power to lay down any laws, rules, or guiding principles for the kingdom of God. The Word of God alone is our only rule of faith and practice.

Remember, that which Peter here confessed is the Rock of Foundation upon which the Church and Kingdom of God is and must be built. Here are five blessed things spoken of in this passage of scripture.

"Thou Art The Christ"

A Blessed Confession

At first glance, the careless reader might pass over the words of vv. 13-16, thinking there is nothing extraordinary in them; but such thoughts arise from great ignorance. Peter's confession here is truly remarkable. The more I study it, the more remarkable and blessed it appears. Consider it carefully.

This confession put Peter at odds with the rest of the world. Few were with Christ in those days. Many were against him. But Peter confessed him. When the rulers of his own nation and all the religious people he knew, the scribes, the Pharisees, the Sadducees, the priests, and the people, all opposed Christ, Peter confessed him. Many would gladly acknowledge him to be a prophet, even a great prophet, even a resurrected prophet. But Peter confessed him to be "The Christ, The Son of the living God".

This confession of faith came from a man of tremendous faith, character, commitment, and zeal. Say what you will about Peter. He had his faults, I know. But do not underrate this man. His heart was under the rule of Christ. Grace is evident in him. Peter was a true-hearted, fervent, faithful servant of our God.

Now, look at the content of Peter's confession. Looking in the face of the Son of man, Peter said to that man, "Thou art the Christ, the Son of the living God". Peter confessed that the Man Christ Jesus is God, the eternal Son; that the despised Nazarene is the Christ, the promised Messiah, the One of whom all the prophets spoke. In a word, he confessed that the Man, Jesus, is God come to save his people from their sins (Matthew 1:21). I do not know all Peter knew or did not know, but he knew Christ and confessed him. Do you?

A Blessed Man

"And Jesus answered and said unto him, Blessed art thou, Simon Bar-jona: for flesh and blood hath not revealed it unto thee, but my Father which is in heaven" (v. 17). Peter was a truly blessed man. His blessedness was manifest, not in his lifestyle, or his freedom from trouble and sorrow, but in the grace of God he had experienced, as was evident in his confession. Like all who are born of God, he was blessed with spiritual understanding (John 6:44, 45; 1 Corinthians 2:11-16; 1 John 2:20). He was blessed by divine decree (Ephesians 1:3-14). And he was distinctively blessed by distinguishing grace (1 Corinthians 4:7).

Who can describe the blessedness of knowing him, whom to know aright is eternal life? As it was in Peter's day, so it is today, and so it is in every age. The people of this world, religious and irreligious, have many and varied opinions about Christ. But only one opinion is right; and that is the opinion formed in the heart by divine teaching and illumination. If we know him, our Saviour says, "Flesh and blood hath not revealed it unto thee". That is to say, we did not come to know him on our own, and no mere man revealed him to you. We do not know Christ after the flesh, or by human learning (2 Corinthians 5:16). "But my Father which is in heaven", God himself, by his Holy Spirit, has revealed him to us and in us by the preaching of the gospel (Matthew 11:25-27; John 6:45, 46; Galatians 1:15, 16; Ephesians 1:17, 18; 3:14; 1 Corinthians 12:3; Romans 10:14-17).

A Blessed Foundation.

The Foundation upon which God's church is built, the Foundation on which our souls are built, the Foundation on which our faith and hope is built is the Rock Christ Jesus. He is the Foundation laid by God's decree (Isaiah 28:16), the sure Foundation, a precious Foundation, an indestructible Foundation (Matthew 7:24-27), and a tried Foundation.

Christ is the Rock upon which we must be built, "For other foundation can no man lay than that is laid, which is Jesus Christ" (1 Corinthians 3:11). He is the precious Corner Stone the Lord God has laid in Zion. Those who believe on him shall never perish, but have everlasting life. Those who build on the sand of their own works shall be buried in the everlasting ruins of their own confusion in hell.

Faith in Christ is compared to the building of a house of refuge (Matthew 7:24). Sooner or later your house will be tested by earthly trials, spiritual trials, rains of trouble, floods of sorrow, and winds of adversity (v. 25). If your house is built on Christ the Rock, it will endure the trial and stand the tests of time. If your house is built on the sand, anything other than Christ, sooner or later the rains and floods and winds will bring it crumbling down around you.

Everything built upon the sand will crumble. Only that which is built upon Christ, the Stone that God has laid, will stand. Our Lord Jesus Christ is the Foundation, and God's elect are the building reared upon that Foundation. He alone is the Rock of our salvation.

A Blessed Promise

"Upon this rock I will build my church; and the gates of hell shall not prevail against it" (v. 18). Perhaps no word in the Bible has been more misunderstood, more abused, and more confusing to men than the word "church". Man's misunderstanding of this word has led to bigotry, sectarianism, strife, isolationism, and even persecution.

What is this Church, which the Son of God calls "my church"? The word "church" is used in three ways in the New Testament. Sometimes, the word "church" is used to describe local, visible assemblies of professed believers in a given place. In every local church there are both believers and unbelievers, wheat and tares, sheep and goats, true possessors of faith and false professors of faith. Every local church has in its membership both the true and the false; but still every local assembly of men and women, who profess faith in Christ and the gospel of God's free grace in him, is set forth as a local church and is called, "the church of God" (Romans 16:1-5).

Sometimes the word "church" is used to describe all true churches at any given time in the world. Obviously I do not suggest that the church of God is made up of all churches and denominations, but it does include all New Testament churches at any given time in the world. We are one in Christ, one in purpose, one in heart, and one in desire. All true gospel churches in this world in Jesus Christ are one (1 Corinthians 10:32; 12:28).

The word church, as it is used here, does not refer to any local church, or any denomination, but to "the church which is his body, the fulness of him that filleth all in all" (Ephesians 1:22, 23), the family of God, the redeemed and called ones of Christ, "of whom the whole family in heaven and earth is named" (Ephesians 3:15). Here, as in many other places in the New Testament, the word "church" is used to describe all true believers of all ages, from the beginning of the world to its end, all the saints of the Old Testament and New Testament ages, all of God's elect upon the earth and in heaven. This is what we call the universal church. It is the mystical body and spiritual bride of the Lord Jesus Christ. It is that spiritual body of which Jesus Christ is the Head (Ephesians 1:22; 5:23-25).

What does the Lord Jesus here promise his church? He promised to build it. "I will build my church". It is his church. He chose it. He redeemed it. And he builds it, calling his elect to life and faith by his Spirit. And he promised to protect it, "The gates of hell shall not prevail against it". Local churches do wither and die. How often we have seen the Lord remove the candlestick from different places! But not one member of Christ's mystical body shall perish (John 10:28).

A Blessed Gift

The Lord Jesus gave to Peter and the Apostles the keys to the kingdom of heaven (v. 19), and he has given them to us by them in the volume of holy scripture. Christ brought in everlasting righteousness by his obedience to God as our

Representative. He put away sin by the sacrifice of himself as our sin-atoning Substitute. And the gospel declares that every sinner who believes on the Lord Jesus Christ "hath everlasting life" (1 John 5:1).

Now, look at verse 20. Here is a charge our Master has reversed. He told his disciples to "tell no man that he was Jesus the Christ", because his hour was not yet come. But now he commands us to tell all men everywhere that he is Jesus, the Christ, the Son of the living God (Matthew 28:18-20). It is the business of his church in this world (the only business of his church) to proclaim the gospel to all. By this means the Lord God our Saviour builds his church.

Chapter 43

"Get Thee Behind Me, Satan"

"From that time forth began Jesus to shew unto his disciples, how that he must go unto Jerusalem, and suffer many things of the elders and chief priests and scribes, and be killed, and be raised again the third day. Then Peter took him, and began to rebuke him, saying, Be it far from thee, Lord: this shall not be unto thee. But he turned, and said unto Peter, Get thee behind me, Satan: thou art an offence unto me: for thou savourest not the things that be of God, but those that be of men. Then said Jesus unto his disciples, If any man will come after me, let him deny himself, and take up his cross, and follow me. For whosoever will save his life shall lose it: and whosoever will lose his life for my sake shall find it. For what is a man profited, if he shall gain the whole world, and lose his own soul? or what shall a man give in exchange for his soul? For the Son of man shall come in the glory of his Father with his angels; and then he shall reward every man according to his works. Verily I say unto you, There be some standing here, which shall not taste of death, till they see the Son of man coming in his kingdom."
(Matthew 16:21-28)

In this passage of holy scripture there are some deep mysteries and profound spiritual truths that need to be both carefully studied and laid to heart. Here we see the eternal God talking about a death he must die, a faithful disciple of Christ rebuking his Master, the Lord Jesus calling one of his beloved servants "Satan", the necessity of self-denial and commitment to Christ, the incomparable value of our souls, the second advent of our Lord and the judgment that shall accompany it, and the spiritual reign and kingdom of our Lord Jesus Christ. Without question, in these verses there are some things hard to be understood. May God the Holy Spirit, who inspired Matthew to write these things, be our teacher as we study them.

"He Must"

"From that time forth began Jesus to shew unto his disciples, how that he must go unto Jerusalem, and suffer many things of the elders and chief priests and scribes, and be killed, and be raised again the third day" (v. 21). First, we see that as a Man, as our Mediator and Substitute, as Jehovah's Servant, there are some things that the Lord Jesus Christ must do.

As God, it could never be written, "He must". But as the Surety of the covenant, in order to fulfil the terms of the covenant, because he is Jehovah's voluntary Servant, there are some things that the scriptures declare the Lord Jesus Christ "must" do. He told his parents that he must be about his Father's business (Luke 2:49). He said, "I come to do thy will, O my God". He said to his disciples, "My meat is to do the will of him that sent me". He told a chosen sinner, at the appointed time of mercy, "I must abide at thy house" (Luke 19:5). He must do so because the time had come when that chosen sinner must be called and saved by his omnipotent grace (Psalm 110:3; John 10:16). We read in John 4:4 that "he must needs go through Samaria", because there was another chosen sinner there for whom "the time of love" had come.

Here our Lord told his disciples that he must go up to Jerusalem, suffer, and die, and rise again the third day. Why must he? It was because the Father ordained it, the prophets revealed it, the types portrayed it, God's justice demanded it, and the time appointed for it had come.

We cannot imagine how shocking this was to the disciples. Like the rest of the Jews, they were not anticipating a Messiah who would suffer and die. They looked for a political Messiah. It seems that all of the disciples were confused about our Lord's teaching regarding his death until it actually happened, all except for the woman who anointed him for his burial. This is what led to Peter's error.

True, But Weak

Second, we are once again taught that a man can be a true disciple and yet be a weak disciple and ignorant about many things (vv. 22, 23). The issue of great importance is not what do you know, but who? It is not doctrine that saves, but Christ. I do not suggest for a moment that a person can be saved trusting a false Christ. But the scriptures do show us, by numerous examples, that people who truly trust Christ are ignorant of many, many things.

Peter was, without a doubt, born again and a true believer (vv. 16-19). He was a man taught of God (v. 17). Who can read the conversation between Christ and

Peter in the preceding verses and imagine that Peter was not yet converted? Such an idea is too ludicrous to mention. Yet, there are some who, attempting to defend an erroneous system of doctrine, dogmatically assert that neither Peter, nor any of the other apostles and disciples of Christ, were converted until after the Lord's resurrection!

This faithful and gracious man behaved very foolishly and ignorantly. "Then Peter took him, and began to rebuke him, saying, Be it far from thee, Lord: this shall not be unto thee". Peter actually rebuked the Lord Jesus and sought, like Satan, to hinder him from doing what he did come to do! This man, who was so faithful in so many, many things, became an instrument of Satan in his time of weakness.

Because he had become an instrument of Satan, the Lord Jesus rebuked his disciple as Satan. "He turned, and said unto Peter, Get thee behind me, Satan: thou art an offence unto me: for thou savourest not the things that be of God, but those that be of men". He spoke to Peter as though he were himself Satan, because he had become Satan's instrument. He said, "Thou art an offence unto me", a stumbling block, "thou savourest not the things that be of God, but those that be of men". Peter was looking at things, judging things, and acting from a purely human, carnal, and emotional point of view. His flesh was in the way. His flesh kept him from seeing, at the time, the blessed necessity for our Saviour's death.

Is this Peter? Is this the same man that our Saviour had just declared "blessed" of God? Yes, he is the same man. Yet, to this man, beloved of God, chosen, redeemed, and called by grace, to this man so highly favoured and blessed of God, the Lord Jesus spoke as he never spoke to any other. "Get thee behind me, Satan: thou art an offence unto me: for thou savourest not the things that be of God, but those that be of men". Let us lay this to heart. If the Lord God is pleased to leave us, even momentarily to ourselves and to our own judgment, we are sure to fall into great and grievous evil.

Perhaps, it is for just this reason that the Holy Spirit inspired Matthew to record both our Saviour's great love for us and Peter's terrible, inexcusable weakness at the same time. So great is our need and so great is the determination of his love for our souls that the Lord Jesus Christ zealously longed for the hour when, by his sufferings and death upon the cursed tree, he would accomplish redemption for us. He was, as he put it, "straitened" until it was finished (Luke 12:50).

Substitution
Third, this exchange between Peter and the Master teaches us that there is no doctrine in the Bible so important as the doctrine of Christ's sin-atoning death as our Substitute. That man who denies the doctrine of Christ's effectual atonement, who denies the merit and efficacy of Christ's death as our Substitute, no matter what else he may say that is true, does not savour "the things that be of God". Commenting upon this, C. H. Spurgeon wrote, "He knows not the taste, the aroma, the essence of spiritual things; and however much he may honour Jesus in words, he is an enemy, a real Satan towards the true Christ." The death of Christ is, as J. C. Ryle stated, "the central truth of Christianity. Right views of his vicarious death and the benefits resulting from it, lie at the very foundation of Bible-religion. If we are wrong here, we are ruined forever. Error on many points is only a skin disease. Error about Christ's death is a disease at the heart."

Whatever we think about the death of Christ, let us always remember four things about it: 1. Our Saviour's death was accomplished by his own sovereign will and purpose (John 10:17, 18). 2. The Lord Jesus Christ died as the Substitute for his elect (2 Corinthians 5:21; John 10:11, 15). 3. When he died for us, bearing our sins in his own body on the tree, being made sin and a curse for us, the Son of God fully satisfied all the demands of divine justice for us (Isaiah 53:10, 11). And 4. he was completely successful in his work of redemption (Isaiah 42:4; Galatians 3:13; Matthew 1:21). Whatever he intended to accomplish, he accomplished. All he intended to redeem, he redeemed.

Self-denial
Fourth, the Lord Jesus teaches us that true, saving faith involves deliberate and persevering, self-denial and consecration (vv. 24, 25). Matthew Henry wrote, "The first lesson in Christ's school is self-denial." Those who deny themselves here for Christ shall enjoy themselves in Christ forever. Grace is free; but it is not cheap. Faith in Christ involves the total surrender of myself to him, to his dominion as my Lord and Saviour, my Priest and King. That is what it is to take up your cross and follow Christ.

Christianity, true Christianity, true saving faith involves a total surrender to Christ the Lord. Either you will be a servant under the dominion of King Jesus, voluntarily giving up all to his claims, or you will go to hell. You may not have to give up anything in actuality. But surrender to Christ must be just as real and complete in your heart as if you had actually given up everything, even down to life itself. Our Lord Jesus Christ requires total and unreserved surrender to himself. Christ will be Lord of all, or he will not be Lord at all. Is Jesus Christ, the Son of God, your Lord? Is he truly your Lord?

We must never imagine that this is a matter dealt with only in the initial experience of grace and in the initial act of faith. Here our Lord Jesus addresses these words to men who had been his faithful disciples for a long time. How graciously he warns us and teaches us to guard against the terrible tendency of our sinful flesh to rebel against his rule and his will. How much evil we bring upon ourselves by our carnal misapprehensions! We are all, like Peter, inclined to judge things by our emotions and personal desires. We must not. Rather, we must seek grace to know and bow to the will of God our Saviour in all things. Oh! for grace to savour the things which are of God, and not those which are of men!

"His Own Soul"

Fifth, we are again taught that there is nothing so precious and valuable as your soul. "For what is a man profited, if he shall gain the whole world, and lose his own soul? or what shall a man give in exchange for his soul?" (v. 26) Here is a question so well known and so often repeated that I fear that few take it to heart. It ought to sound in our ears like a trumpet, whenever we are tempted to neglect our eternal interests. There is nothing the world can offer, nothing money can buy, nothing a man can give, nothing to be named in comparison with our souls. We live in a world where everything is temporal. We are going to a world where everything is eternal. Let us count nothing here more valuable than we shall when we have to leave it forever!

Our Reward

Sixth, in verse 27, our Saviour, having declared the value of our souls, assures his disciples and us that our reward is yet to come. "For the Son of man shall come in the glory of his Father with his angels; and then he shall reward every man according to his works." In the day of judgment, every man will get exactly the reward that he deserves, according to the books, the ledgers of heaven. The wicked shall be judged according to their own works. The righteous shall be judged according to their own works, too, the works of Christ imputed to us in free justification.

The Connection

Seventh, in verse 28 the Lord Jesus shows the connection between his death, his resurrection, and his kingdom, or his spiritual reign as King. "Verily I say unto you, There be some standing here, which shall not taste of death, till they see the Son of man coming in his kingdom." This text has caused much controversy among those visionaries who think they can predict or have figured out what they call God's "prophetic time table". This is not talking about the second coming and a millennial reign, or the destruction of Jerusalem in 70 A.D. The only thing that this text can possibly refer to is Christ's spiritual kingdom, into which he entered when he ascended up to heaven, which was signified by the outpouring of the Holy Spirit on the day of Pentecost (Acts 2:32-36; Galatians 3:13, 14). Have you entered into Christ's Kingdom? Have you come under the rule of the Son of God?

Yet, our Lord seems to blend into one his glorious second coming (v. 27), and his coming in grace (v. 28). The fact is all his works are one. Every coming of Christ is glorious, both when he first comes in grace to awaken our souls and in all the visits of his grace that follow, until he finally comes to take us home to glory (John 14:1-3). As Simeon of old could not die until he had seen the Lord Jesus and held him in his arms, so there are some (a great multitude that no man can number) who shall not taste death until Christ is revealed to them and embraced in their arms of faith. And just as this prophecy was fulfilled on the day of Pentecost, it is fulfilled every time a chosen, redeemed sinner is called to life and faith in Christ.

Chapter 44

The Message Of The Transfiguration

"And after six days Jesus taketh Peter, James, and John his brother, and bringeth them up into an high mountain apart, And was transfigured before them: and his face did shine as the sun, and his raiment was white as the light. And, behold, there appeared unto them Moses and Elias talking with him. Then answered Peter, and said unto Jesus, Lord, it is good for us to be here: if thou wilt, let us make here three tabernacles; one for thee, and one for Moses, and one for Elias. While he yet spake, behold, a bright cloud overshadowed them: and behold a voice out of the cloud, which said, This is my beloved Son, in whom I am well pleased; hear ye him. And when the disciples heard it, they fell on their face, and were sore afraid. And Jesus came and touched them, and said, Arise, and be not afraid. And when they had lifted up their eyes, they saw no man, save Jesus only. And as they came down from the mountain, Jesus charged them, saying, Tell the vision to no man, until the Son of man be risen again from the dead. And his disciples asked him, saying, Why then say the scribes that Elias must first come? And Jesus answered and said unto them, Elias truly shall first come, and restore all things. But I say unto you, That Elias is come already, and they knew him not, but have done unto him whatsoever they listed. Likewise shall also the Son of man suffer of them. Then the disciples understood that he spake unto them of John the Baptist."
(Matthew 17:1-13)

In Matthew 17, the Holy Spirit takes us up on the mount of transfiguration. He does not tell us which mountain it was, lest foolish men make it an idolatrous "holy place". But it was one of the high mountains around Jerusalem. There our Lord Jesus Christ was transfigured before Peter, James and John. They saw his majesty and his excellent glory. The order in which this event is recorded is beautiful and full of instruction. It was six days after the events recorded in chapter 16. In that chapter the Lord Jesus warned his disciples to beware of the leaven of the Pharisees and Sadducees (v. 6), and reproved their unbelief (vv. 8-12); Peter made his great confession of Christ (vv. 13-20); Our Lord gave words of instruction about his sufferings, death, and resurrection (v. 21); Peter rebuked the Son of God and was rebuked by him (vv. 22, 23); Our Lord spoke of the cost of following him (vv. 24-26) and he spoke of his coming glory (vv. 27, 28)

"And After Six Days"

The disciples thought on these things for six days. Then the Lord called Peter, James and John to himself and took them up on the mount. He had told them about his suffering. Now he would show them something of his glory. The hearts, which had been saddened by those plain statements regarding his sufferings and death, must be gladdened by the vision of his reward and glory.

"Jesus taketh Peter, James, and John his brother, and bringeth them up into an high mountain apart". Luke tells us that they came up into this high mountain "to pray". What a prayer meeting it was! Did you notice that Peter is still in the favoured circle? Six days earlier he had greatly sinned in rebuking his Master. But Christ did not remember it. He did not bear the offence in mind. He freely forgave Peter's sin. He loved Peter still. How thankful we ought to be for such a Saviour! He will not impute sin to his own (Romans 4:8).

The Transfiguration

Much in verses 2-5 is shrouded in mystery; and we will leave it there. That which God has not revealed we are content not to know. We will not pry curiously into God's secrets. Robert Hawker wrote:

> We know that 'the Word was made flesh, and dwelt among us' (John 1:14). And we know also, that 'in him', that is, Christ, 'dwelleth all the fulness of the Godhead bodily' (Colossians 2:9). All that we can possibly frame to ourselves of this transfiguration therefore is, that the Godhead shone forth in the manhood in a more than ordinary manner. The Son of God was pleased to manifest himself in his double-nature glory more than in the usual appearances of Christ in the days of his flesh. It was a moment of peculiar manifestation of the glories of his person. It was the personal glory of the God-Man, as God-Man.

Still, there is much in these verses which is intended for our instruction and edification. We have before us a striking demonstration of the glory in which Christ and his people will appear when he comes the second time. The transfiguration was a revelation of our Lord's true dignity. Here the corner of the veil was lifted to show Peter, James and John the glory which awaited Christ as the reward of his agony upon the cross (2 Peter 1:16; John 1:14). It was also a picture of the glory which awaits every believer. J. C. Ryle said, "There is laid up for Jesus, and all that believe on him, such glory as the heart of man never conceived" (1 John 3:1, 2).

These verses also give us a clear, factual demonstration of life after death and of the resurrection of the body. Moses had been dead and buried for 1500 years. Elijah "went up by a whirlwind into heaven" 900 years before this time. Yet, here they stood on the mount talking to the Lord Jesus. Peter, James and John saw them and heard them; and they knew immediately who they were, though they had never seen them or even a picture of them. That fact clearly demonstrates the universal teaching of holy scripture that there is life after death and that there is a coming day of resurrection. I think we may safely infer from this that God's elect will know one another in the resurrection.

Something Better

When the Lord Jesus was transfigured before Peter, James and John, his face shone like the sun and his garments were as white as the light. Peter later tells us that they were "eyewitnesses of his majesty" (2 Peter 1:16) and heard God's voice "from the excellent glory" (2 Peter 1:17). But there is something better than that. Peter tells us that the written Word of God is a more sure and dependable revelation than his experience upon the mountain of transfiguration (2 Peter 1:19). In this day of imaginary extra-biblical revelation, Peter's words need to be remembered. We must never interpret the written Word of God by our experiences, no matter how glorious. Rather, we are to interpret our experiences by God's written Word.

Peter's Proposal

"Then answered Peter, and said unto Jesus, Lord, it is good for us to be here: if thou wilt, let us make here three tabernacles; one for thee, and one for Moses, and one for Elias" (v. 4). Peter was simply overwhelmed. Who can blame him for making his proposal that three tabernacles should be made? Who would not wish to abide in such a mountain and in such a state?

After seeing and hearing the things he saw and heard upon the mount of transfiguration, and after hearing such a testimony "from the excellent glory", and after having made such a great confession of faith regarding the Lord Jesus Christ (16:15-19), who would ever have imagined that Peter would later deny his God and Saviour? But he did (Matthew 26:69-75). And there is not a more blessed example in all the Word of God of that which he was later inspired to write. We "are kept by the power of God, through faith unto salvation" (1 Peter 1:5). Who could write those words with more force and gratitude than Peter? He knew, by blessed experience, that the safety and security of God's elect is altogether, at all times, and in all circumstances, a matter of pure, free grace.

God The Son

This event is recorded to show us, by divine testimony, that the Lord Jesus Christ is infinitely superior to all who are born of women (vv. 4, 5). Peter, bewildered by the heavenly vision, suggested that three tabernacles ought to be built: one for Moses, one for Elijah, and one for Christ. In his confusion, Peter seems to have placed the lawgiver and the prophet side by side with Christ, as though they were equal to him. Immediately, Moses and Elijah were engulfed in a cloud, and a voice came forth from the cloud saying, "This is my beloved Son, in whom I am well pleased; hear ye him." That voice was meant to teach Peter and us that Jesus Christ alone is the Son of God, the Saviour of men, and the One in whom and by whom God is well-pleased.

As the rising of the sun eclipses every star and causes them to fade away, even so the rising of Christ, the Sun of Righteousness, in the earth eclipses all who ever came before him. Once Christ has come, Moses, the law, has nothing more to say. He met the law's demands. The words of the prophets, represented by Elijah, are no longer to be pried into as mysterious secrets. He fulfilled all the prophets.

"This is my beloved Son". With those words, God the Father publicly owned and identified himself with Jesus, the Son of Mary, as his own dearly beloved Son. The babe of Bethlehem, the man of Nazareth, the suffering One of Calvary is himself "God over all, blessed forever". Christ is the only begotten Son of God (John 3:16), the eternally begotten Son of God (Proverbs 8:22, 23), and the Son co-equal with his Father (John 5:18, 10:33; 1 John 5:7).

Christ is co-essential with the Father, so essentially one with the Father that without Christ there would be no God (John 1:1-3). We who believe are the sons of God by adoption and grace; but Christ is the Son of God by nature and essence. He is the Son as none others are. This voice from heaven announced the fulfilment of the prophecies, which foretold the coming of One who would be both God and man in one Person (Isaiah 7:14, 9:6; Micah 5:2; Zechariah 13:7).

The Lord Jesus Christ is the Beloved Son of God. God the Father loves the Son as the Son. Particularly, this is spoken to show us that the Father loves and delights in the Son because of his obedience as the Mediator and Substitute for sinners (Proverbs 8:30; John 3:35; 10:17). The Lord Jesus Christ is the embodiment, revelation, and medium of divine love. God loves sinners in Christ and because of Christ (John 17:23, 24; Romans 5:8; 1 John 3:16; 4:8-10).

This is the first, essential thing to be learned: Jesus Christ our Saviour is himself God, the eternal Son, well-beloved by his Father. It is his Godhead that gives infinite merit and efficacy to all that he does. He who is God is an all-sufficient, effectual Substitute for sinners.

Well-Pleased

"This is my beloved Son, in whom I am well-pleased". God the Father speaks from heaven to Peter, James and John, and by them to us, declaring that he is well pleased with his dear Son, and only with his Son. Moses was there; but God was not pleased with him. Elijah was there; but God was not pleased with him. Peter was there; but God was not pleased with him. James was there; but God was not pleased with him. And John was there; but God was not pleased with him. God never has been and never can be pleased with any sinful man. But God always has been and always must be well pleased with his dear Son, the God-man.

It goes without saying that God the Father is essentially well pleased with his Son as his Son. But here we are told that God the Father is well pleased with his Son as the God-man Mediator. God was well pleased with his Son eternally, as our Surety and Mediatoral Representative in the covenant of grace (Isaiah 42:21). He is well pleased, honoured by, and delights in the representative life of his Son, by which he brought in everlasting righteousness for us (Matthew 3:13-17). God is well pleased with the substitutionary, sin atoning death of his Son, by which he both satisfied divine justice and put away the sins of his people (Isaiah 53:10; Psalm 85:9-13). He is well pleased with the heavenly intercession of his Son as our Advocate and great High Priest (1 John 2:1, 2). God is well pleased with the providential rule of his Son as the sovereign King of the universe (Isaiah 42:1-4). As our Saviour said of his earthly life, he might say of his heavenly rule, "I do always those things that please him" (John 8:29). And God shall be well pleased with the results of his Son's covenant engagements and mediatoral rule (1

Corinthians 15:24-28). Christ, as the Mediator, as the God-man, shall present his kingdom to the eternal Father, that God the Father, the Son, and the Holy Spirit may be forever glorified (Revelation 19:1-7).

But the voice that was heard from heaven did not say, "This is my beloved Son with whom I am well pleased", but "This is my beloved Son in whom I am well pleased". God is well pleased with his people in his Son. Imagine that! The holy, righteous, just, and true God, Lord of heaven and earth, is honoured by, delights in, and is well pleased with us in his Son! In our natural condition we are all displeasing to God. This is our miserable state by nature. But our God is well pleased with us for Christ's sake, because he is well pleased in Christ. He was well pleased with us in Christ eternally (Ephesians 1:6). He is well pleased with all that we offer to him and do for him in Christ (1 Peter 2:5). Furthermore, he is always, immutably, well pleased with us in Christ (Jeremiah 23:6; 33:16).

Hear Him

"Hear ye him." The God of glory commands us to hear Christ our Surety, to hear all that he declares and reveals, as our Prophet, Priest, and King, and to hear him with confident faith; to receive and accept him in all the fulness of his person and work as the God-man, our Saviour. Our God here tells us to be completely well pleased with him as the Lord our Righteousness, just as he is completely well pleased with him. He would have us, by faith, to look upon ourselves in Christ, just as he looks upon us in Christ. To reckon ourselves to be what he reckons us to be: justified, righteous, holy, accepted, without sin, blameless, spotless, unreproveable, well-pleasing to God (Romans 6:11).

Are you well pleased with Christ? He who is well pleased with Christ alone as his Wisdom, Righteousness, Sanctification, and Redemption, accepts Christ as all, looks to Christ for all, pleads Christ in all, makes Christ to be what God makes him, the whole of salvation, as the sole means of salvation. When the Holy Spirit declares of God's elect that we are "accepted in the Beloved" (Ephesians 1:6), he is not merely telling us that God accepts our repentance, our faith, our prayers, and our works for Christ's sake (though that is true). He is telling us that we are accepted as one with the Beloved. As such, because we are in him and one with him, "the fulness of him that filleth all in all", we are well pleasing to our God in him. And that can never change! As John Kent put it:

Christ exalted is our song,
Sung by all the blood-bought throng;
To His throne our shouts shall rise,
God with us by sacred ties.

Shout, believer, to thy God!
He hath once the wine-press trod;
Peace procured by blood divine;
Cancelled all thy sins and mine.

Here thy bleeding wounds are healed;
Sin condemned and pardon sealed;
Grace her empire still maintains;
Love without a rival reigns.

In thy Surety thou art free;
His dear hands were pierced for thee;
With His spotless garment on,
Holy as the Holy One!

Oh, the heights and depths of grace!
Shining with meridian blaze;
Here the sacred records show
Sinners black, but comely too.

Saints dejected, cease to mourn,
Faith shall soon to vision turn;
Ye the kingdom shall obtain,
And with Christ exalted reign.

"Hear ye him." With these words, God the Father also informs us that Christ alone is the great Prophet and Teacher in his kingdom. No voice is to be heard in the church and kingdom of God, but the voice of Christ. His doctrine alone is the doctrine of his church. His Word alone is our authoritative rule of faith and practice.

Grace Experienced

In verses 6-8, Matthew gives us a beautiful picture of the experience of grace. I am certain that I am not stretching the text when I tell you that the scene described in these three verses is a beautiful, spiritual picture of what happens when the Lord Jesus comes to sinners in his saving power and performs his saving operations of grace. Here is the power by which sinners are born of God in regeneration, "Jesus came and touched them". When touched by his omnipotent hand, we were called by his omnipotent voice. "Arise". And being called, he assures us that all is well, saying, "Be not afraid". And, as soon as sinners are born of God, raised up from the dead by him, hearing his voice, "They see no man, save Jesus only" as Saviour and Lord (1 Corinthians 1:30).

"Oh! for grace", wrote Hawker, "to possess such faith in Jesus, as may raise our souls above all fears, while conscious of a union with Christ, and acceptance in Christ. The sudden departure of Moses and Elias may serve to teach us, that none but Jesus can be our abiding comfort. Everything here below is short and transitory. Oh! What a blessed thought it is. Jesus hath said, 'Lo! I am with you always' (Matthew 28:20)".

Elijah

In verses 10-13 our Lord explains the ministry of John the Baptist. Malachi prophesied that prior to the Messiah's coming, Elijah would come again to prepare the way for him (Malachi 4:5, 6). Here, our Lord states plainly that Malachi was talking about John the Baptist. Indeed, like Elijah and John the Baptist, all true Gospel preachers are sent of God as forerunners to prepare the way of the Lord by declaring to men the gospel of God's free, sovereign, saving grace in Christ (Isaiah 52:7; Romans 10:14-17).

Chapter 45

"Jesus Only"

"And when they had lifted up their eyes, they saw no man, save Jesus only." (Matthew 17:8)

Peter, James and John were with the Lord Jesus "in the holy mount". There they saw the Saviour transfigured before them. We do not know what that vision was like. But we do know that it was a dazzling display of his divine glory and majesty (2 Peter 1:16-18; John 1:14; 1 John 1:2). Suddenly, Moses and Elijah appeared on the mountain with them and talked to Christ about the death he must accomplish at Jerusalem (Luke 9:32). Needless to say, Peter, James and John were awestruck! When Peter saw and heard Moses and Elijah, he blurted out, "Lord, it is good for us to be here: if thou wilt, let us make here three tabernacles, one for thee, one for Moses, and one for Elijah"! The Lord Jesus said nothing. But while Peter was yet talking, "A cloud overshadowed them". God simply took Moses and Elijah out of the picture. "And behold a voice spoke out of the cloud, which said, This is my beloved Son, in whom I am well pleased; hear ye him".

Moses and Elijah were removed from the scene for a reason. The Old covenant was vanishing away. The dawn of a new day and a new covenant had come. When the Lord God said, "This is my beloved Son in whom I am well pleased; hear ye him", he was saying to Peter, James and John, and to you and me, "Moses and Elijah have been fulfilled. Moses and Elijah have nothing more to say or do. All that they said and all that they did was in preparation for and pointed to the coming of my beloved Son. Here he is. 'Hear ye him!' Moses and Elijah, the Law and the Prophets have no other function."

At Sinai the people were forbidden to make any approach to the presence of God. They were not allowed to even touch the mountain. In the tabernacle and in the temple a thick, thick veil stood before the most holy place, constantly separating the people from God. The law did nothing to bring sinners into God's presence. It never could (Romans 8:33, 34; Hebrews 10:1-4, 12, 14). In fact, it did just the opposite. The law forbade men from even trying to approach the holy Lord God! No one could ever approach the God of heaven and earth until the law was fulfilled, its curse removed, and sin was put away by the satisfaction of God's justice. The Lord Jesus, so to speak, came down the mountain to the people, tore down the veil, and by the blood of his cross opened to fallen men a way of access to the Lord God (Hebrews 10:19-23).

When the disciples saw Christ in his glory and heard God speak from heaven, they fell on their faces. They realized that they were in the awesome presence of the glory of God and were terrified by it. That is always what happens when a sinner realizes who he is before the holy Lord God (Job 40:3-5; 42:5, 6; Isaiah 6:1-5; Daniel 10:8).

Then, after they fell before him in utter terror, we read that "Jesus came and touched them, and said, Arise, and be not afraid" (v. 7). God the Son, having assumed our nature for the express purpose of redeeming us and, thereby, showing us how greatly he loves us, here reveals that his whole heart towards his own is love, and bids his chosen never to be afraid.

When the law has been honoured, fulfilled, and silenced and you look up to see the One by whose obedience it has been fully satisfied, you will see "Jesus only". When you are made to understand that all the prophets have been fulfilled and you look up to see who fulfilled all those prophetic visions and promises given in the Old Testament, you will see "no man, save Jesus only". The Lord Jesus Christ alone is our salvation, comfort, strength, and hope.

Our Saviour

"Jesus only" is Our Saviour (Matthew 1:21; Acts 4:12; 1 Corinthians 1:30, 31). In the matter of salvation Christ stands entirely alone. We put no trust in the flesh, in ourselves, or in anything we do or experience. We trust "Jesus only" (Philippians 3:3; Romans 11:6; Galatians 5:2-4). We trust Christ alone for righteousness (Romans 3:24-26; 4:25-5:1; Jeremiah 23:6; 33:16). "Jesus only" is that Holiness we must have, without which none can see God (Hebrews 12:14). We trust "Jesus only" for redemption (2 Corinthians 5:21; Galatians 3:13; 1 Peter 1:18-21; 3:15). We trust "Jesus only" for sanctification (1 Corinthians 1:30; Hebrews 10:10-14). We trust "Jesus only" for preservation in grace (2 Timothy 1:12). We trust "Jesus only" for our resurrection and glorification (Psalm 16:9-11; Romans 6:5; 8:30).

Either Christ alone is my Saviour, or I have no Saviour! Either he completely saves, or he does not save at all. If so much as the will to be saved depends upon me, I cannot be saved (John 5:46; Romans 9:15, 16). If, after having been saved for fifty years, I should be required to reach back and drag my foot across the threshold of heaven, I would sink at last into hell. "Salvation is of the Lord"! "By the grace of God I am what I am"!

Our Lord

"Jesus only" is our Lord and Master. "Grace and peace be multiplied unto you through the knowledge of God, and of Jesus our Lord" (2 Peter 1:2). I know that the Lord Jesus Christ is the sovereign Monarch of the universe and the Ruler of all men, the wicked as well as the righteous. But he is the Lord of his people willingly, by our voluntary consent (1 Corinthians 12:3). True faith voluntarily surrenders all things to the rule of Christ (Luke 14:25-33). True faith trusts Christ's providential rule of all things, saying, "Thy will be done". True faith is obedient to Christ the Lord.

The Church of God is a Kingdom under the rule of Christ by voluntary consent, willingly obedient to his Word, his ordinances, and his will. He is our Master, and we are happy and thankful that he is.

Our Rule

"Jesus only" is our rule of life. We are not slaves under the dominion of the law. We are children, walking in the path of our Elder Brother because we love him and seek the honour of his name (John 13:15). Our rule of life is not the ten commandments, but the whole revealed will of God given to us in holy scripture. It is summarized in two commandments, two motivating forces by which we are governed in all things: faith and love (1 John 3:23).

Our Hope

"Jesus only" is our hope before God (Colossians 1:27; Lamentations 3:24-26). Our only assurance and peace is Christ (Romans 5:1). All who know him gladly confess, "I am a poor sinner and nothing at all; but Jesus Christ is my all in all"! Christ alone is our plea before and advocate with the Father (1 John 2:1, 2). Christ alone is able to present us faultless before the presence of God's glory. And he will do it (Ephesians 5:25-27; Jude 24, 25).

Bold shall I stand in that great day,
For who aught to my charge shall lay,
While through Christ's blood absolved I am
From sin's tremendous guilt and blame?

Our Reward

"Jesus only" is our reward in heaven. "Whom have I in heaven but thee? and there is none upon earth that I desire beside thee. My flesh and my heart faileth: but God is the strength of my heart, and my portion for ever" (Psalm 73:25, 26). In heaven's eternal glory we want nothing and hope for nothing but "Jesus only". He is the Crown we seek and the beauty we desire (Isaiah 28:5). "When my father and my mother forsake me, then the LORD will take me up" (Psalm 27:10). Soon we shall be with Christ (John 14:1-3). Soon we shall see his face (Revelation 22:4). When we see him, we shall be like him (1 John 3:2). We shall be fully satisfied with him (Revelation 21:1-4). And the Son of God shall be fully satisfied with us! (Isaiah 53:11). Imagine that!

Our All

"Jesus only" is our all. As the Spirit of God states it in Colossians 3:11, "Christ is all, and in all". To him every knee shall bow. Christ is all in all in creation, redemption, providence, grace, glory. He is all in all in his church and in the hearts of all his people. Christ is all in the Book of God, the sum and substance of the whole Bible. He is the living Word of whom the written Word speaks. The Lord Jesus Christ is not one of many revelations. He is the revelation of the One invisible God. Christ is not one of many words. He is the One True Word of God (John 1:1-3, 18). You and I cannot see God, know God, speak to God, be spoken to by God, or come to God except by Christ (John 14:6: Matthew 11:25-27). Christ is the Way. Without him, there is no going to God. Christ is the Truth. Without him, there is no knowing God. Christ is the Life. Without him, there is no living before God. There is no prophet like Christ our Prophet. He is unrivalled in his excellence as the revelation of the invisible God.

When we read the promises of God, we understand that Christ is the first promise in the sacred Word, and the whole of every promise that follows. In him all the promises of God are yea and amen. When we read the law of God, we rejoice to know that "Christ is the end of the law for righteousness to every one that believeth". When we read of the sacrifices, we rejoice to know that Christ has, by his one sacrifice fulfilled them all, for by that one sacrifice he has "perfected forever them that are sanctified". When we read the prophets, our hearts leap with joy because "to him give all the prophets witness, that through his name whosoever believeth in him shall receive remission of sins" (Acts 10:43).

Chapter 46

Only By Prayer And Fasting

"And when they were come to the multitude, there came to him a certain man, kneeling down to him, and saying, Lord, have mercy on my son: for he is lunatick, and sore vexed: for ofttimes he falleth into the fire, and oft into the water. And I brought him to thy disciples, and they could not cure him. Then Jesus answered and said, O faithless and perverse generation, how long shall I be with you? how long shall I suffer you? bring him hither to me. And Jesus rebuked the devil; and he departed out of him: and the child was cured from that very hour. Then came the disciples to Jesus apart, and said, Why could not we cast him out? And Jesus said unto them, Because of your unbelief: for verily I say unto you, If ye have faith as a grain of mustard seed, ye shall say unto this mountain, Remove hence to yonder place; and it shall remove; and nothing shall be impossible unto you. Howbeit this kind goeth not out but by prayer and fasting."
(Matthew 17:14-21)

In this passage of scripture we have the healing of the lunatic by the word of our Lord. It was a miracle that the disciples were not able to perform because of their unbelief. While the Lord Jesus was in the mount of transfiguration, a certain man brought his epileptic son to the disciples. But the disciples were unable to help him.

Mark's more detailed account of this event (Mark 9) shows us that this all took place in the midst of a large crowd of jeering adversaries. The disciples tried in vain to cast out the evil spirit and cure the child of his seizures. You can imagine the father's disappointment. When the Lord Jesus appeared, he immediately appealed to him, saying, "Lord, have mercy on my son: for he is lunatick, and sore vexed: for ofttimes he falleth into the fire, and oft into the water. And I brought him to thy disciples, and they could not cure him."

This is one of those miracles that is recorded by Matthew, Mark, and Luke. It is reported to us three times because the Holy Spirit intends for us to recognize the importance of it, and learn the spiritual lessons taught by it. So, without introduction, let me show you what these lessons are.

A Good Father

Blessed are those children who have such a good father. The best parents are those who seek the mercy of God for their children. This young man's father recognized the great need of his son. He recognized that his son's needs were primarily spiritual, not physical. He realized that his boy was possessed of a devil (Mark 9:17, 25, 26; Luke 9:39-42). Blessed is that son, blessed is that daughter whose parents earnestly seek the salvation of their souls.

This man recognized his son's great need was the mercy of God found in Christ (v. 15). He brought his needy son to the Lord's disciples, hoping for his cure (v. 16). These were the men he knew had been used of God for the healing of many. Therefore, he brought his son to them. Blessed are those children who have parents who bring them to the house of God, whose parents see to it that they hear the preaching of the gospel. That is the means by which God gives life and faith to chosen sinners, the means by which he communicates mercy to the needy (Romans 10:17; 1 Peter 1:23-25).

But it took more than the work of the disciples to cast out the evil spirit and cure the child; and it takes more than the voice of a preacher to save a sinner. The Word preached must be accompanied by the power of God, or it will accomplish nothing. Let us, like this man, take our children and their needs directly to the Saviour, making intercession, earnest intercession, on their behalf (vv. 14, 15).

Here is something that must not be overlooked, when this man brought his child to the Saviour, he obtained the mercy he craved for his son (v. 18). I would not make more of this fact than is warranted by the scriptures; but it is a fact that ought to encourage every believing mother and father to bring their children, in the arms of faith, to the Son of God by prayer. I do not find a single example of anyone bringing a needy soul to Christ during his earthly ministry who did not obtain the mercy craved for the one brought to the Saviour.

Satan's Influence

We have before us a pitiful example of the destructive power of Satan upon those who are under his influence. This young man was possessed of a devil. During the days of our Lord's earthly ministry, demon possession was a very common thing. One reason it was allowed was to give clear evidence of Christ's power over hell. Another reason why God allowed that horrible evil was to teach us that Satan's influence is always destructive (v. 15).

Like a roaring lion, he seeks to devour the souls of men (1 Peter 5:8). The old serpent appears to seek the destruction of young souls especially. Thousands upon thousands of young men and women seem to be wholly given over to Satan's influence, and are "taken captive at his will" to the destruction of their souls (2 Timothy 2:26).

Ignorant, indulgent parents often look upon the reckless rebellion of their children as a passing phase. They excuse a child's disregard for authority, moral perversity, and pleasure seeking behaviour as "sowing the wild oats" of youth. How foolish! How irresponsible!

Do not overlook the fact that this young man was raised by a man who believed and worshipped and loved the Lord Jesus Christ. Many look upon parents whose children are rebels as though the parents themselves must be bad parents. Such thoughts arise from hearts full of pride and self-righteousness. David was a man after God's own heart. Yet, his sons and daughters were all, except Solomon, reprobate rebels.

Though this man's son had been under Satan's dominion for a long time, though it appeared that he would ultimately be destroyed (or destroy himself) by Satan's devices, he obtained mercy. What a blessed, sweet revelation that fact is! Satan was given permission to torment this young man to make way for the greater manifestation of Christ's glory in healing him. As God gave Satan permission to afflict Job, that he might show his goodness and grace more gloriously, he often allows the fiend of hell to cast his chosen into the fires of their own lusts for a season, that he may snatch them as brands from the fire by his omnipotent mercy.

We must never despair of those who seem most in need of mercy. When the Son of God spoke to this young man, he was immediately cured, immediately healed, immediately saved from the grasp of Satan. When we read of our Lord's miracles like this one, we should be encouraged to believe that he may yet repeat his wonderful work in the lives of others today.

Faithless And Perverse

In verse 17 we read, "Then Jesus answered and said, O faithless and perverse generation, how long shall I be with you? how long shall I suffer you? bring him hither to me." These words are often misunderstood. Our Lord Jesus was not here speaking to his disciples, but to the jeering multitude, and specifically to the scribes and Pharisees who had mocked his disciples for their failure. Those words, "O faithless and perverse generation", he never used in speaking to or about his disciples. Like his followers today, the disciples' faith was often weak, but they were not faithless. Neither were they a perverse, rebellious, and stubborn generation; though, like us, there was much perversity in them. The Pharisees, on the other hand, though they were highly respected religious leaders, were just that, a "faithless and perverse generation", just as their fathers and forefathers had been (Deuteronomy 32:5). The Lord Jesus demanded that the child be brought to him publicly, before those "faithless and perverse" people, that he might publicly shame them.

Faith And Unbelief

Yet, when the disciples asked why they could not cast out the evil spirit, our Saviour said plainly, "Because of your unbelief" (vv. 19, 20). Sadly, there is much unbelief in the most faithful believers. These disciples were believers. Yet, they could not perform the work before them because of their unbelief. The weakness of their faith is often set before us, in many ways, in the scriptures. It is set before us for the encouragement of God's people in every age (Romans 15:4).

It is faith in Christ, not great faith, just faith in Christ that is the evidence and assurance of a God-wrought salvation in our souls (Hebrews 11:1, 2; 1 John 5:1). The weakest faith in Christ is as truly the evidence of grace as is the strongest faith. A raindrop is as truly water as all the mighty rivers of the world. It is of the same nature and quality, though not the same in quantity. So it is with God-given faith. That faith, which is the gift and operation of God the Holy Spirit, is the evidence and proof of our union with Christ, of our election, redemption, and regeneration by his grace (Acts 13:39, 48).

Yet, we must not fail to see that nothing so greatly hinders our usefulness as our unbelief. These disciples truly trusted Christ as their Saviour and Lord. Yet, their unbelief made it impossible for them to perform the miracle they had been commissioned to perform (Matthew 10:8). I am fully aware of God's sovereignty, divine predestination, and eternal election. I know that the purpose of God stands forever, and that it is altogether immutable. But we must never blame God for our failures. The word of God lays the blame upon our unbelief, and nowhere else. Peter sank because of unbelief (Matthew 14:31). Israel's failure to obtain the blessedness that might have been theirs was because of their unbelief (Isaiah 48:18; Matthew 13:58; Mark 6:5, 6). The disciples failed to grasp the good news of Christ's resurrection because "they believed not" (Mark 16:11-14). I often wonder what blessings I have missed, what works I have been unable to perform, and what wonders I have failed to see because of my unbelief (John 11:40).

Let us not pass over this matter lightly. Faith is the key to success in our warfare. Unbelief is the path to heartache, trouble, and defeat. As faith languishes, usefulness languishes. The same Israelites, who went through the Red Sea in triumph, became cowards on the borders of Canaan, and could not enter the land because of unbelief (Hebrews 3:19).

Faith's Power

Our Saviour says, "If ye have faith as a grain of mustard seed, ye shall say unto this mountain, Remove hence to yonder place; and it shall remove; and nothing shall be impossible unto you" (v. 20). I think there is an obvious reference here to Zechariah 4:7. "Who art thou, O great mountain? Before Zerubbabel thou shalt become a plain". Zerubbabel, of course, typified our Lord Jesus Christ. And our Saviour here declares that if we look to him, if we trust him, no obstacle will be too great for us to overcome, no work too difficult for us to perform, and nothing shall be impossible to us.

That is not to be understood as a blanket promise that we can do anything we want to do, or have anything we want to have, if we just believe and our faith is strong enough. This promise is made to the smallest grain of faith, not to strong faith. If we have true faith in Christ, nothing shall prevent us from glorifying our God, doing the work he has given us to do, and overcoming every obstacle that opposes us or would hinder us in this world.

Faith in Christ is the most powerful influence in the world (1 John 5:4). The Word of God gives constant testimony to the power of faith in the lives of God's elect. It was faith in Christ that caused Joshua and Caleb to give a good report (Numbers 13:30). It was faith in Christ that sustained Job in hope (Job 13:15, 16). It was faith in Christ that caused Shadrach, Meshach, and Abednego to remain faithful (Daniel 3:17, 18). It was faith in Christ that caused the woman who was a sinner to love her Saviour (Luke 7:47-50). Hebrews 11 gives us example after example of the power of faith, showing us that faith honours God and God honours faith.

In verse 20, our Lord once more compares faith to a grain of mustard seed. Mustard seed faith is little faith with a big Object: the Omnipotent Christ!

God's Work
God's work must never be attempted by the arm of the flesh or with careless indifference. "Howbeit this kind goeth not out but by prayer and fasting" (v. 21). These words were addressed as a gentle rebuke to the disciples, who had perhaps become overly confident of their powers as the servants of Christ (Luke 10:17). Like Israel, puffed up with the fall of Jericho, we are all quick to say, "The men of Ai are but few there is no need for us to put forth all our strength" (Joshua 7:3). But it is a mistake, a fatal mistake, to underestimate our foes (Ephesians 6:12). Satan will not be unseated without a fight. "This kind goeth not out but by prayer and fasting." So long as we are in this world and seek by faith to serve our God and Saviour, let us do so "by prayer and fasting", by faith in Christ, denying ourselves.

As always, we must interpret this statement in verse 21 in its context. Our Saviour is still referring to the message of Zechariah's vision in Zechariah 4. The vision was about God's work, the building of his house, the saving of his people, which is the very thing portrayed in the mercy performed upon this demon-possessed boy. God's message to his prophet then is his message to his disciples here, and his message to us today. The work is all God's. He uses men to perform his work. He allows us to lay brick, take away stones, and preach the gospel. But nothing depends upon, or is determined by man. The work is all his. "This is the word of the LORD unto Zerubbabel, saying, Not by might, nor by power, but by my spirit, saith the LORD of hosts. Who art thou, O great mountain? before Zerubbabel thou shalt become a plain: and he shall bring forth the headstone thereof with shoutings, crying, Grace, grace unto it" (Zechariah 4:6, 7). Let us, therefore, serve him with prayer, trusting him, and fasting. By fasting (if I understand it correctly) I mean denying any strength, goodness, power, or ability in ourselves, seeking not our will but his, seeking not our own gratification but his glory.

Chapter 47

"Lest We Should Offend Them"

"And while they abode in Galilee, Jesus said unto them, The Son of man shall be betrayed into the hands of men: And they shall kill him, and the third day he shall be raised again. And they were exceeding sorry. And when they were come to Capernaum, they that received tribute money came to Peter, and said, Doth not your master pay tribute? He saith, Yes. And when he was come into the house, Jesus prevented him, saying, What thinkest thou, Simon? of whom do the kings of the earth take custom or tribute? of their own children, or of strangers? Peter saith unto him, Of strangers. Jesus saith unto him, Then are the children free. Notwithstanding, lest we should offend them, go thou to the sea, and cast an hook, and take up the fish that first cometh up; and when thou hast opened his mouth, thou shalt find a piece of money: that take, and give unto them for me and thee."
(Matthew 17:22-27)

During the last six months of his public ministry, our Lord spent less and less time with the multitudes and more and more time in private with his disciples. During these last six months, he constantly gave them intense, careful instruction, both about his betrayal, death, and resurrection for the redemption of our souls and about the principles of his kingdom, the principles of grace, faith, and love by which we are to live in this world for the glory of his name and the advancement of his kingdom. Some of these momentous words and the events surrounding them are recorded by all four gospel writers. But some were recorded only by one. Matthew 17:22-27 describes an event and a word of instruction recorded by Matthew alone.

Christ's Determination
The first thing that demands our attention is Christ's determination to suffer and die for his elect. Our Lord's heart was focused upon his death from eternity. He came into the world to suffer and die for his people. Every step he took moved him with predetermined pace to the appointed place and hour when he would lay down his life for the people he loved from everlasting and had come to save.

The Lord Jesus seemed to delight in the prospect of his death as our Substitute, because the joy set before him of our everlasting salvation would be accomplished by his great sacrifice (Matthew 16:22, 23; Luke 2:48, 49; 12:50; John 12:27, 28; 13:27). Because his heart was fixed upon us from eternity, he was determined to die upon the cursed tree and spoke often of the event. Here he tells his disciples, now for the third time, how that he must go to Jerusalem, be betrayed into the hands of men, and die (Matthew 16:21; 17:12).

Our Saviour was not the helpless victim of circumstances beyond his control. He voluntarily laid down his life for his sheep (John 10:17, 18), and did so by the will, purpose, and determinate counsel of God the Father (Acts 2:23). But let it never be forgotten that the Lord of Glory was betrayed and slain by the hands of wicked men. The Son of man came into the world to save men, and was by a man "betrayed into the hands of men". For men he lived, and by man he was betrayed. For men he died, and by men he died. Nothing would satisfy the rage of men against him but his blood. God-hating man ever cries, "Give us his blood"! Yet, nothing could satisfy the wrath and justice of God but his blood. When justice found our sins upon him, justice cried, "Give me his blood"! (Hebrews 9:22). By his precious, sin-atoning blood divine justice is fully and forever satisfied.

As our Saviour kept his death in the forefront of all his teachings, so too must his servants. "We preach Christ crucified" because nothing is so needful, so vital, so comforting to our souls and so glorious as this: "When we were yet without strength, in due time Christ died for the ungodly … God commendeth his love toward us, in that, while we were yet sinners, Christ died for us" (Romans 5:5-8). Then, our Lord assured the disciples that he would, according to the type and prophecy of the Old Testament, rise from the dead on the third day (Psalm 16:9-11; Isaiah 26:19; 1 Corinthians 15:3, 4).

The last line of verse 23 reads, "And they were exceeding sorry". Many excuses are offered by which to make less of this than the Holy Spirit does. Some say they sorrowed because they loved the Saviour. No doubt that is true. Others say they sorrowed because they were confused and did not understand his doctrine. That, too, is certainly true. But the Holy Spirit tells us by Mark, that they sorrowed because of their ignorance (Mark 9:32). And their ignorance was rooted in a lack of faith. John Gill explains how their grief might arise from their ignorance of the Lord's doctrine:

> They seem to have overlooked, and to have taken no notice of his rising again from the dead; which might have administered comfort

> to them, and have relieved them under their melancholy apprehensions of things; but this they understood not, nor indeed truly any part of what he had said; so Mark and Luke intimate. But then it may be said, how came they to be so very sorrowful, if they did not know what was said? To which may be replied, that this might be the reason of their sorrow, because they did not understand what he said, and they were afraid to ask. They could not tell how to reconcile the betraying of him into the hands of men, and his sufferings and death, with their notions, that the Messiah should abide forever, and should set up a temporal kingdom, in great splendour and magnificence. And what he meant by rising again from the dead, they could not devise. They could not tell whether all this was to be understood in a literal, or mystical sense.

How often we grieve when there is no cause! Christ's death was for the glory of God, by the will of God, and according to the purpose of God. It was the means of their ransom and ours. Our Saviour's death upon the cursed tree was the revelation of God's glory. It was our Saviour's path to glory, joy, and everlasting dominion, and the accomplishment of their everlasting redemption and ours! Yet, they were exceeding sorry! Why? Because they had counted on an earthly kingdom, with earthly joys, and earthly honours.

These faithful men were so greatly influenced by the religion of the Pharisees that they never questioned the Pharisees' traditions regarding the Saviour's kingdom. Blinded by tradition, they remained ignorant of his plain teaching, until he was raised from the dead. Therefore, he set the truth before them again and again, in almost the same words. His purpose was to banish from their thoughts, and ours, all dreams of an earthly, Jewish millennial kingdom. His death would be a painful, heavy trial to them and he took great care to prepare them for it.

Temple Tax

Next, we read about a dispute some raised with Peter over paying the Jewish temple tax. Matthew, who was himself a tax-collector, is the only one of the inspired writers who mentions it. But the tribute money here, the tax being discussed was not a tax imposed by Caesar or a political government. That is discussed later on (Matthew 22:17). This tribute money was a temple tax, which the Roman government allowed the Jews to collect. It was a Jewish custom.

Originally, it was based upon God's law. It was the ransom money that every man was to pay for the maintenance of the tabernacle and temple sanctuary (Exodus 30:12-14; 2 Chronicles 24:6-9). From the payment of this redemption money there was no exemption. But it was not a tax levied every year. It was a free gift made by every man numbered among the children of Israel. It was not "tribute" money but "ransom" money.

The Jews, by custom, had made the ordinance of God a fashionable, annual ceremony, imposed upon and expected of all professedly religious people. It was a matter of custom which they practised, as usual, with great show. Religious people in that day, as in ours, who did not know God, made certain that everyone saw their acts of "devotion". Consequently, when they asked Peter, "Doth not your master pay tribute?" he answered, without hesitancy, though he did not really know for sure, "Yes! Of course he does."

Christ's Divinity

That brings us to the third thing in our text, which is the marvellous demonstration of our Saviour's divine majesty. In verses 25-27 we see a clear, instructive demonstration of his omniscience and omnipotence as God. These two divine attributes are full of very practical instruction. We cannot be reminded too often that the Lord Jesus Christ, our God and Saviour, knows everything that is thought, said, and done in this world (v. 25). When Peter came into the house, apparently to discuss this matter with the Saviour, the Lord "prevented him"[4]. He showed Peter that he had heard every word of his conversation with the tax collectors from the temple.

All things are naked before him. Nothing is secret (Hebrews 4:13). A more solemn realization cannot be imagined. Hypocrisy is useless! Concealment is impossible! Christ sees everything, hears everything, and knows everything. We live in the immediate presence of God! We will be wise always to realize that fact. J. C. Ryle wrote,

> Let us measure every difficult question as to right and wrong by one simple test. 'How would I behave if Jesus was standing by my side?' Such a standard is not extravagant and absurd. It is a standard that interferes with no duty or relation of life. It interferes with nothing but sin.

[4] Here prevent carries the older meaning to anticipate.

As he is omniscient (all-knowing), so too our Saviour is omnipotent (all-powerful). This is demonstrated by his power over all creation. He told Peter to go catch a fish, assuring him that the first fish caught would have the money needed to pay the tax (Psalm 8:6-8).

Here is a blessed fact we must never overlook. Our God will provide for his own. We may safely serve him and confidently trust him. God our Saviour is also God our Provider. His name is Jehovah-jireh. "The Lord will provide" (Genesis 22:14). He often provides our needs supernaturally. And he often does so through the instrumentality he has appointed, by our faith in and obedience to him. (Because he trusted Christ, Peter got his fishing pole and went fishing.) But the provision is God's and God's alone!

No Offence

In these last three verses of Matthew 17 (vv. 25-27), our Saviour and Master demonstrated a great willingness to make concession in matters of indifference, rather than give offence. First, he showed Peter that neither he, nor Peter, was under obligation to pay the customary tribute (vv. 24-26).

Do kings require their own children to pay taxes? Of course not. The king's family is always exempt. But his subjects, and especially the immigrants in his kingdom, are required to pay tribute. Should the Lord Jesus pay redemption-money for himself to God? Should he, who is himself the King's Son, come under poll-tax to his Father? Even if the tribute money had become a tax to be levied by law, still "are the children free". Neither the Lord Jesus, nor Peter, was obliged to pay. Our Lord was free; he was not obliged to pay, because he is the Son of God. His disciples were free, in him they were (and are) the sons of God!

Then, the Master gave a lesson that needs to be often repeated about matters of indifference. It was his right not to pay the tribute. But rather than cause needless offence, as he put it, "Lest we should offend them", he said to Peter, "Go get the money and pay the tribute". We must never give up God's rights as God. But we must always be willing to give up our own. If we must quarrel, we ought to make certain that it is worth it; and the only thing worthwhile is Christ, his cause, his glory, and his gospel. God's people should never engage in anything that disturbs the peace of society or the lives of other people that is of mere temporary importance. And in the house of God and our own homes we ought to be even more lenient. In all matters of indifference we should be ready and willing to yield to others, especially to our brethren.

Sometime ago, a local church with which I have intimate connection, suffered a terrible split. Both groups were faithful men and women I have known for years. There were no gospel issues at stake, nothing involving moral or spiritual compromise. The whole division began with small, personal quibbles. Being asked by both groups to help, I personally called each man in both factions and reasoned with him. I said, "I do not know and do not want to know what the strife is all about; but let me give you my assessment. Please correct me if I am wrong. There is no division over doctrine, or over moral or spiritual evil, is there?" Each one answered, "No, not really." So I said, "This whole thing is about personal quibbles?" The reply, without exception, was "Yes. Really, that's all." Then I asked, "Would you be willing to break up your family over these things?" "No, of course not", was the reply. So I urged my friends to each call the other and eat crow. They did. The church has since not only survived, but thrived.

Our Master, by example and by precept, teaches us to bend over backwards to avoid offending even self-righteous, legalistic, lost religionists. How much more we should do so among those who are of the household of faith (Ephesians 4:1-7; 5:18-21; Philippians 2:1-5). "Give none offence, neither to the Jews, nor to the Gentiles, nor to the church of God" (1 Corinthians 10:32).

Tribute Paid

Beyond those things plainly revealed in this passage there are beautiful blessed spiritual truths beneath the surface. Our Lord Jesus Christ willingly came under tribute for our sakes (Galatians 4:4-6; 2 Corinthians 8:9). By his one payment, a payment which he provided, typified in the ransom money required under the law (Exodus 30:12-14), by the sacrifice of himself, he cleared our debt completely.

There were not two coins in the fish's mouth, one for Peter and one for the Lord Jesus, our Substitute. There was one piece of money, which made payment for both Peter and his Saviour. What a picture this is of our complete union with Christ in redemption. Our debt became his. His payment was and is ours. By his one sacrifice both the Surety and those for whom he died must go free!

In all things seek the glory of God (1 Corinthians 10:31). Let us live in the awareness of his presence. Let us live to honour his name. Let us seek to help others by our behaviour, moulding our lives to Christ's example.

If our Saviour performed a miracle then to pay tribute for Peter, we ought to be confident that he will not now fail to supply all our needs. Robert Hawker wrote, "Oh! how blessedly doth every incident in the life of Christ, minister instruction, grace, and comfort?"

Chapter 48

"As Little Children"

"At the same time came the disciples unto Jesus, saying, Who is the greatest in the kingdom of heaven? And Jesus called a little child unto him, and set him in the midst of them, And said, Verily I say unto you, Except ye be converted, and become as little children, ye shall not enter into the kingdom of heaven. Whosoever therefore shall humble himself as this little child, the same is greatest in the kingdom of heaven. And whoso shall receive one such little child in my name receiveth me. But whoso shall offend one of these little ones which believe in me, it were better for him that a millstone were hanged about his neck, and that he were drowned in the depth of the sea. Woe unto the world because of offences! for it must needs be that offences come; but woe to that man by whom the offence cometh! Wherefore if thy hand or thy foot offend thee, cut them off, and cast them from thee: it is better for thee to enter into life halt or maimed, rather than having two hands or two feet to be cast into everlasting fire. And if thine eye offend thee, pluck it out, and cast it from thee: it is better for thee to enter into life with one eye, rather than having two eyes to be cast into hell fire. Take heed that ye despise not one of these little ones; for I say unto you, That in heaven their angels do always behold the face of my Father which is in heaven. For the Son of man is come to save that which was lost. How think ye? if a man have an hundred sheep, and one of them be gone astray, doth he not leave the ninety and nine, and goeth into the mountains, and seeketh that which is gone astray? And if so be that he find it, verily I say unto you, he rejoiceth more of that sheep, than of the ninety and nine which went not astray. Even so it is not the will of your Father which is in heaven, that one of these little ones should perish."
(Matthew 18:1-14)

The Word of God uses many names to describe and identify the Lord's people. But more frequently than anything else the name that is used is "children". We are called "children of promise", "children of light", "dear children", beloved children", "children of the day", and "little children". This is a great privilege and a matter of great joy. All who believe on the Lord Jesus Christ are the children of

God, chosen in eternity, adopted in love, "accepted in the Beloved", "heirs of God and joint-heirs with Christ", and always under the Father's tender care. "Behold, what manner of love the Father hath bestowed upon us, that we should be called the sons of God ... Beloved, now are we the sons of God, and it doth not yet appear what we shall be: but we know that, when he shall appear, we shall be like him; for we shall see him as he is" (1 John 3:1, 2).

However, the word "children" not only expresses the idea of great privilege and highest honour, it also is a word that implies our nature and state, our condition in this world. Children are weak, dependant, very ignorant, unable to care for themselves, and immature. Moreover, children are easily persuaded, tender-hearted, and quick to forgive.

Matthew 18 tells us that all who are converted by the grace of God become as "little children" in this world. Of course, there are babies, young men, and old men in the kingdom of God (1 John 2:12, 13). But there is a very real sense in which it may be said that as long as we are in this world, in this body of flesh, we are in a state and condition of spiritual childhood. This eighteenth chapter of Matthew should be read and understood as a single sermon, one of the greatest and most important sermons ever to fall from the lips of the Lord Jesus Christ. The subject of the sermon is "children", the children of God. The purpose of the message is to teach us, the church of God as a family of imperfect, weak children, how to get along with each other in this world. Our blessed Saviour teaches us five distinct lessons in this message.

1. All who enter the kingdom of heaven must do so as little children (vv. 1-14)
2. All of God's children are to be treated by us as God's children (vv. 5-9)
3. They are all to be cared for as God's children (vv. 10-14)
4. When they require it, all must be disciplined as God's children (vv. 15-20)
5. They must all be forgiven as God's children (vv. 21-35)

The thing that inspired this sermon was a question that seemed to have been a constant matter of debate among our Lord's disciples, even as it is to this day "Who is the greatest in the kingdom of heaven?" These poor disciples were still looking for Christ to establish an earthly kingdom; and each one wanted a carnal place of prominence in that kingdom. Their question is one that revealed terrible ignorance, terrible arrogance, and terrible ambition in these men. And it is a question that still reveals terrible ignorance, arrogance, and ambition.

"As Little Children"

There is only one Great One in the Kingdom of God; and that Great One is Christ. All believers are equal in him. There are no "degrees of reward" among the redeemed (John 17:24). But this question inspired our Lord to give the message contained in this chapter. And the method our Lord took to correct their error was as gentle and affectionate as it was wise and instructive.

The Necessity Of Conversion

Our Lord's response to this question reveals the necessity of conversion. He said, "Verily I say unto you, Except ye be converted, and become as little children, ye shall not enter into the kingdom of heaven" (v. 3). It is impossible for anyone to be saved without being changed, not outwardly changed, but inwardly changed. "Ye must be born again"! By nature there is no fear of God in our hearts, no love for God in our souls, and no faith toward God in us, only corruption and sin. By nature, we are unfit for God's presence (Isaiah 64:6). We deserve God's wrath, and we are unfit to enter into his presence. Conversion is as necessary as election and redemption. Without it there is no salvation (Revelation 21:27).

The Nature Of Conversion

In verses 2-4, our Saviour teaches us the nature of true conversion. Conversion is a change, the turning of a sinner to God. It is not something we do, but something that is done to us. The language of holy scripture is not, "Except ye convert yourself", but "Except ye be converted, and become as little children, ye shall not enter into the kingdom of heaven" (Jeremiah 31:18, 19; Lamentations 5:21).

Someone once wrote, "Conversion is a change. It is a change of natures (2 Corinthians 5:17), a change of masters (Luke 14:25-33), a change of motives (1 Corinthians 8:9), and a change of manners (Galatians 5:22, 23)." This change is begun in regeneration (Ephesians 2:1-4). When a sinner is born again he enters into an entirely new world, an entirely new life. Christ enters into him and he enters into Christ in such a real way that he is made a partaker of the divine nature (2 Peter 1:4). But conversion is an on-going, continual operation of grace. Regeneration is the commencement of life. Conversion is the continual movement of the soul toward God, the believer's continual coming to Christ (1 Peter 2:4; Romans 6:11-18; Philippians 3:4-14).

The illustration our Master used to exemplify conversion is clear and instructive. "Jesus called a little child unto him, and said, Except ye be converted, and become as little children, ye shall not enter into the kingdom of heaven." What did he intend to convey by this child and these statements? Children are completely dependent. So we must be completely dependent upon him, living by faith, trusting him alone as our Saviour. Children are modest, humble, and unassuming. So those who are converted by the grace of God, knowing and confessing their sin before him, are modest, humble, and unassuming. Children are sincere and honest. And grace experienced in the soul makes people sincere and honest. Children are relatively free of envy and ambition. And grace teaches us to deny such lusts of the flesh. Children are quick to forgive. And those who have experienced forgiveness forgive one another. In a word, conversion in time (our experimental and vital union with Christ by faith) is the fruit and evidence of our union with Christ from eternity.

Receive Them

In verses 5 and 6 our Lord Jesus teaches us that we are to receive his children, just as we would receive him. He warns us to carefully avoid offending any of his darlings. Those who receive God's children receive Christ himself. He regards anything done to one of his children as being done to him (Matthew 10:41, 42). But those who offend his children are regarded by him as his marked enemies. To offend is to cause to stumble, to lead astray, or to discourage. We can offend directly by our acts, and words, and attitudes. Sometimes we offend others indirectly by an example of inconsistent behaviour.

It is impossible for us to measure (this side of eternity) the harm that is done by one person who professes faith in Christ, and yet behaves inconsistently. He gives the infidel ammunition. He stands in the way of those who seek the Lord. He discourages God's saints. Our lives affect a lot of people and a lot of things. None of us lives unto himself. Everything we say and everything we do affects other people. Our companions, our children, our brethren, our neighbours, our friends, and our enemies are watching us. What we say and do affects them.

The scandalous lives of people who profess faith in Christ and the scandalous actions of people who possess faith in Christ is a matter of grave concern, because it gives men occasion to blaspheme the name of our God. The more prominent and influential a person is the more severe the consequences of his sin (Romans 2:23, 24).

These lessons are clearly demonstrated in David's terrible fall. Though God did not punish David personally for his sin (his sin was punished in Christ!), he did chasten him publicly. God had to vindicate his honour and show his displeasure with David's sin. The consequences of David's sin were far reaching. The name of the Lord was blasphemed (2 Samuel 12:14). The child of David's lust was killed (2 Samuel 12:18). The sword has never departed from his house (2 Samuel 12:10). And David reaped the consequences of his sin in his children (2 Samuel 12:11, 12; 16:22). Absalom learned to despise his father by his father's deeds. Ahithophel learned to betray his trusted friend by David's deeds.

Let us take care never to offend any of God's children. So earnest is our blessed Saviour for the present and everlasting welfare of his redeemed ones, that he declares, "Whoso shall offend one of these little ones which believe in me, it were better for him that a millstone were hanged about his neck, and that he were drowned in the depth of the sea."

Hell Fire

In verses 7-9 the Son of God speaks plainly about the judgment of God and of his everlasting wrath poured out upon the damned in hell. Two strong, strong expressions are used here to get our attention. "everlasting fire" and "hell fire". There is a place of unspeakable misery and fiery indignation, where reprobate, unbelieving men and women will spend eternity suffering the horrible, unmitigated wrath of God. Many foolish dreamers and religious deceivers have joined ranks with the infidel and scoffer, denying the doctrine of everlasting punishment. They repeat the devil's lie "Ye shall not surely die" (Genesis 3:4). Do not allow their logic and reasonings to deceive you, no matter how plausible they sound, hell is real! Hell is horrible! Hell is forever! Your conscience verifies that fact. Noah's flood verifies that fact. The ashes of Sodom verify that fact. There is such a thing as "the wrath of the Lamb" (Revelation 6:16, 17). "God is love." God is merciful and gracious. God is good and kind. And God is just and true. That means, "The soul that sinneth, it shall die". The only way to escape the wrath of God in hell is to find refuge in a Substitute God has accepted, the Lord Jesus Christ.

The hand, the foot, and the eye are used metaphorically to represent our strongest earthly desires and our dearest earthly possessions. All are to be denied and renounced rather than that we, by indulging ourselves, offend our brothers and sisters in Christ. Rather than gratifying ourselves, let each submit to the other, each esteeming the other better than himself. What redeemed sinner would not count it his great honour to personally sacrifice his dearest possession, or surrender his most ardent desire to Christ? That is the great privilege and high honour afforded us, every time we have opportunity to serve the interests of another believer, either by receiving him, or by taking care not to offend him.

Blessed Security

In verses 10-14 the Lord Jesus returns to and teaches us one of his favourite subjects. Here, once more, he asserts the blessed and absolute security of his elect. Christ is the Good Shepherd who tenderly cares for every soul committed to his charge. The youngest, the weakest, the most sickly of his flock are as dear to him as the strongest. They shall never perish. Not one of them can perish because their angels watch over them (v. 10), Christ came to save them (vv. 11-13), and it is the will of God that they all be saved (v. 14).

Chapter 49

The Parable Of The Lost Sheep

"Take heed that ye despise not one of these little ones; for I say unto you, That in heaven their angels do always behold the face of my Father which is in heaven. For the Son of man is come to save that which was lost. How think ye? if a man have an hundred sheep, and one of them be gone astray, doth he not leave the ninety and nine, and goeth into the mountains, and seeketh that which is gone astray? And if so be that he find it, verily I say unto you, he rejoiceth more of that sheep, than of the ninety and nine which went not astray. Even so it is not the will of your Father which is in heaven, that one of these little ones should perish."
(Matthew 18:10-14)

This passage begins with our Lord Jesus telling us that we must never look down upon one of God's elect. To despise the redeemed is to despise the Redeemer. To despise the saved is to despise the Saviour. The Lord Jesus considers anything we do to his people, for them or against them, as being done to him. In addition to that, the angels of God are their companions, friends, and protectors (v. 10). John Calvin wrote, "It's no light matter to despise those who have angels for their companions and friends."

God uses his angels to take care of and protect his elect (Hebrews 1:14). These angels guard and watch over God's saints with deep interest and love, carrying them in their very hearts (Luke 15:10; 16:22). I am certain that none of us are sufficiently aware of the work which God has appointed to his angels for us. Therefore, we are not as thankful as we ought to be for them. The scriptures clearly teach us seven things about the angels of God.

They are constant attendants of Christ (Isaiah 6:1-5; 2 Thessalonians 1:7).
They were the first to bring good tidings of Christ's incarnation (Luke 2:13, 14).
They are heavenly choristers (Revelation 5:11, 12).
They are protectors of chosen sinners (Hebrews 1:14).
They are defenders of God's saints (Psalm 34:6, 7; Acts 5:19).
They exemplify obedience (Matthew 6:10; 1 Corinthians 11:10).
They are executioners of divine justice (1 Peter 1:12; Revelation 20:1-3).

We must not worship angels. We must never pray to angels. But let us never ignore them. They are our unfailing companions, unseen protectors, and constant helpers.

In verse 11 our Lord Jesus Christ declares the purpose for which he came into the world, "The Son of man is come to save that which was lost". The mission, the work for which he was sent into this world, that work which he has undertaken and for which he is responsible as our Surety is the salvation of God's elect who were lost through the sin and fall of our father Adam (John 10:16; Matthew 1:21; Isaiah 42:4). The scriptures universally declare all God's lost ones, all whom the Lord Jesus Christ came to save, shall be saved because that is the will of God (v. 14); and God almighty always does his will (Isaiah 46:10).

In order to illustrate this fact our Lord Jesus gives us the parable of the lost sheep in verses 12 and 13. This is an abbreviated account of the parable. It is given more fully in Luke 15:4-7. In order to understand the parable we must read both Matthew's account of it and Luke's. This parable of the lost sheep shows us the deep, self-sacrificing love of the Lord Jesus Christ for perishing sinners. It opens the very heart of the eternal God to us, and shows us how pleasurable it is to him to save sinners, because "He delighteth in mercy"!

There are obvious differences in the account given by Matthew and that given by Luke; but nowhere do they contradict one another. Matthew simply was not inspired to write out the entire parable, and for obvious reasons: 1. As Luke records it, the parable was originally spoken by our Lord to condemn self-righteous Pharisees, the "ninety and nine just persons who need no repentance" (Luke 15:1-3). 2. Matthew's record shows our Lord using the same parable to comfort his saints and to teach us to tenderly regard his elect, even as he does. 3. In both places, the object is to assure us that Christ has come to save sinners, to seek and to save that which was lost (Luke 5:31, 32).

The Shepherd

In this parable the Lord Jesus portrays himself as a Shepherd. He is not a hireling-shepherd, who does not care for the sheep, but our owner-shepherd. He is one who both owns and cares for his sheep. One of the most beautiful and most frequently used descriptions of Christ is that of a Shepherd. How we rejoice to say with David, "The Lord is my Shepherd"!

A shepherd is a man who tends and serves sheep. He knows his own sheep. He knows how many he has and where to lead them. He knows how to protect them and where to feed them. He knows how to nurse them. He leads them out in the morning, tends them all through the day, and folds them when the day is done. Throughout the scriptures our Lord Jesus Christ is spoken of as the Shepherd of his sheep.

He is also Jehovah's Shepherd, smitten by the sword of divine justice so that his sheep might go free and be saved (Zechariah 13:7-9; John 18:7-9). Christ is the Good Shepherd who willingly, voluntarily laid down his life for the sheep (John 10:11, 15). He is the Great Shepherd who rose in triumph and victory from the dead (Hebrews 13:20). He is the Chief Shepherd who shall soon appear the second time, without sin, unto salvation (1 Peter 5:4). Christ is the Shepherd and Bishop of our Souls who saves us and preserves us unto life everlasting (1 Peter 2:25). The Lord Jesus is our Covenant Shepherd, under whose care we have peace (Ezekiel 34:22-25). And he is the Shepherd of the sheep who gathers his little lambs in his arms and carries them in his bosom (Isaiah 40:11).

Christ is the Shepherd; and all the sheep belong to him. We are his sheep by covenant agreement (John 6:39) and lawful purchase (1 Peter 1:18). And the Lord Jesus Christ knows his sheep (John 10:14). He knows his sheep with a peculiar knowledge of love and grace. He knows all about us. But there is more. He knows us! He shall say to the wicked, "I never knew you". But he says, "I know my sheep". He knows who they are, where they are, what they have been, all they have done, what he will make of them, what they need, how to protect them, and how to bring them home.

The Sheep

Now, consider the Lord's sheep. I am sure Benjamin Keach is correct in the analysis he gives of this parable. Mr Keach suggests that the one hundred represent all mankind in Adam. All the human race belongs to Christ who created it. All are his property. The ninety and nine represent the self-righteous. The Pharisees of this world, who are just and righteous in their own eyes, having no need of repentance, and are left to perish in the wilderness of their ignorance. And the one lost sheep represents all of God's elect in this world who are brought by divine grace to see their lost and ruined condition. Our Saviour said, "I am not sent but to the lost sheep of the house of Israel."

God's people in this world are set forth as silly, lost, helpless, ignorant sheep. "All we like sheep have gone astray; we have turned everyone to his own way" (Isaiah 53:6). We were all lost by the sin and fall of our father Adam (Romans 5:12). We went astray as soon as we were born speaking lies (Psalm 58:3). And, if left to themselves, the sheep would surely perish. Silly sheep have no sense of direction. They roam and wander, straying further and further from home, until the Shepherd finds them.

The Search

The Shepherd leaves the ninety and nine in the wilderness and goes out to search for his one lost sheep. His search will continue until he finds that one lost sheep. He knows the sheep that is missing. He has a picture of it in his mind. He thinks nothing of the ninety and nine who need no Shepherd. His heart is all wrapped up in that one lost sheep. This one thought seems to possess his entire Being: "One of my sheep is lost." Immediately the search begins.

It is an all-absorbing search. That one lost sheep consumes the Shepherd's tender heart. He can neither eat nor sleep until he finds his lost sheep. The poor, wandering sheep has no thought for the Shepherd. But the Shepherd seems to think of nothing else but that one lost sheep. He loves his sheep, and he cannot bear the thought of it being lost. He knows all the pits into which the sheep will fall, and all the wolves that are thirsty for its blood. And he knows that the poor sheep is both defenceless and senseless.

That one lost sheep belongs to the Shepherd. God the Father gave it to him in eternity. He purchased it with his own precious blood; and he will not lose it. The Shepherd is responsible for the sheep. His honour as a Shepherd is bound up in the welfare of that sheep. He assumed all responsibility for it when the Father entrusted him to save it (Ephesians 1:12).

It is a definite search. The Shepherd goes after his sheep, that one, definite, particular sheep. It is an active search. No hill is too difficult to climb. No mountain is too high. No valley is too low. No precipice is too rocky. No distance is too far. The Shepherd must have his sheep. It is a persevering search. He will search for that lost sheep "until he find it". It is a personal search. It is Christ himself who goes after the sheep. Though they ever flee from him, the sheep are pursued by Christ, pursued by the Son of God, by the eternal Lover of their souls, and pursued by him until he finds them.

Furthermore, it is a successful search. Not everyone who hears the gospel will believe. All men will not be saved. It may be that many that I love and for whom I labour with a heavy heart will perish at last. But of this one thing I am certain: not one of Christ's sheep shall ever perish. Not one of those lost ones for whom he suffered and died will be lost in the end (John 10:16).

The Salvation

Luke 15:5 speaks of the salvation of the sheep, "when he hath found it". What sweet words those are! One of the old writers said, "In his incarnation Christ came after his lost sheep. In his life he continued to seek it. In his death he laid it upon his shoulders. In his resurrection he bore it on its way. And in ascension he brought it home rejoicing."

Picture that lost sheep, he has fallen over the edge of a high cliff on a dark stormy night. Overhead, he sees the terrifying storm of God's wrath. The lightning seems to strike out at him saying, "The soul that sinneth, it shall die". Below, he sees the gaping jaws of hell wide open to engulf him. He fears he is losing his footing, slipping into hell! But the Shepherd has found his sheep. What does he do? He reaches down the long arm of his almighty grace, and lays hold on the sheep (Ephesians 2:1-9). He lays his sheep upon his shoulders. This is a place of rest for the sheep. This is a place of security for the sheep (John 10:28, 29; Deuteronomy 1:30, 31).

Once my soul was astray from the heavenly way,
And was wretched and vile as could be;
But my Saviour above, gave me peace from above,
When He reached down His hand for me.

I was near to despair when He came to me there,
And He showed me that I could be free;
Then He lifted my feet, gave me gladness complete,
When He reached down His hand for me.

How my heart doth rejoice when I hear His sweet voice
In the tempest to Him now I flee;
There to lean on His arm, where I'm safe from all harm.
Since He reached down His hand for me.

I can almost picture it. There is the Good Shepherd. The sheep is on his omnipotent shoulders, wrapped around his neck, held firmly in the hands of divine grace. And now the Shepherd carries his sheep all the way home!

The Satisfaction
Read Luke 15:5-7, and see the satisfaction of both the Shepherd and his sheep:

> And when he hath found it, he layeth it on his shoulders, rejoicing. And when he cometh home, he calleth together his friends and neighbours, saying unto them, Rejoice with me; for I have found my sheep which was lost. I say unto you, that likewise joy shall be in heaven over one sinner that repenteth, more than over ninety and nine just persons, which need no repentance.

This man whose sheep was lost is filled with joy in finding it. And the sheep is the sole source of his joy! His soul, his heart, his mind, his body had all been absorbed in finding the sheep that was lost. Now he finds great joy and satisfaction in that sheep which he has found. The Shepherd is satisfied (Isaiah 53:11). This was the joy set before him, for which he endured the cross, despising the shame (Hebrews 12:2). There is a holiday in heaven over one sinner who repents. God our Saviour is he of whom the prophet wrote, "He delighteth in mercy". And the sheep is satisfied (Psalm 65:4). He has Christ, and having Christ he has all. Child of God, as Christ gave himself to save you, now give yourself to him. As we have filled his heart, may he fill our hearts, now and forever.

Chapter 50

The Matter Of Church Discipline

"Moreover if thy brother shall trespass against thee, go and tell him his fault between thee and him alone: if he shall hear thee, thou hast gained thy brother. But if he will not hear thee, then take with thee one or two more, that in the mouth of two or three witnesses every word may be established. And if he shall neglect to hear them, tell it unto the church: but if he neglect to hear the church, let him be unto thee as an heathen man and a publican. Verily I say unto you, Whatsoever ye shall bind on earth shall be bound in heaven: and whatsoever ye shall loose on earth shall be loosed in heaven. Again I say unto you, That if two of you shall agree on earth as touching any thing that they shall ask, it shall be done for them of my Father which is in heaven. For where two or three are gathered together in my name, there am I in the midst of them. Then came Peter to him, and said, Lord, how oft shall my brother sin against me, and I forgive him? till seven times? Jesus saith unto him, I say not unto thee, Until seven times: but, Until seventy times seven. Therefore is the kingdom of heaven likened unto a certain king, which would take account of his servants. And when he had begun to reckon, one was brought unto him, which owed him ten thousand talents. But forasmuch as he had not to pay, his lord commanded him to be sold, and his wife, and children, and all that he had, and payment to be made. The servant therefore fell down, and worshipped him, saying, Lord, have patience with me, and I will pay thee all. Then the lord of that servant was moved with compassion, and loosed him, and forgave him the debt. But the same servant went out, and found one of his fellowservants, which owed him an hundred pence: and he laid hands on him, and took him by the throat, saying, Pay me that thou owest. And his fellowservant fell down at his feet, and besought him, saying, Have patience with me, and I will pay thee all. And he would not: but went and cast him into prison, till he should pay the debt. So when his fellowservants saw what was done, they were very sorry, and came and told unto their lord all that was done. Then his lord, after that he had called him, said unto him, O thou wicked servant, I forgave thee all that debt, because thou desiredst me: Shouldest not thou also have had compassion on thy fellowservant, even as I had pity on thee? And his lord was

wroth, and delivered him to the tormentors, till he should pay all that was due unto him. So likewise shall my heavenly Father do also unto you, if ye from your hearts forgive not every one his brother their trespasses."
(Matthew 18:15-35)

In this passage our Lord and Saviour anticipates two things. First, he anticipates the fact that differences would arise among his disciples, causing offences. It is a sad fact, but a fact nonetheless, that God's people in this world are sinners still. We love one another; but those who are the objects of our most ardent love are the very people we are most apt to offend. The offences are without excuse. We ought to exercise great care not to offend. But offend we do. What husband, wife, son, or daughter has not wept bitterly after needlessly offending one in the family dearly loved? Paul and Barnabas were both brethren, faithful servants of God. But they had a falling out over John Mark. Yes, God's people, true believers, often trespass against one another.

Second, the Saviour anticipates the gathering of his saints as local congregations. At the present time, they assembled in synagogues and in the temple. But that would soon cease to be. Shortly after the resurrection local churches were formed, visible societies of baptized believers. Our Saviour had already spoken of building his church in his commendation of Peter's confession (Matthew 16:18). So the disciples were already familiar with the term. The things our Lord teaches in this passage are not instructions about the Jewish synagogues, but instructions about local churches. Particularly, he is giving us instruction about the matter of church discipline (1 Corinthians 5:1; 6:1; 1 Timothy 1:20). John Gill asserts, correctly, that these words are "spoken not to the apostles as such, but as believers in Christ, and concern everyone that stands in the relation of a brother, or church member to each other". In this passage of scripture, our Saviour gives us a direct command for the discipline of his house and lays down general guidelines that are to be followed.

Caution

Because men are ever prone to extremes a word of caution is in order. Church discipline is not a prominent issue in the New Testament. It is rarely mentioned. The only place in the New Testament in which fairly full instructions about it are given is here in Matthew 18. Yet, men commonly run to one of two extremes regarding this matter. Some ignore it altogether. Others go to great lengths to write out rules and regulations for discipline far exceeding the teachings of the

New Testament, and to enforce them rigorously. Personally, I am far more concerned about getting sinners converted and into the kingdom of God than I am about getting sinners out of it. Throughout this chapter our Saviour tells us to love one another. He tells us that we must always deal with our brethren in kindness, showing tenderness and affection. All believers are members of Christ's body, brothers and sisters of Jesus, and to one another in Christ. In Christ we are all one (1 Corinthians 12). Robert Hawker wrote:

> To the little infirmities, which from the remains of indwelling corruption, may, and will, occasionally break out, how precious is the direction of Jesus. Oh! that it were more generally adopted in the Church of Christ! And what an unanswerable argument doth the Lord here leave upon record, for the constant meeting together of his whole body, both in private and public ordinances (Zechariah 2:5, 10, 11; Matthew 20:28).

Guidelines

First, our Saviour gives us a word of instruction about church discipline, and lays down specific guidelines that are to be followed (vv. 15-18). Without question, there are many difficulties surrounding the whole issue of church discipline. I know that I am not going to settle these difficulties in this study. That is not my intention. I only want to show you that which is obvious in the passage. I will say no more than the text says and no less. But I must show you what is taught in this passage of scripture. In these verses our Lord Jesus gives us three admirable, simple rules for the healing of differences among brethren. And the rules are accompanied with a blessed promise.

Sinners in this world, though washed in the blood of Christ and sanctified by his spirit, are sure to offend one another from time to time. The offences spoken of in our text are not petty gripes, personality clashes, and silly spats, about which it is utterly ridiculous and totally unchristian for grown men and women to be divided. The offences spoken of here are radical and, if left unsettled, destructive. All matters of insignificance are to be treated as such (Matthew 5:38-42). Because our Lord does not name the offences, we must look elsewhere in the New Testament where discipline was practised or exercised to see what disciplinary offences are. The disciplinary offences set forth in the New Testament may be summarized in four groups.

Financial, Business Offences (1 Corinthians 6:1-8)
Divisive, Bickering Offences (1 Corinthians 3:17; Ephesians 4:29-5:1)
Clearly Established, Publicly Known Moral Offences. The Incestuous Man (1 Corinthians 5:1-5)
Heretical, Doctrinal Offences (1 Timothy 1:20; 2 Timothy 2:17, 18; Titus 3:10)

These are issues that must be dealt with, because they are things that endanger the welfare of the whole church, things that harm the family of God, and bring reproach upon the cause of Christ. Sometimes, in a household, a father who loves his family is forced by a rebel son to put the son out of the house. A loving father would never do so because he is embarrassed by his son's behaviour, or personally shamed by it. But, when the rebel son's behaviour endangers the welfare of the family, a loving father is forced to put him out of the house. He does not disown his son, or cease to love his son. And he will receive his son back into his home with open arms and joyful heart at any time, if the son's behaviour changes (Luke 15:20). He cannot allow one child, that he dearly loves, to endanger the wellbeing of the whole family. So it is with the family of God.

The steps to be taken in discipline are clearly established, so that those who have offended may be most easily won with the least public scandal. The object is to win your brother, not to punish him, reproach him, or destroy him. Therefore, every effort must be made to correct the erring brother. All matters of offence are to be handled as privately as possible, making every effort to avoid humiliation and embarrassment.

As a last resort, our Lord says, "tell it unto the church". That does not necessitate a public hearing. I cannot imagine anything more contrary to the whole New Testament than having a public trial, parading the offences of erring members! And these words, "tell it unto the church", forbid discipline by a church council. Discipline is a matter for each local church, to be handled by the appointed pastors and elders of that local assembly.

The promise of verse 18 must be understood properly. "Verily I say unto you, Whatsoever ye shall bind on earth shall be bound in heaven: and whatsoever ye shall loose on earth shall be loosed in heaven." This does not mean that men can bend the will of God to their own will, but that God has a clearly revealed principle to which the church must conform. The text could be better translated, whatsoever you shall bind on earth *shall have been* bound, etc.. In other words, when the church of God follows Christ's instruction in this matter, it conforms in its decisions to that which God has already done. This kind of discipline may be laughed at or ignored by men, but it is done with God's authority and approval.

Public Worship

In verse 19 our Saviour shows us the blessedness of public prayer. In verse 20 he shows us the blessedness of public worship. Verse 19 gives encouragement to united, public prayer. Remember, the whole context is talking about the local church. This verse is not calling for the confusion of many voices in prayer, but the union of believing hearts in prayer. "Again I say unto you, That if two of you shall agree on earth as touching any thing that they shall ask, it shall be done for them of my Father which is in heaven." Matthew Henry wrote, "Besides the general regard God has to the prayers of the saints, he is particularly pleased with their union and communion in these prayers (2 Chronicles 5:13, 14; Acts 4:31)".

In verse 20 the Lord Jesus promises his presence with his people whenever they come together for worship in his name. "For where two or three are gathered together in my name, there am I in the midst of them." Numbers mean everything to men. They mean nothing to God. Our Saviour here promises his presence whenever and wherever ransomed sinners meet together to worship God, though they are as few in number as two or three. Whenever and wherever two or three come together in his name (that is to say, trusting his blood and righteousness, calling upon his name, and seeking to honour his name), to pray, give praise to God, to hear his word, to attend his ordinances, and to seek his grace, the Son of God says, "there am I in the midst of them".

When God's saints thus meet together in public worship, the local church is "an habitation of God through the Spirit" (Ephesians 2:22), and the temple of God's presence (1 Corinthians 3:16). Our Saviour is always present in the assembly of his saints. He presides over all our meetings, rules in our midst, directs our hearts, and bestows his blessings in his holy place. Do not fail to observe that the only place in this world where men are assured of Christ's presence is in the assembly of his saints. That makes public worship vital to our souls and a matter of highest honour and blessing. It is a privilege never to be despised (Hebrews 10:25, 26).

Forgiveness

In verses 21 and 22 our Lord answers a question raised by Peter about the matter of forgiveness. Remember the context. Everything here is directly related to believers in general and to matters concerning local churches in particular. These two verses have nothing to do with civil law or civil government. The welfare of society demands law and order, which cannot be maintained without the punishment of crime. Our Lord does not suggest that we are to tolerate thefts, assaults, or injuries to property with impunity. As J. C. Ryle stated, "All that he means is that, we are to study a general spirit of mercy and forgiveness towards our brethren. We are to learn much and put up with much rather than quarrel. We are to look over much and submit to much, rather than have any strife". Because such a spirit of mercy, forgiveness, and longsuffering is contrary to the flesh, we struggle with it. But it is absolutely essential to Christianity (Matthew 6:15).

A Parable

After telling Peter, and us, that we should constantly forgive one another, our Saviour gives us a parable about forgiveness in verses 23-35. He compares our sins to a debt we owed to God and the forgiveness of our sins by the blood of Christ to the cancellation of the debt. Sin is a debt we cannot pay. But God our Father has freely forgiven us. He is ready, willing, and able to forgive guilty sinners of their debt, granting forgiveness to all who seek it by faith in Christ (1 John 1:9). He grants forgiveness on the satisfaction of his justice by the death of our Saviour (Romans 3:24-26). The cause of forgiveness is his mercy and love toward sinners. All who sue for mercy receive forgiveness (Isaiah 55:6, 7).

The object of our Lord in giving this parable is obvious. The parable is given to show us, sinners who have obtained (and continually obtain) the free and full forgiveness of countless sins by Christ, that we ought to readily and freely forgive one another. It is both our reasonable responsibility and our great privilege to forgive all offences committed against us. It is a reasonable duty because we are forgiven. It is also a blessed privilege, because in forgiving one another, we are allowed to imitate our great and gracious God in his most glorious work of forgiveness! "And be ye kind one to another, tender-hearted, forgiving one another, even as God for Christ's sake hath forgiven you. Be ye therefore followers of God, as dear children; And walk in love, as Christ also hath loved us, and hath given himself for us an offering and a sacrifice to God for a sweetsmelling savour" (Ephesians 4:32-5:1).

Would you win a fallen brother? Show him forgiveness. Would you prove your faith? Forgive those who trespass against you. Would you grow in grace? Practise forgiveness. Would you be like God? Forgive those who offend you. Forgive, and forgive, and forgive, relentlessly, freely, and sincerely. The best discipline in all the world is the discipline of forgiveness (2 Corinthians 2:7, 8).

Chapter 51

The Sin Debt

"Then came Peter to him, and said, Lord, how oft shall my brother sin against me, and I forgive him? till seven times? Jesus saith unto him, I say not unto thee, Until seven times: but, Until seventy times seven. Therefore is the kingdom of heaven likened unto a certain king, which would take account of his servants. And when he had begun to reckon, one was brought unto him, which owed him ten thousand talents. But forasmuch as he had not to pay, his lord commanded him to be sold, and his wife, and children, and all that he had, and payment to be made. The servant therefore fell down, and worshipped him, saying, Lord, have patience with me, and I will pay thee all. Then the lord of that servant was moved with compassion, and loosed him, and forgave him the debt. But the same servant went out, and found one of his fellowservants, which owed him an hundred pence: and he laid hands on him, and took him by the throat, saying, Pay me that thou owest. And his fellowservant fell down at his feet, and besought him, saying, Have patience with me, and I will pay thee all. And he would not: but went and cast him into prison, till he should pay the debt. So when his fellowservants saw what was done, they were very sorry, and came and told unto their lord all that was done. Then his lord, after that he had called him, said unto him, O thou wicked servant, I forgave thee all that debt, because thou desiredst me: Shouldest not thou also have had compassion on thy fellowservant, even as I had pity on thee? And his lord was wroth, and delivered him to the tormentors, till he should pay all that was due unto him. So likewise shall my heavenly Father do also unto you, if ye from your hearts forgive not every one his brother their trespasses."
(Matthew 18:21-35)

Sin is set forth in the word of God under a variety of pictures and metaphors. Sometimes it is described as a loathsome disease, such as leprosy. Sometimes it is compared to bondage, slavery, or imprisonment. Frequently sin is represented by death and compared to an obnoxious, rotting corpse. In this passage sin is compared to a debt that we owe.

How thankful we ought to be that Peter asked this question! "Lord, how oft shall my brother sin against me, and I forgive him? till seven times?" It was in response to Peter's question about forgiveness the Lord Jesus gave us this rich and blessed parable, comparing the kingdom of heaven to a king who graciously forgives the enormous debt of his servant. It was our Saviour's purpose in this parable to teach Peter and each of us both the boundless, incomprehensible fulness of God's free grace to us in him and how we are to forgive one another. He shows us that both the pattern and the motive for forgiveness among believers is the infinite, incalculable forgiveness of our sins by our God. In chapter 6 he taught us to pray, "Forgive us our debts, as we forgive our debtors" (v. 12). Now he teaches us that our sins are debts cancelled and forgiven by God, and that as we have been forgiven, even so we ought to forgive one another.

Christ's Purpose

Our Lord's purpose in giving this great parable is obvious. Here our all-merciful Saviour shows us that we are to forgive one another of all evil done against us, just as our God has forgiven us for Christ's sake (Ephesians 4:32-5:1). What a vast, immeasurable debt sin is! Our Lord compares it to "ten thousand talents", using a definite number to represent a debt that is indefinite and incalculable. He is telling us that the offences of men against us are nothing, compared to our offences against our God. As God's forgiveness is free and without limit, so we ought to forgive one another freely and without limit. As Benjamin Keach wrote:

> O what have sinners done, and in what a poor, miserable, and wretched state are all men naturally? Owing so much, and not having one farthing to pay. What is any debt owing to us, compared to this?

The example our Saviour gives, by which he motivates such brotherly kindness, as in all things spiritual, is himself, and the grace of God that is ours in him. The God of all grace freely forgives all who seek his mercy in Christ. If the love, grace, and mercy of God to us is so infinite and boundless, how utterly unthinkable it is for forgiven sinners not to forgive one another! "It was", as Don Doezema states, "to underscore that all-important principle of the kingdom of heaven that Jesus told the parable of the unmerciful servant".

All Debtors

The "certain king" in this parable represents the Lord God. We are all debtors to him. There are certain, moral obligations due to God from all his creatures. We are all debtors to the Almighty. Creatures owe a debt of obedience to their Creator. All that God required of Adam in the Garden of Eden was obedience. Certainly, the Creator deserves that much!

God is our Creator, our Preserver, our Provider, our Benefactor. "It is he that hath made us, and not we ourselves; we are his people and the sheep of his pasture". He is "the living God, who giveth us richly all things to enjoy". Every breath of our nostrils is the gift of God. We live upon his bounty. All of us owe our lives to him. As our Creator and Benefactor, God demands two things from us. His law is not extreme. His demands are not unreasonable. They are perfectly righteous demands (Matthew 22:37-39). First, "Thou shalt love the Lord thy God with all thy heart, and with all thy soul, and with all thy mind" (Exodus 20:3-11). Second, "Thou shalt love thy neighbour as thyself" (Exodus 20:12-17). In a word, we all owe the Lord God a life of perfect righteousness, a life of perfect obedience. He requires it. Failure to render such a life unto him is the incurrence of a very great debt.

Not only have we failed to obey him, we have further indebted ourselves by sin, by the wilful transgression of his law. What a debt sin is! It is compared in verse 24 to "ten thousand talents". That is millions of dollars in modern currency! And the debt increases every day. It is a debt of infinite proportion, beyond calculation, a debt that will go on swelling as long as we live, unless it can be removed from us by some power greater than our own. Sin is a debt with tremendous consequences. It is written, "The wages of sin is death" (Romans 6:23). "The soul that sinneth, it shall die" (Ezekiel 18:20). The consequence of sin is death: legal death (Romans 5:12), spiritual death (Ephesians 2:1-4), physical death (Hebrews 9:27), and the second, everlasting death in hell (Revelation 20:6, 13-15).

Truly, saved sinners, those who have been pardoned and forgiven of all their sins by the grace of God through the blood of Christ are debtors who owe a mighty, deep debt of gratitude and love to God. Let us never forget it. Let us ever be keenly aware of it (1 Corinthians 6:19, 20; 2 Corinthians 8:9; Romans 12:1, 2).

When I stand before the throne, dressed in beauty not my own
When I see thee as thou art, love Thee with unsinning heart,
Then, Lord, shall I fully know, not till then, how much I owe.

Sin is that which makes us debtors to God. These days debt is not so shameful and embarrassing as it once was. Most people today seem to think, "The more I owe, the more I own", ignoring the word of wisdom, which declares, "the borrower is servant to the lender" (Proverbs 22:7). Still, debtors and sinners have much in common with one another.

Debtors are very likely to get more deeply into debt. One of the terrible facts about sin is that it breeds so quickly and profusely. You can never say to sin, "Hitherto shalt thou come, and no further". Sin, like a great debt, causes uneasiness in people when they are aware of it. If a man has a spark of honesty about him, he cannot rest when he knows he has debts he cannot pay. Even so, a sinner awakened by the grace of God to see his debt to God begins to be greatly disturbed and troubled by sin. He cannot find rest for his soul because he cannot pay his debt. Debtors and sinners alike shun their creditors. When a man is in debt and has nothing to pay, he tries to hide from his creditors. So men and women in debt to God try to hide from him, just as Adam and Eve, after the fall, made fig leaf aprons to cover themselves and tried to hide from God in the Garden. And sinners, like debtors in earlier times, are in very great danger. The law of the land these days says, "You do not have to pay anyone you owe, unless you want to. Instead of paying your bills, if you like, you can file bankruptcy". It was not always that way; and it shall never be that way with regard to our sin debt. God demands that the debt be paid (Matthew 5:25, 26).

We are all debtors to God; but some have greater debts than others. This thought must not be pressed beyond what is revealed. Yet, it is clearly represented in this parable. Here is one man who owed "ten thousand talents" (millions of dollars), another owed "an hundred pence" (about 15 dollars). The implication is obvious. We have all sinned; but we have not all sinned alike, or to the same degree. Therefore, we are not all debtors to the same extent. Some sins are greater than others; and the consequences, both in this world and in the world to come, are greater (John 19:11; Matthew 11:20-24). Every sin is an infinite evil, deserving of eternal ruin. Any sin will destroy the soul forever. Yet, there are some sins that have a special venom in them, a special vileness of offence to God. The scriptures clearly teach that there are degrees of punishment in hell. Punishment is always in exact proportion to the crime committed. But the Word of God does not teach degrees of reward in heaven. Heavenly glory is the inheritance of grace. Sinners go to hell by their own merit and are rewarded accordingly. But do not imagine that God measures sin by man's yardstick.

It may surprise you to read the Book of God and discover who God says are in the greater condemnation. Those who are placed in positions of greater trust and influence, but neglect or abuse it shall suffer greater condemnation (James 3:1). Those who have been given greater light, but refuse to walk in that light shall suffer greater wrath (John 15:22, 24). Those who hear, but refuse to believe the gospel of Christ shall have the greater punishment (1 John 5:10). Unbelief, the wilful rejection of God's mercy and grace in Christ, is the most glaringly hideous evil in the world. It is written, "He that believeth shall not be damned". "He that believeth not is condemned already, because he hath not believed in the name of the only begotten Son of God" (John 3:18).

Unbelief is man's highest crime against God. Unbelief says that God is a liar! Unbelief is man's stubborn denial of his own sin and his obstinate claim of personal righteousness. Unbelief is blasphemy against the Holy Spirit. Unbelief is despising the grace of God. Unbelief says that Christ accomplished nothing. By unbelief, sinful men and women, ever clinging to their fig-leaf righteousness, attempt to justify themselves, hide from God, and refuse to submit to – to trust, Christ, the sinners' Substitute, for righteousness (Romans 9:31-10:13). C. H. Spurgeon wrote of unbelief, "That is the sin which, above all others, drops the black wax upon (your) death warrant, and sets the seal of divine wrath there". Not even the sins of Sodom can be compared to the sin of unbelief (Matthew 11:23, 24). Do you see what debtors we are to God? We are sinners and our sin involves us in a very great debt.

Payment Demanded

"But forasmuch as he had not to pay, his lord commanded him to be sold, and his wife, and children, and all that he had, and payment to be made" (v. 25). The sin debt must be paid. Some disposition must be made of our debt. We may try to ignore it; but God will not. We may deny that our debt exists; but the debt still stands. And it must be paid. God is just. Our obligations to him must be met, or we must suffer the consequences forever in hell. God will deliver the debtor to the prison to suffer at the hands of his tormentors in hell forever. Our sin debt must be paid (Romans 6:23; Ezekiel 18:20).

Nothing To Pay

But, like the man in the parable, we have no ability to pay our debt. "He had not to pay". We must see this. No one will ever seek forgiveness until he realizes that he has nothing with which to pay. We are all insolvent debtors. Repentance can never satisfy our debt. Good works cannot erase our debt. Not even the sufferings of hell can satisfy the infinite justice of God. The sufferings of the damned in hell are everlasting torments, because the sufferings of finite creatures can never satisfy the demands of infinite justice. God demands perfect righteousness; but we have none (Isaiah 64:6). He demands complete satisfaction, atonement for sin; but we cannot give it. Silver and gold cannot ransom our souls (Psalm 49:6-8). Sacrifice and offering cannot purge away sin (Psalm 40:6; Hebrews 10:1-3). We are all bankrupt debtors before God. The sooner we realize it, the better. We have "not to pay". Nothing with which to pay our debt.

Our Great Surety

If the sin debt must be paid and the sinner has nothing with which to pay, then someone else must pay it for him. The only way the sinner's debt can be paid is by an infinitely great, blessed, and all-sufficient Surety. That Surety is our Lord Jesus Christ, the Son of God (Hebrews 7:22). Nothing but the blood of Christ can satisfy the justice of God and cancel our debt. There is no other way for our sin debt to be liquidated.

Among the many descriptions used in holy scripture to describe our Saviour's glorious person and redemptive work, none can be more instructive, consoling, and assuring than the fact that the Lord Jesus Christ is our Surety, the Surety of the everlasting covenant. As Judah became surety for Benjamin (Genesis 43:8, 9), the Lord Jesus Christ became Surety for God's elect in the covenant of grace. That is to say, the Lord Jesus Christ, the Son of God, willingly, voluntarily assumed the total responsibility of our souls before his Father, making himself honour bound to save us!

A surety is one who makes himself liable and responsible for the debts of another, for debts that he himself did not make. Someone else accrued the debts. The surety pays them. And the one who made them goes free. The only possible way for sinners to be saved and God's law be honoured; the only way God could ever save us and still be consistent with his justice and truth, is through a Surety. Unless there is someone able and willing to pay our debt, we are all without hope, doomed forever! But, blessed be God, there is such a Surety! The Lord Jesus Christ, the Son of God, our Surety, has fully paid the sin debt for his people.

In one of his sermons, C. H. Spurgeon told a story that illustrates this beautifully. A young man in the army of Nicholas the Great was addicted to gambling. He had gambled so much that he had lost everything he owned and had accumulated a very great debt, which he could not pay. He had come from a good family. But he brought shame upon his family's name by his deeds. At last, he reached the end of his rope. Completely hopeless, he sat at a table and added up his debts. When the overwhelming sum was known, he wrote these desperate words across the bottom of the page, "Who is able to pay all this?" Exhausted and hopeless, he fell asleep at the table where he sat. As he slept, the Emperor walked through the barracks. When he saw the paper on the table, the great debt, and the question, "Who is able to pay all this?" he leaned over and wrote one word "Nicholas"!

Even so, when I saw my debt, I cried, "Who can pay my debt? Who can atone for my sin?" And I heard these words echo through my soul: Jesus paid it all! All the debt I owed! Sin had left a crimson stain, He washed it white as snow!

The Son of God disposed of the sin debt owed by his people, paying it off completely, by the sacrifice of himself (Galatians 3:13).

If we would obtain forgiveness for our sin, we must sue for mercy (v. 26). There is a time coming when the King of heaven shall "take account" of all men. God must reckon with us regarding our debt, either by his grace through the gospel, or in his wrath on the day of judgment. Blessed are those sinners whom God calls to account now by his grace and compels to sue for mercy.

God Ready To Forgive

The God of all grace, against whom we have sinned, is ready, very ready, because of his infinite, free love, mercy, and grace, to forgive the sins and cancel the debts of all who call upon him, because he "delighteth in mercy" (Micah 7:18; Matthew 18:27). "The Lord was ready to save me: therefore we will sing my songs to the stringed instruments all the days of our life in the house of the Lord" (Isaiah 38:20). Blessed be his name, the God of all grace is "a God ready to pardon" (Nehemiah 9:17).

In this parable, it looks as though the king is moved with compassion and forgives the debt in response to the debtor's plea. That is how forgiveness is first viewed by us. But, in reality, the sinner's suit for mercy is the result of God's mercy, love, and grace. But I do like the way verse 27 reads. "Then the lord of that servant was moved with compassion, and loosed him, and forgave him the debt." What a picture that is of our God!

Substitution

Though this wicked servant was just that, a wicked servant, he was the representative of all the king's servants. His debt, being cancelled, all their debts were cancelled. That is a great picture of Christ our Substitute. As this one servant represented all, so our Lord Jesus Christ is the Representative of all God's elect. As the representative of all in the kingdom, this man had incurred a great, immeasurable debt. So our Lord Jesus Christ was made sin for us. He incurred all our debt before God, a debt that would have sunk us forever into hell! Yet, just as all the king's servants were forgiven when that one servant was forgiven, so when Christ was "justified in the Spirit", released from all the debt he incurred as our Substitute, all God's elect were justified in him and forgiven of all things forever!

Once the man was loosed from all obligation and responsibility and forgiven his debt, it could never be recalled. His cruelty to his fellow-servant made him liable for another offence, but the debt forgiven could not be unforgiven. Here is the superiority of our blessed Saviour and the forgiveness of our sins by his great sacrifice. Our God has forgiven all our sins, all our debt, (past, present, and future), by the precious blood of Christ. The parable certainly is not intended to teach us that our everlasting salvation depends upon our forgiveness of those who offend us. The scriptures clearly declare that God's forgiveness of our sins is free, eternal, and irreversible.

The teaching of our Lord in this parable is that men and women who are hard hearted, merciless, and unforgiving have never known God's forgiveness. Our Lord here tells us that as we hope for mercy, we ought to show mercy, as we have been forgiven, we ought to forgive one another. The consciousness of pardoned sin in Christ ought to make us gracious, kind, and forgiving. In a word, grace experienced makes saved sinners gracious. Christ in us is manifest to our brethren when we imitate the goodness and love of God that is ours in him (Ephesians 4:32-5:1). The intent of our Lord Jesus in this parable is set forth beautifully in Robert Hawker's comments regarding it. May God be pleased to give you and me such grace that his words are echoed in our hearts.

> Thanks to my dear Lord for this beautiful and instructive Parable, Yea, Lord! my debt was so great, in ten thousand talents as made me insolvent forever. In vain were it for me to say, Lord have patience with me and I will pay thee all. Never to all eternity, could I have done it. Oh! then add a grace more to the merciful forgiveness of all; and incline my heart to be merciful, even as my Father which is in heaven is merciful! Precious Jesus! help me to imitate thee in all things.

Chapter 52

Marriage, Divorce, Eunuchs, And Children

"And it came to pass, that when Jesus had finished these sayings, he departed from Galilee, and came into the coasts of Judaea beyond Jordan; And great multitudes followed him; and he healed them there. The Pharisees also came unto him, tempting him, and saying unto him, Is it lawful for a man to put away his wife for every cause? And he answered and said unto them, Have ye not read, that he which made them at the beginning made them male and female, And said, For this cause shall a man leave father and mother, and shall cleave to his wife: and they twain shall be one flesh? Wherefore they are no more twain, but one flesh. What therefore God hath joined together, let not man put asunder. They say unto him, Why did Moses then command to give a writing of divorcement, and to put her away? He saith unto them, Moses because of the hardness of your hearts suffered you to put away your wives: but from the beginning it was not so. And I say unto you, Whosoever shall put away his wife, except it be for fornication, and shall marry another, committeth adultery: and whoso marrieth her which is put away doth commit adultery. His disciples say unto him, If the case of the man be so with his wife, it is not good to marry. But he said unto them, All men cannot receive this saying, save they to whom it is given. For there are some eunuchs, which were so born from their mother's womb: and there are some eunuchs, which were made eunuchs of men: and there be eunuchs, which have made themselves eunuchs for the kingdom of heaven's sake. He that is able to receive it, let him receive it. Then were there brought unto him little children, that he should put his hands on them, and pray: and the disciples rebuked them. But Jesus said, Suffer little children, and forbid them not, to come unto me: for of such is the kingdom of heaven. And he laid his hands on them, and departed thence."
(Matthew 19:1-15)

Marriage
The matter of marriage, divorce, and remarriage was as hotly debated among religious people in our Lord's day as it is today (vv. 3-9). The importance of our

Lord's words in these verses cannot be over stressed. The wellbeing of nations, the happiness of society, and welfare of the church greatly depends upon the strength of families. And family values, family strength, family wholeness depends upon a proper understanding of the teachings of God's Word about marriage. In these verses our Lord teaches us that marriage is for life. The marriage union of a husband and wife is never to be dissolved, and cannot be lawfully dissolved, except upon the most serious grounds.

In the days of our Lord's earthly ministry, during the zenith of the Roman Empire, moral decadence was much the same as it is in western society today. Divorces were permitted and marriages were dissolved, even among the Jews, for the most frivolous and trifling reasons. The Pharisees did not simply ask, "Is it lawful for a man to put away his wife?" They asked, "Is it lawful for a man to put away his wife for every cause?" It is true, because of the hardness of men's hearts, to prevent the abuse of and murder of women, Moses did permit men to divorce their wives, but not for "every reason" (Deuteronomy 24:1-4). Yet, by long tradition and great laxity, that which Moses permitted was so commonly practised, that marriage had become nothing more than a whimsical thing, regarded with utmost disdain.

When men and women abandon God's law and look contemptuously upon marriage, they produce a generation of children who are utterly without conscience (Malachi 2:14). The disciples' comment in verse 10 "If the case of the man be so with his wife, it is not good to marry", gives us some idea of just how bad things were. They as good as said, "If a man cannot get rid of his wife whenever he wants to, he would be better off not to marry at all"!

Marriage is a relationship of greater importance and greater influence than any other earthly relationship. It was established by God in Paradise before sin entered into the world (Genesis 2:18-25). It was chosen to be typical of the relationship that exists between Christ and his church (Ephesians 5:25-33). Marriage is a relationship superior even to the relationship between parents and children (Ephesians 5:31). Marriage involves commitment, the loving devotion of a man and a woman to one another. It involves sacrifice and self-denial. It is giving, never taking. It is yielding, not demanding. It is unconditional, never qualified. Marriage involves a dissolution of other relationships, and a blessed isolation of a man and woman with one another.

Our Lord here teaches us that this blessed relationship of marriage is a life-long union. Today, few people enter into a marriage with the determination that it is forever. Many write out prenuptial agreements in anticipation of divorce. And many do not even bother with a wedding ceremony. They just "shack up" together like wild animals until something more attractive comes along. "From the beginning it was not so ... What God hath joined together, let no man put asunder". All who violate God's Word in this matter are guilty of adultery, and cause those who are recklessly abandoned and put away to do the same.

Divorce

This life-long marriage union can be dissolved lawfully, biblically, only for the most extreme reasons. In this passage our Lord cites fornication as the basis of divorce. As it is used here, the word "fornication" refers to sexual infidelity. The Master is not teaching that men and women ought to get a divorce if one or the other commits an act of infidelity. Indeed, we ought to forgive. But he is teaching that in such cases the marriage union may be permanently dissolved. The apostle Paul, writing by divine inspiration, also allows that abandonment dissolves the marriage union (1 Corinthians 7:15). In such cases, the person abandoned, or the one against whom the infidelity was committed, is perfectly free to marry again in the Lord (Deuteronomy 24:1-4).

Many of God's saints have already experienced divorce and remarriage, some several times, before the Lord was pleased to save them by his grace? The question is sometimes raised, "How should we deal with them?" We are to deal with them as forgiven sinners, just like the rest of us! Like us, they are sinners saved by God's free grace in Christ, born of God, washed in the blood of the Lamb, forgiven of all sin, free from all condemnation, and new creatures in Christ (Romans 8:1).[5]

Union With Christ

The scriptures clearly teach us that marriage was ordained of God to be an instructive and beautiful picture of the union of Christ and his church (Genesis 2:18-21; Ephesians 5:23-33). Moses, the law, permitted the union of a man and his wife to be dissolved by divorce because of adultery. He did so because of the hardness of men's hearts. But, blessed be his name, God our Saviour "hateth putting away" (Malachi 2:16). He has betrothed his elect to himself for ever (Hosea 2:19, 20). His word is, though "thou hast played the harlot with many lovers, yet return unto me saith the Lord" (Jeremiah 3:1). Therefore, he recovers

[5] 1 Timothy 3:2 has nothing to do with divorce and remarriage! There Paul is dealing with the issue of polygamy.

his adulterous wife by his free and sovereign grace. When he does, he causes the object of his love to willingly put away her lovers and return to him, saying, “I will return unto my first husband” (Psalm 65:4; 110:3; Hosea 2:6, 7).

Eunuchs

In verses 10-12 our Saviour gives us a word of instruction about eunuchs, or about the matter of celibacy. The word “eunuchs” here does not merely refer to an emasculated man. Nowhere does the word of God approve of physical disfigurement in the name of worship! As it is used here, the word refers to men who have no interest in marriage. Yet, it has nothing to do with effeminacy! Our Saviour tells us that some are eunuchs by birth. Some (particularly those who were slaves) were forced to be eunuchs. Others choose to be eunuchs, to remain celibate, so that they may be freer to serve Christ’s interests in this world.

Our Lord is not here teaching that celibacy is a more spiritual or more desirable state than marriage (1 Corinthians 7:1, 2; 1 Timothy 4:3). He is simply telling us that some men do not have the need to marry. And he is telling us that some men voluntarily forgo marriage that they may more freely serve Christ (1 Corinthians 7:32, 33). Such men are not to be held in suspicion. Having said that, I must add, in this day of rampant homosexuality, it seems best (in my opinion) for any man who is not impotent to take a wife with whom he can serve Christ, particularly if he is a minister of the gospel.

Children

Our Saviour uses children to exemplify his own humility and to teach us what humility is (vv. 13-15). These little children were brought to the Lord Jesus, just as sick and diseased people were, that he might lay his hands upon them and pray for them. There is no more and no less in this incident than that. There is not a word about whose children they were. There is not a word about baptism, much less sprinkling! And there is not a word about the common practice these days of having a dedication service for babies.

Very few passages in the New Testament have been so perversely twisted to teach false doctrine as these three verses. Papists and those who continue to practise Roman rituals commonly refer to these verses as a defence of sprinkling water on babies. If there were any place in the Bible where we might expect to find some mention or example of “infant sprinkling” this would be the place; but that is not the case. This practice of what is called “infant baptism” is totally without foundation in holy scripture. There is not so much as one word in the

Bible that teaches, or even implies it. And there is not a single example of it in the entire Bible. It is a tradition purely of Roman Catholic origin. It is vainly hoped by those who practise infant sprinkling, that the baby sprinkled with a little water is thereby regenerated, or at least given one foot up toward God. The practice is, of course, totally contrary to the plainest declaration of holy scripture, both with regard to salvation and baptism.

It is a complete contradiction of the gospel of God's free and sovereign grace in Christ. Salvation does not come by water, be it much or little, but by grace. It is not the result of some man's priestly pretence, but of God's sovereign operation. Infant sprinkling is also totally contrary to the teaching of holy scripture about baptism. Baptism is immersion, picturing the death, burial and resurrection of Christ and our death, burial, and resurrection with him (Romans 6:3-6). It is called believer's baptism because only believers are to be baptized. Baptism is the believer's symbolic confession of faith in Christ.

"Then were there brought unto him little children, that he should put his hands on them, and pray: and the disciples rebuked them." They brought these children to the Master that he might, as was his custom, heal them of their diseases by touching them. But the disciples rebuked those who brought these sick children to the Master. We are not told why the disciples rebuked them. They may have had what they thought were good reasons for doing so. In fact, that appears to have been the case, because the Lord Jesus did not, in any way scold them for their action. But this much is certain. They did not bring the children to the Saviour to be baptized by him. As John Gill observes:

> From this rebuke and prohibition of the disciples, it looks plainly as if it had never been the practice of the Jews, nor of John the Baptist, nor of Christ and his disciples, to baptize infants. Had this been then in use, they would scarcely have forbidden and rebuked those that brought them, since they might have thought they brought them to be baptized. But knowing of no such usage that ever obtained in that nation, neither among those that did, or did not believe in Christ, they forbad them.

"But Jesus said, Suffer little children, and forbid them not to come unto me". Our Lord Jesus was such a gracious, humble, accommodating man that he readily seized the opportunity to tenderly embrace young children, take them onto his knee, and minister to them. He was so gracious, gentle and kind that young children were perfectly comfortable in approaching him.

"For of such is the kingdom of heaven". It is as if our Lord said, "Don't drive these children away from me. Let them come, and I will teach you something. These children are a good picture of what I require all my children to be: trusting and dependent, harmless and inoffensive, free from bitterness and malice, meek, modest and humble, without pride, arrogance and ambition, having no desire for greatness, just children". In a word, our Saviour here tells us that there is no true faith, except that faith that is exemplified in childlike qualities. What a profound, needful, vital lesson that is! May God give us grace to receive it. "Verily I say unto you, Whosoever shall not receive the kingdom of God as a little child shall in no wise enter therein" (Mark 10:15).

Infant Salvation

I am compelled to give a word of comfort and instruction concerning infants. As I was preparing to write this chapter, I received a lengthy, sad letter from a dear friend. She and her husband married fairly late in life, just two or three years ago. They have been trying to have a child. You can imagine their elation when they learned that she was pregnant. Then, my friend miscarried. In her great sadness and disappointment she wrote to ask me three things. Was my unborn child a human being? At what point is an unborn child a living person? Is my child in heaven? I wrote back and said, "Yes, your baby is one of Christ's jewels, taken from your womb into his everlasting arms and into his glory."

John Newton once said, "The majority of persons who are now in the kingdom of God are children." I would not argue the point. When I think of all the multitudes of babies who have died in infancy, who are now swarming the streets of glory, I rejoice in God's great wisdom and goodness. Though adults, generation after generation, die in rebellion and unbelief; but countless multitudes of infant children have entered into the kingdom of heaven, saved by the grace of God, through the death of Christ, and forever sing the high praises of their great Redeemer and Friend before the eternal throne of his glory. "Of such is the kingdom of heaven."

I have no hesitancy in asserting that infants dying in infancy, including infants slain in abortion, burned on heathen altars, the infants of Papists, Mohammedans, and Buddhists, enter the kingdom God. I am fully convinced that all of our race who die in infancy are the objects of God's eternal love, are redeemed by the blood of Christ, and born again by God the Holy Spirit. Let others object, if they please. For my part, I am delighted with this. Everything I read in the Book of God convinces me of it. All who leave this world as babies are saved.

How are they saved? How do they enter the kingdom? By works? By the exercise of their will? Of course not! They enter the kingdom by the mighty operations of God's free grace. And if we enter the kingdom of God, that is exactly the way we will enter it.

However it is that they receive the kingdom of heaven, that is the way we must receive it (Luke 18:17). Certain it is that children do not receive the kingdom by birth or blood, for we are expressly told in John's gospel that the children of God are born not of blood nor of the will of the flesh. No baby enters into heaven because it was born of godly parents, neither shall any be shut out because his parents are atheists, or idolaters, or ungodly. If saved, as I am convinced the scriptures teach they are, infants must be saved simply according to the will and good pleasure of God, because he has made them his own by election, redemption, and regeneration.

Notice this, too, these children were "brought unto him". These young children were brought to Christ. The word means "brought and presented". So sinners, if ever they enter into the kingdom of God, must be brought by God the Holy Spirit, brought by omnipotent, irresistible grace and power, and presented to Christ, presented to him as the reward of his soul's travail. Thus, "He shall see of the travail of his soul, and shall be satisfied."

When we think of marriage, let our hearts be drawn to Christ, who has married himself to us, and has caused us to be married to him for ever. When we think about eunuchs, may the thought of such inspire us not with curiosity, but with devotion to Christ. When we see a child, let us pray for grace to be as a child before Christ, our God and Saviour.

Chapter 53

"What Lack I Yet?"

"And, behold, one came and said unto him, Good Master, what good thing shall I do, that I may have eternal life? And he said unto him, Why callest thou me good? there is none good but one, that is, God: but if thou wilt enter into life, keep the commandments. He saith unto him, Which? Jesus said, Thou shalt do no murder, Thou shalt not commit adultery, Thou shalt not steal, Thou shalt not bear false witness, Honour thy father and thy mother: and, Thou shalt love thy neighbour as thyself. The young man saith unto him, All these things have I kept from my youth up: what lack I yet? Jesus said unto him, If thou wilt be perfect, go and sell that thou hast, and give to the poor, and thou shalt have treasure in heaven: and come and follow me. But when the young man heard that saying, he went away sorrowful: for he had great possessions. Then said Jesus unto his disciples, Verily I say unto you, That a rich man shall hardly enter into the kingdom of heaven. And again I say unto you, It is easier for a camel to go through the eye of a needle, than for a rich man to enter into the kingdom of God. When his disciples heard it, they were exceedingly amazed, saying, Who then can be saved? But Jesus beheld them, and said unto them, With men this is impossible; but with God all things are possible."
(Matthew 19:16-26)

Here is a man who was anxious about his soul and concerned about eternal life. Such men are rare. He was rich; but he was concerned about his soul. He was young; but he was interested in eternity. He was a ruler of men; but he came to be taught by the Lord Jesus Christ. This rich young ruler came running up to Christ, and said, "Good Master, what good thing shall I do, that I may have eternal life?" Our Lord knew the man's heart. He knew that this young man was thoroughly familiar with the law of Moses. And he knew that the young man thought, like most people do, that eternal life could be gained by outward morality, by obedience to the law. Therefore, he answered this young man according to the law. He told him to keep the commandments. The rich young ruler responded, "All these things have I kept from my youth up". Then he asked, "What lack I yet?"

Perhaps some who read these lines ask the same question in their own minds, "What lack I yet?" You are very moral, and respectable in the eyes of men. You believe in God. You believe the Bible is the Word of God. And you believe in the Lord Jesus Christ. You believe that he is God. You believe in his death, burial, and resurrection as the sinner's Substitute. You even know that Jesus Christ the Lord is the sinner's only hope of salvation before God. Yet, for all that, you know that you are not a child of God, a saved sinner, and an heir to eternal life. Knowing all these things the question of great concern in your heart is just this "What lack I yet?"

Many very moral and religious people yet lack that one thing which is essential to eternal life. They lack faith in Christ. There are three questions raised in this passage of scripture that I want to answer from the Word of God.

1. "What Good Thing Shall I Do, That I May Have Eternal Life?"
The rich young ruler asked our Saviour this question. Looking at the question by itself, it appears to be a very noble one, one that we all should ask. We find this question many times in the scriptures. Those who asked it became saved men. They were given eternal life. On the day of Pentecost, a large number of men, after they heard the gospel message, were pricked in their hearts, and they cried, "Men and brethren, What shall we do?" The Philippian jailor, with a broken and submissive heart cried, "Sirs, what must I do to be saved?"

But when this rich young ruler asked the question, his heart was not broken with conviction. His soul was not humbled with a sense of sin. He was a terribly proud, self-righteous man. He felt that he was sufficient in himself to meet whatever requirements God himself might demand of him. In essence, he was saying to the Lord, "You tell me what God requires, and I will do it"! He had a zeal for righteousness; but going about to establish his own righteousness he had not submitted himself to the righteousness of God (Romans 10:3). How many there are like this rich young ruler: Very moral, very proud, and very lost!

There is much about this young man that is commendable. He was not a base, profligate rebel. He was moral, religious, and devout. He had been a respectful and obedient son to his parents. He was a good husband, a good father, a good provider for his family. He was a hardworking, honest man, who had acquired much wealth. He was a good neighbour, a respected community leader.

In a day of abounding unbelief he came to Christ of his own accord. He came, not to have some disease healed, not to plead for a helpless child, not to see some great miracle, but out of concern for his immortal soul. He was earnest and sincere. Mark tells us that he came running to Christ. He was orthodox in his creed. He was a religious leader. He believed in God. He believed the holy scriptures. He believed in the reality of eternal life. He was very strict and devoted in his practice of religion. Since the days of his youth, he had outwardly kept the law of God. His life was meticulously moral and precise. He even worshipped Christ. Mark tells us that when he came to Christ, he knelt before him. Like Nicodemus, this young man realized that Jesus Christ was a teacher come from God. He seems even to have acknowledged our Lord’s deity. When the Lord Jesus asserted that no man is good, but God only, the young ruler did not withdraw his statement. He seems to have acknowledged that Christ is God.

Yet, this young man demonstrated two very sorrowful characteristics. Two things about this rich young ruler’s character show us that he was a lost, ruined, unregenerate man. First, he was ignorant of all spiritual truth. He knew much in a natural sense, but spiritually, regarding spiritual things, he was as ignorant as a man who had never heard of God. He was ignorant of God’s holy character. He was ignorant of his own sinfulness. He was ignorant of the law’s spiritual nature. He obviously thought that the law only required outward obedience. And he was altogether ignorant of the gospel of Christ (Ephesians 2:8, 9).

Second, the rich young ruler was, as already stated, dreadfully self-righteous. Beware of self-righteousness! No sin is more deadly, and more likely to keep you from Christ than the sin of self-righteousness. And no sin is more common to man. All men, by nature, are self-righteous. It is the family disease of all the sons of Adam. From the heights to the depths of society, we all think more highly of ourselves than we should. We secretly flatter ourselves that we are not so bad as some, and that we have something that will recommend us to the favour of God. The wise man said, “Most men will proclaim every one his own goodness” (Proverbs 20:6). We forget the plain testimony of holy scripture: “In many things we offend all” (James 3:2). “There is not a man upon the earth, that doeth good and sinneth not” (Ecclesiastes 7:20). “What is man that he should be clean, or he that is born of woman that he should be righteous” (Job 15:14). “They are all under sin; as it is written, there is none righteous, no not one” (Romans 3:9, 10).

Ever since man became a sinner, he has been self-righteous. When man had a perfect righteousness before God, he did not glory in it or cherish it. But ever since the fall, when we lost all righteousness, man has pretended to be righteous. Immediately after his fall, Adam wrapped himself in a fig leaf apron and began to defend himself by blaming his troubles on God who gave to him the woman, and the woman for giving him the fruit.

As it was with Adam, so it is with us all. We justify ourselves before God and men. Self-righteousness is born within us. We may, to a degree, control our lusts and wicked behaviour, but our self-righteousness will not allow us to confess our sins and come to God for mercy. Millions of sermons have been preached against self-righteousness, but it remains the number one sin that keeps men from coming to Christ. One old preacher said, "I scarcely ever preach a sermon without condemning self-righteousness, yet I find I cannot preach it down. Men still boast of who they are, what they have done, what they have not done, and mistake the road to heaven to be one paved by their own works and merit." God help us!

Our Lord Jesus answered this man's question plainly. He had asked what he could do to win God's favour; and the Saviour told him. "If you want salvation by human merit, you must keep the law." As far as he understood the law, in its outward requirement, he had kept it. He was like Saul of Tarsus, "as touching the law, blameless". But he was not all that he thought he was. He did not, in reality, love his neighbour as himself. The law must be kept perfectly. It must be kept in all points. It must be kept at all times. It must be kept outwardly. And it must be kept inwardly. God never intended the law to be a basis of salvation. Its design is to show man God's holy character and his own guilt. Nothing else. But those who attempt to obtain righteousness by the works of the law do not understand what the law requires. It requires perfect, complete obedience (Galatians 3:10).

2. "What Lack I Yet?"

Though our Saviour answered the rich young ruler's question so plainly that he should have been convinced of his inability to produce righteousness for himself, his pride and self-righteousness compelled him to press the matter further. He asked the Master, "What lack I yet?" Who would dare be so bold? The man must be either mad or blind. Yet, this man, like most, was very confident that he was righteous. He appears to be saying, "If there is any deficiency in me, I do not know what it could be. I have done all that God requires of a man."

He did appear to lack very little. If a modern soul-winner could find a young man like this, he would have him under the water, dried off, and in the pulpit in no time. But the Lord Jesus was not trying to get another decision to put on his promotional charts as a "soul winning evangelist". He laboured for the souls of men, not their applause. He was both compassionate and honest. Therefore, he showed the young man exactly what he lacked. He was not lacking in morality, religious duty, orthodoxy, sincerity, or zeal. But he was lacking one essential thing. He had no faith in Christ.

“What Lack I Yet?”

“Jesus beholding him loved him, and said unto him, One thing thou lackest” (Mark 10:21). He boasted that he loved his neighbour as himself. Therefore, Christ put him to a test. “Jesus said unto him, If thou wilt be perfect, go and sell that thou hast, and give to the poor, and thou shalt have treasure in heaven; and come and follow me.” Our Lord commanded this young man to surrender to his authority as his Lord. “Go and sell all that thou hast, and give to the poor.” He commanded the man to trust him. He said, “Come”. Coming to Christ is an act of faith. “He that cometh to God must believe that he is, and that he is the Rewarder of them that diligently seek him.” Mark adds the words “Take up the cross”. That is to say, our Lord commanded the man to confess him. And he commanded this young man to obey him. He said, “Follow me”. These are the things which our Lord requires of all his people: submission, faith, confession, and obedience.

The Lord had a good reason for giving this command to this particular man. He was probing at his heart. He wanted to expose his point of rebellion. He was determined to show this young man exactly what he was lacking. God always meets the sinner at his point of rebellion. This man’s money was his god. Therefore, the Master commanded him to give it away. This command was designed to expose the evil of his heart, destroy his self-confidence and pride, show him the impossibility of salvation by the works of the law, and to show him the necessity of the gospel. By this one, pointed command, our Saviour stripped away the fig leaves of the rich young ruler’s self-righteousness, exposed the foolishness of his pride, and showed him his need of God’s grace.

The rich young ruler’s one fatal deficiency was a deficiency of the heart. Like Simon Magus, his heart was not right in the sight of God. He was yet unregenerate. He was in the gall of bitterness and in the bond of iniquity. His heart was not broken. His Spirit was not humbled. He would not surrender to Christ as Lord. God met him at his point of rebellion, and he would not bow. He would not come to Christ, trusting him alone for salvation. He would not confess Christ to be Lord. He would not obey the Son of God.

Are you like this young man? If so, our Saviour’s words to him must be addressed to you, “one thing thou lackest”. You have one fatal deficiency. Your heart is not right before God. If ever you are saved, your heart must be broken (Psalm 51:17; Isaiah 66:2). And the only way your heart will ever be broken is if God is pleased to reveal himself to you in the fulness of his grace and glory in Christ (Zechariah 12:10; 2 Corinthians 4:3-6). Unless God himself breaks your heart, it will never be broken; and you will never be saved. You must be born again by almighty grace. A new heart must be created within you.

3. "Who Then Can Be Saved?"

When the disciples saw and heard these things, they were astonished, and cried "Who then can be saved?" Our Lord gives us a plain answer to that question. "With men this is impossible, but with God all things are possible" (v. 26). Salvation is not a work of man. It is not, in any way, or to any degree, dependent upon or determined by man (John 1:12, 13). Salvation is altogether the work of God's sovereign and irresistible grace (Romans 9:16; Ephesians 2:8-10). None but God can save sinners in a way that is suitable to satisfy his holy law (Romans 3:24-26). None but God can give a lost sinner a new heart. None but God can break a sinner's stubborn will. None but God can give life to the dead and faith to the unbelieving. None but God can reveal Christ in us.

With men salvation is impossible, "but with God all things are possible". Salvation is accomplished entirely by his omnipotent, effectual, irresistible grace (Psalm 65:4). If ever the almighty God puts his hand upon a sinner, that sinner will be saved.

"Who then can be saved?" Let me tell you who can, who will, who must be saved. All who are redeemed by the blood of Christ, all who are born-again by God the Holy Spirit, all who are called by almighty grace, all who come to Christ must and shall be saved. The Lord Jesus Christ has declared, and it shall never be reversed, "All that the Father giveth me shall come to me; and him that cometh to me I will in no wise cast out" (John 6:37).

Come to Christ, no matter who you are, no matter how vile your transgressions are, and he promises that he will receive you just as you are; that he will never cast you out, that he will give you eternal life, and that you shall never perish. Come, then, to Christ without any preparations to make yourself worthy of coming, without making change to qualify you for acceptance. Come to Christ without delay. Sinner, come and welcome! The Saviour's word is, "Come unto me, all ye that labour and are heavy laden, and I will give you rest. Take my yoke upon you, and learn of me; for I am meek and lowly in heart: and ye shall find rest unto your souls. For my yoke is easy, and my burden is light" (Matthew 11:28-30). If you are lost, it is not because there is no love in Christ for sinners. It is not because Christ is not able, willing, and ready to save sinners. If you are not saved, it is as the Lord himself said, "Ye will not come to me, that ye might have life" (John 5:40). If you die in your sins, it will be entirely your own fault. If you do come, if you are saved, if you do trust the blessed Saviour it will be entirely because of and entirely the work of God's free grace.

Chapter 54

A Foolish Question Graciously Answered

"Then answered Peter and said unto him, Behold, we have forsaken all, and followed thee; what shall we have therefore? And Jesus said unto them, Verily I say unto you, That ye which have followed me, in the regeneration when the Son of man shall sit in the throne of his glory, ye also shall sit upon twelve thrones, judging the twelve tribes of Israel. And every one that hath forsaken houses, or brethren, or sisters, or father, or mother, or wife, or children, or lands, for my name's sake, shall receive an hundredfold, and shall inherit everlasting life. But many that are first shall be last; and the last shall be first."
(Matthew 19:27-30)

After seeing and hearing our Lord's conversation with the rich young ruler, who refused to give up all and follow Christ, the disciples appear to have had another discussion about rewards and prominence in the kingdom of heaven. Though Peter was the spokesman, he was clearly speaking for the rest of the disciples. We know this because, when the Lord answered his question, we are told, "Jesus said unto them" (v. 28) When Peter said, "Behold, we have forsaken all, and followed thee; what shall we have therefore?" it was as though he said, "Master, we have done what the rich young ruler refused to do. What shall be our reward for forsaking all and following you?" Foolish as the question was, our Lord graciously answered it and by it gives us much needed instruction in the way of life and faith.

Though the cost of following Christ may, at times, appear to be very high, the reward of following him is infinitely beyond measure, both in this world and in the world to come.

Forsake All

If we would follow Christ, we must forsake all and follow him. Faith in Christ is such trust in him, such confidence in him, that those who are born of God, who are true believers are, in the totality of their lives, committed to him. Faith in

Christ surrenders all to him. He is that Pearl of Great Price for which a person gladly sells all that he has (Matthew 13:44-46; Luke 14:25-33).

Faith in Christ is much more than simply believing facts about Christ. It is believing Christ. It is not trusting that he will save you, but trusting him. It is the surrender of my life to the rule, dominion, and disposal of the Son of God. Until we can truthfully say, "We have forsaken all and followed thee", we are lost, without life, without faith, without hope, under the wrath of God (Matthew 4:18-20; 19:27; Luke 5:11). Spurgeon rightly observed:

> No man has truly given himself to Christ unless he has said, 'My Lord, I give thee this day my body, my soul, my powers, my talents, my goods, my house, my children, and all that I have. Henceforth, I hold them at thy will, as a steward under thee, thine they are. As for me, I have nothing. I have surrendered all to thee.

Faith in Christ basically involves three things: first, the knowledge of Christ, his person and work, which comes to men by the preaching of the gospel (Romans 10:14-17), second, assent to God's revelation concerning his Son (1 John 5:1), and third, surrender, or commitment to Christ the Lord.

That which most effectually keeps people from this commitment of faith to Christ is the love of the world (Matthew 19:23, 24; James 4:4; 1 John 2:15). "No man can serve two masters: for either he will hate the one, and love the other; or else he will hold to the one, and despise the other. Ye cannot serve God and mammon" (Matthew 6:24). Nothing on the earth is more dangerous to a man's soul than riches (Matthew 13:22). Read the Saviour's words again (vv. 23, 24).

"Then said Jesus unto his disciples, Verily I say unto you, That a rich man shall hardly enter into the kingdom of heaven. And again I say unto you, It is easier for a camel to go through the eye of a needle, than for a rich man to enter into the kingdom of God." Commenting on those verses J. C. Ryle wrote:

> Few of our Lord's sayings sound more startling than this; few run more counter to the opinions and prejudices of mankind; few are so little believed; yet, this saying is true, and worthy of all acceptation. Riches, which all desire to obtain, riches, for which men labour and toil, riches are the most perilous possession!

Beware of the love of money! Wealthy people are not to be envied, but pitied. It is possible to use riches well and do much good with it. But few people do. For every one who uses wealth for the glory of God and the good of men's souls there are thousands who make a god of their gold and serve it. Money does not make a man good. Only grace can do that. God does not measure a man by the money he has in the bank, but by the grace he has put into his heart. Make certain that your treasure is in heaven.

Yet, we must never presume that the rich cannot be saved (Matthew 19:25, 26). God's grace is sufficient for the rich as well as for the poor. God the Holy Spirit can cause even the richest of men to seek treasure in heaven. He can cause kings to cast down their crowns at the feet of Christ. He can compel even rich men to count all things but loss for Christ. Abraham was rich. Yet, he was the father of the faithful. Job was rich. But he loved Christ. Moses was rich. Still he followed the Saviour. David, Solomon, Jehoshaphat, Josiah, and Hezekiah all stand as monuments of sovereign grace. They forsook all and followed Christ. Though God gave them riches, he graciously enabled them not to set their hearts upon their wealth, and taught them to use what he put in their hands for his glory. When he called for them to make sacrifices, they made them willingly. We must carry the gospel to the rich and to the poor. God has his elect everywhere, for "with God all things are possible" (Isaiah 43:13). He saves both the rich and the poor, as it pleases him.

Nothing Lost

Those who forsake all and follow Christ shall lose nothing by doing so. God's people do not serve him for gain. Those who preach the health, wealth, and prosperity gospel of greed are false prophets. Let that be stated emphatically. And those who attempt to inspire holiness, devotion, and sacrifice among God's saints by the promise of reward in heaven betray a base falseness to their own religion. Yet, I affirm, without hesitation, to all who have forsaken all and do forsake all to follow Christ, that you shall incur no lose by doing so, not in this world, nor in the world to come (1 Samuel 2:30; Romans 8:18, 26-39; 1 Corinthians 3:22, 23).

I am not suggesting God will make you wealthy, healthy, or even comfortable in a physical, material sense in this world. Such a condition probably would not be best for you or me. But I do make you this assertion in the name of God as you forsake all and follow Christ, "My God shall supply all your need according to his riches in glory by Christ Jesus" (Philippians 4:19; Luke 18:28-30). Our Lord promised his Apostles that in the world to come (the regeneration) they would sit upon twelve thrones judging (ruling over) the twelve tribes of Israel (v. 28). Frankly, I have no idea what that means. It is nowhere explained in the Bible. But, as there are different positions of service in the kingdom of heaven now, there shall be different positions of service when God makes all things new. We will all possess the full reward of grace. But we will still be individuals with personal services to render to Christ (see Revelation 4:9-11; 5:8-10).

All who have forsaken family and property for Christ's sake, shall receive a hundredfold in this world. If your family abandons you for your devotion to Christ, do not forget that you have a father and brother in every believing man, a mother and a sister in all the women of Christ's kingdom. If your faith costs you property and possessions, do not fret. To be at home everywhere is to be the richest person imaginable. To have family everywhere is to be rich indeed.

Moreover, in the world to come you who forsake all and follow Christ "shall inherit everlasting life", all the glory, bliss, and joy of heaven (John 17:5, 22; Romans 8:17, 18). As Spurgeon put it, "They who lose all for Christ will find all in Christ, and receive all with Christ."

In Luke 22:31 the Lord Jesus had just declared to Peter, and declared it publicly before all his disciples, that Satan desired to have them all that he might sift them as wheat. Then, he told Peter plainly that he had prayed for him that his faith fail not; assuring him that, though he must be sifted and suffer a great fall, he would be converted and made an instrument of usefulness to his brethren. Peter protested. He said, "Though all men shall be offended because of thee, yet will I never be offended … Though I should die with thee, yet will I not deny thee" (Matthew 26:33-35). Then, the Lord said to him plainly, "I tell thee, Peter, the cock shall not crow this day, before that thou shalt thrice deny that thou knowest me" (Luke 22:34). Then, the Lord Jesus spoke to all the disciples, Peter included. "He said unto them, When I sent you without purse, and scrip, and shoes, lacked ye any thing? And they said, Nothing" (v. 35).

The Lord Jesus had sent these men out to preach the gospel without any visible means of sustenance. They were not even given the necessities of life. They had no property, no accommodations, no supplies, and no money. And now, the Lord Jesus asked, "Lacked ye anything? And they said, Nothing". They lacked nothing at all. Wherever they went, they found someone ready to put them up, feed them, and give them a change of clothes and a little travelling money. Though they were sent out empty and destitute with nothing, wherever they went, the Lord Jesus went before them, opened the hearts of men to them, and graciously supplied them with everything they needed, and did so bountifully.

All this was done, as if to say to Peter, and to the rest of the disciples, and to you and me, "Though Satan will sift you as wheat, and though you will often fail and often fail miserably, though you may fall, fall often, and fall very low, you are mine, and you shall never lack anything."

Let all who have forsaken all to follow Christ, hear and answer this question. It is a question your Saviour asks of you and me. "Lacked ye anything?" I know your answer. It is the answer all God's saints are sweetly compelled by the blessed experience of grace to give. "Nothing." He "Who daily loadeth us with benefits" (Psalm 68:19) has seen to it that we have lacked nothing. And as it has been yesterday, so it shall be tomorrow. Those who trust the Lord Jesus shall lack nothing. "The LORD is my Shepherd; I shall not want … For there is no want to them that fear him … they that seek the LORD shall not want any good thing" (Psalm 23:1; 34:9, 10). We sing with John Newton:

Through many dangers, toils, and snares
I have already come,
'Tis grace hath brought me safe thus far
And grace will lead me home.

The Lord has promised good to me,
His Word my hope secures.
He will my shield and portion be
As long as life endures.

And, when this heart and flesh shall fail,
And mortal life shall cease,
I shall possess within the veil,
A life of joy and peace.

The richest man in the world is the man who is content. If a man is content, he can never be made richer or poorer. And those who have Christ ought to be perfectly content, because Christ is contentment. It is written, "I will satiate the soul of the priests with fatness, and my people shall be satisfied with my goodness, saith the LORD" (Jeremiah 31:10-14). Having Christ, we lack nothing.

In him we have all. There is such infinite fulness in him that we can lack nothing. "Lacked ye anything" that God requires? "Nothing" (Colossians 1:12). "Lacked ye anything" needed to perform the work he has given you? "Nothing". His grace has been sufficient. "Lacked ye anything" when, like Peter, you have fallen? "Nothing". He has come to us again and again. "Lacked ye anything" when your heart has been most heavy? "Nothing". Christ has been our Comfort and our Strength. "Lacked ye anything" when you have been utterly empty? "Nothing". Christ is our fulness. "Lacked ye anything" when you have been utterly weak before him? "Nothing". His strength is made perfect in our weakness. "Lacked ye anything" when your love for him has waned? "Nothing". His love for us is perfect, free, and immutable. "Lacked ye anything" when your faith has been small? "Nothing". Our hope is not in our faith, but in his faithfulness.

As we have lacked for nothing in days past, be assured, we shall lack nothing tomorrow (John 14:1-3). When tomorrow's trials come, his grace will be sufficient. When tomorrow's sickness comes, his grace will be sufficient. When tomorrow's sorrow comes, his grace will be sufficient. When tomorrow's death comes, his grace will be sufficient. When, on the appointed tomorrow, we must stand before our God to give account, even then we shall lack nothing. His grace will be sufficient.

Last First

God does not view things as we do. Our Saviour declares that "the first shall be last, and the last shall be first" (v. 30). God is no respecter of persons. Those who are counted first by men (the wealthy, the learned, the powerful) are counted last by God. And those whom men look upon as nothings and nobodies shall be first (1 Corinthians 1:26-31).

Chapter 55

The Last First And The First Last

"For the kingdom of heaven is like unto a man that is an householder, which went out early in the morning to hire labourers into his vineyard. And when he had agreed with the labourers for a penny a day, he sent them into his vineyard. And he went out about the third hour, and saw others standing idle in the marketplace, And said unto them; Go ye also into the vineyard, and whatsoever is right I will give you. And they went their way. Again he went out about the sixth and ninth hour, and did likewise. And about the eleventh hour he went out, and found others standing idle, and saith unto them, Why stand ye here all the day idle? They say unto him, Because no man hath hired us. He saith unto them, Go ye also into the vineyard; and whatsoever is right, that shall ye receive. So when even was come, the lord of the vineyard saith unto his steward, Call the labourers, and give them their hire, beginning from the last unto the first. And when they came that were hired about the eleventh hour, they received every man a penny. But when the first came, they supposed that they should have received more; and they likewise received every man a penny. And when they had received it, they murmured against the goodman of the house, Saying, These last have wrought but one hour, and thou hast made them equal unto us, which have borne the burden and heat of the day. But he answered one of them, and said, Friend, I do thee no wrong: didst not thou agree with me for a penny? Take that thine is, and go thy way: I will give unto this last, even as unto thee. Is it not lawful for me to do what I will with mine own? Is thine eye evil, because I am good? So the last shall be first, and the first last: for many be called, but few chosen."
(Matthew 20:1-16)

This parable was given by our Lord in response to the disciples' question in the latter part of chapter 19, verses 27-30. In fact, it appears to be a continuation of our Lord's conversation with them. In chapter 19, verse 30, he says, "Many that are first shall be last; and the last shall be first." There is no need for us to guess what that means. This parable is the Saviour's explanation and illustration of that statement.

Our Lord's parables are earthly stories, or illustrations, by which he demonstrated his doctrine. Always look at the parables as you would the use of an illustration in a sermon. The illustration is not the sermon. It is an illustration of the sermon, or of some point in the sermon. Even so, our Lord's parables are not the basis of our doctrine. We do not build our doctrine upon parables. We build our doctrine upon the plain statements of holy scripture. The parables are earthly illustrations of spiritual, heavenly truths. We do not need to search for hidden meanings in the parables. Instead of doing that, we must look for the obvious. When we have discovered the obvious message of a parable, we have discovered all that it is intended to reveal. We should not look for more.

The obvious message of this parable has to do with following Christ, serving him, and the reward of doing so. That is what our Lord is dealing with in the context. The message of the parable is this, "The last shall be first, and the first shall be last". That simply and obviously means that all true believers are the servants of Christ, all are equal in the eyes of God, and all shall have an equal, infinite fulness of reward in heaven.

The Labourers

First, the parable describes all who follow Christ as "labourers". "For the kingdom of heaven is like unto a man that is an householder, which went out early in the morning to hire labourers into his vineyard" (v. 1).

The parable is about the kingdom of heaven, or the church of God, the household of faith. The labourers hired to work in the Master's vineyard are all true believers. This is not a parable about pastors, missionaries, and evangelists. It is a parable about believers. In the church of Christ there is no such thing as clergy and laity. All true believers are the servants of God. Some serve in one capacity and some in another; but all true believers are God's servants. We are all in the ministry. Faith in Christ, in its essence, involves surrender to Christ as our Lord, our Master, and our King. It is the giving up of our lives to the rule and service of Christ (Matthew 10:37-39; Luke 14:25-33).

The place of labour is "his vineyard", the church of God. Without question, God sovereignly uses all things according to his purpose to accomplish his will. He sometimes uses people who do not behave in normal order. But God's order is not to be despised by us. There is no excuse for neglecting God's order of things. He will hold us accountable (1 Chronicles 15:13). If we would serve God and serve our generation by the will of God, we must find our place in his vineyard, in his church, and serve him there.

The whole affair of serving Christ, as it is set forth in this parable, is a manifestation of God's free and sovereign grace. Wholehearted devotion in the service of the Lord Jesus Christ is a very reasonable thing (Romans 12:1, 2). Religious exercise without heart, doctrine without devotion, and religious conversation without real commitment are inexcusable evils. The very best service that we can give our Master is in itself altogether unworthy of him and unacceptable to him (Isaiah 64:6). Even our prayers and sacrifices are acceptable to God only when they are washed in the blood of Christ and robed in his righteousness (1 Peter 2:5).

Having said that, we must never forget that any gifts, talents, and abilities we have, with which to serve God, are the gifts of his free grace (Ephesians 4:7). If one person has greater mental abilities than another, he has them by the gift of God. If any man is gifted for the work of the ministry, the gift is God's. If one has greater means to support the work of the gospel than another, it is God who gave him the means. There is no room for boasting or for envy in the kingdom of Christ (1 Corinthians 4:7).

So, too, every opportunity to serve God by serving men is the gift of his grace, arranged by special providence. Even the length of our labour and service in the kingdom of God is altogether determined by God's sovereign grace. Some are called in the dew of their youth. Others are called in the middle of the day, as grown men and women. And some are called in old age, at the eleventh hour of the day. But all who are called to life and faith in Christ are called at the appointed "time of love". Robert Hawker says:

> What a beautiful similitude is here, of the kingdom of grace! Such is the Church of Jesus, as a vineyard gathered out of the world's wide wilderness; chosen (as scripture expresseth it) by God the Father; purchased by God the Son; and set apart in the regenerating and purifying grace of God the Holy Ghost. At what age are you standing? Hath the Lord called you at the early morning of life, the mid-day, the afternoon, or evening? Are you in the vineyard of the Lord of Hosts? or are you still idle in the market-place? Oh! the unspeakable blessedness of knowing, under divine teaching, that we are 'saved and called with an holy calling, not according to our works, but according to his own purpose and grace given us in Christ Jesus before the world began' (2 Timothy 1:9).

The Reward
Second, this parable is intended to teach us about the reward of God's saints, the reward of those who labour in the Master's vineyard (vv. 8-12). This was a real problem with our Lord's disciples. They judged, by carnal reasoning, that since they had sacrificed more than others and had done more than others (at least in their opinion), they deserved a greater reward (Matthew 18:1; 19:27, 28; 20:20-22). How very sad it is to see faithful men seeking great things for themselves, and sadder still to see them seeking positions of superiority over their brethren!

The God of Glory does not measure things the way we do. He will reward every labourer in his vineyard, but not as men judge that he should. He will reward his people in a way that will exalt his grace, exalt his Son, and give no room for the flesh to boast. He has no regard to the time of our service, or the amount of ground covered. God does not measure out reward according to the abilities of his servants. Heaven's reward will not be given according to the judgment and estimation of men. God will not be impressed with the impressions we make upon men. He will not deal out his reward according to the measure of our apparent success. God will not reward us according to the measure of our gifts, neither our gifts of grace and usefulness, nor our monetary gifts for the cause of Christ.[6] God will not even reward us according to the measure of our faithfulness.

The reward that God gives to his servants at the end of the day, in heaven's glory, will be a matter of pure grace, and will be one that makes all his people equal. Those servants who had laboured the whole day "murmured against the goodman of the house, Saying, These last have wrought but one hour, and thou hast made them equal unto us, which have borne the burden and heat of the day." And the Lord Jesus replied "the last shall be first, and the first last" (vv. 11, 12, 16). And so it shall be (Romans 8:16, 17; John 17:5, 22). God will reward us according to the merit of Christ, which has been imputed to us (Revelation 20:12; 22:11, 12). Hawker's comments on this verse give us the teaching of scripture regarding the rewards of God's saints in heaven.

---

[6] Men applaud and honour very wealthy people who make large gifts out of their abundance to churches and charitable causes, while poorer people who give far greater gifts (though utterly insignificant in the eyes of men) out of their meagre supply are ignored. The Lord Jesus measured the gifts of those who "*cast money into the treasury*" not by the amount they gave, but by the amount they kept for themselves (Mark 12:41-44).

> The equality of wages, is a beautiful illustration of the free and sovereign grace of God; because, strictly and properly speaking, it is all free: no merit, no pretensions of merit, in one more than another, making the smallest claim to favour. The Vineyard, the Church, and the labourers in the Church, all the gift of God the Father, the purchase of God the Son, and the whole cultivation from the work of God the Holy Ghost. And however different the measures of grace, and strength, and ability given; yet the whole is the Lord's not theirs; and every thing speaks aloud that the whole efficiency is of him. 'Not by might, nor by power, but by my Spirit, said the Lord of hosts' (Zechariah 4:6).

Degrees Of Reward

Will there be degrees of reward in heaven? If we read this parable in its context (Matthew 19:27-20:21), it is obvious that the parable was given to put an end to all questions about degrees of reward among God's saints. Yet, multitudes continue to teach the absurd doctrine. Many men, whose doctrine has been thoroughly biblical in other areas, have been in grave error concerning rewards.

The issue by which this question must be settled is clear. Is God's salvation, in its entirety, the work of his free grace in Christ, or is it not? If, as the scriptures everywhere assert, our salvation is altogether the work of God's free grace, if our works have nothing to do with it, and heavenly glory is but the consummation of that salvation, then there can be no degrees of reward in heaven[7].

Without question, salvation is by grace alone, through faith alone, in Christ alone. No part of salvation can be, in any measure, attributed to the will, worth, or works of man (2 Timothy 1:9; Ephesians 2:8, 9; Romans 11:6). If it is possible to separate heavenly rewards from salvation, then one might imagine that there shall be degrees of reward in heaven; but if heaven and the glorious inheritance of the saints in heaven is only the consummation of salvation, then the doctrine that there shall be degrees of reward in heaven is but another subtle way of teaching salvation by works! It is impossible to separate heavenly glory from salvation.

---

[7] Salvation involves all that is required to bring a sinner from the ruins of the fall into the glory of heaven.

The Doctrine
What is the doctrine of those who teach degrees of reward in heaven? I realize that some who teach that there are degrees of reward in heaven may have slightly different opinions than others; but basically their doctrine is the same. I do not wish to put words into the mouths of others. So, I will give you the doctrine in the words of one of its leading proponents, Merrill F. Unger.

> Rewards are offered by God to a believer on the basis of faithful service rendered after salvation. It is clear from scripture that God offers to the lost salvation and for the faithful service of the saved, rewards. Often in theological thinking salvation and rewards are confused. However, these two terms must be carefully distinguished. Salvation is a free gift (John 4:10; Romans 6:23; Ephesians 2:8, 9), while rewards are earned by works (Matthew 10:42; Luke 19:17; 1 Corinthians 9:24, 25; 2 Timothy 4:7, 8). Rewards will be dispensed at the Judgment Seat of Christ (2 Corinthians 5:10; Romans 14:10). The doctrine of rewards is inseparably connected with God's grace. A soul being saved on the basis of divine grace, there is no room for the building up of merit on the part of the believer. Yet, God recognizes an obligation on his part to reward his saved ones for their service to Him. Nothing can be done to merit salvation, but what the believer has achieved for God's glory God recognizes in His great faithfulness with rewards at the Judgment Seat of Christ.

Here are five things involved in the teaching that there will be degrees of reward in heaven, as stated by Mr Unger:

1. *Salvation is limited to the initial experience of conversion.* In the Word of God salvation is presented as the work of God's free grace in bringing sinners into heavenly glory, and includes election, redemption, justification, sanctification, preservation, and glorification in and with Christ (Matthew 10:22; Romans 8:28-30; 13:11; 2 Corinthians 2:10; 2 Timothy 1:9; 1 Peter 2:4, 5).

2. *It is possible for a person to be saved and not be a faithful servant of Christ.* Nothing can be more contrary to the words of our Lord (see Luke 14:25-33). There is no such thing as a believer who does not live in submission to Christ as his Lord. Believers do not always act faithfully; but they are all faithful. To be

a believer is to be one who is a saint (sanctified) and numbered among "the faithful in Christ Jesus" (Ephesians 1:1).

3. *Men and women, by their service to God, put God under obligation to reward them.* What an atrocious statement! Is it possible for a sinful man or woman to do anything to merit God's favour, to earn God's blessing? Can a mere man oblige the Almighty? We are debtors to God. He is not, and cannot be made to be, a debtor to us![8]

4. *There will be two judgment days, one for believers and another for unbelievers.* The Word of God never hints at the idea that Christ will come again twice, once in secret and then openly, or that there will be two distinct resurrection days, or that there will be two separate days of judgment. Such fabrications are but the inventions of men, in an attempt to make the Word of God fit into their theological systems.

5. *Believers will yet have to suffer for their sins!* The doctrine of degrees of reward in heaven unashamedly declares that those for whom Christ has suffered all the wrath of God, whose sins he put away, will yet suffer in heaven for their sins after God saved them; that they will suffer the everlasting shame of heaven's loss in the presence of those who earned a greater measure of glory, those who by their great goodness obliged God to give them a greater inheritance! The Lord God says otherwise. He declares that he will never charge his people with sin (Romans 4:8; 8:33, 34). The doctrine of degrees of reward in heaven is nothing less than a Protestant version of purgatory. Heavenly glory is not everlasting sorrow, but everlasting bliss.

Implications

Such doctrine is not without unavoidable implications. If the doctrine of degrees of reward in heaven is accepted, then it must be acknowledged that heaven's glory is not the reward of grace, but the payment of a debt. It must also be acknowledged that heaven is not a place of unmingled joy, as the scriptures assert (Revelation 7:15-17; 21:1-5; 22:2-5), but a place of mingled joy and grief. If the doctrine of degrees of reward is accepted, it must also be accepted, contrary to the plainest statements of divine revelation, that God does withhold some good things from them that walk uprightly, and some evil shall fall upon the just (Psalm

---

[8] Let the reader ask himself: "What have I ever done, or thought, that is worthy of God's acceptance?" If, as every child of God humbly acknowledges, sin is mixed with all we are and do (1 John 1:8-10), and our very righteousnesses are filthy rags in the sight of the infinitely holy Lord God (Isaiah 64:6), we certainly cannot "oblige" the Almighty by our deeds!

84:11; Proverbs 12:21). Again, if the doctrine of degrees of reward in heaven were accepted, then we would be forced to conclude, in direct opposition to the clear teaching of holy scripture, that the blood and righteousness of Christ will not alone be sufficient for our acceptance with God; that some part of God's favour, some element of his blessings, must be earned by us; that salvation is partly a matter of works and not altogether the gift of God's free grace in Christ. These implications are inescapable, and utterly blasphemous. Yet, they are the unavoidable consequence of the doctrine of degrees of reward in heaven.

Why has this issue been contradicted so dogmatically? Why deal with it so pointedly? Here are five reasons for my decision to write as I have on this matter.

The doctrine of degrees of reward in heaven is totally without foundation in the Word of God. Not one passage referred to in support of this doctrine even hints that some saints will have more and some have less in heaven. Not one of the crowns mentioned in the Bible are said to be given only to certain believers. All the saints before the throne have the same golden crowns, crowns which they gladly cast before the feet of the Lamb (Revelation 4:10).

But not only is the doctrine without foundation in holy scripture, it is totally contrary to the plain statements of God's word (Romans 8:17, 29; Ephesians 1:3; 5:25-27; 1 John 3:1, 2; Jude 24, 25). Can there be degrees of holiness, degrees of perfection, degrees of faultlessness, degrees of glorification? Never!

1. The doctrine of degrees of reward, and rewards earned by personal obedience, makes service to Christ a legal, mercenary thing. Such doctrine promotes pride. If one person could obtain a brighter crown than another, a higher rank, or greater nearness to God by his works, he would have every reason to strut around heaven, and have crownless people bow and scrape before him.

2. Not only does the doctrine promote pride, it threatens punishment. It attempts to put God's people upon a legal footing before him, threatening the loss of reward and everlasting shame for non-compliance with what is expected of us. This horrendous doctrine makes God's saints mere hirelings. It solicits obedience and faithfulness upon threat of punishment and promise of reward. I challenge anyone to find a single example of such base, carnal threats against redeemed sinners in the New Testament. Such doctrine is as offensive as it is unscriptural. It dishonours God and assumes God's people act out of personal ambition and not out of love for Christ. It assumes they are motivated and governed by something other than the love of God and concern for his glory.

3. This base, carnal doctrine of earned reward in heaven robs Christ of the glory of his grace and makes room for human flesh to boast before God.

4. If you and I do something that puts God almighty in obligation to reward us, then we have a right to boast in his presence. If we do something by which we merit a higher standing than others in glory, why should we not boast about it?

5. The doctrine of degrees in glory has the obnoxious odour of works about it; and there is no room for works in the kingdom of grace. The God of Glory will not be worshipped upon an altar of hewn stone (Exodus 20:25). He will not be worshipped upon an altar built by our hands. There is no room for the baggage of works in the strait and narrow way.

No Tears

There is a text of scripture that destroys the doctrine of degrees of reward and assures every believer of an everlasting fulness of joy in glory. The text is Revelation 21:4, "And God shall wipe away all tears from their eyes; and there shall be no more death, neither sorrow, nor crying, neither shall there be any more pain: for the former things are passed away." Do you see what this is saying? There shall be no tears in heaven!

Without question, there is much weeping in the way to heaven. Faith in Christ brings deliverance from all curse and condemnation, but not from pain and sorrow. There are many things that believers suffer in this world along with other men. Because the world is a world of sin, it is a world of sorrow. God's saints are not immune but suffer physical pain and sickness, domestic troubles, financial losses, and bereavement, just like all other people in this world.

Added to these earthly sorrows, there are many things that bring tears to our eyes, about which the world knows nothing. We struggle incessantly with inward sin and unbelief. There is a warfare in our souls, a warfare between the flesh and the spirit, a fight from which there will never be a moment's truce, until we have left this world.

There are even some precious tears that we shed here that will be dried on the other side of Jordan. Here we shed bittersweet tears of repentance, but not in glory! Here we often weep in sympathy because those we love are in pain or trouble, but not in eternity! Here we weep with broken-hearted concern for others, but not in heaven. Here our hearts break and our eyes swell with tears because we long for Christ's manifest presence, but not in the land of our inheritance!

Even now, our heavenly Father does much to dry our tears. The believer's life is not a morbid, sorrow-filled existence. Not at all! But we do have our sorrows. Yet, even in the midst of sorrow, our Lord gives us great comfort (Isaiah 43:1-7).

As our days require, he gives us grace sufficient to meet our every need. He gives us a measure of resignation to his will. He teaches us to trust his providence. He reminds us of his gracious purpose. He causes us to remember his promises. He blesses us with the sense of his presence. He floods our hearts with the knowledge of his love (Ephesians 3:19). He reminds us that the cause of our pain is his fatherly love for his erring children (Hebrews 12:5-14). And he causes our hearts to be fixed upon better things (Colossians 3:1-3; 2 Corinthians 4:15-18).

Yet, in heaven's glory our God will wipe all tears from our eyes. Impossible as it is for us to imagine, there is a time coming when we shall weep no more, when we shall have no cause to weep. Heaven is a place of sure, eternal, ever-increasing bliss; and the cause of that bliss is our God. Heaven is a place of joy without sorrow, laughter without weeping, pleasantness without pain. In heaven there are no regrets, no remorseful tears, no second thoughts, no lost causes, no sorrows of any kind!

Without question, if our God did not wipe away all tears from our eyes, there would be much weeping in heaven. We would forever weep over our past sins, over unconverted souls forever lost in hell, over all our wasted opportunities, over our unkindness and lack of love to our brethren here, and over the terrible price of our redemption. These things and many others would cause us to weep forever. But God will wipe away all tears from our eyes. It is written, "There shall be no more death, neither sorrow, nor crying; neither shall there be any more pain, for the former things are passed away"!

Our great God shall in heaven's glory remove us from all sin, remove all sin from us, and remove us from all the evil consequences of sin. He will remove us from every cause of grief. He will bring us at last into the perfection of complete salvation, and every desire of our hearts will be completely gratified. We will be like Christ! We will be with Christ! We will see Christ! We will love Christ perfectly! We will serve Christ unceasingly! We will worship Christ without sin! We will rest in Christ completely! We will enjoy Christ fully! We will have Christ entirely!

Will you be among the blessed company of the redeemed? Will you be with Christ in glory? You will only enter into glory if you are worthy of heaven. You can only be made worthy by the merits of Christ. If you are worthy of everlasting glory, you shall have all the glory of heaven itself, without degrees, perfectly. The very glory that God the Father gave to the God-man Mediator, that great Mediator has given to his people (John 17:5; 22). Trust Christ and all the glory of Christ in heaven is yours. All who believe on the Son of God are heirs of God, and more. We are joint heirs with Christ! In Christ we are one. Christ is our Reward. "In that day shall the LORD of hosts be for a crown of glory, and for a diadem of beauty" (Isaiah 28:5).

The Master

Third, this parable reveals much about the character of our God and Saviour represented by "the householder". He is just in everything he does (vv. 7, 13). He is faithful (v. 13). And he is sovereign in all things, doing with his own what he will, especially in the exercise of his grace (v. 15). Every blessing and privilege of grace is God's free gift. He bestows his gifts upon whom he will. And it is right for him to do so.

Free Election

Fourth, in verse 16 our Saviour once more declares one of his choice themes, the free and sovereign grace of God in election. "So the last shall be first, and the first last: for many be called, but few chosen." He asserts that he has, indeed, made all his servants equal. When we stand before him in glory, "the last shall be first, and the first last". There shall be no distinction of honour, place, or reward among the glorified. The reason for this is clearly stated. "For many be called, but few chosen." Salvation is, in its entirety, the result of God's eternal, electing love.

"Many are called" by the preaching of the gospel. But being called by the preaching of the gospel, and being chosen by God's eternal purpose of grace are very distinct things. When the gospel is preached to sinners, every one within the sound of the preacher's voice and all who hear are called by the gracious sound. All are, by the authority of God's Word, commanded of the sovereign God to hear and obey. But this outward call that is issued to all in the preaching of the gospel differs greatly from the inward work of grace, wrought by God the Holy Spirit in the hearts of the chosen. That effectual call of the Spirit, wrought in the redeemed, comes "not in word only, but also in power, and in the Holy Ghost, and in much assurance" (1 Thessalonians 1:5). That call is the result of God's election. As the Apostle Paul puts it, "We are bound to give thanks alway to God, for you brethren beloved of the Lord, because God hath, from the beginning, chosen you to salvation, through sanctification of the Spirit and belief of the truth, where unto he called you, by our gospel, to the obtaining of the glory of our Lord Jesus Christ" (2 Thessalonians 2:13, 14; Ephesians 1:3, 4; 2 Timothy 1:9). The whole work of grace, from regeneration to glorification, is the result of God's everlasting love for his elect in Christ (Jeremiah 31:3; Romans 8:28-30).

Chapter 56

Divine Sovereignty

"Is it not lawful for me to do what I will with mine own? Is thine eye evil, because I am good?"
(Matthew 20:15)

With those words, the Son of God plainly declares the glorious fact of God's absolute sovereignty over all things. No attribute of our great God is more comforting and delightful to his children than that of divine sovereignty. No doctrine in the Bible is more important, or more blessed. Under the most adverse circumstances, in the most severe troubles, when carrying our heaviest burdens, we believe and are sure that God has sovereignly ordained our trials, that he sovereignly controls them, and that he will sovereignly sanctify them to our souls. There is no doctrine in the Bible more basic to our faith, more fundamental or more absolutely asserted than the doctrine of divine sovereignty. It is essential to the very character of God.

To declare that God is sovereign is simply to declare that he is God. It is no less criminal or blasphemous to deny God's holiness, justice, omnipotence, truth, or even his very Being, than it is to deny his sovereignty. Those who deny that God is sovereign declare that God is, in reality, irrelevant!

Biblical Doctrine

Divine sovereignty is not merely a point of logic, or an old, out of date religious system dug out of the books of old reformers, puritans, and theologians. We believe what we do because we believe God. Our doctrine is based upon and arises from the plain statements of holy scripture. If you have a Bible and can read, you will have no difficulty at all in seeing that holy scripture universally declares God's sovereignty (Psalm 115:3; 135:6; Isaiah 14:24-27; 40:13-25; 45:7; 46:10; Daniel 4:35-37; Romans 9:11-24; 11:33-36). God is sovereign in creation, in providence, and in grace. He is sovereign over men and angels, good and bad. He is sovereign in heaven, earth, and hell.

I do not particularly care for the name, but all who believe the scriptures believe what men have nicknamed “Calvinism”, because those five grand, old gospel truths commonly called “Calvinism” are written out plainly in the word of God.

Total Depravity (Jeremiah 17:9; Romans 5:12; Ephesians 2:1-3)
Unconditional Election (John 15:16; Romans 9:11-13)
Limited Atonement (Isaiah 53:8)
Irresistible Grace (Psalm 110:3)
Perseverance of the Saints (John 10:28).

These delightful, soul cheering gospel truths cannot be gainsaid. Let religious rebels hoot and holler all they may. These things are written out in simple English in the Word of God for all to read. Let men read any translation of the Bible they may. No translation can be found that does not plainly assert these things. They are so thoroughly woven into the whole of divine revelation that even the most determined efforts of unbelieving religionists cannot extricate them from the Book of God. We insist upon them with dogmatic tenacity, because they are written plainly in the scriptures, because our God has pinned his glory to them, and because they are vital to the gospel. “Salvation is of the Lord” (Jonah 2:9). That is the language of the Bible. He planned it. He purchased it. He performs it. He preserves it. He perfects it. And he shall have the praise of it. As I stated, he has pinned his glory to it (Ephesians 1:3-14).

All Things Are His

“Is it not lawful for me to do what I will with mine own?” All things belong to God our Saviour. It is his sovereign right to do what he will with them. It is his right, as he will, to give them all to all, to give them all to some, to give some things to some and other things to others, or give them to none.

All temporal blessings are the gifts of God sovereignly bestowed upon men as he sees fit. All personal traits and abilities, mental powers, and earthly conditions are distributed among the sons and daughters of Adam according to God’s will alone (1 Corinthians 4:7; 1 Samuel 2:6-9). All the gifts of God’s saving grace are bestowed upon sinners in this world according to his sovereign, eternal purpose (Matthew 11:20-24; Romans 8:28-30; Hebrews 2:16).

Divine Sovereignty

The illustrations of God's sovereignty in the gifts of his grace are strewn across the pages of scripture. He chose some angels, and passed by others. He chose Israel alone, in the Old Testament, to be the people to whom he would give his Word and ordinances. The gospel is sent to some, and withheld from others (Acts 16:6, 7). He chose some to salvation, and not others, according to his own sovereign will (Romans 9:11-24). In his family, the church, God sovereignly bestows his gifts as he will (1 Corinthians 12:18-25; Ephesians 4:7).

Some believers have greater knowledge and deeper experience than others. Some are gifted to serve as deacons, while others are not. Some have gifts of ministry in one area, and others in another. Some have many gifts. Some have few. Some are gifted to preach the gospel; others are not. Even among preachers, the gifts vary: some are eloquent, some are analytical, some are passionate, some are cool, some are brilliant, some are not so brilliant. But all are gifted for the work to which God has ordained them, according to his infinite wisdom, goodness, and purpose. That means that there is no place in the church and kingdom of God for pride or envy.

All gifts of usefulness in this world are sovereignly dispensed to us as local churches or individuals by God. Yes, God honours those who honour him. Yes, he blesses faithfulness. But our usefulness in his hands is not determined by us. It is his sovereign gift. Gifts of spiritual comfort are distributed also among God's saints according to his sovereign will. Some enjoy great assurance, and some do not. Some, who struggle with assurance all their life, have its blessedness in the end. Some who have had assurance all their lives have none in the end.

"Whatsoever the Lord pleased, that did he in heaven, and in earth, in the seas, and all deep places" (Psalm 135:6). With those words the Psalmist David both declares God's absolute, universal sovereignty and calls upon us to trust, worship, and praise him because he is the sovereign God of the universe. The very foundation of our confidence and faith in our God is his sovereignty. Were he not sovereign, absolutely, universally sovereign, we could not trust him implicitly, believe his promises, or depend upon him to fulfil his Word. Only an absolute sovereign can be trusted absolutely. We can and should trust our God implicitly because he is sovereign. Nothing is more delightful to the hearts of God's children than the fact of his great and glorious sovereignty. Under the most adverse circumstances, in the most severe troubles, and when enduring the most heavy trials, we rejoice to know that our God has sovereignly ordained our afflictions, that he sovereignly overrules them, and that he sovereignly sanctifies them to our good and his own glory.

A Matter Of Great Joy

We rejoice to hear our Saviour say, "Is it not lawful for me to do what I will with mine own?" We rejoice to know that "our God is in the heavens: he hath done whatsoever he hath pleased" (Psalm 115:3). Yet, in this day of religious darkness and confusion there is no truth of holy scripture for which we must more earnestly contend than God's dominion over all creation, his sovereignty over all the works of his hands, the supremacy of his throne and his right to sit upon it. We rejoice in God's sovereignty. Yet, there is nothing revealed in the Bible that is more despised by worldlings and self-righteous religionists.

Natural, unregenerate, unbelieving men and women are happy enough to have God everywhere, except upon the throne of total, universal sovereignty. They are happy to have God in his workshop, creating the world and naming the stars. They are glad to have God in the hospital to heal the sick. They are pleased to have God to calm the raging seas of life. And they are delighted to have God in the funeral parlour to ease pain and sorrow. But God upon his throne is, to the unregenerate man, the most contemptible thing in the world. And any man who dares to preach that it is God's right to do what he will with his own, to dispose of his creatures as he sees fit, and save whom he will, will be hissed at, despised, and cursed by this religious generation. Still, it is God upon the throne that we love, trust, and worship. And it is God upon the throne that we preach.

Sovereignty Or Idolatry

God's sovereignty is so basic and fundamental that it is impossible to understand any doctrine taught in the Bible until we recognize, and have some understanding of the fact that God is sovereign. A God who is not sovereign is as much a contradiction as a God who is not holy, eternal, and immutable. A God who is not sovereign is no God at all. If the god you worship is not totally sovereign, you are a pagan, and your religion is idolatry. You would be just as well off worshipping a statue of Mary, a totem pole, a spider, or the devil himself as to worship a god who lacks total sovereignty over all things.

In one of his letters to the learned and scholarly Erasmus, Martin Luther said, "Your thoughts of God are too human." No doubt Erasmus resented the remark. But it exposed the heart of his heretical theology. And it exposes the heart of all false religion. I lay this charge against the preachers and theologians of our day, and against the people who hear them, follow them, and support them. Their thoughts of God are too human. I know the seriousness of what I have written.

But it must be stated with emphatic clarity. The God of the Bible is utterly unknown in this religious generation.

God's charge against apostate Israel was, "Thou thoughtest that I was altogether such an one as thyself" (Psalm 50:21), and that is his indictment against the religious world of our day. Men today imagine that God is moved by sentiment, rather than by the determination of his sovereign will. They talk about omnipotence, but imagine that it is such an idle fiction that Satan can thwart the power of God. They think that if God has a plan, it must, like the plans of men, be subject to constant change. They tell us that whatever power God does possess must be limited, lest he violate man's free-will and make him a machine. The grace of God is thought by most people to be nothing but a helpless, frustrated desire of God to save men. The precious sin-atoning blood of Christ is thought by most to be a waste, shed in vain for many. And the invincible, saving power of the Holy Spirit is reduced by most to a gentle offer of grace, which men may easily resist. All such thoughts about God are the blasphemies of idolaters.

The god of this generation no more resembles the sovereign Lord of heaven and earth than a flickering candle resembles the noon-day sun. The god of modern religion is nothing but an idol, the invention of men, a figment of man's imagination. Pagans in the dark ages used to carve their gods out of wood and stone and overlay them with silver and gold. Today, in these much darker days, pagans inside the church carve their god out of their own depraved imaginations. In reality, the religionists of our day are atheists, for there is no possible alternative between a God who is absolutely sovereign and no God at all. A god whose will can be resisted, whose purpose can be frustrated, whose power can be thwarted, whose grace can be nullified, whose work can be overturned has no title to Deity. Such a god is not a fit object of worship. Such a puny, pigmy god merits nothing but contempt.

When I say that God is sovereign, I am simply declaring that God is God. I repeat myself deliberately. He is the most High, the Lord of heaven and earth, overall, blessed forever. He is subject to none. And he is influenced by none. God is absolutely independent of and sovereign over all his creatures. He does as he pleases, only as he pleases, and always as he pleases. None can thwart him. None can resist him. None can change him. None can stop him. None can hinder him. He declares, "My counsel shall stand, and I will do all my pleasure" (Isaiah 46:10). "He doeth according to his will in the army of heaven, and among the inhabitants of the earth, and none can stay his hand, or say unto him, What doest thou?" (Daniel 4:35). Divine sovereignty means that God sits upon the throne of universal dominion, directing all things, ruling all things, and working all things "after the counsel of his own will" (Ephesians 1:11). This is a subject about which hundreds of books have been written, and yet "the half hath not been told". Divine sovereignty is not some isolated doctrine, taught in a few verses of scripture. It is revealed, literally, upon every page of Inspiration.

Predestination

God's sovereignty is irrefutably revealed in the eternal predestination of all things. Does the Bible teach predestination? Of course it does! Anyone who attempts to deny it is either totally ignorant of the Word of God, or a liar. God chose some men and women in eternity to be the objects of his saving grace and predestinated those elect ones to be conformed to the image of his dear Son (Romans 8:28, 29). Before the world began God sovereignly determined that he would save some, who they would be, and when he would save them. Having determined these things, our great God infallibly secured his eternal purpose of grace by sovereign predestination.

Yes, God predestinated from eternity everything that comes to pass in time to secure the salvation of his elect. That is the plainly stated doctrine of holy scripture (Ephesians 1:3-6, 11; Romans 11:36). It is written, "All things are of God" (2 Corinthians 5:18). "The Lord hath made all things for himself" (Proverbs 16:4). Eternal election marked the house into which God's saving grace must come. Eternal predestination marked the path upon which grace must come. And sovereign providence led grace down the path to the house at the appointed time of love.

Creation

No one can reasonably deny the revelation of God's sovereignty in his marvellous work of creation (Genesis 1:1; Revelation 4:11). Nothing moved God to create, except his own sovereign will. What could move him when there was nothing but God himself? Truly, "the heavens declare the glory of God" (Psalm 19:1-4). God created the heavens and the earth as a stage upon which he would work out his purpose of grace (Psalm 8:1-9). He created the angelic host to be ministering spirits to those who shall be the heirs of salvation (Hebrews 1:14). God created the sun, the moon, and the stars for the benefit of his elect. He created all plants and animals to provide food, comfort, and pleasure for man. At last, God created man in his own image and after his own likeness, that he might show forth the glory of his grace in man. Adam was created in the image of

Christ, "the figure of him who was to come", our eternal Surety and Substitute (Romans 5:12-21). He was created in conditional holiness. In God's wise, holy, and good purpose of grace, Adam was permitted to fall, and we all fell in him that we might be raised to life again in Christ the last Adam.

Providence

We see God's sovereignty in all the works of his daily providence (Romans 8:28; 11:36). In divine providence God Almighty sovereignly accomplishes his eternal purpose of grace in predestination. The Holy Spirit showed John a beautiful picture of this. It is recorded in the Book of Revelation. He saw the Lord Jesus Christ as our Mediator, the Lamb of God, taking the book of God's purpose, opening the book, and fulfilling all that was written in it in all the world (Revelation 5:1-10; 10:1-11). He who is God our Saviour, the Lord Jesus Christ, rules all things in providence by the book of God's predestination.

God's sovereign rule of providence extends to all his creatures. Inanimate matter, irrational creatures, and all things in this world perform their Maker's bidding. It was by the will of our God that the waters of the Red Sea divided (Exodus 14). By his word the earth opened up her mouth to swallow his enemies (Numbers 14). When he willed it, the sun stood still (Joshua 10) and went backward ten degrees on the sundial of Ahaz. Once, he even made an axe head float. Ravens carried food to his prophet (1 Kings 17). Lions were tamed by God's decree for his servant Daniel. He made the fire refuse to burn his faithful servants when they were cast into the fiery furnace. All things come to pass, or not, at his pleasure.

God's rule of providence extends even to the thoughts, and wills, and actions, and words, even of wicked men. He kept Abimelech from adultery with Sarah. He kept the Canaanites from desiring the possessions of Israel when they went to worship him (Exodus 34:23, 24). The hearts of all men, their thoughts, intents, and passions are in the hands of our God (Proverbs 21:1). Shimei was sent of God to curse David. Even the wrath of man shall praise him, and the remainder of wrath, that which he chooses not to use for his praise, he restrains (Psalm 76:10).

The object of God's providence, in all that he does, or allows to be done, is threefold. It is for the salvation of his elect, the eternal, spiritual good of all his people, and the glory of his great name. Here is a resting place for every believer's troubled heart. Neither Satan, the demons of hell, nor men, nor sickness, nor war, nor pestilence, nor the whirlwind is beyond the reach of God's sovereign throne (Matthew 10:30). Our times are in his hand (Psalm 31:15).

Salvation
God's indisputable sovereignty is conspicuously revealed in the salvation of sinners by his almighty grace (Romans 9:8-24). God chose to save some, but not all. He gave Christ to die for some, but not all. He gives his Spirit to some, but not all. He causes some to hear his voice, but not all. He saves some who seek him, but not all. He saved the woman with the issue of blood, but not the rich young ruler; the one leper, but not the nine; the publican, but not the Pharisee. "Salvation is of the Lord"!

Spiritual Gifts
God's sovereignty is, as we have already seen, conspicuously revealed in the various spiritual gifts he bestows upon his people (1 Corinthians 12:14, 18, 28-30). That is specifically what Matthew 20:15 asserts. He sees to it that his church has everything she needs to carry out the work he has for her to do. We need missionaries, and pastors, too. We need preachers, and deacons, as well. We need faithful witnesses; and we need the prayers of God's saints. We need workers; and we need givers. We need some to do great things, and some to do small things. In a word, we need Marthas and Marys, Johns and Jameses, Peters and Pauls, Lydias and Lucases. God gives each when they are needed and where they are needed for the accomplishment of his will. Let each child of God covet earnestly the best gift, the gift of love one for another. If we have that, we will serve God and his people well in our place, using all other gifts accordingly (1 Corinthians 12:31-13:13).

"Our God is in the heavens. He hath done (and is doing) whatsoever he hath pleased". Let us, therefore, believe him confidently, walk with him in peace, submit to him cheerfully, serve him faithfully, and honour him supremely. Gladly, we bow before God our Saviour, and worship with joy, he who asks, "Is it not lawful for me to do what I will with mine own?"

Chapter 57

"Ye Know Not What Ye Ask"

"And Jesus going up to Jerusalem took the twelve disciples apart in the way, and said unto them, Behold, we go up to Jerusalem; and the Son of man shall be betrayed unto the chief priests and unto the scribes, and they shall condemn him to death, And shall deliver him to the Gentiles to mock, and to scourge, and to crucify him: and the third day he shall rise again. Then came to him the mother of Zebedee's children with her sons, worshipping him, and desiring a certain thing of him. And he said unto her, What wilt thou? She saith unto him, Grant that these my two sons may sit, the one on thy right hand, and the other on the left, in thy kingdom. But Jesus answered and said, Ye know not what ye ask. Are ye able to drink of the cup that I shall drink of, and to be baptized with the baptism that I am baptized with? They say unto him, We are able. And he saith unto them, Ye shall drink indeed of my cup, and be baptized with the baptism that I am baptized with: but to sit on my right hand, and on my left, is not mine to give, but it shall be given to them for whom it is prepared of my Father."
(Matthew 20:17-23)

Evangelist Rolfe Barnard used to say, "You ought to be careful what you pray for. God just might answer your prayer." So often we pray and ask God to do things for us, or give things to us, without considering what weighty things might be involved in God's compliance with our requests. Such was the case with the mother of Zebedee's children. Our Saviour said to her, "Ye know not what ye ask." There are five very important lessons to be learned from these verses.

Our Saviour's Death

The first thing we see in this passage is the fact that our Lord Jesus Christ suffered and died at Calvary by his own choice and determination, by his own voluntary will. We should never fail to realize our Saviour's delight in speaking of his approaching death. This is the third time our Lord told his disciples how that he must suffer and die at Jerusalem (16:21; 17:22, 23). Though he told them frequently and plainly how he must be betrayed, delivered by the Jews into the hands of the Romans, and condemned to die as a common criminal, yet Luke tells us, "They understood none of these things" (Luke 18:34). He told them plainly that he must go to Jerusalem; there to be betrayed, condemned, and crucified, and that he must rise from the dead on the third day.

These were not bare possibilities, but absolute certainties. The death of our blessed Saviour at Calvary was a matter of divine predestination. Indeed, Christ's death at the cross was the focal point of God's purpose from eternity and is the focal point of all God's works in time (John 12:31, 32; Acts 2:23; 1 Peter 1:18-20). Robert Hawker says:

> Every act of Jesus testified his promptness to the work, as though he longed for it. Lo? I come (said Jesus,) to do thy will: O God. I delight to do it: yea, thy law is in the midst of my bowels; And when Peter, out of love (though a mistaken love) for his Master, wished it to be otherwise; Jesus rebuked him, yea, called him Satan, for what he said. Never did the meek and loving Saviour ever drop such an expression before: so very intent was he on finishing the work his Father gave him to do, and so much displeased was he with any one who wished it to be otherwise. Precious Lord Jesus! Was this thine ardent love to thy spouse the Church, as one longing to bring her out of the prison-house of sin and Satan, though all the cataracts of divine wrath for sin were broken up, to be poured on thy sacred head?

Our Lord Jesus Christ died as a voluntary victim of horrible, ignominious cruelty and of divine wrath, as our Substitute. He knew from the beginning all that he must suffer: Judas' betrayal, Peter's denials, the beatings and humiliation, being made sin, the wrath of God, and his cursed death upon the tree. What a great aggravation to his soul the foreknowledge of his suffering must have been! Yet, none of these things moved him from his gracious purpose (Isaiah 50:5-7). J. C. Ryle wrote, "He saw Calvary in the distance all his life through, and yet walked calmly up to it, without turning to the right hand or to the left." As no sorrow can be compared with the sorrow he anticipated and finally endured as our Substitute (Lamentations 1:12), no love can be compared with his love for us (John 13:34; 15:13)

Why did the Son of God voluntarily lay down his life for us at Calvary? He knew that it was his Father's will (John 10:16-18; Hebrews 10:5-10). He knew that divine justice must be satisfied, that without the shedding of blood is no remission of sins (Hebrews 9:22). He knew that he was the Lamb of God who must be sacrificed for the sins of his people (Revelation 13:8). He knew that without his death, his life, though perfect, holy, and gracious, would be useless to his people. He knew that the whole of God's law, the whole book of the writings of God's prophets, and the whole revelation of God's glory could be fulfilled and revealed only by his death as the Sinner's Substitute. Blessed is everyone to whom God the Holy Spirit has revealed these things. Blessed are those eyes that see and hearts that understand the meaning and necessity of Christ's sufferings and death.

Our Sinfulness

Second, we have before us another of the many examples in holy scripture of the fact that true believers often behave in a very foolish, sinful manner. One clear evidence of the divine inspiration is that the Word of God never attempts to hide the sins, weaknesses, and foolishness of it's most prominent characters.

James and John, the sons of Zebedee, apparently persuaded their mother to ask the Lord Jesus to give them the places of highest honour and glory in his kingdom. Historians tell us that this woman was sister to Joseph, Mary's husband. She and her sons were true disciples, genuine believers, followers of Christ. But they behaved very foolishly. James and John, as well as their mother, were truly spiritual people; but they behaved in a very carnal manner. They were more concerned about their crowns than Christ's cross (Galatians 6:14). They were unbelievably presumptuous, confidently asserting that they were able drink of the cup and be baptized with the sufferings the Lord Jesus was about to endure, when they should have been overwhelmed with wonder and humbled (v. 22). They were more concerned about themselves than about Christ and their brethren. Yet, these son's of Zebedee, James and John, were in time to become pillars of the church and kingdom of our Lord.

There are many true believers like this woman and her sons. Indeed, in some areas at different times, we all are very much like them. It is written, "The flesh lusteth against the spirit and the spirit against the flesh". True faith is often found beneath a pile of trash. We are all weak and sinful. We are all terribly proud, and horribly self-serving. And we are very ignorant of the very things we think we clearly understand.

Our Lord's Reproof

Third, our Lord Jesus teaches us that we are all terribly ignorant by the gentle reproof he gave to James, John and their mother. He said, "Ye know not what ye ask". They had asked to share Christ's glory, never stopping to consider that they must first share his sorrow (1 Peter 4:13).

How much like this woman and her sons we are! We ask for God to save our sons and daughters. But are we willing for the Lord to teach us patience, trusting him even with those most precious to us? Are we willing to endure trials? We ask for God to set our hearts on things above. But are we willing to be weaned from this world by affliction? We ask the Lord to teach us to trust him. But are we willing to be cast upon him? We ask our God to make Christ precious to us. But are we willing to have every rival to Christ taken from us? We ask for God to use us. But are we willing to be used as he sees fit?

These words apply to us all far more than we realize. "Ye know not what ye ask". God the Holy Spirit teaches us to weigh our words before the throne of God. "Be not rash with thy mouth, and let not thine heart be hasty to utter anything before God" (Ecclesiastes 5:2). Let us ever come to the throne of grace with open hearts, seeking mercy and grace in every time of need (Hebrews 4:16); but we must always remember that we do not know what we should pray for as we ought. We need God's grace continually, that we may pray in the Spirit and with understanding (Romans 8:26, 27).

Substitution

Fourth, we are assured, in verse 23, that all the Lord Jesus Christ did and suffered, all that he endured, and all that he accomplished was as the Representative of his people. He lived, died, and rose again as our Substitute.

Both James and John suffered greatly for Christ's sake. James was the first of the Apostles who bore testimony to Christ with his blood (Acts 12:2). And John was exiled to the Isle of Patmos "for the testimony of Jesus Christ" (Revelation 1:9). But there is only one way that it can be truthfully said that these disciples drank the cup of wrath the Lord Jesus drank and were baptized in the sea of woe into which he was baptized. They did so, just as all God's elect did, representatively. In Christ all God's elect are completely and perfectly saved by his representative work as our Substitute.

With regard to the request that they might sit one on his left and the other on his right hand in glory, the Saviour said, "It is not mine to give, but for whom it is prepared of my Father". The words added by our translators, "it shall be given to them", should never have been added. They were added to make the text read more smoothly, but the indication that some will have superiority over others in heavenly glory is totally contrary to everything revealed in holy scripture about that blessed inheritance of grace. All who were given to Christ in the eternal covenant of grace shall come to him in time. And those who, in time, come to him by faith, he "shall in no wise cast out" (John 6:37). This is a matter of absolute certainty, because God the Father has given him, our covenant Surety, "power over all flesh: that he should give eternal life to as many as thou hast given him" (John 17:2). And all who come to him by faith shall sit with him in his throne (Revelation 3:21).

This is the provision our God has prepared for and given to his elect from eternity, as "heirs of God and joint-heirs with Christ" (Romans 8:17). It is the gift of pure, free, sovereign grace, in no measure determined by or dependent upon us. He who gave us his own dear Son gave us all things in his Son, withholding nothing (1 Corinthians 3:22, 23; Ephesians 1:3-7; Psalm 84:11). "Thanks be unto God for his unspeakable gift"!

Jehovah's Servant

Fifth, we see here that the Lord Jesus Christ became a voluntary servant to God the Father in order to accomplish our redemption, subjecting himself in all things to the Father's will. He is God the eternal Son, in all things equal with the Father (1 John 5:7). Yet, he willingly became our Surety and Mediator, Jehovah's Servant, to save us by his obedience to the Father. The law describes a man who would voluntarily make himself a bond servant to his master for life; and that Man is the Lord Jesus Christ our Saviour (Exodus 21:1-6; Isaiah 42:1; John 10:16-18; Philippians 2:1-11; Hebrews 10:1-14).

We understand and rejoice to know that this Servant is himself God, one with the Father in being, glory, and greatness, in all things equal with the Father. In his eternal Deity as God the Son, our Saviour is altogether equal with the Father. But he became a man, became our Surety, became our Mediator, that he might subject himself to and obey his Father's will as a man.

The Son of God cannot possibly be inferior to the Father in his divine nature. If Jesus Christ is God manifest in the flesh, as the scriptures declare, there cannot be, in anyway, an inequality between the Father and the Son. Augustus Toplady, wrote, "The uncreated and eternally begotten Son of the Father Almighty is and must be as truly a divine being as the Father who begat him."

When we read in the scriptures of Christ being the Servant of God, subjecting himself to the will of God, and obeying the commandment of God, we are assured that his servitude is and must be by his own free and voluntary consent. He is indeed Jehovah's Servant; but his service was not a forced subjection. "He gave himself for us, that he might redeem us from all iniquity, and purify unto himself a peculiar people, zealous of good works" (Titus 2:14). "Christ also loved the church, and gave himself for it" (Ephesians 5:25). Our Lord himself declares, "As the Father knoweth me, even so know I the Father: and I lay down my life for the sheep" (John 10:15). From the moment of his birth, until his final breath in this world, the Lord Jesus served. He was ever Jehovah's righteous and faithful Servant. He said to his disciples, "I am among you as he that serveth" (Luke 22:27).

There was a perfect understanding between the Father and the Son from eternity. Let there be no misunderstanding in our own minds. Christ became the Servant of Jehovah by his own will.

"The Lord GOD hath opened mine ear, and I was not rebellious, neither turned away back. I gave my back to the smiters, and my cheeks to them that plucked off the hair: I hid not my face from shame and spitting. For the Lord GOD will help me; therefore shall I not be confounded: therefore have I set my face like a flint, and I know that I shall not be ashamed" (Isaiah 50:5-7).

As he served the will of God for us, let us now serve the will of God for him.

Chapter 58

“Whosoever Will Be Great Among You”

“And when the ten heard it, they were moved with indignation against the two brethren. But Jesus called them unto him, and said, Ye know that the princes of the Gentiles exercise dominion over them, and they that are great exercise authority upon them. But it shall not be so among you: but whosoever will be great among you, let him be your minister; And whosoever will be chief among you, let him be your servant: Even as the Son of man came not to be ministered unto, but to minister, and to give his life a ransom for many.”
(Matthew 20:24-28)

True greatness is exactly the opposite of what the world calls greatness. The world assesses greatness by the number of people under a man’s control, how many are at his beck and call, how much money he has in the bank, how much property is listed under his ownership, how many titles and degrees he has appended to his name, how many committees and boards he is a member of, or how widely his reputation extends. But in the assessment of the Lord Jesus Christ all those things are totally irrelevant. In Matthew 20:24-28, he shows us what true greatness is.

This instructive passage of holy scripture is crystal clear. It needs less explanation, and more emulation by all who “follow the Lamb whithersoever he goeth”. The message of these verses is as plain as the nose on your face. The path to greatness in the kingdom of God is humble service to the people of God.

A Great Problem

The Lord’s disciples, like us, constantly struggled with a very great problem; and that problem was pride. When the rest of the disciples heard what James and John requested for themselves, they were indignant. But their indignation was far from righteous. They were not moved with indignation because they thought such a desire was out of place. They were indignant because each of them thought himself deserving of the high honour James and John openly sought.

The disciples' indignation toward James and John vividly displays the depravity of our fallen nature. No man on earth has ever known, or can know, the vastness of the injury the human race sustained by Satan's seduction of Adam and Eve in the garden of Eden. Every time we think of the depths of our natural depravity, it should inspire us with greater appreciation for the immense, infinite mercy of our Lord Jesus Christ in restoring that which he took not away. The indignation of the disciples toward their brethren demonstrates that God's saints, in this world, dwell in the body of sin and death, though saved by his free grace in Christ. The disciples were men of like passions with ourselves.

The greatest problem we have is pride. It is the root of all sin, the cause of all strife, and the most destructive of all passions. Even among true believers, pride, jealousy, and the love of pre-eminence is a horrible passion that must constantly be held in check. This horrible evil was found among the apostles of our Lord.

The disciples were not upset with James and John because they sought pre-eminence, but because they sought it above them. Like these disciples, we are all very proud and love pre-eminence. We love power, prestige, property, and position. We love them and seek them, because we are all very proud. Pride is the oldest of all sins and the most destructive. Pride inspired Lucifer's revolt (Isaiah 14:12-14). Pride brought down one third of the angels (Jude 6). Pride seduced Eve. Pride destroyed Adam. Pride divides men (Psalm 10:2).

What separates and distinguishes men from one another according to race, rank, riches, and recognition? Pride! What separates families? Pride! What is the cause of war? Pride! Seldom ever do men go to war for principle. We go to war over property and concoct principles to justify our stupid pride.

Even among God's saints in this world, our greatest difficulties, our greatest injures, and our greatest troubles arise from pride. J. C. Ryle quoted Thomas Hooker as saying, "Pride is a vice that cleaveth so fast unto the hearts of men, that if we were to strip ourselves of all faults one by one, we should undoubtedly find it the very last and hardest to put off." It is pride that keeps sinners from seeking the Lord (Psalm 10:4). Of all things named in the Bible that God hates, pride is number one (Proverbs 6:16-19).

A Great Precept

In verses 25-27 we see that a life of self-denying kindness and service to others is the measure of true greatness. The standard of the world and the standard of our Lord are exact opposites. In the kingdom of God a person is considered great who devotes himself to the temporal and the spiritual welfare of others. Greatness is not receiving, but giving. Greatness is not seen in what we gather to ourselves, but in what we dispense to others. Greatness is not being served, but serving.

If we desire to be truly great in the kingdom of God, we must find the place where we are needed and be a minister, a servant to others. The word translated "minister" is the word that is elsewhere translated "deacon". It refers to a person who does menial labour, house cleaning, serving tables, gardening, etc.. It is the least recognized, but the most needed and certainly the most basic service.

If we really want to be great, if we want to be chief, we must make ourselves servants, slaves to the church and kingdom of God. The word "servant" in verse 27 means "slave". A servant does not have much; but a slave has nothing. And this slavery is altogether voluntary. The cost of true greatness is humble, self-denying, sacrificial service. It is service rendered to others for Christ's sake by men and women who have learned that, "It is more blessed to give than to receive" (Acts 20:35).

May God enable us to shun the world's greatness and seek true greatness. The angels of God see far more greatness in the work of a missionary or pastor in some remote, insignificant place, than in all the celebrity of the rich and famous. They see more greatness in a poor widow giving her two mites for the cause of Christ than in all the combined works of bankers, lawyers, doctors, and presidents; and we should, too.

When greatness sees weakness in others, it is moved with compassion. Greatness covers the frailties and acknowledges the strengths it sees in another. Greatness weeps with those who weep, and rejoices with those who rejoice. Greatness overlooks neglect, forgives offence, and returns kindness for injury.

A Great Pattern

If you want an example to follow look to the Lord Jesus Christ himself. "Even as the Son of man came not to be ministered unto, but to minister, and to give his life a ransom for many" (v. 28). Our blessed Redeemer shows us what true greatness is by his own example. "He that saith he abideth in him ought himself also so to walk, even as he walked" (1 John 2:6). He who was Jehovah's righteous Servant was the servant of men (John 13:3-5, 12-17; Luke 22:27). In the circle of his own disciples, our Lord always assumed a position of servitude. Where he was most Master, he was most Servant. He was like a shepherd, the servant to the sheep. He was like a nurse, servant to the child. In the whole course of his life on earth our great God and Saviour took the place of a servant, or slave. If we are the servants of God, we are the servants of men.

Lord, help me to live from day to day
In such a self-forgetful way
That even when I kneel to pray
My prayer shall be for others.
Help me in all the work I do
To ever be sincere and true,
And know that all I'd do for You
Must needs be done for others.
Saviour, help me in all I do
To magnify and copy You.
That I may ever live like You,
Help me to live for others.

A Great Ransom

Not only has the Son of God given us a noble example of self-denying love by his obedience, he has by his sacrifice ransomed us. He gave "his life a ransom for many". The Lord Jesus gave life to ransom, redeem, and deliver God's elect, the many he came to save, from the guilt, curse and condemnation of God's law and justice, and to bring us into "the glorious liberty of the sons of God".

The ransom price he paid was his own precious blood (Ephesians 1:7; 1 Peter 1:18-20; Revelation 5:9). It was paid for "many", and paid for them in particular, as the objects of his special love. The many for whom the Lord gave his life are the many ordained to eternal life (Acts 13:48), those given to him in the covenant of grace (John 6:37-40), for whom Christ makes intercession (John 17:9, 20), who are called by God the Holy Spirit (Revelation 19:9), and who are saved by God's free and sovereign grace (John 1:12, 13). If you would live for Christ, live for others; if you would serve Christ, serve one another. Make Christ the example your life is governed by. Make Christ your rule of life. Here is your motive: you are not your own, you are bought with a price. Glorify God in your body and in your spirit, which are God's (1 Corinthians 6:19, 20). Robert Hawker says,

> How many heart aches would it have saved me in days past, had I learnt of Jesus the humbling lesson he here taught them, in what the growth of grace consists: namely, in being more and more lowly in heart, from a conviction of unworthiness, and more and more to see my need of Jesus.

Chapter 59

The Day The Sun Stood Still

"And as they departed from Jericho, a great multitude followed him. And, behold, two blind men sitting by the way side, when they heard that Jesus passed by, cried out, saying, Have mercy on us, O Lord, thou Son of David. And the multitude rebuked them, because they should hold their peace: but they cried the more, saying, Have mercy on us, O Lord, thou Son of David. And Jesus stood still, and called them, and said, What will ye that I shall do unto you? They say unto him, Lord, that our eyes may be opened. So Jesus had compassion on them, and touched their eyes: and immediately their eyes received sight, and they followed him."
(Matthew 20:29-34)

We read in the tenth chapter of Joshua how that he, by whom the walls of Jericho fell, commanded the sun to stand still in the midst of heaven. At the command of a man "the sun stood still"! We are told, "There was no day like that before it or after it, that the Lord hearkened unto the voice of a man" (Joshua 10:14). But here the Spirit of God inspired Matthew to describe something even more remarkable than that. Matthew tells us about a day when the Sun, not the created star in heaven that Joshua caused to stand still, but Christ the Sun of Righteousness, the Son of God, stood still. As he was coming up out of Jericho on his way to Jerusalem to redeem his people, the Son of God heard two blind beggars crying for mercy. At the sound of their cry, we are told, "Jesus stood still"!

What a wonderful, amazing picture we have before us in these verses! Here is the omnipotent God stopped in his tracks, held fast by two needy souls crying out for mercy. He was on his way to Jerusalem to accomplish the redemption of his people, to fulfil the will of his Father. Nothing could stop him. Nothing could cause him to pause. Nothing could divert him from his work. Herod could not stop him. Satan could not hinder him. The scribes and Pharisees failed in all their efforts to impede him in his determined course. Not even his disciples or his own mother could stop him as he made his way to the appointed place. But two blind beggars crying for mercy; two helpless souls, looking to him for help, believing him, crying to him, stopped the Son of God in his tracks. "Jesus stood still"!

What an encouragement this passage of holy scripture ought to be to any sinner who needs his mercy. It is encouragement to pour out our need to the Lord Jesus Christ. The Son of God will never ignore the cry of a sinner seeking mercy.

Three Miracles

Luke tell us about our Saviour healing one blind man as he approached Jericho (Luke 18:35-43). Here, Matthew tells us that he healed two more blind men, "as they departed from Jericho". Mark was inspired to describe the same event Matthew speaks of; but only mentions the healing of one of these men, a man by the name of "Bartimaeus, the son of Timaeus" (Mark 10:46-52). Obviously, there is no contradiction in inspired accounts of that momentous day. Three blind men were publicly healed by the Son of God as he passed through Jericho on his way to Jerusalem to accomplish our redemption. It is that fact that Matthew, Mark, and Luke were inspired to record for our learning. Here are three great miracles performed by the Lord Jesus Christ, "the Light of the world", as he was going to Calvary to die in the room and stead of poor, blind, helpless sinners.

Gospel Lessons

These things are written not merely to inform us that the Lord Jesus has the power to perform miracles. They are not just to teach us to look to him as the great Physician for the healing of our bodily infirmities; though both things are true. These three great miracles are object lessons, proclaiming the gospel of God's free, omnipotent grace in Christ. May God the Holy Spirit bring the lessons home to our hearts. Robert Hawker suggests four points of instruction:

The mighty miracles were themselves a proof of our Saviour being the Messiah (Isaiah 35:5). The fact that our Lord performed these miracles near Jericho, the cursed city (Joshua 6:26; 1 Kings 16:34), may have reference to what he would accomplish as our Substitute upon the cursed tree. All the blessings of grace come to chosen sinners because the Lord Jesus Christ was made a curse for us, that we might be made the righteousness of God in him (Galatians 3:13; 2 Corinthians 5:21). Hawker further suggested:

> The sovereign act of Jesus, in the freeness and fulness of his mercy, was a testimony of his Godhead; for on the supposition of an eyeless socket, it is not simply giving sight to the blind but a new creation. And who but God himself can do this?

> The conduct of those blind, also hold forth many sweet instructions. They were in the highway begging. It is good to be found in the highway of ordinances, where Jesus passeth by. The cry of those men under a sense of their misery, and Jesus' power afford great lessons to teach men how to pray, and not to faint. But who taught them that Jesus was the Son of David; that is the Messiah which should come? Who indeed, but he to whom they came could lead them to himself?

Faith In Christ

These blind men are, also, great examples of faith in Christ. Faith is frequently found where it is least expected. There were great multitudes who followed the Lord Jesus as he walked along and taught the people, some for loaves and some for love, some out of curiosity and some out of conviction, some for greed and some for grace. But there were few, very few, who believed on Christ. Many saw his miracles, yet believed him not (Matthew 11:20-24; John 2:23, 24). But here are three blind men who had never seen our Lord's miracles. They knew him by hear-say, by the testimony of others. Yet, they believed him. They heard others talking about the Saviour. They heard people in the streets talking about the great works of mercy he performed. Then "they heard that Jesus passed by" (v. 30). Spurgeon called that "blessed gossip". Would to God we had more of it!

We know that faith comes by hearing and hearing by the Word of God (Romans 10:17). It was "when they heard that Jesus passed by" that "they cried out, saying, Have mercy on us, O Lord, thou Son of David". Perhaps they had heard how the Master had healed a blind man on his way into Jericho (Luke 18:35-43). Without question, they had heard who he is. They called him, "Jesus", Saviour, and openly acknowledged him to be both their God and the Messiah.

John Gill tells us the things stated by these men declare their faith in Christ, "calling him 'Lord', expressing their sense of his deity, dominion, and power; and 'Son of David', thereby owning and professing him to be the Messiah" (see Isaiah 35:5; 42:6, 7; 61:1). They looked to him as their God and Saviour, the only One from whom they hoped to obtain mercy. Mercy that only God could perform. They looked to him, hoping that he would cause their blind eyes to see. No doubt, they heard about his mighty miracles of mercy. And they heard that "Jesus passed by". Knowing that he might never pass their way again, they seized the opportunity before them and sought his mercy.

Yes, the cry of these blind men was the cry of faith. They believed on the Son of God. Their faith puts me to shame. I have books of evidence, a library full of good commentaries and books of theology, volumes of biographies. Yet, how little there is of this childlike confidence and faith in Christ! Even among true believers; simple, confident, unhesitating faith is found where we least expect it. The humble soul believes God and walks in peace; while learned, well-read theologians are often harassed with doubts and questions.

Use Of Means

The blind men healed by our Saviour along the Jericho road clearly teach us that sinners in need of mercy ought to avail themselves of every means of good to their souls. I know that God is sovereign. I know that salvation is of the Lord. I know that every chosen, redeemed sinner shall be saved. I am fully aware of these facts. Yet, the scriptures teach us that every man is responsible for his own soul. We are responsible to use the means of grace God gives us. When these two blind men heard that "Jesus passed by", they were found "sitting by the way".

What wisdom they displayed! They took up a hopeful position "by the way". There they would be likely to hear any good news that might be spread among the people. There they were most likely to meet with and be seen by the compassionate One. Though they were blind, they were not deaf; and they used what they had for good.

Do not forsake the assembly of God's saints and the preaching of the gospel (Hebrews 10:25). Do not forsake the reading of holy scripture (2 Timothy 3:15). Do not forsake private prayer (Luke 18:1). These are God's ordained means of grace. To despise them is to despise his grace. To neglect them is to neglect his grace. To use them is to be in the path of mercy (Matthew 18:20).

Blessed Violence

These blind men seem to be vivid examples of our Saviour's doctrine in Matthew 11:12. As "the kingdom of heaven suffereth violence", so "the violent take it by force". These men were earnest. They needed mercy. They wanted to see. Therefore, though they were rebuked by the crowd, who urged them to be quiet, they held on, like Jacob of old (Genesis 32:26). We ought to be just as earnest before the throne of grace. Such importunity is the fruit of great need before God, knowing that he can supply the mercy needed (Hebrews 4:16). It is the forerunner of the mercy itself (Luke 11: 8-13). Hawker again says,

> And do thou blessed Master and Lord, give the grace to thy children, both to be sensible of our spiritual blindness; and to be as earnest in the cry of the soul for deliverance from it: and may that grace of thine in our hearts be more powerful to lead to thee, than all the world, or sin, or unbelief, to keep from thee. But may all thy redeemed, though blinded by sin, be so taught by grace, that they may besiege thy throne night and day, until the Lord hath heard and answered prayer; and then follow thee in the regeneration, 'beholding with open face, as in a glass, the glory of the Lord, and be changed into the same image, from glory to glory, even as by the spirit of the Lord' (2 Corinthians 3:18).

These men needed mercy. They knew that Christ could give them the mercy they needed. They knew that they might never get this opportunity again. Consequently, the opposition they met with was hardly noticed by them. Rather, "they cried the more, saying, Have mercy on us O Lord, thou Son of David"!

Christ's Compassion

We read, first, that "Jesus passed by". What a marvellous picture this is of God's prevenient grace! These men were born blind, that they might be found "sitting by the wayside" on that day when "Jesus passed by". Then, "Jesus stood still". He "made a full stop, when he was near, or right against where these blind men sat. Which shows the strength of faith, the force of prayer, and the great regard Christ has to both" says John Gill. Then, he "called them". He called them personally, them and only them, and said, "What will ye that I shall do unto you?" They answered, "Lord, that our eyes may be opened".

"So Jesus had compassion on them". He who stood still, when he heard their plaintive cry, was moved to his heart with pity for them. Their need drew forth his tenderness; and he "touched their eyes". "And immediately their eyes received sight". With all the ease of omnipotent divinity, the Son of God caused these poor, blind men to see. How merciful our Saviour is to our souls! Truly, "the love of Christ passeth knowledge" (Ephesians 3:19). Faith always gets what it seeks from him! Having obtained mercy, "they followed him". He who gave sight to their eyes gave life to their souls, and they followed him. May God ever give us eyes to see and hearts to desire our Saviour, that we may follow him by faith here, until, with open vision, we shall see him as he is and dwell with him forever.

Chapter 60

"Who Is This?"

"And when they drew nigh unto Jerusalem, and were come to Bethphage, unto the mount of Olives, then sent Jesus two disciples, Saying unto them, Go into the village over against you, and straightway ye shall find an ass tied, and a colt with her: loose them, and bring them unto me. And if any man say ought unto you, ye shall say, The Lord hath need of them; and straightway he will send them. All this was done, that it might be fulfilled which was spoken by the prophet, saying, Tell ye the daughter of Sion, Behold, thy King cometh unto thee, meek, and sitting upon an ass, and a colt the foal of an ass. And the disciples went, and did as Jesus commanded them, And brought the ass, and the colt, and put on them their clothes, and they set him thereon. And a very great multitude spread their garments in the way; others cut down branches from the trees, and strawed them in the way. And the multitudes that went before, and that followed, cried, saying, Hosanna to the Son of David: Blessed is he that cometh in the name of the Lord; Hosanna in the highest. And when he was come into Jerusalem, all the city was moved, saying, Who is this? And the multitude said, This is Jesus the prophet of Nazareth of Galilee."
(Matthew 21:1-11)

These verses of scripture, at first glance, appear to be out of sync with the rest of our Lord's earthly life. The narrative reads like the account of some royal conqueror returning to his own city. "A great multitude" swelled quickly to "multitudes", accompanying the Lord Jesus Christ in what is described as his "triumphal entry" into Jerusalem. Loud cries of praise and expressions of adulation rang through the air. "All the city was moved." Everyone wanted to know, "Who is this?"

Everything in these eleven verses seems to run counter the whole tenor of our Lord's earthly life and ministry. It seems to be altogether unlike him who would not cry, nor strive, nor lift up his voice in the streets. He always withdrew from the crowd, hid from applause, and urged those who were healed by his power to tell no one what he had done for them.

Yet, our Lord's public, triumphal entry into Jerusalem at this time is just what we should expect to see. He knew well that the hour of his death, the hour of his glory, the hour of his manifestation was near. The time of his humiliation and earthly ministry was drawing to a close. The hour was rapidly approaching when he must finish the work he had come into this world to do. His last great, climactic work was before him. There was nothing left for him to do except make atonement for and redeem his people by the sacrifice of himself upon the cursed tree. Having assumed our nature, and having fulfilled all other things written in the Book of God concerning him, the Lord Jesus must now finish his work; he must fulfil all righteousness by his sin-atoning death. Now, he must satisfy justice and put away our sins by the sacrifice of himself.

He deemed it proper that every eye should be fixed upon him as he came to be offered up as the Lamb of God. He would have his great work of redemption known and advertised by everyone in Jerusalem. The sin atoning blood of the Son of God was about to be shed. And this great deed was not to be "done in a corner" (Acts 26:26). Therefore, he who had deliberately spent most of his life in secrecy, secluded from public view; he who would not allow his admirers to make him a king, now comes to announce himself King in the most public manner imaginable. His death would be his entrance into his kingdom. Therefore, he made a royal procession through the streets of Jerusalem. This royal procession was our Lord's public declaration that he is indeed the Christ of God, and that he was about to enter into his kingdom.

All four of the Gospel writers were inspired of God to describe our Lord's triumphal entrance into Jerusalem five days before his death, verifying the prophecies of Isaiah and Zechariah (Isaiah 62:11; Zechariah 9:9). We should not fail to observe the fact that none but Christ ever made such an entrance. The conclusion to be drawn from that fact is obvious and undeniable: This is the Christ, Zion's King, of whom all the prophets spoke!

The Omniscient God

All the city asked, "Who is this?" The answers to that question were before them, and are clearly set before us in this passage. This King is distinguished from all others in that he made his entrance in humility. Yet, as he did, he demonstrated both his omniscience and sovereignty as our great God. Truly, this man, "Jesus of Nazareth", is himself God who sees all, knows all, and rules all. He ordered two of his disciples to go into a specific village nearby, where they would find an ass and her colt. Then, he said, "Loose them, and bring them", assuring them that the owner would immediately surrender his property to them for his sake.

"The Lord hath need". I am sure that those four words have a far greater depth of meaning and significance than I am able to grasp. But that which is obvious is profoundly instructive. Taking upon himself our nature, our blessed Saviour, while he was in this world, was a man full of needs, yet, he never relinquished his deity in the least. He had need of the animals, yet, he exercised absolute sovereignty over them and their owner. He sovereignly requisitioned this man's property and made him perfectly willing to comply with the request.

Obedience To Christ

"All this was done … And the disciples went, and did as Jesus commanded them" (vv. 4 and 6). To all human reason, the Lord's orders to these disciples would appear terribly difficult, even dangerous. They might be taken for thieves and dealt with accordingly. Yet, the disciples obeyed the Master without the least hesitancy, completely trusting him to prepare the way before them and make them successful in their task. That is the way we ought to obey our Lord. If he sends us on an errand in his name, he will both prepare our way and make us successful in performing the work to which he sends us. Obedience to Christ must be unquestioning and unhesitating. Genuine obedience, that obedience which arises from true faith, must be blind obedience (John 2:5; Proverbs 3:5-10).

Scripture Fulfilled

"All this was done", not because our Lord Jesus was incapable of walking the distance to Jerusalem, but "that it might be fulfilled which was spoken by the prophet". Then, our Lord Jesus puts two Old Testament passages together (Isaiah 62:11; Zechariah 9:9).

"Behold, the LORD hath proclaimed unto the end of the world, Say ye to the daughter of Zion, Behold, thy salvation cometh; behold, his reward is with him, and his work before him" (Isaiah 62:11).

"Rejoice greatly, O daughter of Zion; shout, O daughter of Jerusalem: behold, thy King cometh unto thee: he is just, and having salvation; lowly, and riding upon an ass, and upon a colt the foal of an ass" (Zechariah 9:9).

The Bible is, without question, the Word of God, fully and perfectly inspired and without error (2 Timothy 3:16, 17; 1 Peter 1:20). Zechariah's prophecy made more than 550 years earlier; is here fulfilled in every detail. Once more, we see a clear example of the complete harmony of the Old and New Testament scriptures.

“Hosanna”

In verses 5-9 Matthew shows that the Lord Jesus Christ is King over all things by virtue of his obedience to God as our Substitute (John 17:2; Romans 14:9; Ephesians 1:21, 22; Philippians 2:9-11). Let us ever worship and obey him as our great King. Let us ever throw off our filthy garments of self-righteousness before him and worship him, saying, “Hosanna to the son of David: Blessed is he that cometh in the name of the Lord; Hosanna in the highest”!

The word “Hosanna” is an exclamation of adoration and praise; but it is more. The word means “save me”. We worship and adore Christ as Saviour only when we bow to him as our King; and we bow to him as our King only when we worship and trust him as our Saviour, laying all at his feet. As the multitudes “spread their garments in the way” and “cut down branches from the trees, and strawed them in the way” before the Lord, let us also bow before our King.

Robert Hawker suggested, “The Feast of Tabernacles was so celebrated, to denote holy joy in the gathering in of all the Lord’s blessings; and some have thought, that this feast was particularly typical of this entry of the Lord Jesus; for it is somewhat remarkable, that at this feast they carried branches, which they called Hosannas”.

“Who Is This?”

“And when he was come into Jerusalem, all the city was moved, saying, Who is this? And the multitude said, This is Jesus the prophet of Nazareth of Galilee” (vv. 10, 11). Our Saviour had been here before; but never had such enthusiastic crowds surrounded him with acclamations of praise. It seems that they were moved by some secret impulse to go out to meet the King who came into their streets. Perhaps it was nothing more than curiosity. Perhaps they had only some passing interest. Whatever their motives, the Lord’s appearance here stirred the whole city to such a degree that “all the city was moved, saying, Who is this?”

“Who is this?” No better, more needful question was ever raised. Let none find rest until he knows in the experience of faith that “this is Jesus the prophet of Nazareth”, until he is made to know that this man, who is God our Saviour and King, is the Nazarite of God, who has fulfilled all the will of God as the sinner’s Substitute, by whom alone all the blessings of God come upon men (Numbers 6:1-27). I do not suggest that the majority of this multitude had any real idea what they were saying. Yet, like Caiaphas the high priest (John 11:49-52), they identified the Lord Jesus Christ as Jehovah’s righteous Servant and our Mediator, the only true Nazarite of God.

Chapter 61

The House Of Prayer

"And Jesus went into the temple of God, and cast out all them that sold and bought in the temple, and overthrew the tables of the moneychangers, and the seats of them that sold doves, And said unto them, It is written, My house shall be called the house of prayer; but ye have made it a den of thieves. And the blind and the lame came to him in the temple; and he healed them. And when the chief priests and scribes saw the wonderful things that he did, and the children crying in the temple, and saying, Hosanna to the Son of David; they were sore displeased, And said unto him, Hearest thou what these say? And Jesus saith unto them, Yea; have ye never read, Out of the mouth of babes and sucklings thou hast perfected praise? And he left them, and went out of the city into Bethany; and he lodged there. Now in the morning as he returned into the city, he hungered. And when he saw a fig tree in the way, he came to it, and found nothing thereon, but leaves only, and said unto it, Let no fruit grow on thee henceforward for ever. And presently the fig tree withered away. And when the disciples saw it, they marvelled, saying, How soon is the fig tree withered away! Jesus answered and said unto them, Verily I say unto you, If ye have faith, and doubt not, ye shall not only do this which is done to the fig tree, but also if ye shall say unto this mountain, Be thou removed, and be thou cast into the sea; it shall be done. And all things, whatsoever ye shall ask in prayer, believing, ye shall receive."
(Matthew 21:12-22)

This passage of holy scripture sets before us two of the most remarkable events in our Lord's earthly life and ministry. They are remarkable in that they are displays of the wrath and judgment of almighty God. Judgment is God's strange work. Therefore, our Lord's works primarily display the love, mercy, grace and goodness of God toward sinners. But judgment is as truly the work of God as redemption. Christ came both to redeem and save his people and to establish judgment in the earth (Isaiah 42:4) Usually, we see him displaying works and miracles of mercy. But here we see him displaying wrath and judgment. Both in driving the moneychangers out of the temple and in cursing the fruitless fig-tree, our Saviour shows his willingness and his power to execute judgment.

Both of these acts of judgment are emblems of spiritual things. Both were eminently figurative and typical. J. C. Ryle said, "Beneath the surface of each lie lessons of solemn instruction". Yet, in the midst of wrath, our Lord remembers mercy. How like him that is! He drove out the moneychangers; but he healed the needy. He refused the services of the priests, but accepted the praises of children. He left the cavilling scribes, but went to his friends in Bethany. He who is our God and Saviour is both furious in wrath and glorious in goodness.

As we go through these verses together, I want you to see seven things here recorded by divine inspiration for our comfort, learning, and edification.

The Cleansing Of The Temple

We saw our Lord do a similar thing in the beginning of his ministry (John 2:14, 15). During those days the temple of God, the priesthood, and all the ordinances of divine worship had degenerated into a sham, a show and a pretence. Religion was nothing but an outward service. Religious leaders were money-grubbing, self-serving professionals who, like most religious leaders today, made a business out of doing what men call "the work of the ministry", and "the work of God".

When our Lord came into the temple, he found the house built in God's name where God's glory was once revealed, where sacrifice was made and the law of God expounded, disgracefully profaned. Everything was out of order. Our Lord saw it all with utter indignation. In fury, he drove out the religious merchandisers, who callously made a profit on God.

This is a vivid display of our Saviour's holy sovereignty and power in judgment. Among all the miracles our Lord performed, this must be viewed as one of the clearest displays of his eternal Godhead. Here is a man, the most humble man who ever lived, casting out those who bought and sold in the temple, overthrowing the tables of the moneychangers and the seats of them that sold doves. He did this with such authority and zeal that no one dared oppose him. When he publicly announced that he had done this as God, publicly claiming that he was himself God, calling the temple "My house", no one raised a voice of objection. What an invincible proof this is of his divinity! No one resisted him or his claim. So shall it be in the day of judgment. When the Son of God comes to judge the wicked, none shall be able to resist him (Malachi 3:2).

There is a day coming when the Son of God will purge and cleanse his church and temple thoroughly. "He shall thoroughly purge his floor". In that day, all chaff shall be burned. All the wood, hay, and stubble of man's works shall be consumed with the fire of his holy wrath.

The Church of God, the assembly of God's saints in public worship is a place of worship, "the house of prayer" (Isaiah 56:7). "Prayer" is the worship of God and in the worship of God, small things matter (1 Chronicles 15:13). It is an act of abomination to make it anything else. Every true local church, every assembly of men and women in the name of Christ, is the house of God (1 Timothy 3:15). This is the place where Christ meets his people (Matthew 18:20). This is the place of worship. There is no room in the house of God for anything except the worship of God. Worship involves preaching the gospel, prayer and praise, the reading of his Word, the attentive hearing of his Word, and the observance of the gospel ordinances of believer's baptism and the Lord's supper. Anything else is out of place in God's house.

The Compassion Of Our Saviour

"And the blind and the lame came to him in the temple; and he healed them" (v. 14). It is ever the character of our God that in wrath he remembers mercy. When the blind and the lame came to him for healing, "he healed them". Do not imagine that our Saviour is not merciful because he is just and true. He has no tolerance for religious con-men and hucksters; but he is full of compassion to needy souls. Never did anyone come to him for mercy, while he walked on this earth, who did not obtain the mercy sought. And he has not changed. All who seek mercy from him obtain mercy.

The place of mercy is still the temple of God, the divinely appointed place of worship, the church and house of God. I once came into God's house as a blind, lame, helpless soul. There, in the house of worship, the Son of God healed me. In that place where his word is preached, I obtained mercy from him, and left the house healed, and praising God my Saviour. If you want mercy, put yourself in the place where mercy is found. If you are interested in others obtaining mercy, get them to the place where Christ dispenses mercy.

The Children's Confession

"The children crying in the temple" (v. 15) is another remarkable display of our Saviour's divinity. When our Lord Jesus received worship from these children in the house of God, his acceptance of their praise was an open claim that he is God. He, as well as those in the temple, knew that this cry, "Hosanna to the Son of David", was praise reserved for no one but the Messiah.

When the priests and scribes heard the praise of these children, and saw the Saviour's wonderful works of mercy, they were furious. Nothing that glorifies the Lord Jesus escapes the eyes of religious legalists and ritualists. Wherever Christ alone is honoured as Saviour, religionists are soon in a rage. Ecclesiastical pretenders are enraged by the simple preaching of Christ crucified, which is the constant exaltation of Christ in his house.

How can the praise of these children be accounted for, except by the fact that their minds were seized and ruled by divine power, and sweetly forced to bear testimony to our Saviour? This singular, unified act of adoration and praise from the children of those men our Lord had just thrown out of the temple, and of the scribes, chief priests, and Pharisees standing before him, cannot be accounted for any other way. They did not learn what they heard confessed from their parents. They learned who Christ was and how to praise him, being taught of God himself (John 6:45).

Religionists Confused

The Jews were quick to accuse the children, but the Lord rose to their defence. "And Jesus saith unto them, Yea; have ye never read, Out of the mouth of babes and sucklings thou hast perfected praise?" (v. 16). The chief priests and scribes were amazed, as well as angered by the fact that our Lord accepted the simple, sincere praise of children, and showed utter contempt for their ornate, gaudy, well prepared services. They were confused because they understood nothing concerning the things of God. They did not understand that worship is spiritual, a matter of the heart (Isaiah 1:10-20; Philippians 3:2, 3; Luke 16:14, 15).[9]

True religion is not man centred, but Christ centred. True religion is not ceremonial, but spiritual. True religion is not a matter of creed, but of conviction. True religion is not outward, but inward. "For we are the circumcision". We are God's true, covenant people, the Israel of God, Abraham's true children, who "worship God in the Spirit". We worship God as he is revealed in the scriptures, by the power of his Holy Spirit, in our spirits, and in a spiritual manner. True worship is spiritual worship, not carnal, ceremonial ritualism (John 4:23, 24). "And rejoice in Christ Jesus". We trust the Lord Jesus Christ alone, placing all our confidence in him as our Saviour, with joy. We are complete in him (1

---

[9] In Isaiah 1:10-20, the prophet describes just how abominable and meaningless Israel's worship had become. So much so that God calls his nation Sodom and likens it to Gomorrah. How much more so today when sodomy is tolerated and even openly approved in many parts of the visible church.

Corinthians 1:30, 31; Colossians 2:9, 10). “And have no confidence in the flesh”. We place absolutely no confidence in our flesh, the experiences, emotions, or (imaginary) excellencies of our flesh. The privileges of the flesh, the feelings of the flesh, and the works of the flesh are no basis for confidence before God. Christ alone is our confidence and joy. To lost religionists, that is utterly infuriating and confusing.

The Contrast

What a contrast there is in verse 17! The Lord Jesus left these cavilling religionists to themselves, and went to Bethany. No greater judgment can befall human beings on this earth than for the Lord of Glory to leave them to themselves! But, there is always a remnant, according to the election of grace, to whom he ever comes in mercy. Do you remember who lived in Bethany? He went to the home of Mary and Martha, and their brother Lazarus. Because he loved them, he went to lodge with them. What a blessing!

Our Master despised the company of quibbling religionists. Because he knew that debate with them was useless he left them to themselves. We would be wise to follow his example. In Bethany, in the home of his friends, the Friend of sinners was at home. Spurgeon wrote, “A day of excitement was followed by an evening of retirement in a country home. He spent the night of that most eventful day with his faithful friends. What a contrast between his entry into Jerusalem and his visit to his friends at Bethany! Lord, lodge with me! Make my house thine abode”. Let us pray the same.

The Fig Tree Cursed

The fig tree is an unusual fruit tree. It first bears fruit and then puts forth its leaves. Most fruit trees put forth their leaves and then their fruit. So when the Saviour came, he saw leaves on the tree, a sign that it had put forth fruit early, but there was none. Having shown us clear displays of his deity, our Saviour here shows us his real humanity. “He hungered”.

The Saviour’s curse upon this barren fig tree is a picture of God’s coming judgment upon all who have a form of godliness but no substance of life, no fruit of grace. It was, no doubt, as Robert Hawker wrote, our Saviour’s intention in this miracle “to preach by it to the people. The leaves of mere profession, without fruit from Christ, will not satisfy in the day of enquiry. Nothing short of union with Christ’s person, can bring behind it communion and interest in what belongs to Christ”. He cursed the fig tree, and it withered. Is your religion all leaves?

Prayer And Faith

Clearly, these words in verses 21 and 22 had specific reference to those men to whom our Lord Jesus gave the power to perform miracles in that apostolic age. There are none who have such gifts in this age. Yet, the Lord's instruction here is for us. In these two verses our Saviour teaches us great lessons about prayer. Prayer involves faith in Christ, confidence in him, and confidence in God's revelation of his will. And prayer involves submission to and seeking the will of God (John 14:13, 14; James 4:3; 1 John 5:14).

I do not pretend to understand all that our Lord teaches us here. However, I am confident that his instructions in these two verses are to be understood in connection with everything we have seen in this passage, and have a particular reference to the withered fig tree. Believing him, his church shall see the barren systems of false religion wither away. Babylon shall fall before us. The gates of hell shall never prevail against us. The obstructing mountains of difficulty shall be removed, and cast into the sea. How often we have seen it; and we shall yet see it! Those who do not know and trust our Saviour consider his words here unbelievable. Those who know him, to whom he has given, as Mark puts it, "faith in God", know they are words filled with hope, and inspire expectation (Revelation 18:2; 19:1-7).

Chapter 62

Two Questions And A Parable

"And when he was come into the temple, the chief priests and the elders of the people came unto him as he was teaching, and said, By what authority doest thou these things? and who gave thee this authority? And Jesus answered and said unto them, I also will ask you one thing, which if ye tell me, I in like wise will tell you by what authority I do these things. The baptism of John, whence was it? from heaven, or of men? And they reasoned with themselves, saying, If we shall say, From heaven; he will say unto us, Why did ye not then believe him? But if we shall say, Of men; we fear the people; for all hold John as a prophet. And they answered Jesus, and said, We cannot tell. And he said unto them, Neither tell I you by what authority I do these things. But what think ye? A certain man had two sons; and he came to the first, and said, Son, go work to day in my vineyard. He answered and said, I will not: but afterward he repented, and went. And he came to the second, and said likewise. And he answered and said, I go, sir: and went not. Whether of them twain did the will of his father? They say unto him, The first. Jesus saith unto them, Verily I say unto you, That the publicans and the harlots go into the kingdom of God before you. For John came unto you in the way of righteousness, and ye believed him not: but the publicans and the harlots believed him: and ye, when ye had seen it, repented not afterward, that ye might believe him."
(Matthew 21:23-32)

The passage we have before us begins the last three days of our Lord's earthly ministry prior to his arrest in Gethsemane. It is simply astonishing to consider how much work our Saviour pressed into those three days. All that is recorded from Matthew 21:23 through chapter 25, all that is recorded by Luke in chapters 20, 21, and 22, and all that we read in John's gospel from chapters 12 through 18 was done in those last three days before his arrest. His food and drink was to do his Father's will. What an example he has given us! May God give us grace to follow it as men and women who know that "time is short".

In these verses we see the priests and elders of the people, the religious leaders of the day, attempting to discredit the ministry of the Son of God. These bitter enemies of righteousness, these bitter, envious, insecure, religious men swarmed around the Son of God like a swarm of bees, trying to find some weakness in him. The question by which he silenced their quibbles, and the parable by which our Master forced them to condemn themselves are by divine inspiration here recorded for our comfort, learning, and admonition. May God the Holy Spirit, who inspired Matthew to write these words, inscribe their lessons upon our hearts.

Satan's Strategy

The question raised by our Lord's adversaries demonstrates the fact that Satan's strategy never changes. While the Lord Jesus was preaching the gospel in the temple (Luke 20:1), the chief priests, with the scribes and elders, rudely blurted out, "By what authority doest thou these things; and who gave thee this authority?" (Mark 11:27, 28).

Their obvious insinuation was that our Saviour obtained his power to perform the miracles he had performed from Satan. From the beginning of time, Satan's most constant weapon against Christ and his people has been slander. Eve was seduced by the serpent's slander of God's character. Once the Lord God was discredited in her eyes, she was snared. Whenever it is impossible to disprove the work of God or deny the truth of God, Satan's weapon of choice is to discredit the messenger of God by slander.

These hell-inspired religionists could not refute our Lord's doctrine nor deny his power. The fig tree withered before their eyes! They could not find fault with his life or the lives of his disciples. The only way to defend themselves and justify their opposition to the Son of God was to discredit him by casting some slander upon him. Often they slandered the Saviour by his association with sinners; but here they attempted to discredit his authority. They ignored the good he did healing the sick, cleansing the temple, raising the dead, and teaching the people the Word of God, and quibbled about his authority to do what he did.

Commenting on the actions of these men, J. C. Ryle observed, "Too many care nothing for the manifest blessings of God upon a man's work, so long as he is not sent forth by their own sect or party." These religious leaders had all the right credentials; but they knew nothing of the power of God. The Lord Jesus had no earthly credentials; but his words and works manifested the very wisdom and omnipotence of God. Credentials, degrees, and letters of authority mean nothing in the church and kingdom of God. Any man who is being used of God can expect to be the object of hellish slander. Wolves never attack a painted sheep, only living ones. Even so, artificial preachers are rarely the objects of spite, ridicule, and persecution, but faithful ones.

The pope offered to make Luther a cardinal if he would just keep quiet. Luther refused. Then men called him a proud fool. He said, “Let me be counted fool or anything, but I will not be guilty of cowardly silence.” When the papists could not silence him, they said, “Luther is an apostate”. Luther replied, “I am an apostate, but a blessed and holy apostate, one that has fallen off from the devil”! When men said, “Martin Luther is a devil”, he replied, “So be it. Luther is a devil; but Christ liveth and reigneth. That is enough for Luther.”

The most common accusations by which God’s servants are slandered today are the same as were hurled against the Son of God. Many are ridiculed because they lack the backing of recognized religious leaders, or impressive academic degrees. William Huntington, always signed his name “William Huntington, S.S.”. He once said, “The degree S.S., or sinner saved, is more needful to teach others than an M.A. or a D.D.”. Commenting on that degree, Spurgeon said, “Huntingdon’s degree of S.S., or Sinner Saved, is more needful for a soul winning evangelist than either M.A. or D.D. The pardoned sinner’s matter will be good, for he has been taught in the school of experience, and his manner will be telling, for he will speak sympathetically, as one who has felt what he declares.”

Others are slandered by name-calling. Gospel preachers are often called antinomians. In the religious world no one is so quickly identified as wicked as that one against whom the charge of “Antinomianism” is laid. But, the fact is, no man ever preached the gospel of God’s free and sovereign grace who was not accused of antinomianism! Pharisees accused our Lord of being a glutton and a drunk. Legalists accused Paul of teaching, “Let us sin, that grace may abound”.

When wicked men, religious or irreligious, cannot refute that which is taught by another, slander is the tool they most commonly use to discredit the man. Nothing in this world is more base, more vile, more hellish and demonic than gossip and slander! Slander comes from an evil heart (Luke 6:45). It is characteristic of Satan, the slanderer (Revelation 12:10). Slanderers are wicked, base hypocrites (Psalm 50:19, 20; Proverbs 11:9). Slander inflicts deadly wounds (Proverbs 18:8), stirs up strife and separates friends (Proverbs 16:28; 17:9). It causes discord among brethren (Proverbs 6:19). The tongue of slander is a scourge (Job 5:21) that is venomous (Psalm 140:3; Ecclesiastes 10:11) and destructive (Proverbs 11:9).

Believer's Baptism

Our Saviour's question in verses 24 to 27, by which he confounded the religious quibblers, clearly teaches us that believer's baptism is a divine ordinance. If they had been honest the question which our Lord put before these men would have been very simple to answer. But they were not honest men. Though they pretended to serve God, they were men-pleasers. And men-pleasers are like politicians. They never commit themselves to anything until they know which way the wind is blowing and what the political cost will be.

Obviously, our Lord could easily have answered their question. He had already told them many times who he was and by what authority he acted. But now he shakes off the dust of his feet against them. He showed his contempt for them publicly because they were public men. We must always be ready to give answer to anyone who desires to know the reason of our hope (1 Peter 3:15). We ought never shrink from any inquiry from people seeking to understand gospel doctrine or practices. Yet, our Saviour's example plainly shows us that we have no obligation to answer the cavilling complaints of those who oppose the gospel.

Our Master's primary instruction in this question was for the benefit of his disciples. The ministry of John the Baptist, particularly his practice of immersing those who professed repentance toward God, was a matter of great controversy in those days, just as believer's baptism is today. Here, our Lord Jesus teaches us that John's baptism was of heavenly origin. John Gill wrote, "By 'the baptism of John' is meant the ordinance of water-baptism, which was first administered by him." No one had ever done anything like this before. Believer's baptism began to be practised by divine ordinance with the ministry of John the Baptist.

Many talk about baptism as a matter of choice, or indifference. It is neither. Believer's baptism is a divine ordinance essential in the worship of God. This gospel ordinance is so clearly taught in scripture that any confusion about it is inexcusable. Baptism is for believers only (Acts 8:37, 38). Infant baptism has no foundation in the Word of God. Baptism is by immersion only (Matthew 3:15-17). Immersion is not the "mode" of baptism, it is baptism. It is what the word means. Baptism is a symbolic burial and resurrection (Romans 6:3-6; Colossians 2:12). Until you can bury a corpse by throwing a few grains of sand on its face, you cannot baptize a person by throwing a few drops of water on their head. Baptism is a symbolic picture of the gospel (Romans 6:4-6). It is not a picture of regeneration, or of circumcision, or of renewal, or of cleansing. It is a picture of redemption, a picture of death, burial, and resurrection with Christ our Substitute.

God's Saving Grace

In the parable about the two sons (vv. 28-32), our Saviour teaches us that the Lord our God graciously saves every penitent sinner, even the most base and vile. This parable is very brief, but very instructive. All who are wise will learn what it teaches. All men belong to God. God is not the Father of all men in a gracious, covenant way; but he is the Father of all and the Owner of all as the Creator of all (Matthew 20:15). As the sovereign Owner of all, God almighty has the right to do what he will with all. And he has chosen some to salvation and passed by others, loved some and hated others (Romans 9:13-18).

All men are commanded to repent (Acts 17:30, 31). In the Word of God, and particularly in this passage (vv. 28, 29, 32), repentance, obedience, and faith are used synonymously. Repentance is neither more nor less than faith in Christ; and faith in Christ is neither more nor less than obedience to him as Lord. We preach the gospel to all, and call all who hear our voices to faith in Christ. Because God commands all to repent, all who hear the gospel are responsible to repent.

And the Lord our God is infinitely willing and able to save every sinner who bows to his dear Son, the Lord Jesus Christ, in true repentance and faith. It matters not how bad the sinner has been. All who believe on the Lord Jesus Christ shall be saved. It matters not how good you appear to be, or imagine yourself to be, if you do not trust the Son of God, you must perish forever. God is no respecter of persons. None are too bad to be saved; but many are too good in their own eyes to be saved.

Robert Hawker wrote, "From our Lord's giving the preference to publicans and harlots, to that of self-righteous scribes and Pharisees, we may safely conclude that nothing was more offensive to the Lord of life and glory, than a frame of mind which, of all others, is more immediately levelled against the leading doctrines of his gospel. Oh! for grace to be always aware of the leaven of the scribes and Pharisees, which the Son of God himself declares to be hypocrisy (Luke 12:1)". In the day of judgment I would rather stand before God as a publican, or a harlot, or anything, rather than stand before him as a self-righteous hypocrite (Romans 9:31-10:4). Beware of self-righteousness!

When you are slandered let it have no effect upon you, except to drive you into your Father's arms. If you would be saved, you must "believe on the Lord Jesus Christ". If God has saved you, if he has given you faith in Christ, confess him in believer's baptism.

Chapter 63

The Parable Of The Wicked Husbandmen

"Hear another parable: There was a certain householder, which planted a vineyard, and hedged it round about, and digged a winepress in it, and built a tower, and let it out to husbandmen, and went into a far country: And when the time of the fruit drew near, he sent his servants to the husbandmen, that they might receive the fruits of it. And the husbandmen took his servants, and beat one, and killed another, and stoned another. Again, he sent other servants more than the first: and they did unto them likewise. But last of all he sent unto them his son, saying, They will reverence my son. But when the husbandmen saw the son, they said among themselves, This is the heir; come, let us kill him, and let us seize on his inheritance. And they caught him, and cast him out of the vineyard, and slew him. When the lord therefore of the vineyard cometh, what will he do unto those husbandmen? They say unto him, He will miserably destroy those wicked men, and will let out his vineyard unto other husbandmen, which shall render him the fruits in their seasons. Jesus saith unto them, Did ye never read in the scriptures, The stone which the builders rejected, the same is become the head of the corner: this is the Lord's doing, and it is marvellous in our eyes? Therefore say I unto you, The kingdom of God shall be taken from you, and given to a nation bringing forth the fruits thereof. And whosoever shall fall on this stone shall be broken: but on whomsoever it shall fall, it will grind him to powder. And when the chief priests and Pharisees had heard his parables, they perceived that he spake of them. But when they sought to lay hands on him, they feared the multitude, because they took him for a prophet."
(Matthew 21:33-46).

The parable contained in these verses was spoken by our Saviour to the Jews and applies directly to that nation upon which the judgment of God has fallen. They are the husbandmen described in the parable. Their sins are set before us in plain words. They persecuted God's prophets. They killed other prophets. And, at last, they murdered God's darling Son! There can be no doubt that the parable was directly intended to be a word of condemnation against the Jewish nation. "When the chief priests and Pharisees had heard his parable, they perceived that he spake of them" (v. 45). But it is a serious mistake for anyone to read these words and say, "That applies to the Jews. It has no reference to me."

"A godly man", wrote John Trapp, "reads the scriptures as he doth the statute-book. He holds himself concerned in all that he reads. He finds his name written in every passage and lays it to heart, as spoken to him. The wicked, on the other side, put off all they like not, and dispose of it to others." Let us not be so foolish. The parable of the wicked husbandmen is a parable by which the Son of God speaks to us. "He that hath an ear, let him hear". The Jews who heard this parable fall from the lips of the Son of God refused to heed its lessons. Therefore that nation is to this day under the curse of God's holy wrath and just judgment. When they had the light, they refused to walk in the light. Therefore God has sent blindness and darkness upon them. Let us beware lest the same thing happen to us. "If God spared not the natural branches, take heed lest he also spare not thee" (Romans 11:21).

The message of this parable is obvious. It warns us of the danger of despising gospel privileges. Those who despise the privileges of the gospel court the wrath of God.

A Word Of Warning

The nation of Israel, and the blindness God has sent upon that reprobate nation that was once so greatly blessed of God, stands as a beacon to warn all who despise his goodness. God almighty sovereignly and graciously bestows upon some very great opportunities and privileges, and withholds them from others, as he sees fit (Matthew 11:20-26; Acts 16:6, 7). He chose Israel alone to be a peculiar people unto himself. He separated Israel from all other nations. He counted the Jews alone to be his vineyard. He built a tower in it: that is to say, God established his worship in Israel alone. To Israel alone he gave his law, his ordinances, his tabernacle, his altar, his priesthood, his sacrifices, and his prophets. The great privileges the nation of Israel once enjoyed, as well as the judgment of God described in this parable, were the subjects of Isaiah's song:

> Now will I sing to my wellbeloved a song of my beloved touching his vineyard. My wellbeloved hath a vineyard in a very fruitful hill: And he fenced it, and gathered out the stones thereof, and planted it with the choicest vine, and built a tower in the midst of it, and also made a winepress therein: and he looked that it should

> bring forth grapes, and it brought forth wild grapes. And now, O inhabitants of Jerusalem, and men of Judah, judge, I pray you, betwixt me and my vineyard. What could have been done more to my vineyard, that I have not done in it? wherefore, when I looked that it should bring forth grapes, brought it forth wild grapes? And now go to; I will tell you what I will do to my vineyard: I will take away the hedge thereof, and it shall be eaten up; and break down the wall thereof, and it shall be trodden down: And I will lay it waste: it shall not be pruned, nor digged; but there shall come up briers and thorns: I will also command the clouds that they rain no rain upon it. For the vineyard of the LORD of hosts is the house of Israel, and the men of Judah his pleasant plant: and he looked for judgment, but behold oppression; for righteousness, but behold a cry.
> (Isaiah 5:1-7).

The greatest blessing and privilege God can bestow upon any people is to establish his Word and his worship in their midst. How thankful men and women ought to be for the privilege and blessing of a gospel church and a regular gospel ministry (Amos 8: 11, 12). After attending one of the annual Bible conferences hosted by our assembly, a friend in New Jersey who had no gospel church near his family wrote, "If the people of Danville only knew what an opportunity and privilege God has given them, that little hillside would be covered with people, seeking to hear the Word of God."

It is our privilege and responsibility to avail ourselves of the blessing God has given us. I wonder how we would react if we knew we were in danger of having the Word of God removed from us. If we knew that God had threatened to remove his candlestick from its place among us, so that neither we, nor our neighbours, nor our children, nor our grandchildren could ever again hear the gospel of his grace, would such a warning be of real concern to us. Well, he has given us warning. "Remember therefore from whence thou art fallen, and repent, and do the first works; or else I will come unto thee quickly, and will remove thy candlestick out of his place, except thou repent" (Revelation 2:5).

God says, "Thou hast despised mine holy things" (Ezekiel 22:8). It is a well-deserved word of reproof. It is impossible for me to understand how men and women who claim to love the gospel of Christ can willingly absent themselves from the ministry of the Word. It is one thing to despise the labours of a pastor who faithfully seeks a message from God and diligently preaches the gospel. But a willing neglect of the gospel is much, much more than despising the labours of a man. It is despising God's holy things: his Word, his ordinances, his praise, and his people. The Lord Jesus promised that wherever and whenever two or three gather together in his name he will be with them. To neglect that assembly is to neglect Christ's company!

I know many people who have no place of public worship and no one to minister to their souls. They get excited when a gospel preacher comes within a hundred miles. They gladly drive the distance to hear him. They plan their vacations around Bible conferences, special meetings, or places of worship. They listen to tapes every day. When they get a chance to meet with God's saints and hear his Word, they are the first to arrive and the last to leave. They simply cannot get enough of the gospel. They soak it up like a dry sponge soaks up water. When the message is over, they talk about it enthusiastically.

I know others, many others, who have faithful pastors and regular places of worship, who act as though they could not care less. If they attend the worship of God once a week and give a little money to pay the light bill, they are more than content. In many places where people claim to love the gospel, it goes begging for a hearing. The evening services and mid-weak services could be held in a closet without being over crowded. If you are too busy to attend the worship of God, you are too busy! If you are too tired, then you need to give up something else, but not this! If you despise God's holy things, he will take them away from you and give them to someone else (Romans 11:21).

It is a sad fact that multitudes, like the Jews in our text, despise the privileges God gives them. God gave Israel his word; but they mingled with the heathen, and learned their works (Psalm 106:35). God sent them his prophets; but they chose darkness rather than light. God showed them the path of righteousness and life; but they hardened their hearts in unbelief and sin. God revealed himself to them; but they turned aside after idols. At last, God sent them his Son, the Lord Jesus Christ; and they crucified him!

What are you doing with the privileges God has given you? You have his Word. Do you read it, study it, and seek to know its message? If you have a gospel church and a regularly established, faithful gospel ministry, do you avail yourself of God's ordinance? Do you value God's people, his family? Do you cherish their company, or despise it? It is either one or the other. There is no middle ground.

J. C. Ryle wrote, "Nothing offends God like the neglect of privileges." I cannot adequately warn you of the danger of despising the worship of God. It is the first step toward apostasy (Hebrews 3:10-14; 10:25, 26). If you despise the kingdom of God, "the kingdom of God shall be taken from you" (v. 43). The time came when the cup of Israel's iniquity was full and God would tolerate them no more. In AD 70, just 40 years after this parable was uttered, God sent Titus and the armies of Rome into Jerusalem to destroy the holy city, the temple, and the nation. From that day to this, the Jews have been scattered over the face of the whole earth, and grope about in spiritual darkness, as blind men; but as blind men who are completely confident that they alone have light, and see.

The churches of Asia Minor, once so strong, are now gone. Africa, once the cradle of light, is now the house of darkness. England, once so full of light and life, is now a graveyard of religious relics and memories. The same is true of the United States. Much, much has been given to us, and much shall be required of us! As John Trapp put it, "The gospel is that inheritance we received from our forefathers. It must be our care to transmit the same to our posterity."

"They Perceived"

When our Lord spoke, even these proud priests and Pharisees could not help but understand he spoke of them (v. 45). Even in wicked men, the conscience is strong to condemn. But it takes something more than a guilty, condemning conscience to produce repentance and faith in the heart. That is the gift of God's saving goodness and grace (Romans 2:4; Ephesians 2:8, 9).

Recently, I read an article in which a man stated, "Mental assent itself is equal to faith". When I read those words, I was shocked. The mere perception of truth is not saving faith. Saving faith is more than understanding and agreeing with gospel truths. Saving faith involves love for him who is the Truth. Anyone who is well taught by another man can be persuaded of doctrinal, gospel truth. But it takes more than the teaching of a man, and more than personal study for a lost sinner, dead in trespasses and in sins, to become a living saint, savingly united to Christ by faith. Saving faith is the supernatural gift of God the Holy Spirit, the operation of his grace in us (Colossians 2:12). It is not something we arrive at by natural reason, something we merely perceive and agree to, or something we can be persuaded to perform by a slick "soul-winner". Faith in Christ is that which springs up in the heaven-born soul by the mighty operation of God's free grace (Ephesians 2:1-9).

"Marvellous In Our Eyes"

"Jesus saith unto them, Did ye never read in the scriptures, The stone which the builders rejected, the same is become the head of the corner: this is the Lord's doing, and it is marvellous in our eyes?" (v. 42). Here, speaking of himself, our Saviour quotes Psalm 118:22, 23, and pointedly applies these words to the chief priests and Pharisees standing before him. Those who were supposed to be the builders of God's house had rejected the Foundation Stone, Christ Jesus, whom God has made "the Headstone of the corner".

Throughout scripture our Lord Jesus Christ is likened to a stone. He is called "the stone of Israel" (Genesis 49:24). He is the Foundation Stone God has laid in Zion (Isaiah 28:16). He is the One Stone laid before God's elect in conversion, upon which we are built (Zechariah 3:9). Christ is the Stone "cut out of the mountain without hands" (Daniel 2:45), that will fall on his enemies in judgment. To the unbelieving, he is "a stone of stumbling and rock of offence" (Isaiah 8:14; Romans 9:32; 1 Peter 2:8). But, to all who trust him, Christ is "a living stone", and the "chief corner stone, elect and precious" (Isaiah 28:16; 1 Peter 2:4, 6).

Christ is the Foundation on which we are built and upon which we build. All who build upon him are safe and secure. All who build upon anything else build upon sand; and every house built upon sand will fall. Yet, there are multitudes, like the chief priests and Pharisees mentioned here, who reject the Foundation God has laid and build upon another. Rejecting his eternal deity, his sin-atoning sacrifice, his perfect righteousness, his effectual intercession, and omnipotent grace, they build upon a false foundation of "another Jesus". Rejecting his work, they build on their own works and religious ceremonies. Worse, they build their house of hope upon their own, imaginary freewill; and great will be the fall of it!

Faith in Christ is compared to the building of a house of refuge (Matthew 7:24). Sooner or later our house will be tested by earthly trials, spiritual trials, rains of trouble, floods of sorrow, and winds of adversity (Matthew 7:25). If your house is built on Christ the Rock, it will endure the trial and stand the test of time. If your house is built on the sand (anything other than Christ), sooner or later the rains and floods and winds will bring it crumbling down around you.

Thanks be unto God forever, man's rejection of Christ can never disannul the purpose and work of God! "The stone which the builders rejected, the same is become the head of the corner"! Though men reject him, God has accepted him and made him the Head of all things and the Head Stone of the Corner. This "stone, cut out of the mountain without hands", is the Stone by which antichrist shall be destroyed (Daniel 2:34, 35, 45).

Zechariah describes our Saviour's exaltation as the Chief Corner Stone with exultation (Zechariah 4:6-10). He is the chief corner stone; he is higher than the kings of the earth. He is infinitely superior to angels, and the chief among ten thousands of his saints. He is exalted above all creatures, angels, and men. Like the corner stone in a building, Christ knits and cements his building, his church together. Chosen angels and chosen men, chosen Jews and chosen Gentiles, Old Testament saints and New Testament saints, saints above and saints below, all are joined together in him. It is Christ, the Chief Corner Stone, who strengthens and supports the building and holds it together.

"This is the Lord's doing and it is marvellous in our eyes" (v. 42). It is marvellous in the eyes of all who believe; for the exaltation of Christ as our Mediator and Redeemer is a marvellous and wonderful display of the wisdom, goodness, justice, grace, mercy, truth, power, and faithfulness of God (Romans 3:24-26; 4:25-5:1; Philippians 2:9-11). Christ is Head of the corner. Christ is the Heir of all things, Ruler of all things, and Disposer of all things; and in him we have all things.

Salvation By A Fall

"Whosoever shall fall on this Stone shall be broken" (v. 44). Salvation is obtained by a fall. You must fall upon Christ, the Stone, and be broken upon him. If you do not fall upon him, this Stone will fall upon you and grind you to powder. Falling upon him, sinners are broken. Our Lord did not say, "Be broken and fall", but, "Fall and be broken". Faith is falling on him. It is a long, hard fall. We must fall from our loftiness and self-righteousness upon Christ alone as our hope before God. Trusting his blood alone for atonement, his righteousness alone for acceptance with God, his grace alone to save us, trusting Christ alone as our Saviour (1 Corinthians 1:30, 31). Falling on this Rock, sinners are broken. Yet, to the broken, God's Word gives this assurance. "A broken spirit: a broken and a contrite heart, O God, thou wilt not despise" (Psalm 51:17).

Just Judgment

"But on whomsoever it shall fall, it will grind him to powder. And when the chief priests and Pharisees had heard his parables, they perceived that he spake of them" (vv. 44, 45). If you refuse to trust Christ, if you will not fall on him for mercy, he will fall on you in wrath. God's judgment is always just.

Judgment and wrath are always presented in scripture as God's response to man's sin. "The wages of sin is death". Judgment is something you earn. "But the gift of God is eternal life". If you go to hell, it will be your fault, the result of what you have done. If you go to heaven, it will be God's gift, the result of what he has done. If a person walks in the light God gives him, God will give him more light. The Ethiopian eunuch (Acts 8), Cornelius (Acts 10), and Lydia (Acts 16), are three great examples of that fact. If you despise the light God gives you, the light will be turned into darkness; and when light becomes darkness, how great is that darkness! There is no darkness like spiritual darkness; and there is no spiritual darkness like the darkness of reprobation (Hosea 4:17; Romans 11:8-10, 21, 22). Yet, man's unbelief will not thwart, but shall only serve, the purpose of God (Romans 3:3, 4; 11:33-36).

Chapter 64

"All Things Are Ready; Come Unto The Marriage"

"And Jesus answered and spake unto them again by parables, and said, The kingdom of heaven is like unto a certain king, which made a marriage for his son, And sent forth his servants to call them that were bidden to the wedding: and they would not come. Again, he sent forth other servants, saying, Tell them which are bidden, Behold, I have prepared my dinner: my oxen and my fatlings are killed, and all things are ready: come unto the marriage. But they made light of it, and went their ways, one to his farm, another to his merchandise: And the remnant took his servants, and entreated them spitefully, and slew them. But when the king heard thereof, he was wroth: and he sent forth his armies, and destroyed those murderers, and burned up their city. Then saith he to his servants, The wedding is ready, but they which were bidden were not worthy. Go ye therefore into the highways, and as many as ye shall find, bid to the marriage. So those servants went out into the highways, and gathered together all as many as they found, both bad and good: and the wedding was furnished with guests. And when the king came in to see the guests, he saw there a man which had not on a wedding garment: And he saith unto him, Friend, how camest thou in hither not having a wedding garment? And he was speechless. Then said the king to the servants, Bind him hand and foot, and take him away, and cast him into outer darkness; there shall be weeping and gnashing of teeth. For many are called, but few are chosen."
(Matthew 22:1-14)

We have before us the parable of the marriage feast. It is the third in a trilogy of judgment parables, parables by which our Lord describes the basis of God's judgment upon those who despise the blessings and privileges of grace. In the parable of the two sons (Matthew 21:28-32), the parable of the husbandmen (Matthew 21:33-45), and this parable of the marriage feast, our Saviour shows us why God cast off the nation of Israel and sent the gospel to the Gentiles. Without question, it was God's purpose from eternity to save his elect among the Gentiles. Without question, God predestinated the fall of the Jews as the very means by which he would save his elect among the Gentiles (Romans 11:11, 25, 26). There are no accidents in God's universe (Romans 11:33-36). Yet, the cause of divine judgment upon that nation was and is their unbelief.

The gospel was first revealed to the Jews, the nation of Israel, in the types and shadows of the Mosaic economy. To Israel alone God gave his law, the priesthood, the tabernacle, and his prophets. When Christ came, he preached the gospel to none but the lost sheep of the house of Israel. Yet, that nation, being blinded by their religious leaders, despised the privileges of mercy God gave them; the gospel of his grace and his dear Son. Though they feverishly adhered to the rites and ceremonies of the law, they had long rejected the message of God's prophets. When John the Baptist came preparing the way of the Lord, they ignored him. When God's own Son came, they hung him up on the cursed tree to die. And when God sent the apostles and disciples of Christ to proclaim the message of Christ, the risen Lord and ascended King, they rejected their message, imprisoned them, beat them and murdered them.

Therefore, in AD 70 the Lord God sent the Roman army, under the command of Titus, into Jerusalem. By the hand of Titus, God destroyed both Jerusalem and the nation of Israel. This was the fulfilment of Daniel's "seventy weeks" prophecy (Daniel 9:23-27), the house of Israel was left desolate. Their light was turned into darkness. Never again would that nation have a word from God or a visitation of his grace. God said to his servants, "Israel will not hear. Leave her alone. Go ye therefore into the highways of the world, and as many as you find, whether Jew or Gentile, bid them come. And whosoever shall call upon the name of the Lord shall be saved.

Israel rejected God. Therefore God rejected Israel. Israel despised the light God had given her. Therefore God withdrew the light. Israel despised and rejected God's Son. Therefore God cast her off forever. God's judgment upon the nation of Israel stands as a beacon to warn us. God will not trifle with those who trifle with his Son and the gospel of his grace. An awesome weight of responsibility lies upon the shoulders of all who hear the gospel of Christ faithfully preached to them. It will not be heard without consequence. It will be to all either a savour of life unto life or of death unto death (2 Corinthians 2:15-17; Romans 11:21; Proverbs 1:23-33). The same sun that melts the candle hardens the clay. And the same message that melts the believer's heart before God hardens the unbeliever's heart in judgment. In this parable of the marriage feast our Saviour plainly teaches us seven things.

The Marriage Feast

First, the salvation proclaimed in the gospel is comparable to a marriage feast. "The kingdom of heaven is like unto a certain king, which made a marriage for his son" (v. 2). At a marriage feast everything is provided for the guests. They are not expected to bring anything. It would be an insult for them to do so. In the gospel there is complete provision for all the needs of a man's soul before God. Everything needed to relieve spiritual hunger and thirst is found in Christ. The pardon of sin, peace with God, and the hope of eternal life are all spread before us in rich abundance in the gospel. This is truly "a feast of fat things".

All this bounty comes to needy sinners through the love, grace, and mercy of God, by the sacrifice of the Lord Jesus Christ. By the preaching of the gospel, Christ himself speaks to sinners. He calls sinners to himself. The Son of God calls sinners into marriage union with himself! And every sinner who comes to him by faith, he clothes with the wedding garment of his own righteousness, gives a place in his kingdom, and will present faultless before the presence of his Father's glory in the last day (Matthew 11:28-30; John 7:37; Jude 24, 25).

The gospel of Christ truly is "glad tidings of good things"! The God of glory calls sinners into union with himself through his dear Son. He calls for rebel sinners to be reconciled to him by faith in his Son; and he does so upon the basis of reconciliation accomplished by his Son (2 Corinthians 5:17-21).

"Come To The Marriage"

Second, our Lord Jesus here reminds us that the invitations of the gospel are full, free, and unlimited. "All things are ready, come to the marriage" (v. 4). There is nothing lacking. No barriers are set before us. No conditions are to be met by us. "All things are ready"! The gospel sets an open door of mercy, love, and grace before all fallen sinners, and says, "Come". No one is excluded from the range of its invitation. "Whosoever will, let him come and take of the water of life freely". Though only few enter in by the straight gate, all are bidden to enter. And all who enter find that "all things are ready". There is nothing to be made ready by us, or even by God. All is ready by the eternal purpose of God and the finished work of Christ, our Substitute. Pardon by blood atonement is ready! Righteousness is ready! Peace and reconciliation are ready! Sonship by adoption is ready!

An Unworthy Refusal

Third, yet, our Saviour also teaches us that the gospel of the grace of God is flatly rejected by many who hear it. "But they made light of it, and went their ways, one to his farm, another to his merchandise: And the remnant took his servants, and entreated them spitefully, and slew them. But when the king heard thereof, he was wroth: and he sent forth his armies, and destroyed those murderers, and burned up their city. Then saith he to his servants, The wedding is ready, but they which were bidden were not worthy" (vv. 5-8).

Most people who hear the gospel receive no spiritual benefit from it. Many who hear the gospel of Christ week after week, year after year yet refuse to trust him. The preaching of the gospel profits them nothing. They see no beauty in Christ. They feel no need for Christ. Such rebels may not openly scoff and ridicule the message of grace, or outwardly oppose the gospel. They show their contempt by their preference for other things, by their love of the world, which is enmity against God. Their hearts are full of this world, so full of the pleasures and cares of the world that there is no room for Christ. Money and property, fashion and pleasure, happiness and popularity are the things that interest them. Christ and his gospel simply have no appeal to them. The sad fact is, multitudes will find themselves in hell, not because they were grossly immoral, but because they loved the world and gave no consideration to the Son of God.

While this is, as we have said, a judgment parable, it is a parable full of grace, too. Robert Hawker wrote with regard to it:

> We shall enter, through the teaching of God the Holy Ghost, into the beautiful design of our Lord, in this parable, if we take with us, all the way through it, the leading features the Son of God hath drawn. The kingdom of heaven is uniformly meant to describe the kingdom of grace, in the present gospel state of the church. The certain king, here spoken of, is God our Father. And the marriage is that union the Son of God hath been mercifully pleased, at the call of God his Father, to make with our nature, and with each person in that nature whom God the Father hath given to him, whose redemption Christ hath purchased, and God the Holy Ghost hath regenerated, for the purpose of grace here, and glory hereafter.
>
> This marriage took place, in the plan and counsel of Jehovah, before all worlds. The church was then presented by the Father, and fore-viewed by the Son, and sanctified in the will and design of God the Holy Ghost when Christ betrothed her to himself forever. And although, in the ordination of the divine will, this church of Jesus was to be involved in the Adam-fall of our nature, in common with

the whole race of men, yet the original connection could not be dissolved by this spiritual adultery, but rather afforded occasion for the Son of God to get more glory and honour by her recovery, in the wonderful means he accomplished in time, by the salvation he wrought for this purpose.

The church, therefore, departing from her glorious husband, and having lost the image of God by sin, and having mingled with the heathen, and learned their works; this parable represents the King as sending forth his servants to bring his church home to her lawful Lord and Husband again, notwithstanding all her baseness and unworthiness of departure.

The invitation to this purpose is represented under the image and similitude of a great dinner, in which a plentiful table is spread, the richest food is provided, servants are in waiting, and all with one voice say, all things are ready, come to the marriage! ... The servants being again and again sent, and the contempt shown by some, and the cruelty by others; are meant to set forth the various ages of the church, in which Patriarchs, Prophets, and Apostles, have ministered to this one end, and the events which have followed. These things are so plain, that every one who is acquainted with the Bible, cannot but know them ... The final issue of the Lord’s design, can neither be frustrated, nor unaccomplished. The Lord Jehovah, in his threefold character of persons, Father, Son, and Holy Ghost, hath made, for this, an effectual security. The church is One with Christ, her Head and Husband, from all eternity. Hence every individual which constitutes a part in that mystical body, notwithstanding the after act in the Adam-nature, and Adam-fall, is secured from a pre-union with the Lord, her Husband, from everlasting ruin. Hence their effectual call and conversion is engaged for in covenant settlements. A secret union subsisted between Christ and his members from all eternity. And this brings up after it an open espousal of every one of them at the season of their conversion. Thy people shall be willing in the day of thy power. And hence they are carried safely on through all the periods of time, and will be brought home to a more public display of the divine love, at the marriage supper of the Lamb in heaven (Revelation 19:9).

The Wedding Garment
Fourth, our Master tells us plainly that many who profess to believe the gospel are yet without faith and under the wrath of God. C. H. Spurgeon said, "This man without the wedding garment is the type of those who pretend to be Christians, but do not honour the Lord Jesus, nor his atoning sacrifice, nor his holy name. They are not in accord with the design of the gospel feast, namely, the glory of the Lord Jesus Christ in his saints. They came into the church for gain, for honour, for fashion, or for the purpose of undermining the faith of others."

Yes, the vast majority of those who take up a profession of religion are walking in the broad way that leads to destruction (Matthew 7:13, 14, 21-23). This man without a wedding garment is the representative of all who are found in the last day without the garment of Christ's righteousness. Our Lord did not say that he was without a garment. No doubt he was clothed, as many are, in a righteousness of his own. His crime was that he was not wearing *the* wedding garment, the garment of Christ's righteousness.

Many would have us believe that this wedding garment is the good works of a holy life. Thanks be to God, that is not the case! Hawker states,

> If our acceptance at Christ's table upon earth, or at his marriage supper in heaven, rested upon what some are so fond of talking of, but not a single son or daughter of Adam's fallen race ever knew; I mean good works and an holy life, no guests would be found for either. Neither doth this wedding garment consist in the adorning of a renewed soul by the graces of the Holy Spirit, such as faith, repentance, or any, or all of the sweet effects of the Lord's work in the soul. These are all blessed and essential things in the life of grace, and every child of God, called by grace, will be blessed in the enjoyment of them, but they are not Christ. These are the effects, not the cause; the fruits of regeneration, but not the root of salvation. The wedding garment, therefore, is none of these. And though it is blessed, yea very blessed, when grace is in lively exercise, to behold how true believers in Christ, from an union with Christ, act faith upon him, and live to him, and his praise; adorning, the doctrine of God our Saviour in all things: yet these form no part in the wedding garment, which is wholly of Christ, wrought out by Christ, and is; put on the believer by Christ. Every act of theirs is

> polluted, and must be cleansed in the blood of Christ, as well as their persons; for without this cleansing, neither the one, nor the other, can find acceptance before God.

Let us be sure we have this wedding garment. If we appear before God in any other at that great day, we shall, like this man, be speechless, and shall be cast "into outer darkness; there shall be weeping and gnashing of teeth". But the possession of this garment, the righteousness of Christ, proves that we were eternally betrothed to Christ, and that we are, by his grace, a part of his chosen bride, adorned for her Husband and by her Husband, "members of his body, of his flesh, and of his bones" (Ephesians 5:23-32).

The Guests

Fifth, still, our Saviour assures us that man's unbelief will not alter, thwart, or in any way hinder the purpose of God. "The wedding was furnished with guests" (v. 10). The purpose of God does not depend upon man. Though the Jews rejected God's Son, he had a "remnant according to the election of grace", who gladly embraced him.

Though many refuse to believe on the Lord Jesus Christ, every chosen, redeemed, and regenerated sinner in this world, everyone purposed by God from eternity to be saved, shall be saved by him and shall believe on him (Romans 3:3, 4; 11:11, 24-26).

The Day Of Judgment

Sixth, in the last day, on the day of judgment, all false professors will be detected, exposed, and eternally condemned (vv. 12, 13). In this life a profession of faith and a fairly moral life is enough to secure a name and reputation as a Christian. But when we stand before God, he will examine us thoroughly and judge us according to strict justice by those things written in the court books of heaven (Revelation 20:11, 12).

If we are not washed in the blood of Christ and robed with his righteousness, we will be lost forever. None shall enter into everlasting bliss whose names were not written in the Lamb's book of life by divine election before the world began. And all whose names are in that book shall enter in, because they are made perfectly holy and righteous in Christ (Revelation 21:27).

Special Call
Seventh, in verse 14 the Son of God declares that the source and cause of true faith is God's sovereign, electing love. "For many are called, but few are chosen". If you and I are true believers, if we truly believe the gospel of Christ, if we truly rest our souls upon the Lord Jesus Christ alone, it is because God, from all eternity, chose us as the objects of his special love and grace (Jeremiah 31:3). All who believe God gladly confess, with Josiah Conder:

'Tis not that I did choose Thee,
For, Lord, that could not be;
This heart would still refuse Thee,
Hadst Thou not chosen me:
Thou, from the sin that stained me,
Hast washed and set me free,
And to this end ordained me,
That I should live to Thee.

'Twas sovereign mercy called me,
And taught my opening mind,
The world had else enthralled me,
To heavenly glories blind.'
My heart owns none before Thee,
For Thy rich grace I thirst.
This knowing, if I love Thee,
Thou must have loved me first!

Called And Called
"Many are called". This statement refers to the general call that goes forth to all who hear the gospel. But there is another call. There is an inward, personal, particular, divine call, which is issued by God the Holy Spirit to God's elect and to them alone (John 10:3). This call of the Holy Spirit is always effectual and irresistible. God the Holy Spirit effectually draws chosen, redeemed sinners to Christ by almighty grace (Psalm 65:4). This call always produces faith in Christ. It always results in salvation. This inward, irresistible call is given only to God's elect, those who were chosen, predestinated, and redeemed (Romans 8:28, 29; 1

Corinthians 1:21-24; 2 Timothy 1:9, 10). The examples of this call are numerous (Ezekiel 16:6-8; 37:1-14; Matthew 4:18-22; Luke 19:5, 6; John 11:43, 44).

Were it not for this effectual call of the Spirit, no one would ever be saved (John 6:44, 45). But this is not the call mentioned in our text. The call, which our Lord speaks of here, is the earnest proclamation of the gospel by his servants. Every time a true servant of God preaches the gospel of God's electing love, redeeming mercy, and saving grace, sinners are called to faith in Christ (2 Corinthians 5:20). The call of the gospel is universal in its scope. It goes forth to all who hear the gospel preached. It is a sincere and gracious call (Romans 10:1-4), issued by divine authority which all who hear it are responsible to obey (Proverbs 1:22-33).

The question is often asked, "If only God's elect are going to be saved, why do we preach the gospel to all men?" The scriptures give us three clear answers to that question: 1. Our Lord commands us to preach the gospel to all (Matthew 10:27; 28:19; Mark 16:15; Acts 1:8). 2. The preaching of the gospel is God's ordained means of salvation for his elect (1 Corinthians 1:21-25). And 3. we have no way of knowing who the elect are until they believe the gospel (1 Thessalonians 1:4, 5). Therefore, we preach the gospel to all. And when we have done so, when we have faithfully preached the gospel to all, we are free of their blood (1 Corinthians 9:16; Ezekiel 33:7-9).

Sinners respond to the preaching of the gospel in many ways. Some flatly reject the gospel call (v. 3). Some lightly esteem it (v. 5; Lamentations 1:12). Others are enraged by it (v. 6). Some pretend to obey it, taking up a profession of religion (vv. 10, 11). And some, those to whom the gospel comes in divine power, believe on the Lord Jesus Christ.

Divine Election

Why? Why do some believe, while others believe not? It is because "few are chosen". The difference between those who believe and those who believe not is the choice of God. There are some people in this world whom God has chosen to salvation. Sooner or later, they shall be saved. They shall believe on the Lord Jesus Christ. The rest are left in their sins. God has done them no injustice. He does not violate their will. He does not force them to do what they choose not to do. He simply leaves them to themselves. And you can be sure of this, if God leaves a man to himself, if God leaves a man to his own free-will, that man will never believe on the lord Jesus Christ and be saved (John 6:37-40; 10:16, 26; Acts 13:46-48).

Thank God, he does not leave all men unto themselves! He has chosen to save some. There is yet “a remnant according to the election of grace”, of whom he says, “I will be their God, and they shall be my people”. Let me make just four statements about this matter of election, as it is presented in this fourteenth verse.

1. It is a fact beyond dispute that the Bible teaches the doctrine of God’s sovereign, unconditional, election of his people unto salvation in Christ (John 15:16; Romans 9:11-13; Ephesians 1:4-6; 1 Thessalonians 1:4; 2 Thessalonians 2:13, 14; 2 Timothy 1:9; 1 Peter 1:2). 2. It is also a fact beyond dispute that the Bible declares that God’s elect in this world are few. Our Saviour said, “Few are chosen”. I solemnly admonish you to make your calling and election sure (2 Peter 1:10). Trust the Son of God. Believe on the Lord Jesus Christ. 3. If we are among the number of those chosen, redeemed, and called to salvation and eternal life in Jesus Christ, we ought to be filled with wonder, praise, and gratitude before the holy Lord God (Romans 11:33-36; 1 Corinthians 4:7; 15:10). 4. Election has secured for us a place with Christ in glory. And in the end, it shall be said, “The election hath obtained it”.

Who shall condemn to endless flames
The chosen people of our God.
Since in the Book of life their names
Are clearly writ in Jesus’ blood?

He, for the sins of the elect,
Hath a complete atonement made;
And justice never can expect
That the same debt should twice be paid.

His sovereign mercy knows no end,
His faithfulness shall still endure;
And those who on His Word depend
Shall find His Word forever sure.

Chapter 65

Trappers Trapped

"Then went the Pharisees, and took counsel how they might entangle him in his talk. And they sent out unto him their disciples with the Herodians, saying, Master, we know that thou art true, and teachest the way of God in truth, neither carest thou for any man: for thou regardest not the person of men. Tell us therefore, What thinkest thou? Is it lawful to give tribute unto Caesar, or not? But Jesus perceived their wickedness, and said, Why tempt ye me, ye hypocrites? Shew me the tribute money. And they brought unto him a penny. And he saith unto them, Whose is this image and superscription? They say unto him, Caesar's. Then saith he unto them, Render therefore unto Caesar the things which are Caesar's; and unto God the things that are God's. When they had heard these words, they marvelled, and left him, and went their way. The same day came to him the Sadducees, which say that there is no resurrection, and asked him, Saying, Master, Moses said, If a man die, having no children, his brother shall marry his wife, and raise up seed unto his brother. Now there were with us seven brethren: and the first, when he had married a wife, deceased, and, having no issue, left his wife unto his brother: Likewise the second also, and the third, unto the seventh. And last of all the woman died also. Therefore in the resurrection whose wife shall she be of the seven? for they all had her. Jesus answered and said unto them, Ye do err, not knowing the scriptures, nor the power of God. For in the resurrection they neither marry, nor are given in marriage, but are as the angels of God in heaven. But as touching the resurrection of the dead, have ye not read that which was spoken unto you by God, saying, I am the God of Abraham, and the God of Isaac, and the God of Jacob? God is not the God of the dead, but of the living. And when the multitude heard this, they were astonished at his doctrine. But when the Pharisees had heard that he had put the Sadducees to silence, they were gathered together. Then one of them, which was a lawyer, asked him a question, tempting him, and saying, Master, which is the great commandment in the law? Jesus said unto him, Thou shalt love the Lord thy God with all thy heart, and with all thy soul, and with all thy mind. This is the first and great commandment. And the second is like unto it, Thou shalt love thy

neighbour as thyself. On these two commandments hang all the law and the prophets. While the Pharisees were gathered together, Jesus asked them, Saying, What think ye of Christ? whose son is he? They say unto him, The Son of David. He saith unto them, How then doth David in spirit call him Lord, saying, The LORD said unto my Lord, Sit thou on my right hand, till I make thine enemies thy footstool? If David then call him Lord, how is he his son? And no man was able to answer him a word, neither durst any man from that day forth ask him any more questions."
(Matthew 22:15-46)

In the passage before us the Holy Spirit has recorded a series of subtle snares laid by our Lord's enemies during the last days of his earthly ministry. By their deceitful questions, asked with the pretence of seeking to honour God and understand his truth, these hell-inspired religionists were trying to entangle our Lord, trying to trick him into saying something they could use as an accusation against him. Obviously, their schemes failed. They were taken in their own snare, and retreated in utter confusion. There is much to be learned from this event.

Religious knowledge is not spiritual knowledge. Spiritual knowledge comes only by faith in Christ (Hebrews 11:3). It is attained by divine revelation (1 Corinthians 2:11-16). A saving knowledge of Christ is not a carnal apprehension of the intellect, but the gift and revelation of God the Holy Spirit. "Wherefore henceforth know we no man after the flesh: yea, though we have known Christ after the flesh, yet now henceforth know we him no more" (2 Corinthians 5:16). Let us be sure we understand what the Spirit of God tells us. Our knowledge of Christ is not a carnal apprehension of the intellect, but the gift and revelation of God the Holy Spirit. Being born again by the omnipotent grace and irresistible mercy of God the Holy Spirit, all who are taught of God, know Christ after the Spirit, and not after the flesh. John Owen wrote:

> Of all the poison which at this day is diffused in the minds of men, corrupting them from the mystery of the gospel, there is no part that is more pernicious than this one perverse imagination, that to 'believe in Christ' is nothing at all but to 'believe the doctrine of the gospel!'

A Question About Taxes

The Herodians obviously had some connection with both Herod and with the Pharisees. It is really unknown to us who they were, what their connections were, and what their beliefs were. Many have tried to figure out who these men were. I will leave that to them. I want you to see the message the Holy Spirit of God would have us to learn. The Herodians hoped to entangle our Saviour with a political question, asking whether it is lawful to pay taxes.

The word "then" in verse 15 directs our attention to the preceding parables given by our Lord. In the parable of the two sons our Saviour told them that their religious works would profit them nothing before God (21:31). In the parable of the husbandmen the Pharisees "perceived that he spake of them" (21:45), when he said, "The kingdom shall be taken from you", and judgment shall fall upon you (21:42-45). Then, the parable of the marriage feast plainly declared the message of God's sovereign, electing love and irresistible, saving grace (22:1-14). That message of grace was the clincher. The Pharisees, the Herodians, and the Sadducees were all enraged by it, and sought to destroy the Son of God for preaching it.

Here is the first thing set before us in this passage. The cross of Christ, the gospel of God's free, sovereign, saving grace in Christ is an offence to all natural men, and more so to lost religious people than to anyone else (Galatians 5:11).

Why is the gospel of Christ so offensive to self-righteous people? The gospel of Christ declares that man is totally depraved, that all men are spiritually dead, evil at heart, and utterly incapable of doing good before God (Romans 5:12; Ephesians 2:1; Mark 7:20-23; Romans 3:10-20). The gospel doctrine of unconditional election makes salvation to be a matter wholly determined by the immutable will of God, not the will of man (John 15:16; Ephesians 1:3-6; 2 Thessalonians 2:13, 14). The sweet message of redemption accomplished by Christ alone, of limited atonement, of salvation merited by and effectually secured by Christ alone, takes man out of the work altogether (2 Corinthians 5:17-21; Galatians 3:13; Ephesians 1:7; Hebrews 9:12). The gospel proclaims grace that is free, irresistible, and effectual, making the new birth and faith in Christ the gifts and operations of God the Holy Spirit, not the work of man's imaginary free will (Psalm 65:4; 110:3; Ephesians 2:8, 9; Colossians 2:12). And the gospel of Christ assures every believing sinner of an everlasting, salvation by Christ (John 10:27-30). The perseverance of the saints makes salvation, grace, and eternal life entirely dependent upon the work of God, and in no way dependent upon the works of man.

Second, we see in verse 16 how Satan often comes against us as a flattering friend, rather than an enraged enemy. The Herodians, who hated our Saviour, said to him, "Master, we know that thou art true, and teachest the way of God in truth, neither carest thou for any man: for thou regardest not the person of men. Tell us therefore, What thinkest thou?" Many may be deceived by seductive kindness and flattery of deceitful men, who would never be moved by direct opposition. Samson, Solomon, and Hezekiah are well-known examples of that fact. Sweet things cause more sickness than bitter things. The warm, balmy sunshine of a bright summer day is far more likely to make a man shed his protective armour than the freezing blasts of winter. Satan is never so dangerous as when he appears to be our friend.

The third lesson, the primary lesson taught by our Lord's answer to the Herodians is the fact that in all matters of civil law it is our duty to be obedient to civil government. "Render therefore unto Caesar the things which are Caesar's; and unto God the things that are God's" (v. 21; Romans 13:1-7). I do not approve of many things, indeed, of most things promoted and encouraged by the institutions of government in our country. I am thankful for the nation, love it, and am willing to fight to the death to defend the land and liberty God has given us. But those laws of the land that tend to destroy the very fabric of society, I do not and cannot condone.

Yet, wherever the laws of the land do not demand that I violate the Word of God, I am and must be obedient to the laws of civil government. We must be obedient to God, regardless of cost or consequence, even when law forbids our obedience (Acts 4:18-20). But, where Caesar does not demand disobedience to Christ, we must render unto Caesar the things that are his. That includes paying taxes (Matthew 17:27).

A Question About The Resurrection

In verses 23-33 the Sadducees attempted to entangle the Son of God with a question about the resurrection. The Sadducees were the liberals of the day. They denied the resurrection. The Sadducees and the Pharisees were not at all friendly with one another. But they were willing to put aside their differences when it came to opposing Christ. They were happy to work together against him, as in verses 15-22. There are three things in these verses that are as obvious as the sun.

First, in verses 23-29 we see how utterly dishonest people can be while pretending to sincerely serve God. These men pretended to honour Moses, the scriptures, and God, though they sought honour only for themselves. And, in their attempt to destroy the doctrine of Christ, they fabricated a story. Imaginary suppositions are the strongest weapons of religious infidels. While ignoring obvious evidences of divine truth, they pile up suppositions and hypothetical situations to cast reproach upon the revealed truth of the God they despise. When we are confronted with such people, we should simply ignore them. We must never be drawn into debate (which God the Holy Spirit calls the work of the flesh) with people who are "ever learning, and never able to come to the knowledge of the truth" (2 Timothy 3:7). There are some things we know (1 Peter 1:18-25), and some things we do not know (Acts 1:7). Spiritual things can be known only by the Word of God and the power of God the Holy Spirit (v. 29). They are never learned by carnal debate.

In verse 30 our Saviour shows us something of the blessedness of the resurrection "For in the resurrection they neither marry, nor are given in marriage, but are as the angels of God in heaven". In that blessed, glorious state we shall be as the angels of God. We know very little about the life that awaits us in the resurrection. But there are some things about that which awaits us in resurrection glory that the Lord our God has graciously revealed; and those things are sure: The glory awaiting us is beyond imagination (1 Corinthians 2:9). No consequence of sin shall follow us into eternity (Revelation 21:4). We shall be "as the angels of God". We shall forever enjoy the immediate presence of our Lord! In heavenly glory we shall be forever perfectly obedient to his will, serving him perfectly, giving him all glory, without sin, and without the restraints or needs of these carnal bodies!

Second, in verses 31-33 the Lord Jesus speaks about his eternality as God our Saviour. Our Saviour quotes Exodus 3:6 in the present tense: "I am (not was) the God of Abraham, Isaac, and Jacob". Remember, the God who spoke those words to Moses out of the burning bush is Christ himself, the Angel of the Lord. Then he adds these words "God is not the God of the dead, but of the living". He is telling us that he is the eternal God, and assures us that all who die in him are not dead, but living. Because he is the Resurrection and the Life, those who trust him shall never die (John 11:25, 26).

A Question About The Law

Third, the Pharisees sent one of their lawyers to tempt the Saviour with a question about the law in verses 34-40. The word "lawyer" here does not refer to the kind of lawyer you might find in a court of law. This man was not a trial lawyer, or a civil lawyer, but a religious lawyer, the worst kind of lawyer! He was a man whose life and business was to study and teach the Mosaic law, with all the customs and traditions appended to it by men.

Again, there are three things in these verses that must be understood: 1. The law of God is holy, just, and good. What a blessed place this world would be if all men loved God and one another! But, 2. No sinful man is capable of obeying God's holy law. The grace of God teaches us to love God and one another (1 John 3:16, 17; 4:9-11), and enables us in a measure to do so; but our best love is full of sin! 3. The only way any sinner can obey and fulfil God's holy law is by the doing and dying of Christ, our Representative and Substitute (Romans 8:1-4). He obeyed the law for us. He paid our debt to the full satisfaction of divine justice. We fulfil the law by faith in him – by trusting only in him (Romans 3:28).

One Significant Question

In verses 41-46 the Son of God puts forth one question before which all other questions fade into insignificance. "What think ye of Christ?" With this question of all questions, he snared the fowlers and trapped the trappers. These learned religious men were put to silence by this question. To answer it honestly, they would have been compelled to acknowledge that the Messiah must be both God and man. But, rather than be honest, they held to their religious traditions and went to hell!

I put this question to you. "What think ye of Christ?" Let me answer for myself and for every saved soul, according to the scriptures. The Man Christ Jesus is the mighty God (1 Timothy 3:16). Yet, he is really and truly man, the woman's Seed (Galatians 4:4-6). He is the Lord our Righteousness! (Jeremiah 23:6; 33:16). He is our all-sufficient Substitute! (2 Corinthians 5:21). He is our omnipotent Saviour! (Hebrews 7:25; Matthew 1:21). He is our all-prevailing Advocate with the Father! (1 John 2:1, 2). And he is precious (1 Peter 2:7).

Overruling Providence

Once more, we see how our Lord takes the duplicity of wicked men, inspired by Satan himself, meant for evil, and turns it for good. We should never miss an opportunity to admire the overruling providence of our God, who constantly works all things together for the everlasting salvation of his elect (Genesis 50:20; Psalm 76:10; Romans 8:28).

The malice of the Herodians, Sadducees, and Pharisees was sweetly overruled to the glory of Christ and the comfort of our souls. Had those wicked men not raised their trivial questions of strife, we would never have had the precious things revealed in this passage. We certainly could never have known the meaning of those words spoken to Moses out of the burning bush had our Saviour not explained it to us here. “God in Christ”, wrote Robert Hawker, “is not the God of the dead, but of the living”. Speaking of those who have died in Christ, Hawker continued, “All live to him; their souls among the spirits of just men, made perfect, and their bodies, from an union with Christ, resting in this covenant hope of being raised at the last day. For if the spirit of him that raised up Jesus from the dead, dwell in you, he that raised up Christ from the dead, shall also quicken your mortal bodies by his Spirit that dwelleth in you.”

What a sweet, delightful thing it is to realize that our great God made the malice of these wicked men an occasion to put forth that one question of indescribable importance, “What think ye of Christ?” Again, I am compelled to give you Mr Hawker’s tremendous comments on that question:

> What think ye of Christ? What think ye of his person, of his offices, characters, relations? What think ye of the completeness, fulness, suitableness, all-sufficiency of his salvation? What think ye of Christ as to his worth, preciousness, beauty, glory? What, as to his value, importance, his absolute necessity, and the living without knowing him, and the dying without enjoying him? Oh! for the proper apprehension of Jesus! Oh for the absolute and certain union with him, and interest in him! The soul that hath so learned Christ, will best know how to enter into the full sense of our Lord’s question; and will best appreciate the being found in him, so as to render all other knowledge of no value, but the knowledge of Christ, the power of God, and the wisdom of God, for salvation to every one that believeth.

Chapter 66

A Form Of Godliness Condemned

"Then spake Jesus to the multitude, and to his disciples, Saying, The scribes and the Pharisees sit in Moses' seat: All therefore whatsoever they bid you observe, that observe and do; but do not ye after their works: for they say, and do not. For they bind heavy burdens and grievous to be borne, and lay them on men's shoulders; but they themselves will not move them with one of their fingers. But all their works they do for to be seen of men: they make broad their phylacteries, and enlarge the borders of their garments, And love the uppermost rooms at feasts, and the chief seats in the synagogues, And greetings in the markets, and to be called of men, Rabbi, Rabbi. But be not ye called Rabbi: for one is your Master, even Christ; and all ye are brethren. And call no man your father upon the earth: for one is your Father, which is in heaven. Neither be ye called masters: for one is your Master, even Christ. But he that is greatest among you shall be your servant. And whosoever shall exalt himself shall be abased; and he that shall humble himself shall be exalted."
(Matthew 23:1-12)

That which the Word of God calls "godliness" is the worship of God. "Godliness with contentment is great gain" (1 Timothy 6:6). Blessed are they who, being born of God, worship God in Spirit and in truth! Blessed is that person who, trusting Christ as his Saviour and Lord, worships God, ever coming to God by Christ Jesus! But, when the Bible speaks of "a form of godliness" (2 Timothy 3:5), the reference is to the mere practice of religion. "A form of godliness" is going to church. "A form of godliness" is engaging in religious activity. "A form of godliness" is saying your prayers. How few there are who have the blessed great gain and sweet contentment of godliness! What multitudes there are who have a form of godliness! The apostle Paul warned us that in the last day the vast majority of the religious world would have a mere form of godliness, an outward show of religion, while denying the very power of true godliness, which is the gospel of Christ (2 Timothy 3:5). In the days of our Lord's earthly life and ministry Judaism had already withered into a mere form of godliness; and the Son of God abhorred it.

Matthew 23 records the very last words ever spoken by the Son of God in the temple at Jerusalem. Judgment was about to fall on that nation. In just a short while God would destroy the city, the nation, and the temple. In this chapter our Lord tells the multitude and his disciples why such judgment must come. The first twelve verses of this chapter show us how utterly contemptible a mere form of godliness is to the Son of God.

In these verses, and in those that follow, our Saviour gives a withering exposure of the religion of the scribes and Pharisees, and of their disciples today. He sharply rebukes them, both for their doctrine and their practices. Their religion retained the Word of God and the name of God; but it was nothing less than an utter denial of God. By this time, Judaism had been reduced to little short of idolatry! Will worship, ritualism, and legalism prevailed. Our Lord despised it. Knowing well that his time on earth was almost done and that soon his followers must be left alone like sheep among wolves, he warns us plainly against the false shepherds and false religion that surrounds us in this world.

Nothing is more abominable in the sight of God than a self-righteous form of godliness. Here are five important lessons to be learned from these twelve verses.

Beware False Teachers

First, it is the solemn responsibility of every faithful servant of God to warn his hearers of the false teachers and false religion that surrounds them. It is not meekness, but cowardice, that causes men to hold back in denouncing false doctrine. No man was ever more meek, more gracious, or more loving than the Lord Jesus Christ, the God-man. Yet, no man ever more boldly denounced false religion (Matthew 7:15-23).

That man who refuses to identify heresy and heretics is unfaithful to his charge as God's messenger and God's watchman (1 Timothy 4:1-8; 2 Timothy 2:16-18; 3:1-5; 4:1-4; Philippians 3:17-19; Colossians 2:8-23). No sin is more sinful than silence when alarm is needed! All preachers of free-will, works religion are false prophets. All who make salvation dependent upon man's will, man's works, or man's worth are destroyers of men's souls and must be treated by us as God's enemies (2 John 10).

"Try The Spirits"

Second, it is the responsibility of every man to try the spirits and judge preachers and their message by the Word of God (vv. 2, 3). "Beloved, believe not every spirit, but try the spirits whether they are of God: because many false prophets are gone out into the world. Hereby know ye the Spirit of God: Every spirit that confesseth that Jesus Christ is come in the flesh is of God: And every spirit that confesseth not that Jesus Christ is come in the flesh is not of God: and this is that spirit of antichrist, whereof ye have heard that it should come; and even now already is it in the world. Ye are of God, little children, and have overcome them: because greater is he that is in you, than he that is in the world" (1 John 4:1-4).

Those who sit in Moses' seat are responsible to teach what Moses taught. And they are to be obeyed, followed, and honoured, only as they obey, follow, honour, and teach the Word of God (Hebrews 13:7, 17; 1 Thessalonians 5:12, 13). But we must not allow any man to be our pope. Like the noble Bereans, we are responsible to search the scriptures for ourselves. We must receive nothing taught by any man that we do not find written in the Book of God.

Self-righteousness

Third, nothing in all the world is more obnoxious, abominable, and damning to the souls of men as an outward, self-righteous form of religion. In verses 3-7 our Saviour identifies self-righteous religion by four common traits. It may have many names, varied ordinances, and conflicting ceremonies, but false religion can always be identified by these four things. There are many other things to identify it, as we have seen; but these four common characteristics of false religion are observable by everyone, except those involved.

1. False religion always seeks to bring people into some form of legal bondage. "All therefore whatsoever they bid you observe, that observe and do; but do not ye after their works: for they say, and do not. For they bind heavy burdens and grievous to be borne, and lay them on men's shoulders; but they themselves will not move them with one of their fingers" (vv. 3, 4). Obviously, when our Lord said, "Whatsoever they bid you observe, that observe and do", he was speaking sarcastically. He had already declared that by their traditions they had transgressed the commandment of God and made it of none effect (Matthew 15:3). The gospel of Christ proclaims liberty to sinners in captivity. All human religion seeks to bind the captive more securely. Like the Gadarenes had often bound the demoniac with fetters and chains, religious people seek to bind the souls of men in the chains of the Mosaic law, the fetters of religious customs, and the bonds of religious superstition. When the Lord Jesus comes in the saving operations of his grace, he sets the captive free (Mark 5:1-15). His word to his servants, with regard to all he has raised from death to life, is "Loose him, and let him go" (John 11:44). Hymnwriter John Kent says it beautifully,

Till God the sinner's mind illume 'tis dark as night within;
Like Lazarus in the dreary tomb bound hand and foot by sin.

Yet though in massy fetters bound, to God's free grace a foe,
The gospel has a joyful sound: 'Loose him, and let him go.'

Sinners shall hear this joyful sound when God designs it so;
Grace shall beyond their sins abound; 'Loose him, and let him go.'

Justice, beholding his attire no more appears his foe;
He says, 'I've all that I require; Loose him, and let him go.'

He stands accepted in his name whose blood for him did flow;
The holy law proclaims the same: 'Loose him, and let him go.'

I was once in bondage, cursed and condemned by my sin. I lived under the galling yoke of the law, bound by the heavy chains of guilt, the willing captive of Satan. But the Lord Jesus saw me, had compassion upon me, came to my dark dungeon, and said, "Loose him, and let him go"!

The Lord Jesus Christ has brought me into the blessed liberty of his free grace. My soul overflowed with unspeakable joy, "looking for the mercy of our Lord Jesus Christ unto eternal life" in "the glorious liberty of the sons of God". It is this blessed liberty of grace that I want you to know and enjoy. I urge you to count as your soul's enemy every preacher, and every form of religion that seeks to bring you into bondage.

2. False religion is always marked by the glaring hypocrisy of those who seek to impose it upon you. "They say and do not". They bind heavy burdens and lay them on others, "but they themselves will not move them with one of their fingers". They talk about obeying the law; but they know they do not obey it. They require from others things they do not practise themselves.

Their religious rules and regulations, their rituals and ceremonies, their sabbath days and duties are bound together in creeds, by-laws, church covenants, and constitutions like huge intolerable burdens. They form a yoke that no man can bear. Like the scribes and Pharisees, false religion piles its great load upon ignorant men and demands obedience, but offers nothing to help the needy soul. The Lord Jesus is not like them. His servants are not like them. Our Saviour says,

"Come unto me, all ye that labour and are heavy laden, and I will give you rest. Take my yoke upon you, and learn of me; for I am meek and lowly in heart: and ye shall find rest unto your souls. For my yoke is easy, and my burden is light" (Matthew 11:28-30). His sweet yoke of grace gives rest to weary sinners.

3. False religion in all its outward works is designed only "to be seen of men" (v. 5). Such works are performed by false religionists so that men will approve of them and applaud them as godly, devoted people, and admire them as great lovers of God. False religion is very imaginative in finding ways to appear holy. False religion teaches people to dress in a way that will show others their godliness. False religion teaches people to find a way to demonstrate their giving, so that people will know how sacrificial they are. False religion teaches people to advertise the amount of time they spend reading the Bible and praying, so that others can observe their devotion. False religion teaches people to "humbly" let people know when they fast, so that their spiritual gravity can be applauded.

All these things, our Saviour tells his disciples to do in secret (Matthew 6:16-18). How often have you heard someone say, "I want the world to see Jesus in me". What they really mean is, "I want the world to think I am a good man, not like them". The world did not see Jesus in Jesus. It certainly will not see him in you and me! False religion teaches people to "make broad their phylacteries and enlarge the borders of their garments", to put "I love Jesus" and "WWJD?" (What Would Jesus Do?) bumper stickers on their cars, so that the world can acknowledge them as devoted people.

Throughout the New Testament, our Lord and his apostles teach us the very reverse of these things. True godliness, true worship, true faith in Christ is a matter of the heart. It causes saved sinners to seek the will of God and the glory of God in all things. Its works are always portrayed as works of love and faith. Those who perform them are totally unaware of having done so (Matthew 25:34-40), while those who boast of performing them never do (Matthew 25:41-46). Beware of every form of religion that teaches you to do "for to be seen of men".

4. False religion encourages the love of recognition (vv. 6, 7). It says, "Stand up and testify". The Word of God teaches us to bow before the throne of grace and worship. The scribes and Pharisees loved the best place in public meetings. "The upper most rooms at feasts". They sought the most prominent place of recognition in church. "The chief seats in the synagogues". They craved the recognition of men, having their names recognized and honoured. "Greetings in the markets". They loved titles of distinction, by which they were pretentiously elevated above others. "To be called of men, Rabbi, Rabbi", or "Reverend", or

"Father". Religious hucksters love to be first and foremost. God's servants teach, by practice and precept, the unity of God's saints in Christ as brethren.

Titles And Honours

Fourth, it is absolutely wrong for believers to give any man the names, titles, and honours that belong to our God and his Son alone. "But be not ye called Rabbi: for one is your Master, even Christ; and all ye are brethren. And call no man your father upon the earth: for one is your Father, which is in heaven. Neither be ye called masters: for one is your Master, even Christ" (vv. 8-10).

C. H. Spurgeon wrote, "In the church of Christ, all titles and honours which exalt men and give occasion for pride are here forbidden". To call a man "Father" is to rob God of his supremacy and Fatherhood as God. To call a man "Reverend" is to rob God of his supremacy and holiness as the "Holy One". "Holy and reverend is his name" (Psalm 111:9). To speak of a man as "your priest" or "intercessor" is to rob Christ of his Priesthood. To call a man "Doctor" or "Rabbi", or "Master" is to rob Christ of his glory as our Teacher.

A Servant To The Church

Fifth, the secret of greatness in the kingdom of God is service to the kingdom of God (vv. 11, 12). Richard Baxter said, "Church greatness consisteth in being greatly serviceable". The desire of the Pharisee is to receive honour, and to be called "Master". The desire of the believer is to do good, devoting himself and all he has to the glory of God and the service of his people, each esteeming the other better than himself. What a solemn passage this is! If there were no other passage in the whole Book of God to warn us of man-centred, self-righteous, works religion, this should be sufficient to alarm us and cause us to abhor it. It seems that our Saviour considered no language sufficiently strong to express his utter contempt for man's religion and religious customs. Pretentious sanctity and the outward show of religion, a mere form of godliness, are things detested by the Son of God! Our attitude toward such should be the same.

"If there be therefore any consolation in Christ, if any comfort of love, if any fellowship of the Spirit, if any bowels and mercies, Fulfil ye my joy, that ye be likeminded, having the same love, being of one accord, of one mind. Let nothing be done through strife or vainglory; but in lowliness of mind let each esteem other better than themselves. Look not every man on his own things, but every man also on the things of others" (Philippians 2:1-5).

Chapter 67

Eight Stern Words Of Condemnation

"But woe unto you, scribes and Pharisees, hypocrites! for ye shut up the kingdom of heaven against men: for ye neither go in yourselves, neither suffer ye them that are entering to go in. Woe unto you, scribes and Pharisees, hypocrites! for ye devour widows' houses, and for a pretence make long prayer: therefore ye shall receive the greater damnation. Woe unto you, scribes and Pharisees, hypocrites! for ye compass sea and land to make one proselyte, and when he is made, ye make him twofold more the child of hell than yourselves. Woe unto you, ye blind guides, which say, Whosoever shall swear by the temple, it is nothing; but whosoever shall swear by the gold of the temple, he is a debtor! Ye fools and blind: for whether is greater, the gold, or the temple that sanctifieth the gold? And, Whosoever shall swear by the altar, it is nothing; but whosoever sweareth by the gift that is upon it, he is guilty. Ye fools and blind: for whether is greater, the gift, or the altar that sanctifieth the gift? Whoso therefore shall swear by the altar, sweareth by it, and by all things thereon. And whoso shall swear by the temple, sweareth by it, and by him that dwelleth therein. And he that shall swear by heaven, sweareth by the throne of God, and by him that sitteth thereon. Woe unto you, scribes and Pharisees, hypocrites! for ye pay tithe of mint and anise and cummin, and have omitted the weightier matters of the law, judgment, mercy, and faith: these ought ye to have done, and not to leave the other undone. Ye blind guides, which strain at a gnat, and swallow a camel. Woe unto you, scribes and Pharisees, hypocrites! for ye make clean the outside of the cup and of the platter, but within they are full of extortion and excess. Thou blind Pharisee, cleanse first that which is within the cup and platter, that the outside of them may be clean also. Woe unto you, scribes and Pharisees, hypocrites! for ye are like unto whited sepulchres, which indeed appear beautiful outward, but are within full of dead men's bones, and of all uncleanness. Even so ye also outwardly appear righteous unto men, but within ye are full of hypocrisy and iniquity. Woe unto you, scribes and Pharisees, hypocrites! because ye build the tombs of the prophets, and garnish the sepulchres of the righteous, And say, If we had been in the days of our fathers, we would not have been partakers with them in the blood of the prophets. Wherefore ye be witnesses unto yourselves, that ye are the children of them which killed the prophets. Fill ye up then the measure of your fathers. Ye serpents, ye generation of vipers, how can ye escape the damnation of hell?" (Matthew 23:13-33)

Standing in the midst of the temple, after addressing his own disciples and the multitude around him, while he had the ear of the people, our Lord Jesus Christ turned to the scribes and Pharisees and in the most public manner possible denounced and condemned them with these scathing words. The words were not spoken secretly. Our Lord did not call the scribes and Pharisees aside for a private conversation. Rather, he went into the temple, where they regularly taught and were most highly respected, and publicly condemned them and their religion in the most emphatic terms. Eight times he uses the solemn expression, "Woe unto you"! Seven times he calls them "hypocrites". Twice he calls them "blind fools". And at last he denounces them as "serpents and a generation of vipers".

Why such sternness? Why such public condemnations? Why such scathing language? Could he not have said the same thing in a more polite, more civil, more acceptable tone? Of course, he could have done so. But it was not his intention to be polite, civil, and acceptable. It was his intention to be heard. Remember, these are the words of the one man, the one preacher whose love and goodness cannot be called into question. Why did our Lord choose to use such scathing language to denounce and condemn these men and the religion they taught? Because the glory and truth of God, and the souls of men were at stake. The solemn truth to be learned from this passage is clear: The doctrines, religion, spirit, and practices of the scribes and Pharisees are abominable in the sight of God. The religion of the world is contemptible to God and should be to us.

Shut Up The Kingdom

First, our Lord condemns these religious leaders for shutting up the kingdom of heaven. "But woe unto you, scribes and Pharisees, hypocrites! for ye shut up the kingdom of heaven against men: for ye neither go in yourselves, neither suffer ye them that are entering to go in" (v. 13). Of course, no man is able literally to shut up the kingdom of heaven. That kingdom which God almighty builds, no man shall hinder. Yet, many do all they can to keep sinners out of the kingdom, persuading them not to hear those who preach the gospel and not to believe the truth of holy scripture. That is what the scribes and Pharisees did. They rejected the message of John the Baptist. They refused the doctrine of Christ. They tried to keep everyone from hearing and believing the Lord Jesus Christ, the Son of God.

Pretentious Religion

Second, our Saviour condemned these men for being pretentious, abusive and self-serving. "Woe unto you, scribes and Pharisees, hypocrites! for ye devour widows' houses, and for a pretence make long prayer: therefore ye shall receive the greater damnation" (v. 14). These men, masked in piety and devotion, devoured widows houses and took advantage of the unsuspecting. Pretending to be devoted, spiritual leaders, true servants of God, they (like the hucksters of our day) took everything they could get from weak, unprotected, elderly women. The slickest and most vile conmen in the world are those who run a scam upon the souls of men to enrich themselves! Men who enrich themselves by the work of the ministry are not God's servants; and they are not ministering to people. They are using them. God's servants come to serve the souls of men, not to be served by them (Matthew 20:26-28; 2 Corinthians 2:17; 4:5).

False Religion

Third, the Son of God condemns the scribes and Pharisees (and all their successors today) for destroying the souls of men with false religion. "Woe unto you, scribes and Pharisees, hypocrites! for ye compass sea and land to make one proselyte, and when he is made, ye make him twofold more the child of hell than yourselves" (v. 15). Be sure you understand this verse correctly. Our Lord is not condemning what is commonly called proselytizing. If you care for men's souls, you will do everything within your power to make proselytes of them; that is, to bring them out of false religion into the knowledge of the Lord Jesus Christ. It is not the encompassing of land and sea to make a disciple that our Lord condemns. He commands that (Matthew 28:18-20). What he condemns is the destruction of men's souls by false religion: getting sinners to believe a false gospel (Galatians 3:1), getting people to make a profession of faith who have not experienced grace, giving people a false peace and false assurance in a false hope.

Religious hucksters do not do what they do from a desire to benefit the souls of men, or bring them to the knowledge of the living God. Not in the least! Their only object is to swell their own ranks, build their churches, increase the number of their disciples, and make themselves a name. Their religious zeal arises not from a desire for the glory of God or the salvation of men's souls, but from their own, self-serving interests.

Categorizing Sin
Fourth, the Lord condemns the scribes and Pharisees for categorizing sin (vv. 16-22). Our Lord plainly declared that we are not to swear at all (Matthew 5:34-36). But the scribes and Pharisees taught that some swearing was alright, that it was acceptable to take God's name in vain (Exodus 20:7), so long as one did not swear by the gold in the temple's coffers or the gifts upon the altar! Let a man, a church, or a denomination forsake the teachings of Christ and it is impossible to place a limit upon the heresies and foolishness to which they will run.

Certainly some sins are more grave than others and will be punished more severely. But, whenever self-righteous men start defining and categorizing sin, they make the Word of God of none effect and imply that certain sins, lesser sins, are permissible. Someone once said, "The ten commandments are not ten suggestions, but ten commandments; and they are not multiple choice"!

Strain At A Gnat
Fifth, the scribes and Pharisees, like the religionists around us, exalted trifles, while ignoring the most important things. For that, they were to be condemned (vv. 23, 24). They put the last things first and the first things last. They made a great issue about tithing, even on the herbs of their gardens. That would have been okay, except for one thing. They ignored "judgment, mercy and faith", the justice of God, the mercy of God, and faith in Christ.

I cannot imagine anything that more properly describes this religious generation. Religious people t day are meticulous about the outward form of godliness. They place great importance on outward behaviour, dress code, tithing, church attendance, and countless customs and traditions, but ignore the most basic elements of the gospel: the satisfaction of justice by the sacrifice of Christ (Romans 3:24-26), the mercy of God flowing to sinners by his sacrifice (Ephesians 1:7), showing mercy (James 3:17), faith in Christ (2 Timothy 1:9-13).

Outward Not Inward
Sixth, the religion of the scribes and Pharisees was condemned by Christ because it was an outward religion of rituals and ceremonies, rather than the inward, spiritual, heart worship of God (vv. 25, 26). For most people, Christianity is an outward system of creeds, confessions, and ceremonies. But true Christianity, while never ignoring God's doctrine or his ordinances, is primarily an inward, spiritual matter of the heart (1 Samuel 16:7; Proverbs 23:26; Joel 2:13; John 4:23, 24; Romans 10:9, 10; 14:17; Philippians 3:3).

Human Approval
Seventh, our Lord condemns as hypocrisy all religion that has for its object the approval of men (vv. 27, 28). Those religious works and ceremonies which are performed and promoted to show men how holy, zealous, or devoted we are, are an abomination to God (Matthew 6:3-16; Luke 16:15). We are neither ashamed nor ostentatious. We simply walk with and serve our God and Saviour. We seek to live for his glory and do all things for his glory. And, really, it does not matter whether anyone, other than God himself, sees that. We want to glorify our Father before men, to live honestly, do justly, and to walk humbly with our God by faith in Christ; but we do not want men to look at us and say, "There is a truly humble man or woman, who lives for the glory of God". If we seek the approval of men, we are not seeking the honour of God and cannot believe God (John 5:44).

Despise The Gospel
Eighth, the Son of God, in verses 29-33, condemned as a crooked and perverse generation of snakes and vipers, all who exalt the names and honour of dead prophets, while despising those who preach and teach the gospel, the message of those prophets. The scribes and Pharisees built monuments to dead prophets and revered the memories of God's saints who lived in other ages. But, by their treatment of Christ, his disciples, and his people, they demonstrated that they were of one mind with those who "killed the prophets".

Religious Serpents
Here are eight solemn woes pronounced upon men who trusted in themselves that they were righteous. These stern words of condemnation were spoken by the Lord Jesus, the meekest man who ever walked the earth, the very embodiment of gentleness and humility. They were made by that man by whom God shall judge the world in righteousness in the last day (Acts 17:31). He calls these men, and all who follow them, by names which identify them as a people whose father is that old serpent, the devil, whose damnation is sure. "Ye serpents, ye generation of vipers, how can ye escape the damnation of hell?"

Nothing is more damning to the souls of men than self-righteous, works religion. We read in the Word of God about many who were converted by God's almighty grace. Idolaters, harlots, thieves, publicans, soldiers, and many who were possessed of devils have become everlasting trophies of God's omnipotent grace. But in all the Word of God we find only two Pharisees who were converted: Nicodemus and Saul of Tarsus (John 3:1-20; 7:50; 19:39; Philippians 3:1-14). Two Pharisees, only two, are set before us in holy scripture who escaped the damnation of hell. Thank God, there were two, lest any despair. But there were only two, that none presume.

How did these religious serpents manifest their serpentine hatred of the Son of God? They were not immoral in their outward behaviour. They could not be charged with any open vices. They prided themselves in being very moral. They did not neglect the ordinances of divine worship, either in public or in private. They prayed three times a day, fasted twice a week, paid tithes on everything they obtained, and went to church every time the doors were open.

What was it then that brought upon these men the Lord's most severe words of condemnation? It was their proud self-righteousness, their legal righteousness. Following after the righteousness of the law, going about to establish their own righteousness, such men show both their ignorance of God's righteousness and their determination never to submit themselves to the righteousness of God in Christ. "For Christ is the end of the law for righteousness to every one that believeth" (Romans 10:4). Teaching others to do the same, they "shut up the kingdom of heaven against men".

They compassed sea and land, the Lord told them, to make one proselyte, and when this was done, they made him two-fold more the child of hell than themselves. That is, they laboured to establish a righteousness of their own by undermining the necessity of salvation by faith in Christ alone, and setting up a system teaching others to do the same. By denying the fall of man and the necessity of a recovery by grace alone, they set up Satan's kingdom. As children of hell they fought against the kingdom of heaven.

Nothing is so completely opposed to the gospel of the grace of God than self-righteousness. Nothing is so opposed to the cross of Christ, nothing so despises the blood and righteousness of Christ, nothing is so hardening to the heart of man, nothing is so damning to the souls of men, nothing is so obnoxious to God in heaven! When teachers, preachers, and religious leaders of any age are engulfed in the darkness and delusion of self-righteous, good works religion, how great is the darkness of that generation! God hates hypocrisy and the show of religion! Let us ever pray as David did, "Let my heart be sound in thy statutes; that I be not ashamed" (Psalm 119:80). Let us be found in Christ, not having any righteousness of our own, but only that which was accomplished by the faithfulness of Christ our Surety, "the righteousness which is of God by faith" (Philippians 3:9).

Chapter 68

The Master's Last Public Words

"Wherefore, behold, I send unto you prophets, and wise men, and scribes: and some of them ye shall kill and crucify; and some of them shall ye scourge in your synagogues, and persecute them from city to city: That upon you may come all the righteous blood shed upon the earth, from the blood of righteous Abel unto the blood of Zacharias son of Barachias, whom ye slew between the temple and the altar. Verily I say unto you, All these things shall come upon this generation. O Jerusalem, Jerusalem, thou that killest the prophets, and stonest them which are sent unto thee, how often would I have gathered thy children together, even as a hen gathereth her chickens under her wings, and ye would not! Behold, your house is left unto you desolate. For I say unto you, Ye shall not see me henceforth, till ye shall say, Blessed is he that cometh in the name of the Lord."
(Matthew 23:34-39)

We have before us the last words ever spoken in public by our Lord Jesus Christ, not the last words he spoke, but the last words he spoke in public to the multitudes and particularly to the Jewish nation. These words are some of the most solemn and stern words ever spoken by him. They are words of judgment from the God-man, whose heart was full of pity.

This passage of scripture, so often twisted and perverted by Arminians in their vain attempts to disprove the gospel of God's free grace in Christ, is in fact not a passage showing that salvation is by man's will, but rather a passage declaring that man's ruin and everlasting destruction is by his will. In these verses our Lord declares to the scribes, and Pharisees, and Jewish people that the basis of God's judgment and the cause of their spiritual ruin was their obstinate, wilful unbelief.

That which our Lord asserts concerning the nation of Israel is equally true of our own day. There is nothing that keeps a man out of heaven but his own unwillingness to bow to Christ, receive him, and believe on him as Lord and Saviour (John 5:46; 6:37-40; 7:37, 38). Israel did not enter into the land of promise for one reason only: unbelief! (Hebrews 4). That nation perished, not because God would not be gracious to them, but because they would not trust him

(Isaiah 48:18, 19). If you and I miss heaven it will be because of our own, wilful unbelief. Nothing keeps a man out of heaven but his own will. And there is nothing that keeps a man out of hell but God's will. The decree of God opens the door of heaven for a great, innumerable multitude of sinners. But the decree of God does not shut the doors of heaven against anyone. Be sure you understand this: Eternal life is by God's will, God's gift, and God's work (Romans 9:16; 2 Timothy 1:9). But eternal death is the result of man's will, man's work, and man's just deserts. "The wages of sin is death" (Romans 6:23; 1:22-32; 10:21).

Space For Repentance

Our Lord first teaches us that God almighty graciously gives wicked men and women space for repentance. Our great King's earthly life and ministry was to end soon. But, before this world, he delivered a royal and prophetical message. "Wherefore, behold, I send unto you prophets, and wise men, and scribes: and some of them ye shall kill and crucify; and some of them shall ye scourge in your synagogues, and persecute them from city to city" (v. 34). In this verse, our Lord speaks of his apostles as prophets, wise men, and scribes. And there is a sense in which all true gospel preachers may be described as such. Prophets declare what God will do. Wise men are made wise unto salvation and have wisdom to declare God's salvation to others. Scribes interpret and teach the Word of God.

These "prophets, and wise men, and scribes" are Christ's ascension gifts to his church. Here he declared the kind of reception his servants would have among the Jews. "And some of them ye shall kill and crucify, and some of them shall ye scourge in your synagogues, and persecute them from city to city".

Pastor Henry Mahan wrote, "God's mercy forgives sin, his grace bestows favour, his longsuffering and patience give space for repentance and faith." As God sent his servants to the Jews and gave them repeated warnings; message, after message, after message, so he does today. God does not allow men to sin without rebuke. He does not allow iniquity to go unchecked in anyone. With every transgression, with every breach of God's law, man must trample under his feet the hedge of warnings God has planted about him.

Your conscience is God's law written on your heart, by which God speaks to those who have not had their consciences seared (Romans 2:14, 15). The Lord God, as it were, knocks at the door of conscience and variously gets a person's attention by sickness, afflictions, bereavements, and fearful brushes with death but rebels harden their hearts, and persist in their defiance of the Almighty. God opens the grave under their eyes, destroys their idols, and stirs their souls; but they ignore his warning. Like cattle in a field when one of the herd is slaughtered, they look up for a moment then return to grazing on the grass beneath their feet.

How often the Lord God gives a summons to sinners by the preaching of the Word. Frequently, men and women experience soul trouble, but do not know what is happening. Blind, deaf, and dead, they do not understand the Lord's ways. So, they harden their hearts, as Pharaoh of old. But soon everyone will see and understand, "God speaketh once, yea twice, yet man perceiveth it not" (Job 33:14). In the day of judgment, when it is too late, everyone will realize that there is a voice in every event of providence, saying, "Turn ye, turn ye! Why will ye die?" (Ezekiel 33:11).

God's servants today put the prophet's question before eternity bound sinners, crying to perishing men, "Why will ye die?" Justice has been satisfied by Christ. Righteousness has been brought in by the Son of God. All who trust the Lord Jesus are saved by him (John 6:40; Hebrews 7:25). Still, unless the Lord Jesus himself grants the rebel sinner repentance by his almighty grace, none will obey the gospel.

Relentless Persecution

Second, the Lord God takes notice of and remembers the relentless persecutions of his people by wicked men (vv. 34-36). Our Saviour's prophecy was literally fulfilled among the Jewish people. He said, "Verily I say unto you, All these things shall come upon this generation". And, before that generation had passed away, Jerusalem was besieged and destroyed. There was a sufficient interval granted for the full proclamation of the gospel and the gathering out of God's elect among them, who were made to know that the crucified Christ is the Messiah. Then came the awful end, which the Saviour foretold.

But our Lord's warning here was not for the Jewish people alone. It speaks to this generation as well. As Cain, the first murderer, began to show this hardness of heart and bitterness of spirit against Abel, so every persecution and blood shedding suffered in the cause of Christ, from the days of Cain to the end of that holy war between the seed of the serpent and the woman's Seed, will be required of the serpent's generation (1 John 3:12; John 8:44).

God's servants in this world are often lied about and scandalized by those who oppose them, held in contempt by those they serve, and despised and abused by some who pretend to love them. Frequently, people who would not openly abuse God's messenger will abuse his wife and children. Such people think, "No one really knows what I am doing". What fools!

This is so serious for any who would raise a hand against the Lord's people. There is a day of reckoning coming, if not in this world, then in the next when those men and women will see that their actions were observed by God. They will understand how they were punished by God providentially in their own experience in time, in their own families, and through their own woes. And it shall be a matter of eternal ruin, not only for themselves but for their children, and their children's children.

Who would ever have imagined that the dying words of Zacharias would find their fulfilment not only when he was murdered (2 Chronicles 24:19-23), but 800 years later in his murderers' descendants? Our Lord declares that anything done to one of his servants is done to him (1 Samuel 8:7; Matthew 10:40-42). On one occasion, some children were mocking God's prophet, Elisha, and God sent two bears to destroy forty-two of them at one time (2 Kings 2:23-25).

Be warned, God will destroy those who would destroy his church and kingdom (1 Corinthians 3:16, 17). God's servants should find great satisfaction in this. The God we serve will not allow any to get away with the abuse of his servants. There is an Eye that sees, an Ear that hears, and a Hand that records everything done against God's servants. He who lives forever says, "He that toucheth you toucheth the apple of mine eye" (Zechariah 2:8). Yes, "God requireth things that are past" (Ecclesiastes 3:15).

False Prophets

Third, this passage of holy scripture declares that false prophets are murderers of men's souls (v. 37). Our Lord did not say, "How often would I have gathered you, and you would not". Neither did he say, "How often would I have gathered thy children, and they would not". Rather he says, "How often would I have gathered thy children and ye would not." This verse of scripture must be understood in its context. Our Lord was condemning the scribes and Pharisees. He is saying the same thing here as he said in verse 13. "Woe unto you, scribes and Pharisees, hypocrites! for ye shut up the kingdom of heaven against men: for ye neither go in yourselves, neither suffer ye them that are entering to go in."

Our Lord Jesus Christ exemplified what a true preacher of the gospel is and must be; one who is full of compassion and care for men's souls. The words of verse 37 express the tenderness and compassion of Christ as a man, not his immutable will as God. They display our Lord's human affection for his fellow men (Mark 10:21). Our Lord's understanding of God's absolute sovereign election, particular redemption, and irresistible grace did not keep him from caring about the souls of men (Romans 9:2-4; 10:1). He knew the wickedness of that city. He knew what crimes they had committed. He knew the prophets they had murdered. He knew what they wanted to do to him. Yet, he pitied them!

Still, it must be asserted plainly that any who represent our Lord's words in verse 37 as a frustration of his will, purpose, and grace toward chosen sinners are greatly mistaken. Our Lord, obviously, is not suggesting that he desired the spiritual and eternal salvation of multitudes that he could not save, or did not save because they chose to reject his grace. There was not another people on earth for whom so much had been done, to whom so much had been given. The tabernacle, the temple, the priesthood, all the ordinances of divine worship in the Old Testament, and the many preincarnate appearances of Christ were theirs.

By all these things our blessed Lord displayed his great love for his elect among that nation and people, watching over them by the secret workings of his Holy Spirit throughout those days of old. Oh, what great love is in our Saviour's heart today, by which he comes to us yet does not come to the world (John 14:18-23). Every ordinance of worship, every blessing of providence is given to lead chosen, redeemed sinners into the knowledge, apprehension, and experience of his love for them and his grace to them. All are revelations of "the good will of him that dwelt in the bush" (Deuteronomy 33:16). With all the tenderness of a hen, spreading her wings over her brood to protect them from danger, our blessed Saviour watches over his elect, gathers them unto himself, and protects them from all danger. He has always done so, he is doing so now, and ever shall do so. It is written, "There shall no evil happen to the just" (Proverbs 12:21).

It is delightful to seize every opportunity to observe our Saviour's grace and goodness, love and care, and ceaseless mercy toward his elect. But, here our Redeemer is describing the ruin of Jerusalem and the nation of Israel, among whom his beloved people were preserved and blessed throughout the Old Testament age. How often he would have gathered their children together; but their religious leaders (the scribes and Pharisees), like false prophets in every age, "shut up the kingdom of heaven against them" and would not have any to enter it.

Remember, our Saviour is here addressing the scribes and Pharisees, condemning them for their treachery in destroying the souls of men. He is not suggesting that he would have gathered them to himself in grace. They were never the objects of his grace. Yet, had the Jewish people, as a nation, received him as the Christ of God, instead of crucifying the Lord of life and glory, they would have been saved as a nation, and the Romans would not have been sent by him to destroy the nation.

A Willing Saviour

That which is spoken here is not a word of grace, but of judgment. Yet, I cannot fail to take this opportunity to show that our Lord Jesus Christ is a willing Saviour. Oh, what a willing Saviour our Saviour is! He is a God who "delighteth in mercy"! The Lord Jesus Christ, the Son of God, is as willing to save as he is mighty to save (Isaiah 45:22; 55:1-3, 6, 7; 59:1, 2; Matthew 11:28-30; John 5:40; 7:37, 38). Are you not thankful? The Lord Jesus came into the world to save lost sinners. He said, "I am come to seek and to save that which was lost". The Son of God died in the room and stead of the ungodly. The Lamb of God is seated upon the throne of grace in heaven, waiting to be gracious, waiting to save sinners.

Salvation is the work of God. All will be saved in the end who were chosen to salvation from the beginning, they and none else. All will be with Christ in glory for whom Christ made atonement and satisfaction at Calvary, only them and no others. All of them will be crowned with the heavenly hosts who have been effectually called by the Holy Ghost. Yet, he who is God our Saviour is ready and willing to save all who come to God by him, and will most assuredly save them.

If I should die with mercy sought,
When I the Lord have tried,
This were to die,
(Delightful thought!),
As sinner never died!

Cause Of Ruin

Fifth, these words from the Master teach us that all who are lost are lost and ruined forever because of their own, wilful rebellion and unbelief. "O Jerusalem, Jerusalem, thou that killest the prophets, and stonest them which are sent unto thee, how often would I have gathered thy children together, even as a hen gathereth her chickens under her wings, and ye would not! Behold, your house is left unto you desolate. For I say unto you, Ye shall not see me henceforth, till ye shall say, Blessed is he that cometh in the name of the Lord" (vv. 37-39).

It is written, "O Israel, thou has destroyed thyself; but in me is thine help" (Hosea 13:9). If we are saved, we will be saved by grace alone. If we are destroyed, we must destroy ourselves. The judgment of God is always just. Three things are clearly established in these last three verses of Matthew 23.

1. The cause of man's ruin is his own will. J. C. Ryle wrote, "Impotent as man is by nature, unable to think a good thought of himself, without power to turn himself to faith and call upon God, he still appears to have a mighty ability to ruin his own soul." 2. Often eternal ruin begins in this world with judicial reprobation (v. 38; Hosea 4:17). And 3. there is a day coming when all men shall see and acknowledge who Christ is and what he has done (v. 39; Philippians 2:9-11). In the last day, in that great day of judgment, he will be completely vindicated and honoured, even by those who perish under his wrath.

"Behold, your house is left unto you desolate"! This is what you have chosen. You shall forever eat the fruit of your own ways. The God you have despised and forsaken has despised and forsaken you forever! "Jerusalem", wrote Spurgeon, "was too far gone to be rescued from its self-sought doom". Their city, their houses, and their temple would be abandoned and destroyed forever; and they would be forever cast into hell.

"I say unto you, Ye shall not see me henceforth, till ye shall say, Blessed is he that cometh in the name of the Lord." You shall see me no more until you see me glorified by all as the Christ of God, in my glorious second advent when you shall say, as the gaping pit of hell opens wide its mouth to swallow you up, "Here is the Blessed One who comes in the name of the Lord"! (Revelation 1:7; Philippians 2:9-11; Isaiah 45:22-25).

> Ye sinners, seek His grace, whose wrath ye cannot bear;
> Fly to the shelter of His cross, and find salvation there.
> So shall the curse remove, by which the Saviour bled;
> And that last, awful day shall pour His blessings on your head!

If we are saved, go to heaven, enjoy eternal life and glory in the bliss of God's presence, it will be by God's will, and God's work alone. If we are lost, perish under the wrath of God, and go to a dark, Christless, eternal hell, it will be altogether our fault alone, because of our will, our unbelief, and our sin!

Chapter 69

"When Shall These Things Be?"

"And Jesus went out, and departed from the temple: and his disciples came to him for to shew him the buildings of the temple. And Jesus said unto them, See ye not all these things? verily I say unto you, There shall not be left here one stone upon another, that shall not be thrown down. And as he sat upon the mount of Olives, the disciples came unto him privately, saying, Tell us, when shall these things be? and what shall be the sign of thy coming, and of the end of the world? And Jesus answered and said unto them, Take heed that no man deceive you. For many shall come in my name, saying, I am Christ; and shall deceive many. And ye shall hear of wars and rumours of wars: see that ye be not troubled: for all these things must come to pass, but the end is not yet. For nation shall rise against nation, and kingdom against kingdom: and there shall be famines, and pestilences, and earthquakes, in divers places. All these are the beginning of sorrows. Then shall they deliver you up to be afflicted, and shall kill you: and ye shall be hated of all nations for my name's sake. And then shall many be offended, and shall betray one another, and shall hate one another. And many false prophets shall rise, and shall deceive many. And because iniquity shall abound, the love of many shall wax cold. But he that shall endure unto the end, the same shall be saved. And this gospel of the kingdom shall be preached in all the world for a witness unto all nations; and then shall the end come."
(Matthew 24:1-14)

Matthew 24 is a chapter filled with prophetic things. Much of the prophecy of this chapter is yet unfulfilled. Some of it has been fulfilled already. But all of it is of great interest and very instructive to us. Whenever we approach any portion of scripture, we should do so with deep humility, realizing that we are reading, studying, and seeking to understand the Word of God. Therefore, we must earnestly pray for the illumination, direction, and teaching of the Holy Spirit, who alone can give us understanding in the Word of Truth.

I suppose that there has been more disagreement among true gospel preachers about the proper interpretation of Matthew 24 than any other passage of holy scripture. That is terribly regrettable. Yet, men who truly love Christ, his Word, and the gospel of his grace sometimes find it impossible to labour together in the cause of Christ because one holds to one interpretation of this passage and one another. I do not pretend to have the answers to all the questions that are raised about the prophecies contained in these verses. I do not think that our Lord intended for us to fully comprehend them until they come to pass. Otherwise, he would not have answered the disciples' questions so ambiguously. It was our Lord's disciples who asked, "When shall these things be?" I am certain that the question itself revealed a weakness and an improper curiosity in those faithful men, even as it reveals a weakness and an improper curiosity in those who are overly concerned about prophetic issues today (see Acts 1:6-8). Prophecy cannot be fully and clearly understood until the thing foretold has come to pass (compare Acts 2:16 with Joel 2:28-32).

This entire chapter is the answer that our Lord gave to the question the disciples asked in verse three: "When shall these things be?" It is a question relating to three things specifically: the judgment of God upon Jerusalem, the second coming of Christ, and the end of the world. Some parts of this chapter deal with one of these things, some another, and some the third. Much of what our Lord said in response to the disciples question may be applied to two of those events; and some of his answers must be applied to all three. Spurgeon was exactly right when he wrote, "When we have clearer light, we may possibly perceive that our Saviour's predictions on this memorable occasion had some connection with all three of these great events."

Our Lord was always practical in his instruction. When he preached, he always gave his hearers practical doctrine. Though they were curious about when these things would happen, he knew that it was far more important for them to know both what to expect in this world and what was expected of them. Rather than directly answering their question, the Master gave them some general hints as to when they might expect to see these things come to pass and seized the opportunity to teach them very important, practical lessons which he knew they needed to learn. Seven of these lessons are found in the first fourteen verses of the chapter. These seven lessons are as applicable to us as they were to them. And they shall be applicable to every generation of believers who shall follow us until time shall be no more.

External Things

First, we must never judge God's blessings, or God's works by external things (vv. 1, 2). When our Lord Jesus went out of the temple, never to return to it, the glory was departed from it. The prophet Haggai wrote, "The glory of this latter house should be greater than the former". And it was truly made so by the presence of the incarnate God, when he entered it, in substance of our flesh (Haggai 2:9). Yet, the second temple built at Jerusalem, after the Babylonian captivity, lacked much of the glory that was in the original temple built by Solomon. It did not have the Urim and Thummim, the ark of the covenant, the constantly burning fire upon the altar, the manifest presence of God (the Shechinah), or the spirit of prophecy. When the Lord Jesus entered the temple, the presence of the incarnate God was the sum and substance of that glory to which all those things faintly pointed, and fulfilled Haggai's prophecy.

When the Lord Jesus left the temple, that which he declared in the previous chapter was fulfilled. "Your house is left unto you desolate" (Matthew 23:38). As they walked away, those words must have echoed in the disciples' ears. "Behold, your house is left unto you desolate". They turned back to look at that spectacular building, with its great stones, beautiful gates, and rich adornments, and came to show it to the Master. To them it was a glorious thing to behold. To him it was a sad, sad sight. That which had been his Father's house, which ought to have been a house of prayer, had become a den of thieves. That place, where once God dwelt and manifested his glory, was now the object of his judgment and must soon be destroyed.

How much like these disciples we are. We delight in the temporal prosperity of the church, her buildings, her wealth, her numbers and those things that impress men, as though such things really matter, as though they will last. That is a great mistake. All that is external will perish. "The things which are seen are temporal" (2 Corinthians 4:18). Only that which is wrought of God is substantial (1 Samuel 16:7; 1 Corinthians 3:11-15).

Our Lord's prophecy of the temple's destruction was fulfilled when Titus destroyed Jerusalem in AD 70. Not one stone of that magnificent structure was left standing upon another. Micah prophesied, "Zion for your sake be plowed as a field, and Jerusalem shall become heaps" (Micah 3:12); and his prophecy was fulfilled. Let every redeemed sinner, when he reads of the Saviour forever abandoning that physical temple and destroying it, rejoice that he will never leave his people (his church), who are his true temple (Hebrews 13:5; Matthew 28:20). None shall destroy those he has bought with his blood (Romans 8:1, 35-39).

False Prophets

Second, if we care for our souls, we must always exercise great care not to be deceived by false prophets and false religion (vv. 4-12). Our Lord's plain words are, "Take heed that no man deceive you". Those are the first words out of his mouth in response to the disciples' question. Do not take them lightly. It is absolutely wrong to try to make the things described in these verses fit any single period of time. These things could be applied to every age, including the one in which we live. Therefore, this warning is as needful today as it was in the New Testament era and as it shall be in the ages of time that may yet come.

I cannot imagine a more needful warning. "Take heed that no man deceive you". Satan knows how easily people are deceived. Robert Hawker wrote:

> False Christs and false prophets are signs always to be noticed in the Church history. Wars, and rumours of wars are all ministering to Christ's kingdom. Every period in the Church to the present hour hath been marked with these things. They are exercises to the faithful, and truly profitable, under the Spirit's teaching, to establish the heart in grace.

We must take heed not to be deceived by false Christs (v. 5). There were many in the days prior to the destruction of Jerusalem who arose, claiming to be the Lord's Anointed One. Multitudes followed them, just as multitudes follow the Russells, the Campbells, the Jones, the Moons, and the Koreshes of our day. But there is a far greater deception than that of any mere man claiming that he is the Christ. Modern religion presents men with a false Christ in the preaching of Arminian, free will, works religion. There is but one true Christ. He is that Christ, who is, according to the infallible testimony of God the Spirit in holy scripture, God the Son (John 1:1-3; 1 John 1:1-3). He who is the Christ is the Surety of an everlasting covenant (Hebrews 7:22), who came to save his people from their sins (Matthew 1:21); and he has accomplished all that he came into this world to do (Galatians 3:13; Hebrews 10:10-14). He who is the Christ is the Substitute and Redeemer, who shall be satisfied with the results of his redemptive, saving work (Isaiah 53:10-12). A Christ who tries to save but fails, who tries to redeem but fails, who seeks but does not find, who calls any who do not obey his call is a false Christ, an impostor, and antichrist!

We must not be deceived by the trials of life we are called to face, or by the opposition we endure from the religious world around us (vv. 6-11). When wars, and famines, and persecutions come, by which many are offended, we must continue looking to Christ, clinging to Christ, trusting Christ. When others fall, we must not allow Satan to get an advantage of us. Skirmishes may be lost but the battle will be won and the war is Christ's.

We must not allow ourselves to be deceived by any of the many false prophets Satan raises up to destroy our souls (v. 11). Beware of false prophets and false religion (Matthew 7:13-15; 2 Corinthians 11:3, 13-15; Galatians 1:6-8; 3:1-3; 5:1-4; Colossians 2:8-23). Do not be deceived by the doctrine of the day. That doctrine which exalts the flesh, making man feel and think well of himself, is antichrist. Any doctrine that abases God our Saviour, robbing him of his absolute holiness, sovereignty, justice, and efficacy in all his works, is antichrist. Though heretics come performing miracles and speaking in tongues, though all the world runs after them, our all-wise Master says, "Take heed that no man deceive you"!

We must not allow ourselves to be deceived by the apostasy of others (v. 12). When iniquity abounds among those who profess to be followers of Christ, and those who once appeared to burn with love and zeal for his name have become altogether indifferent to it, let us seek the company and companionship of those who yet seek to honour our Master, lest we be drugged by the poison that is in the hearts of the apostate.

Satanic Warfare

Third, we must never expect to see the triumph of the gospel and the kingdom of God until the warfare between the serpent and the Saviour is over. This is a warning every bit as important as the last one. Far too often men get discouraged in the work of the ministry, and church members get discouraged in the service of Christ, because they expect to see the fruit of their labours in this world. Do not expect peace on this earth until the Prince of Peace has made all things new. Do not expect moral purity from people who do not know God. Do not expect the world to be converted to Christ.

Our Lord teaches us plainly that these things will not happen while time shall stand. Troublesome days lie before us. Heresies and persecutions will continue to abound. Doors that are now open to us may soon be shut. These are the facts plainly revealed in these verses. But there are other lessons here, too.

Be Not Troubled

Fourth, we must not allow these things to trouble our hearts. "See that ye be not troubled: for all these things must come to pass" (v. 6). None of these things will ever cause any injury to Christ, his church, or his people. Anything that appears to be injurious to God's elect, or appears to be overturning his will and purpose will ultimately prove otherwise, and will be seen to have been only the instrument by which our God has wisely and graciously accomplished his will and that which is best for his people. "For there must be also heresies among you, that they which are approved may be made manifest among you" (1 Corinthians 11:19). When the apostle Paul had explained, by divine inspiration, the very things our Saviour spoke of in Matthew 23 and 24, he was overwhelmed by the wisdom and goodness of our God in sovereignly overruling evil for good.

"O the depth of the riches both of the wisdom and knowledge of God! how unsearchable are his judgments, and his ways past finding out! For who hath known the mind of the Lord? or who hath been his counsellor? Or who hath first given to him, and it shall be recompensed unto him again? For of him, and through him, and to him, are all things: to whom be glory for ever. Amen." (Romans 11:33-36).

Persevere

Fifth, we must persevere and endure all these things in faith. "But he that shall endure unto the end, the same shall be saved" (v. 13). Though tempted, tried, persecuted, and troubled by many things, we must persevere, we must continue looking to Christ. If we are truly his, we shall. Grace will keep us still! "The righteous shall hold on his way", because all the righteous are held in the grip of God's omnipotent grace (John 10:27, 28; Philippians 1:6; 1 Peter 1:7). Every true believer shall endure in the pure doctrine of the gospel, though many are deceived by false religion. And enduring in the faith of Christ, being kept by the power of his grace, they shall be saved from all temporal trouble, and with everlasting salvation.

Though we are weak, helpless, defenceless sheep, the Lord Jesus Christ, the Son of God, is our Shepherd, wise, good, and strong. Because Christ is our Shepherd, we are secure in him. This is what the Son of God, our dear Shepherd, says concerning all his sheep: "They shall never perish"! With those words, the Son of God declares the absolute, infallible, unwavering security of God's elect in Christ.

Those who are born of God must and shall persevere. They will continue in the faith of Christ. God's elect both believe and keep on believing. The true believer begins in faith, lives in faith, and dies in faith. True faith never quits, never succumbs (Matthew 10:20; John 8:31; 1 Corinthians 15:1; Colossians 1:23; Hebrews 3:6, 14). The Word of God is very clear in this matter: Only those who continue in the faith shall enter into glory. This is the doctrine of the final perseverance of the saints.

Believers persevere in faith, because we are preserved in Christ by almighty grace. Not one of God's elect shall ever perish. The Word of God teaches the preservation of the saints just as plainly, fully, and forcibly as it teaches the perseverance of the saints. Perseverance is the believer continuing in faith. Preservation is God keeping his people in faith. Perseverance is the believer holding Christ by the hand of faith. Preservation is Christ holding the believer by the hand of grace.

Jesus is our God and Saviour,
Guide, and Counsellor, and Friend:
He will never, never leave us,
Nor will let us quite leave Him.

Having Christ as our Shepherd, all of God's sheep are absolutely secure in his hands. It is not possible for any true believer to perish, because we are preserved by the grace of God in Christ.

The End Is Coming

Sixth, we must learn to look upon this world and everything in it like scaffolding to a building. This world exists only for the building of God's church and kingdom. Like scaffolding, it must come down once the building is complete. "Then shall the end come". Long ago the playwright William Shakespeare wrote, "The world is a stage". Perhaps he said more than he knew, but he was exactly right. This world is a stage for action, a scaffold upon which God does his work, and a place for graves, in which the bodies of sleeping saints are laid to rest in hope of the resurrection. When the human race shall have performed their various predestined parts, when the building of mercy (the Church of God) is complete, when the appointed day of resurrection has come, time shall be no more (Revelation 10:5-7). That will bring on the long-awaited midnight cry, "Behold, the Bridegroom cometh" (Matthew 25:6). Then this stage shall come down. The scaffolding will be put away. All that "sleep in their graves shall awake, some to everlasting life, and some to everlasting shame and contempt" (Daniel 12:2). At last, when all that must be has been, the Sun of Righteousness shall arise! His glorious beams shall bring on the blessed morning of that great, eternal day, "in which the upright shall surely have dominion" (Psalm 49:14, 15). In that day, when the Son of God makes all things new, the wicked, the unbelieving, who seem always to prosper in this world, shall be turned into hell; and the righteous, the believing, who seem always to suffer, "shall inherit all things" (Revelation 21:5-7).

"Then shall the end come". The very last thing that shall be done, the very last act of Christ as the Saviour of his people shall be the deliverance of his Church and Kingdom up to the Father, perfect, complete, and glorious, without spot or wrinkle, "that God may be all in all" (1 Corinthians 15:24-28). Then our God will make all things new!

Preach The Word

Seventh, it is the duty, responsibility, and privilege of God's people to preach the gospel in all the world. "And this gospel of the kingdom shall be preached in all the world for a witness unto all nations; and then shall the end come" (v. 14). This is the means by which God will save his elect (Romans 1:15-17). And this will be the basis of divine judgment in the last day (2 Corinthians 2:14-17). Let us be stedfast and unmoveable, always abounding in the work of the Lord, obeying the commission he has given us, knowing that our labour is not in vain (1 Corinthians 15:58).

"And Jesus came and spake unto them, saying, All power is given unto me in heaven and in earth. Go ye therefore, and teach all nations, baptizing them in the name of the Father, and of the Son, and of the Holy Ghost: Teaching them to observe all things whatsoever I have commanded you: and, lo, I am with you alway, even unto the end of the world. Amen" (Matthew 28:18-20).

Chapter 70

Where The Carcass Is: Eagles Gather

"When ye therefore shall see the abomination of desolation, spoken of by Daniel the prophet, stand in the holy place, (whoso readeth, let him understand:) Then let them which be in Judaea flee into the mountains: Let him which is on the housetop not come down to take any thing out of his house: Neither let him which is in the field return back to take his clothes. And woe unto them that are with child, and to them that give suck in those days! But pray ye that your flight be not in the winter, neither on the sabbath day: For then shall be great tribulation, such as was not since the beginning of the world to this time, no, nor ever shall be. And except those days should be shortened, there should no flesh be saved: but for the elect's sake those days shall be shortened. Then if any man shall say unto you, Lo, here is Christ, or there; believe it not. For there shall arise false Christs, and false prophets, and shall shew great signs and wonders; insomuch that, if it were possible, they shall deceive the very elect. Behold, I have told you before. Wherefore if they shall say unto you, Behold, he is in the desert; go not forth: behold, he is in the secret chambers; believe it not. For as the lightning cometh out of the east, and shineth even unto the west; so shall also the coming of the Son of man be. For wheresoever the carcase is, there will the eagles be gathered together."
(Matthew 24:15-28)

In these verses our Lord is answering the questions his disciples asked about the destruction of the temple, his second coming, and the end of the world (v. 3). The verses that are now before us have specific application to the destruction of Jerusalem and our Lord's second coming. But we must not make the mistake of imagining that they contain no message for us. These things, too, were written for our learning and admonition.

The Lord Jesus Christ so graciously cares for his own that he tenderly prepares them for the trials they must face in this world; and the means by which he does this is his Word. There are several things we should learn from these words of our Saviour.

A Complete End

When the Lord God destroyed Jerusalem, the temple, and the nation of Israel, he made a complete end of the old, Mosaic, legal system of worship (vv. 15-21). As we have seen the primary subject of these verses is the destruction of Jerusalem in AD 70 by the Romans. The horrors and miseries endured by the Jews at that time of destruction exceeded anything recorded in the history of the world. Josephus, the Jewish historian, gives a graphic, detailed account of the havoc inflicted upon the Jewish nation by Titus. More than a million Jews were slaughtered and another 100,000 were carried into slavery. That truly was a time of "great tribulation, such as was not since the beginning of the world".

Those men and women who blasphemously cried, "Let his blood be upon us and upon our children", had no idea what they were doing. But the Lord God heard their cry and answered it in the severity of his strict justice. With the destruction of their city, he destroyed their entire system of worship.

Jerusalem and the temple were at the heart of Old Testament worship. The daily sacrifices, the yearly feasts, the mercy-seat, the holy of holies, the priesthood, the altar, the table of shewbread, all were essential parts of worship during the legal dispensation. But once Christ came, the legal system ceased to have any function. God destroyed it forever. "Christ is the end of the law" (Romans 10:4; Colossians 2:8-23). We have no earthly temple because Christ is our temple. We have no material altar because Christ is our altar. We have no physical mercy-seat because Christ is our mercy-seat. We observe no sabbath days because Christ is our sabbath. In Christ we are totally free from the yoke of legal bondage (Romans 7:4; 10:4; Galatians 3:13-26).

Exercise Wisdom

Did you notice in verse 16 that our Lord told his disciples to flee from death at the hands of persecuting tyrants? Sometimes, our wisest and most proper course of action is to flee. Prudence is always proper. Many think that fleeing from persecution is an indication of cowardice. It is not. Without question, we are to confess Christ before men, and be willing to die for him should providence demand it in the path of duty. But there are times when more grace is required to be quiet than to act rashly. Let us never walk away from known duty. Let us never deny or compromise the gospel of Christ. But it is altogether proper for us to exercise wisdom and use good, sound judgment in all matters.

In our day, at least in Western countries, the violence of physical persecution is not an immediate threat to the followers of Christ. Yet, the Saviour's instruction is just as applicable to us as it was to those who heard him speak these words. When trouble arises, let us flee to our Refuge (Psalm 143:9; Proverbs 18:10). When controversies rage among men, where the glory of God is not at stake, rather than engaging in them, we would be wise to flee from them.

God's Constant Care

God's elect are always the objects of his special love and tender care (vv. 22-24). I remind you that the world is but scaffold for the building of God's church and kingdom. The reprobate reap many of the benefits of providence. But the objects of providence are "the elect". Those days of tribulation were shortened "for the elect's sake". This will be of tremendous help if you can get hold of it. God's care is for his elect. He hears their prayers. He keeps them by his Spirit. He orders all the affairs of the world for their good (Romans 8:28). He allows neither men nor devils to harm them. He sacrifices men and nations for them (Isaiah 43:5-7). Be wise and make your calling and election sure. Tribulation and trouble are sure to attend our lives in this world. But in the midst of earthly woes, here are three soft pillows for your aching head: 1. Electing Love, 2. Our Crucified Saviour, and 3. Divine Providence. God does everything "for the elect's sake".

Many Antichrists

"For there shall arise false Christs, and false prophets, and shall shew great signs and wonders; insomuch that, if it were possible, they shall deceive the very elect. Behold, I have told you before. Wherefore if they shall say unto you, Behold, he is in the desert; go not forth: behold, he is in the secret chambers; believe it not." (vv. 24-26).

There are many antichrists in this world (1 John 4:1-4). I have no problem in stating, as did our forefathers, that the pope is antichrist and the church of Rome is antichrist. I do not restrict this to apostolic times. I mean that now, today, *his unholiness*, the Pope, is Antichrist and Roman Catholicism is Antichrist. That fact cannot be stated too often, or too emphatically.

However, it is a serious mistake to limit antichrist to one man, or one religious sect. Antichrist was already at work in the Apostolic age. John said many antichrists had gone out into the world. Paul had to contend with antichrists at Galatia, Colosse, Corinth, and Jerusalem. 2 Thessalonians 2:3 describes antichrist as "the man of sin, the son of perdition". Antichrist is anyone who opposes God, exalts himself above God, or sets himself up in the temple of God to be worshipped as God, showing that he is God.

That is to say, antichrist is any system of religion, any man, any preacher, any church, any denomination that makes salvation to be dependent upon or determined by the will, works, and worth of man, rather than the will, works, and worth of Christ. It does not matter whether that system of religion is conservative or liberal, a mainline Protestant Church or a wild cult, Baptist or Methodist, Pentecostal or Presbyterian. Any church, doctrine, preacher, or religious system that makes man the centrepiece is antichrist.

Let me be understood. Those who teach that God's will can be altered, hindered, or thwarted by man's will, are, according to Colossians 2, will worshippers, not God worshippers. They are antichrists. Those who teach that the merit and efficacy of Christ's atonement resides in man's will, man's decision, and man's faith are antichrists. Those who teach that the gracious operations of the Holy Spirit may be successfully resisted by man are antichrists. Those who teach that grace can be forfeited or taken away as the result of something a man does are antichrists.

Any religion, doctrine, or gospel that turns you away from Christ alone as Saviour is antichrist. A Christ who loves but cannot save is a useless Christ, an antichrist. A Christ who redeems but does not save is a useless Christ, an antichrist. A Christ who calls but does not convert is a useless Christ, an antichrist. A Christ whose work depends on the will or work of the sinner to make it effectual is a useless Christ, an antichrist. A Christ who wills the salvation of any who are not actually saved is a useless Christ, an antichrist.

Christ's Advent

Our Lord's second coming will be a sudden, climatic, glorious event. "For as the lightning cometh out of the east, and shineth even unto the west; so shall also the coming of the Son of man be" (v. 27). Contrary to the "prophecy experts" of our day, there is no such thing as a secret rapture. When our Lord appears, his coming will be as startling and sudden as a bolt of lightening. He will be seen by all men at once (Revelation 1:7). His coming will terrify the wicked. But it will be the delight of the believer. Let us live every moment in the hope and expectation of his glorious advent (Titus 2:14; Jude 21).

Where The Carcass Is

"For wheresoever the carcase is, there will the eagles be gathered together" (v. 28). There are two common interpretations given to this verse by sound, orthodox men. I do not know which is strictly correct; but since both are theologically sound, I will give them both to you. Most commentators teach that the carcass here refers to empty, dead Judaism, and the eagles to the flocks of lost religious men and women who clung to it feverishly, even to the destruction of their lives and of the lives of their sons and daughters. So it is today. Find a church that is utterly dead, void of the knowledge of God, his gospel, his Word, his grace, his Son, and his glory, and you will find a church full of lost religionists. Foul, unclean birds feed upon a dead carcass. Where there is no life, people cling to rituals, ceremonies, creeds, and emotionalism.

But there is another interpretation, one that I think is better. Perhaps the carcass here refers to our Lord Jesus Christ, who was slain for our sins, and the eagles refer to chosen sinners like you and me who flee to him for salvation and life. In that case the lesson is this: Christ crucified is the great magnet by which God draws chosen sinners to himself. Whether that is the teaching of this verse or not, I will not attempt to say; but it is the teaching of holy scripture (John 12:32; 1 Corinthians 1:21-23). And that is clearly our Saviour's teaching in Luke 17:32-37 (cf. Isaiah 40:31), where he makes a similar statement. "Wheresoever the body is, thither will the eagles be gathered together". Notice the use of the definite article. Our Lord said, "Wheresoever the body is (not wheresoever bodies are), thither will the eagles be gathered together". Also, notice that he speaks of eagles (not buzzards) in the plural.

"The body" of the One slain is our Lord Jesus Christ. "The eagles" are God's elect who are gathered to him in faith. This is the teaching of holy scripture (Deuteronomy 32:8-12) and the teaching of our Saviour here. God's elect are spoken of in the scriptures as eagles. His church is given "the wings of the eagle, that great eagle" (Revelation 12:14). "They that wait upon the Lord shall renew their strength; they shall mount up with wings as eagles" (Isaiah 40:31).

Wherever Christ crucified is set forth in the preaching of the gospel, wherever Christ is revealed to men by the power and grace of his Spirit through the preaching of the gospel, there his elect will be gathered unto him "in the day when the Son of man is revealed".

Christ's eagles "gather" to him who is their food (Job 9:25, 26). He is the One upon whom we live. He is to us life eternal. The body of our slain Saviour, Christ crucified, is the meeting-point of his elect. He is the great attraction, drawing needy souls, like eagles to the carcass. He said, "I, if I be lifted up from the earth, will draw all men unto me".

God our Creator in the Book of Job says of the eagle, his creature, "She abideth upon the rock from thence she seeketh the prey; her eyes behold afar off

… where the slain are, there is she". God our Saviour here tells us, "As the eagles gather round the body, so the souls of men, chosen, redeemed, and called by my grace, are gathered unto me." Keen and swift as eagles for the prey are God's elect for Christ crucified. These are the words of our blessed Saviour. Let not one of them fall to the ground. "Wheresoever the body is, thither will the eagles be gathered together".

The eagle is a bird of prey. In all birds of prey, we are told, there is great sense of smell. Added to its sense of smell, the eagle has a ravenous appetite. Compelled by hunger and its sense of smell, it flies quickly, at every opportunity to its feast. But the eagle is not a vulture. It does not feed on dead things, but living. And the crucified Christ, upon whom our souls feed, though once slain as our Substitute, is alive for evermore (John 6:53-58)!

If Christ has given us life in himself, if he has made us alive by his grace, he gives us a continually increasing appetite and hunger for himself. Does he not? Do you not hunger for him, for his grace, for his embrace, for his face, for his righteousness, for his blood, for his presence? Hungering for him, his eagles fly to the place where he is, like famished birds hastening to the prey. They fly with eager anticipation to his house, his Word, his ordinances, and his throne of grace.

As David longed for the waters of Bethlehem when he was thirsty, O let our souls long for Christ. "As the hart panteth after the water brooks", so he longed for his God. May the same be true of you and me. Oh for grace to have our souls hungering for Christ crucified day and night! As the eagles gather together unto the prey, so should we be found feasting upon Christ crucified relentlessly. In him, in his glorious excellencies is everything our souls need. His name is our Salvation and High Tower. His blood is our atonement. His righteousness is our dress. His perfections are our delight. His promises are our meditation. His grace is our assurance. His visits are our sweet memories. His presence is our joy. His strength is our comfort. His glory is our ambition. His coming is our hope. His company forever is our heaven!

Crave him! Crave him! Like birds of prey crave their food, let us crave our Saviour. If we have tasted that the Lord is gracious, let us feast upon him. May God give us an insatiable, constant, ever-increasing hunger for Christ, a hunger for everything he is, for everything he gives, for everything he has done, for everything that belongs to him, touches him, and smells of him, a hunger that graciously forces us ever to fly to him, like an eagle to the prey! Wherever Christ is, there will his people fly, as eagles to the prey and as doves to their windows (Isaiah 60:8).

Chapter 71

False Christs And The True

"And Jesus answered and said unto them, Take heed that no man deceive you. For many shall come in my name, saying, I am Christ; and shall deceive many … For then shall be great tribulation, such as was not since the beginning of the world to this time, no, nor ever shall be. And except those days should be shortened, there should no flesh be saved: but for the elect's sake those days shall be shortened. Then if any man shall say unto you, Lo, here is Christ, or there; believe it not. For there shall arise false Christs, and false prophets, and shall shew great signs and wonders; insomuch that, if it were possible, they shall deceive the very elect."
(Matthew 24:4, 5, 21-24)

The Word of God warns us plainly and repeatedly that in the last days, the days in which we now live, many false Christs will appear, that many will claim to be Christ who are impostors, false Christs and deceivers, and that many false prophets will arise pointing us to these false Christs, saying, "Lo, here is Christ, or there." As you care for your own soul, the souls of your family, the souls of perishing men and women, I urge you to give earnest heed to the words of the Son of God in this passage.

The plain fact is there are many false Christs, many antichrists, by whom the souls of men are deceived and damned. I want to be as charitable and gracious as I can; but charity and grace will not allow me to be silent while immortal souls are deceived and God's glory is trampled beneath the feet of men. If you trust a false Christ, you cannot be saved any more than you could be saved by trusting a tadpole. We are called of God to trust, love, follow, and obey the true Christ and him only. Salvation is promised to none but those who trust the true Christ. Therefore, we are clearly warned, "Take heed that no man deceive you." We must take heed to the teachings of holy scripture, lest we be deceived by some false Christ.

The Liberals' Christ
The false Christ presented by liberals was a social do-gooder. "Of course", we are told, "he is not God". The virgin birth, the incarnation, the resurrection must all be understood allegorically. In fact, the Christ of the liberals is considered by many to be a man of very questionable moral character. Any who are deceived by liberal theology and the Christ of the liberals are willingly deceived. We are not deceived by the Christ of the liberals. Only a prating fool would pretend to be a Christian while teaching what liberals do concerning Christ. The Christ of the liberals is a false Christ. All who trust the Christ of the liberals are lost.

The Cults' Christ
The false Christ of various cults is presented to us as a good man, a prophet, a teacher of morality, the first and greatest creation of God, even a secondary god. But the Christ of the cults is never represented as the true and eternal God. Their Christ receives his existence from another god, one who is greater than he is. This, of course, is not the Christ of the Bible. We are not deceived by him. The Christ of the cults is a false Christ. All who trust the Christ of the cults are lost.

The Papists' Christ
Roman Catholicism proclaims another false Christ. The papists profess that Jesus Christ is God, that he came into the world as a man, that he suffered the wrath of God as a substitute for sinners, died, was buried, rose again the third day, ascended to heaven, and is coming again. But the Christ of Romanism is not a complete Saviour. The Christ of Rome cannot save sinners without their own good works, the intercessions of priests, and the sacraments of the church. The Christ of Rome is not the Christ of the Bible. We are not deceived by him. The Christ of the papists is a false Christ. All who trust the Christ of Rome are lost.

The Arminians' Christ
However, there is a false Christ much more dangerous than the antichrists of the liberals, the cults, and the papists. A false Christ by whom the souls of men have been deceived for years and by whom millions are being deceived today. I am compelled to say, the vast majority of those who profess faith in Christ are followers of this false Christ, who will lead them to eternal ruin. This Christ, this antichrist, is so dangerous and deceptive that our Lord tells us he would deceive the very elect, were it possible for God's elect to be deceived (Matthew 24:24). The Christ I speak of is the false Christ of Arminian, freewill, works religion.

False Christs And The True

Few think it is uncharitable to denounce the false Christs of liberals, cults, and papists as antichrists, or to warn men that following those false Christs will result in everlasting damnation. Yet, whenever anyone boldly asserts that the Christ of Arminian, freewill, works religion is a false Christ, and that all who trust him are lost, he is castigated as an evil man. Be that as it may, as a watchman upon the walls of Zion, I am responsible to warn you of the danger of this antichrist.

The Christ of Arminian, freewill, works religion is extremely dangerous because in many ways he appears to be the true Christ. The free-willers and work-mongers tell us that Christ is the true God, in every way equal with the Father and the Holy Spirit. They assert that he saves by grace alone, without the works of man. They insist that good works play no part in their salvation. The devotees of this Christ will have nothing to do with the Christ of the liberals, the cults, or the papists. But "take heed that no man deceive you". Do not be fooled. The Christ of Arminian, freewill, works religion is not the Christ of the Bible. He is a false Christ. All who trust this false Christ are lost, too.

The Issue

Be sure you understand the issue. It is not what or how much a person has to know to be saved. The issue is who must I know? The answer to that question is plainly stated in John 17:3. We must know the true God and the true Christ. Let me make five comparisons of the false Christ of modern religion, the Christ of Arminian, freewill, works religion, and the Christ of the Bible. When you have considered these five comparisons in the light of holy scripture, I have no doubt that you will see the obvious distinctions between the false Christs and the true.

1. The Christ of modern, freewill, works religion loves everyone in the world and wants to save them. We are told that Christ loves all men alike, desires the salvation of all men alike, and is gracious to all men alike. But as multitudes are not saved that means the love, will, and grace of Christ is in itself ineffectual to save. That language cannot be applied to the Christ of the Bible. If God loves all men equally yet some men are not saved, the love of God cannot be the determining factor in the salvation of a sinner. Yet God says his love is saving love (Jeremiah 31:3, 38-40). It cannot be both saving and universal. Thank God, he does love many; but he does not love everyone (Romans 9:13).

The Christ of the Bible, loves his people, wills and prays for their salvation and is gracious to them. They are his people, unconditionally elected to salvation from eternity. He came to save them (Psalm 5:5; 7:11; 11:5; Matthew 1:21; 11:27; John 10:16; John 17:9, 10; Acts 13:48; Romans 9:21-24; Ephesians 1:3-6).

2. The Christ of modern, freewill, works religion tries to save everyone. We are told that he offers salvation to every sinner and does everything he can to save them all; but his offer is rejected and his work frustrated by the will of those who refuse to come to him and be saved. If God the Holy Spirit calls all sinners alike to life and faith in Christ and yet some die without faith, there can be no life-giving power in that call! If his grace can be resisted, it is not the distinguishing factor in salvation. But God says it is (John 6:63; 1 Corinthians 4:7).

The Christ of the Bible does not merely offer salvation, he performs it. Grace is not an offer, it is an operation. The Son of God effectually calls to himself all his elect, his sheep, and sovereignly works salvation in them by the irresistible power and grace of his Holy Spirit. Not one of them will be lost (Psalm 65:4; 110:3; Isaiah 55:11; John 5:21; 6:37-40; 10:3, 25-30; 17:2; Philippians 2:13).

3. The false Christ of Arminianism cannot regenerate and save anyone who does not first choose to be saved by him. We are told that man's will is free but Christ's will is bound by and must wait upon man's will because it would not be right for him to violate man's freewill. The will of God to save all is frustrated, defeated and reversed. But God says his will is absolute and unalterable (Isaiah 14:24). Salvation comes only by God's irresistible will (Romans 9:16).

The true, saving Christ does defy man's will; and I am very thankful that he does. Had he not overwhelmed my will, I would be lost or in hell right now. The same is true of you. He sovereignly regenerates and saves every chosen, redeemed sinner. His operations of grace are totally independent of the will and choice of the sinner. Apart from his work of grace in us, spiritually dead sinners never would come to him in faith. Faith is not our contribution to the work of salvation. Faith is the result, not the cause of God's saving operations. "Let God be true, but every man a liar" (John 3:3-7; 6:44, 65; 15:16; Acts 11:18; Romans 2:4; 9:16; Ephesians 2:1-9; Philippians 1:6, 29; Colossians 2:12; Hebrews 12:2).

4. The false Christ of this modern, man-centred religion died on the cross for everyone in the world, to make it possible for all to be saved. He made salvation possible, we are told, but actually secured no one's salvation by his death. If Christ, by dying, merely made it possible for men to be redeemed, justified, and saved, clearly there is no inherent efficacy and saving power for anyone until they believe on him. Once again it is the will of the individual that rules and the Son of God died in vain for all who perish in unbelief. He tried to save them but failed.

If Christ died to redeem everyone and some yet die under the wrath of God, the blood of Christ does not secure salvation! If Christ died for those in hell as well as those in glory, his blood is of no value at all. It saves no one. It does not wash away sin and was shed in vain! But God says all for whom Christ's blood was shed shall be saved by it (Isaiah 53:10, 11; John 10:15, 26; Romans 8:34).

The Christ of God is not a frustrated failure. He died for God's elect and effectually put away our sins by the sacrifice of himself. Having satisfied the justice of God for us, he obtained eternal salvation for us. We are actually and forever pardoned, justified, and sanctified by his blood (Isaiah 42:4; 53:8; Matthew 20:28; John 10:14, 15, 26; Acts 20:28; Romans 5:9, 10; Ephesians 5:25; Hebrews 9:12; 10:10-14; 1 Peter 3:18; Revelation 5:9, 10).

Here then, are three inescapable conclusions which must be accepted by all who believe the Arminian doctrine of universal redemption, or general atonement i.e. that the Lord Jesus Christ shed his blood for every person in the world and that the intention of Christ in his death was the eternal salvation of all men.

1. If it was the intention of the Son of God to redeem and save all men yet some are not saved, Christ's purpose in dying has been therefore been frustrated.

2. If the Lord Jesus Christ shed his blood to save every person in the world and some of those for whom He died go to hell, then for those who perish, Christ died in vain.

3. If Christ died to make atonement for all men and some yet perish under the wrath of God, then the work of redemption failed.

These blasphemous absurdities no true child of God can tolerate. They rob Christ of his glory in redemption, destroy the foundation of hope for sinners, and call into question the very divinity of our Saviour. If he is a failure, if he fails to save all for whom he died, he is not God. Yet, if the doctrine of universal, general redemption is believed, these blasphemous conclusions must be accepted.

Indeed, there are many who acknowledge these blasphemous absurdities, while claiming to be the servants of God. Noel Smith was my first theology professor. He taught biblical interpretation and theology at Baptist Bible College in Springfield, Missouri. As he endeavoured to describe hell, this is what he wrote …

> "What is hell? It is an infinite negation. And it is more than that. I tell you, and I say it with profound reverence, hell is a ghastly monument to the failure of the triune God to save the multitudes who are there. I say it reverently. I say it with every nerve of my body tense. Sinners go to hell because God almighty himself couldn't save them! He did everything he could. He failed"!

Even as an eighteen year old boy, I found that statement shocking. But it is not unique. Jerry Falwell, pastor of Thomas Road Baptist Church in Lynchburg, Virginia, one of Mr Smith's earliest pupils in Springfield, also asserts that God is a failure. Several years ago, I heard him say, "If you go to hell, you will go to that awful place, in spite of the fact that God himself has done everything he possibly could to save you". Shortly after hearing Falwell's statement, Al Geisler, who was at the time, pastor of the First Baptist Church in Danville, Kentucky made this statement, as he begged sinners to let Jesus save them at the end of a radio sermon. "Jesus loved you, died for you, and has done everything he can to save you; but it will all be in vain unless you believe. What a shame it will be that Jesus' death will be in vain for so many." I agree. It would be a terrible shame, not for the lost sinner, but for Christ! It would not be a failure on the sinner's part, but a failure on Christ's part, if he died to save anyone he fails to save! This is no less than the denial of Christ's deity. If he is a failure, he is not God.

5. The false Christ of Arminianism looses many who have been saved by him because they do not hang on, hold out, or persevere to the end. Some do grant that the saved sinner has what they call "eternal security". But it is not security based upon the will, work, and purpose of God in Christ. It is not security based upon the blood of Christ, or the operations of his Spirit. According to the freewiller, all these things are done for all people alike. Their doctrine of "eternal security" is security based on the will of man, not the choice and will of God.

The Christ of the Bible preserves his chosen, redeemed, called ones by his almighty grace so that they cannot fall away and perish at last. We are kept in life, grace, and faith by the immutability of his will, the power of his blood, the efficacy of his grace, the seal of his Spirit, and the perfection of his intercession (Malachi 3:6; John 5:24; 10:26-30; Romans 8:28-39; 1 Peter 1:2-5; Jude 24, 25).

At a glance, the Christ of freewill may seem to resemble the true Christ of scripture. He does not. He is a false Christ, weak and helpless, bowing to the will of man. Those who serve the false Christ reject the Christ of the Bible. They are deceived. They shall forever perish under the wrath of God, unless they come to know and trust the Christ of God who saves his people from their sins by himself. We must, as we fear God and care for the souls of men, have no fellowship with and give no credibility to Arminian, freewill, works religion (2 Corinthians 6:14-7:1; Revelation 18:4). We must, in these days of darkness, deception, and delusion, proclaim the Christ of God in all his saving fullness, grace, and glory. He alone is able to save (Romans 1:15-17). Let us ever adore, praise, and extol the Lord Jesus Christ alone and completely as our great Saviour (Isaiah 59:16).

Chapter 72

Christ's Second Coming And The Parable Of The Fig Tree

"Immediately after the tribulation of those days shall the sun be darkened, and the moon shall not give her light, and the stars shall fall from heaven, and the powers of the heavens shall be shaken: And then shall appear the sign of the Son of man in heaven: and then shall all the tribes of the earth mourn, and they shall see the Son of man coming in the clouds of heaven with power and great glory. And he shall send his angels with a great sound of a trumpet, and they shall gather together his elect from the four winds, from one end of heaven to the other. Now learn a parable of the fig tree; When his branch is yet tender, and putteth forth leaves, ye know that summer is nigh: So likewise ye, when ye shall see all these things, know that it is near, even at the doors. Verily I say unto you, This generation shall not pass, till all these things be fulfilled. Heaven and earth shall pass away, but my words shall not pass away."
(Matthew 24:29-35)

Our Lord seems to have deliberately mingled the prophecies of the destruction of Jerusalem and his own second coming. Thus, he carefully avoided satisfying the carnal curiosity of his disciples' questions, while at the same time encouraging them to live in watchful anticipation of his glorious second advent.

The fact is, our Saviour does not intend for us to know the day and hour of his second coming (Acts 1:4-7). "But of that day and hour knoweth no man, no, not the angels of heaven, but my Father only" (v. 36). While assuring us of his coming and inspiring our hearts with the blessed hope of that great day, our Saviour wisely hides from us any information regarding the time of his advent.

Without question, much that is contained in these verses has direct bearing upon the coming of the Roman armies into Jerusalem as the instruments of God's judgment upon that city and the nation of Israel. Immediately after the great tribulation fell upon that nation, spiritual blindness engulfed them. Their sun, moon and stars, all the spiritual light they had, was turned to darkness. The very things that had once been to them symbols of heavenly power and favour were shaken to the very foundation, and became to them a snare and a stumbling block.

However, it would be a great mistake to limit the words of our Lord in these verses to that terrible day of judgment upon the nation of Israel. The verses now before us speak also of Christ's glorious second coming to judge the world.

The Second Coming Of Christ

The first thing spoken of here is the second coming of our Lord Jesus Christ (vv. 29-31). The darkening of the sun and moon, and falling of the stars are to be understood figuratively, having reference to the prophecy of Amos (Amos 8:8-14). Those terms speak of God taking away the light he had given to Israel, casting them off, and shutting the nation up in the darkness of divine judgment (Romans 11:8-10). When our Lord speaks here of the Son of man coming to judgment, he is not speaking of the day of final judgment, but of the judgment that fell upon the nation of Israel for rejecting the Lord of life and glory. The sending of "his angels with the great sound of a trumpet" to gather his elect refers to him sending forth gospel preachers to preach the gospel, by which he gathers in his chosen (Isaiah 27:13; Revelation 14:6).

Yet, as he came in judgment upon that nation in AD 70, so he shall come again in the last day to judge the world in righteousness. There will be no need for the sun, the moon, and the stars when he who is the brightness of the glory of the invisible God and the express image of his person shines forth in the fulness of his indescribable glory. Christ's second coming will be a glorious event, universally known and acknowledged, both by the righteous and the wicked, the believing and the unbelieving (Revelation 1:7; 2 Thessalonians 1:7-10).

"Christ's coming", wrote C. H. Spurgeon, "will be the source of untold joy to his friends; but it will bring unparalleled sorrow to his foes". Without trying to expound the doctrine of the second advent, let me show you what our Lord teaches us in these verses about his coming.

First, the Lord Jesus Christ really is coming again. Scoffers abound who think our faith is foolishness and that our hope is a dream. Do not allow their infidelity to rub off on you. There is a day of reckoning yet to come. Christ is coming again. There is yet to be a day of resurrection and of judgment (Acts 1:11; 17:30, 31; 1 Corinthians 15:19, 51-58; 1 Thessalonians 4:13-18; 2 Thessalonians 1:7-10; Titus 2:13; Hebrews 9:27, 28; Revelation 1:7; 22:20).

Second, when the Lord Jesus returns to this world, it will not be in secrecy or in humiliation, but in power and in great glory. There is no such thing as a secret coming of Christ, or a secret rapture. Our Lord declares that all men "shall see the Son of man coming in the clouds of heaven with power and great glory" (v. 30).

When Christ comes again, the very sun, moon, and stars will melt before him. The heavens, being on fire, shall melt with a fervent heat (2 Peter 3:10-14).

Our Lord's second advent will be as different as possible from his first coming. At his first advent, our Saviour came into the world as "a man of sorrows and acquainted with grief". He came here in humiliation, born in a stable, laid in a manger, the child of a poor, insignificant woman. He took upon himself the form of a servant. He was despised and rejected of men. He was betrayed into the hands of wicked men by the kiss of a friend. Condemned by a mockery of justice, beaten, crowned with thorns, and covered with the spit of vile humanity, the Son of God was at last crucified between two thieves.

But when he comes again, he shall come in the full display of his royal majesty as the King of glory, the King of heaven, and the King of the earth. All the nations of the world shall be gathered before his august majesty to be judged by him. Before him every knee shall bow. Every tongue shall acknowledge and confess that he is Lord. Whatever ungodly men and women say and do now, things will be different in that day. There will be no scoffing then. Every mouth will be stopped. We need to constantly remember these things, so that we may wait patiently for our Saviour's arrival. Our Master will one day soon be acknowledged by all the world; and we shall see him with joy (Job 19:25-27).

Third, when our Lord comes again, his first concern and his first order of business will be the security, salvation, and glory of his elect. "And he shall send his angels with a great sound of a trumpet, and they shall gather together his elect from the four winds, from one end of heaven to the other" (v. 31). As it always has been, so it shall be then: our Master's great concern shall be his people. When he comes to judge the world, he will first take care of his elect. Not a hair of their heads shall fall to the ground. Not a bone of his mystical body shall be broken.

When God destroyed the world in the flood, there was an ark for Noah and his family. When he poured fire and brimstone down upon Sodom, Lot found refuge in Zoar. And when the wrath of God at last bursts out against the wicked to destroy this world, his elect shall first be gathered by his holy angels to their blessed hiding place, Christ Jesus. Those holy angels, who rejoiced over each repenting sinner, who ministered from the beginning to those who were chosen to be the heirs of salvation, shall gladly gather them all out of the earth in one mighty sweep of grace! Our Saviour has gone to prepare a place for us. When the place is ready and the time has come for us to be glorified together with him, he will come again and gather his elect from the four corners of the earth.

East and west, and south and north,
Speeds each glorious angel forth,
Gathering in with glittering wing
Zion's saints to Zion's King!

Fourth, the day of our Lord's second advent will be a great and terrible day of judgment and wrath for all the wicked; but for believers it will be a day of great glory and great joy. This is a point that needs emphasizing. Nowhere in the Word of God is the second coming of Christ set forth as a matter of fear and dread for believers. Not at all! This is the one day we ought to look forward to and anticipate with great joy. When Christ comes in his glory, all God's elect shall be gathered together as one; and we shall be one. The saints of every age and every tongue shall be assembled at once before his glory. All shall be there, from righteous Abel down to the very last soul to be converted to God, from the oldest patriarch down to the smallest infant to be aborted by wicked hands. What a happy gathering that will be, when all the family of God meets together in perfection and glory! Our little meetings and reunions, our assemblies for worship and our conferences here are matters of great delight to us. How we look forward to meeting God's saints here. Just try to imagine what that will be when we meet that great multitude which no man can number!

John Newton once wrote, "When I get to heaven, I shall see three wonders there. The first wonder will be to see people there whom I did not expect to see. The second wonder will be to miss many people whom I did expect to see. The third and greatest wonder of all will be to find myself there"!

After commenting on these things, J.C Ryle wrote, "Surely, we may be content to carry the cross, and to put up with partings for a few years. We travel on towards a day, when we shall meet to part no more."

The Parable Of The Fig Tree

In verses 32-34 our Lord illustrates his doctrine using the parable of the fig tree. There has been much speculation about this parable of the fig tree. Numerous sermons have been preached about it; and far too many books have been written about it. But there is nothing really mysterious about it. Our Lord simply drew another illustration from nature, as was his custom, to enforce what he was teaching. As men know that summer is near when they see the trees, in this case a fig tree, putting forth their leaves, so our Lord said this generation would know that God had come upon the nation of Israel in judgment when the Roman armies left Jerusalem as a heap of ashes in a pool of blood.

The key which must determine our interpretation of this parable is verse 34. Our Saviour said, "Verily I say unto you, This generation shall not pass, till all these things be fulfilled". Spurgeon explained, "It was just about the ordinary limit of a generation when the Roman armies compassed Jerusalem, whose measure of iniquity was then full, and overflowed in misery, agony, distress, and bloodshed such as the world never saw before or since."

So the second coming of Christ will be a summer of joy and comfort to the saints. Christ will be glorified by his saints and in them. We shall see him as he is and admire him. Grace will consummate in glory. Then we will enjoy full redemption and salvation. The winter of sorrows, afflictions, and persecutions, and of coldness, darkness, and indifference will be over. The sun shall no more go down, nor the moon withdraw itself, but the Lord will be the everlasting light of his people!

The Infallibility Of Holy Scripture

In verse 35 our Saviour declares the absolute infallibility of holy scripture. "Heaven and earth shall pass away, but my words shall not pass away". The Word of God is infallible. It will stand forever. Everything written upon the pages of Inspiration must and shall be fulfilled (Isaiah 40:8; 1 Peter 1:25).

Our Lord's predictions will be fulfilled. He knew that scoffers would come, saying, "Where is the promise of his coming?" He knew that when he comes again faith will be a rare thing among men. He knew how terribly prone we are to unbelief. Therefore, he gives this word of assurance concerning his Word. Let us be wise and hear what he says. Every promise he has made of mercy, grace, and pardon shall be fulfilled. Every prophecy of wrath, judgment, and everlasting punishment must be fulfilled. When heaven and earth have passed away, as they must, the Word of our God, and the purpose for which he created the heavens and the earth shall stand forever.

"The Lord is not slack concerning his promise, as some men count slackness; but is longsuffering to us-ward, not willing that any should perish, but that all should come to repentance. But the day of the Lord will come as a thief in the night; in the which the heavens shall pass away with a great noise, and the elements shall melt with fervent heat, the earth also and the works that are therein shall be burned up. Seeing then that all these things shall be dissolved, what manner of persons ought ye to be in all holy conversation and godliness, Looking for and hasting unto the coming of the day of God, wherein the heavens being on fire shall be dissolved, and the elements shall melt with fervent heat? Nevertheless we, according to his promise, look for new heavens and a new earth, wherein dwelleth righteousness. Wherefore, beloved, seeing that ye look for such things, be diligent that ye may be found of him in peace, without spot, and blameless." (2 Peter 3:9-14).

Chapter 73

Are You Ready?

"But of that day and hour knoweth no man, no, not the angels of heaven, but my Father only. But as the days of Noe were, so shall also the coming of the Son of man be. For as in the days that were before the flood they were eating and drinking, marrying and giving in marriage, until the day that Noe entered into the ark, And knew not until the flood came, and took them all away; so shall also the coming of the Son of man be. Then shall two be in the field; the one shall be taken, and the other left. Two women shall be grinding at the mill; the one shall be taken, and the other left. Watch therefore: for ye know not what hour your Lord doth come. But know this, that if the goodman of the house had known in what watch the thief would come, he would have watched, and would not have suffered his house to be broken up. Therefore be ye also ready: for in such an hour as ye think not the Son of man cometh. Who then is a faithful and wise servant, whom his lord hath made ruler over his household, to give them meat in due season? Blessed is that servant, whom his lord when he cometh shall find so doing. Verily I say unto you, That he shall make him ruler over all his goods. But and if that evil servant shall say in his heart, My lord delayeth his coming; And shall begin to smite his fellowservants, and to eat and drink with the drunken; The lord of that servant shall come in a day when he looketh not for him, and in an hour that he is not aware of, And shall cut him asunder, and appoint him his portion with the hypocrites: there shall be weeping and gnashing of teeth."
(Matthew 24:36-51)

Our Lord Jesus admonishes us to make certain that we are prepared for his coming. "Therefore be ye also ready: for in such an hour as ye think not the Son of man cometh" (v. 44). Are you ready for the Son of God to appear?

While this passage is speaking specifically of Christ's glorious second advent, we must not look upon the things spoken in this passage as having no reference to any except those who happened to be living upon the earth when the Lord comes again. In fact, as we have already seen, these verses also apply to Christ's coming in judgment to destroy Jerusalem in AD 70. The Lord Jesus Christ comes upon men and women in judgment and in grace in many ways. He is said to come upon the wicked in judgment whenever he brings providential wrath upon them, as he did upon Sodom. He comes to his elect in grace in conversion. The Lord comes again for both the righteous and the wicked in the hour of death. But, in this passage the Lord Jesus is talking about his glorious second advent.

Are you ready? Are you prepared to meet God? Soon you must meet the Lord God in judgment. When you do, he will judge you upon the grounds of absolute righteousness (Revelation 20:11, 12). Whatever state you are in then, you will be in forever (Revelation 21:27; 22:11). If you are righteous, you will be righteous forever. If you are saved, you will be saved forever. If you are wicked, you will be wicked forever. If you are lost, you will be lost forever! In these closing verses of Matthew 24 the Son of God urges us to make certain we are ready to meet him.

No One Knows

"But of that day and hour knoweth no man, no, not the angels of heaven, but my Father only (v. 36). The language could not be clearer. No one knows when Christ will come again. Yet, every few years, some religious fool predicts the time of our Lord's coming, and multitudes are duped by them. Such predictions began as early as the apostolic era (2 Thessalonians 2:1-5), and continue to this day; but the teachings of scripture are specific and clear. No one knows when Christ will come again. Such knowledge God gives to no one (Acts 1:6, 7).

Usually, these imaginary prophets wrest verse 36 from its obvious meaning, and say, "Though we cannot know the day and hour of Christ's coming, we can know the year, the month, and even the week." Then, by some intricate, elaborate scheme of days, numbers, and events linked together, they make a prediction, which always proves to be wrong. It only takes a little time for their folly to be demonstrated; but they never give up. No sooner is one date-setter fallen than another rises to repeat his error. Not even the angels of heaven know about the hour of Christ's second advent. "We need not", wrote C. H. Spurgeon, "be troubled by idle prophecies of hair-brained fanatics, even if they claim to interpret the scriptures; for what the angels do not know has not been revealed to them."

Even our Saviour, while he walked on this earth in our nature, voluntarily limited his own capacity to know the time of his second advent (Mark 13:32). Surely, we ought to be content not to know what he chose not to know. It is enough for us to know that our Lord is coming again. Knowing that, let us be ready for him to appear at any moment, ever "looking for the mercy of our Lord Jesus Christ unto eternal life" (Jude 21).

No Change

Fallen man never changes. When the Lord Jesus comes again, the world will be in the same condition it is in now. That is what our Saviour tells us in verses 37-39. The world will not be converted before Christ comes. It will be in the same condition it was in when God sent the flood: absorbed in worldly, sensual pursuits, oblivious to eternal, spiritual things, and despising the warnings of God's faithful servants and the gospel of his grace. Therefore, judgment shall fall upon it (Proverbs 1:23-33).

Our Lord is not here declaring that marriage and its privileges are evil, any more that he is telling us that eating and drinking is evil. He is simply telling us that fallen man is completely absorbed with temporal things, living as if he had no soul to lose, no judgment to face, and no eternity before him. Yet, it must be stated that those things which are perfectly lawful in normal circumstances, "eating and drinking, marrying and giving in marriage", become great evils and snares to our souls, if they keep us from seeking, knowing, and serving Christ (Matthew 13:22). As Spurgeon stated, "Woe unto those whose eating and drinking do not include the bread and the water of life; and who marry or are given in marriage, but not to the heavenly Bridegroom"!

A Great Separation

"Then shall two be in the field; the one shall be taken, and the other left. Two women shall be grinding at the mill; the one shall be taken, and the other left" (vv. 40, 41). In that great day, when Christ comes again, there will be a great separation. The godly and the ungodly, the righteous and the wicked, the elect and the reprobate are mingled together in this world. In the church, in the factory, in the field, and in the family the children of God and the children of the devil are side by side. But it shall not always be so. When Christ comes again, there shall be a great separation made. In a moment, in the twinkling of an eye, at the last trumpet's sound these two groups shall be forever separated. In that great and terrible day the separation of the godly from the ungodly will be decisive, immediate, and everlasting. Husbands and wives, mothers and children, brothers and sisters, pastors and their hearers shall be forever separated from one another.

There will be no time for repentance. There will be no opportunity for grace. As we are in that day, so we shall be forever! Believers shall be caught up to heaven, glory, honour, and eternal life. Unbelievers shall be snatched away and cast into hell, damnation, and eternal destruction and death. Let us therefore make our calling and election sure (2 Peter 1:4-11; James 2:14-26). J. C. Ryle wrote:

> Blessed and happy are they who are of one heart in following Christ! Their union alone shall never be broken: it shall last for ever more. Who can imagine the happiness of those who are taken, when the Lord returns? Who can imagine the misery of those who are left behind? May we think on these things, and consider our ways!

Our Responsibility

It is our responsibility to be always watchful (vv. 42-44), ready for and anticipating the Lord's coming. This is a point which our Master frequently presses upon us. He seldom mentions his second coming without urging us to be watchful. He knows the slothfulness of our nature. He knows how quickly we forget the most solemn things. He knows how worldly-minded we are by nature. He knows how Satan seeks to destroy us, and with what cunning devices. So, he arms us with heart-searching exhortations to be awake and alert, lest we be found at last among the damned (1 Thessalonians 5:6; Revelation 3:11).

We will be wise, like the spouse in the Song of Solomon 7:12, to rise up early, shake off all carnal security, determine not to be slothful and sluggish, and stand watchful over our souls, that we may be prepared at any moment to meet our Lord and Master. We do not know, we cannot even guess in what watch of the earth's long night Christ will come. But we do know that he may come at any moment. Therefore, we ought to be as watchful as if we knew that Christ would come tonight, ever standing on the tip-toe of expectation, "looking for the coming of our Lord Jesus Christ" (Titus 2:13).

Our Lord commands that we be ready and watchful at the prospect of his second coming, and to every man's departure out of life, whether it be by death or at the day of judgment. To be ready is to be one with Christ, in union with him by grace, born again by his Spirit, washed in his blood, robed in his righteousness. To be watchful is to dwell in the lively exercise of faith and hope in the expectation of his coming. Only those who live by faith in Christ are ready; and they are always ready. Whether their Lord comes at midnight or at the rising of the morning sun, they shall arise at the joyful call, and shall meet the Lord in the air, and shall be forever with the Lord. "Blessed is that servant, whom his Lord when he cometh shall find so doing"! C. H. Spurgeon said,

> Oh, to be ready for his appearing, watching and waiting for him as servants whose Lord has been long away from them, and who may return at any hour! This will not make us neglect our daily calling; on the contrary, we shall be all the more diligent in attending to our earthly duties because our hearts are at rest about our heavenly treasures.

Are you ready? Are you ready now to meet the Son of God in judgment? What an awesome thought that is. Yet, it is a thought that I pray will never cease to rouse our hearts. Soon we must meet God in judgment. Are we ready? We are ready only if we are in Christ (1 Corinthians 1:30; Philippians 3:4-14).

Justly Rewarded

In that great day, every faithful servant of God shall be publicly recognized, honoured, and rewarded by Christ; every false prophet shall be publicly exposed and damned (vv. 45-51). Our Lord gives us a brief description of his faithful servant in verses 45-47. All are God's servants, some willingly and others unwillingly; yet all are his servants. The true servant of Christ is faithful and he shall be rewarded as a faithful servant. There are rewards for faithful service, both in this world and in the world to come. These are not rewards of debt, but of grace, not according to the rules of law, but of love. John Trapp said, "Christ is a liberal pay-master, and his retributions are more than bountiful."

While there is no indication anywhere in scripture that there are degrees of reward among the saints in heaven, we are encouraged to faithfulness by the promise of being rewarded by our God. As faithfulness honours God, so God honours faithfulness. Here, faithfulness in one form of service is rewarded by greater opportunities of service. Faithfulness in small things is rewarded by greater responsibilities (Luke 19:17). In the world to come we shall inherit all the bounty of life everlasting and see the results of our faithfulness around the throne of our God. What more could we desire?

The unfaithful servant is also described (vv. 48-51). He says, "My lord delayeth his coming", and abuses his fellow servants, beating them and putting them under the law. Rather than comforting them (Isaiah 40:1, 2), he threatened and beat them. He lives for pleasure, to the gratification of his lusts, rather than for the glory of God and the good of men's souls. Such people, the unbelieving and unfaithful, will be taken by surprise when Christ comes again (v. 50), because they are not looking for him. And they shall be forever ruined (v. 51). They pretend to be the servants of God, while serving Satan and themselves. Therefore, they shall justly have their portion with hypocrites in hell forever.

Let us live in this world as watchmen, as sentinels of an army in enemy territory, resolved by God's grace never to be found asleep at our post. Let us live as the servants of the Son of God, ever looking for our Master's immediate return. Let us make certain that we are in the faith (2 Corinthians 13:5).

Chapter 74

God's Servants – The Faithful And The Evil

"Who then is a faithful and wise servant, whom his lord hath made ruler over his household, to give them meat in due season? Blessed is that servant, whom his lord when he cometh shall find so doing. Verily I say unto you, That he shall make him ruler over all his goods. But and if that evil servant shall say in his heart, My lord delayeth his coming; And shall begin to smite his fellowservants, and to eat and drink with the drunken; The lord of that servant shall come in a day when he looketh not for him, and in an hour that he is not aware of, And shall cut him asunder, and appoint him his portion with the hypocrites: there shall be weeping and gnashing of teeth."
(Matthew 24:45-51)

In these verses our Lord gives us a parable in which he describes two servants, one faithful, the other evil. This parable is a word of instruction, inspiration, and warning to those men who stand in the house of God as his servants. It speaks of both the faithful and the evil as the Lord's servants. The fact is all things serve the gracious purposes of God toward his elect (Proverbs 16:4; 21:1; Psalm 76:10). Satan is as much the servant of God, though unwillingly, as Gabriel is willingly. The fallen angels, the very demons of hell, are as fully the servants of God, though they despise him, as are the angels of heaven who adore him. Every human being is the servant of God, too. Some of us rejoice in that fact. What a privilege it is for believing men and women to serve the living God! Others despise the thought of God's dominion; but they are, nevertheless, under his dominion and serve his purposes (Romans 8:28; 11:36; Ephesians 1:11). Our God rules everywhere, everything, and everyone, totally and absolutely. Even those evil men, false prophets and messengers of Satan, who deceive the souls of men with their perverse doctrine, even they are the servants of our God, sovereignly used by him to accomplish his purpose (1 Corinthians 11:19).

Faithful Servants

In verses 45-47 our Lord gives us a description of God's faithful servants. Without question, the instruction in this parable may be applied to every believer in his particular calling in life. We who believe on the Lord Jesus Christ gladly bow to his dominion as our Lord. We are his servants. Our lives are spent in his service. Whatever your particular gifts are, whatever your station in life may be, that is the place of your calling and service in the kingdom of God, the place in which you are to use your gifts for the glory of Christ and the good of his people. Be God's faithful servant where you are.

Those men who are gifted of God to be preachers and teachers in his church, but are not called and gifted as pastors are also his servants, and ought to be highly regarded as such. God sometimes gives a congregation men who are clearly gifted by his grace as preachers and teachers of the Word, gifted to preach the gospel of his free grace in Christ. They are gifted teachers in his church, though not called of God to be pastors. They are to be heard and treated with the respect that their gifts demand as the servants of God. But, in this parable, our Saviour is talking about that specific group of men who are trusted with the care of God's household as pastors of local churches (v. 45).

You may never be a pastor; but you will, as long as you are in this world, need the services of a faithful pastor. You will be wise to know what to expect from God's servant, how to pray for him, and how best to assist him in the work God has put in his hands. And you need to know how to recognize and distinguish between a faithful and an evil servant. So the message of this parable is a message of importance to you.

In these verses our Lord Jesus Christ describes his faithful servant, a faithful gospel preacher, a faithful pastor by four things in which he is distinguished from a self-serving, false prophet. These four characteristics describe God's true servants in every age of the church and in every place where gospel churches are found.

His Position

God's servant is here described as one "whom his Lord hath made ruler over his household". The church of God is his household, the household of faith, and the household of his Son, the Lord Jesus Christ. It is God's family and God's church, not the pastor's, not yours, not this or that denomination's, but the Lord's household! It is God's house and temple (1 Corinthians 3:16, 17; Ephesians 3:15; 1 Timothy 3:15).

In the family of God there are fathers, young men, and children. There are some who are strong and some who are weak. There are some who are very independent and need little attention, and some who need a good bit of attention. Each one has been placed in his house and family exactly according to the Master's will. God ordained pastors have been placed by him as rulers over his household. They are not tyrants, dictators, or lords over God's household, but rulers placed over the house to govern it as stewards under Christ (Acts 20:28; 1 Timothy 3:4, 5; Hebrews 13:7, 17).

In Kentucky, we have June bugs every summer, big green beetles that appear in June. When I was a boy in North Carolina, we had them, too. As boys we loved to catch them, tie threads around one of their legs, and fly them. The bugs flew with great eagerness; but they could not fly anywhere the boy holding the string did not want them to fly. Most preachers these days are what I call, "June bug preachers". The church, the board of deacons, the elders, or the denomination has a string tied to their pastor and, like a little boy with a string around a June bug, controls everything they do. But not God's servants, God's servants serve his people; they are not controlled by them.

Where in the Word of God can you find a prophet, or a preacher who is ruled, governed, or even influenced by the will of the people to whom he is sent to preach? The only preacher like that you can find in this Book is a hireling prophet. God's servants are responsible under God to rule his house in exactly the same way as a husband is responsible under God to rule his household (1 Timothy 3:4, 5). They rule the house of God by the Word of God, according to the will of God; and do so in love for Christ and his people; but they rule.

A faithful steward rules his Master's house exactly according to his Master's will. As he does, all in the house are expected to honour and obey the steward in charge of the house. And that household is most honourable and most happy that is well-governed, with each member of the family knowing his place, working together with every other member in love, for the welfare of the whole family.

His Work

The pastor's work is "to give them meat in due season". It is the work, the calling, and the responsibility of gospel preachers to feed the church of God with knowledge and understanding, with the meat of gospel truth (Jeremiah 3:15; Acts 20:28). It is not the pastor's work to be a good socialiser, an analyst, a social worker, a therapist, a counsellor, a priest, or a community door knocker. God's servants are preachers! They feed the house of God by preaching the gospel, by opening the bread of life and dispensing it to the family. If a pastor does that, he has to spend time in his study, not running the roads (2 Timothy 2:15). It is the work of the pastor "to give", not to take (Ezekiel 34:7, 8). What is to be given is meat: the strong and soul nourishing gospel doctrine of grace.

It is not our business to enact laws, but to give meat. It is not our business to regulate the lives of men, but to feed their souls. And that with which God's servants feed his children is the sweet meat of the gospel, not the husks of intellectualism, the mists of mysticism, the stones of useless doctrinal speculation, or the poison of heresy. God's servants come with the meat of saving grace in the knowledge of Christ, declaring ruin by the fall, redemption by the blood, and regeneration by the Holy Spirit!

The pastor is to feed the saints of God with "meat in due season". The Word of God must be rightly divided; and each member of the family must be fed with the meat that is suitable for him at the time: grace for the guilty, pardon for the fallen, redemption for the ruined, righteousness for the wicked, cleansing for the defiled, reproof for the wayward, comfort for the troubled, strength for the weak, and Christ for all.

His Character

Our Lord describes his servants as men with these two traits of character: "faithful and wise". God's servants are faithful men (1 Corinthians 4:2). They are stewards of the mysteries of God, of the manifold grace of God, the unsearchable riches of Christ (1 Corinthians 4:1; 1 Peter 4:10; Ephesians 3:8). John Gill wrote, "They are faithful to the trust reposed in them ... They preach the pure gospel of Christ, and the whole of it; conceal no part, nor keep anything of it; seek not to please men, but God; neither seek their own things, their ease, honour, and profit, but the glory of God, the honour of Christ, and the good of souls; and abide by the truths, cause, and interest of the Redeemer at all costs." Matthew Henry's comments on the faithfulness of God's servants are of equal importance. "A faithful minister of Jesus Christ is one that sincerely designs his Master's honour, not his own; delivers the whole counsel of God, not his own fancies and conceits; follows Christ's institutions and adheres to them; regards the meanest, reproves the greatest, and doth not respect persons."

As they are faithful, God's servants are wise. They are neither faithful nor wise by nature; but God has made them both faithful and wise by grace and by his gifts upon them, making them fit and able ministers of the gospel. They are well instructed in the things of God, given a clear understanding in the doctrines of the gospel, and wisely exercise their talents and gifts for the glory of God. They seek constantly to improve their knowledge, make the best use of their time, and manage their lives to best serve Christ and his people. God graciously gives his servants wisdom to guide and direct his people, and to care for them, like a father guides and cares for his family.

The faithful and wise pastor is a man who is doing what God called him to do (v. 46). He always has something to do; and he is always found doing what he has been sent and called of God to do, doing his Master's will and work, feeding his sheep. The faithful and wise servant is constant in his labour, persevering in the work God has put into his hands.

His Reward

"Verily I say unto you, That he shall make him ruler over all his goods" (v. 47). As we have seen, the scriptures nowhere teach that there will be degrees of reward in heaven. That is contrary to everything taught in the gospel (Romans 8:17). Nor does our Lord exalt one servant in his kingdom above another. However, God does reward faithfulness, both in this world and in the world to come. Those who are faithful over a few things shall be made Lord over many things (Luke 19:17). Frequently, God honours faithful service by giving greater service to perform. God's servants shall find great reward in seeing those for whom they have laboured around the throne of Christ in glory (1 Thessalonians 2:19). And God's faithful and wise servants shall themselves inherit all things with Christ in glory (John 17:5, 20).

Evil Servants

In verses 48-50 our Lord describes those men who are evil servants in the house of God. Here, again, our Lord gives us four things, which are descriptive of that man who is a false prophet, an evil servant in the house of God. First, he is a man of unbelief, saying "My Lord delayeth his coming". That is his character.

Then, in his conduct, he is abusive. The unfaithful servant is judgmental. Presuming he is superior to those he serves, rather than feeding them, he beats them (v. 49). Because he can be controlled and motivated only by law, he beats others with the threats of the law, trying to get them to serve him. The false prophet has no interest in persuading anyone to serve God. He only uses the name of God to get people to serve him, and calls serving him honouring God.

Third, when the Lord Jesus comes, he will be taken by surprise. The faithful servant labours for Christ upon the tip-toe of faith and expectation, "looking for the mercy of our Lord Jesus Christ unto eternal life" (Jude 21), "looking for that blessed hope, and the glorious appearing of the great God and our Saviour Jesus Christ" (Titus 2:13). But self-serving, unfaithful servants, while they may talk much about his coming, do not look for his coming (v. 50). They are only looking for what they can get for themselves.

Fourth, he shall be cast into hell when the Lord comes. "And shall cut him asunder, and appoint him his portion with the hypocrites: there shall be weeping and gnashing of teeth" (v. 51).

An Admonition

In the light of these things I urge you, "to know them which labour among you, and are over you in the Lord, and admonish you and to esteem them very highly in love for their work's sake. And be at peace among yourselves" (1 Thessalonians 5:12, 13). Pray for them, "that the word of the Lord may have free course, and be glorified, even as it is with you" (2 Thessalonians 3:1). Faithful gospel preachers are God's gift to his church. They are to be highly esteemed for their work's sake. They are men God has set as watchmen over your soul upon the walls of Zion. They never hold their peace, but ever preach Christ to you (Isaiah 62:6, 7).

"How beautiful upon the mountains are the feet of him that bringeth good tidings, that publisheth peace; that bringeth good tidings of good, that publisheth salvation; that saith unto Zion, Thy God reigneth! Thy watchmen shall lift up the voice; with the voice together shall they sing: for they shall see eye to eye, when the Lord shall bring again Zion." (Isaiah 52:7, 8).

The evil servants, self-serving false prophets, are messengers of Satan, "transformed as the ministers of righteousness; whose end shall be according to their works" (2 Corinthians 11:15). Isaiah describes them well: "His watchmen are blind: they are all ignorant, they are all dumb dogs, they cannot bark; sleeping, lying down, loving to slumber. Yea, they are greedy dogs which can never have enough, and they are shepherds that cannot understand: they all look to their own way, every one for his gain, from his quarter" (Isaiah 56:10, 11).

Chapter 75

The Parable Of The Ten Virgins

"Then shall the kingdom of heaven be likened unto ten virgins, which took their lamps, and went forth to meet the bridegroom. And five of them were wise, and five were foolish. They that were foolish took their lamps, and took no oil with them: But the wise took oil in their vessels with their lamps. While the bridegroom tarried, they all slumbered and slept. And at midnight there was a cry made, Behold, the bridegroom cometh; go ye out to meet him. Then all those virgins arose, and trimmed their lamps. And the foolish said unto the wise, Give us of your oil; for our lamps are gone out. But the wise answered, saying, Not so; lest there be not enough for us and you: but go ye rather to them that sell, and buy for yourselves. And while they went to buy, the bridegroom came; and they that were ready went in with him to the marriage: and the door was shut. Afterward came also the other virgins, saying, Lord, Lord, open to us. But he answered and said, Verily I say unto you, I know you not. Watch therefore, for ye know neither the day nor the hour wherein the Son of man cometh."
(Matthew 25:1-13)

Matthew 25 is a continuation of our Lord's sermon on the Mount of Olives, which began in chapter twenty-four at verse three. The purpose of the sermon is to teach us that when the Lord Jesus comes again we must be ready to meet him. We must exercise diligence and care, always watching, that we may always be ready to meet the Master at his appearing. When the midnight cry is heard, "Behold, the bridegroom cometh; go ye out to meet him", whether at his second advent or at death, let us be found ready. This readiness consists not in gazing idly into the heavens, but in doing the Master's will. Someone once said, "They are always ready who are always doing his will". "Blessed is that servant, whom his lord when he cometh shall find so doing" (24:46).

A wife may watch for her husband because she is anxious to see him, but a good and faithful wife will have the house cleaned and dinner prepared. She has been anxiously watching for her husband as she performed her daily responsibilities. Her watchfulness is readiness. That is the kind of watchfulness and readiness with which we are to look for our Saviour.

This twenty-fifth chapter of Matthew is divided into three parts. All three sections have a definite reference to the second coming of Christ. In the parable of the ten virgins (vv. 1-13) our Lord uses his second coming as an argument for watchfulness, showing us the necessity of heart faith, heart worship, and heart obedience. In the parable of the talents (vv. 14-30) our Saviour uses his second coming as an argument for diligence and faithfulness. In verses 31-46 our Lord concludes his sermon with a description of the great and terrible Day of Judgment, and does so in language of unparalleled greatness and beauty.

The parable of the Ten Virgins contains lessons that are peculiarly solemn, which ought to awaken and stir our souls. The five wise virgins represent all true believers and the five foolish virgins represent all professed believers, who are yet without the grace of God.

A Mixed Multitude

First, our Lord is teaching us that his church and kingdom in this world is always a mixture of believers and unbelievers. I do not mean that any are to be received into the fellowship of the church who do not personally profess faith in Christ. That must never be done. But our Lord constantly taught us that in his visible church, in his earthly kingdom, there are both true believers and those who merely profess to be believers. The ten virgins represent these two groups.

We must never be surprised to find goats among the Lord's sheep, tares among the wheat, bad fish mixed with the good, foolish builders alongside the wise, and hypocrites mingled with true believers. That has always been the case, and always shall be. And we must never try to separate the bad from the good. That is God's business. We do not know the one from the other. If we try to separate them, we will throw out the good and keep the bad every time (Matthew 13:28-30). Yet, we must not be too surprised and disappointed when God separates the bad from the good (1 John 2:19).

After all our preaching and praying, witnessing and visiting, teaching and exhortation, and despite all the missionary endeavours expended abroad and all the labours put forth at home, in the last day, when the Lord Jesus comes again, many will be found inside the walls of Zion who are dead in trespasses and sins! It is horrible to be found in the streets of Sodom without Christ; but it will be indescribably more horrible to be found in Zion without him!

Be Warned

Read this parable and be warned. All these virgins had lamps of profession; but only five had the oil of grace in their lamps. It is one thing to be baptized, but something else to be baptized into Christ. It is one thing to have a profession of faith in Christ, but another thing altogether to have the grace of Christ. It is one thing to wear the Master's name, but something else to have his nature. It is one thing to be in Christ's church, but another thing altogether to be in Christ. It is one thing to be religious, but another thing to be righteous. It is one thing to sing about the blood, and another thing entirely to be washed in the blood.

All ten of these virgins were outwardly moral, pure and upright; but only five were made righteous in Christ. A mere outward righteousness will be of absolutely no benefit to your soul in the day of judgment. We must be washed in the blood of Christ, forgiven of all our sins (Hebrews 9:22). We must be robed in Christ's spotless robe of perfect righteousness (Revelation 21:27; 22:11).

All ten of the virgins went out to meet the Bridegroom. The wise separated themselves from family and friends, but so did the foolish. The wise professed to trust, love and follow Christ, but so did the foolish. The difference was that the wise had an inward principle of grace, while the foolish had nothing but a name, a profession, and an outward show of religion. Let us make our calling and election sure. We must have a God-given, heart faith in Christ (Romans 10:9, 10). We must be born again by God the Holy Spirit (Galatians 5:22-25). We must have Christ formed in us, being made "partakers of the divine nature", or we have no hope of everlasting salvation (Colossians 1:27; 2 Peter 1:4).

Both Asleep

Second, we learn from this parable that both the wise and the foolish will be taken by surprise at Christ's second coming. Both the wise and the foolish shall be found asleep. While the bridegroom tarried, that is, while waiting in the ordinances of divine worship, they all slumbered and slept. The Church of God describes herself in such a sad condition, saying, "I sleep, but my heart waketh" (Song of Solomon 5:2). But the sleep of God's saints is not the sleep of spiritual death. Rather, it is a deadness that causes lamentation. The sleep of the foolish virgins is the sleep of spiritual death, the sleep of those who have never been awakened from being "dead in trespasses and sins" (Ephesians 2:1-5). Without question, there is a vast and vital difference between the two. The believer sleeps, but his heart wakes (Song of Solomon 5:2), while the unbeliever sleeps the sleep of death in carnal ease. Because both "slumbered and slept", both the wise and the foolish were surprised when their lord appeared.

I know that we are commanded to watch, always to watch and be ready. That is our responsibility. That is what I want to stir up in you and in myself. But our Lord plainly teaches us that at the last day, when he comes again, all ten virgins, both the righteous and the wicked, both the true believer and the carnal professor will be asleep. When Christ comes again, he will find the great majority of mankind unbelieving and unprepared; and he will find the vast majority of his own people, his true saints, in a state of slothfulness, indolence and sleep. Business, politics, farming, buying, selling, and pleasure seeking will consume the care and attention of men; just as they do now. The Lord Jesus, when he comes again, will find his church in the very same state as the angels found Lot in Sodom, asleep in the lap of the world. "There is something unspeakably awful in the idea", wrote J. C. Ryle, "but thus it is written, and thus it shall be". One of God's servants long ago described the church today, as well as the church of his own day, when, on his deathbed, the faithful pastor said to those gathered around him, "We are none of us more than half awake."

Christ Tarries

Third, this parable teaches us that our Lord tarries in his coming. I was once asked by a friend, "Is it right to say, 'If the Lord tarries?'" I suspect it is. That is the language our Lord used to describe his physical absence. "While the bridegroom tarried, they all slumbered and slept" (v. 5). The fact that our Lord is not yet here is proof enough that he tarries.

But do not imagine that he tarries haphazardly. He tarries for a purpose. The Lord tarries to exercise our patience. He tarries to arouse our desires after him. Our Saviour tarries to gather in his elect (2 Peter 3:9; Romans 11:25, 26). He tarries that the mystery of iniquity may be fulfilled (2 Thessalonians 2:7). Our Lord tarries to accomplish his Father's purpose (Romans 8:28-30).

Too Late

Fourth, when our Lord does come, many will discover the value of heart faith, heart worship, and heart obedience; but they will discover it too late. The virgins all went forth with their lamps to meet the bridegroom, to meet the Lord Jesus Christ, the Bridegroom of his Church. They went forth to meet him with a profession of faith in him. The foolish took their lamps, but had no oil. What multitudes will be found like them when Christ comes! They have a profession of faith, but no oil of grace. They have religion, but not Christ. They are yet without life, without the Spirit of God, without the Saviour, and lost. Yet, they are ignorant of their own lost estate before God. Though professing faith in Christ, they know nothing of his saving power and grace in their hearts. Whereas the wise, having been made wise unto salvation, know their need of Christ and earnestly seek him. Robert Hawker writes:

> The foolish virgins, destitute of all vital godliness, unawakened, unregenerated, unacquainted with the plague of their own heart, and ignorant of the person, work, and glory of Christ; in all his saving offices, characters, and relations; and having nothing but a lamp of profession, were found in utter darkness, at the Lord's approach. While on the contrary, the wise virgins being furnished with the oil of grace, under the teaching of God the Holy Ghost, and brought into an union with Christ, and communion in all that belonged to Christ, in regenerating, converting, justifying, and sanctifying mercy; thus prepared by the Lord, for the knowledge and enjoyment of the Lord; arise with holy joy, at the bridegroom's coming, and enter with him into the marriage and the door is shut.

The parable tells us that when the bridegroom came, the foolish virgins said to the wise, "Give us of your oil", for "our lamps have gone out". The wise virgins told them to go buy oil for themselves. But while they were gone, the bridegroom came, and they were shut out. Then their opinion was drastically changed. Then they would have given anything in the world for true, vital godliness, anything for Christ. There is much to be learned from this. Let me just mention two or three things that must be understood by all.

True Christianity is a personal thing. No one can trust Christ for you, secure the grace of God for you, or convey grace to you. If you would be saved, you must seek the Lord.

The oil of grace can be bought (Isaiah 55:1-7). C. H. Spurgeon wrote, "There is a proper place where the oil can be bought at the right time: we are bidden to 'buy the truth,' grace is sold in God's market on gospel terms, 'without money and without price;' but when the midnight cry is heard, the day of grace has closed, and buying and selling are over for ever."

But true, saving faith is more than a decision for Jesus. If faith is simply deciding to get saved, these foolish virgins would have been saved with the wise. They decided to get some oil, but could not. Saving faith is the gift and operation of God the Holy Spirit, by which our souls are wed to Christ.

Shut Out

Fifth, this parable teaches us that when Christ comes, the door will be shut and sinners shall be shut out of his kingdom forever. The door is open now. Sinners are bidden and urged to enter into the kingdom of God by the door, Christ Jesus; but soon the door will be shut.

In that great day, all true believers will receive a great reward of grace (v. 10). Those who are ready will be carried to glory, to the marriage supper of the Lamb. The 'ready' are those who are washed in the Saviour's blood, robed in his righteousness, and born again by his Holy Spirit.

All mere professors of religion shall be cast away into hell with the rest of the damned, as those who are unknown to the Son of God (v. 12). The foolish virgins professed to be the bridegroom's beloved, but proved at last not even to have been acquainted with him. They represent all the multitudes of lost religionists in every age, who wear the name of Christ, but have neither part nor lot in his great salvation.

When the Master says, "I know you not", his meaning is, "You are not the object of my love and care. I never chose you. I do not approve of you. I will not accept you."

When Christ comes again, the door will be shut forever. What a blessing this will be for God's elect! The door will at last be shut, shut upon all sickness, sorrow, sin and pain; shut upon a tempting world; shut upon a roaring devil; shut upon all doubts and fears; shut upon bereavement and death; shut never to be opened again! What terror this will be for the wicked! The door shall be shut upon all mercy, love, grace, righteousness, happiness, life and joy; shut forever, shutting you out from God and his kingdom!

Are you a wise or a foolish virgin? Let us constantly prod our hearts and souls, lest we sleep (v. 13; 1 Thessalonians 5:6-9).

Chapter 76

The Parable Of The Talents

"For the kingdom of heaven is as a man travelling into a far country, who called his own servants, and delivered unto them his goods. And unto one he gave five talents, to another two, and to another one; to every man according to his several ability; and straightway took his journey. Then he that had received the five talents went and traded with the same, and made them other five talents. And likewise he that had received two, he also gained other two. But he that had received one went and digged in the earth, and hid his lord's money. After a long time the lord of those servants cometh, and reckoneth with them. And so he that had received five talents came and brought other five talents, saying, Lord, thou deliveredst unto me five talents: behold, I have gained beside them five talents more. His lord said unto him, Well done, thou good and faithful servant: thou hast been faithful over a few things, I will make thee ruler over many things: enter thou into the joy of thy lord. He also that had received two talents came and said, Lord, thou deliveredst unto me two talents: behold, I have gained two other talents beside them. His lord said unto him, Well done, good and faithful servant; thou hast been faithful over a few things, I will make thee ruler over many things: enter thou into the joy of thy lord. Then he which had received the one talent came and said, Lord, I knew thee that thou art an hard man, reaping where thou hast not sown, and gathering where thou hast not strawed: And I was afraid, and went and hid thy talent in the earth: lo, there thou hast that is thine. His lord answered and said unto him, Thou wicked and slothful servant, thou knewest that I reap where I sowed not, and gather where I have not strawed: Thou oughtest therefore to have put my money to the exchangers, and then at my coming I should have received mine own with usury. Take therefore the talent from him, and give it unto him which hath ten talents. For unto every one that hath shall be given, and he shall have abundance: but from him that hath not shall be taken away even that which he hath. And cast ye the unprofitable servant into outer darkness: there shall be weeping and gnashing of teeth."
(Matthew 25:14-30)

This parable, like so many of our Lord's parables, teaches us that in this world the church and kingdom of God is a mixed multitude. There are many among the professed people of God, who have been baptized in the name of Christ, who are confident they have a saving interest in Christ who yet do not know Christ at all. In the parable of the ten virgins, five were wise and five foolish. Here, among those who claim to be people of God and servants of Christ, two are represented as being faithful; the other is described as wicked and slothful. Both parables are intended to remind us that among the multitudes who profess to be the people of God, there are but few who shall enter into the kingdom of heaven. The warnings of scripture in this regard are abundant both in number and in clarity (Matthew 7:21-23; 13:18-23; 22:14; Luke 13:23-25; 17:32, 33; 2 Corinthians 13:5).

Applicable To All

The parable is applicable to those who are pastors, preachers and teachers, in the church of God. Some have greater talents and apparently greater spheres of usefulness than others, according to the decree of God and by the gift of Christ. Yet, all who are God's servants are faithful in the place of their calling and in the use of the talents entrusted to them. Do not miss this: the servant who was faithful over two talents received the same reward and entered into the same joy as the servant who was faithful over five (vv. 20-23). The man to whom two talents were given was not expected to do the same thing as the man to whom five were given; but both worked with what they had. All who do what they can with the gifts of grace are rewarded as good and faithful servants (Mark 14:8).

However, it would be a great mistake to apply the parable to none but those who are responsible to teach and preach the gospel of Christ. This parable speaks to us all. In the day of judgment we shall be held accountable to God for every blessing, benefit, and privilege he has given us in this world.

Talents And Rewards

The lord in this parable portrays the Lord Jesus Christ, who gives different talents to his servants and shall in the day of judgment justly reward each for his use or abuse of the things committed to his charge. The two servants to whom great charges were entrusted are represented as making good use of their time and talents. They were approved of at the coming of their lord and rewarded. The one to whom less was committed proved himself an unprofitable servant, and was condemned at his lord's coming. The talent entrusted to him was taken from him and given to the servant who had best used what was entrusted to him.

Robert Hawker very properly warns, "The rewards given to the faithful servant, must not be considered in a light contrary to the whole tenor of the gospel, as if any man merited divine favour." When we have done all, we are still unprofitable servants. We do not make God our debtor by anything we do for his honour. The Lord God is not moved, or compelled, to bestow blessings because of anything a man does that might be called good. His blessings of grace can never be restrained by, or withheld from, any because they are undeserving. "The gifts and callings of God are without repentance" (Romans 11:29).

The talents given to the two faithful servants portray the gifts of grace bestowed upon God's elect, by which they are made faithful. Being gifts of grace, they are not meritorious! The original gifts of grace and the increase of grace are God's. "LORD, thou also hast wrought all our works in us" (Isaiah 26:12).

The one talent received by the unprofitable servant cannot represent anything other than those gifts a man receives from God's hand by creation, nature, and providence. Grace is that "good part" which cannot be taken away (Luke 10:42). But every good thing of nature, both created and providential, enjoyed by men in this world, shall be taken from the ungodly and given to God's elect when Christ comes again. It is written, "All things are yours. Whether Paul, or Apollos, or Cephas, or the world, or life, or death, or things present, or things to come; all are yours; and ye are Christ's; and Christ is God's" (1 Corinthians 3:21-23).

Seven Obvious Lessons

Seven lessons are clearly set before us in this parable. Certainly there are more; but the following lessons should be obvious to all who read this parable.

First, this parable shows us how readily religious men and women wrest the scriptures to their own destruction (vv. 24, 25). The wicked servant described in this parable twisted the Master's sovereignty into a doctrine that represented him as an unjust tyrant, and sought to excuse his disobedience and sin by blaming God for it. That is exactly what Adam did in the garden. In effect he said to God, "The real problem here is 'the woman thou gavest me'".

Many, attempting to justify doctrines that are clearly contrary to the message of holy scripture, turn to this very passage and wrest the scriptures to their own destruction. They would have us to believe that this parable teaches that God's grace and salvation may be taken away from one who truly has been saved. Others point to this parable and assert that believers, by diligently improving God's gifts of grace, earn for themselves a greater degree of acceptance with God and a greater reward and eternal happiness in heaven.

We do not build our doctrine upon parables. Our doctrine must be built upon the plain statements of holy scripture, not upon parables, illustrations, and obscure texts. Any honest man will build his doctrine not by piecing verses and phrases together, but by the plain statements of God's Word. The clear, obvious message of holy scripture is this: "Salvation is of the Lord" (Jonah 2:9), by grace alone (Ephesians 2:8; Titus 3:5), through faith alone (Romans 3:28, 31; 4:16), and in Christ alone (Romans 3:24-26; 1 Corinthians 1:30, 31)

Wherever there appears to be a conflict between the obvious and the obscure, we must always interpret the obscure by the obvious. Only dishonest men ignore the obvious, plain statements of holy scripture, and interpret the scriptures by pointing to imaginary proof texts, found by diligently searching a concordance, or digging out a minute rule of grammar in the Hebrew or Greek text to validate their doctrine. Such self-serving teachers are not to be followed or even heard. They cannot be reasoned with because they do not bow to the authority of the Word of God. Their authority is the traditions of men, held forth in creeds, confessions, catechisms, liturgies, and historic church dogmas. Our only authority is the Word of God (Isaiah 8:20; 2 Timothy 3:16, 17). You do not need to know Hebrew and Greek to understand God's Word. He has providentially given it to you in your own language, and has done so in simple, easily understood words.

Second, the Lord Jesus Christ is the sovereign Master of all things; and all men are his servants (v. 14). Here our Lord Jesus calmly speaks of his death and the sorrow and suffering he must endure to save us, as a well planned long journey, a journey he was determined to take. He presents himself as the sovereign Lord; Master, Owner, and Possessor of all things. The servants are his, the bad as well as the good (2 Peter 2:4). The goods are his. The kingdom is his.

Third, this parable teaches us that all men have received certain talents from the Lord, with which to serve him (v. 15). Anything given to us by which we may glorify God is a talent given to us to use for him. The word "talent", as it is used here, does not refer to special abilities, but to any ability or opportunity by which we may glorify God. Our gifts, our money, our health, our strength, our time, our knowledge, our senses, our memory, our affections, our privileges, even our families, are talents loaned to us by God. We are responsible to use them for God.

All these talents are given to us by the Lord Jesus Christ, not according to our ability, but according to his ability. The words, "according to his several ability", do not refer to the servants' ability, but to the Master's ability. The talents he gives determine our ability (Psalm 68:18, 19; Ephesians 4:8-11).

Fourth, our Lord shows us that many who profess to be his servants terribly abuse the talents he gives them (v. 18). This man represents many in the visible church. They do not use their talents for evil. They are not adulterers, murderers, or riotous people. They simply hide their talents. Rather than using the opportunities God has given them to know, worship, serve, and glorify him, they neglect them. Does this man represent you? He represents anyone who has a Bible, but does not read it, anyone who has opportunity to hear the Word of God, but chooses not to do so. He represents anyone who uses his powers, abilities, and talents for sensual pleasure, rather than the glory of God.

If this man's behaviour is representative of you, then Daniel's words to Belshazzar must be addressed to you, too. "The God in whose hand thy breath is, and whose are all thy ways, hast thou not glorified" (Daniel 5:23). Daily you rob God by using for yourself what he has given you to honour him.

Fifth, we are again taught that, when our Lord comes again, there will be a great day of reckoning with God (v. 19). Soon we must meet God before the Great White Throne in judgment. We shall all give account before him of every privilege that was granted to us, and of every ray of light that we enjoyed. In that great day we will be dealt with as accountable and responsible men and women. And to whomsoever much is given, of them much will be required. Be wise and remember this. Live every day in the prospect of that great day. Let us judge ourselves that we be not condemned with the world (cf. 1 Corinthians 11:31, 32).

"After this the judgment" (Hebrews 9:27). What solemn words those are! There is a day coming in which God shall judge all men. Every man will be judged according to exact truth, righteousness, and justice. The standard by which we shall be judged is the holy law of God himself. We shall be judged according to the books of God, in which are recorded all our earthly thoughts, words, and deeds (2 Corinthians 5:10, 11; Revelation 20:11, 12; Matthew 25:31-46). In that great and terrible day of the Lord everyone will receive exactly what is justly due to him. None will be punished who do not deserve to be punished. None will be received into heaven's eternal glory who do not deserve to enter in. Those who are found guilty of any sin, or infraction of God's holy law, shall be cast into hell. Those who are perfectly holy, holy as God himself, shall enter into heaven (Psalm 24:3, 4; Revelation 21:27; 22:11).

In that day the Judge of all the earth, who must do right, will do right. He who sits upon the Great White Throne will not show any leniency, partiality, or favouritism. He will not bend his law. At the bar of God there will be no mercy and no grace. The judgment seat is not a place of mercy. It is a place of strict, unbending, unwavering, immutable justice. Only the facts will be considered when we stand before God. Guilty or not guilty, righteous or unrighteous, holy or unholy, these will be the only matters of consideration in that day. "Evil pursueth sinners: but to the righteous good shall be repayed" (Proverbs 13:21). "The soul that sinneth, it shall die" (Ezekiel 18:20). He that "hath done that which is lawful and right; he shall surely live" (Ezekiel 33:16). God will by no means clear the guilty. And he will not punish the righteous.

In the light of these facts the only hope any sinner has of eternal life and acceptance with God is salvation by the infinite merits of an able, all-sufficient Substitute. That substitute is the Lord Jesus Christ, the Son of God! Christ, by his precious blood, has completely washed away the sins of his people, so that they are no longer recorded in the book of God's law and justice against us (Isaiah 43:25; 44:22; Jeremiah 50:20). His righteous obedience to God is imputed to all who believe on him, making us worthy of eternal life (Romans 5:19; Colossians 1:12). Again, I say, let us "judge ourselves that we be not condemned with the world" (1 Corinthians 11:31, 32).

Sixth, the parable shows that all true believers receive the same joyful reward from their Master (vv. 21-23) in the day of judgment. Every faithful servant of Christ, that is to say, every believer, every sinner saved by his grace, washed in his blood and robed in his righteousness shall hear the Saviour say, "Well done, thou good and faithful servant: thou hast been faithful over a few things, I will make thee ruler over many things: enter thou into the joy of thy Lord."

Perhaps you think, "How can that be?" The answer is as simple as it is glorious. Christ's obedience to God is our obedience. Just as he was rewarded for our sins, when our sins were made his at Calvary, so we shall be rewarded for his righteousness, which has been made ours by his grace. The glory he earned by his obedience unto death for us (John 17:5), our Saviour has given to us by his grace (John 17:22). And we shall possess it with him. In that great day he will say to every saved sinner, "Enter thou into the joy of thy Lord"!

Seventh, our Lord once more shows us that in that great and terrible day of reckoning every unprofitable servant will be cast away and condemned by the Son of God (vv. 26-30). In that great and terrible day every condemned soul will acknowledge that his damnation is fully deserved. Each will be judged by the things that he now knows, but will not obey. As he casts the wicked into everlasting hell, the Judge will say, "Thou knewest"!

You and I are the stewards of God. Let us be found faithful (1 Corinthians 4:2), using what he has put in our hands for the glory of his name.

Chapter 77

"When The Son Of Man Shall Come"

"When the Son of man shall come in his glory, and all the holy angels with him, then shall he sit upon the throne of his glory: And before him shall be gathered all nations: and he shall separate them one from another, as a shepherd divideth his sheep from the goats: And he shall set the sheep on his right hand, but the goats on the left. Then shall the King say unto them on his right hand, Come, ye blessed of my Father, inherit the kingdom prepared for you from the foundation of the world: For I was an hungred, and ye gave me meat: I was thirsty, and ye gave me drink: I was a stranger, and ye took me in: Naked, and ye clothed me: I was sick, and ye visited me: I was in prison, and ye came unto me. Then shall the righteous answer him, saying, Lord, when saw we thee an hungred, and fed thee? or thirsty, and gave thee drink? When saw we thee a stranger, and took thee in? or naked, and clothed thee? Or when saw we thee sick, or in prison, and came unto thee? And the King shall answer and say unto them, Verily I say unto you, Inasmuch as ye have done it unto one of the least of these my brethren, ye have done it unto me. Then shall he say also unto them on the left hand, Depart from me, ye cursed, into everlasting fire, prepared for the devil and his angels: For I was an hungred, and ye gave me no meat: I was thirsty, and ye gave me no drink: I was a stranger, and ye took me not in: naked, and ye clothed me not: sick, and in prison, and ye visited me not. Then shall they also answer him, saying, Lord, when saw we thee an hungred, or athirst, or a stranger, or naked, or sick, or in prison, and did not minister unto thee? Then shall he answer them, saying, Verily I say unto you, Inasmuch as ye did it not to one of the least of these, ye did it not to me. And these shall go away into everlasting punishment: but the righteous into life eternal."
(Matthew 25:31-46)

Few passages in the Bible are more solemn and heart-searching than Matthew 25:31-46. Here our Saviour speaks to us about his glorious second advent and the day of judgment. What a solemn passage this is! In that great day every son and daughter of Adam shall be present. Each one shall "receive the things done in his body, according to that he hath done, whether it be good or bad. Knowing therefore the terror of the Lord, we persuade men" (2 Corinthians 5:10, 11). Every thing here spoken by our Master is plain and clear. There are no parables here. It is impossible to misunderstand our Saviour's words in this passage.

When He Appears

This passage begins with the fact of our Lord's glorious second advent. Verse 31 identifies three things about our Saviour's second coming.

First, his coming: "When the Son of man shall come in his glory". He states the fact of his coming again as a well-known, commonly acknowledged fact. With his disciples, Christ's second coming is not a speculative matter. We have no idea when he will come again. But we do know that he is coming. We rejoice in the hope of it. And we know that when he comes again, our great God and Saviour will appear in all the splendour, grandeur, and majesty of his glory as the God-man, our Saviour. Not only is he coming, but "the Son of man shall come in his glory"!

Second, his companions: when Christ comes again, he will not come alone, but "all the holy angels with him". Elsewhere we are told that he will come with all his saints, too. This will be no secret rapture, but the glorious appearing of the great God, who is our Saviour. The holy angels, who sang his praise at his first advent, will accompany him in his second advent.

Third, his character: "Then shall he sit upon the throne of his glory". When our Saviour comes again, there will be no more debate about his sovereignty. The throne of judgment upon which he shall sit will be "the throne of his glory". Every knee shall bow before "the throne of his glory". All his enemies shall be made the footstool of "the throne of his glory". Everyone will worship before "the throne of his glory".

Two Groups

"And before him shall be gathered all nations: and he shall separate them one from another, as a shepherd divideth his sheep from the goats: And he shall set the sheep on his right hand, but the goats on the left" (vv. 32, 33). We are once more reminded of the fact that all the human race is divided into only two families, two groups and two races, the one called "the sheep", the other called "the goats". You will never understand the Bible, or any of the workings of God, until you understand this fact. Earthly distinctions of race, nationality, social status, mental aptitude, and even religious affiliation are of absolutely no significance before God. We are all either sheep or goats.

Sheep have always been sheep; and goats have always been goats. Sheep never become goats; and goats never become sheep. Some sheep are saved, and some are yet lost; but all sheep shall be saved (John 10:11, 14, 15, 27-30). Goats never shall be saved (John 10:26). Everything God does in this world, he does for the sheep, to save his sheep. He chose his sheep. Christ redeemed, seeks, and finds his sheep. And, finding them, he fetches them to himself by his omnipotent grace in the effectual call of his Spirit. When Christ comes again, the sheep shall be set on his right hand, the place of highest honour and blessing. The goats shall be set on his left hand of contempt, judgment, and destruction.

Blessed Of God

God's elect, the sheep set on the Saviour's right hand, are described as a people "blessed" of God the Father, and are bidden to come and inherit the kingdom prepared for them "from the foundation of the world" (v. 34). In verse 31 our Saviour calls himself "the Son of man". Here he calls himself "the King". He is the King of kings and Lord of lords, the King of his church, the saints, and the King of the whole earth. He will appear in his glory as the King, sitting upon his throne of glory as the Judge of all the earth.

In that great day he will speak as gently, tenderly, and lovingly to his sheep as he does today in the gospel, saying, "Come, ye blessed of my Father". He will call those on his right hand to come before his great white throne with boldness and confidence, entering into and taking possession of heavenly glory as a people "made meet to be partakers of the inheritance of the saints in light" (Colossians 1:12), "which he had afore prepared unto glory" (Romans 9:23).

When we stand before Christ in judgment, he will call us a people "blessed of my Father". What reason have any who are blessed of God to fear that day? God's eternal choice of us as his people declares that we are loved of him with an everlasting love, accepted of him in Christ from eternity, and blessed of him with all spiritual blessings in Christ before the world began. Being blessed of God, we are redeemed by Christ's blood, forgiven of all sin, justified, and sanctified by his grace. Having given us his grace, the Lord will give us glory, too (Psalm 84:11).

A Kingdom Prepared

The happiness of God's elect in the world to come is described as a "kingdom", because of the glory, riches, grandeur, and majesty of it. It is a kingdom prepared and suitable for a people who have been made kings and priests unto God by Christ. It is "an inheritance" obtained by the gift of our heavenly Father. It is ours by right of adoption as the children of God, by right of purchase by the blood of Christ, and by right of our union with the Lord Jesus Christ, who has already taken possession of it as our Forerunner.

Heavenly glory is a kingdom "prepared" by God's free grace and everlasting favour. Being prepared, it is both sure and made ready. As John Gill wrote, "It is a kingdom erected, an inheritance reserved, and a crown of righteousness laid up in heaven, a glory really provided and secured in an everlasting covenant, and that for you … the peculiar favourites of God, the objects of his love and choice, the redeemed of the Lamb, and that are born of the Spirit."

That kingdom into which we shall enter at last was prepared for us "from the foundation of the world". Heavenly glory is a kingdom prepared for God's elect from all eternity. That fact alone should convince all that the blessings of eternity do not, and cannot be dependent upon or determined by the things we do in time. The whole of heavenly glory is the gift of God in Christ. It is written, "The gift of God is eternal life" (Romans 6:23). Nothing connected with eternal life is earned and merited by those who shall possess it. "But plainly", as Robert Hawker put it, "the whole is the result of free, sovereign grace, and not an atom of merit in man, contributing, in the least degree, to the accomplishment".

What can be so truly blessed than to contemplate this provision of grace our God has made for us, not only before we were born, but before the foundations of the earth were laid? How delightful our Saviour's words are! It appears to me that his intent is to convey to us the greatest possible peace and joyful hope as we anticipate his glorious appearing, "looking for the mercy of our Lord Jesus Christ unto eternal life" (Jude 21). He seems to be saying here, as he did in Luke 12:32, "Fear not little flock, for it is your heavenly Father's good pleasure to give you the kingdom."

The Day Of Judgment

In verses 35-46 our Lord Jesus Christ describes the day of judgment. Let no one be deceived, there is a day appointed by God when all men shall stand before his righteous bar, "the throne of his glory", to be judged by him. There is a day of reckoning. Put it out of your mind, if you dare. Try to dismiss it from your thoughts, if you like. But there is a day fixed by God almighty when you and I must give account to him. It is written, "after this", after this life is over, after we have finished our little space of appointed time in this world, "after this the judgment" (Hebrews 9:27). Therefore, I make no apology for echoing that which all men by nature prefer never to hear, "Prepare to meet thy God"!

Consider this sober fact seriously: You must soon meet God in judgment! How will it go for you in that great and terrible day? Where will you spend eternity? Do not be so foolish as to ignore these questions. Let me show you four things taught in these verses by the Son of God about the day of judgment.

First, our Saviour assures us that he will himself be the Judge in that great day. Understand this: everything God does he does through the Son, for the honour of the Son, that the Son may have all pre-eminence and glory. The saving of men is the work of the Son; and the judgment of men shall be the work of the Son (John 5:22; Acts 17:30, 31; 2 Corinthians 5:10, 11; Philippians 2:9-11).

That same Jesus who was born at Bethlehem, who was raised in Nazareth, who preached and performed mighty miracles of mercy in the days of his humiliation, who was despised and rejected of men, and who was at last betrayed, beaten, scourged, stripped naked, and nailed to the cursed tree by the hands of wicked men, that same Jesus shall himself come again in power and in great glory to judge this world. You and I will soon be gathered before his august throne of glory to answer for our lives upon this earth.

Believers have every reason to look upon this solemn event with comfort and joy. He who shall sit upon the throne in that great and dreadful day is our Saviour, Redeemer, Good Shepherd, mighty Advocate, great High Priest, Elder Brother, and Faithful Friend. I do not suggest for a moment that he will bend the law on our behalf. He will never do that! But I do mean for you to understand that so long as we have such an Advocate as Christ in the court, indeed, upon the very bench of judgment, we have no reason to fear the proceedings of that bench.

If you are without Christ, if you are an unbeliever, unconverted, and living in rebellion to our great God, every thought of this great and terrible day should fill your soul with terror. Your Judge in that day will be the very Christ whose gospel you now despise, whose gracious invitations you scorn, whose blood you trample beneath your feet. If you go on and die in your rebellion and unbelief, how great will be the wrath poured out upon you in that day! To be condemned by anyone would be terrible; but to be condemned by him who is "the Saviour of the world", who is able, willing, and ready to save all who come to God by him is unthinkable! I urge you in the words of the psalmist, "Kiss the Son, lest he be angry, and ye perish from the way" (Psalm 2:12).

Second, our Master tells us that everyone will be judged by him in that day. "Before him shall be gathered all nations" (v. 32). All who ever lived shall in that day give account of themselves before the Son of God. When the King of heaven issues his summons, his holy angels like a great hosts of deputies will fetch you before his throne. Each one will be forced to step forward to receive his sentence from Christ himself. J. C. Ryle wrote, "Those who would not come to worship Christ on earth, will find that they must come to his great assize, when he returns to judge the world."

In that great day all the human race shall be publicly divided into two groups. "And he shall set the sheep on his right hand, but the goats on the left" (v. 33). In that day earthly distinctions shall be meaningless. Rich and poor, the learned and the unlearned, black and white, religious and irreligious men and women, moralists and rogues shall all be lumped together as goats. All former, earthly distinctions, for which people contend and strive, will have passed away.

In that day nothing will matter to you or to God except this: are you or are you not in Christ? Grace or no grace, faith or no faith, converted or unconverted, saved or lost are the only distinctions that will matter when you stand before the bar of God. If you trust the Son of God, you shall be seated with Christ on his right hand, with his sheep, in "the throne of his glory". If you die without faith in Christ, you will in that day be found among the goats at his left hand.

Third, our Lord here shows us that the judgment of that great day will be totally righteous, just, and equitable. No one will challenge the proceedings of that court. When the judgment is over, even the damned will acknowledge that it was right. The judgment will be conducted upon the basis of evidence.

We recognize that we are justified by grace through the redemption Christ accomplished at Calvary. Our only righteousness before God is his righteousness, that which he has made ours and given to us, the righteousness of God in Christ. Our works have nothing to do with our everlasting acceptance with God. When God opens the books on that day, he will bring us into heaven because no sin is recorded against us; but only righteousness, perfect righteousness is recorded under our names in heaven (Revelation 20:11, 12; Jeremiah 50:20; Numbers 23:21; Romans 8:33, 34).

However, God will in that day demonstrate that grace made his elect to be truly new creatures in Christ. Their works, which follow them into heaven, shall be witnesses brought forward by Christ himself as to why they should be admitted into his heavenly kingdom. Above all else, their works of charity, kindness, and hospitality shall be brought forth as evidences of their faith. Our faith is proved to be either false or true by our lives. In that sense, and only in that sense, the Spirit of God declares, "by works a man is justified" (James 2:24).

Believers show the reality of their faith by their works (James 2:18). The fact is, "faith without works is dead" (James 2:11-14, 20-26). The great test of godliness, the evidence of faith in Christ is love. "He that loveth not knoweth not God".

The day of judgment will bring great, eternal joy to every believer (v. 34). The Saviour will say to each of his elect, to every believing sinner, "Well done, thou good and faithful servant ... Enter thou into the joy of thy Lord" (Matthew 25:21, 23). The wages God shall give to his faithful servants shall be the full kingdom of grace and glory. The least, the lowest, the poorest, the weakest, and the youngest shall have the same reward as the greatest, the richest, the highest, the strongest, and the oldest. We shall all receive "a crown of glory that fadeth not away" from the King of glory.

The day of judgment will bring utter confusion to all unbelievers (v. 41). Those who will not heed the Saviour's call now, "Come unto me", will obey with terror when he says, "Depart from me, ye cursed"! That day will demonstrate the character of all the saved and the character of all the lost in a striking manner. Believers, the saved, Christ's sheep, will be clothed with humility, never imagining that they had done anything worthy of his notice and approval. When the Lord speaks of their good deeds, they will be astonished by his words.

"Then shall the King say unto them on his right hand, Come, ye blessed of my Father, inherit the kingdom prepared for you from the foundation of the world: For I was an hungred, and ye gave me meat: I was thirsty, and ye gave me drink: I was a stranger, and ye took me in: Naked, and ye clothed me: I was sick, and ye visited me: I was in prison, and ye came unto me. Then shall the righteous answer him, saying, Lord, when saw we thee an hungred, and fed thee? or thirsty, and gave thee drink? When saw we thee a stranger, and took thee in? or naked, and clothed thee? Or when saw we thee sick, or in prison, and came unto thee? And the King shall answer and say unto them, Verily I say unto you, Inasmuch as ye have done it unto one of the least of these my brethren, ye have done it unto me." (vv. 34-40).

Whenever we think of "good works", we ought to think of works of kindness, mercy, and love. Nowhere in holy scripture are good works spoken of under any other terms. And, it appears, judging from our Saviour's words here, that those who perform such works are totally oblivious to having done so. Whereas, those who never perform such works, but only live in the delusion of self-righteousness, presume that they do good all the time. The lost, the unbelieving, will yet be blind and self-righteous, never imagining that they had failed to make themselves worthy of God's acceptance.

In that great day (vv. 41-46), our Lord will make all men see how highly he regards his people. He considers anything done for them or against them as being done to him. It seems to me that no man alive is able to conceive how real is the union of Christ and his people. The astonishment here expressed, both by the redeemed and the reprobate, at our Lord's words, seems to suggest that the real union of Christ and his church will be comprehended by none until we stand before him in that great day.

Fourth, the Son of God tells us that the results of that judgment will be final and immutable. "These shall go away into everlasting punishment: but the righteous into life eternal" (v. 46). Everything after the judgment will be eternal. There will be no changes in eternity. The blessedness of the saved will be everlasting. We shall enjoy eternal life, eternal rest, eternal peace, eternal joy, eternal satisfaction, eternal righteousness, eternal communion with the Lord Jesus Christ!

The misery of the damned shall also be eternal! Who can describe the woe of the damned? It is eternal wrath, everlasting fire, undying torment, "the second death", everlasting hell! It is unceasing separation from God and all good! All the lost shall be required to endure eternal agony, eternal sin, eternal want, eternal company with the most vile, wicked, abominable creatures; eternal separation from all that is good and pleasant.

Let us solemnly consider these things. Soon, you and I must meet God in judgment. "For we must all appear before the judgment seat of Christ; that every one may receive the things done in his body, according to that he hath done, whether it be good or bad. Knowing therefore the terror of the Lord, we persuade men; but we are made manifest unto God; and I trust also are made manifest in your consciences" (2 Corinthians 5:10, 11).

Chapter 78

A Good Work Done For Christ

"And it came to pass, when Jesus had finished all these sayings, he said unto his disciples, Ye know that after two days is the feast of the Passover, and the Son of man is betrayed to be crucified. Then assembled together the chief priests, and the scribes, and the elders of the people, unto the palace of the high priest, who was called Caiaphas, And consulted that they might take Jesus by subtilty, and kill him. But they said, Not on the feast day, lest there be an uproar among the people. Now when Jesus was in Bethany, in the house of Simon the leper, There came unto him a woman having an alabaster box of very precious ointment, and poured it on his head, as he sat at meat. But when his disciples saw it, they had indignation, saying, To what purpose is this waste? For this ointment might have been sold for much, and given to the poor. When Jesus understood it, he said unto them, Why trouble ye the woman? for she hath wrought a good work upon me. For ye have the poor always with you; but me ye have not always. For in that she hath poured this ointment on my body, she did it for my burial. Verily I say unto you, Wheresoever this gospel shall be preached in the whole world, there shall also this, that this woman hath done, be told for a memorial of her."
(Matthew 26:1-13)

Commenting on this passage, J. C. Ryle wrote, "We now approach the closing scene of our Lord Jesus Christ's earthly ministry. Hitherto we have read of his sayings and doings. We are now about to read of his sufferings and death. Hitherto we have seen him as the great Prophet. We are now about to see him as the great High Priest."

I would not exalt one portion of scripture above another; but the last three chapters of Matthew's Gospel, along with the accounts given by Mark, Luke, and John of our Saviour's sufferings and death as our Substitute, ought always to be read with peculiar reverence and careful attention, and ought to be read often. This truly is "holy ground". Here we see the Seed of woman crushing the serpent's head. Here we see that one great Sacrifice to which all the sacrifices of the Old Testament pointed. Here we see that blood shed which “cleanseth us from all sin”, and that Lamb slain who “taketh away the sin of the world”.

In the substitutionary death of our Lord Jesus Christ the Holy Spirit shows us how God can be both just and the Justifier of the ungodly. The things contained in these chapters are of such peculiar importance that all four gospel narratives contain a detailed account of them. Frequently, with regard to other matters, when one of the gospel writers refers to something, the other three say nothing about it; but when it came to the events surrounding our great Saviour’s great sacrifice for sin, the Holy Spirit inspired all four Gospel writers to describe it in great detail.

The Message Of The Bible

“And it came to pass, when Jesus had finished all these sayings, he said unto his disciples, Ye know that after two days is the feast of the passover, and the Son of man is betrayed to be crucified” (vv. 1, 2). Throughout his earthly ministry the Lord Jesus carefully and constantly called the attention of his disciples to his sin-atoning death at Calvary.

The connection of these first two verses with the preceding chapter is not accidental. Our Redeemer had just been talking about his glorious second advent, the end of the world, the day of judgment, and the eternal states of the righteous and the wicked. Then, without the least pause, he directs our attention to his own crucifixion and death. While the wondrous predictions of the end were still ringing in their ears, he tells his disciples once more of his sin-atoning death. He reminds them that before he reigns as the King of Glory, he must die as the Substitute for sinners. Before he takes his crown of universal monarchy, he must endure and satisfy the wrath of God as our sin-offering. Before he could sit down on the right hand of the Majesty on high, he must put away the sins of his people by the sacrifice of himself.

We can never attach too much importance to the sin-atoning death of our Lord Jesus Christ. The focal point of scripture, upon which our minds ought to ever be fixed, is the death of Christ. Without the shedding of his blood, there is no remission of sins. This is the foundation doctrine of holy scripture. Without it there is no gospel in the gospel. Without the doctrine of the cross, the Bible is a meaningless book. It is, as Ryle stated, “like a clock without a dial or a spring, a building without a foundation, or a solar system without a sun”.

We must never minimize our Lord’s incarnation, fail to follow his example, ignore his parables, forget his miracles of mercy, or despise his words of instruction; but he intends for us, above all things, to make much of his cross. I delight to think of his second coming, heavenly glory, and the day when our God shall make all things new; but these things, great and glorious as they are, are meaningless without our Saviour's death upon the cursed tree. The doctrine of the atonement is the master-truth of holy scripture. This is our daily bread. "Christ died for our sins"! What can be more marvellous? What can be more inspiring? What can be more instructive? Some, like the Greeks of old, sneer at this message and call it foolishness. Others, like the Jews of Paul's day, looking for signs and wonders, stumble over it and perish; but to those who are saved by the grace of God, Christ crucified is the power of God and the wisdom of God.

The message of the Bible is the gospel of Christ' substitutionary atonement (Luke 24:27, 44-47; 1 Peter 1:25). That is the message God's servants are sent to preach (1 Corinthians 2:1, 2). The sacrifice of Christ for us is the motive and inspiration for devotion, faith, godliness, worship, and obedience (1 Corinthians 6:19, 20). The doctrine of the cross is the glory of the redeemed (Galatians 6:14).

Vicious Hypocrisy

What a display we have, in verses 3-5, of the hypocrisy and viciousness of self-righteous, lost religionists! Little needs to be said about these men. They were lost, religious zealots. They were the religious leaders of the day. They spent their lives in religion. They did all that they did in the name of God. But they were lost. And you can mark this down as a general rule, the most vicious people in this world are lost religionists. Here are "men of the cloth", as they say, consulting on the business of trumping up an excuse for murdering the Son of God because they despised his doctrine; and they did it in the name of God!

Weak Brethren

"Now when Jesus was in Bethany, in the house of Simon the leper, There came unto him a woman having an alabaster box of very precious ointment, and poured it on his head, as he sat at meat. But when his disciples saw it, they had indignation, saying, To what purpose is this waste? For this ointment might have been sold for much, and given to the poor" (vv. 6-9).

God's people in this world are sinners still. We all, at different times and in different ways, behave in such a way that we make manifest what weak, sinful creatures we are. Such shameful weakness we see in the response of our Lord's faithful disciples to the humble devotion of another, as she bows before and worships the Lord Jesus.

Remember, these were our Lord's disciples: loving John, bold Peter, and faithful James. They, along with the rest, were indignant at this dear women; but they were led astray by the actions of one wicked man, whom they mistakenly respected. When Judas spoke against this woman, so did the others (John 12:4, 5). Judas was perhaps the most prominent and highly respected man in the church at this time. His word and opinions carried weight.

Observing the bad behaviour of these saints, as it is recorded here, we should learn two things and lay them to heart. First, we should never harshly and rashly condemn one another when our own weaknesses are many. Frequently, genuine believers are led into evil actions by the influence of others, actions contrary to their character. I do not excuse the evil done by these disciples. It was a horrible thing they did to this woman. But their actions did not reflect their true character.

Second, self-denying, self-sacrificing acts of devotion and commitment to Christ are seldom understood by others, not even by other believers. Can you imagine how shocked this woman was when she heard the response of her brethren to what she had done? She only intended to honour her Lord. She wanted to show, in some public way, how much she loved him and how thankful she was for his goodness and grace to her. The sad fact is, if you are committed to Christ, and inclined out of love and gratitude to him, to do some unusual thing for his honour and the interest of his kingdom, you need not expect the approval of others. Others will always consider what is done for Christ a waste.

Honoured Of Christ

Others rarely recognize and honour that which is truly done for Christ. But God our Saviour declares, "Them that honour me I will honour" (1 Samuel 2:30). And he honoured this woman who honoured him (vv. 10-13).

In these verses our Lord Jesus shows us what high regard he has for anything that is done for him. Others found fault with what she had done; but the Master quickly rebuked the fault-finders and honoured the woman. Those who honour him, he will honour. Not only did he approve of her sacrifice and accept it, he gave her the highest honour imaginable in this world for what she had done. He called her work a good work (v. 10). She had done what she could, what she was able to do and had opportunity to do for him. And our Saviour established her work as a memorial to be proclaimed throughout the world (v. 13).

Since Christ was pleased with her action, I am sure this dear soul was indifferent to the opinions of others about what she had done for her Lord. Their opinions mattered nothing. Her faith, love, and devotion to Christ gave her courage and boldness in the face of opposition.

If I am conscious that I am doing something as unto the Lord, for the glory of Christ, in the interests of his kingdom, and for the furtherance of the gospel, the opinions of men, be it their approval or their disapproval, are of no consequence to me. As David said to his envious, cowardly brothers, we ought to say to those who would oppose our work for our Master. "Is there not a cause?" If we would serve Christ, we simply must not allow the opinions of men to rule, or even influence our actions (John 2:5; Galatians 1:16).

This woman is held before us as a noble example to follow. Our Lord holds her up as an example of what we should be and do as his servants in this world. Let me show you several things about what this dear lady did, by which her work shows itself to be indeed a good work done for Christ.

1. It was a work done for the glory of Christ alone. She was wrapped up in, absorbed with, and consumed by, the Lord Jesus Christ. She cherished him. This perfume was meant for no one but him. She had no regard for herself, the consequences of her actions, what she might lose, or what she might gain. She wanted nothing but to honour Christ.

2. This was an act of pure love. This is exactly what Luke's narrative of this event teaches us (Luke 7:36-50). The one thing that motivated this woman to do what she did was love for Christ (1 John 4:19; 2 Corinthians 5:14). When our hearts and lives are ruled by love for Christ, they are well ruled.

3. This was a work requiring considerable cost, self-denial and sacrifice. If you read the accounts of Mark and John, you will find that this ointment was worth nearly a year's wages (300 pence – cf. Matthew 20:9-13).

4. This sacrifice was the result of thoughtful, deliberate preparation. It was something she had been planning for some time. She had been saving this rich, costly perfume specifically to use it for Christ's honour at the appropriate opportunity.

5. This woman's sacrifice was made silently. She said nothing; she drew as little attention to herself as she possibly could. She said nothing about what she would like to do, what she planned to do, what she was doing, or what she had done. She just did what she could.

6. This was the response of a believing heart to the sacrifice of her Lord. This woman appears to have been the only one of the Lord's disciples who clearly understood at the time how he must accomplish our redemption by his death as our Substitute.

7. This was an act of faith. She anointed him for his burial, but she did so in anticipation of his resurrection (Isaiah 53:10-12). The primary motivation of embalming was and is a belief in the resurrection of the dead.

I see in this incident a blessed foretaste of the honour that shall be given to God's elect on the day of judgment. In that great and glorious day, no honour done to Christ shall be forgotten. The speeches of orators, the feats of warriors, the deeds of the greatest politicians, the trophies of athletes, the poetry and literature and art produced by men, all shall be forgotten; but this work, and the least work of any and every believing man and woman, even the giving of a cup of cold water in Christ's name shall be remembered and honoured before men by God himself! Let us do what we can for our Redeemer and his honour as he gives us opportunity (1 Corinthians 6:19, 20; 10:31; Romans 12:1, 2; 1 Corinthians 15:58).

Chapter 79

Lessons From The Betrayer

"Then one of the twelve, called Judas Iscariot, went unto the chief priests, And said unto them, What will ye give me, and I will deliver him unto you? And they covenanted with him for thirty pieces of silver. And from that time he sought opportunity to betray him. Now the first day of the feast of unleavened bread the disciples came to Jesus, saying unto him, Where wilt thou that we prepare for thee to eat the passover? And he said, Go into the city to such a man, and say unto him, The Master saith, My time is at hand; I will keep the passover at thy house with my disciples. And the disciples did as Jesus had appointed them; and they made ready the passover. Now when the even was come, he sat down with the twelve. And as they did eat, he said, Verily I say unto you, that one of you shall betray me. And they were exceeding sorrowful, and began every one of them to say unto him, Lord, is it I? And he answered and said, He that dippeth his hand with me in the dish, the same shall betray me. The Son of man goeth as it is written of him: but woe unto that man by whom the Son of man is betrayed! it had been good for that man if he had not been born. Then Judas, which betrayed him, answered and said, Master, is it I? He said unto him, Thou hast said."
(Matthew 26:14-25)

Commenting on this passage, C. H. Spurgeon wrote:

> What a contrast to the incident we have just been considering! The anointing of Jesus is to be the theme of admiration wherever the gospel is preached, but his betrayal by Judas will be a subject for execration to all eternity. It was one of the twelve, who went unto the chief priests, to bargain for the price of his Lord s betrayal. He did not even mention Christ's name in his infamous question, 'What will ye give me, and I will deliver him unto you?' The amount agreed upon, thirty pieces of silver, was the price of a slave, and showed how little value the chief priests set upon Jesus, and also revealed the greed of Judas in selling his master for so small a sum. Yet many have sold

> Jesus for a less price than Judas received, a smile or a sneer has been sufficient to induce them to betray their Lord.
>
> Let us, who have been redeemed with Christ's precious blood, set high store by him, think much of him, and praise him much. As we remember, with shame and sorrow, these thirty pieces of silver, let us never undervalue him, or forget the priceless preciousness of him who was reckoned as worth no more than a slave.

Matthew 26:14-25 is the record of one of the blackest events in the history of the world. There is no greater evidence of the wickedness of man than the character and conduct of Judas Iscariot, betrayer of our Lord. These verses speak of things we would prefer not to consider; but are written for our instruction. If God the Holy Spirit will be our Teacher, we will find much in them that will bring joy to our hearts. I want to show you five lessons to be learned from them.

The Word Of God

First, these verses confirm that the Bible is the inspired Word of God. You ask, "Where is that taught in this passage?" The inspiration of scripture is established by the precise fulfilment of the prophecies of scripture. Here we see Old Testament prophecy fulfilled to the letter, not by one who was attempting to bring honour to the Word of God, but by one who was inspired by the devil himself.

The scriptures clearly predicted that our Saviour would be betrayed by one of his most intimate companions, one who ate bread with him. "Yea, mine own familiar friend, in whom I trusted, which did eat of my bread, hath lifted up his heel against me" (Psalm 41:9). The Old Testament specifically prophesied that the Lord Jesus would be betrayed for thirty pieces of silver, which would then be cast down in the temple, and that the money would be used to buy a place in the potter's field (Zechariah 11:12, 13).

Ever reverence the Bible as the inspired Word of God. This Book alone is God's Word. This Book alone is authoritative in the church and kingdom of God. This Book is our rule of faith and practice, able to make us wise unto salvation. Treasure this Book. Seek to know this Book. Believe this Book. Obey this Book.

Religious, But Lost

Second, we learn by the example of Judas Iscariot that a person may enjoy great religious privileges and yet be an unregenerate reprobate. Judas Iscariot was religious, but lost. He had the highest possible privileges of outward religion. He was a chosen apostle and companion of Christ, an eyewitness of the Lord's miracles. He heard the gospel from the lips of the incarnate God, ate at the same table, dipped his bread in the bowl from which the Master ate. He lived in the society of the Lord Jesus, preached with Peter, James and John. Yet, Judas was lost. He was, it appears, a man of highest reputation and esteem among men. He appears to have been a man who was, in outward appearance, quiet and unassuming. We read of very little that he ever said or did; but he was trusted by all to be the treasurer of the early church. When the Master said, "One of you shall betray me", no one suspected Judas. Yet, Judas was a hypocrite.

Like Lot's wife, Judas is held before us as a warning. Think of this base, vile man often. Do not imagine he was outwardly wicked. He was not. Outwardly, he was an example of what men call "purity", "holiness", and "godliness". But Judas was a devil. Whenever we think of Judas, we ought to pray, "Search me, O God, and know my heart: try me, and know my thoughts: And see if there be any wicked way in me, and lead me in the way everlasting" (Psalm 139:23, 24).

Do not be content with mere outward religion. Do not be satisfied with the approval of men. Make certain that your religion is a matter of the heart, a union of your very soul with the Son of God, by faith. Spurgeon warned, "A man may get very near to Christ, ay, may dip his hand in the same dish with the Saviour, and yet betray him. We may be high in office, and may apparently be very useful, as Judas was, yet we may betray Christ."

The Root Of All Evil

Third, the Holy Spirit shows us here a vivid picture of the fact that "the love of money is the root of all evil". I cannot conceive of a clearer proof of this fact than Judas Iscariot. The wretched question, "What will ye give me?" betrayed the evil that ruled his heart. Judas had given up much to follow Christ. Outward sacrifices he was prepared to make. But he could not and would not give up his covetousness. Money was his god and ruled his heart. We have many illustrations of the corrupting influence of the love of money. It is not the lack of money or the possession of money that is the root of all evil, but the love of money. It was for money that Joseph was sold into Egypt, Samson was betrayed by Delilah, Gehazi deceived Naaman and lied to Elisha, Ananias and Sapphira lied to the Holy Spirit, and Judas betrayed the Son of God.

Be warned, the love of money will destroy your soul. If ever it gets control of you, it will harden, paralyze, freeze, and sear your heart and conscience. It destroyed Judas; and it will destroy you and me, if ever it gets hold of our hearts.

"What shall it profit a man if he gain the whole world, and lose his own soul?" (Proverbs 30:8, 9). Be wise and pray daily, "Give me neither poverty nor riches; feed me with food convenient for me". The rich in this world often find in the end, like Esau and Judas, that the bargain they made was the worst of bargains. All that said, recognized too that many have betrayed the Son of God at a far lower price than thirty pieces of silver. Many, especially those who claim to be preachers, have sold him for no more than the smile and approval men!

Our Sovereign God

Fourth, these verses reveal the Lord Jesus Christ as the sovereign God of the universe. Notice the language our Saviour used to speak of Judas' betrayal. He speaks as One who is in total control of all around him. This Man who was about to be betrayed is the eternal God who made, ruled, and disposed of his betrayer.

His divine omniscience is evident in the fact that our Master knew what his disciples would do, what the certain man in the city would do, what Judas had done and would do. He knew it because he predestinated it and controlled it all.

Everything and everyone in this world is moving according to a precise schedule to a predestined end. Even the actions of wicked men, the very demons of hell, and the devil himself do nothing to thwart, hinder, or disturb God's purpose. They are servants, used to accomplish his purpose (Psalm 76:10; Romans 8:28-30; 11:36). Even Judas was an instrument in the hands of our God for the purposes of redemption and grace for his elect. Nowhere is the fact of our Lord's absolute and total sovereignty seen more clearly than in the events surrounding his betrayal and crucifixion (Acts 2:23; 4:27, 28; 13:28, 29).

Better Not To Have Been Born

Fifth, our Lord Jesus here teaches us that it would be better never to live at all than to live and die without Christ (v. 24). Judas stands before us in the Word of God as a glaring warning. He would this day give anything simply never to have been born. Judas is in hell! He lived and died without Christ as an unbeliever and an enemy of God. Now he suffers the wrath of God in hell. So, too, shall you if, like Judas, you live and die without Christ. Be warned. If you are yet without Christ, you are just like Judas. Your heart is exactly the same as Judas Iscariot's (Matthew 15:19). You may be taken captive by Satan at his will, and led by him to do things you never dreamed you were capable of doing (2 Timothy 2:26). Unless you repent, unless you look to Christ by faith, you shall be with Judas forever in hell, suffering the terrible wrath of almighty God.

Chapter 80

The First Communion Service

"And as they were eating, Jesus took bread, and blessed it, and brake it, and gave it to the disciples, and said, Take, eat; this is my body. And he took the cup, and gave thanks, and gave it to them, saying, Drink ye all of it; For this is my blood of the new testament, which is shed for many for the remission of sins. But I say unto you, I will not drink henceforth of this fruit of the vine, until that day when I drink it new with you in my Father's kingdom. And when they had sung an hymn, they went out into the mount of Olives. Then saith Jesus unto them, All ye shall be offended because of me this night: for it is written, I will smite the shepherd, and the sheep of the flock shall be scattered abroad. But after I am risen again, I will go before you into Galilee. Peter answered and said unto him, Though all men shall be offended because of thee, yet will I never be offended. Jesus said unto him, Verily I say unto thee, That this night, before the cock crow, thou shalt deny me thrice. Peter said unto him, Though I should die with thee, yet will I not deny thee. Likewise also said all the disciples."
(Matthew 26:26-35)

By God's purpose and by his providence, the Jewish passover of the Old Testament melted into the Lord's supper as the stars of the night dissolve into the light of the rising sun. The ordinance could not have been established with greater simplicity. There was absolutely nothing of ceremonial pageantry about it.

"And as they were eating, Jesus took bread, and blessed it, and brake it, and gave it to the disciples, and said, Take, eat; this is my body" (v. 26). With those simple, unpretentious words our Master established the blessed ordinance of the Lord's supper. He knew all that was before him. He knew what he must suffer. He knew what would happen with his disciples. He knew the turmoil that was coming. Wisely and graciously, he chose this last quiet evening before his crucifixion to bestow this parting gift to his church. How precious the memory of this night must have been to those disciples every time they met around the table afterward! Yet, the misunderstanding and abuse of this blessed ordinance has been the cause of strife, controversy and division, and of much heresy throughout church history. How sad! If there is anything that ought to unite all who profess faith in Christ, the Lord's supper is it; but sinful men have so perverted the teachings of Christ regarding this ordinance that it has become an opportunity for controversy to many, rather than an ordinance of communion. Let every saved sinner seek grace to observe this blessed ordinance as it was originally established. Indeed, if we would worship God in this ordinance, or in any other, it must be observed as it was established by our Lord.

The Elements

It is important to understand the meaning of the elements our Lord used in giving us the ordinance of the Lord's supper. Our Saviour simply took the unleavened bread and wine of the passover supper and incorporated them into the elements to be used in the Lord's supper. He said, of the bread, "this is my body", and of the wine, "this is my blood". We need to understand what this means.

Error concerning the meaning of our Lord's words has led men to serious, deplorable idolatry and superstition. Papists tell us that in the mass the bread and wine literally change their substance and become the actual body and blood of Christ, so the mass becomes, in the idolater's mind, a sacrifice and a re-crucifixion of Christ to make atonement for sin! Martin Luther taught that the bread and wine are mystically and spiritually transformed into the body and blood of Christ, so that the elements themselves become holy and convey grace to the communicants. Many today have a view similar to Luther's. They attach a pagan, idolatrous meaning to the bread and wine of the Lord's table. I have friends who used to bury any bread and wine that was left over after communion. They had been taught that once consecrated, it could never be used again. Others make the ordinance, Christ's established symbol of his finished work, to be a sacrament, a means by which grace is conveyed to the soul.

However, the meaning of our Lord's statement is clear: "This bread represents my body. This wine represents my blood". There is absolutely no indication that he meant any more than that. In the scriptures things are often said to be what they represent. This is a simple device of language to express symbolism and is common in other portions of scripture where it is readily understood without the need to use words like "signify", "denote", "portray", "typify", or "represent". For example, when Moses writes in Genesis 40:12, "The three branches are three days" it is clear he is saying that the three branches represent three days. Similarly, in Genesis 41:26, "The seven kine are seven years" means that the kine signify seven years. In Daniel 7:24, "The ten horns are (or represent) ten kings", in Matthew 13:38, "The field is (or represents) the world". In Revelation 1:20

John writes, "The seven stars are the angels of the seven churches, and the seven candlesticks which thou sawest are the seven churches" and it is again clear that symbols are said to be the things they portray and represent.

The Bible is full of expressions similar to these, and we would never think of taking them in a literal sense. Good sense demands that they be interpreted allegorically. Our Saviour is called "the Lamb of God", "the Door of the sheep", "the Lion of Judah", and "the Vine". No one would ever think of saying that he is literally those things! And no one, whose mind has not been perverted by religious nonsense, would ever imagine that the bread and wine of the Lord's supper are anything but representative of our Redeemer's body and his blood. All you have to do is taste the bread to know that it is bread, not flesh! All you have to do is drink the wine to know that it is wine, not blood!

The unleavened bread represents the holy human body of our Saviour. We dare not use soda crackers or light bread. Our Lord used unleavened bread for a reason. Leaven represents sin; and our Saviour had no sin. Therefore, he used unleavened bread to represent his body. The wine represents his precious, sin-atoning blood. Many today have found excuses for using grape juice and other liquids in the celebration of the Lord's supper. But no excuse will justify such behaviour in the house of God. Wine is used because, like the unleavened bread, it is free of corruption, and thus a proper representation of our Saviour's blood.

In Matthew 26:28 our Lord tells us four things about his blood. 1. He says it is "my blood", the blood of that man who is God: infinitely meritorious blood, sin-atoning, precious blood. 2. This is "the blood of the new testament", the everlasting, new covenant (Hebrews 13:20). 3. His blood was "shed for many". It was not shed for all, but for many; the many who are the objects of his mercy, love, and grace; the many who are redeemed and saved by it. 4. His blood was shed "for the remission of sins". There was no other way by which God could, in his holiness, justice, and truth, forgive the sins of his people. Only by the shedding of Christ's blood can he be both "a just God and a Saviour", both just and the Justifier (Isaiah 45:21; Romans 3:24-28).

When we come together around the Lord's table, we should take great care to focus our attention on the incarnation, life, and death of Christ as our Substitute. That is what is represented to us by the unleavened bread and wine.

The Purpose

When he established the Lord's supper as a standing ordinance of divine worship, our Saviour plainly stated the purpose of the ordinance. The Holy Spirit tells us in

1 Corinthians 11:24 that he said, "This do in remembrance of me". The Lord's supper was established by Christ to be a memorial of him and his sacrifice of love for us, by which he redeemed his elect, no more and no less. Immense harm has been done by those who teach God's people that this is a mysterious, complex thing. As we have seen, it could not have been established with greater simplicity.

The Lord's supper is not a sacrifice. Not a word is mentioned about a sacrifice in connection with the establishment or the observance of this ordinance. No mention is made of priests or altars. The fact is, once Christ was offered as a sacrifice for our sins, all sacrifices, all altars, and all priests ceased (Hebrews 10:14). We have no sacrifice but Christ. We have no altar but Christ. We have no priest but Christ. If you have any other altar, priest, or sacrifice, you do not have Christ and cannot partake of Christ (Hebrews 13:10).

The Lord's supper is not a sacrament. Those who speak of the ordinances of Christ as sacraments are in error. The bread and wine are not sacred. The table is not sacred. The act of eating and drinking the bread and wine is not sacred. No grace is conferred upon us by our observance of the Lord's supper. It is not a means by which God conveys his grace to sinners. God's grace is conveyed to us through Christ alone and by faith alone. The word sacrament implies a means of grace. By definition, a sacrament is "a solemn religious ceremony enjoined by Christ, to be observed by his followers, by which their special relation to him is created, or their obligations to him are renewed and ratified". A sacrament is a piece of Roman Catholic idolatry retained by Protestant churches who still imagine that the grace of God can be obtained by ceremonies, rituals, and works.

The Lord's supper is a symbolic memorial ordinance of public worship. It is not an ordinance to be observed privately, but publicly. It is an ordinance for redeemed sinners, for believers, for men and women who are born again by the power and grace of God the Holy Spirit. By our public observance of this ordinance, eating the bread and drinking the wine, we openly declare to all that we are sinners in need of Christ alone as our sin-atoning Saviour, looking to him alone for salvation and eternal life; trusting him just as we did in our baptism when we were symbolically buried with him in the watery grave and arose with him to walk in the newness of life.

The Lord's supper is a solemn, but joyful ordinance of worship. At the end of the supper, our Lord and his disciples sang a hymn. Every remembrance of our redemption accomplished by Christ should fill us with joy. John Trapp suggested that we ought to leave the Lord's table with "shouting as a giant after his wine, singing and making melody to the Lord in our hearts. We should come from the

Lord's table, as Moses did from the mount, with our faces shining; as the good women did from the sepulchre, 'with fear and great joy'; as the people went to their tents from Solomon's feast, 'joyful and glad of heart' (1 Kings 8:66). If those in the wilderness were so cheered by their idolatrous feast before the golden calf that they 'eat and drink, and rise up to play' (1 Corinthians 10:7), how much more should we by this blessed banquet?"

Those Present

This passage also shows us the character of those who were present with our Saviour at the first observance of the Lord's supper. Let me state emphatically that we do not and must not make the celebration of the Lord's supper a community or family service. It is not a gathering to which unbelievers are invited, or encouraged to join in. Anyone who does not trust the Lord as Saviour is disqualified from both baptism (Acts 8:36, 37) and the Lord's supper (1 Corinthians 11:27-29). Unbelievers are unworthy of the Lord's ordinances because they do not discern (or understand the necessity of) the Lord's body. But, it is not up to the pastor, the elders, the deacons, or the church to decide who shall partake of the Lord's supper. The burden of examination and responsibility is upon the individual. Each one must examine himself (1 Corinthians 11:28). This is obvious when we see who first observed this blessed ordinance with our Lord.

Those present all professed to be believers and followers of Christ and all who profess faith in Christ are welcome. The scriptures do not teach closed communion, or even restricted communion. Yet, though all professed to be believers, one was a devil; and the Lord knew it (vv. 21-23; Luke 22:14). The Lord Jesus knew what Judas had done but he did not refuse him a place at the table. The reason appears obvious. He would give no precedent for the practice of fencing the table, which gained prominence by the legality of puritan theology.

We must never attempt to set barriers around the table to keep people away. It is the responsibility of the individual who eats the bread and drinks the wine to examine them self, to be certain that he or she is a believer who discerns the Lord's body. But be warned, all who eat and drink unworthily, that is, without faith in Christ, eat and drink damnation to themselves (1 Corinthians 11:27-30). Only you can determine whether you are in the faith. If you profess faith in Christ, it is the responsibility of God's people to look upon your profession as genuine and to receive you "without doubtful disputations", without suspicion (Romans 14:1). Our Lord knew Judas was a devil yet, when he passed out the bread and wine, he gave it to Judas as well as to Peter, James and John.

In a few hours Peter would curse and deny the Master yet the Lord spread the bread and wine before him. He knew all who sat with him would forsake him but not one was exempted from his supper. God never sends his erring children to bed without supper. Let no child of God look upon the Lord's supper as unnecessary. Let no believer imagine he is unworthy to receive it. Our worthiness is Christ. He who is unfit for an ordinance of Christ is unfit for the company of Christ. Let us never be more strict in these things than Christ himself.

Immutable Grace

In verses 31-35 our dear Redeemer, knowing that his disciples would soon need to be reminded of it, declares the blessed immutability of his saving grace. He assures us that because of his one great sacrifice for sin, God will never charge his people with sin (Romans 4:8). As was prophesied by Zechariah (Zechariah 13:7), when the Shepherd was smitten by the rod of divine justice, the sheep would all be scattered. So it came to pass. All of them were confident that they would never be offended by him and would never forsake him. But they were all offended by the Saviour, and all forsook him. How deceitful are our hearts!

But Zechariah said more. The Lord declared, "Awake, O sword, against my Shepherd, and against the man that is my fellow … Smite the Shepherd, and the sheep shall be scattered". That much of the prophecy we often hear quoted. But God's word by Zechariah continues. The first part of Zechariah 13:7 announced the death of Christ as our sin-atoning Substitute, the Good Shepherd who laid down his life for his sheep. The next line announced the weakness, sin and unbelief of the smitten Shepherd's poor, depraved sheep. "And the sheep shall be scattered". But the last line of Zechariah 13:7 gives a blessed word of grace, assuring us of the immutability of God's grace to us in Christ, though we are but weak, sinful, straying sheep. "And I will turn mine hand upon the little ones"!

Those precious words of grace were in the heart and mind of our Saviour as he anticipated the shameful behaviour of his disciples. In verse 32 he assures them, and us, that his grace is unaltered even by our sin. He says, "I will turn mine hand upon the little ones"! "After I am risen, I will go before you into Galilee". The Lord Jesus was saying to his people, "I will go before you in grace to recover you, wherever you may in weakness and sin stray from me" (see Mark 16:7; John 21:15-19). "If we believe not, yet he abideth faithful: he cannot deny himself" (2 Timothy 2:13). "Blessed is the man to whom God will not impute sin" (Romans 4:8). What we celebrate in the Lord's supper is salvation by the grace of God in Christ, by whom our sins have been put away forever!

Chapter 81

Lessons From Gethsemane

"Then cometh Jesus with them unto a place called Gethsemane, and saith unto the disciples, Sit ye here, while I go and pray yonder. And he took with him Peter and the two sons of Zebedee, and began to be sorrowful and very heavy. Then saith he unto them, My soul is exceeding sorrowful, even unto death: tarry ye here, and watch with me. And he went a little further, and fell on his face, and prayed, saying, O my Father, if it be possible, let this cup pass from me: nevertheless not as I will, but as thou wilt. And he cometh unto the disciples, and findeth them asleep, and saith unto Peter, What, could ye not watch with me one hour? Watch and pray, that ye enter not into temptation: the spirit indeed is willing, but the flesh is weak. He went away again the second time, and prayed, saying, O my Father, if this cup may not pass away from me, except I drink it, thy will be done. And he came and found them asleep again: for their eyes were heavy. And he left them, and went away again, and prayed the third time, saying the same words. Then cometh he to his disciples, and saith unto them, Sleep on now, and take your rest: behold, the hour is at hand, and the Son of man is betrayed into the hands of sinners. Rise, let us be going: behold, he is at hand that doth betray me."
(Matthew 26:36-46)

Now we follow the Lord Jesus Christ into Gethsemane. Let us do so with great reverence, gratitude and wonder. Robert Hawker's opening comments on this portion of holy scripture express the attitude with which we ought to approach it. Hawker wrote:

> We have here Christ's entrance upon his sufferings, in the garden Gethsemane. The whole life of Jesus had been a life of sorrow, for of him, and him only, by way of emphasis, can it be said, that he was a 'man of sorrows and acquainted with grief.' But here he is entering more especially upon the great work of sorrow, for which he became the Surety of his people. And here it is therefore, that we need most eminently the teaching of God the Holy Ghost. I am

> aware how very little a way our discoveries carry us, when following the steps of Jesus by faith, into the garden of Gethsemane. If Peter, James and John, whom Christ took with him there, fell under such a drowsiness as is described, how shall we hope to watch the footsteps of Jesus to any great discoveries of such an awful scene? Nevertheless, looking up for the teachings and leadings of the Holy Ghost, I would beg the Reader to accompany me, in following by faith, the Lord Jesus to Gethsemane's garden, in this dark and gloomy hour; and may the Lord be our Teacher in beholding the glory of Christ, even in the depth of his soul travail, when he drank the cup of trembling to the dregs, that we might drink the cup of salvation and call upon the name of the Lord.

As we read this passage, we must remember that everything our Lord Jesus did, and all that he suffered, was as the Surety and Representative of his elect, whom he came into the world to save. That fact should fill us with reverent adoration, and should keep us from vain curiosity. If it were possible for a man to remove a deadly virus from his wife by drawing it into himself, I cannot imagine her trying to figure out the chemical and biological reactions of his body and mind as he suffered and died with her disease. Somehow, such curiosity would seem out of place. Would it not? It would be far more reverent and honouring to her husband for her simply to adore his great love for her.

Let us, therefore, reverently remember and adore our Saviour's great love for us and draw from his agony in Gethsemane some practical lessons by which we may honour him who loved us and gave himself for us. I will not attempt to explain to what extent our Lord's agony here was the result of Satan's temptations. I do not know. I cannot tell you how much agony a holy, sinless person, like our Redeemer, would endure at the prospect of being made sin for us. That is altogether beyond human imagination. Nor will I attempt to explain what appears to many to be a conflict between the human and divine wills of our Saviour. It is sufficient for us to know that he is perfectly God and perfectly man. I leave these points alone, because I know any attempt of mine to explain them would merely "darken counsel by words without knowledge" (Job 38:2).

However, I am certain that all that our Saviour endured and did in Gethsemane is recorded here by divine inspiration for our comfort and learning that we might walk in his steps. Therefore, I want to show you seven thing set before us in this paragraph.

The Necessity Of Satisfaction

The first thing that is obvious in these verses is the fact that there is absolutely no way for the holy, just, and true God to forgive sin and save sinners apart from the sin-atoning death of his own dear Son as our Substitute. Why was our Lord so sorrowful? Why was his heart so heavy? Why was his soul so troubled? Why did he fall on his face and cry out to his Father three times with strong crying and tears? What is the meaning of the bloody sweat, sore amazement and astonishment described by the other Gospel writers? Why is the almighty, the omnipotent Son of God so apparently helpless? Why is that One who raised the dead, that One who performed astonishing miracles for multitudes suddenly disturbed and cast down in his own soul? Why is the Lord Jesus Christ who came into this world to die for sinners by the will of God suddenly filled with agony and astonishment at the prospect of death?

It certainly was not the fear of physical pain, the fear of death, or even the fear of dying upon the cross. Many men, even women and children have endured terrible pains without crying out and without dread. Our Saviour was not weaker than such men. Something more than the prospect of a horrible, painful death pressed down upon him. It was not death on the cross that our Redeemer agonized over in Gethsemane. Our Lord full well that, "Without shedding of blood is no remission" (Hebrews 9:22). That is the reason why it was impossible for the cup of God's wrath to pass from his darling Son. God almighty could not forgive sin; he could not save his people without the shedding of Christ's precious blood. God cannot save sinners apart from the satisfaction of justice (Romans 3:24-26). He stated very emphatically that he came for the purpose of dying as our Substitute upon the cursed tree.

What was the cause of this great heaviness and sorrow, this grief and agony of our blessed Redeemer's soul? If not the prospect of death by crucifixion, what was it that crushed our Master's heart and so greatly disturbed him? It was the prospect of being made sin for us (2 Corinthians 5:21; 1 Peter 2:24). No man, not even an angel, can comprehend that weight upon his holy soul! As he anticipated being made sin for us, our Saviour said, "My soul is exceeding sorrowful, even unto death". The sorrow of his soul was the very soul of his sorrow.

It was the enormous load of our sin and guilt that crushed our Saviour's heart in Gethsemane, the sin and guilt of all God's elect which was about to be made his. Our Saviour's great sorrow was caused by his anticipation of being made sin for us. "It was", wrote J. C. Ryle, "a sense of the unutterable weight of our sins and transgressions which were then specially laid upon him". He who knew no sin was about to be made sin for us. He who is the only man who really knows what sin is, the only man who sees sin as God, was about to become sin. He who is the holy, harmless, undefiled Lamb of God was about to be made a curse for us. The holy Son of God was about to be forsaken by his Father.

Our Lord Jesus Christ, the Son of God, "began to be sore amazed", to be in great consternation and astonishment, at the sight of all the sins of his people coming upon him, the black storm of divine wrath gathered thick over him, the sword of justice about to be drawn against him, and the curse of God's holy law and inflexible justice about to be poured out upon him when he would be made sin for us! In consideration of these things our Saviour began "to be very heavy"! What crushed our Saviour's very heart and soul was the very thing for which he came into the world, the prospect of what he must endure as our Substitute.

No Exemption From Sorrow

Second, we are here taught that holiness of life is no exemption from trouble and sorrow. Our Lord Jesus Christ was "holy, harmless, and undefiled". He never did anything but good. He loved God perfectly. He loved men perfectly. "He knew no sin". Yet, never was there a human being who suffered like the "man of sorrows". The fact is, "Man that is born of a woman is of few days, and full of trouble" (Job 14:1). There are no exceptions. While we live in this world, trouble and sorrow will always be the portion of our cup. We are, all of us, "born unto trouble as the sparks fly upward" (Job 5:7). No creature in this world is so vulnerable as man. Our bodies, our minds, our families, our jobs, our daily responsibilities, our businesses, our friends, all are doors of trouble and sorrow. Let us, in the midst of sorrow, try to remind ourselves that our troubles and sorrows are light in comparison with what we deserve, what others have suffered, what our Saviour suffered for us, and with the glory that awaits us in heaven. Compared with eternity, they are but for a moment (2 Corinthians 4:18-5:1).

Cure For Care

Third, we should learn from our Saviour's conduct here that prayer is the best cure for care. When Job was troubled, he fell down and worshipped God (Job 1:20). When Hezekiah was faced with great sorrow and trouble, he spread his matters before the Lord (2 Kings 19:14). When our Lord Jesus was "exceeding sorrowful", he turned to God his Father in prayer. The very first Person to whom we should turn with our sorrows and troubles and cares is our God and Father.

Nothing that concerns us is too trivial, and nothing too great for him who bids us cast all our care upon him, assuring us that he cares for us (Hebrews 4:16; 1 Peter 5:7; 2 Corinthians 12:9). As we look to the Lord our God for help, he will either remove our trouble or he will give us grace sufficient to bear it for his glory.

Submission To God's Will

Fourth, submission to the will of God is one characteristic of true faith. The words of our Saviour give us a marvellous example of faith, an example of what our attitude ought to be in all things. May God give me grace always to surrender to him and say, "Not as I will, but as thou wilt ... Thy will be done". Someone once said, "He who abandons himself to God will never be abandoned by God."

We all think we want to have our own way. But we do not know what is best for us, best for the glory of God, best for the people of God, or best for the cause of God. Only God knows what is best. We will be wise, like old Eli, ever to say, "It is the Lord: let him do what seemeth him good" (1 Samuel 3:18). Blessed is that person who is so well taught of God that he has learned to be content with the purpose of God and with the providence of God (Philippians 4:11-13).

Watch And Pray

Fifth, our Lord also shows us here that the strongest and most faithful believers are very weak in this world and always need to watch and pray. Here are Peter, James and John, chosen Apostles, three of the strongest, most exemplary believers ever to walk upon the earth. Here they are with the Son of God in Gethsemane, yet fast asleep! When they ought to have been watching and praying, they were sleeping. The sad fact is, that is the common sin of God's elect in this world (Song of Solomon 5:2, 3). We are a people with two distinct, opposing natures, "flesh" and "spirit" (Romans 7:14-24). Yet, our weakness is never to be looked upon as an excuse for sin, but always as a reason for watchfulness and prayer (Galatians 5:17).

We must always live like soldiers in enemy territory, watchful, alert, and on guard. We cannot be too careful. We cannot be too jealous of our souls. The world is cunning. The devil is crafty. Our flesh is weak. In such a condition it is utterly foolish for us not to watch and pray that we enter not into temptation.

Our Tender, Forgiving Saviour

Sixth, we are taught that our Lord Jesus Christ is a very gracious, tender, forgiving God and Saviour. "Then cometh he to his disciples, and saith unto them, Sleep on now, and take your rest: behold, the hour is at hand, and the Son of man is betrayed into the hands of sinners" (vv. 45, 46). Our Lord did not speak those words in sarcasm. He simply told Peter, James and John to rest while he kept watch. He saw the glare of the torches approaching. The stillness of the night was broken by the trampling feet of the betrayer and the blood-thirsty mob he led. But the Lord Jesus speaks to these sleeping disciples, not for their sake but for ours, (They could not hear him. They were asleep!), as if to say, "There is no need for you to be disturbed. I will take care of this." May God the Holy Spirit graciously and constantly teach us to look to Christ in faith, confident that he is watching for us and over us, that we might take our rest in him.

A Willing Sacrifice

Seventh, we should learn from this passage of scripture that the Lord Jesus Christ willingly laid down his life for his people. He died as a willing sacrifice for our sins. He said to his beloved servants, "Rise, let us be going: behold, he is at hand that doth betray me" (v. 46). Our Redeemer did not die as the helpless victim of circumstances beyond his control. He had come into the world to come to this hour that he might die in our place as our sin-atoning Substitute. This is "how" Christ died for our sins according to the scriptures. He died vicariously, in the place of God's elect (John 10:11). He died voluntarily, by his own will (John 10:17, 18). And he died victoriously, triumphing over death, hell, and the grave, having accomplished eternal redemption for us (John 19:30). Hawker said:

> Oh! Gethsemane! Sacred, hallowed spot! Did Jesus oft-times resort thither with his disciples? And wilt thou now, O LORD, by thy sweet Spirit, aid my meditations, that I may take the wing of faith and often traverse over the solemn ground? It was a garden in which the first Adam began to break through the fence of God's holy plantation. And in a garden the second Adam, so called, shall begin the soul-travail of sorrow, to do away the effects of it. And, oh! What humiliation, what agonies, what conflicts in the arduous work? Oh! How vast the glory, when smiting to the earth his enemies, the LORD JESUS proved his GODHEAD by the breath of his mouth! Sweetly do I see thee, LORD, by faith, going forth a willing sacrifice. Lo! I come! said JESUS. So come, LORD, now, by grace.

Chapter 82

The Betrayal

"And while he yet spake, lo, Judas, one of the twelve, came, and with him a great multitude with swords and staves, from the chief priests and elders of the people. Now he that betrayed him gave them a sign, saying, Whomsoever I shall kiss, that same is he: hold him fast. And forthwith he came to Jesus, and said, Hail, master; and kissed him. And Jesus said unto him, Friend, wherefore art thou come? Then came they, and laid hands on Jesus, and took him. And, behold, one of them which were with Jesus stretched out his hand, and drew his sword, and struck a servant of the high priest's, and smote off his ear. Then said Jesus unto him, Put up again thy sword into his place: for all they that take the sword shall perish with the sword. Thinkest thou that I cannot now pray to my Father, and he shall presently give me more than twelve legions of angels? But how then shall the scriptures be fulfilled, that thus it must be? In that same hour said Jesus to the multitudes, Are ye come out as against a thief with swords and staves for to take me? I sat daily with you teaching in the temple, and ye laid no hold on me. But all this was done, that the scriptures of the prophets might be fulfilled. Then all the disciples forsook him, and fled."
(Matthew 26:47-56)

Nothing in human history more vividly portrays the depravity, blackness, vileness and deceit of the human heart than the betrayal of our Lord Jesus Christ into the hands of his enemies by Judas Iscariot. Nothing more woefully displays the evil of the hypocrite's heart than this vile deed of Judas. Nothing more fearfully exemplifies the hardness of heart that is produced by a profession of faith in Christ without the possession of the grace of God and the knowledge of Christ. If we are wise, we will read the passage before us with fear and trembling, lest we should at last be found with Judas.

What a sad picture the Holy Spirit has painted with these words. Here we see the beginning of our Lord's sorrows. The cup of his woe is beginning to be filled. One of his disciples betrays him. All of his disciples forsake him. He is arrested like a common thief by his enemies. Behold these things, the beginning of his sorrows, and know that there never was or ever shall be any sorrow like his sorrow. May we never forget that the cause of all his sorrows was our sin. The Son of God was "delivered for our offences" (Romans 4:25). In the verses before us we are given clear instructions concerning both our Redeemer and ourselves. May God the Holy Spirit take the things of Christ and show them to us.

Kiss Of Treachery

Who is not familiar with the kiss of hypocrisy, called "the Judas kiss"? All are familiar with the event; but few, I fear, pause to consider its implications. The most abominable and dangerous men in the world are those who betray Christ with the kiss of friendship. Judas betrayed the Lord of glory with a kiss! Though treachery was in his heart, familiarity, kindness, peace, and love was what he wished to convey. In eastern countries a kiss is a common form of greeting. It suggests respect, friendship, affection, and a wish that the one kissed may enjoy every blessing. Judas' kiss was the kiss of a betrayer, a kiss of treachery and hypocrisy. When he said, "Hail, master", he was saying, "Joy and happiness to you, my master". Thus, the hypocrite, with brazenness and hardness of heart, pretended to worship, honour, love, and serve Christ, even in the act of betraying him! May God save us from the treacherous kisses of self-righteousness, false religion, idolatry, and hypocrisy.

This kiss of treachery is also manifest in all who pretend to serve and honour our Lord Jesus, while betraying him with false doctrine, by which they deny the saving operations of the triune God: the work of God the Father in the accomplishment of our salvation by his eternal decree (Romans 8:29, 30; Ephesians 1:3-6), the work of God the Son in accomplishing righteousness and redemption at Calvary (Ephesians 1:7-12), and the works of God the Holy Spirit imparting righteousness to us, making us partakers of the divine nature in regeneration, sanctifying chosen, redeemed sinners by his grace in the gifts of life and faith in Christ. Our Saviour's warning needs to be rung out often and heard distinctly. He said, "Beware of false prophets, which come to you in sheep's clothing, but inwardly they are ravening wolves" (Matthew 7:15). These wolves would not be so dangerous if they did not come in sheep's clothing (2 Corinthians 11:1-15). C. H. Spurgeon wrote, "This sign of Judas was typical of the way in which Jesus is generally betrayed. When men intend to undermine the scriptures, how do they begin their books? Why, always with a declaration that they wish to promote the truth of Christ"!

An Accessible Saviour

The Lord Jesus Christ is such a friend of sinners that he is readily accessible to them. I recognize that we are never told that any of the other apostles kissed the Saviour; but that does not mean that they did not. In fact, it would be a very strange thing if they had failed to do so. As I said, this was then, as it is now, a common form of greeting in eastern countries (Exodus 18:7; 1 Samuel 20:41). Our Lord rebuked Simon the Pharisee because he did not greet him in this manner (Luke 7:45).

When Judas made his deal of treachery he told them to arrest the one that he kissed. His object was to betray the Master in a way that would appear the least suspicious. Therefore, he said, "Whomsoever I shall kiss, that same is he". Apparently, this was the common way in which our Lord was greeted by his disciples after a time of absence. It was a custom maintained by the disciples long afterward. Paul frequently admonishes believers to greet one another with a "holy kiss". Peter urges us to greet one another with a "kiss of charity".

There is a word of instruction, comfort, and encouragement in this. Our Lord Jesus Christ is gracious. He condescends to be accessible to and approached by sinners such as we are in the most intimate manner. In fact, we are commanded to "kiss the Son". What a blessed commandment of grace that is! What the Son of God was to sinners in his humiliation, he is in his exaltation. He is just as ready to save, just as accessible today as he was when he walked upon the earth. Sinners may freely come to the Son of God without fear of being rejected or cast off by him (John 6:37; Hebrews 4:16). "Sinners Jesus will receive, sound this word of grace to all!"

Spiritual Warfare

Let all who seek to serve the cause of Christ in this world learn from verses 51-53 that the cause of Christ and his kingdom cannot be established, maintained, defended, or even helped by carnal means. In verse 51 we see Peter acting very rashly. He drew out his sword and began to take on a band of soldiers single-handedly. While we may admire his courage, we must not fail to see his folly in this. Our Lord rebuked him for it. He did not commend him. John Trapp wisely observed: "A wonderful work of God it was surely, that hereupon he was not hewn in a hundred pieces by the barbarous soldiers." Two things need to be understood here.

1. Our Lord does not condemn the lawful use of the sword, of deadly arms and force. There are many that make this verse an argument against believers

going to war in defence of the nation, or against a man arming himself to defend his family and property against criminal intruders, or against the exercise of capital punishment by the state. While I am not interested in debating any of those issues, I will state that the Word of God does, without question, allow the use of the sword, of deadly force, in such circumstances. But that is not the subject here, either for or against.

2. Our Lord is here teaching us that his cause, his kingdom, his church, his gospel can never be established, maintained, defended, or even helped by carnal weapons. "The weapons of our warfare are not carnal, but mighty through God to the pulling down of strong holds" (2 Corinthians 10:4). While he specifically speaks of the sword, the sword is but a symbol for all carnal things. The church and kingdom of God cannot be established by carnal means; and we must never attempt it. Christ builds his church by the power of the Holy Spirit, through the preaching of the Gospel. Every other means by which men attempt to advance the cause of Christ in this world; civil law, political power, religious entertainment, religious philosophy, human reason, the doctrines of men, eloquent speech, etc., is but wood, hay, and stubble that will be burned (1 Corinthians 3:13-15).

A Voluntary Sacrifice

All that our Lord Jesus Christ endured as our Substitute he endured freely and voluntarily. One great feature in the redemption of our souls is the freeness with which our Redeemer performed the work. In fact, in great measure it was the voluntariness of our Saviour's sacrifice that gave it merit and efficacy. Our Saviour said, "Therefore doth my Father love me, because I lay down my life that I might take it again. No man taketh it from me. I have power to lay it down, and I have power to take it again. This commandment have I received of my Father" (John 10:17, 18).

Our Lord Jesus was not taken captive against his will, or because he could not escape. That would have been a very easy thing for him to do. But he had come here on purpose to fulfil the will of God, to fulfil the types and prophecies of the Old Testament, and to fulfil all righteousness for the salvation of his people. His heart was set upon accomplishing this great work. He was a voluntary Scapegoat, a willing Victim, and a willing Sacrifice for us.

The Lord Jesus said, "Thus it must be". Why? Why must it thus be? It "must be", because it was ordained by God the Father, it was agreed upon in the covenant of grace, and it was prophesied in the Old Testament scriptures. Every detail of our Lord's sufferings and death, from this vile betrayal to the piercing of his holy side, was foretold in the Old Testament. It “must be”, because it was typified in the sacrifices and ceremonies of the law. There was no other way for God in his holy justice to forgive and pardon the sins of his people.

Depraved Sinners Still

“Then all the disciples forsook him, and fled” (v. 56). We see in the conduct of our Lord’s disciples a clear picture of that which the Word of God constantly holds before us with regard to saved sinners. Though loved and chosen of God, though redeemed and justified by the blood of Christ, though born of his Spirit, sanctified, and given a new, righteous nature by him, God’s saints in this world are sinners still. None of us really knows what evils we are capable of committing. How little we know of the weakness and sin of our own hearts! All these disciples had, just a few hours earlier, protested against our Lord’s prophecy, and said, “We will not forsake you” (v. 35).

There was no reason for their fear. The Lord Jesus had already demanded of these soldiers that they let his disciples go (John 18:8). They had witnessed his sovereign power over these soldiers. Yet, when left to their own strength, all the disciples forsook their Master. In the time of testing they forgot everything. They forgot God’s goodness, grace, and power, their past experiences, their fervent resolutions, and their Master’s love. They forgot it all.

This is here recorded to remind us again that there is no evil we are not capable of committing or will not commit if left to ourselves, and that salvation is by grace alone. Our only righteousness is Jesus Christ our Redeemer. Our only hope of preservation is that God, who saved us by his grace, will keep us by his grace. J. C. Ryle said,

> Let us learn from this passage lessons of humiliation and self-abasement. Let us resolve, by God’s grace, to cultivate a spirit of lowliness and self-distrust. Let us settle in our minds, that there is nothing too bad for the very best of us to do, unless he is held up by the grace of God; and let it be one of our daily prayers, ‘Hold thou me up, and I shall be safe’ (Psalm 119:117).

A Final Thought From The Garden

We should read the account of our Saviour’s private agony in the Garden of Gethsemane, his desertion by his friends and his betrayal and arrest by his enemies all in the light of his earlier temptation in the wilderness. After that temptation, Satan left him for a season, awaiting another opportunity to assault him (Luke 4:13). In Gethsemane the prince of this world launched his final assault upon the Lord Jesus. Just as he assaulted the first Adam in the garden of Eden, he assaulted the last Adam in the garden of Gethsemane. In Gethsemane the serpent bruised the heel of the woman's Seed, and the woman's Seed again overthrew his assault.

Here on the Mount of Olives, in the garden of the olive press, olives were grown, harvested and crushed to produce valuable oil for food, light and warmth. Here too, our Lord was crushed to provide his people with spiritual comfort and eternal joy. And after these things, after suffering the wrath of men, our Saviour yet had to endure the wrath of God to save us. That, too, he voluntarily endured for us as our Substitute (2 Corinthians 5:21; Galatians 3:13, 14).

Those for whom the Lord Jesus Christ was made to be sin, for whom he suffered and died, are most assuredly made the righteousness of God in him, and shall be saved by his almighty grace. All for whom the Son of God died under the wrath of God shall be saved by the grace of God. His blood was not shed in vain (Isaiah 53:10-12).

Chapter 83

The Son Of God Excommunicated And Condemned

“And they that had laid hold on Jesus led him away to Caiaphas the high priest, where the scribes and the elders were assembled. But Peter followed him afar off unto the high priest’s palace, and went in, and sat with the servants, to see the end. Now the chief priests, and elders, and all the council, sought false witness against Jesus, to put him to death; But found none: yea, though many false witnesses came, yet found they none. At the last came two false witnesses, And said, This fellow said, I am able to destroy the temple of God, and to build it in three days. And the high priest arose, and said unto him, Answerest thou nothing? what is it which these witness against thee? But Jesus held his peace. And the high priest answered and said unto him, I adjure thee by the living God, that thou tell us whether thou be the Christ, the Son of God. Jesus saith unto him, Thou hast said: nevertheless I say unto you, Hereafter shall ye see the Son of man sitting on the right hand of power, and coming in the clouds of heaven. Then the high priest rent his clothes, saying, He hath spoken blasphemy; what further need have we of witnesses? behold, now ye have heard his blasphemy. What think ye? They answered and said, He is guilty of death. Then did they spit in his face, and buffeted him; and others smote him with the palms of their hands, Saying, Prophesy unto us, thou Christ, Who is he that smote thee?”
(Matthew 26:57-68)

See the Lord of glory dragged before the ecclesiastical court of the Jews, before Caiaphas, the chief priests, the scribes, and the elders. Everybody who was anybody among the Jews was represented in this assembly of madness. The religious world of the day, all who claimed to reverence the Word of God, honour the law of God, walk in the ways of God, and worship in the name of God were represented in this blood-thirsty mob. These men were not the religious kooks and crackpots, but the leaders of mainstream religion, conservative and liberal, both the orthodox and the unorthodox. All of them had come together now for the third time in one week (John 11:47-52; Matthew 26:3, 4) to excommunicate the Lord of glory and condemn him to death. They were determined to get rid of

Christ and his Gospel, while maintaining their religious status quo. They wanted to keep their temple, and priesthood, their religious customs, and the name of God; but they were determined to put an end to the influence of the Son of God and his Gospel of grace. Do not missed the point. This is what I want you to see. It is as evident as the noonday sun throughout the scriptures. The religious world, the mainstream religious world, in all its branches and denominations, is now and always has been opposed to Christ, his gospel, and his kingdom.

Every church in the world is acceptable in the religious world, except the church of God. Every religious notion in the world is acceptable in the religious world, except the Gospel of God's free and sovereign grace in Christ. Every way of salvation promoted by the perverse imaginations of men is acceptable in the religious world, except the declaration that Christ is the only Way, the declaration that salvation is to be had only by the shedding of his blood for the satisfaction of divine justice, that righteousness can be obtained only by divine imputation, and that salvation is the gift and operation of God's free, sovereign, effectual grace.

The Sacrifice Bound

"And they that had laid hold on Jesus led him away to Caiaphas the high priest, where the scribes and the elders were assembled". It was fitting that our Saviour be brought before the high priest of the Jews at this time. The great day of atonement was at hand. The wondrous types of the paschal lamb, the mercy-seat, and the scapegoat were about to be fulfilled. Now, before he is led forth to be crucified, the high priest, by the arrangement of providence, pronounces sin to be upon the head of the innocent Lamb of God (Leviticus 16:21; cf. John 11:49-52).

Our Saviour's sufferings were voluntarily endured. He, who by his mere word smote the band of soldiers who came to arrest him (John 18:6), was not bound and led away against his will. This, too, came to pass according to the purpose of God, that the scriptures might be fulfilled. In Psalm 22 our Saviour cried, "Many bulls have compassed me: strong bulls of Bashan have beset me round … Dogs have compassed me: the assembly of the wicked have enclosed me."

Our blessed Saviour was bound as the sacrifices of old, just as Isaac was bound and put on the altar (Genesis 22:9), and all the sacrifices of the law were bound at the horns of the altar (Psalm 118:27). The binding of the sacrifices in the Old Testament typically pictured the sins and iniquities of God's elect binding the Lord Jesus. Robert Hawker observed, "For as chains and fetters tie down the body, so sin and iniquity bend down the soul". And our blessed Saviour cried, as one whose soul was bound, when he was restoring that which he took not away,

"O God, thou knowest my foolishness; and my sins are not hid from thee ... Innumerable evils have compassed me about: mine iniquities have taken hold upon me, so that I am not able to look up; they are more than the hairs of mine head: therefore my heart faileth me" (Psalm 40:12; 69:5). Perhaps, the binding of our Substitute was intended of God to set forth the binding of all the sins of his people to him, when the Lord God had "laid on him the iniquity of us all", making him "sin for us, who knew no sin, that we might be made the righteousness of God in him". But Hawker makes another observation concerning the binding of our sins to our Saviour that is a matter of certainty. He wrote:

> It is a very, very precious thought, to the soul of every truly regenerated believer, that all the sins of his redeemed, without the omission of a single infirmity or sin; in thought, or word, or deed, were laid upon Christ, as the sacrifice was bound on the altar. Hence, the High Priest, under the Jewish dispensation, was commanded to be thus particular, on the great day of atonement. And Aaron shall lay both his hands upon the head of the live goat, and confess over him all the iniquities of the children of Israel, and all their transgression in all their sins, putting them upon the head of the goat: and shall send him away by the hand of a fit man (a man of opportunity, as the margin hath it, and as Christ was) into the wilderness, as Christ was led away when bound (Leviticus 16:21).

When our blessed Saviour was bound, led away, and, at last, put to death as our sin-atoning Sacrifice, he fulfilled all the typical sacrifices of the law that foreshadowed and represented him. Thus, he who was made sin for us put away all the sins of all his people by the sacrifice of himself.

Caiaphas And The Sanhedrin

Caiaphas represents the very worst of lost, unregenerate religious leaders. John Gill tells us that his name means "one that vomits at the mouth". Though he had all the proper outward credentials of a high priest, he obtained his office by the appointment of the Roman governor, either as the result of bribery or as a favour done to him, not by the appointment of God.

Like most religious leaders who obtain their offices and positions by the appointment of men, Caiaphas was a pragmatic leader for the people. He knew, at least in theory, certain aspects of divine truth; but he was a subtle politician.

When it was to his advantage to do so, he could act very manly and speak truth in the face of others. I do not know how much, if anything, he understood about what he said; but he certainly spoke the truth in John 11:47-52. He had no interest in the glory of God, the people of God, or the souls of men; but he did on occasion speak the truth. There are many like him in pulpits and positions of leadership and influence around the world today.

High office in the church is no indication that a man is God's servant. Read the Bible with your eyes open. The chief agents of our Lord's death were the priests, the elders, and the scribes of Israel. These priests could trace their lineage back to Aaron. They held the highest offices of religion. They led the people in acts of worship. They lived austere lives of devotion. At least they publicly appeared to live such lives. But these men were the murderers of the Son of God! Beware, hold no man in high esteem because he is reputed as a great preacher or religious leader. The teaching of any man who comes in the name of God must be tested by the standard of holy scripture (Isaiah 8:20; 1 John 4:1-6).

Peter And The Lord's Enemies

"But Peter followed him afar off unto the high priest's palace, and went in, and sat with the servants, to see the end" (v. 58). I do not want to say more than is suggested by this verse; it is placed here by divine inspiration to prepare us for what is later revealed about Peter's denial of the Lord Jesus.

After first forsaking the Lord with the rest, Peter and John turn back to follow him. Peter alone is mentioned here because it is Peter who is being considered. But we must not be too severe in our judgment of Peter. John Gill wrote, "Peter's following Christ showed love to him. He was loth (reluctant) to leave him. His bowels (heart) moved towards him. He wanted to know how it would fare with him, and what would become of him". But, sadly, that is not all that we are told. "Peter followed him", but he "followed him afar off". As Matthew Henry observed, "Some sparks of love and concern for his Master were in his breast, and therefore he followed him; but fear and concern for his own safety prevailed, and therefore he followed him afar off ... Here began Peter's denying him; for to follow him afar off is, by little and little, to go back from him".

Next we are told that Peter "went in and sat with the servants". He went in not to speak for Christ, but to screen himself, hoping not to be identified with Christ and his disciples. In fear and unbelief this bold disciple played the hypocrite. Foolishly and needlessly, he put himself in the way of temptation. He had no intention when he came to the high priest's house of denying his Lord; but he put himself in the path of danger by putting himself in the company of the Lord's enemies. C. H. Spurgeon says, "When a servant of Christ by his own choice sits with the servants of the wicked, sin and sorrow speedily follow."

The reason why Peter followed and went in was to gratify his curiosity about the most sacred of all things, the death of Christ. Look what the Holy Spirit tells us. He went in "to see the end". Peter went in to indulge his curiosity! He wanted to see what was happening. He wanted to see how the Lord would be condemned and delivered up to die. Perhaps he wanted to see what no one else would see. Whatever the case, his curiosity nearly destroyed him. Let us be warned.

The Chief Priests And Their False Witnesses

Even though they were plotting the murder of the Lord of Glory, these men were meticulous in their religious duty. They knew that the law required at least two witnesses for conviction of a capital crime. Before long, two men were found who perverted the Lord's words into an accusation of blasphemy. The two false witnesses could not get their stories to agree (Mark 14:56-59), but they served to soothe the consciences of these religious murderers (vv. 59-62).

Falsehood and ridicule are Satan's favourite weapons. The old serpent is a liar and the father of lies (John 8:44). Throughout our Lord's earthly ministry he was constantly accused of being an evil man and of doing wicked deeds. We must not be surprised to find men and women who oppose the gospel of the grace of God falsely accusing God's saints of wickedness.

Do not believe the evil reports that reprobate men give of God's saints. Gospel preachers particularly are the objects of scandalous gossip inspired by Satan. That has always been the case. I have never known any man to be used of God who was not the object of scandalous rumour at one time or another. More often than not, the rumours are started by religious people pretending to seek the honour of God and promote the cause of righteousness. Do not be surprised when you attempt to serve God if you are falsely accused of evil; and do not be surprised when faithful gospel preachers are accused of evil. Those who despise, but cannot repudiate our doctrine, try to repudiate our names.

Bloodthirsty Religionists

Here (vv. 63-68) we see the Son of God enclosed by the assembly of the wicked (Psalm 22:16). When accused by these false witnesses, our Lord held his peace. When he saw that his enemies were determined to have his blood, he choked their spite with silence. But "Jesus held his peace" because the scripture must be fulfilled which said, "He was oppressed, and he was afflicted, yet he opened not his mouth: he is brought as a lamb to the slaughter, and as a sheep before her shearers is dumb, so he openeth not his mouth" (Isaiah 53:7). Caiaphas was infuriated by the Saviour's composure and silence.

Then, in verse 64 our Saviour declared himself to be the Christ, God the Son. He told this enraged mob he would be seated upon the right hand of power, of omnipotence, and they would see it; that is to say, it would be made manifest to them. The right hand of power is the right hand of God. Being seated there signified that his work was finished and was accepted by God. Here our Saviour made a claim of deity, which the Jews understood. Indeed, if Jesus of Nazareth is not God, he was guilty of blasphemy and did deserve to die (Leviticus 24:16).

Then our Master boldly declared his second coming and how these godless reprobates would see him in judgment. Almost the last word spoken by our Lord before his crucifixion was about his second coming. Let us never question it.

After that, in great pomp and pretence, the high priest contemptuously condemned our Redeemer to be crucified, ripping his garments as he screamed "blasphemy"! (vv 65-68). Caiaphas ripped his clothes in a pretence of "righteous indignation" and to hide the malignity of his murderous heart. He denounced the Son of God as a blasphemer to disguise his own blasphemous heart.

The penalty for blasphemy was death by stoning; but our Lord had foretold that he would be crucified. Therefore, rather than stoning him on the spot, these men spit upon him, as they beat and mocked the Son of God. Then they delivered him up to the Romans to be crucified. All of this the Son of God voluntarily endured as our Substitute. John Trapp wrote: "Christ was content to be spit upon to cleanse our faces from the filth of sin, to be buffeted with fists and beaten with rods to free us from that mighty hand of God (1 Peter 5:6), and from those scourges and scorpions of infernal fiends."

The Good Shepherd laid down his life for his sheep as a voluntary sacrifice and sin-offering (John 1:15-18); and he did it according to the will and purpose of God almighty (Acts 2:23). All that was done to our Saviour was done according to the purpose of God, and had been beforehand revealed in the Old Testament scriptures (Acts 4:27, 28; 13:27-29). After suffering the wrath of men, our Saviour yet had to endure the wrath of God to save us. That, too, he voluntarily endured as our Substitute (2 Corinthians 5:21). The day shall soon come when the Lord of Glory will respond to the challenge of mockery in verse 68. "Prophesy unto us, thou Christ, Who is he that smote thee?" (2 Thessalonians 1:7-10; Revelation 1:7; 20:11-13).

Chapter 84

Peter's Fall And Restoration

"Now Peter sat without in the palace: and a damsel came unto him, saying, Thou also wast with Jesus of Galilee. But he denied before them all, saying, I know not what thou sayest. And when he was gone out into the porch, another maid saw him, and said unto them that were there, This fellow was also with Jesus of Nazareth. And again he denied with an oath, I do not know the man. And after a while came unto him they that stood by, and said to Peter, Surely thou also art one of them; for thy speech bewrayeth thee. Then began he to curse and to swear, saying, I know not the man. And immediately the cock crew. And Peter remembered the word of Jesus, which said unto him, Before the cock crow, thou shalt deny me thrice. And he went out, and wept bitterly."
(Matthew 26:69-75)

Here is a picture of God's servant Peter which is humbling and instructive. The fall of Peter is set before us as a beacon. It has many warnings and lessons for us. Peter's fall is recorded at considerable length by all four of the gospel writers. Matthew, Mark, Luke, and John were inspired to write out the details of this sad event. Yet, not one of them offers a word of excuse or explanation in defence of their friend and brother. This is one of those things which indirectly demonstrates the truthfulness of holy scripture. If the Bible were nothing but the compositions of men, it would never have been written that the great apostle to the Jews was so weak and sinful that he shamefully denied his Lord and Master. This story of Peter's fall was written by the inspiration of God the Holy Spirit for our learning and admonition. Here are four things that appear to me to be obvious reasons why so much attention is given to Peter's fall.

First, Peter's denial of the Lord Jesus must have greatly increased the pain and grief of our Saviour's sufferings. Second, the Holy Spirit here sets before us in a most emphatic way both the power and the immutability of God's saving grace. Third, the divine Comforter knew that we would all be subject to the same temptations by which Peter was overcome. Fourth, this fourfold record of Peter's fall is intended by God to be an instructive lesson for us concerning the frailty of the very best of men.

The Word of God does not tell us much even about the best of those men who lived in Bible times. The history of God's saints is scanty. Yet, the Bible very particularly and meticulously records the faults of God's elect. It seems that the Holy Spirit goes out of his way to remind us that the very best of men are only men at best. Peter was not the infallible bishop of Rome, as the papists pretend. He was a frail, fickle, fallible, sinful man. The only thing the pope has in common with Peter is his denial of Christ.

Peter's fall seems to say to each of us: "You, too, are weak. You, too, will fall if left to yourself. Do not trust yourself, trust Christ. Lean on him. Do not rely upon your experiences or the imaginary strength and firmness of your faith. Satan has desired to have you that he may sift you as wheat. Christ alone can hold you up. Christ alone can keep you". As we care for our souls and the honour of our God, let us never cease to be prayerfully watchful over our souls, ever seeking grace from God to keep us from the evil that is in us. All who know God's saving grace in Christ want to magnify and honour their Lord in this world. We want to live for the honour and glory of Christ. Our hearts shudder and tremble at the thought of bringing reproach upon the name of our blessed Redeemer. Yet, we know that unless the Lord himself preserves us, we will surely profane his name.

The Circumstances

Think about the circumstances of Peter's fall. This is not the fall of a hypocrite or an apostate. Peter was not a lost man, but a saved man, even when he fell. Not only was he a saved man, he was an apostle of Christ, a gospel preacher, a man who loved the Lord Jesus. Peter was a believer, a child of grace, pardoned and accepted in Christ. He was a man of strong faith, firm conviction, and zeal. But he was a man, just like you and me, a man whose heart was by nature full of sin. On this particular night the evil of his heart broke out in an unrestrained denial of Christ, a denial that was accompanied with foul oaths. As we consider the nature of Peter's fall, you will notice there were no extenuating circumstances to excuse his guilt. In fact, there appears to have been no reason for it at all. Everything recorded about it only aggravates Peter's guilt in the matter.

Peter's fall seems very strange because he was one of the Lord's most highly favoured and honoured disciples. We might have expected this from any of the other disciples before we would have expected it from Peter. The Lord had done so much for Peter. Peter was one of the first to whom the Lord Jesus revealed himself in this world, one of the first to be saved by the power of his grace (John 1:40-42) He was in the inner circle of the Master's friends and appears to have been chief spokesman for the early church. Let all who are honoured of God in this world be warned. The greater our privileges and the higher our honours, the greater our responsibilities and the more horrible our offences.

Peter's fall is especially sad because he had been plainly and faithfully warned of his great danger. The Saviour told Peter exactly what was going to happen to him in the plainest terms possible. He knew the danger to which he was exposing himself when he walked into the high priest's palace (Matthew 26:31; Luke 22:31-34). Satan desired to have him. His faith would be fiercely attacked. He must watch and pray that he enter not into temptation. But Peter walked headlong into his sin, rejecting the light and counsel God had given him. He ignored the light of God's revelation. Furthermore, Peter's guilt is aggravated in that it came so soon after he had declared his loyalty and faithfulness to Christ, at least implying he was confident he was more loyal and dependable than any of his brethren. "Peter answered and said unto him, Though all men shall be offended because of thee, yet will I never be offended … Peter said unto him, Though I should die with thee, yet will I not deny thee" (vv. 33-35). Just an hour or two after making this bold and arrogant profession of love and commitment to Christ, Peter cursed and denied that he even knew him!

The Apostle's fall did not come at once, but by degrees. Great, life-threatening sicknesses seldom come upon men without warning. Usually there are symptoms to warn us that something is wrong. Even so, believers seldom experience sudden falls into grave sin. Usually there are symptoms that something is wrong. The problem is we ignore the symptoms. J. C. Ryle wrote:

> The Church and the world are sometimes shocked by the sudden misconduct of some great professor of religion; believers are discouraged and stunned; the enemies of God rejoice and blaspheme: but if the truth could be known, the explanation of such cases would generally be found to have been private departure from God. Men fall in private long before they fall in public.

Notice that the Holy Spirit records a specific series of steps by which this man of great faith descended into such a low condition. He was far too confident and proud (vv. 31-33). The Lord told him to watch and pray. Instead, he slept! He followed the Lord afar off (v. 58). He chose to sit with scorners (v. 58; Luke 22:55; John 18:18). He denied his Master by degrees (Mark 14:68-71). At first, he pretended not to understand the maiden's words. Then, he denied that he knew the man (a denial of his own confession Matthew 16:16; John 6:69). At last, he took up the oaths of a profane man, cursing as he denied his Redeemer, as if to prove his point by foulness. There are many, many ways by which men and women deny the Lord Jesus Christ; but usually the falls of God's saints are not sudden. Normally, great falls are preceded by smaller inconsistencies. It takes very little to make a great saint fall into great sin, if God leaves him to himself. Peter's trial was nothing but the word of a weak young woman, who said, "Thou also wast with Jesus of Nazareth".

Here is another aggravation of Peter's terrible sin: All of this was done very close to the place where his Lord and Master was at that very time suffering for him! The Lord Jesus was standing right before Peter's eyes, hearing every word!

Some Reasons

How can we account for all of this? How did such a great man come to commit such grievous evil? I remind you, Peter was not a lost man, but a child of God, redeemed by blood, justified in Christ, saved by grace, and sanctified by the Spirit. Peter was a faithful giant among faithful giants. Few before him, and few after him could stand shoulder to shoulder with him. He was a man strong in faith, firm in conviction, bold in preaching, and unrelenting in his zeal for Christ.

This man was eminent, even among the Apostles, a leader among leaders, an example among examples. How did this man, great, unique in so many ways come to commit such an offence? Because, this man, great as he was, was just a man. Like you and me, he was a man whose heart by nature is full of sin, whose flesh is weak. Peter was too proud, too confident of his own strength. He was overcome by the fear of man; or in this case, the fear of a woman, who had no obvious power against him. He neglected to watch his heart and soul (Proverbs 4:23). And, I suspect, like Eve, Peter had begun to doubt the Saviour's word.

Peter's Preservation

Peter fell; but he did not perish. His faith weakened; but it did not die. He sinned; but he was not cast off nor forsaken. He denied the Lord; but the Lord did not deny him. Peter belonged to Christ; and Christ can never lose one of his own. The Good Shepherd keeps his sheep. Peter fell; but Christ graciously raised him up.

It is written in the scriptures, "The righteous falleth seven times a day; but the LORD raiseth him up". Peter belonged to Christ. He was one of those sheep to whom the Son of God gave eternal life and promised, "They shall never perish". Therefore, Peter was graciously preserved and restored by the hand of God. How did the Lord God restore his fallen child? Here are four means by which God restored Peter. They are the same means he uses to restore his fallen ones today.

First, the Saviour performed a special work of providence to preserve his fallen. "And immediately the cock crew" (v. 74). The Lord God has many ways to reach the hearts of his chosen. There are many roosters he can cause to crow to awaken his erring children. Psalm 107 describes some of them.

Second, there was a work of grace. Providence is made effectual only by the Lord's work of grace in and upon the heart. "The Lord turned and looked upon Peter" (Luke 22:61). What a look that must have been! The Lord turned to Peter. Peter did not turn to the Lord. The Lord turned and looked upon Peter, not in anger, disgust, and wrath, but in mercy, love, and grace! That look reflected all the tenderness, compassion, and faithfulness of Christ toward his fallen, sinful children. With that look, the Lord Jesus spoke silently, but effectually, to Peter's heart. He seems to have said, "Peter, I have loved you with an everlasting love. Ye have not chosen me, but I have chosen you. I have given to you eternal life; and you shall never perish. I will never leave thee, nor forsake thee. Fear not, for I have redeemed thee. I, even I am he that blotteth out thy transgressions. In me is thy righteousness found. I am thy strength. Return, return unto me and I will pardon. Greater love hath no man than this, that a man lay down his life for his friends. I am the LORD, I change not; therefore ye sons of Jacob are not consumed. Blessed is the man to whom the Lord will not impute sin."

Third, the Word of the Lord performed its work in Peter. "And Peter remembered the word of Jesus" (v. 75). If we do not remember the Word that has been preached unto us, all is lost (1 Corinthians 15:1, 2). We cannot escape the wrath of God if we let the gospel slip through our ears without effect (Hebrews 2:1-3). Yet, we are sure to do so, unless God the Holy Spirit be our Remembrancer. It was the Word of God, graciously and effectually brought home to Peter's heart, that worked repentance in him.

We must never presume that the Word of God has no effect because it has no immediate effect upon the hearts of those who hear it (Isaiah 55:11; Ecclesiastes 11:1). Peter was not immediately restored by the Word he had heard, even when he was made to remember it. But he was restored. The Word of God never returns to him void.

Fourth, Luke tells us of the Saviour's work as Peter's Advocate and Intercessor. "I have prayed for thee, that thy faith fail not" (Luke 22:32). As a great High Priest and Intercessor, the Lord Jesus Christ prayed for Peter's preservation in faith and restoration by grace, even before he fell! That same great High Priest is our Advocate on high. He intercedes for us now, and has interceded for us from eternity (1 John 2:1, 2).

Peter's Restoration

The Lord's work for Peter and upon Peter was effectual. It accomplished its design. Peter's heart was restored. Satan had run him through his sieve, but Peter lost nothing in the process but chaff. Thus Satan himself was used as an instrument of good for Peter.

Peter's trial and his fall were not accidents. Satan ran God's child through his rough sifter; but Peter lost nothing. He came out of this thing a much better man than he was before, as is clearly displayed in Acts chapters 2 and 4. Even this tragic affair was under the control of God's sovereign providence and according to his purpose of grace. The devil is God's devil. That fiend of hell is the unwilling, unwitting vassal of the Almighty (Isaiah 14:12-27). The dragon of hell is as much included in all things working together for good to God's elect as the angels of light (Romans 8:28). Nothing can ever separate us from our Saviour's mercy, love, grace and favour. Nothing can ever tear us from his hands or his heart, not even our own corruptions (John 13:36-14:1).

"Peter went out". Once the fire was restored in his soul, he no longer wanted or needed the brazier, which the Lord's enemies had kindled. He immediately forsook those who had turned his heart from his Lord.

As he went out of the place, Peter "wept bitterly". Sin is no light thing to the regenerate soul. Convulsive weeping came upon Peter when he realized what he had done. He could not stand himself. His heart was crushed within him (Psalm 51:17; 1 John 1:9). Then, at the time appointed, the Lord Jesus came to Peter, just as he said he would, made himself known to Peter, and made Peter to know himself (Mark 16:7; John 21:15-19; 1 John 4:19). If you are a believer, if truly you trust Christ alone as your Lord and Saviour, nothing shall ever separate you from him, not even your sins (Romans 4:8).

These thoughts thrill my heart and flood my soul with joy, gratitude, and praise. The Lord Jesus Christ is full of tenderness and mercy. His compassions fail not. They are new every morning! Jesus Christ is a faithful Saviour! If you are a true believer, you may be assured of this fact: Your sins will never separate you from your Saviour! You never shall, for any reason or by any means, be separated from his love, banished from his presence, put outside his favour, lose his mercy, cease to be the object of his care, or fail to be kept by his saving power!

Needed Lessons

Obviously, there are some lessons in this sad piece of history that we need to learn, lessons we ought to ask God the Holy Spirit to graciously apply to our hearts. Remembering Peter's fall, let us learn something about ourselves. We are all too much like Peter. We are fickle, sinful wretches by nature. There is no evil in the world of which you and I are not capable. Let us not be presumptuous, proud, and self-confident; but watch and pray (1 Corinthians 4:7; 10:12). Knowing that we are such sinful creatures ourselves, we should never be severe with our erring, fallen brethren.

Here we are again reminded that, "Salvation is of the LORD". From start to finish, salvation is by the grace of God alone. Our only standing, our only acceptance, our only righteousness is Jesus Christ, our Redeemer. God's grace is free and immutable. It is effectual and indestructible. Bless his name, God's grace is sufficient! What blessed security our souls have in Christ! Nothing can ever severe us from our Saviour. "Once in Christ, in Christ forever"! All who are saved by grace are kept infallibly secure in Christ. All who are in Christ are as secure as the very throne of God (John 10:27-30).

We are secure because God our Saviour is faithful (2 Timothy 2:13). His grace is sure (Mark 16:7). The Lord Jesus Christ will not leave his own; and he will not let his own leave him (Jeremiah 32:37-40). "He abideth faithful"! Even in the teeth of our most horrible sins against him, the Son of God urges us to confidently trust him. It was in anticipation of this very fall that the Lord Jesus said to Peter, "Let not your heart be troubled: Ye believe in God, believe also in me" (John 13:36-14:1).

"Keep yourselves in the love of God, looking for the mercy of our Lord Jesus Christ unto eternal life." Cling to Christ always. As often as you fall, return quickly to your Saviour. He will receive you. He has forgiven you. He will be gracious to you. He will forget your fall.

Chapter 85

Remember Judas

"When the morning was come, all the chief priests and elders of the people took counsel against Jesus to put him to death: And when they had bound him, they led him away, and delivered him to Pontius Pilate the governor. Then Judas, which had betrayed him, when he saw that he was condemned, repented himself, and brought again the thirty pieces of silver to the chief priests and elders, Saying, I have sinned in that I have betrayed the innocent blood. And they said, What is that to us? see thou to that. And he cast down the pieces of silver in the temple, and departed, and went and hanged himself. And the chief priests took the silver pieces, and said, It is not lawful for to put them into the treasury, because it is the price of blood. And they took counsel, and bought with them the potter's field, to bury strangers in. Wherefore that field was called, The field of blood, unto this day. Then was fulfilled that which was spoken by Jeremy the prophet, saying, And they took the thirty pieces of silver, the price of him that was valued, whom they of the children of Israel did value; And gave them for the potter's field, as the Lord appointed me."
(Matthew 27:1-10)

As we read the Bible, we cannot help noticing that there are numerous examples of men and women who appeared to fear God and walk with him, who in time forsook him altogether and perished under his wrath. There are multitudes in hell today who were once considered saints of God. Lot's wife, Korah, Dathan, Abiram, Achan, King Saul, Ananias and Sapphira, Demas, and Diotrephes are all names that ought to be alarming. Like the multitude in John 6, though they professed to be disciples and were considered by all, except the Lord himself, to be his disciples, they "went back and walked no more with him". They are beacons placed before us in scripture to warn us of the danger of hypocrisy and carnal security. All is not gold that glitters. "They are not all Israel which are of Israel". Many who profess faith in Christ and are confident their faith is genuine shall betray and forsake Christ in time and perish under the wrath of God in hell.

No one more fearfully and glaringly demonstrates this fact than Judas, the son of perdition, our Lord's betrayer. He is the principle subject of this paragraph.

Judas was once numbered with the apostles of Christ. He once preached the gospel, performed mighty miracles, and carried the treasurer's bag for the first church ever to exist in this world. Yet, Judas betrayed the Son of God. Afterward, though he repented, confessed his sin, and made restitution, he committed suicide, perishing under the terror of God's justice and wrath. Today that man, who once was thought to be such a great man, such an eminent believer, burns in hell, suffering the wrath of God! Let no one who read these lines follow him.

God's Word

First, the Bible is the inspired, inerrant Word of God. I stress this again because we must never entertain the idea there may be some error in the Book of God, or that it is not to be depended upon implicitly. The Bible alone is inspired. It alone is God's Word. The Bible alone is authoritative. The Bible alone is our rule of faith and practice, able to make us wise unto salvation through faith which is in Christ Jesus (2 Timothy 3:16, 17; 2 Peter 1:21; Revelation 22:18, 19). Yet, there are many who, daring to defy God, love to point out supposed discrepancies in the scriptures. Learned infidels are only educated fools; their folly is evident when they attempt to discredit the Word of God. Many have suggested that Matthew 27:9 is an example of a mistake found in the Bible.

If you read your Bible carefully, you know the quotation attributed to Jeremiah in verse nine cannot be found in the Book of Jeremiah. It is found in Zechariah's prophecy (Zechariah 11:12). Did Matthew make a mistake? If so, the veracity and inspiration of the Bible falls to the ground. Find a single error in holy scripture and our faith is destroyed. Prove the Bible is not verbally inspired, and Christianity is proved to be a lie! But Matthew did not make a mistake. He wrote what the Holy Spirit inspired him to write. Jeremiah's prophecy is not all Jeremiah ever spoke or even all that he wrote. Zechariah quoted Jeremiah's words as they were handed down to him. How do we know? We know because the Holy Spirit here tells us he did. There are, of course, other examples of this in the scriptures (Acts 20:35; Jude 14). God has placed stones of stumbling in the Book of Inspiration over which blind and ignorant men stumble into hell.

The chief priests and elders bound Christ and delivered him into the hands of the Gentiles (vv. 1, 2) because the scriptures must be fulfilled. Our Lord had prophesied that he must be delivered by the Jews into the hands of the Gentiles. Therefore, the Jews did what they did because the scriptures must be fulfilled (Acts 4:27, 28; 13:27-29). Those wicked men did exactly what they wanted to do (Acts 2:23). Their crimes cannot be excused. The chief priests and elders, headed by Annas and Caiaphas, were so intent upon murdering the Lord Jesus that they sat up all night in council in pursuit of their wicked scheme (Luke 22:66). But they could do nothing, except that which God had purposed from eternity (John 19:10, 11). Let us ever remember that it is the hand of our God that controls all things, even the evil that men do, and that he does so exactly according to his eternal purpose of grace (Psalm 76:10; Romans 8:28-30; 11:33; Ephesians 1:11).

As Isaac was bound to the altar of sacrifice, so the Lord Jesus Christ, of whom Isaac was a type, was bound for us as the Lamb of God to the altar of sacrifice. He was already bound with cords of love to his elect, bound by his will to redeem us. Otherwise, he would have broken these bonds more easily than Samson broke the bonds of the Philistines. Matthew Henry wrote, "We were fettered with the bond of iniquity, held in the cords of our sins (Proverbs 5:22); but God bound the yoke of our transgressions upon the neck of the Lord Jesus (Lamentations 1:14), that we might be loosed by his bonds, as we are healed by his stripes."

It was prophesied from Israel's earliest days that Shiloh would not come, that the Messiah and Redeemer promised in the Old Testament would not come, until the sceptre of civil government had departed from Judah (Genesis 49:10). This prophecy was manifestly fulfilled by this act. These enraged Jews would never have turned the Lord Jesus Christ over to Pilate to be crucified had it not been for the fact that they were now no longer a nation with civil authority. Two years before this event the Romans had stripped them of their last remnant of national power. They had no legal power to put a man to death. If Christ were to be legally murdered by them, the Romans would have to do it. Thus, God almighty arranged for the fulfilment of his Word to the letter.

God's Work

Second, we have before us a vivid illustration of the fact that "all things are of God" (2 Corinthians 5:18). The finger of God was in this matter. The hand of God ruled the whole affair. Nothing was left to chance, fate, accident, or the will of man. The Jews were not in charge. Pilate was not in charge. The Gentiles were not in charge. God almighty was in charge. The betrayal by Judas, the scheming of the Jews, the deliverance of Jesus to the Romans, the spinelessness of Pilate, and the barbarianism of the soldiers and the people, were all under the total rule of our God. These men, doing only what their wicked hearts and wills desired, did nothing but what God almighty ordained and arranged for the redemption of his people and the glory of his own great name. "Surely the wrath of man shall praise thee: the remainder of wrath shalt thou restrain" (Psalm 76:10).

Our Holy Saviour

Third, Judas himself gives us a glaring proof that the Lord Jesus Christ was totally innocent of the trumped up charges laid against him. I cannot imagine any evidence more compelling to honest men of our Redeemer's complete innocence than the fact that when the Jews were trying to hire false witnesses to testify against him, Judas was silent. If anyone could have given evidence against the Master, Judas was the man. He was one of the Lord's chosen apostles, a constant companion for more than three years. Judas heard everything Christ taught in public and in private. If our Lord had done anything amiss, in word or deed, Judas would have known. And it would have been in his own interest to tell it. If he could produce one incident of evil, his betrayal would have been justified.

Why did he not do it? Why was he silent? Why did neither the Jews nor Pilate call him to their courts and question him? There can be only one reason: Judas did not bear witness against Christ because he knew nothing against him. Wicked, base, and vile as he was, the apostate apostle knew that Jesus Christ was an innocent man; holy, harmless, undefiled, and separate from sinners (Hebrews 7:22-27). This is a matter of huge importance. The Holy Spirit takes great care to prove that Jesus is the Lamb of God who takes away the sins of his people.

The Betrayer

Fourth, Judas shows us that a person may experience, know and do much that appears to be spiritual and yet perish at last. Salvation is an experience; but it is more than an experience. It involves knowledge; but it is more than knowledge. Salvation produces good works; but it is much more than good works. In those matters, neither you nor I come close to Judas. Until he betrayed the Master, he was never once, insofar as the scriptures reveal, reprimanded for anything. Even after he had been identified as the betrayer by the Master (John 13:26-30), no one was suspicious of him. Yet, Judas never knew God.

Salvation is "Christ in you" (Colossians 1:27). Salvation is a living union of faith with the Son of God. Salvation is a heart work, a work of God in our hearts. Salvation is not something you can muster. It is not something the preacher can bestow. It is not something parents can bequeath. "Salvation is of the LORD"! Salvation is the complete surrender of a sinner to the rule, dominion, and will of God by faith in Christ. When a person comes to know Christ, the last Adam, he does willingly what the first Adam refused to do. He bows to God as God, acknowledging his right to be God and thus to do what he will (Luke 14:25-33).

False Repentance

Next, Judas shows us that there is a repentance that needs to be repented of. Judas' repentance in verses 3-5 was not the repentance of faith, but the remorse of a horrified man, conscious of the fact that he had committed a damning deed, and terrified by the wrath of God. Judas was horrified "when he saw that he was condemned". It appears that he thought he could never have done such a thing. He may have thought the Lord Jesus would, by some miracle, escape from the Romans, as he often had from the Jews. It may be Judas never dreamt that the Son of God would be crucified as a result of his betrayal. But "when he saw that he was condemned", in utter terror, he tried to undo the mischief of his crime. We are plainly told that Judas "repented himself". He confessed, "I have betrayed innocent blood". He even made restitution of the money he had taken. But Judas' repentance was a fearful example of that repentance which needs to be repented of! "For godly sorrow worketh repentance to salvation not to be repented of: but the sorrow of the world worketh death" (2 Corinthians 7:10).

This matter deserves special attention. Multitudes have a form of repentance that, like Judas', will bring them at last to hell. Solomon warns us that many shall call upon God, but he will not answer; they shall seek him early, but they shall not find him (Proverbs 1:28). Judas did not repent because he had seen the glory of God in Christ, but because he was terrified at the prospect of God's wrath. He wanted salvation, but not the Saviour. He wanted mercy, but not the Master. He wanted grace, but did not care for the glory of God. Jesus Christ will not be a fire escape. There is a difference between being afraid of God and fearing God. There is a difference between awareness of guilt and conviction of the Holy Spirit. Repentance is the gift of God's goodness, not the fear of his wrath (Romans 2:4).

Judas warns us that the things of this world give no comfort to an immortal soul. "The treasures of the wicked profit nothing" (Proverbs 10:2). The money Judas wanted so desperately, and earned so wickedly brought him nothing but bitterness and sorrow. "What shall it profit a man if he should gain the whole world and lose his own soul?" Judas teaches us that no sinner is so great a sinner as that sinner who sins against light, and knowledge, and privilege. He went out and hanged himself. What a sad, sad tale the life of Judas is! Here is an apostle of Christ hanged by his own hands. He came to the very Door of heaven, handled the Door, showed others the Door; but he went to hell! Be wise and remember Judas! "He, that being often reproved hardeneth his neck, shall suddenly be destroyed, and that without remedy" (Proverbs 29:1).

Chapter 86

Our Saviour's Mock Trial

"And Jesus stood before the governor: and the governor asked him, saying, Art thou the King of the Jews? And Jesus said unto him, Thou sayest. And when he was accused of the chief priests and elders, he answered nothing. Then said Pilate unto him, Hearest thou not how many things they witness against thee? And he answered him to never a word; insomuch that the governor marvelled greatly. Now at that feast the governor was wont to release unto the people a prisoner, whom they would. And they had then a notable prisoner, called Barabbas. Therefore when they were gathered together, Pilate said unto them, Whom will ye that I release unto you? Barabbas, or Jesus which is called Christ? For he knew that for envy they had delivered him. When he was set down on the judgment seat, his wife sent unto him, saying, Have thou nothing to do with that just man: for I have suffered many things this day in a dream because of him. But the chief priests and elders persuaded the multitude that they should ask Barabbas, and destroy Jesus. The governor answered and said unto them, Whether of the twain will ye that I release unto you? They said, Barabbas. Pilate saith unto them, What shall I do then with Jesus which is called Christ? They all say unto him, Let him be crucified. And the governor said, Why, what evil hath he done? But they cried out the more, saying, Let him be crucified. When Pilate saw that he could prevail nothing, but that rather a tumult was made, he took water, and washed his hands before the multitude, saying, I am innocent of the blood of this just person: see ye to it. Then answered all the people, and said, His blood be on us, and on our children. Then released he Barabbas unto them: and when he had scourged Jesus, he delivered him to be crucified."
(Matthew 27:11-26)

Here the Judge of all the earth stood before wicked men to be judged by them! He that shall soon judge the world in righteousness was judged most unrighteously. He that shall one day sit upon the throne of judgment, with ten thousands of his saints and angels, stood as a prisoner before the bar of reprobate men. Never in the pages of history was justice so violently and deliberately abused. The Son of

God was denied the rights of justice given to a common thief or murderer. Before one witness was produced to testify against him, before any evidence was weighed, the Lord of glory was beaten, mocked, stripped, and abused by vile, God-hating men. Who can comprehend the depths of humiliation endured by the God-man? That one "Who, being in the form of God thought it not robbery to be equal with God", now "made himself of no reputation, and took upon him the form of a servant, and was made in the likeness of men: and being found in fashion as a man, he humbled himself, and became obedient unto death, even the death of the cross".

Judas made good on his bargain to betray our Lord. No sooner did he kiss the Saviour than the high priests had his hands bound and led him away. These wolves of the night were thirsty, longing to be sucking the blood of the Lamb of God. Their revenge and malice would not allow any delay. They could not sleep until they had his precious, innocent blood. Therefore, they resolved to kill him as soon as possible. But, so that it would not look like downright murder, they formalized it with a mock trial.

The Background

Our Redeemer was arrested in the Garden of Gethsemane, and hurried along the road which crosses the brook of Kidron, like David before him, who passed over that brook, weeping as he went. The brook Kidron was a sewer into which all the filth of the temple sacrifices was thrown. Our blessed Saviour was led to that black stream, as though he were some foul and filthy thing. He was led into Jerusalem by the sheep-gate, the gate through which the passover lambs were led.

Little did those men understand that they were fulfilling to the very letter those types which God had ordained by the law of Moses. These wicked men led the Lamb of God to slaughter. May the Lord himself sanctify our hearts as we follow our Redeemer through his trial and cruel mockery. First, they led Immanuel to the house of Annas, the ex-high priest, to gratify that bloodthirsty wretch with the sight of his victim. Then, they hurriedly brought the Son of God to the house of Caiaphas, where the members of the Sanhedrin were assembled, to take counsel against the Lord and against his Anointed. Next, they took the Lamb of God through the streets to Pilate's judgment hall. There they sought a legal sentence of execution to be pronounced upon God's Holy One. Pilate sent the bloodthirsty mob to Herod, the governor of Galilee. Finally, the Lord of Glory was returned to Pilate's judgment hall, where he was tried, beaten, mocked, and sentenced to die. This is where we find him in the passage before us. Though nothing worthy of bonds or of death could be found in him, our Lord Jesus Christ was condemned to be nailed to a cross and there to hang until he died.

Innocence Proved

It was the intention of these wicked men to make it appear that Jesus Christ was a sinful man, worthy of death. But, by their deeds, God proved his complete innocence, and showed beyond every shadow of doubt that our Lord Jesus Christ is "holy, harmless, undefiled, and separate from sinners".

Remember, our Lord was about to be offered up as the Lamb of God, a sacrifice for sin. The sacrificial lamb must be examined to be sure that it had no blemish. So it was necessary that the Lamb of God be found by those who crucified him to be "a Lamb without blemish and without spot". The over-ruling hand of God so ordered the events of his trial that even when his enemies were his judges, they could find no fault and prove nothing against him.

The Son of God was examined on three separate occasions. They took him from one judge to another, from one court to another, seeking some grounds for putting him to death. He was first examined by an ecclesiastical court in the house of Caiaphas the high-priest.

The court here was the Jewish Sanhedrin. They were the most honoured and respected men of the nation. They were supposed to be a court of seventy honourable, sober, learned, and faithful men (Numbers 11:16, 17). But it was now reduced to a pack of malicious scribes and Pharisees. Over this mob of bloodthirsty, self-righteous men, Caiaphas was the head. It was Caiaphas who led the examination. They questioned the Saviour about his doctrine and his assertions that he is both the Messiah and God the Son. And they sought false witnesses against him. When he gave answer, they began to mock him, spit on him, and beat him (Mark 14:61-65).

It was here, at this point concerning the divinity of the Lord Jesus, that these religious leaders rebelled. The Jews would gladly have received Christ as a saviour to deliver them from Roman bondage; but they would not worship him as God and bow to him as Lord. That is still the point of man's rebellion (Luke 14:25-33). There are multitudes who pretend to honour our Saviour as a good, moral man and a good religious teacher, while denying his eternal deity as God the Son. But, surely, if he were not the Son of God, if the Jews had misunderstood his claims, this trial was his opportunity to explain himself and put things right. Surely, if this was all a mistake, he would have said so here!

Caiaphas

Caiaphas was a self-serving religious leader, the high priest in Israel, who curried favour with the Romans. It was Caiaphas who gave counsel that it was expedient for one man to die for the nation, lest the Romans destroy the whole nation. He considered the sacrifice of a man's life a matter of insignificance, if by the sacrifice the Romans were pacified.

We know, of course, that it was God the Holy Spirit who compelled him to speak prophetically (John 11:47-52). Yet, his words display clearly the devious, political character of the man himself. At the same time, they show us the moment had come that was prophesied in Genesis 49:10. The sceptre of civil government had departed from Judah, because Shiloh, the Messiah, had come.

The Sanhedrin was now nothing but an insignificant band of Jewish religious leaders, who had no legitimate authority or power to judge anything. Herod took all authority from them in the beginning of his reign. So they were compelled to seek a death sentence against the Lord Jesus at Pilate's judgment hall. This fact they stated plainly in John 18:31, saying to Pilate, "It is not lawful for us to put any man to death".

Pilate

In a pretence of righteousness, the Jews refused to enter Pilate's house, lest they should defile themselves on the passover. So Pilate came out onto the pavement where they stood, to examine the Lamb of God (John 18:28, 29). The Jews brought three charges against our Redeemer: 1. They accused him of refusing to pay tribute to Caesar. 2. They accused him of stirring up sedition. 3. They accused him of blasphemy. But they could produce no proof of their charges.

Then Pilate personally examined the Saviour. He asked him about his claims as King of the Jews. He asked the Saviour, "What is truth?" (John 18:38). Perhaps he said this sarcastically, but the Truth was standing before him; and he knew it. Pilate then sent the Lord Jesus to Herod. Here again, our Lord was examined; but nothing was found against him. Herod and his soldiers mocked and beat God's eternal Son, and sent him back to Pilate.

Matthew describes the scene of our Saviour's mock trial before Pilate. Pilate had the immaculate Lamb of God severely beaten, humiliated, mocked, and scourged. He hoped by this means to satisfy the anger of the mob; but it would not do. Finally, the verdict was passed. Immanuel was found innocent of all charges. But these men cared nothing for that. Pilate then presented the Lord Jesus to the crowd proclaiming, "Behold Your King" (John 19:14).

Do you get the picture? There is the bleeding Lamb of God. A crown of thorns is upon his head. A reed is in his hand. A mock robe is on his back. And Pilate says, "Behold your King"! He is, indeed, the King. But these wicked men despised God's anointed King. They clamoured for his blood, crying, "Crucify him! Crucify him!" And they assumed full responsibility for the shedding of Immanuel's blood, saying, "His blood be upon us and upon our children."

It appears that Pilate's conscience was alarmed by the things that transpired before him. His wife was alarmed as well. She had a fearful dream concerning the matter. So Pilate tried to reason with the chief priests and elders, hoping to spare himself from murdering the Christ of God. But the Jews would not be pacified. At last, Pilate consented to the will of the Jews. Obviously horrified and unable to conceal the wickedness of ordering the crucifixion of a completely innocent man, he publicly washed his hands, as if to show that he bore no responsibility for what he was about to do. Then, probably as he was drying his hypocritical hands, he pronounced the sentence of death against the Saviour and proclaimed his innocence! What a mockery!

Sweet Consolation

Yet, this proof of our Lord's innocence ought to be a sweet consolation and comfort for our hearts. We should be deeply thankful that our great Substitute was in all respects proved to be perfect and innocent, that our Surety was pronounced faultless by the very man who ordered his crucifixion.

Who among us can number his sins? We leave undone the things we ought to do and do the things we ought not to do every day of our lives. But here is our comfort. "Jesus Christ the righteous" stood in our place to pay the debt we owed and fulfil the law we have broken. He fulfilled the law completely. He satisfied all its demands. He accomplished all its requirements. He was the last Adam, who had "clean hands and a pure heart", and could enter with boldness into God's holy hill. He is our Righteousness. In him God's elect have perfectly fulfilled all the law. The eyes of a holy God beholds us in Christ, clothed with Christ's perfect righteousness, and made the righteousness of God in him. For Christ's sake, God can now say of the believing sinner, "I find no fault in him at all".

Truly, the Son of God, our Substitute, "knew no sin". And God compelled those who crucified him to confess his perfect innocence. The Lamb of God was examined publicly and privately, and he was without blemish and without spot. It must be so, because he who undertakes to be a Substitute for sinners must be sinless.

Mercy And Judgment

I cannot avoid directing your attention to the great mercy of our great God and Saviour toward the men who shed his blood. When Pilate said, "I am innocent of the blood of this just person, see ye to it: Then answered all the people and said: His blood be upon us and on our children." The Jews defiantly pronounced God's judgment upon themselves. Yet, our Saviour sent great mercy to many of those very men. In Acts 2, when the enthroned Christ poured out his Spirit on the day of Pentecost, Peter declared that the men of Israel had with wicked hands crucified and slain Jesus of Nazareth, whom God had made both Lord and Christ. When they heard Peter's message, they were pricked in the heart, and cried, "Men and brethren what shall we do?" Upon many of those present, the Lord God performed his great work of grace. And the precious blood of Christ graciously put upon them, sprinkled their hearts to the purging of their consciences by the Spirit of God.

The very first word spoken by the Lord Jesus Christ from the cross was for them. He prayed, "Father! forgive them, for they know not what they do." In Acts chapter 2 God the Father and God the Holy Spirit graciously answered his prayer on their behalf. There is always a perfect and gracious correspondence between the intercession of Christ and the gifts of God the Holy Spirit. Robert Hawker wrote, "Even the Jerusalem sinners, who imbrued their hands in the blood of Christ are made partakers in the blessedness of salvation in his blood." That fact should be a great encouragement to sinners everywhere to come to him who has promised, "Him that cometh unto me I will in no wise cast out" (John 6:37-45).

Yet, upon others the Lord God poured out his furious wrath. The Jewish nation is to this day a nation reeling under the judgment of God. The guilt of Immanuel's blood is still upon the children of those who crucified him! As it is written, God has "mercy on whom he will have mercy, and whom he will he hardeneth". Salvation is his sovereign prerogative (Romans 9:11-24).

Depravity Displayed

The innocence of Christ had no bearing with the angry mob. They wanted his blood, so the death sentence was passed upon him, proclaiming the guilt and depravity of man. "And Pilate gave sentence that it should be as they required." As Luke tells us, Pilate "delivered Jesus to their will" (Luke 23:25). The crowd cried, "Crucify him! Crucify him"! Pilate, willing to please the crowd, sentenced our Redeemer to die upon the cursed tree.

I am certain Pilate knew what he was doing. There, standing before him, was the embodiment of meekness, innocence, love, and purity. Pilate tried in vain to wash his hands of the innocent blood. I expect that those bloodstained hands still torment his conscience in hell. But he gave the sentence, nevertheless. Jesus of Nazareth must be nailed to a cross and hung up to die. This was the most unjust and unrighteous sentence ever passed. It was an indescribably cruel sentence. The Lamb of God was sentenced to die a violent, cruel, tormenting death. It was as merciless as it was unjust.

Never was there such a glaring display of the guilt and depravity of the human heart! The Pharisees and the Roman soldiers, Jews and Gentiles, Pilate and Herod were all complicit in this matter; they hated the Son of God, and determined to murder him. We all had a hand in the crucifixion of Christ. Those men are true representations of humanity. Every rebel sinner, by his wilful unbelief, continues to cry, "Crucify him! Crucify him! Let his blood be upon me and upon my children." Unbelief is but man's continuing repetition of this hellish crime! Unbelief declares that Christ our God is a liar (1 John 5:10), the assertion that he deserved to be crucified, trampling under foot the blood of the Son of God! Unbelief is the relentless cry of man's wicked free-will, "Crucify him! Crucify him! We will not have this man to rule over us"!

God's Purpose

Still, we must never forget that, though they knew it not, these men were under the dominion and control of that One whom they sentenced to die. They fulfilled the very words of holy scripture, doing no more and no less than was ordained by him whom they executed (Acts 4:26-28; 13:27-29). By their wicked hands, with all the malice of their wicked will, they did exactly what our Lord had declared they would do (Daniel 9:26; Isaiah 53:1-12). Our Lord's tormenters used the very words and performed the very deeds he had predicted by his prophets. A casual reading of Psalm 22 alone will demonstrate this fact. Those very words used by wicked men in the betrayal, shame, mockery, deceit, and cruelty heaped upon the Lord Jesus were the fulfilment of the Old Testament scriptures (see also Psalms 22, 40 and 69). The Son of God did not die as a helpless victim of circumstances. He did not die because the Jews would not let him be their king! He died by his own, voluntary will, accomplishing the eternal purpose of the triune God, as the Surety and Substitute for his people.

Substitution Portrayed

By the arrangement of divine providence, a substitution was made, portraying the nature of Christ's atonement. Pilate "released unto them Barabbas". He condemned the innocent and released the guilty. That is a picture of real substitution. It wonderfully portrays the nature of our Lord's sacrifice. The innocent One died in the place of the guilty and the guilty one went free.

Barabbas was a justly condemned man. He was guilty. He was sentenced to die. But the Lord Jesus Christ took his place on the cursed tree. He took Barabbas' shame and torment. He died in Barabbas' place. He died in Barabbas' stead. And Barabbas went free.

That is exactly what the Son of God did for us. "For he hath made him to be sin for us, who knew no sin; that we might be made the righteousness of God in him" (2 Corinthians 5:21). "Christ hath redeemed us from the curse of the law, being made a curse for us: for it is written, Cursed is every one that hangeth on a tree" (Galatians 3:13). We were guilty. Christ took our place. He died in our stead under the furious wrath of God. Now we go free!

Who can imagine the depths of our Saviour's humiliation? What infinite love is the love of Christ for us! O the blessedness of substitutionary redemption! Because the Son of God was arraigned and condemned before Pilate's bar, and before the bar of divine justice, no believer shall ever be arraigned, or condemned, or even charged with sin before the bar of God! As Augustus Toplady wrote:

> If Thou hast my discharge procured,
> And freely in my room endured
> The whole of wrath divine,
> Payment God cannot twice demand,
> First at my bleeding Surety's hand,
> And then again at mine.

Chapter 87

Barabbas: A Picture Of Substitution

"Now at that feast the governor was wont to release unto the people a prisoner, whom they would. And they had then a notable prisoner, called Barabbas. Therefore when they were gathered together, Pilate said unto them, Whom will ye that I release unto you? Barabbas, or Jesus which is called Christ? For he knew that for envy they had delivered him. When he was set down on the judgment seat, his wife sent unto him, saying, Have thou nothing to do with that just man: for I have suffered many things this day in a dream because of him. But the chief priests and elders persuaded the multitude that they should ask Barabbas, and destroy Jesus. The governor answered and said unto them, Whether of the twain will ye that I release unto you? They said, Barabbas. Pilate saith unto them, What shall I do then with Jesus which is called Christ? They all say unto him, Let him be crucified. And the governor said, Why, what evil hath he done? But they cried out the more, saying, Let him be crucified. When Pilate saw that he could prevail nothing, but that rather a tumult was made, he took water, and washed his hands before the multitude, saying, I am innocent of the blood of this just person: see ye to it. Then answered all the people, and said, His blood be on us, and on our children. Then released he Barabbas unto them: and when he had scourged Jesus, he delivered him to be crucified."
(Matthew 27:15-26)

There is nothing revealed in holy scripture that is more important than the gospel doctrine of Substitution, so we shall look again carefully at this teaching. Men everywhere talk about substitutionary atonement, and speak much about Christ being the sinner's Substitute. But their language is vague. Few seem to understand what the Bible teaches about substitution. In this study we will take a close look at the story of Barabbas. Here we have a clear illustration of the nature of Christ's death. Our blessed Saviour died as a substitutionary sacrifice to make atonement for the sins of his people, to redeem us from the curse of the law. Because Christ died in the place of God's elect, all God's elect must go free.

The story of Barabbas is recorded by all four gospel writers. During the days of Israel's subjection to Rome, a strange custom was regularly practised. On the day of the Passover, the Roman governor released a guilty prisoner. No doubt, this was intended to be an act of benevolence on the part of the Roman authorities toward the Jews. The Jews probably accepted it as a significant compliment to their Passover celebrations. Since on that day the Jews were themselves delivered out of the land of Egypt, they may have thought it a most fitting thing for a prisoner to obtain his freedom. Since some prisoner must be released at Passover (John 13:1), Pilate thought that he now had opportunity to allow the Saviour to go free, without compromising himself in the eyes of his superiors at Rome. So he asked the people which of the two they preferred, a notorious criminal or the holy Saviour. Without hesitation or dissension, the crowd cried for the release of Barabbas and the death of Christ. Pilate's last effort to release Christ had failed. "Then released he Barabbas unto them: and when he had scourged Jesus, he delivered him to be crucified".

The Man Barabbas

Who Barabbas was we do not know. His name signifies, "His father's son". Some mystics think that there is an indication here that he was particularly and specially the son of Satan. Others suppose that it was an endearing name, a name given to him because he was his father's darling, a child indulged by his father, or as we would say, his daddy's boy.

It is certain that overly indulged, spoiled children are likely to become griefs to their parents and a burden to society. Look at the cases of Eli's two sons, Absalom, and Barabbas, and be warned. Do not be too excessive in indulging and pampering of your children. John Trapp wrote, "How many a Barabbas, brought to the gallows, blameth his fond father, and haply curseth him in hell"!

Barabbas appears to have committed at least three crimes. He was imprisoned for murder, sedition, and robbery. We might well pity the father of such a son. This wretch is brought out and set in competition with the holy Son of God. And the poor inhabitants of Jerusalem were so hardened in their unbelief and sin, so thirsty for the innocent blood of Christ that they preferred this obnoxious creature to the man who is God's own Fellow!

The Picture

In this act of freeing the guilty and binding the innocent, we have a vivid example of salvation by substitution. The guilty is set free and the innocent is put to death in his place. Barabbas is spared, and Christ is crucified. We have in this striking event a display of the manner in which God pardons and justifies the ungodly. He does it because Christ has suffered and died in their stead, the Just for the unjust. We deserve to die as the punishment for our sins; but a mighty Substitute has suffered our punishment. Eternal death is our due; but a glorious Surety has died for us. We are all in the position of Barabbas by nature. We are guilty, wicked, condemned, and shut up under the law. But, when we were without hope and without strength, "in due time Christ died for the ungodly". Now God, for Christ's sake, can be just and yet "the Justifier of him which believeth in Jesus".

In the Old Testament rite of cleansing lepers two birds were used. One bird was killed and its blood poured into a basin. The other bird was dipped into the blood of the slain bird, and then, with its wings covered with crimson, set free to fly into the open air. The slain bird typified our Saviour, whose blood was shed at Mount Calvary. The released bird typifies every soul that by faith is plunged into the "Fountain filled with blood, drawn from Immanuel's veins". The soul set free, owes its life and liberty to the Saviour, who was once for sinners slain. This is substitution. It comes to this: Barabbas must die, or Christ must die. You the sinner must perish, or Christ, the immaculate Lamb of God, must be slain. The incarnate God died that we might be delivered. The Lord Jesus Christ suffered in the place of sinners like Barabbas, satisfying the wrath and justice of God; and, like Barabbas, all those sinners for whom Christ made satisfaction must go free.

A Guilty Man

Barabbas was a man guilty of many offences. We sometimes say that a man is "as guilty as sin". Barabbas was as guilty as sin. His life was a life of riotousness and sin. He was tried in a court of law and found guilty of robbery, sedition, and murder. As such he is a fair representative of all men by nature. We could all be named "Barabbas". We are all the sons of our father Adam. His image, his nature, and his character are reflected in us all. Like Barabbas, we are rebels. Barabbas stirred up sedition. He was a revolutionary. That is a modern name for a rebel. He would not submit to authority. This is the problem with our race. We are proud, self-willed rebels. We hate authority. In our father Adam we rebelled against God's command. We are born with a rebellious nature. In pride and self-will we rebel all our lives against God's throne. We sinfully rebel against God's holy law. As children, we rebel against parents and teachers. As adults, we rebel against moral and civil authority. Even as believers, we have a nature within us that rebels against everything holy and good (Romans 7:14, 15, 18).

Like Barabbas, we are robbers. It was Adam's determination to rob God of his authority, of his creation, and of his glory. We have robbed God of his glory, refusing to worship him. We have robbed God of his honour, refusing to believe his Word. We have robbed God of his creation, stealing that which God has made for himself and using it for ourselves, without regard to him. We have robbed ourselves and our children of the benefits of our original creation, of fellowship with God, of the image of God, of true freedom, of the favour of God, of life itself. By sin, our race is reduced to emptiness and vanity. Once we were princes of God's creation. Now we are empty handed thieves (Ephesians 2:11, 12).

Like Barabbas, we are murderers. In his rebellion and robbery Barabbas committed murder. So have we all. There is not a guiltless one among us. We have all committed multiple murders in our hearts. Envy, hatred, anger, wrath, and malice are in the eyes of God's law equal to murder (Matthew 5:21, 22). We have infected our children with the disease of sin. Sin is a plague of the heart, passed from generation to generation. What is more, we are all guilty of the blood of the Son of God. Yes, we are guilty of slaughtering the Lord of Glory!

We must never forget what we are by nature (Matthew 15:19). There is not an evil deed, or atrocious crime, or an infamous sin recorded on the pages of human history which does not reside in the heart of every man, woman, and child in the world. We are all named "Barabbas". We are the descendants of Adam. We are of our father the devil. We are all, by nature, children of wrath. Read the book of God's holy law. Read every commandment of the Almighty. By the law we stand judged. The verdict is guilty. Like Barabbas, we are men guilty of many offences.

A Cursed Man

Barabbas was a prisoner, under the sentence of the law. He had been found guilty. The sentence was passed. Barabbas must die. On the day when the Jews observed their Passover, two thieves were to be crucified; and Barabbas would be crucified in the midst of them as the vilest of the three. He was cast into prison, to be held there as a cursed, condemned man until the day of his execution.

Try to picture Barabbas in prison. He expected very soon to be taken out, nailed to a cross, and hung up to die, as the just payment for his crimes. He was held under the sentence of the law. That is the state of everyone in the world by nature. "He that believeth on the Son hath everlasting life: and he that believeth not the Son shall not see life; but the wrath of God abideth on him" (John 3:36). "Now we know that what things soever the law saith, it saith to them who are under the law: that every mouth may be stopped, and all the world may become guilty before God" (Romans 3:19) "For as many as are of the works of the law are under the curse: for it is written, Cursed is every one that continueth not in all things which are written in the book of the law to do them … The scripture hath concluded all under sin, that the promise by faith of Jesus Christ might be given to them that believe. But before faith came, we were kept under the law, shut up unto the faith which should afterwards be revealed" (Galatians 3:10, 22, 23). We all "were by nature the children of wrath, even as others" (Ephesians 2:3).

Man's bondage is as cruel and terrible as it is sure. Men today like to boast of their independence and freedom. We are told, "I'm going to do my own thing". But they are only doing exactly the same thing that men have been doing throughout history. Man is not free. He is in bondage to sin. He is in bondage to religious tradition, social custom, and peer pressure. He is in bondage to his own nature, and the lusts of his own heart. "Can the Ethiopian change his skin, or the leopard his spots? Then may ye also do good, that are accustomed to do evil" (Jeremiah 13:23). Men are taken captive by Satan at his will (2 Timothy 2:26). Man by nature is prone to every kind of evil. It is only the restraining hand of God that keeps you and me from practising the wicked things that we pretend to abhor. All who are without Christ are bound under the chains of darkness. Their will is held in captivity by the fetters of iniquity.

Christ alone can set guilty prisoners free. "If the Son therefore shall make you free, ye shall be free indeed"! We were "such as sit in darkness and in the shadow of death, being bound in affliction and iron". Then we cried unto the Lord in our trouble, and he saved us out of all our distresses. "He brought us out of darkness and the shadow of death, and brake our bands in sunder! (Psalm 107:10-14).

Man's sentence is fixed and immutable. "The soul that sinneth, it shall die"! God has spoken. There is no reprieve. There is no amnesty. There is no repeal. God's law says the guilty must die. God's holiness demands that the sinner must be slain. God's justice requires the death of every transgressor. Man by nature is under the sentence and curse of God's holy law. Fallen man is not on probation. He is on death row. God judges him guilty. His own conscience consents to the verdict. The sentence is passed. The only thing lacking is the appointed day of execution. We died spiritually in our father Adam (Romans 5:12). Physical death is the consequence of sin. And every unbelieving sinner must die eternally, because of God's immutable law. Every sinner out of Christ is dead at law.

Is there, therefore, no hope for a sinner like Barabbas? Must all the guilty forever perish? Will God not have mercy? Is there any way whereby God can be faithful to his holy law and yet pardon sin? Is there any means whereby God can both satisfy his justice and let the sinner live? God will not show mercy at the expense of justice. But he will show mercy if justice is satisfied in a Substitute. Blessed be the name of the Lord, there is hope, for God has found a Substitute!

A Substitute Provided

A substitute was provided to die in Barabbas' place. The One who suffered and died as Barabbas' Substitute is our Substitute. His name is Jesus Christ, the Lord. He is God's own, well-beloved Son. He is the only Substitute God can or will accept (Romans 3:24-26; 2 Corinthians 5:21; 1 Peter 2:24). The sinner's Substitute must be a suitable person, able and willing to redeem. Whoever reconciles a holy God and sinful men must himself be both God and man. He must be God, for only God is able to make infinite satisfaction. Yet, he must be man, for man must be punished. The Lord Jesus Christ is such a One. Being God, he is able to redeem. Being man, he is able to suffer. Being the God-man, he is an all-sufficient Redeemer, able and willing to save. Someone once said, "God could not die, and man could not satisfy; but the God-man has both died and satisfied."

In order to be a Substitute for others, our Redeemer must be perfect and sinless; and our blessed Saviour "knew no sin". Yet, the sinless One, the Lord Jesus Christ, was made sin for us and suffered the just punishment due to our sins as our Substitute. When the holy Lord God made Christ sin for us, sin was imputed to him, and he was slain in our place. God took his Son without the camp. God hung his Son up in our place between two thieves. God forsook his well-beloved Son. God killed his Son as our Substitute. And by a marvellous transfer of grace, all for whom Christ Jesus was made sin are made (caused to become) the very righteousness of God in him.

Barabbas Set Free

Because the Lord Jesus Christ died in his place, Barabbas was set free. The Son of God took Barabbas' place at Calvary. Therefore, Barabbas did not die. There is a glorious truth here. All of those for whom the Son of God died at Calvary must be set free. It is not possible for the law to punish my Substitute and punish me too. Justice will not allow it. Not one soul for whom Jesus Christ died shall be found in hell. "He shall see of the travail of his soul, and shall be satisfied." That is real substitution. Any doctrine that teaches that God will punish Christ and punish those for whom Christ died is not substitution and is not the gospel.

Chapter 88

"Then The Soldiers"

"Then released he Barabbas unto them: and when he had scourged Jesus, he delivered him to be crucified. Then the soldiers of the governor took Jesus into the common hall, and gathered unto him the whole band of soldiers. And they stripped him, and put on him a scarlet robe. And when they had platted a crown of thorns, they put it upon his head, and a reed in his right hand: and they bowed the knee before him, and mocked him, saying, Hail, King of the Jews! And they spit upon him, and took the reed, and smote him on the head. And after that they had mocked him, they took the robe off from him, and put his own raiment on him, and led him away to crucify him. And as they came out, they found a man of Cyrene, Simon by name: him they compelled to bear his cross."
(Matthew 27:26-32)

Here is a short, but very solemn description of the scourging, mockery, and shame inflicted upon our Lord Jesus Christ by the Roman soldiers before he was crucified. May God the Holy Spirit fill our hearts with reverence and gratitude as we are again reminded of all that our Redeemer endured at the hands of wicked men, and are reminded again that he endured it all for us according to the will and appointment of God, "that he might redeem us from all iniquity and purify unto himself a people zealous of good works". The Lord of Glory was humiliated, scourged, and mocked by men, that we might be exalted, embraced, and honoured by God.

The Scourging Of Our Saviour

"Then released he Barabbas unto them: and when he had scourged Jesus, he delivered him to be crucified" (v. 26). When Pilate had scourged the Saviour, he delivered him to be crucified. Barabbas was released; and the Lord Jesus took his place, was scourged, and crucified in the place of a vile criminal, a man who was condemned as one worthy of death. Thus, by an act of divine providence, we are given a vivid picture of our own salvation by substitution. "For he hath made him to be sin for us, who knew no sin; that we might be made the righteousness of God in him" (2 Corinthians 5:21).

Luke tells us that Pilate tried to appease the Jews by scourging the Lord Jesus rather than crucifying him (Luke 23:22). But the Jews wanted his death. Therefore, we read here that the order was given first for our Lord to be scourged and then crucified. The indignities heaped upon the Lord Jesus, as the prelude to his crucifixion, must never be considered lightly. These things were also a part of his physical sufferings and deep anguish of soul as our Substitute, and demand our reverent attention. John Trapp wrote:

> Christ was scourged when we had offended, that he might free us from the sting of conscience, and those scourges and scorpions of eternal torments, that he might make us a plaster of his own blessed blood, for by his stripes we are healed, by the bloody weals (welts) made upon his back we are delivered.

This act of scourging was almost as cruel, inhumane, and barbaric as crucifixion. It was done with a whip with multiple strands. The cords were made of something like rawhide. Each strand had numerous pieces of bone fragments tied into it. When the whip was dragged across a man's back, it literally ploughed it up. One lash would be indescribably painful. Our Lord Jesus received thirty-nine lashes from the scourge! Thus the scriptures were fulfilled "The plowers plowed upon my back: they made long their furrows" (Psalm 129:3). "I gave my back to the smiters, and my cheeks to them that plucked off the hair: I hid not my face from shame and spitting" (Isaiah 50:6). "But he was wounded for our transgressions, he was bruised for our iniquities: the chastisement of our peace was upon him; and with his stripes we are healed" (Isaiah 53:5). "And shall deliver him to the Gentiles to mock, and to scourge, and to crucify him: and the third day he shall rise again" (Matthew 20:19).

The scourging of Christ was an emblem of the strokes of divine justice, which he endured in his soul as our Surety, when he was stricken, smitten, and afflicted by the sword of divine justice as our Substitute. But scourging was not enough. We could not be saved if Christ had only been scourged for us. He must be slain for us, and slain in a manner identifying him as one cursed of God. So, once Pilate had scourged him, "he delivered him to be crucified". No peace could be made, except by the blood of his cross (Colossians 1:20).

The Sport Of The Soldiers

Notice the first word of verse 27 – "Then". Normally, a convicted felon, even in those barbaric times, was given some time between being sentenced to death and his execution. Usually, he had a few days to be visited by family members. But the Son of God was hurried off by the soldiers to be tormented as soon as he had been scourged. While they were preparing the place of execution, an entire band[10] of Roman soldiers got together in Pilate's palace to have a little fun with this man who was to be executed.

The Lord of glory became an object of sporting torment for a band of depraved men! Yet, even this was according to the will of God for the fulfilment of scripture, both to assure us that Jesus is the Christ and that he has ransomed our souls by his great sacrifice for sin. These barbarians, hardened by a lifetime of bloodshed, tried to make our Lord's death a thousand deaths in one. These things are written for our comfort and learning. May God the Holy Spirit both teach us and comfort our hearts by them. We are specifically told by Matthew of seven things, seven acts of barbarism these soldiers did to the Son of God.

1. "They stripped him" (v. 28). It appears that the only thing in this world that belonged to him, were the clothes on his back; but now he was stripped even of them. The shame of nakedness came into the world with sin (Genesis 3:7). Therefore, when Christ came to be made sin for us, to satisfy the justice of God for it, and to put it away, he was stripped naked and put to public shame! He was put to shame that we might be given honour. He was stripped that we might be clothed with the white raiment of his perfect righteousness (Revelation 3:18).

2. They "put on him a scarlet robe" (v. 28). They took some old red coat of one of the soldiers, or some old red blanket, and draped it over Immanuel in mockery, because he claimed to be the King. Thus, they derided him. Yet, in their derision of him, they fulfilled the will of God and the Word of God. This is he of whom the prophet declares, he was "red in his apparel" (Isaiah 63:1, 2), who "washed his garments in wine" (Genesis 49:11). Our sins are described as being both scarlet and crimson (Isaiah 1:18). Thus, as he was about to be made sin, our Lord was here providentially draped in the scarlet robe as our sin-bearer.

3. "They platted a crown of thorns and put it on his head" (v. 29). Continuing to mock his claims as the Messiah and King of Israel, they made a crown for his

[10] The word used is the technical word for a cohort, or sub-division of a legion. Some commentators suggest the soldiers involved may have numbered over 500 men and even in excess of a thousand. Our Lord's torture and humiliation was a very public spectacle!

head, but a crown of thorns designed to torture him. Had they made the crown merely for laughter, they would not have chosen thorns. It was made specifically by them to cause our blessed Saviour as much pain as possible. What horrible pain it must have caused when shoved into his sacred head!

Yet, this too was done according to the purpose of our God. Thorns are the result of sin and part of God's curse upon it (Genesis 3:18). Therefore, when Christ was being made a curse for us and would remove the curse from us, he wore the emblem of the curse. This was a fulfilment of the typical ram caught in the thicket that Abraham sacrificed for Isaac (Genesis 22:13). These thorns drew forth blood upon the brow of our great High Priest, which flow down from his head as precious ointment (Psalm 133:2).

4. "They put a reed in his right hand" (v. 29). Again, this was mockery of our Master. They gave him a bamboo sceptre, as if to imply that his claim to a throne and his kingdom was no more than a reed shaken in the wind. How mistaken they are who fail to see that Jesus Christ is King forever! "Thy throne, O God, is for ever and ever: the sceptre of thy kingdom is a right sceptre" (Psalm 45:6; Hebrews 1:8).

5. "They bowed the knee before him and mocked him, saying, Hail, King of the Jews" (v. 29). Like Joseph's brethren, they said, "Shalt thou indeed reign over us?" Like multitudes today, they mocked his claims to sovereignty and dominion. But man's mockery will not last for long. "Wherefore God also hath highly exalted him, and given him a name which is above every name: That at the name of Jesus every knee should bow, of things in heaven, and things in earth, and things under the earth; And that every tongue should confess that Jesus Christ is Lord, to the glory of God the Father" (Philippians 2:9-11).

6. "They spit upon him" (v. 30). Robert Hawker wrote, "Their spitting on him was intended to manifest the highest indignation and contempt. Among the Jews it was the greatest indignity, imaginable. If a father spit in his daughter's face, so filthy was she considered thereby, that like the leper, the law enjoined the being shut out of the camp seven days (Numbers 12:14)". I do not know which is more shocking: that men should dare spit upon his holy face, or that the Son of God should stoop to being spit upon as one who is utterly contemptible! Yet, to this great depth our God condescended for the salvation of our souls. "For ye know the grace of our Lord Jesus Christ, that, though he was rich, yet for your sakes he became poor, that ye through his poverty might be rich" (2 Corinthians 8:9).

7. "They took the reed, and smote him on the head" (v. 30). They beat him on the head, while he was wearing the crown of thorns, inflicting all the pain they

could upon him. Why? Why was all this done? Why did the Lord of glory submit to it? FOR US! The Son of God endured this misery, this shame, this torture, that he might purchase for us everlasting life, and joy, and peace, and glory! But these things were not sufficient to save us. These torments could never satisfy the justice of God. He must be crucified. Therefore, we read, “And after that they had mocked him, they took the robe off from him, and put his own raiment on him, and led him away to crucify him” (v. 31). They put his own clothes back on him, that all might recognize him, and led him away, as a lamb to the slaughter, to crucify him.

Carefully read what the Lord Jesus said by the Spirit of prophecy in Psalms 22 and 49 about the sorrow of his soul in suffering these things, and worship him who loved us and gave himself for us. John Trapp admonished, “We should read with regret for our sins, the weapons and instruments of all his sufferings; and see through his wounds the naked bowels, as it were, of his love to our poor souls”. As our blessed Saviour was led away to suffer for us, “that he might sanctify us with his own blood”, suffering “without the gate, let us go forth unto him without the camp bearing his reproach” (Hebrews 13:12, 13).

The Service Of Simon

“And as they came out, they found a man of Cyrene, Simon by name: him they compelled to bear his cross” (v. 32). This man Simon was one of the Lord’s disciples (Mark 15:21; Romans 16:13). Whether the soldiers knew it, or not, we do not know. He was compelled to carry the Master’s cross, because they feared they might be robbed of their final sport of crucifying him. Yet, even in this, our God was ruling and overruling to teach us spiritual lessons. If we would follow Christ, we must take up his cross and do so daily (Luke 14:25-33). It is certain the cross of Christ is so contrary to our flesh that, if we take up his cross and follow him, we must be compelled to do so by the grace of God. C. H. Spurgeon said:

> Oh, that we were as willing to bear Christ’s cross as Christ was to bear our sins on his cross! If anything happens to us by way of persecution or ridicule for our Lord’s sake, and the gospel’s, let us cheerfully endure it. As knights are made by a stroke from the sovereign’s sword, so shall we become princes in Christ’s realm as he lays his cross on our shoulders.

The Substitute For Sinners

All that our Lord Jesus Christ suffered, he suffered vicariously, as the sinner's Substitute, because he was made sin for us. This is a matter of the deepest importance. Until we understand the purpose of our Redeemer's sufferings and death, we can never understand what he accomplished by his sacrifice. The Lord Jesus Christ died in place of and instead of chosen sinners, that sinners loved by him from everlasting might be made the righteousness of God in him.

He bore our sins in his own body on the tree. He died the just for the unjust that he might bring us to God in perfect reconciliation. He was made sin for us, who knew no sin, that we might be made the righteousness of God in him. The holy Lamb of God was made a curse for us, that he might redeem us from the curse of the law. He was once offered to bear the sins of his elect, that we might bear them no more. He was wounded for our transgressions, and bruised for our iniquities, as the Lord God laid upon him all the sins of all his people (1 Peter 2:24; 3:18; 2 Corinthians 5:21; Galatians 3:13; Hebrews 9:28; Isaiah 53:5, 6).

As we read of his sufferings, let us follow our Saviour through all his agony, viewing him as our sin-atoning Substitute and Surety, who voluntarily undertook from eternity the redemption of our souls. Was he scourged? It was that through his stripes we might be healed. Was he condemned, though innocent? It was that we might be acquitted, though guilty. Did he wear a crown of thorns? It was that we might wear the crown of glory. Was he stripped? It was that we might be clothed in his perfect righteousness. Was he mocked and reviled? It was that we might be honoured and blessed. Was he reckoned a sinner and numbered among transgressors? It was that we might be reckoned righteous and numbered among the holy. Could he not save himself? It was that he might be able to save others to the uttermost. Did he die the painful, shameful, ignominious death of the cross? It was that we might have eternal life and be exalted to the highest glory.

"Thanks be unto God for his unspeakable gift"! Our sins are many and great. But our blessed Christ has put them all away forever by the sacrifice of himself. There is infinite merit and efficacy in his sufferings and death. He who suffered and died as our sin-atoning Substitute is God as well as man. It is written of him, "He shall not fail … He shall see of the travail of his soul and shall be satisfied". Let this picture of Christ crucified, as it is set before us by God the Holy Spirit upon the pages of Inspiration, be stamped upon our hearts by that same Spirit's almighty grace, compelling us to trust and love our great Saviour!

Chapter 89

The Crucifixion

"And when they were come unto a place called Golgotha, that is to say, a place of a skull, They gave him vinegar to drink mingled with gall: and when he had tasted thereof, he would not drink. And they crucified him, and parted his garments, casting lots: that it might be fulfilled which was spoken by the prophet, They parted my garments among them, and upon my vesture did they cast lots. And sitting down they watched him there; And set up over his head his accusation written, THIS IS JESUS THE KING OF THE JEWS. Then were there two thieves crucified with him, one on the right hand, and another on the left. And they that passed by reviled him, wagging their heads, And saying, Thou that destroyest the temple, and buildest it in three days, save thyself. If thou be the Son of God, come down from the cross. Likewise also the chief priests mocking him, with the scribes and elders, said, He saved others; himself he cannot save. If he be the King of Israel, let him now come down from the cross, and we will believe him. He trusted in God; let him deliver him now, if he will have him: for he said, I am the Son of God. The thieves also, which were crucified with him, cast the same in his teeth."
(Matthew 27:33-44)

These verses describe the sufferings of our Lord Jesus Christ when he was made to be sin for us and hanged upon the cursed tree. It is an amazing, marvellous record. It is amazing and marvellous in our eyes when we realize who suffered these things. It was the Lord Jesus Christ, the Son of God, the Lamb of God, the only truly holy and good man ever to live in this world. It is amazing and marvellous in our eyes when we are made to know for whom he suffered. "For when we were yet without strength, in due time Christ died for the ungodly. For scarcely for a righteous man will one die: yet peradventure for a good man some would even dare to die. But God commendeth his love toward us, in that, while we were yet sinners, Christ died for us" (Romans 5:5-8). It is amazing and marvellous in our eyes when we remember why he suffered. The cause of his great sorrow and agony of body, soul, and spirit was the fact that the Son of God suffered for sin, as the sin-bearer. "Christ died for our sins"!

We have seen our Saviour's sorrow in Gethsemane when he prayed three times, "O my Father, if it be possible, let this cup pass from me: nevertheless not as I will, but as thou wilt". Such was the shock of his holy soul at the thought and prospect of being made sin that our Redeemer broke out into a sweat of blood. Luke describes it in these words: "Being in an agony he prayed more earnestly: and his sweat was as it were great drops of blood falling down to the ground" (Luke 22:44). We have seen the scourging of Pilate's judgment hall, too. There our Lord was condemned in a mockery of justice (John 19:12, 13). There he was delivered into the hands of cruel, barbaric Roman soldiers to be scourged. They took him into the common judgment hall where they gathered an entire band of soldiers, between five and twelve hundred of them, to scourge our Saviour. They stripped him. They mercilessly whipped him with a Roman scourge. They mocked him. And they spit upon him! "Then they led him away to crucify him."

Golgotha

"And when they were come unto a place called Golgotha, that is to say, a place of a skull" (v. 33). Calvary, the place chosen for the slaughter of God's dear Son, is called by Matthew, "Golgotha". "Golgotha" means "place of a skull". It was called Golgotha because in this place, people who were executed were simply covered over with a little dirt. In a matter of time skulls and bones were seen everywhere. Our blessed Saviour was slaughtered in this hideous place of infamy where the carcasses of dead bodies were exposed as dung abhorred by God and men. God's prophet, speaking of one cursed of God, said of him, "They shall not lament for him, saying, Ah my brother! or, Ah sister! they shall not lament for him, saying, Ah lord! or, Ah his glory! He shall be buried with the burial of an ass, drawn and cast forth beyond the gates of Jerusalem" (Jeremiah 22:18, 19).

When our Saviour came to redeem us from the curse of the law, being made a curse for us, he put himself in the place of one cursed of God. "Christ hath redeemed us from the curse of the law, being made a curse for us: for it is written, Cursed is every one that hangeth on a tree" (Galatians 3:13). He took our curse and was made a curse for us, that he might redeem us from it.

Sovereignty Displayed

In this scene of slaughter at Golgotha the Holy Spirit shows us a tremendous display of God's glorious sovereignty in three things. First, we see God's sovereignty displayed in the fulfilment of holy scripture by men who had no regard for the scriptures. These soldiers had no more regard for the scriptures than hogs have for diamonds. Yet they did exactly what God ordained they would do and said they would do (Acts 4:27, 28; 13:27-29). Thus, the Lord God makes even his Son's murderers to be his witnesses!

"They gave him vinegar to drink mingled with gall: and when he had tasted thereof, he would not drink" (v. 34). This mixture of vinegar (flat wine that had gone sour and bitter) mixed with gall was thought to prolong one's life. It was given by the soldiers because they must, according to God's decree, fulfil the prophecy of Psalm 69:21. "They gave me also gall for my meat; and in my thirst they gave me vinegar to drink". John Gill wrote, "This potion of vinegar with gall was an aggravating circumstance in our Lord's sufferings, being given to him when he had a violent thirst upon him; and was an emblem of the bitter cup of God's wrath he had already tasted of in the garden, and was about to drink up." But, "When he had tasted thereof, he would not drink". Our Lord refused to drink this mixture because he was determined to suffer the wrath of God for us without any distraction or intoxication of mind. He would make all to know that he did nothing to prolong his life, but willingly died now that his hour had come. The fulness of time had come, and he laid down his life.

"And they crucified him, and parted his garments, casting lots: that it might be fulfilled which was spoken by the prophet, They parted my garments among them, and upon my vesture did they cast lots" (v. 35). Again, we are reminded that the Lord God was in total control on this day of infamy. The barbaric soldiers did nothing except what God had long before said they would do. This parting of our Lord's garments was a fulfilment of Psalm 22:18. "They part my garments among them, and cast lots upon my vesture." Then, "sitting down they watched him there" (v. 36). After they had scourged him, mocked, beaten, and crucified him, these hardened men sat down to watch the Lamb of God die. Like little boys cruelly throw a worm into a fire just to watch it wriggle, squirm, and die, they watched the Son of God; but to their utter astonishment, there was no wriggling, no squirming, and no dying until he gave up the ghost by his own sovereign will!

Second, we see a display of God's sovereign, distinguishing grace in the two thieves crucified with our Lord. "Then were there two thieves crucified with him, one on the right hand, and another on the left" (v. 38). Our Lord Jesus was crucified between two thieves, just as the prophet Isaiah declared he must be. "He was numbered with the transgressors" (Isaiah 53:12). One of these thieves was plucked as a brand from the burning, out of the very jaws of hell by God's sovereign grace, while the other was left to suffer the just consequences of his sin. Let it never be forgotten by us that if we are saved, we are saved because God did it. The only distinction between you and me and the damned in hell is the distinction that grace has made (1 Corinthians 4:7; 15:10; Romans 9:16).

Third, we see in these verses a great display of God's sovereignty in causing reprobate, unbelieving men to declare his truth, to declare the very essence of the gospel, though they never knew it themselves. We do not know for certain, but it may be that it was the testimony of spineless Pilate, the testimony of these wicked, taunting, jeering Jews, and the testimony of the mocking chief priests, scribes, and elders that became the instruments by which God taught that elect thief the gospel and brought him to faith in Christ.

Pilate declared, "THIS IS JESUS THE KING OF THE JEWS" (v. 37). Pilate, by the order of divine providence, announced that the crucified Christ is the King of the Jews, and refused to alter it, though urged to do so. This proclamation was made in Hebrew, the language of religion, in Greek, the language of philosophy, and in Latin, the language of science. That was no accident. There is no true religion, no true philosophy, and no true science that does not begin with the acknowledgment and confession that Jesus Christ is King. The priests, scribes, elders, and people, danced in a drunken, hellish party around Immanuel's cross, and in their blasphemy spoke the truth of God as distinctly as inspired apostles. In verse 40 they jeered, "Thou that destroyest the temple and buildest it in three days". Though they knew it not, these religious ritualists proclaimed the fact of our Lord's death and resurrection. He destroyed the temple of his body in death and raised it up again in three days.

Again, they mocked the Lord of Glory, saying, "He saved others; himself he cannot save" (v. 42). That is the very essence of the gospel! The Son of God died as our Substitute. If he would save us, he could not save himself. Those "fools and blind" did not know they were proclaiming Immanuel's greatest glory. It was because he saved others that he could not save himself. Were he willing to let chosen sinners perish, he could easily have saved himself. But he bore, not only the cruel nails and spear, but their more cruel mockeries, rather than give up his self-imposed task of saving his people by the sacrifice of himself.

"He trusted in God" (v. 43). Our Lord Jesus Christ, as a man, lived by faith, in all things trusting God his Father. He taught us that the only way we can honour, obey, and live for God in this world is by faith. And by his faith, as God the Holy Spirit declares in Galatians 3:22-26, we were justified. It is not our believing that fulfilled God's covenant promise and brought in the blessed righteousness by which we now stand before him in life. The promise is given to all who believe. But the promise was fulfilled and comes to us "by faith of Jesus Christ". It was

Christ to whom the promise was made as our Surety in the everlasting covenant upon condition of his obedience unto death as our Substitute. And it is Christ who obtained the promise by his faithful fulfilment of his covenant engagements as our Surety (Hebrews 10:5-14).

It is this, "the faith of Jesus Christ", that is revealed to us by the gospel. We are shut up to Christ, who is the faith that is now revealed in the gospel. Our faith in Christ is not revealed to us; it is given to us and worked in us by the mighty operations of God the Holy Spirit (Ephesians 1:19, 20; 2:8, 9; Colossians 1:12). It is Christ ("the faith of Christ") who is revealed. When God the Holy Spirit comes to chosen sinners in the saving power of omnipotent grace, he convinces them of all that Christ accomplished by his faithful obedience as our Substitute. When he reveals Christ in an individual, he convinces him that his sin has been put away by Christ's atonement, that righteousness has been brought in by Christ's obedience, and that justice has been satisfied by Christ's blood (John 16:7-11). The sinner, being convinced of these things, trusts Christ.

Again they taunted our Redeemer, saying, "He said, I am the Son of God" (v 43). Modern infidels choose to ignore it; but these people heard his doctrine plainly. Jesus Christ of Nazareth openly, publicly declared himself to be the Son of God. And that is who he is! He is God and man in one glorious Person the God-man, our Mediator. He was the God-man in Mary's womb, while he lived on earth in obedience to the Father's will, and when he died as our Substitute on the cursed tree. He is now, and forever the God-man, exalted to save his redeemed!

The Sufferings Of Our Saviour

When we think about the crucifixion and death of our Lord Jesus Christ, we ought always to bear in mind, to the best of our ability, the extent and reality of his sufferings. Our Lord Jesus endured all the hell of God's wrath for us when he bore our sins in his body on the cross. He suffered all the wrath of God that we deserved in his body, in his soul, and in his spirit. The bare listing of his agonies is torturous to read. What must it have been to experience! The most savage barbarians in history have not been able to equal the tortures heaped upon the Son of God by the Jews and the Romans who crucified him. J. C. Ryle wrote, "Never let it be forgotten that he had a real human body, a body exactly like our own, just as sensitive, just as vulnerable, just as capable of feeling intense pain."

Without question, many place too much emphasis upon the physical, bodily sufferings of Christ, trying to get people to feel sorry for "poor, helpless Jesus". That is not my aim. Jesus Christ did not die a helpless victim of circumstances.

He is the God of circumstances. Let us weep for the sins that made his death necessary. But he does not need or desire our pity. In fact, he said, "Weep not for me, but for yourselves, and for your children". Yet, others seem to think our Lord's bodily sufferings were of little importance. The Word of God records the physical suffering of Christ in great detail in all four gospels, in several Psalms, and in Isaiah 53, as well as in numerous other Old and New Testaments passages. Isaiah describes in considerable detail what our Saviour suffered for us. In Psalm 22, David tells us what he said as he suffered the wrath of God for us. These things are recorded by divine inspiration for our learning and edification, because it is important for us to know what the Son of God suffered for us at Calvary.

Crucifixion was the most horrid form of execution ever forced upon a human being. The person crucified was stretched out on his back on a piece of timber. His hands were stretched out on the cross piece, and nailed through the wrists to the wood with spikes. His feet were crossed one on top of the other and nailed together with a huge mallet driving the spike through them both and fastening them to the wood. Thus impaled the Lord Jesus was raised on the cross, and it was dropped into a socket three or four feet deep, his body attached to it! There he hung, not dying suddenly for no vital organ was touched, for six long hours. He hung, naked, shamed, covered head to foot with the excrement of other men's foul throats and his own holy blood. His head, hands, feet, and back, oozing blood, throbbing in pain. There the Lord of Glory hung for six long hours of hell.

Yet, his agony of soul was infinitely more excruciating to him than the suffering of his body. I understand the biblical doctrine of the atonement. I know that "without the shedding of blood is no remission", not because God is vengeful and cruel, but because he is good, righteous, holy, and just. I understand the agony of our Saviour's tormented body. I can even, to some degree, understand the torments of his broken heart. But the sufferings of our Saviour's holy soul, I simply cannot comprehend (Isaiah 53:10, 11).

The Son of God was made sin for us! Our sins were imputed to the Son of God! That fact in itself is overwhelming. But I am certain that there is more to the sufferings of our Lord for us than the mere legal, or forensic term "imputation" implies. His heart was not broken simply because he was made to be legally responsible for the debt of our sins. Our sins were not pasted on him, or merely placed to his account. The Lord Jesus Christ was "made sin for us"! He was not merely made legally responsible for sin, or merely made to be a sin-offering. The language of holy scripture is crystal clear "He hath made him sin for us" (2 Corinthians 5:21).

When he was made sin for us, the Lord God made his soul an offering for sin. Then, when our Saviour was most obedient to God as our Representative, his Father forsook him. Martin Luther was right, when he declared, "God forsaken of God, my God, no man can understand that"! The Lamb of God was made sin for us. He was forsaken by his Father. He was slain by the sword of his own holy justice. Robert Hawker's comments on this portion of Matthew's Gospel are as instructive as they are precious:

> Here let us pause over the solemn subject; and again look up by faith, and 'behold the Lamb of God which taketh away the sin of the world!' Methinks we may, as we look up and behold that wondrous sight, contemplate Jesus as thus with arms extended, inviting his redeemed to come to him, as his arms are stretched forth to embrace them. And while his arms are thus open to receive, his feet are waiting for their coming. And with his head reclining, he looks down with his eyes of love, as welcoming their approach. And what a thought is it for every true believer in Christ to cherish, and never to lose sight of: Jesus in all this, hung on the cross not as a private person, but as the public head of his body the Church. For as certain as that you and I, were both in the loins of Adam, when he transgressed in the garden, and were alike implicated in his guilt and punishment; so equally are all the seed of Christ crucified with Christ, and interested in his salvation. For so the charter both of justice and of grace runs: 'In the Lord shall all the seed of Israel be justified and shall glory' (Isaiah 45:25).

How Christ Died

When we think about the crucifixion and death of our Lord Jesus Christ, we ought always to remember with deep reverence, gratitude, and praise "how that Christ died for our sins according to the scriptures" (1 Corinthians 15:3). The gospel is much more than the mere declaration of the fact that Christ died. The gospel is the declaration of "how" he died. The gospel has not been preached until it has been told, "how that Christ died for our sins according to the scriptures". It can be summarize in three words.

Voluntarily
Our Lord Jesus Christ died as a voluntary victim. He was made sin; but his own hand laid our sins upon him. He was slain by the sword of justice; but his own hand held the sword (John 10:14-18).

Vicariously
All our Lord's sufferings were vicarious. He suffered not for his own sins, but for ours. He died as a Substitute in the room and stead of chosen sinners (Isaiah 53:5, 6, 8-10; Matthew 1:21; 2 Corinthians 5:21; Galatians 3:13; Hebrews 9:28; 1 Peter 2:22-24; 3:18). Do not allow yourself to be satisfied with vague, general ideas about substitution and atonement. Everything our Saviour did and endured as a man was for us, as our vicarious Sacrifice. He was scourged but "With his stripes we are healed". He was stripped and we were clothed with righteousness. He was condemned and we went free. He was mocked that we might be blessed. He was numbered with the transgressors that we might be numbered with the sons of God. He was unable to save himself because death was the penalty that must be paid to save us. He was made sin so we might be made the righteousness of God in him. He died that we might live through him.

Victoriously
When the Word of God asserts that the Lord Jesus Christ was and is triumphant and victorious in his death, the meaning is just this: He shall have that for which he died. His people shall be saved. His Father shall be glorified. He shall be exalted forever (Isaiah 53:10-12; Hebrews 10:10-14).

"There is therefore now no condemnation to them which are in Christ Jesus, who walk not after the flesh, but after the Spirit. For the law of the Spirit of life in Christ Jesus hath made me free from the law of sin and death. For what the law could not do, in that it was weak through the flesh, God sending his own Son in the likeness of sinful flesh, and for sin, condemned sin in the flesh … Who shall lay any thing to the charge of God's elect? It is God that justifieth. Who is he that condemneth? It is Christ that died, yea rather, that is risen again, who is even at the right hand of God, who also maketh intercession for us" (Romans 8:1, 33, 34).

Chapter 90

Three Hours Of Darkness

"Now from the sixth hour there was darkness over all the land unto the ninth hour. And about the ninth hour Jesus cried with a loud voice, saying, Eli, Eli, lama sabachthani? that is to say, My God, my God, why hast thou forsaken me? Some of them that stood there, when they heard that, said, This man calleth for Elias. And straightway one of them ran, and took a spunge, and filled it with vinegar, and put it on a reed, and gave him to drink. The rest said, Let be, let us see whether Elias will come to save him. Jesus, when he had cried again with a loud voice, yielded up the ghost. And, behold, the veil of the temple was rent in twain from the top to the bottom; and the earth did quake, and the rocks rent; And the graves were opened; and many bodies of the saints which slept arose, And came out of the graves after his resurrection, and went into the holy city, and appeared unto many. Now when the centurion, and they that were with him, watching Jesus, saw the earthquake, and those things that were done, they feared greatly, saying, Truly this was the Son of God. And many women were there beholding afar off, which followed Jesus from Galilee, ministering unto him: Among which was Mary Magdalene, and Mary the mother of James and Joses, and the mother of Zebedee's children."
(Matthew 27:45-56)

Samuel Stennett wrote:

Yonder, amazing sight! I see
Th' incarnate Son of God
Expiring on th' cursed tree,
And weltering in His blood.

Behold, a purple torrent run
Down from His hands and head,
The crimson tide puts out the sun;
His groans awake the dead.

The trembling earth, the darken'd sky,
Proclaim the truth aloud;
And with th' amazed centurion, cry,
'This is the Son of God!'

So great, so vast a sacrifice
May well my hope revive:
If God's own Son thus bleeds and dies,
The sinner sure may live.

Oh that these cords of love divine
Might draw me, Lord, to Thee!
Thou hast my heart, it shall be Thine!
Thine it shall ever be!

In the verses before us we have Matthew's account of our Saviour's last three hours of agony upon the cursed tree, the last three hours of torture he endured for us as our Substitute, because he was made sin for us. This inspired narrative should always be read with reverence, with hearts broken over sin, and yet rejoicing at the forgiveness of sin obtained at such a price. May God the Holy Spirit sanctify our eyes, our hearts, and our minds as we attempt to meditate upon our Lord's sufferings and to worship him who suffered all the hell of God's holy wrath for us. After suffering the wrath of God as our Substitute, in his body, in his soul, and in his spirit, the Lord Jesus Christ became obedient unto death and "yielded up the ghost". While everything in these verses is utterly amazing, here are seven that are particularly remarkable.

The Darkness

"Now from the sixth hour there was darkness over all the land unto the ninth hour" (v. 45). First, Matthew calls our attention to an extraordinary darkness that covered the land. This was not a natural solar eclipse, but a supernatural one, an eclipse specifically performed by God on this occasion. It was an eclipse that the prophet Amos prophesied. "It shall come to pass in that day, saith the Lord God, that I will cause the sun to go down at noon, and I will darken the earth in the clear day" (Amos 8:9). It lasted for three hours and was attested to by men in other parts of the world who had no idea what was going on in Jerusalem. One Dionysius, living in Egypt at the time, said, "Either the Divine Being suffers, or suffers with him that suffers, or the frame of the world is dissolving". This was a remarkable, three hour eclipse. From noon until three o'clock, the sun refused to shine. Thus, the Lord God gives a vivid, symbolic display of four things.

1. The darkness covering the land indicates the heinousness of the crime being committed. Wicked men were murdering the Lord of Glory! Though our Saviour died and was slaughtered by the hands of wicked men exactly according to the purpose, will, and decree of God for the salvation of his elect, God's decrees did in no way excuse their sin in crucifying him.

2. The darkness indicated the blackness, darkness, and blindness of men's hearts by nature. No impression was made upon these men, though God performed miracles, unheard of before or since, all around them. The fact is, man's heart by nature is so blind that no acts of providence, either in goodness or in judgment, can be seen by him, unless God takes the scales off his eyes.

3. Surely, this darkness was designed to declare the emptiness and darkness of Christless religion. Judaism had become mere ritualism. As such it was altogether darkness. Religion without Christ, without life, without faith is darkness, no matter how orthodox it appears (Amos 8:10).

4. The darkness covering the earth was reflective of the darkness that passed upon and engulfed our Saviour's holy soul, when he was made to be sin for us. When the Light of the world was made sin, darkness flooded the world as darkness flooded his soul.

Christ Forsaken

"And about the ninth hour Jesus cried with a loud voice, saying, Eli, Eli, lama sabachthani? that is to say, My God, my God, why hast thou forsaken me?" (v. 46). Second, the Holy Spirit inspired Matthew to record the fact that the Lord Jesus Christ was forsaken by his Father. "And about the ninth hour", about three o'clock in the afternoon, which was about the time of the slaying and offering of the daily sacrifice, which was an eminent type of Christ, "Jesus cried with a loud voice", as one in great distress. In great darkness for three hours he had been silent, patiently bearing all the torment of his Father's furious wrath in utter abandonment, and all the assaults of hell. Who knows the anguish of his soul? At last, he breaks out in a cry of terrible agony, "saying, Eli, Eli, lama sabachthani? that is to say, my God, my God, why hast thou forsaken me?"

Here our Saviour speaks as a man, the man chosen, made, ordained, and anointed by God with the oil of gladness above his fellows. As a man, our Lord was upheld and strengthened by the Father, just as we are. As a man, he trusted God, loved him, and prayed to him, just as we do; only he did so perfectly, without sin! Though now the Father hid his face from him, still he expresses strong faith in him and love for him. When he is said to be "forsaken" of God, the meaning is not that he was separated from the love of God, or did not know the reason for his abandonment. Our Surety now stood in our place, bearing our sins. He, therefore, had to endure abandonment by God the Father to satisfy justice.

This cry, "My God, my God, Why hast thou forsaken me?" expresses the very soul of his sufferings as our Substitute. Indeed, all the wails and howls of the damned in hell to all eternity will fall infinitely short of expressing the evil and bitterness of sin. But here we see how vile a thing sin is. When God found our sin upon his darling Son, he forsook him in wrath! Whenever we read these words, hear them, or think about them "My God, my God, Why hast thou forsaken me?" we ought to be reminded of the fact that the Lord our God is infinitely holy and just. As such, he must and will punish all sin. Our souls should be flooded with a deep appreciation of God's infinite love, indescribable, everlasting, saving love for us! And we ought to be assured that God's elect shall never be forsaken, not in this world or in the world to come.

The Reason He Was Utterly Forsaken

"My God, my God, Why hast thou forsaken me?" (v. 46). Third, these are the words of our blessed Saviour when he hung upon the cursed tree as our Substitute, when he who knew no sin was made sin for us that we might be made the righteousness of God in him. At the apex of his obedience, at the time of his greatest sorrow, in the hour of his greatest need, the Lord Jesus cried out to his Father, "My God, my God, why hast thou forsaken me?" If we look at Psalm 22, where the Holy Spirit gives us prophetically the agonizing cries of our Redeemer in greater detail, we will find him answering his own heart-rending cry.

> My God, my God, why hast thou forsaken me? why art thou so far from helping me, and from the words of my roaring? O my God, I cry in the daytime, but thou hearest not; and in the night season, and am not silent. But thou art holy, O thou that inhabitest the praises of Israel (vv. 1-3).

How utterly forsaken he was! So utterly forsaken that the Father refused to hear the cries of his own darling Son in the hour of his greatest need. "Why art thou so far from helping me, and from the words of my roaring? O my God, I cry in the daytime, but thou hearest not; and in the night season, and am not silent". I read those words with astonishment. I will not attempt to explain what I cannot imagine. But these things are written here for our learning that we might through patience and consolation of the scriptures have hope. And I hang all the hope of my immortal soul upon this fact. When the Lord Jesus Christ was made sin for me, he was utterly forsaken of God and put to death as my Substitute; and by his one great, sin-atoning Sacrifice he has forever put away my sins. He not only bore our sins in his body on the tree, he bore them away!

In Psalm 22:3 our holy Saviour, when he was made sin for us, answers the cry of his soul's agony. He cried, "My God, my God, Why hast thou forsaken me?" "But thou art holy, O thou that inhabitest the praises of Israel". Why was the Lord Jesus forsaken by his Father when he was made sin for us? Because the holy Lord God is of purer eyes than to behold iniquity. Our Saviour was forsaken by the Father when he was made sin for us, because justice demanded it. "Thou art of purer eyes than to behold evil, and canst not look on iniquity" (Habakkuk 1:13).

Here, as he was dying under the wrath of God, our great Substitute justified God in his own condemnation, because he was made sin for us. He proclaims the holiness of God in the midst of his agony. He is so pure, so holy, so righteous, so just that he will by no means clear the guilty (Exodus 34:7), even when the guilty One is his own darling Son! Rather than that his holy character be slighted, our Surety must suffer and die, because he was made sin for us.

Our Saviour had no sin of his own. He was born without original sin, being even from birth "that Holy One" (Luke 1:35). Throughout his life, he "knew no sin" (2 Corinthians 5:21), "did no sin" (1 Peter 2:22), "and in him is no sin" (1 John 3:5). But on Calvary the holy Lord God "made him who knew no sin to be sin for us, that we might be made the righteousness of God in him" (2 Corinthians 5:21). Just as in the incarnation "the Word was made flesh and dwelt among us" (John 1:14), in substitution he who was made flesh "was made sin for us".

I do not know how God could be made flesh and never cease to be God; but he was. I do not know how God could die and yet never die; but he did (Acts 20:28). And I do not know how Christ who knew no sin could be made sin and yet never have sinned; but he was. These things are mysteries beyond the reach of human comprehension. But they are facts of divine revelation to which we bow with adoration.

"Some of them that stood there, when they heard that, said, This man calleth for Elias" (v. 47). While darkness covered them, they were apparently terrified and silent; but as soon as it was light again, their fear abated and they resumed their derision of the Son of God.

Christ our Passover was now being roasted in the fire of his Father's holy wrath. When he cried, "I thirst", they gave him vinegar to drink. We read in verses 48 and 49, "And straightway one of them ran, and took a sponge, and filled it with vinegar, and put it on a reed, and gave him to drink. The rest said, Let be, let us see whether Elias will come to save him." He thirsted and drank the bitter vinegar of divine justice, that we might drink of the water of life and never thirst; as John Trapp put it, "that we might drink of the water of life, and be sweetly inebriated in that torrent of pleasure that runs at God's right hand for evermore".

A Self-inflicted Death

"Jesus, when he had cried again with a loud voice, yielded up the ghost" (v. 50). Fourth, the Spirit of God reminds us that our blessed Saviour died a remarkable, self-inflicted death. His strength was not abated. His last word was not the gasping breath of a failing life, but the triumphant shout of a conquering King. The Son of God voluntarily laid down his life for his sheep. He did not lose his spirit; he dismissed it! His work was finished. His life was complete. Therefore, he laid it down as a voluntary Surety, vicarious Sufferer, and our victorious Saviour. That is exactly how he said he would die.

> I am the good shepherd, and know my sheep, and am known of mine. As the Father knoweth me, even so know I the Father: and I lay down my life for the sheep. And other sheep I have, which are not of this fold: them also I must bring, and they shall hear my voice; and there shall be one fold, and one shepherd. Therefore doth my Father love me, because I lay down my life, that I might take it again. No man taketh it from me, but I lay it down of myself. I have power to lay it down, and I have power to take it again. This commandment have I received of my Father (John 10:14-18).

The Spirit of God emphasizes that our Saviour cried "with a loud voice". He did not speak as a beaten man, but as a conqueror in the field of battle, carrying away the spoils of his conquests (Colossians 2:15). He cried aloud, that all on earth, all in heaven, and all in hell might hear, "It is finished"! What was finished? Redemption's work was finished. The law's curse was finished. Death, hell, and the grave were vanquished. Robert Hawker wrote, "The most glorious views of that life and immortality, which Christ first brought to light by his gospel, were seen from the hill of Calvary, brighter than Moses saw on the heights of Pisgah, of the promised land. And that song was sung in heaven, which the beloved apostle heard in vision. 'Thou wast slain, and hast redeemed us to God by thy blood (Revelation 5:9).'"

Divine Testimonies

Fifth, the Lord God performed several startling, divine testimonies, declaring that this One who died at Calvary more than two thousand years ago is the Christ of God. "And, behold, the veil of the temple was rent in twain from the top to the bottom; and the earth did quake, and the rocks rent; And the graves were opened; and many bodies of the saints which slept arose, And came out of the graves after his resurrection, and went into the holy city, and appeared unto many" (vv. 51-53). All who consider the miracles performed by God's providence at this time must recognize as the centurion did, that "This man was the Son of God"!

The miracles wrought by God as his Son laid down his life for us seem to say, "These are my witnesses, testifying who I am and what I have accomplished." The veil of the temple rent into two pieces, from the top to the bottom, because the Son of God had now opened a way of access to God by his blood (Hebrews 9:6-12; 10:19-25). The earthquake and the rending of the rocks were celebrations of this glorious event. The opening of the graves and the resurrected bodies of the saints were unmistakable displays of the wonders of redemption and salvation by the death of Christ. These resurrected saints were visible demonstrations of Christ's quickening power, whereby he shall soon raise our vile bodies, and make them like his glorified body, spiritual, immortal, and glorious. Truly, by the death of Christ for us, "death is swallowed up in victory"!

The Centurion's Confession

Sixth, Matthew records a remarkable confession made by one of our Saviour's tormentors. "Now when the centurion, and they that were with him, watching Jesus, saw the earthquake, and those things that were done, they feared greatly, saying, Truly this was the Son of God" (v. 54). The centurion was compelled to confess, by all he saw and heard on that infamous, glorious day, "This man was the Son of God". Soon, in the great day of wrath, all shall confess that Jesus Christ is Lord to the glory of God (Philippians 2:9-11).

Exemplary Women

Seventh, we see many, faithful, loyal, exemplary women beholding their Saviour. "And many women were there beholding afar off, which followed Jesus from Galilee, ministering unto him. Among which was Mary Magdalene, and Mary the mother of James and Joses, and the mother of Zebedee's children" (vv. 55, 56). Let us find our place with these women, beholding Christ crucified for us. Behold him afflicted in his body, in his soul, and in his heart, that he might undo our affliction. Behold him wounded for us, that we might never be wounded. Behold him made sin for us, that we might be made the righteousness of God in him. Behold him put to shame for us, that we might never be put to shame. Behold him dying for us, that we might never die. Behold how he loved us!

John Kent wrote:

Sons of peace redeem'd by blood,
Raise your songs to Zion's God;
Made from condemnation free,
Grace triumphant sing with me.

Calvary's wonders let us trace,
Justice magnified in grace;
Mark the purple streams, and say,
Thus my sins were wash'd away.

Wrath divine no more we dread,
Vengeance smote our Surety's head;
Legal claims are fully met,
Jesus paid the dreadful debt.

Sin is lost beneath the flood,
Drown'd in the Redeemer's blood,
Zion, oh! how blest art thou,
Justified from all things now.

Chapter 91

Our Saviour's Burial

"When the even was come, there came a rich man of Arimathaea, named Joseph, who also himself was Jesus' disciple: He went to Pilate, and begged the body of Jesus. Then Pilate commanded the body to be delivered. And when Joseph had taken the body, he wrapped it in a clean linen cloth, And laid it in his own new tomb, which he had hewn out in the rock: and he rolled a great stone to the door of the sepulchre, and departed. And there was Mary Magdalene, and the other Mary, sitting over against the sepulchre. Now the next day, that followed the day of the preparation, the chief priests and Pharisees came together unto Pilate, Saying, Sir, we remember that that deceiver said, while he was yet alive, After three days I will rise again. Command therefore that the sepulchre be made sure until the third day, lest his disciples come by night, and steal him away, and say unto the people, He is risen from the dead: so the last error shall be worse than the first. Pilate said unto them, Ye have a watch: go your way, make it as sure as ye can. So they went, and made the sepulchre sure, sealing the stone, and setting a watch."
(Matthew 27:57-66)

In our study of Matthew's Gospel we have seen, from this inspired narrative, Matthew's declaration of the gospel "How that Christ died for our sins according to the scriptures". Our Lord Jesus Christ died as a voluntary Substitute, a vicarious Sacrifice, and a victorious Saviour.

Whenever we think about the death of Christ upon the cross, we should always think of four words in our minds' association with it: sovereignty, substitution, satisfaction, and success. Our Saviour died by an act of and in accordance with God's sovereign will. He died as a Substitute in the place of God's elect people, his sheep, those who are justified and saved by his blood. The Son of God did not shed his blood in vain or die for the multitudes who perish under the wrath of God. To suggest he did is to make his blood meaningless and of no effect. By his death on the cross our Lord Jesus Christ made atonement particularly and distinctly for his elect. He effectually accomplished and obtained our eternal redemption. This means his sacrifice and death were a success. He shall have all for whom he suffered and died. That is the message of the gospel. That is "How that Christ died for our sins according to the scriptures".

In this portion of Matthew's gospel narrative we are given an inspired account of the fact "that he was buried". Our Lord's burial is usually passed over quickly in commentaries, sermons, Bible studies, and theological material. It is commonly looked at as being only a necessary event between his death and his resurrection. There is a strong tendency to ignore the burial of our Redeemer. We look upon his death as an amazing thing; and it truly is. And we very properly look upon his resurrection as an amazing thing. We should look upon our Saviour's burial as equally amazing.

Every detail recorded about our Lord's burial, including the scheming of his enemies, is a divinely ordered testimony to the fact that our Lord Jesus Christ is exactly who he claims to be: the Messiah, the Christ, the King, the Son of the living God. Matthew's account of the burial of our Lord contains two very important lessons that I want to set before you in this study. The first is a lesson about the people of God. The second is a lesson about the providence of God.

The People Of God

First, the Holy Spirit gives us a lesson in this passage about the people of God. Here we are introduced to a man called Joseph of Arimathaea. We know very little about him. In fact, he is not mentioned before this incident, and he is not mentioned after it. The Gospel writers tell us only six things about him. 1. His name was Joseph, a very common Jewish name. 2. His home was in Arimathaea, probably the city of Ramah. 3. He was a man of considerable wealth. 4. He was a member of the Sanhedrin (Mark 15:43). 5. He took the Saviour's dead body down from the cross, wrapped it in a clean linen cloth, and buried it in his own new tomb. And 6. he "also himself was Jesus' disciple".

Joseph had been until this time a secret disciple. We have no way of knowing how long he had been a believer, how he heard the gospel, or why he had kept his faith a secret from others. Much speculation has been made regarding these things but I will not add to the confusion. If the Holy Spirit had intended for us to know them, he could have informed us as easily as he gave us the man's name. Still, there are some things to be learned from this man.

We should never presume that we know the spiritual condition of others. We do not. Our Lord has disciples and friends in this world who are altogether unknown to us. There may be some true disciples living very near, perhaps even among our own families, who are unknown to us.

I realize that believers confess Christ before men, that they confess him and identify with him and his people in believer's baptism, and that they are known by their fruits. I am aware of all those things. But what is normally the case is not always the case. We must take care not to look upon someone as an unbeliever because he or she does not appear to us to be a believer. We simply do not have the ability to look upon the hearts of other people. We do not have the ability to separate sheep from goats, or wheat from tares. That is why the Lord tells us to leave them alone.

No one would have named Joseph among the Lord's disciples; but he was a man whose love for Christ was demonstrated when none of the strong disciples dared to do what he did. At just the time he was needed, Joseph came forward to do honour to his Saviour. At a time when the apostles had forsaken him, at a time when it was most dangerous to confess him, at a time when there seemed to be absolutely no earthly advantage to professing allegiance to him, Joseph came forward with boldness, begging Pilate to let him have the body of the Son of God, that he might save it from further desecration. He wrapped the Saviour's body in clean linen, carried it in his own arms to his own tomb, and buried it in honour.

Not all believers are alike. Some are bold. Others are timid. Some are strong, others weak. Some are known around the world, others are hardly known at all. Some are very passive. Others are very active. Some build up the church and kingdom of God as zealous witnesses, preachers, missionaries, and evangelists. Others come forward only in times of specific need, like Joseph. Yet, all are led by God the Holy Spirit and glorify their Master in the specific way, time, and place he has ordained.

The fact that we are here told of a disciple like Joseph, unknown to the other disciples, ought to make us both charitable and hopeful. We should be charitable in our opinions of those who profess faith in Christ. I am not suggesting that religious infidels, people who deny the gospel of God's free and sovereign grace in Christ, should be embraced as our brothers and sisters in Christ. But I am saying that those who profess faith in Christ, who profess to believe the gospel of God's grace, should be received and embraced as true believers, as Paul put it, "not to doubtful disputations" (Romans 14:1), though they may behave in ways that we find inconsistent with faith, or form associations we simply cannot fathom.

Joseph's example ought to make us hopeful, too. We are far too often like Elijah, thinking that we alone are left in this world to serve our God. That is never the case. "Many shall (yet) come from the east and west, and shall sit down with Abraham, Isaac, and Jacob in the kingdom of heaven" (Matthew 8:11).

John tells us that Nicodemus, another prominent Pharisee, and another secret disciple, joined Joseph at the tomb. I find that interesting and instructive. Do you not? Those disciples, who had openly followed the Lord during his lifetime, fled from him in the end. But these two men, who had kept their faith in Christ secret while he was alive, came forward publicly to bury him honourably.

God's Providence

The second lesson in these verses is also a very important one to learn. It is a lesson about God's providence. In infinite wisdom our God foresaw the objections that unbelievers, infidels, and atheists would raise against the resurrection of our Lord from the dead. Did the Son of God really die? Did he literally rise from the dead on the third day after his death? Might there not have been some delusion as to the reality of his death? Might there not have been some distortion of truth in reporting his resurrection? These and many other questions have been raised by men; but they are raised without a fabric of a basis in fact.

Our God, who knows the end from the beginning, prevented the possibility of such cavils having a basis in fact. By his over-ruling providence, he fixed it so that the death, burial, and resurrection of our Lord all were established as irrefutable facts. And he did so by overruling the actions of those very men who most desired to stop the influence of Christ in this world: his murderers! The facts recorded in these last verses of Matthew twenty-seven, are recorded by Matthew alone. They make it evident for all to see that the Son of God literally died as our penal Substitute, that he was buried as a dead man in the earth for three days, and that he arose from the dead on the third day after his death.[11]

---

[11] Robert Hawker's comments on Matthew 27:62-66 are excellent. I give them here without comment. "Here is a precious testimony, and from the mouth of Christ's enemies also, in confirmation of the resurrection which followed. And with respect to the story of the disciples taking away the body, it is in itself too childish and ridiculous to deserve even the relation of it. That a few poor timid disciples, who during their Lord's trial, and before any danger to themselves had even appeared, had all forsook Jesus and fled, should project such a scheme, as to come by surprise on a guard of *Roman* soldiers, who were placed at the sepulchre for no purpose but to watch the body of Jesus; and whose military discipline was the strictest in the world; and should actually take away the body, is one of the most extravagant suppositions, which ever entered the human mind.

And to heighten the representation still more, it is added, that this was done while the soldiers

Our Saviour's Burial

The Lord our god is so gloriously sovereign that he makes even the actions of his enemies, even the most wicked acts of men to serve his purpose for the salvation of his elect and the glory of his own great name.

Sometimes God performs notable miracles, by which he alters the course of nature to accomplish his purpose for the good of his elect and the glory of his name. For example: the flood; the plagues in Egypt; the slaying of the firstborn; the crossing of the Red Sea; the drowning of Pharaoh; the manna that fell in the wilderness; water flowing out of the smitten rock; the day the sun stood still; the fallen walls of Jericho; the axe that swam; the ass that spoke; the opening of the ground to swallow Korah; the fish to swallow Jonah; the burning bush; the fire that could not burn Shadrach, Meshach, and Abednego; the lions that would not harm Daniel etc..

But the supernatural miracles performed by God seem almost insignificant, when compared to his sovereign disposition of all things in providence. Consider for a moment the magnitude of God's providence.

The scriptures universally declare that our God rules all things, everywhere, at all times, absolutely (1 Chronicles 29:11, 12; 2 Chronicles 20:6; Job 23:13; Psalm

---

were asleep. Soldiers and sentinels asleep! And so it seems, that the evidence these soldiers gave of this transaction, of what had happened, was while they were asleep. A new way of giving testimony!

Moreover, it is time to enquire, what possible motive these poor fishermen of Galilee could have to take away a dead body? Nothing can be more plain and evident than that the disciples of Jesus, at the time this transaction of Christ's death took place, knew not any more than their enemies, what the resurrection from the dead should mean. They had no other notions of Christ, notwithstanding all that Jesus had said to them, than that of a temporal prince; and when by his death, the hopes they had conceived of this kingdom were over, they would in a few days have returned to their former occupation again. In fact they did so.

Besides, where could they have put the body? Was it stolen, and yet intended to be concealed? And if so what could be then accomplished by it? And can it be supposed for a moment, that when the soldiers all of them awaked from their sleep and found the body gone, and taken away by disciples; would the *Roman* soldiers, aided by the whole Jewish *Sanhedrin,* have suffered this handful of poor fishermen of *Galilee* to have remained a single hour, without giving up their plunder, and bringing them to immediate punishment.

I have not dwelt so circumstantially on this subject from any apprehension of its necessity, for my Reader's confirmation of *the faith once delivered to the saints*; but for the preciousness of any thing, and every thing connected with the resurrection of Jesus. Oh! the blessedness of knowing, and from divine teaching too; the certainty of that glorious truth, Christ *is risen from the dead.* And oh! when the conviction of that glorious truth is secured in the soul, by a testimony founded in the faithfulness of Jehovah; then in Christ's resurrection, the sure resurrection of his redeemed is included. *Blessed and holy is he that hath part in the first resurrection: on such the second death hath no power (*Revelation 20:6).

76:10; 115:3; 135:6; Proverbs 16.4, 9, 33; 21:30; Isaiah 46:9, 10; Daniel 4:34, 35; Romans 11:36; Ephesians 1:11).

The Word of God is filled with examples of God's sovereign providence ruling and overruling even the most vile actions of men for the accomplishment of his purpose: Joseph and His Brethren, Elimelech, Naomi and Ruth, Esther, Haman and Mordecai, David and Bathsheba (Psalm 76:10; Proverbs 16:9; Jeremiah 10:23).

Yet nowhere in scripture is God's incredible and amazing providence more evident than in the burial of our Lord. Every detail, from Joseph's begging for his body, to Pilate's agreement, to the scheming of the Jews to have his tomb sealed under the protection of Roman guards, all are a testimony to the fact that Jesus Christ of Nazareth is indeed the Christ of God, our Saviour, and our Lord, crucified, buried, and raised again for our justification. There is no human explanation of these events.

Let all who truly are the Lord's disciples come forth in this hour when his name is maligned to confess him in believers' baptism. As he was buried for us, we must take our place with him in the watery grave. May God give us grace both to boldly confess our Saviour's name in the midst of his enemies and to calmly trust his wise and adorable providence (Romans 8:28-30).

Chapter 92

The Resurrection Of Our Lord Jesus Christ

"In the end of the sabbath, as it began to dawn toward the first day of the week, came Mary Magdalene and the other Mary to see the sepulchre. And, behold, there was a great earthquake: for the angel of the Lord descended from heaven, and came and rolled back the stone from the door, and sat upon it. His countenance was like lightning, and his raiment white as snow: And for fear of him the keepers did shake, and became as dead men. And the angel answered and said unto the women, Fear not ye: for I know that ye seek Jesus, which was crucified. He is not here: for he is risen, as he said. Come, see the place where the Lord lay. And go quickly, and tell his disciples that he is risen from the dead; and, behold, he goeth before you into Galilee; there shall ye see him: lo, I have told you. And they departed quickly from the sepulchre with fear and great joy; and did run to bring his disciples word. And as they went to tell his disciples, behold, Jesus met them, saying, All hail. And they came and held him by the feet, and worshipped him. Then said Jesus unto them, Be not afraid: go tell my brethren that they go into Galilee, and there shall they see me."
(Matthew 28:1-10)

The resurrection of Christ is the single greatest event in the history of the world. Without it, our Saviour's incarnation, life, and death as our Substitute and Surety would be altogether meaningless. The resurrection of our Lord is so vital a doctrine that those who deny it deny Christianity altogether. Without the resurrection there would be no such thing as Christianity. Without this, we are yet in our sins, our faith is vain, our hope is a delusion, and our religion is a mockery of men's souls! If Christ was not raised from the dead, redemption was not accomplished, justice was not satisfied, he is not God, and we are yet under the wrath and curse of the Almighty (1 Corinthians 15:13-17).

Today, we seldom here anything preached about the resurrection, except at Easter. But that was not the case in the New Testament. Those who had seen the risen Lord and had experienced the power of his resurrection in the new birth went everywhere preaching "Jesus and the resurrection" (Acts 4:2; 17:18). That is to say, they preached salvation accomplished for sinners by the crucified, risen Christ. This is what Peter preached on the day of Pentecost (Acts 2:23, 24), before the Sanhedrin (Acts 4:10), and to the Gentiles (Acts 10:41).

Paul preached the resurrection constantly. Wherever he went, that was his message. This is what he preached in the Synagogue at Antioch of Pisidia (Acts 13:30, 37), before the Sanhedrin in Jerusalem (Acts 23:6), before Felix the Governor (Acts 24:15, 21), before King Agrippa (Acts 26:8), to the Church at Rome (Romans 6:3-6), to the Corinthians (1 Corinthians 15:4; 2 Corinthians 4:14), to the Galatians (Galatians 1:1), to the Ephesians (Ephesians 1:20), to the Philippians (Philippians 3:10), and to the Colossians (Colossians 2:12). The great apostle to the Gentiles longed to know Christ "and the power of his resurrection, and the fellowship of his sufferings, being made conformable unto his death".

Peter spoke of our living hope through the resurrection. "Blessed be the God and Father of our Lord Jesus Christ, which according to his abundant mercy hath begotten us again unto a lively hope by the resurrection of Jesus Christ from the dead, To an inheritance incorruptible, and undefiled, and that fadeth not away, reserved in heaven for you" (1 Peter 1:3, 4).

And in Revelation 1:17, 18 John tells us how that he saw and heard the risen, exalted Christ. "And when I saw him, I fell at his feet as dead. And he laid his right hand upon me, saying unto me, Fear not; I am the first and the last: I am he that liveth, and was dead; and, behold, I am alive for evermore, Amen; and have the keys of hell and of death."

Our Lord himself declares his resurrection to be the foundation and cornerstone of our hope. He says in John 11:25, "I am the resurrection, and the life: he that believeth in me, though he were dead, yet shall he live", and in John 14:19, "Yet a little while, and the world seeth me no more; but ye see me: because I live, ye shall live also."

As you read the New Testament, you cannot avoid seeing that this matter of our Lord's resurrection is vital to Christianity. It is a prominent theme. Unlike most matters of divine revelation, the Holy Spirit pointedly shows us evidence, upon evidence, upon evidence that the resurrection of Christ is an undeniable, irrefutable fact of history. Indeed, of all the facts recorded in holy scripture about our Saviour, the resurrection is the one thing that is proved clearly and fully. The evidence is simply so overwhelming that it would be impossible to prove anything in the world to a person who rejects it. This thing was not done in a corner (1 Corinthians 15:3-9).

The Resurrection Of Our Lord Jesus Christ

Someone once said, "The resurrection of Jesus is the Gibraltar of Christianity and the Waterloo of infidelity and rationalism". J. C. Ryle wrote, "It is the crowning proof that he has paid the debt which he undertook to pay on our behalf, won the battle which he fought to deliver us from hell, and is accepted as our Surety and our Substitute by our heavenly Father in heaven." Thanks be unto God, he who was delivered to death because of our offences was also raised from the dead because of our justification (Romans 4:25). The resurrection of our Lord Jesus Christ from the dead is the proof of our redemption by his blood and the basis of our confident hope that we, too, shall soon be raised up from the dead.

The Glory Of It

As we meditate upon the resurrection of our Saviour, we should always have a sense of the glory of it. The opening verse of chapter 28 reads, "In the end of the sabbath, as it began to dawn toward the first day of the week, came Mary Magdalene and the other Mary to see the sepulchre." The verse quite literally reads, "In the end of the sabbath, as it began to dawn toward the sabbath". I take the verse to mean this: When the Lord Jesus Christ died at Calvary and rose again, the old sabbath of the law ended and the new sabbath of grace began.

Behold our exalted Saviour! Do you see him seated yonder upon his throne in heaven? There he sits in the undisturbed, undisturbable serenity of his absolute sovereignty! His rest is his glory (John 17:2; Philippians 2:9-11; Isaiah 45:20-25). He has finished his work (John 17:4; 19:30). He has brought in everlasting righteousness by his obedience and obtained eternal redemption by his blood. Because Christ has finished his work, the salvation of his people is certain (Hebrews 9:12). The works were finished before the foundation of the world in God's purpose. They were finished in time when the God-man took his seat in heaven as our forerunner (Hebrews 6:20). There is no more work to be done. Christ did it all. Since he has finished his work, he sat down in his glory. There he is resting; and his rest is his glory!

The Lord Jesus Christ has entered into his rest, and his rest is glorious, because he has finished his work (Isaiah 11:10; 2 Corinthians 5:17-21; Romans 8:34; Hebrews 10:11-14), it is glorious, just as Isaiah 11:10 said it would be. Our Saviour's rest in heaven is his glory. As God rested on the seventh day, because his work of creation was finished; so the God-man rested in the seventh day of time and entered into his rest forever. He has finished his work of making all things new for his people (Romans 8:34; Hebrews 10:11-14).

That which is his rest is our rest (Matthew 11:28-30; Hebrews 4:3). We keep the sabbath of faith, a spiritual sabbath, not a carnal one. We rest in Christ, trusting his finished work, by faith entering into his rest.

The believer's life is a perpetual keeping of the sabbath. None of us keeps it perfectly. Our best faith in this world is still unbelief. But we do keep this blessed sabbath rest sincerely, ever looking to Christ, ever coming to Christ, ever resting in Christ. Our all-glorious Christ gives rest to every sinner who comes to him in faith. He says, "Come unto me, all ye that labour and are heavy laden, and I will give you rest."

> I heard the voice of Jesus say,
> 'Come unto me and rest,
> Lay down, thou weary one, lay down
> Thy head upon my breast.'
> I came to Jesus as I was —
> Weary, and worn, and sad:
> I found in Him a resting place,
> And He has made me glad!

The Lord Jesus Christ has given and continually gives us rest. He gives us the rest of complete pardon (Isaiah 45:22; Ephesians 1:6), perfect reconciliation (2 Corinthians 5:17; Colossians 1:20, 21), absolute security (John 10:27-30; Philippians 1:6; 1 Thessalonians 5:24), and of his special providence (Romans 8:28). We do not keep a carnal, legal sabbath, but a perpetual, spiritual sabbath of faith. Christ is our Sabbath. We rest in him.

As the ceremonial sabbath of the law portrayed a strict, universal consecration to God, so this blessed sabbath of faith involves the perpetual consecration of ourselves to our God and Saviour, the Lord Jesus Christ (Matthew 11:29, 30). We keep the sabbath of faith when we wilfully, deliberately take the yoke of Christ. If we would keep the sabbath, it involves much, much more than living in religious austerity one day a week. To keep the sabbath is to bow to Christ's dominion. To keep the sabbath is to learn of him what to believe, how to live, what to do, how to honour God. To keep the sabbath is to bow to his will.

How can a troubled, weary, heavy-laden, tempest-tossed sinner obtain this blessed sabbath rest? I can tell you, both from experience and from the Word of

God, there is only one way we can enter into his rest. We have to quit working! We have to trust Christ alone for everything!

Our Lord's resurrection glory was announced in a remarkable way. We are told by Matthew that, "There was a great earthquake". Then we are informed that, "The angel of the Lord descended from heaven, and came and rolled back the stone from the door, and sat upon it. His countenance was like lightning, and his raiment white as snow."

Our Lord did not need the help of an angel to roll the stone away from his tomb. But God was pleased to make his Son's resurrection a glorious thing, accompanied by signs and wonders. Therefore, when his Son arose as Conqueror of death, hell, and the grave, he shook the earth and sent an angel wrapped in glory to the scene.

I stress this because we need to always remember that our Lord's resurrection was a type, pledge, and picture of our own. As the grave could not hold him beyond his appointed time, it shall not be able to hold us. As the angel of the Lord witnessed his resurrection, the angels of glory shall both witness and be instruments of our resurrection. They shall gather God's elect in the day of harvest. As our Saviour arose with a renewed, glorious body, but still a recognizable material body, so, too, we shall rise with glorious, yet material bodies in the last day (1 John 3:2).

Let all who are taught of God take comfort. Be patient. There is a day soon coming when you and I shall appear with Christ in glory! Here we often meet with trials, sorrows, and persecutions. In this world our lot is one of suffering, weakness, pain, disease, bereavement, and death. But glory awaits us! We shall rise again!

The Terror Of It

Should these lines be read by any who are yet without Christ, I must not fail to remind you of the terror of our Lord's resurrection. Whenever you think of that great day, do not forget the terror that seized these hardened Roman soldiers, or the terror that will seize your soul when Christ shall appear in flaming fire, taking vengeance on his adversaries.

We read in verse 4, "And for fear of him the keepers did shake, and became as dead men." Those soldiers had witnessed many dreadful sights. They were men of blood. Nothing much bothered them. But as soon as they saw God's angel, not the risen Christ, but just his angel, they froze with fear.

How will you react to the blast of God's trumpet, the glorious appearing of our great God Jesus Christ, God's avenging angels, the glory of his saints, and the great white throne? Fear and terror will seize your soul. You will be unable to speak. But your very soul shall wail before the Son of God whom you have despised. When you cannot hide from his presence, you will melt like wax before him. "Behold, he cometh with clouds; and every eye shall see him, and they also which pierced him: and all kindreds of the earth shall wail because of him" (Revelation 1:7). "And the kings of the earth, and the great men, and the rich men, and the chief captains, and the mighty men, and every bondman, and every free man, hid themselves in the dens and in the rocks of the mountains; And said to the mountains and rocks, Fall on us, and hide us from the face of him that sitteth on the throne, and from the wrath of the Lamb" (Revelation 6:15, 16).

May God give you grace to lay these things to heart. Be wise and consider what your last end will be. Remember, there is a resurrection. There is a judgment yet to come. There is a thing such as you have never imagined called "the wrath of God and of the Lamb".

The Comfort Of It

I want you, who are born of God, when you think of the resurrection of our Lord, to draw comfort from it. "And the angel answered and said unto the women, Fear not ye: for I know that ye seek Jesus, which was crucified. He is not here: for he is risen, as he said. Come, see the place where the Lord lay" (vv. 5, 6).

These words were spoken by the angel and recorded by the inspiration of God the Holy Spirit for the benefit of God's elect in every age and in every place. They are full of meaning. They tell us that we have no cause for fear in this world. Whatever may come our way in this world, whatever trouble or trial we may face, let us remember the resurrection of our Lord and be at peace. The best news you will ever hear came from a graveyard. "He is not here: for he is risen, as he said. Come, see the place where the Lord lay."

Child of God, that means that our Saviour is King, our sins are gone, and it is well with our souls! It is certainly true that our Lord shall appear in the clouds of heaven and the earth shall be burned with fire. The graves shall give up their dead. The sea shall give up its dead. The judgment shall be set. The books shall be opened. The dead shall be judged. The angels of God shall divide the good from the bad and the bad shall be burned with everlasting fire. But there is nothing in all this to make believers afraid.

Clothed in the righteousness of Christ and washed in his blood, we shall be found without spot and blameless before him. We shall be found in that Ark which cannot be hurt when the flood of God's wrath is poured out upon the earth. In that great day, "An entrance shall be ministered unto you abundantly into the everlasting kingdom of our Lord and Saviour Jesus Christ" (2 Peter 1:11). That is to say, we shall enter into everlasting life in a blaze of glory! Then, and not until then, shall both the wicked and the righteous understand the Psalmist's words, "Blessed is the nation whose God is the Lord; and the people whom he hath chosen for his own inheritance" (Psalm 33:12).

The Message Of It

What is the message of our Lord's resurrection? The angel said, "And go quickly, and tell his disciples that he is risen from the dead; and, behold, he goeth before you into Galilee; there shall ye see him: lo, I have told you. And they departed quickly from the sepulchre with fear and great joy; and did run to bring his disciples word. And as they went to tell his disciples, behold, Jesus met them, saying, All hail. And they came and held him by the feet, and worshipped him. Then said Jesus unto them, Be not afraid: go tell my brethren that they go into Galilee, and there shall they see me" (vv. 7-10).

First, our Lord appeared to these two faithful women who had come to honour his body. They had been the last to leave him after his death and the first to come to his tomb. How greatly he honoured their faithfulness! These two women were the first to see the risen Lord! They were the first to hear the risen Christ! They were the first preachers of the Resurrection! Our risen Redeemer's first thought and first word was for his people. He said, "Go, tell my brethren". Does that fact not touch your heart? Those words, "my brethren", deserve an eternity of thoughtful contemplation. The disciples were weak, frail, erring, and filled with unbelief and sin, just as we often are. Yet, the Lord Jesus Christ calls them, and us, "my brethren". Just as Joseph comforted his brethren who had sold him, so the Lord Jesus comforts and encourages our hearts. Sadly, the disciples had not lived up to their profession, but had yielded to the fear of man, just as we often do; but Christ is still not ashamed to call them and us "my brethren".

What a joyful meeting that must have been! How unexpected! Yet, it is just what we should expect from him who is not ashamed to call such as we "my brethren". Mark tells us that the angelic messenger was especially concerned for Peter. He seems especially commissioned to give a message of grace and forgiveness to the most fallen of those whom the Master calls "my brethren".

When he was about to enter into his glory, the Lord Jesus made it a point to show himself to his poor disciples repeatedly, as if to reassure them that no change had taken place in his heart. His love for them was still as fresh and as full as when he first embraced them in electing love before the world began. As if to manifest the nearness, dearness, and completeness of his affection for his poor, fearful people, he said to Mary; "Go to my brethren, and say unto them, I ascend unto my Father and your Father; and to my God and your God" (John 20:17).

If the Son of God is not ashamed to call us his brethren, let us never be ashamed to own him as our Lord.

The Assurance Of It

The fact of our Lord's resurrection is so basic and fundamental that it undergirds and assures us of many things. When we look down first into the empty tomb and then up upon the risen Christ in heaven, we are assured that the Word of God is all true. Our Lord rose from the dead exactly as he said he would (Matthew 12:40; 16:21; 17:9, 23). We are assured that our Saviour is himself "the mighty God". Only he who is himself God has power over life and death (Psalm 68:17-20). Our Redeemer's resurrection assures us that redemption is accomplished, justice is satisfied, our sins are pardoned, righteousness is brought in for us.

The resurrection and the empty tomb assures us of the accomplishment of our redemption. It is our assurance that all God's elect shall be saved. "As thou hast given him power over all flesh, that he should give eternal life to as many as thou hast given him" (John 17:2).

We are assured that when our Lord Jesus Christ comes again, there will be another resurrection (John 14:1-3; Job 19:25, 26; Psalm 73:24; Isaiah 26:19; Hosea 6:2; John 5:28, 29; 1 Corinthians 15:21-58; 1 Thessalonians 4:13-18). Then after that great, general resurrection comes the judgment!

Chapter 93

The Great Commission

"Now when they were going, behold, some of the watch came into the city, and shewed unto the chief priests all the things that were done. And when they were assembled with the elders, and had taken counsel, they gave large money unto the soldiers, Saying, Say ye, His disciples came by night, and stole him away while we slept. And if this come to the governor's ears, we will persuade him, and secure you. So they took the money, and did as they were taught: and this saying is commonly reported among the Jews until this day. Then the eleven disciples went away into Galilee, into a mountain where Jesus had appointed them. And when they saw him, they worshipped him: but some doubted. And Jesus came and spake unto them, saying, All power is given unto me in heaven and in earth. Go ye therefore, and teach all nations, baptizing them in the name of the Father, and of the Son, and of the Holy Ghost: Teaching them to observe all things whatsoever I have commanded you: and, lo, I am with you alway, even unto the end of the world. Amen."
(Matthew 28:11-20)

In this last section of Matthew's Gospel the Holy Spirit inspired his servant to relate several important things to us; matters full of spiritual instruction. The passage begins with a picture of the blind absurdities that unbelief will grasp onto when the truth of God is wilfully rejected. Then Matthew shows us that there is in the hearts of true believers much weakness and unbelief. Even when the risen Christ was standing in front of these worshippers "some doubted". Matthew concludes his Gospel narrative of the life and ministry of our Lord Jesus Christ by recording, for our learning, the great commission our Saviour gave to his church just before he ascended into heaven.

In this great commission our Lord Jesus Christ shows us that it is the blessed privilege and responsibility of his church to preach the gospel to all men, to baptize those who profess faith in him, and to teach believers to observe, obey, and keep all that he has commanded and taught.

The Conspiracy
In verses 11-15 the Spirit of God informs us of a conspiracy made by the Jewish religious leaders, demonstrating their dishonesty. These men were highly respected religious leaders. They pretended to have great reverence for God and his law. They pretended to live by the law of God, keeping the commandments with great zeal. But they were corrupt to the core, self-serving dogs.

Matthew makes no comment concerning this conspiracy on the part of the Jews. He simply states it as a matter of fact. When the chief priests and elders heard from the Roman soldiers who guarded the Lord's tomb how that he had in fact risen from the dead on the third day, they never gave the matter a thought. They were not interested in knowing the facts. They were not concerned about truth, or concerned for the people they pretended to serve. In truth, they were not even concerned for the glory of God. All they were interested in was maintaining their position of honour in the eyes of men, power over the lives of others, and personal gain. They gave no consideration to the evidence. All they wanted to do was to protect themselves and their positions. Therefore, they immediately began what is today called "spin control".

They concocted an unbelievable story and bribed the Roman guards to tell anyone who asked a pack of lies. They were to say, "His disciples came by night, and stole him away while we slept"! That is amazing in itself. But what is even more amazing – it worked! The Jews who had so willingly followed their blind leaders swallowed their lie hook, line, and sinker. The lie is all the more ludicrous and unbelievable when you understand the consequences of a Roman sentry sleeping at his post! Yet it was so commonly reported and received that even to this day Jews and others readily grasp it, rather than believing the undeniable evidence of our Lord's resurrection.

However, these things should not surprise us at all. The fact is: the prejudice of blind unbelief is so great that it will grasp, accept and defend the most ridiculous absurdities rather than bow to and receive the revelation of God, no matter how fully and evidently the truth is manifested. When God sends blindness upon those who have deliberately rejected his truth, that blindness is inconceivably great (John 12:37-40; Romans 11:8-10; 2 Thessalonians 2:11, 12).

There is no end to the folly of otherwise smart, even brilliant, educated men and women who wilfully reject the truth of God. Rather than believe that God created all things, as is evident from any basis of rational judgment, most people believe that all things in creation evolved from something, though they have no idea what, and that the evolutionary process began so long ago that no one has any idea when, or where. And they believe these things without so much as a shred of evidence of any kind.

Rather than believe that salvation is by grace alone, in Christ alone, through faith alone, as the scriptures clearly assert, most people believe that salvation can be obtained in any way a person chooses to seek it, so long as he is sincere. They believe that we who insist upon the gospel of God's free and sovereign grace in Christ are divisive, sectarian bigots.

Rather than bowing to the Word of God and the law of God as the standard of right and wrong, of righteousness and sin, most people are willing to tolerate and even promote abortion (the murder of unborn infants), euthanasia (the murder of the weak and sick), homosexuality, fornication, adultery, and pornography in the name of morality and freedom. In our society those who condone the murder of babies crusade for the protection of rattlesnakes! Our government forbids the teaching of God's Word and his law in our schools and demands the teaching of homosexuality, lesbianism, and assorted methods of sexual perversion to our children in the name of sex education! "Woe unto them that call evil good, and good evil; that put darkness for light, and light for darkness; that put bitter for sweet, and sweet for bitter"!

I repeat myself deliberately. There is no end to the folly of otherwise smart, brilliant, educated men and women who wilfully reject the truth of God.

Doubting Worshippers

"Then the eleven disciples went away into Galilee, into a mountain where Jesus had appointed them. And when they saw him, they worshipped him: but some doubted" (vv. 16, 17). Judas was now dead and the apostle Paul had not yet been converted. So there were only eleven apostles at this time. They, along with more than five hundred brethren (1 Corinthians 15:6), went into Galilee to meet the Lord as he commanded them, both before and after his resurrection (Matthew 26:32; 28:10).

When they saw the Lord Jesus, "they worshipped him: but some doubted". Even while the risen Christ stood before them, there were some who doubted. We are not told what they doubted. Therefore I will not speculate about the matter. But we are plainly told that some of the Lord's disciples, some of those five hundred brethren who were there doubted. I call your attention to this fact because I want you to understand, and to be constantly aware of the fact, that God's saints in this world are sinners still. We are forgiven but not faultless, pardoned but not perfect, sanctified but not sinless. Faith and doubt are often found in the same person. We should never have any doubts concerning matters plainly revealed in the Word of God. But the sad fact is, we do. In fact, I have serious questions about the honesty of that man or woman who claims never to have any doubts.

There were some on the mount with the risen Christ who believed and yet doubted. I have had enough doubts at times to drive a man into utter despair. And the very best of the best of God's saints had this same conflict with faith and doubt. Even when he was imprisoned for the testimony of Christ, John the Baptist had some doubts, doubts in the teeth of all that he had personally seen and experienced (Matthew 11:2, 3).

These things are revealed not to excuse or gloss over the horrible evil of our unbelief, but to let us know and to re-enforce the fact that salvation is by grace alone. God's saints, so long as we are in this world, are sinners still. Our only righteousness is the righteousness of Christ. If we truly understand and believe these things, they will teach and compel us to be patient, gentle, long-suffering, and forbearing with one another, helping the weak, lifting the fallen, and encouraging the unbelieving. Sinners who need grace and experience it are gracious.

All Power

"And Jesus came and spake unto them, saying, All power is given unto me in heaven and in earth" (v. 18). Our risen Lord here declares himself Lord, asserting that all sovereignty, power, dominion, and authority over all things had been given to him as our Mediator (Romans 14:9; Philippians 2:9-11; Psalm 2:8; John 17:2). This power was not given to him as God the Son, the second person of the Blessed Trinity. That could never be. As God, he is one with the Father and equal to him in all things from eternity. This power has been given to Christ as our Mediator, because of his obedience unto the Father as our covenant Surety. John Gill wrote, "This is not usurped power, but what is given him, and what he has right to exercise; having finished sin, abolished death, overcome the world, and destroyed the devil."

Our Saviour's power is the power of absolute, universal monarchy. He rules all things everywhere and rules them absolutely. That is the theme of David's song in Psalm 68:17-20:

> The chariots of God are twenty thousand, even thousands of angels: the Lord is among them, as in Sinai, in the holy place. Thou

> hast ascended on high, thou hast led captivity captive: thou hast received gifts for men; yea, for the rebellious also, that the LORD God might dwell among them. Blessed be the Lord, who daily loadeth us with benefits, even the God of our salvation. Selah. He that is our God is the God of salvation; and unto GOD the Lord belong the issues from death.

Christ is King over all. The angels of heaven are dispatched by him (Hebrews 1:14). The Holy Spirit and his gifts of grace are dispensed by him (1 Corinthians 12:4-12). The gifts of the ministry are distributed by him (Ephesians 4:8-16). The people and events of this earth are ruled and disposed of by King Jesus. Indeed, Satan and the very demons of hell can do nothing in the earth but by his permission and his decree.

And our Lord Jesus Christ exercises this dominion at all times for the salvation of his people. He declares, "Thou hast given him power over all flesh, that he should give eternal life to as many as thou hast given him" (John 17:2).

The Commission

"Go ye therefore, and teach all nations, baptizing them in the name of the Father, and of the Son, and of the Holy Ghost: Teaching them to observe all things whatsoever I have commanded you" (vv. 19, 20). This is the great commission our Lord Jesus has given to his church. There is absolutely no question about what the mission and ministry of the church of God in this world is. Our work is clearly defined and established by our Master. This commission is not given just to the apostles. It is not given only to preachers, pastors, evangelists, and missionaries. It is a commission given to the whole church of God. This is not a command to go to mission fields, though that is certainly included in it. Rather, this is a charge to us all to be Christ's witnesses as we go through this world. The text might be read, "Therefore, since I am Lord, as you are going into all the world, teach all nations"! J. C. Ryle correctly asserts, "It is the bounden duty of every disciple of Christ to do all he can in person, and by prayer, to make others acquainted with Jesus."

The church of God in this world is here given a threefold responsibility. All three things are our duty and our privilege. It is not our duty to perform part of this commission. We are commanded and responsible to perform the whole thing.

First, our Lord commands us to teach, or make disciples of all nations. God has an elect multitude scattered among the nations of the world. Christ has his sheep everywhere. It is our responsibility to seek them out. And the only means we have of doing so is by teaching them his gospel. John Gill informs us that the Persic version explains our Lord's commission most accurately, "Bring them to my religion and faith". You and I are responsible in the generation in which we live to make known to all men the gospel of Christ. Only the Holy Spirit can regenerate and save. Only he can give faith in Christ. But we are responsible to tell out the message of grace. We must make all men know who Christ is, what he did, why he did it, where he is now, and how God saves sinners by the merits of his obedience and death as the sinners' Substitute.

Second, we are commanded to baptize all those who become Christ's disciples. The order given is clear. Our Lord does not say baptize all nations and make them my disciples. He says, make disciples and baptize them. Baptism is to be administered only to those who are by their own profession Christ's disciples (Acts 8:37). Baptism, is symbolic of our burial with Christ. As believers are immersed in water they make a public confession of faith in Christ. As such, baptism is the mark of distinction between believers and the rest of the religious world. It is our public oath of allegiance to Christ as our Lord. Baptism, rising up out of the watery grave, portrays and confesses our hope of resurrection glory.

Our Lord Jesus specifically tells us that those who are immersed with him in the watery grave are to be immersed "in the name of the Father, and of the Son, and of the Holy Ghost", as if to declare that the great salvation we are commissioned to proclaim, which we confess in believer's baptism is the gift and operation of the triune God. Baptism is to be performed in the name of the Holy Trinity, the one true and living God, Father, Son, and Holy Spirit.

Third, it is the responsibility of God's church to teach believing sinners all that Christ has commanded us. No local church and no body of churches have any right to alter the doctrine of Christ, dismiss any portion of it as insignificant, or hold back any portion. And none have any right to add anything to the doctrine of Christ, or invent doctrines of their own. It is not our responsibility to decide what people need to hear and know. We are responsible to teach exactly what Christ has commanded in his Word, all of it.

Christ's Promise

After giving his great commission, as if to encourage us in the work, strengthen us for it, and comfort us in the trials sure to accompany it, our Lord Jesus Christ makes this great promise to his church. "And, lo, I am with you alway, even unto the end of the world" (v. 20). With those words, our Saviour inspires us to be faithful to him in all things, assuring us of his presence with us. He is with us everywhere, at all times, forever. He is with us daily to pardon, forgive, and sanctify us. He is with us to lead, guide, and protect us. He is with us to provide for us, strengthen us, and preserve us. He is with us in sorrow and in joy. He is with us in trial and in triumph. He is with us while we live. He will be with us when we go down to the grave. He will be with us forever!

This is our Saviour's word of promise to his church, to you who believe on him, and to me; and he will stand by it. He who is "the Amen", puts his own name to his promise. "Lo, I am with you alway, even unto the end of the world. Amen". Christ himself is the one who made the promise, the thing promised, and the security of the promise.

If the Lord Jesus Christ is with us, compromise is inexcusable, failure is impossible, and whole-hearted devotion to him and his cause is most reasonable (Isaiah 55:11; 1 Corinthians 15:58).

Index of Bible Verses

New Testament

Other books by Don Fortner published by Go Publications:

Basic Bible Doctrine

Discovering Christ In All The Scriptures

Discovering Christ In Galatians

Discovering Christ In Hebrews

All titles available from Go Publications:

www.go-publications.co.uk and www.go-newfocus.co.uk

www.ingramcontent.com/pod-product-compliance
Lightning Source LLC
Chambersburg PA
CBHW021153160426
42812CB00080B/2694

* 9 7 8 0 9 5 4 8 6 2 4 7 3 *